WESTERN
CIVILIZATIONS

W · W · NORTON & COMPANY · NEW YORK · LONDON

EDWARD MCNALL BURNS
ROBERT E. LERNER
STANDISH MEACHAM

WESTERN
CIVILIZATIONS

Their History and Their Culture

VOLUME I   TENTH EDITION

For Joseph R. Strayer;
Edith, Louisa, and Samuel Meacham

Tenth Edition 1984

First Edition, Copyright 1941
Second Edition, Copyright 1947
Third Edition, Copyright 1949
Fourth Edition, Copyright 1954
Fifth Edition, Copyright © 1958
Sixth Edition, Copyright © 1963
Seventh Edition, Copyright © 1968
Eighth Edition, Copyright © 1973
Ninth Edition, Copyright © 1980

BY W. W. NORTON & COMPANY, INC.

Book Design by Antonina Krass
Layout by Ben Gamit

Cartography by Harold K. Faye

W. W. Norton & Company, Inc.,
500 Fifth Avenue, New York, N.Y. 10110
W. W. Norton & Company Ltd.,
37 Great Russell Street, London WC1B 3NU

1 2 3 4 5 6 7 8 9 0

CONTENTS

Part Two   THE CLASSICAL CIVILIZATIONS OF
             GREECE AND ROME

Part Four   THE EARLY-MODERN WORLD

MAPS

PREFACE

The first eight enormously successful editions of *Western Civilizations,* appearing between 1941 and 1973, were brought out single-handedly by Edward McNall Burns. Professor Burns not only had the courage, vision, and fortitude to write a coherent survey of Western history from primeval times to his own day without collaborators, but he was a pioneer in conceiving of his textbook as a history of *civilizations* rather than as a chronicle of events. Thus although he penned a colorful and vigorous narrative, he laid as much stress on the evolution of ideas and institutions as on political developments. Not surprisingly, then, his *Western Civilizations* withstood passing historiographical fads. With periodic revisions it outlasted all its original competitors to become the preeminent and longest lived introductory survey in the field.

In accepting the assignment to revise *Western Civilizations* for the ninth edition in 1977 we accordingly had no doubts that we wished to retain the work's basic physiognomy. Yet the expansion of historical research over previously neglected subject matters as well as the progress of research in more traditional areas made it necessary to revise substantial portions. Realizing that we could not do everything at once, we brought Professor Burns's account up to the most recent state of knowledge wherever we perceived inadequacies, but concentrated our attentions especially on the Middle Ages and the nineteenth and twentieth centuries.

For this tenth edition we have followed the same strategy, concentrating our attentions now on Europe's early-modern era. More specifically, the chapter on the Renaissance (14) has been thoroughly overhauled and the five following chapters completing the early-modern unit have been almost entirely rewritten. The most important changes in Chapter 14 are the introduction of a new section on "The Italian Background," which examines the social and economic contexts of Italian Renaissance developments; the introduction of coverage of Lorenzo Valla and the place of women in the writings of Alberti and Castiglione; revised discussions of Michelangelo and Vesalius; and a fully rewritten treatment of the northern Renaissance which pro-

ceeds topically rather than geographically and emphasizes the central-
ity of Erasmus and Christian humanism. In Chapter 15 overseas
discoveries and the Protestant and Catholic Reformations are brought
together in one unit: whereas treatment of the Portuguese and Spanish
voyages and colonizing activities was slighted in earlier editions of
Western Civilizations, this material is now fully covered in what we
hope is an engaging narrative. Thereafter the Lutheran upheaval is
analyzed from the points of view of theology and politics, and the
succeeding sections on other major developments in sixteenth-century
religious history are fully reconceived with the aims of pursuing new
organizational strategies, distilling the results of the best recent research,
and paying special attention to the effects of the Protestant and Catholic Reformations on the history of women.

Chapter 16 on "the iron century" falling between about 1560 and
1660 is an addition to our table of contents. This chapter attempts to
respond to the challenge of how to treat the period between Luther
and Louis XIV by adopting the prevalent recent scholarly view that
Early-Modern Europe experiences a thoroughgoing "general crisis."
Pursuit of this interpretation has enabled us to unite otherwise refractory material in an integrated manner. Thus Chapter 16 not only presents a narrative of religious wars and constitutional struggles against
the backdrop of economic pressures and regionalist resentments of
nationalizing tendencies but interrelates treatment of thought, literature, and art in ways which hitherto had been impossible.

While Chapters 17 through 19 correspond ostensibly to Chapters
16 through 18 of the Ninth Edition, they too have been substantially
rewritten. Chapter 17 contrasts the dynamic world of the Commercial
Revolution with the traditional institutions and assumptions of an
ordered, hierarchical society, and suggests the dimensions and tensions of the social, economic, and demographic changes that occurred
during the seventeenth and eighteenth centuries. Material on capitalism and mercantilism has been sharpened and expanded, and now
includes a full treatment of the slave trade. The section on agriculture
and industry has been rewritten to emphasize the fact that the Industrial Revolution did not emerge *de novo* at the end of the eighteenth
century, but was a logical conclusion to the economic expansionism
experienced in the Early-Modern period. Recent scholarly research on
demographic trends has been added to the chapter, as have materials
concerning the patterns of daily life within all ranks of society. Poverty, education, and literacy, subjects dealt with heretofore in only the
broadest terms, now receive their due. Chapter 18 contains an extended
and comparative discussion of absolutism. We have expanded our
coverage of the history of eastern Europe and of the important subjects of warfare, diplomacy, and the development of the state system.
We have also attempted to treat the political developments of the eighteenth century in a way that we hope will assist students to master the

historical intricacies of the French Revolution by avoiding a sharp an potentially confusing break with pre-revolutionary Europe.

Chapter 19 represents another major change in the treatment of Early-Modern Europe. It covers seventeenth- and eighteenth-century intellectual achievements but focuses far more sharply than before on the Scientific Revolution and Enlightenment. In this chapter new emphasis is placed on the achievements of Bacon, Descartes, and Newton; treatment of the ways in which the scientific revolution laid the groundwork for eighteenth-century thought is expanded; the coverage of all the foremost Enlightenment thinkers is reconceived (note too that Montesquieu and Adam Smith are now treated here rather than in the French Revolution chapter); and the coverage of art, literature, and music is reconceived (e.g., a new section on the rise of the novel, culminating in Jane Austen) and rewritten in order to convey the fullest possible measure of aesthetic appreciation integrated with historical analysis.

Of course, in concentrating on Early-Modern Europe we have not neglected to review all the rest of *Western Civilizations'* coverage, and where necessary have made some fundamental changes. In the chapter on Ancient Egypt the narrative of political history has been expanded to include treatment of the archaic period, and greater attention has been paid to the role of women. Occasional streamlining and revision of chronology have been introduced in several other chapters of Parts One and Two, and the title of Chapter 6 has been changed from "Hellenic Civilization" to "Greek Civilization" in order to avoid terminological confusion with the Hellenistic Civilization that followed. In view of the prior slighting of early Russian and eastern European history, an entirely new section on "The Formation of the Empire of Russia" has been added to Chapter 13 on the Later Middle Ages.

In the chapters on the nineteenth and twentieth centuries, additions and innovations begin with an expanded treatment of the causes of the French Revolution and the inclusion of a discussion of the Vienna Settlement in Chapter 20. We have also increased our coverage of the social history of women, the spread of literacy, and the demographic shifts of the nineteenth century. The section on imperialism in Chapter 25 has been greatly expanded, as have those on the coming of the First World War in Chapter 27. In both cases we have introduced the historiographical controversies that have arisen over the interpretation of those events. As in earlier chapters we have added to our accounts of the history of eastern Europe, the expanded sections on Russia in the late–nineteenth and twentieth centuries being the most notable examples. Chapter 29 now contains a fuller—and, we hope, clearer—discussion of the varieties of totalitarianism that emerged in Europe during the interwar years. Finally, the treatment of the post–Second World War world has been systematically revised and updated to accommodate new interpretations and recent developments.

In conjunction with the textual revisions the map and illustration programs have received serious attention. Five new maps have been added and the remaining maps have been amended as necessary. Nearly 40 percent of the over 800 illustrations are new to this edition, having been culled from a wide range of European and American archives. The text was the first to include color illustrations and continues to include far more color plates than any other book in the field. The new edition, like its predecessors, is available in a one-volume and a two-volume edition. Both the Instructor's Manual and the Study Guide, which includes numerous extracts from original and secondary sources, have undergone thorough revision as well.

Robert Lerner has had primary responsibility for Chapters 1 through 16 as well as Chapter 19, while Standish Meacham's province has lain with Chapters 17 and 18, and Chapters 20 through 32. The revision of Parts One and Two was facilitated greatly by criticisms offered by Edward W. Kase (Loyola University of Chicago) and Patrick F. O'Mara (Los Angeles City College). Firm bibliographical aid for Chapter 1 was provided by Loretta F. Smith, for Chapter 4 by Robert L. Cohn (Northwestern University), and for Chapters 6 and 7 by Brook Manville. Extraordinarily helpful suggestions for improving the early-modern coverage were provided by Carolyn C. Lougee (Stanford University; who no doubt would still prefer a very different Renaissance chapter than the one here presented), Paul J. Hauben (University of the Pacific), and David Longfellow (Rice University). Expert bibliographical guidance for early-modern art and music history came respectively from Richard Wendorf and William V. Porter (both of Northwestern University), helpful tips for illustrations came from Theresa Gross-Diaz and Klaus Arnold (University of Hamburg), and Vita Maniscalco and Tiina Ruus were argus-eyed readers. The later chapters have benefited from the careful and perceptive criticisms of Lamar Cecil (Washington and Lee University), Maarten Ultee (University of Alabama in Tuscaloosa), Margaret George (Northern Illinois University), John W. Carson (University of Wisconsin–Oshkosh), and John C. Olin (Fordham University). Valuable bibliographical assistance for modern art and music history was supplied by Charlotte Gomolak. At W. W. Norton, Ruth Mandel, as always, has been a resourceful picture-gatherer, and Ben Gamit an imaginative makeup artist. Without question, however, our greatest debt on this round is to Robert E. Kehoe, by title an editor but really Castiglione's ideal diplomat, man of letters, art connoisseur, impressario, and stage manager, all rolled into one.

Robert E. Lerner
Standish Meacham

WESTERN
CIVILIZATIONS

Part One

THE DAWN OF HISTORY

No one knows the place of origin of the human species. There is evidence, however, that it may have been south-central Africa or possibly central or south-central Asia. Here climatic conditions were such as to favor the evolution of a variety of human types from primate ancestors. From their place or places of origin members of the human species wandered to southeastern and eastern Asia, northern Africa, Europe, and eventually, to America. For hundreds of centuries they remained primitive, leading a life which was at first barely more advanced than that of the higher animals. About 3500 B.C., a few of them, enjoying special advantages of location and climate, slowly developed superior civilizations. These civilizations, which attained knowledge of writing and considerable advancement in the arts and sciences and in social organization, began in that part of the world known as the Near East. This region extends from modern-day Iran to the Mediterranean Sea and to the farther bank of the Nile. Here flourished, at different periods between 3000 and 300 B.C., the mighty empires of the Egyptians, the Babylonians, the Assyrians, the Chaldeans, and the Persians, together with the smaller states of such peoples as the Hittites, the Phoenicians, and the Hebrews. The only other very early civilization existed in India in the area of the Indus valley from about 2500 to 1500 B.C. The earliest signs of civilization in China date from about 1800 B.C., and the earliest civilizations in Europe—on the island of Crete and mainland Greece—similarly date from around that time.

The Earliest Development of Humanity

	CULTURE PERIOD	TYPE OF HUMAN	CHARACTERISTIC ACHIEVEMENTS
2 million years ago	Earlier Paleolithic (Early Old Stone Age)	*Homo habilis*	Walking erect; use of objects taken from nature as tools; hunting
500,000 years ago		Java Man; Peking Man	Larger brains: greater intelligence
50,000 years ago		Neanderthal Man: first *Homo sapiens*	Speech; ability to think in the abstract; earliest tool-making
20,000 years ago	Later Paleolithic (Late Old Stone Age)	Cro-Magnon Man	Variety of tools and weapons made from stone and bone; cooked food; cave-painting
12,000 years ago	Mezolithic (Middle Stone Age)	Modern physical types	More settled living conditions; earliest transition from food-gathering to food-raising
7,000 years ago	Neolithic (New Stone Age)		Agriculture; domestication of animals; pottery; earliest village life; origin of states
5,500 years ago	Bronze Age		Earliest civilizations in Egypt and Mesopotamia; writing; bronze metallurgy; developed political, social, and economic institutions

Chapter 1

THE EARLIEST BEGINNINGS

As we turn to the past itself . . . we might well begin with a pious tribute
to our nameless [preliterate] ancestors, who by inconceivably arduous
and ingenious effort succeeded in establishing a human race. They made
the crucial discoveries and inventions, such as the tool, the seed, and the
domesticated animal; their development of agriculture, the "neolithic revolution" that introduced a settled economy, was perhaps the greatest
stride forward that man has ever taken. They created the marvelous instrument of language, which enabled man to discover his humanity, and
eventually to disguise it. They laid the foundations of civilization: its economic, political, and social life, and its artistic, ethical, and religious traditions. Indeed, our "savage" ancestors are still very near to us, and not
merely in our capacity for savagery.

—Herbert J. Muller, *The Uses of the Past*

1. THE NATURE OF HISTORY

Catherine Morland, the heroine of Jane Austen's novel *North-
anger Abbey,* complained that history "tells me nothing that
does not either vex or weary me. The quarrels of popes and
kings, with wars or pestilences in every page; the men all so good for
nothing, and hardly any women at all, it is very tiresome." Although
Jane Austen's heroine said this around 1800, she might have lodged
the same complaint until quite recently, for until deep into the twentieth century most historians considered history to be little more than
"past politics"—and a dry chronicle of past politics at that. The content of history was restricted primarily to battles and treaties, the personalities and politics of statesmen, the laws and decrees of rulers. But
important as such data are, they by no means constitute the whole
substance of history. Especially within the last few decades historians
have come to recognize that history comprises a record of past human
activities in every sphere—not just political developments, but also
social, economic, and intellectual ones. Women as well as men, the
ruled as well as the rulers, the poor as well as the rich, are part of his-

*History more than battles
and treaties*

tory. So too are the social and economic institutions that men and women have created and that in turn have shaped their lives: family and social class; manorialism and city life; capitalism and industrialism. Ideas and attitudes too, not just of intellectuals but also of people whose lives may have been virtually untouched by "great books," are all part of the historian's concern. And, most important, history includes an inquiry into the causes of events and patterns of human organization and ideas—a search for the forces that impelled humanity toward its great undertakings, and the reasons for its successes and failures.

New historical methods

As historians have extended the compass of their work, they have also equipped themselves with new methods and tools, the better to practice their craft. No longer do historians merely pore over the same old chronicles and documents to ask whether Charles the Fat was at Ingelheim or Lustnau on July 1, 887. To introduce the evidence of statistics they learn the methods of the computer scientist. To interpret the effect of a rise in the cost of living, they study economics. To deduce marriage patterns or evaluate the effect upon an entire population of wars and plagues, they master the skills of the demographer. To explore the phenomena of cave-dwelling or modern urbanization, they become archeologists, studying fossil remains, fragments of pots, or modern city landscapes. To understand the motives of the men and women who have made history, they draw on the insights of social psychologists and cultural anthropologists. To illuminate the lives of the poor and of those who have left few written records, they look for other cultural remains—folk songs, for example, and the traditions embodied in oral history.

Necessity for studying past on its own terms

Perhaps the most important lesson historians have learned is that they must no longer condescend to the past, no longer assume that their civilization is worthier than those that have come before. History is primarily the study of change over time, but that does not mean that it is a tale of uninterrupted progress from past to present or that all change was ordained to produce our own modern world. Those who write history and those who study it must look to see how one event led to another and how the entire past is prologue to the present, but they must also appreciate the past on its own terms, examining it, so far as possible, through the eyes and with the minds of those who lived it.

2. HISTORY AND PREHISTORY

The so-called prehistoric era

It is the custom among many historians to distinguish between historic and prehistoric periods in the evolution of human society. By the former they mean history based upon written records. By the latter they mean the record of human achievement before the invention of writing. But this distinction is not altogether satisfactory because it implies that human accomplishments before they were recorded in characters representing words or concepts were not important. On the contrary, however, many of the greatest accomplishments of human technology, and even of social and political systems, were laid before people could write a word. It is preferable, therefore, that the whole period of human life on earth be regarded as historic, and that the era before the invention of writing be designated by a term such as "preliterate." The records of preliterate societies are, of course, not books and documents, but tools, weapons, fossils, utensils, paintings, and fragments of jewelry and ornamentation. These, commonly known as "artifacts," are often almost as valuable as the written word in providing knowledge of a people's deeds and modes of living.

The entire span of human history can be divided roughly into two periods, the Age of Stone and the Age of Metals. The former is roughly coterminous with the Preliterate Age, or the period before the invention of writing. The latter coincides roughly with the period of history based upon written records. The Preliterate Age covered all but the smallest fraction of humanity's existence and did not come to an end until about 3500 B.C., although some Stone Age cultures persisted after that time and a few tribes still exist in remote areas. The Age of Metals practically coincides with the history of civilized nations. The Age of Stone is subdivided into the Paleolithic, or Old Stone Age, and the Neolithic, or New Stone Age. Each takes its name from the type of stone tools and weapons manufactured during the period. Thus during the greater part of the Paleolithic Age implements were commonly made by chipping pieces off a large stone or flint and using the core that remained as a hand ax or "fist hatchet." Toward the end of the period the chips themselves were used as knives or spearheads, and the core thrown away. The Neolithic Age witnessed the supplanting of chipped stone tools by implements made by grinding and polishing stone.

Fist Hatchet

3. THE CULTURE OF THE EARLIER PALEOLITHIC PEOPLES

The Paleolithic period can be dated from roughly 2,000,000 B.C. to 10,000 B.C. It is commonly divided into two stages, an earlier and a later one. The earlier Paleolithic period was vastly the longer of the two, covering about 99 percent of the entire Old Stone Age. During this time at least four species of humanlike creatures inhabited the earth. Momentous discoveries pertaining to the earliest of these have been made very recently by scientific teams working in East Africa. In 1961, the anthropologist Jonathan Leakey uncovered in Tanzania parts

Homo habilis

The Skull (left) *of a Young Woman of the Species Homo habilis,* believed to have lived in Tanzania, East Africa, about 1,750,000 years ago. On the right is the skull of a present-day African. Though *Homo habilis* was smaller than a pygmy, the brain casing was shaped like that of modern humans.

Java Man

of a skull that was about 1.8 million years old, far older than any humanlike skull previously known. (Chemical tests such as the carbon-14 method or the potassium-argon method are used in determining the age of the geological strata in which bones are found and sometimes the age of the bones themselves.) Then, in 1972, a team led by Jonathan's brother Richard discovered in Kenya a similar and nearly complete skull that was more than 2 million years old. The species which left behind these remains has been named *Homo habilis,* or "man having ability." *Homo habilis* may be counted as a true ancestor of modern man because he walked erect, possessed a brain that was larger than that of any apes, and was intelligent enough to use tools. Of course, his tools were extremely primitive. For the most part they consisted of objects taken from nature: bones of animals, limbs from trees, and chunks of stone, perhaps broken or crudely chipped. But they allowed *Homo habilis* to survive in times of food shortage as a hunter rather than as a food gatherer or forager. It must not be thought that reliance on hunting led these earliest ancestors to kill each other. Quite to the contrary, their survival depended upon cooperation. Most likely only after the development of agriculture and herding—more than a million years later—did humans start warring with each other for the possession of territory. The cooperation necessary in hunting made *Homo habilis* the first truly social creature and led toward the use of language. *Homo habilis* was, therefore, clearly in the vanguard of the human race.

Two subsequent inhabitants of the earlier Paleolithic period were Java man and Peking man. Java man was long thought to be the oldest of humanlike creatures, but it is now generally agreed that the date of his origin was about 500,000 B.C. His skeletal remains were found on the island of Java in 1891. The remains of Peking man were found in China between 1926 and 1930. Since the latter date, fragments of no fewer than thirty-two skeletons of the Peking type have been located, making possible a complete reconstruction of at least the head of this ancient species. Anthropologists generally agree that Peking man and Java man are of approximately the same antiquity, and that both probably descended from the same ancestral type.

Peking Man

During the last 25,000 years of the earlier Paleolithic period a fourth species of ancient man made an appearance. He was Neanderthal man, famous as an early caveman. Although first discovered a few years earlier at Gibraltar, Neanderthal man is named after a find of skeletal fragments in 1856 in the valley of the Neander, near Düsseldorf, in Germany. Since then numerous other discoveries have been made, in some cases complete skeletons, in such widely separated regions as Spain, Italy, Yugoslavia, Russia, and Israel. So closely did Neanderthal man resemble modern man that he is classified as a member of the same species, *Homo sapiens*. The resemblance, however, was by no means perfect. Neanderthalers, on the average, were only about five feet, four inches in height. They had receding chins and heavy eyebrow ridges. Although their foreheads sloped back and their brain cases were low-vaulted, their average cranial capacity was slightly greater than that of modern Caucasians. What this may have signified with respect to their intelligence cannot be determined.

Neanderthal Man

Although we know little about Neanderthal culture, it is certain that Neanderthalers progressed far beyond the apes, above all because they had the capacity for speech which enabled them to communicate with their fellows and to pass on what they had learned to succeeding generations. In addition they had some ability to think in the abstract, as evidenced by their burial of their dead with objects intended for use in an afterlife. The Neanderthalers also progressed beyond *Homo habilis* by fashioning their own tools instead of just using the ones they found. They discovered that stones could be chipped in such a way as to give them cutting edges. Thus were developed spearheads, borers, and much superior knives and scrapers. Indications have been found also of a degree of advancement in nonmaterial culture. In the entrances to caves where Neanderthalers lived, or at least took refuge, evidence has been discovered of flint-working floors and stone hearths where huge fires appear to have been made. These would suggest the origins of cooperative group life and possibly the crude beginnings of social institutions.

Cro-Magnon Man

Later Paleolithic Fishhook

4. LATER PALEOLITHIC CULTURE

About 30,000 B.C. the culture of the Old Stone Age passed to the later Paleolithic stage. This period lasted for only about two hundred centuries, or from 30,000 to 10,000 B.C. A new and superior type of human being dominated the earth in this time. Biologically these peoples were closely related to modern humans. Their foremost predecessors, Neanderthal men, had ceased to exist as a distinct variety. What became of the Neanderthalers is not known.

The name used to designate the prevailing breed of later Paleolithic humans is Cro-Magnon, from the Cro-Magnon cave in southern France where some of the most typical remains were discovered. These people lived by hunting reindeer, bison, and mammoths, which freely roamed through southern Europe and Asia because the climate, dominated by glaciers, was very cold. The Cro-Magnon people were tall, broad-shouldered, and walked erect, the males averaging over six feet. They had high foreheads, well-developed chins, and a cranial capacity about equal to the modern average. The heavy eyebrows so typical of earlier species were absent. Whether Cro-Magnon men left any survivors is a debatable question. They do not seem to have been exterminated but appear to have been driven into mountainous regions and to have been ultimately absorbed into other breeds.

Later Paleolithic culture was markedly more advanced than that which had gone before. Not only were tools and implements better made, they existed in greater variety. They were not fashioned merely from flakes of stone and an occasional shaft of bone; other materials were used in abundance, particularly reindeer horn and ivory. Examples of the more complicated tools included the fishhook, the harpoon, and, at the very end of the period, the bow and arrow. That later Paleolithic people wore clothing is indicated by the fact that they invented the needle (made out of bone). They did not know how to weave cloth, but animal skins sewn together proved a satisfactory substitute. It is certain that they cooked their food, for enormous hearths, evidently used for roasting meat, have been discovered. In the vicinity of one at Solutré, in southern France, was a mass of charred bones, estimated to contain the remains of a hundred thousand large animals. Although Cro-Magnon people built no houses, except a few simple huts in regions where natural shelters did not abound, their life was not wholly nomadic. Evidence found in caves that served as homes indicate that they must have been used, seasonally at least, for years at a time.

With respect to nonmaterial elements there are also indications that later Paleolithic culture represented a marked advancement. Group life became more highly organized than ever before. The profusion of charred bones at Solutré and elsewhere probably indicates cooperative enterprise in the hunt and sharing of the results in community feasts.

The amazing workmanship displayed in tools and weapons and highly developed techniques in the arts scarcely could have been achieved without some division of labor. It appears certain, therefore, that later Paleolithic communities included professional artists and skilled craftsmen. In order to acquire such talents, certain members of the communities must have gone through long periods of training and given all their time to the practice of their specialties.

Substantial proof exists that the Cro-Magnons had highly developed notions of a world with supernatural aspects. They bestowed more care upon the bodies of the dead than did the Neanderthalers, painting the corpses, folding the arms over the heart, and depositing pendants, necklaces, and richly carved weapons in the graves. The Cro-Magnons also formulated an elaborate system of sympathetic magic designed to increase their food supply. Sympathetic magic is based upon the principle that imitating a desired result will bring about that result. Applying this principle, Cro-Magnon people

Sympathetic magic

Later Paleolithic Engraving and Sculpture. The two objects at the top and upper right are dart-throwers. At the lower right is the famous Venus of Willendorf.

The Venus of Laussel

*Significance of later
Paleolithic art*

painted murals on the walls of their caves depicting, for example, the capture of reindeer in the hunt. At other times they fashioned clay models of the bison or mammoth and mutilated them with dart thrusts. The purpose of such representation was probably to facilitate the results portrayed and thereby to increase the hunter's success and make easier the struggle for existence. Possibly incantations or ceremonies accompanied the making of these pictures or images, and it is likely that the work of producing them was carried on while the actual hunt was in progress.

In fact, the supreme achievement of the Cro-Magnon people was their art—an achievement so original and resplendent that it ought to be counted among the Seven Wonders of the World. Nothing else illustrates so well the great gulf between their culture and that of their predecessors. Later Paleolithic art included nearly every branch that the material culture of the time made possible. Sculpture, painting, and carving were all represented. The ceramic arts and architecture were lacking; pottery had not yet been invented; and the only buildings erected were of simple design. The Cro-Magnon art par excellence was cave painting. On cave walls were exhibited the greatest number and variety of their talents—their discrimination in the use of color, their meticulous attention to detail, their capacity for the employment of scale in depicting a group, and above all, their genius for imitating natural detail. Especially noteworthy was their skill in representing movement. Almost all of the murals depict animals running, leaping, chewing their cud, or facing the hunter at bay. Ingenious devices were often employed to give the impression of motion. Chief among them was the drawing of additional outlines to indicate the areas in which the legs or the head of the animal had moved. The scheme was so shrewdly executed that no appearance whatever of artificiality resulted.

Cave painting throws a flood of light on many problems relating to primitive mentalities. To a certain extent Cro-Magnon art was undoubtedly an expression of a true aesthetic sense. Cro-Magnon people did obviously delight in a graceful line or symmetrical pattern or brilliant color. The fact that they painted and tattooed their bodies and wore ornaments gives evidence of this. But their chief works of art can scarcely have been produced primarily for the sake of creating beautiful objects. Such an interpretation must be excluded for several reasons. To begin with, the best of the paintings and drawings are usually to be found on the walls and ceilings of the darkest and most inaccessible parts of the caves. The gallery of paintings at Niaux, for instance, is more than half a mile from the entrance of the cave. No one could see the artists' creations except in the imperfect light of torches or primitive lamps, which must have smoked and sputtered badly, for the only illuminating fluid available was animal fat. Furthermore, there is evidence that Cro-Magnon people were largely indifferent to their murals after they were finished. Numerous exam-

Cave Drawings at Lascaux, France. On the left are characteristic examples of the realism of Cro-Magnon art. On the right, a view of the entrance to the caves.

ples have been found of paintings or drawings superimposed upon earlier ones of the same or of different types. Evidently the important thing was not the finished work itself, but the act of making it.

The real purpose of nearly all Cro-Magnon art was apparently not to delight the senses but to increase the supply of animals useful for food. The artist was not an aesthete but a magician, and art was a form of magic designed to promote the hunter's success. In this purpose lay its chief significance and the foundation of most of its special qualities. It suggests, for example, the real reason why game animals were almost the exclusive subjects of the great murals and why plant life and inanimate objects were seldom represented. It aids us in understanding the Cro-Magnons' neglect of finished paintings and the predominant interest in the process of making them. The placing of the art in the most inaccessible part of the cave is further proof of a religious motivation on the part of the artist—the art then becomes secreted in a sacred place.

Art an aid in the struggle for existence

Later Paleolithic culture ended around 10,000 B.C. because of a disappearance of the food supply. As the last glacier retreated north, the climate of southern Europe became too warm for the reindeer, and they gradually migrated to the shores of the Baltic. The mammoth, whether for the same or for different reasons, became extinct. Cro-Magnon people probably followed the reindeer northward, but any later cultural achievements remain unknown to us.

The end of later Paleolithic culture

5. NEOLITHIC CULTURE

From roughly 10,000 B.C. to roughly 5000 B.C., varying very much according to location, ensued the Mesolithic, or Middle Stone Age. This was a transitional period in which peoples became more sedentary and found new sources of food, such as shellfish and edible grasses, now that most of the world was freed from ice. The Mesolithic stage was succeeded by the Neolithic, or New Stone Age. This name is applied because stone weapons and tools were now generally made by grinding and polishing instead of by chipping or fracturing as in the preceding periods. The bearers of Neolithic culture were new varieties of modern peoples who poured into Africa and southern Europe from Asia. Since no evidence exists of their later extermination or wholesale migration, they must be regarded as the immediate ancestors of most of the peoples now living in Europe.

It is impossible to fix exact dates for the Neolithic period because different peoples passed through the Neolithic stage of development at different rates in different areas. Exciting recent archeological discoveries on the west bank of the Jordan River give evidence of Neolithic settlements in their earliest forms around 7500 B.C. Fully developed Neolithic culture existed in Mesopotamia and Egypt by 5000 B.C., but the culture was not well established in Europe until about 3000 B.C. There is also variation in the dates of its ending. It was superseded in Mesopotamia and Egypt by the first literate civilizations around 3500 B.C., but except on the island of Crete it did not come to an end anywhere in Europe before 2000, and in northern Europe much later still. In a few regions of the world it has not ended yet. The peoples of some islands of the Pacific, the Arctic regions of North America, and the jungles of Brazil are still in the Neolithic culture stage except for a few customs acquired from explorers and missionaries.

In many respects the New Stone Age was the most significant in the history of the world thus far. The level of material progress rose to new heights. Neolithic peoples had a better mastery of their environment than any of their predecessors. They were less likely to perish from a shift in climatic conditions or from the failure of some part of their food supply. This decided advantage was the result primarily of the development of agriculture and the domestication of animals. Whereas all of the peoples who had lived heretofore were mere food-gatherers, Neolithic peoples were *food-producers*. Tilling the soil and keeping flocks and herds provided them with much more dependable food resources and at times even yielded them a surplus. The development of agriculture, one of the most important of all transitions in human history, promoted a settled existence and made possible an increase in population. Such were the elements of a great social and economic revolution whose importance it would be difficult to exaggerate.

The new culture also derives significance from the fact that it was the first to be distributed over the *entire* world. Although some earlier cultures, especially those of the Neanderthalers and Cro-Magnons, were widely dispersed, they were confined chiefly to the accessible mainland areas of the Old World. Neolithic culture penetrated into every habitable area of the earth's surface—from Arctic wastes to the jungles of the tropics. Neolithic peoples apparently made their way from a number of centers of origin to every region of both hemispheres. They traveled enormous distances by water as well as by land, and eventually occupied every major island of the oceans, no matter how remote.

Migration over long distances was not the only example of Neolithic achievements. Neolithic peoples developed the arts of knitting and weaving. They made the first pottery and knew how to produce fire by friction. They built houses of wood and sun-dried mud. Toward the end of the period they discovered the possibilities of metals, and a few implements of copper and gold were added to their stock. Since nothing was yet known of the arts of smelting and refining, the use of metals was limited to the more malleable ones occasionally found in the pure state in the form of nuggets.

But the real foundations of Neolithic culture were the domestication of animals and the development of agriculture, for these advances above all made possible a settled mode of existence and the growth of villages and social institutions. The first animal to be domesticated is generally thought to have been the dog, on the assumption that he

The wide diffusion of the Neolithic culture

New tools and technical skills

The domestication of animals

Activities Around a Neolithic Dwelling. This model represents part of a Neolithic village that was located at Troldebjerg, Denmark, about 2700 B.C. Note the hunters, the wood-gatherer, the potter, the weaver, the grain-grinder, and the carver.

Neolithic Flint Sickles

The beginning of agriculture

The nature of institutions

The family

would be continually hanging around the hunter's camp to pick up bones and scraps of meat. Eventually it would be discovered that he could be put to use in hunting, or possibly in guarding the camp. After achieving success in domesticating the dog, Neolithic peoples would logically turn their attention to other animals, especially those used for food. Before the period ended, at least five species—the cow, the dog, the goat, the sheep, and the pig—had been made to serve their needs.

The exact spot where agriculture originated has never been determined. All we know is that wild grasses resembling modern cereal grains have been found in a number of places. Types of wheat grow wild in the Near East and southern Russia. Wild ancestors of barley have been reported in North Africa, the Near East, and central Asia. Though it is probable that these were the first crops of Neolithic agriculture, they were by no means the only ones. Millet, vegetables, and numerous fruits were also grown. Flax was cultivated in the Eastern Hemisphere for its textile fiber, and in some localities the growing of the poppy for opium had already begun. In the Western Hemisphere maize (Indian corn) was the only cereal, but the American Indians cultivated numerous other crops, including tobacco, beans, squashes, tomatoes, and potatoes.

The most important consequence of Neolithic settled life was the development of lasting institutions. An institution may be defined as a combination of group beliefs and activities organized in a relatively permanent fashion for the purpose of fulfilling some group need. It ordinarily includes a body of customs and traditions, a code of rules and standards, and physical extensions such as buildings, punitive devices, and facilities for communication and indoctrination. Since humans are social beings, some of these elements probably existed from earliest times, but institutions in their fully developed form seem to have been an achievement of the Neolithic Age.

One of the most ancient of human institutions is the family. Sociologists do not agree upon how it should be defined. Historically, however, the family has always meant a more or less permanent unit composed of parents and their offspring, which serves the purposes of care of the young, division of labor, acquisition and transmission of property, and preservation and transmission of beliefs and customs. The family is not now, and never has been, exclusively biological in character. Like most institutions, it has evolved through a long period of changing conventions which have given it a variety of functions and forms. No doubt there were primitive families in Paleolithic times, but we know practically nothing about them and they probably were not very stable. In Neolithic times the family clearly emerges and appears to have been dominated by the male patriarch who had one or more wives depending upon region.

A second institution known earlier but developed in more complex form by Neolithic peoples was religion. On account of its infinite variations, it is hard to define, but perhaps the following would be accepted as an accurate definition of the institution in at least its basic character: "Religion is everywhere an expression in one form or another of a sense of dependence on a power outside ourselves, a power which we may speak of as a spiritual or moral power."[1] Modern anthropologists emphasize the fact that early religion was not so much a matter of belief as a matter of rites. For the most part, the rites came first; the myths, dogmas, and theologies were later rationalizations. Primitive people were universally dependent upon nature—on the regular succession of the seasons, on the rain falling when it should, on the growth of plants and the reproduction of animals. Unless they performed sacrifices and rites these natural phenomena, according to this notion, would not occur. For this reason they developed rainmaking ceremonies in which water was sprinkled on ears of corn to imitate the falling of the rain. The members of a whole village or even a whole tribe would attire themselves in animal skins and mimic the habits and activities of some species they depended upon for food. They apparently had an idea that by imitating the life pattern of the species they were helping to guarantee its continuance.

Still another of the great institutions to be developed by Neolithic peoples was the state. This may be defined as an organized society occupying a specific territory and possessing an authoritative government independent of external control. The essence of the state is the power to make and administer laws and to preserve social order by punishing people for infractions of those laws. Except in time of crisis the state does not exist in a very large proportion of preliterate societies—a fact which probably indicates that it originated rather late in the Neolithic culture stage.

The major explanation for the development of states in the Neolithic period lies in the development of agriculture. In areas such as the Nile valley, where a large population lived by cultivating intensively a limited area of fertile soil, a high degree of social organization was absolutely essential. Ancient customs would not suffice for the definition of rights and duties in such a society, with its high standard of living, its unequal distribution of wealth, and its wide scope for the clash of personal interests. New measures of social control would become necessary, which could scarcely be achieved in any other way than by setting up a government of sovereign authority and submitting to it; in other words, by establishing a state.

6. FACTORS RESPONSIBLE FOR THE ORIGIN AND GROWTH OF CIVILIZATIONS

Sometime around 3500 B.C. the earliest *civilizations* emerged out of Neolithic culture. We may say that civilization is a stage in human his-

[1] A. R. Radcliffe-Brown, *Structure and Function in Primitive Society*, p. 157.

torical development when writing is used to a considerable extent; some progress has been made in the arts and sciences; and political, social, and economic institutions have developed sufficiently to conquer at least some of the problems of order, security, and efficiency in a complex society. What causes contributed to the rise of civilizations? What factors account for their growth? Why do some civilizations reach much higher levels of development than others? Inquiry into these questions is one of the chief pursuits of historians and social scientists. Some decide that factors of geography are most important. Others stress economic resources, food supply, contact with older civilizations, and so on. Usually a variety of causes is acknowledged, but one is commonly singled out by historians as deserving special emphasis.

Probably the most popular of the theories accounting for the rise of advanced cultures are those which come under the heading of geography. Prominent among them is the hypothesis of climate. The climatic theory, advocated by such philosophers as Aristotle and Montesquieu, received its most developed exposition in the writings of an American geographer, Ellsworth Huntington. Huntington acknowledged the importance of other factors, but he insisted that no nation, ancient or modern, rose to the highest cultural status except under the influence of a climatic stimulus. He described the ideal climate as one in which the mean temperature seldom falls below 38 degrees or rises above 64 degrees Fahrenheit. But temperature is not alone important. Moisture is also essential, and the humidity should average about 75 percent. Finally, the weather must not be uniform: cyclonic storms, or ordinary storms resulting in weather changes from day to day, must have sufficient frequency and intensity to clear the atmosphere every once in a while and produce those sudden variations in temperature which seem to be necessary to exhilarate and revitalize human beings.[2]

Much can be said in favor of the climatic hypothesis. Certainly some parts of the earth's surface, under existing atmospheric conditions, could never give rise to a superior culture. They are either too hot, too humid, too cold, or too dry. Such is the case in regions beyond the Arctic Circle, the larger desert areas, and the rain forests of India, Central America, and Brazil. Evidence is available, moreover, to show that some of these places have not always existed under climate so adverse as that now prevalent. Desolate sections of Asia, Africa, and America contain unmistakable traces of better days in the past. Here and there are the ruins of towns and cities where now the supply of water is totally inadequate, or which are entrapped by growths of dense foliage. Roads traverse deserts which at present are impassable, or come to an end at the mouth of a jungle.

The best-known evidences of the cultural importance of climatic change are those pertaining to the civilization of the Mayas. Mayan

---

[2] Ellsworth Huntington, *Civilization and Climate*, 3d ed., pp. 220–23.

civilization flourished in Guatemala, Honduras, and on the peninsula of Yucatan in Mexico from about 400 to 1500 A.D. Numbered among its achievements were the making of paper, the perfection of a solar calendar, and the development of a system of writing partly phonetic. Great cities were built; marked progress was made in astronomy; and sculpture and architecture reached advanced levels. At present most of the civilization is in ruins. No doubt many factors conspired to produce its end, including deadly wars between tribes, but climatic change was also probably involved. The remains of most of the great Mayan cities are now surrounded by jungles, where malaria is prevalent and agriculture difficult. That the Mayan civilization or any other could have grown to maturity under present-day conditions is hard to believe.

The Mayan civilization

Related to the climatic hypothesis is the soil-exhaustion theory. A group of modern conservationists has advanced this theory as the primary explanation of the decay and collapse of the great empires of the past and as a universal threat to the nations of the present. At best it is only a partial hypothesis, since it offers no theory of the birth or growth of civilizations. But its proponents seem to think that almost any environment not ruined by humans is capable of nourishing a superior culture. The great deserts and barren areas of the earth, they maintain, are not natural but artificial, created by improper grazing and farming practices. Ecologists discover innumerable evidences of waste and neglect that have wrought havoc in such areas as Mesopotamia, Palestine, Greece, Italy, China, and Mexico. The mighty civilizations that once flourished in these countries were ultimately doomed by the fact that their soil would no longer provide sufficient food for the population. As a consequence, the more intelligent and enterprising citizens migrated elsewhere and left others to sink into stagnation and apathy. But the fate that overtook the latter was not of their making alone. The whole nation had been guilty of plundering the forests, mining the soil, and pasturing flocks on the land until the grass was eaten down to the very roots. Among the tragic results were floods alternating with droughts, since there were no longer any forests to regulate the run-off of rain or snow. At the same time, much of the top soil on the close-cropped or excessively cultivated hillsides was blown away or washed into the rivers to be carried eventually down to the sea. The damage done was irreparable, since about three hundred years are required to produce a single inch of topsoil.

The soil-exhaustion theory

A recent hypothesis of the origin of civilizations is the British historian Arnold J. Toynbee's adversity theory. According to this, conditions of hardship or adversity are the real causes which have brought superior cultures into existence. Such conditions constitute a *challenge* which not only stimulates humans to try to overcome it but generates additional energy for new achievements. The challenge may take the form of a desert, a jungle area, rugged topography, or a grudging soil. The Hebrews and Arabs were challenged by the first, the Indians of the Andes by the last. The challenge may also take the

The adversity theory of Arnold J. Toynbee

form of defeat in war or even enslavement. Thus the Carthaginians, as a result of defeat in the First Punic War, were stimulated to conquer a new empire in Spain. In general it is true that the greater the challenge, the greater the achievement. Nevertheless, there are limits: if the challenge is too severe it will deal a crushing blow to all who attempt to meet it.

7. WHY THE EARLIEST CIVILIZATIONS BEGAN WHERE THEY DID

Egypt and Mesopotamia

Which of the great civilizations of antiquity was the oldest is still a sharply debated question. The judgment of some scholars inclines toward the Egyptian, though a larger body of authority supports the claims of Mesopotamia. These two areas were geographically the most favored sections in the Near East. In both, larger numbers of artifacts of undoubted antiquity have been found than in any other regions. Furthermore, progress in the arts and sciences had reached unparalleled heights in both of these areas as early as 3000 B.C., when most of the rest of the world was backward in the extreme. If the foundations of this progress were really laid elsewhere, it seems strange that they should have disappeared, although of course there is no telling what archeologists may uncover in the future.

A limited area of fertile soil in the Nile valley

Of the several causes responsible for the earliest rise of civilizations in Egypt and Mesopotamia, the existence of fertile river valleys was certainly the most important. Both regions were endowed with a limited area of exceedingly fertile soil. Although the Egyptian valley of the Nile extended for a distance of 750 miles, the valley was only 10 miles wide in some places, and its maximum width was 31 miles. The total area was less than 10,000 square miles, or roughly the equivalent of Maryland. Through countless centuries the Nile had carved a vast canyon, bounded on either side by towering cliffs. Between the river itself and the cliffs lay narrow shores covered with a rich alluvial deposit, which in places reached a depth of more than thirty feet. The soil here was so productive that as many as three crops could be raised each year. This river valley constituted virtually all the arable land of ancient Egypt, for beyond the cliffs lay nothing but desert.

A similar condition in Mesopotamia

In Mesopotamia similar conditions prevailed, although here two rivers—the Tigris and the Euphrates—played the role that the Nile alone played in Egypt. Indeed, Mesopotamia is simply an ancient Greek word for "between the rivers," alluding to the fact that the territory was defined by its position between the roughly parallel flow of the Tigris and Euphrates. Not only was the soil of the region fertile, but the distance between the two rivers at one point was less than twenty miles and elsewhere was not much greater. Since the surrounding country was desert, the Mesopotamian people were kept from scattering over too great an expanse of territory. The result, as in Egypt, was the welding of the inhabitants into a compact society, under conditions that facilitated the interchange of ideas. As the population increased, the need for agencies of social control became ever more urgent. Numbered among these were government, schools, legal and moral codes, and institutions for the production and distribution of wealth. At the same time conditions of living became more complex and artificial and necessitated the keeping of records of things accomplished and the perfection of new techniques. Among the consequences were the invention of writing, the practice of smelting metals, the performance of mathematical operations, and the development of astronomy and the rudiments of physics. With these achievements the first great milestone of civilization was passed.

Climatic influences also played their part in both regions. The atmosphere of Egypt is dry and invigorating. Even the hottest days produce none of the oppressive discomfort which is often experienced during the summer seasons in more northern countries. The mean temperature in winter varies from 56 degrees Fahrenheit in the Nile Delta to 66 degrees in the valley above. The summer mean is 83 degrees and an occasional maximum of 122 is reached, but the nights are always cool and the humidity is extremely low. Except in the Delta, rainfall occurs in negligible quantities, but the deficiency of moisture is counteracted by the annual floods of the Nile from July to October. Also very significant from the historical standpoint is the total absence of malaria in Upper Egypt, while even in the coastal region it is practically unknown. The direction of the prevailing winds is likewise a favorable factor. For more than three-quarters of the year the wind comes from the north, blowing against the force of the Nile current. The effect of this is to simplify immensely the problem of transportation. Upstream traffic, with the propulsion of the wind to counteract the force of the river, presents no greater difficulty than downstream traffic. In ancient times this circumstance must have been of enormous advantage in promoting communication among the Egyptian peoples stretched out along the length of the Nile.

Climatic advantages in Egypt

Climatic conditions in Mesopotamia do not seem to have been quite so favorable as in Egypt. The summer heat is more relentless; the humidity is somewhat higher; and tropical diseases take their toll. Nevertheless, the torrid winds from the Indian Ocean, while enervating to human beings, blow over the valley at just the right season to ripen the fruit of the date palm. More than anything else the excellent yield of dates, the dietary staple of the Near East, encouraged the settlement of large numbers of people in the valley of the two rivers. Furthermore, the melting of the snows in the mountains of the north produced an annual flooding of the Babylonian plain similar to that in Egypt. The effect was to provide the soil with moisture and to cover it over with a layer of mud of unusual fertility. At the same time, it should be noted that water conditions in Mesopotamia were less dependable than in Egypt. Floods were sometimes catastrophic, a factor which left its mark on the development of culture.

Climatic influences in Mesopotamia

Most significant of all of the geographic influences, however, was the fact that the scanty rainfall in both regions provided a spur to initiative and inventive skill. In spite of the yearly floods of the rivers there was insufficient moisture left in the soil to produce abundant harvests. A few weeks after the waters had receded, the earth was baked to a stony hardness. Irrigation was accordingly necessary if full advantage was to be taken of the richness of the soil. As a result, in both Egypt and Mesopotamia elaborate systems of dams and irrigation canals were constructed as long as five thousand years ago. The mathematical skill, engineering ability, and social cooperation necessary for the development of these projects were available for other uses and so fostered the achievement of civilization.

Uncertainty as to which civilization was older

Which of the two civilizations, the Egyptian or the Mesopotamian, was the older? Until recently most historians assumed that the Egyptian one took precedence. Between the two world wars of the twentieth century, however, facts were unearthed which seemed to prove a substantial Mesopotamian influence in the Nile valley as early as 3500 B.C. This influence was exemplified by the use of cylinder seals, methods of building construction, art motifs, and elements of a system of writing of undoubted Mesopotamian origin. That such achievements could have radiated into Egypt from the Tigris-Euphrates valley at so early a date indicated beyond doubt that the Mesopotamian civilization was one of vast antiquity. It did not necessarily prove, though, that it was older than the Egyptian because the achievements mentioned were not taken over and copied slavishly. Instead, the Egyptians modified them radically to suit their own culture pattern. On the basis of this evidence, it would seem that the only conclusion which can be safely drawn is that both civilizations were very old, and that to a large extent they developed concurrently. With them both we begin the story of the history of Western civilizations.

SELECTED READINGS

• *Items so designated are available in paperback editions.*

• Childe, V. Gordon, *What Happened in History?* New York, 1943. Emphasizes materialistic explanations for the emergence of the earliest civilizations. A modern classic.

• Fagan, Brian, *Archaeology: A Brief Introduction,* 2nd ed., Boston, 1983. Defines the terminology and describes some of the basic methods of archeology. Clear and concise.

• ———, *People of the Earth,* 4th ed., Boston, 1982. The most accessible survey of all cultures without written records, ranging from the earliest humans to the Incas.

• Harris, Marvin, *Cannibals and Kings: The Origins of Cultures,* New York, 1977. A materialistic interpretation of the emergence of primitive societies as a process of interaction with environmental and economic determinants.

- Lamberg-Karlovsky, C. C., and J. Sabloff, *Ancient Civilizations: The Near East and Mesoamerica,* Menlo Park, Calif., 1979. A lucid discussion of how the earliest states were formed and of how the earliest civilizations became increasingly complex over time.

  Leakey, Richard E., *The Making of Mankind,* New York, 1981. Describes the most recent discoveries (including Leakey's own) concerning the ancestors of man and posits environmental explanations of the human species. An extremely valuable account.

- Malinowski, B., *Magic, Science and Religion,* New York, 1954. Essays by one of the founders of modern anthropology.

  Marshack, A., *Roots of Civilization: The Cognitive Beginnings of Man's First Art, Symbol, and Notation,* New York, 1972. A basic interpretation of the origins of art and writing as a product of the human capacity for making symbols.

- Mauss, Marcel, *The Gift: Forms and Functions of Exchange in Archaic Societies,* New York, 1967. Originally written in 1927, this book offers enduring insights into the nature of social interaction between individuals and among groups.

  Norbeck, Edward, *Religion in Primitive Society,* New York, 1961. A clear introductory analysis of primitive religious rituals, beliefs, and symbols.

- Pfeiffer, John, *The Emergence of Man,* 3rd ed., New York, 1978. The fullest review of various theories offered by anthropologists to explain human beginnings.

- Sandars, N. K., *Prehistoric Art in Europe,* Baltimore, 1968.

- Turner, Victor, *The Ritual Process,* Chicago, 1969. A concise and fascinating exploration of how rituals can be "read" like a book.

Ancient Civilizations of the Near East and the Aegean World

	POLITICAL	ECONOMIC
3000 B.C.	Archaic period in Egypt, c. 3100–c. 2770 Old Kingdom in Egypt, c. 2770–c. 2200 Supremacy of Sumerian cities in Mesopotamia, c. 2800–c. 2340 Dominance of Akkadian Empire in Mesopotamia, 2334–c. 2200 First intermediate period in Egypt, c. 2200–c. 2050 Sumerian revival, c. 2200–c. 2000 Middle Kingdom in Egypt, c. 2050–1786	Development of irrigation and large-scale farming in Egypt and Mesopotamia, c. 3500–c. 2500
2000 B.C.	Old Babylonian Empire in Mesopotamia, c. 2000–c. 1550 Height of Minoan civilization under leadership of Knossos and Phaistos, c. 2000–c. 1500 Second intermediate period in Egypt, 1786–c. 1560 Mycenaean civilization on mainland Greece, c. 1600–c. 1200 Hittite Empire in Asia Minor, c. 1600–c. 1200 The New Kingdom in Egypt, c. 1560–1087 Kassites overthrow Babylonians, c. 1550	Extended commerce in Egypt and Crete, c. 2000 Slavery in Egypt, c. 1575
1500 B.C.	Mycenaean dominance on Crete, c. 1500–c. 1400 Destruction of Knossos and end of Minoan civilization, c. 1400 Hebrew occupation of Canaan, c. 1300–c. 1025 Trojan War, c. 1250 Collapse of Mycenaean civilization in Greece, c. 1200–c. 1100 Unified Hebrew monarchy under Saul, David, and Solomon, c. 1025–922	Use of iron by Hittites, c. 1500
1000 B.C.	Height of Phoenician civilization, c. 1000–c. 700 Kingdom of Israel, 922–722 Kingdom of Judah, 922–586 Height of Assyrian Empire, c. 750–612 Chaldean Empire, 612–539 Nebuchadnezzar conquers Jerusalem, 586 Persian Empire, 559–330 Height of Lydia under Croesus, c. 550 Persian conquest of Egypt, 525	Mediterranean trade of Phoenicians, c. 1000–c. 700 Invention of coinage by Lydians, c. 625
500 B.C.	Darius the Great, height of Persia, 522–486	Royal Road of Persians, c. 500

CULTURAL	RELIGIOUS	
Egyptian hieroglyphic writing, c. 3100	Egyptian sun worship, c. 3000	**3000** **B.C.**
Sumerian cunieform writing, c. 3000		
Construction of first pyramid in Egypt, c. 2770		
Development of Indus Valley writing, c. 2500	Egyptian belief in personal immortality, c. 2500	
Sumerian legal codes, c. 2100		
Gilgamesh epic, c. 2000		**2000** **B.C.**
Code of Hammurabi, c. 1790	Ethical religion in Egypt, c. 1800	
Egyptian diagnostic medicine, c. 1700		
Egyptian temple architecture, c. 1580–c. 1090		
Development of alphabet by Phoenicians, c. 1500		**1500** **B.C.**
Naturalistic art in Egypt under Akhenaton, c. 1375	Religious revolution of Akhenaton, c. 1375	
	Hebrew worship of Yahweh, c. 1000	**1000** **B.C.**
Realistic sculpture of Assyrians, c. 750	Hebrew prophetic revolution, c. 750–c. 600	
	Astral religion of Chaldeans, c. 600–c. 500	
Deuteronomic code, c. 600	Zoroaster, c. 600	
		500 **B.C.**
Book of Job, c. 400		

Chapter 2

THE EGYPTIAN CIVILIZATION

Thou makest the Nile in the Nether World,
Thou bringest it as thou desirest,
To preserve alive the people of Egypt.
For thou hast made them for thyself,
Thou lord of them all, who weariest thyself for them;
Thou sun of day, great in glory. . . .

—Hymn to Aton, from reign of the Pharaoh Akhenaton

M odern crowds that flood museums to view fabled treasures of Egyptian art are still caught by the spell of one of the oldest and most fascinating civilizations in history. Although the Egyptian civilization was not necessarily the oldest in the ancient world, it was certainly of great antiquity; its origins date from about 3500 B.C. We may consider it here first because somewhat more is known about its accomplishments than about those of most other early peoples. It should be borne in mind while reading this chapter, however, that Mesopotamian and, later, other civilizations were developing simultaneously and sometimes influenced Egyptian developments.

Chronological primacy of Egypt and Mesopotamia

The hallmark of Egyptian civilization was the sense of stability offered by the Nile valley. The fact that the Nile flooded regularly year after year gave Egyptians a feeling that nature was predictable and benign. Moreover, the fertility of the soil in the valley provided for great agricultural wealth, and the fact that the valley was surrounded by deserts and the sea meant that Egypt was comparatively free from threats of foreign invasion. For all these reasons Egyptian civilization was both very advanced and remarkably peaceful. The Greek historian Herodotus was undoubtedly correct when he referred to Egypt as "the gift of the Nile."

Favorable conditions for the development of Egyptian civilization

1. POLITICAL HISTORY UNDER THE PHARAOHS

Stages of Egyptian history

The ancient history of Egypt is usually divided into six eras: the archaic (or "early dynastic") period, the Old Kingdom, the first intermediate period, the Middle Kingdom, the second intermediate period, and the New Kingdom. Even before the beginning of the archaic period the Egyptians had taken some extremely important steps in the direction of creating an advanced civilization. Above all, they had begun their earliest attempts at irrigation and drainage, and they had learned to use copper tools in place of stone ones, thereby benefiting from the advantages that copper was more durable than stone and could easily be sharpened or recast when blunted.

Egyptian unification and the invention of writing

About 3100 B.C. two of the greatest achievements in all Egyptian history occurred: the unification of the country and the invention of writing. Until then separate powers had ruled in Upper (or southern) Egypt, and Lower (or northern) Egypt, but unity was essential for Egypt's future because a single government was necessary in order to ensure centralized direction of irrigation projects along the entire length of the Nile. Tradition attributes the unification of Egypt to one individual, called Menes by the Greeks and Narmer by the Egyptians, but modern experts lean toward the view that the work of unification was accomplished over several generations. Whatever the case, just around the time when one or more rulers of the "First Dynasty" were forging Egyptian unity, the earliest form of Egyptian writing was invented. Probably this was not coincidental, for the use of writing must have been inspired by the record-keeping needs of the new state.

Zoser and the founding of the Old Kingdom

The first two dynasties of united Egypt were succeeded around 2770 by the rule of the mighty Zoser, the first king of the Third Dynasty and therewith the founder of the Old Kingdom. While it is difficult to be certain how the governmental system of the Old Kingdom differed in details from that of the archaic period, there is no doubt whatsoever that Zoser's reign initiated a period of much greater royal absolutism, best symbolized by the fact that Zoser commissioned the first pyramid. Under Zoser and his leading successors of the Old Kingdom the power of the pharaoh, or king, was virtually unlimited. (Egyptian rulers are called "pharaohs" as the result of biblical usage, even though the ancient Egyptians themselves did not use this term.) The pharaoh was considered to be the son of the sun god, and by custom married one of his sisters to keep the divine blood from becoming contaminated. No separation of religious and political life existed. The pharaoh's chief subordinates were priests, and he himself was the chief priest.

The government of the Old Kingdom was founded upon a policy of peace and nonaggression. In this respect it was virtually unique among ancient states. The pharaoh had no standing army, nor was there anything that could be called a national militia. Each local area had its own militia, but militias were commanded by civil officials, and when

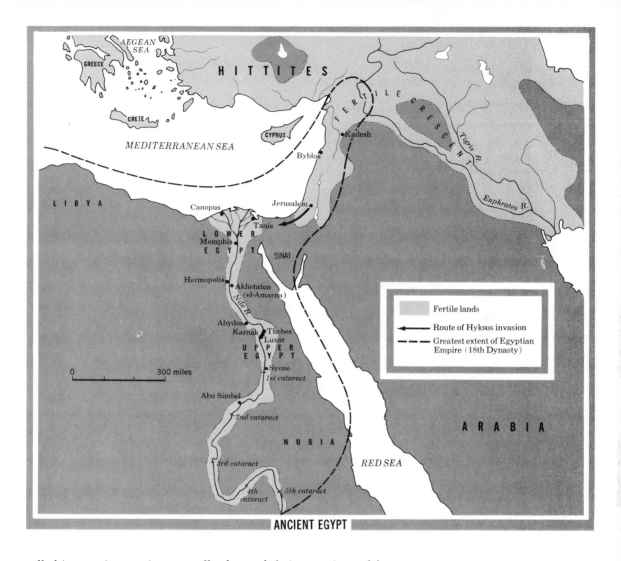

ANCIENT EGYPT

called into active service generally devoted their energies to labor on the public works. In case of a threat of invasion the various local units were assembled at the call of the pharaoh and placed under the command of one of his civil subordinates. At no other time did the head of the government have a military force at his disposal. The Egyptians of the Old Kingdom were content for the most part to work out their own destinies and to let other nations alone. The reasons for this attitude lie in the protected position of their country, in their possession of land of inexhaustible fertility, and in the fact that their state was a product of cooperative need instead of being grounded in exploitation.

The nonmilitaristic character of the Old Kingdom

After centuries of peace and relative prosperity the Old Kingdom came to an end with the downfall of the Sixth Dynasty about 2200 B.C. Several causes were responsible. Governmental revenues became exhausted because the pharaohs invested heavily in such grandiose projects as pyramid-building. To make matters worse, overall Egyp-

End of the Old Kingdom

tian prosperity was adversely affected by climatic disasters which created crop failures. In the meantime provincial nobles usurped more and more power until central authority virtually disappeared. The era which followed is called the first intermediate period. Anarchy now prevailed. The nobles created their own rival principalities, and political chaos was aggravated by internal brigandage and invasion by desert tribes. The first intermediate period did not end until the rise of the Eleventh Dynasty, which restored centralized rule around 2050 B.C. The next great stage of Egyptian history, known as the Middle Kingdom, ensued.

Throughout most of its life the government of the Middle Kingdom was more socially responsible than that of the Old Kingdom. The Eleventh Dynasty could not withstand the power of the nobles, but the Twelfth, which followed around 1990 and lasted until 1786 B.C., ruled strongly by means of an alliance with a middle class composed of officials, merchants, artisans, and farmers. This alliance kept the nobility in check and laid the foundations for unprecedented prosperity. During the rule of the Twelfth Dynasty there were advances in social justice and much intellectual achievement. Public works that benefited the whole population, such as extensive drainage and irrigation projects, replaced the building of pyramids, which had no practical use. There was also a democratization of religion which extended to common people a hope for salvation that they had not been granted before. Religion now emphasized proper moral conduct instead of ritual dependent on wealth. For all these reasons the reign of the Twelfth Dynasty is commonly considered to be Egypt's classical or golden age.

Immediately afterward, however, Egypt entered its second intermediate period. This was another era of internal chaos and foreign invasion which lasted for more than two centuries, or from 1786 to about 1560 B.C. The contemporary records are scanty, but they seem to show that the internal disorder was the result of a counterrevolt of the nobles. The pharaohs were again reduced to impotence, and much of the social progress of the Twelfth Dynasty was destroyed. About 1750 the land was invaded by the Hyksos, or "Rulers of Foreign Lands," a mixed horde originating in western Asia. Their military prowess is commonly ascribed to the fact that they possessed horses and war chariots, but their victory was certainly made easier by the dissension among the Egyptians themselves. Their rule had profound effects upon Egyptian history. Not only did they introduce the Egyptians to new methods of warfare, but by providing them with a common grievance in the face of foreign tyranny they also enabled them to forget their differences and unite in a common cause.

Near the end of the seventeenth century B.C. the rulers of southern (Upper) Egypt launched a revolt against the Hyksos, a movement which was eventually joined by all of Egypt. By about 1560 the last conquerors who had not been killed or enslaved had been driven from the country. The hero of this victory, Ahmose, founder of the Eighteenth Dynasty, thereafter established a regime which was much more highly consolidated than any that had hitherto existed. In the great outpouring of patriotism which had accompanied the struggle against the Hyksos, local loyalties were reduced, and with them the power of the nobles.

The period which followed the accession of Ahmose is called the New Kingdom, and by some, the period of the Empire. It lasted from about 1560 to 1087 B.C., during which time Egypt was ruled by three dynasties of pharaohs in succession: the Eighteenth, Nineteenth, and Twentieth. No longer was the prevailing state policy pacific and isolationist; a spirit of aggressive imperialism rapidly pervaded the nation, for the military ardor generated by the successful war against the Hyksos whetted an appetite for further victories. Moreover, a vast military machine had been created to expel the invader, which proved to be too valuable an adjunct to the pharaoh's power to be discarded immediately.

The first steps in the direction of the new policy were taken by the immediate successors of Ahmose in making extensive raids into Palestine and claiming sovereignty over Syria. With one of the most formidable armies of ancient times, the new pharaohs speedily annihilated all opposition in Syria and eventually made themselves masters of a vast domain extending from the Euphrates to the farther cataracts of the Nile. But they never succeeded in welding the conquered peoples into loyal subjects, and weakness was the signal for widespread revolt in Syria. Their successors suppressed the uprising and managed to hold the Empire together for some time, but ultimate disaster could not be averted. More territory had been annexed than could be managed successfully. The influx of wealth into Egypt weakened the national fiber by fostering corruption and luxury, and the constant revolts of the vanquished eventually sapped the strength of the state beyond all hope of recovery. By the twelfth century most of the conquered provinces had been permanently lost.

The government of the New Kingdom or Empire resembled that of the Old Kingdom, except for the fact that it was even more absolute. Military power now provided the basis of the pharaoh's rule. A professional army was always available with which to overawe his subjects. Most of the former nobles now became courtiers or members of the royal bureaucracy under the complete domination of the king.

The last of the great pharaohs was Ramses III, who ruled from 1182 to 1151 B.C. He was succeeded by a long line of nonentities who inherited his name but not his ability. By the middle of the twelfth century Egypt had fallen prey to renewed barbarian invasions and social decadence. About the same time the Egyptians appear to have lost most of their creative talents. To win immortality by magic devices was now the commanding interest of people of every class. The process of

Ramses II (XIXth Dynasty)

Failures of the Empire

The government of the Empire

The last of the pharaohs

decline was hastened also by the growing power of the priests, who finally usurped the royal prerogatives and dictated the pharaoh's decrees.

The downfall of Egypt

From the middle of the tenth century to nearly the end of the eighth a dynasty of Libyan barbarians occupied the throne of the pharaohs. The Libyans were followed by a line of Ethiopians or Nubians, who came in from the desert regions west of the Upper Nile. In 670 Egypt was conquered by the Assyrians, who succeeded in maintaining their supremacy for only eight years. After the collapse of Assyrian rule the Egyptians regained their independence, and a brilliant renaissance of culture ensued. It was doomed to an untimely end, however, for in 525 B.C. the country was conquered by the Persians. The ancient civilization was never again revived.

2. EGYPTIAN RELIGION

The importance of religion in Egypt

Religion played a dominant role in the life of the ancient Egyptians, leaving its impress upon almost everything. The art was an expression of religious symbolism. The literature and philosophy were suffused with religious teachings. The government of the Old Kingdom was a theocracy, and even the military pharaohs of the Empire professed to rule in the name of the gods. Material resources in considerable amounts were expended in providing elaborate tombs and in supporting priests.

The early religious evolution

The religion of the ancient Egyptians went through various stages: from simple polytheism to the earliest known expression of monotheism, and then back to polytheism. In the beginning each city or district appears to have had its local deities, who were guardian gods of the locality or personifications of nature powers. The unification of the country resulted not only in a consolidation of territory but in a fusion of divinities as well. All of the guardian deities were merged into the great sun god Re. Under the Middle Kingdom, with the establishment of Theban dynasties in control of the government, this deity was commonly called Amon or Amon-Re from the name of the chief god of Thebes. The gods who personified the vegetative powers of nature were fused into a deity called Osiris, who was also the god of the Nile. Thereafter these two great powers who ruled the universe, Amon and Osiris, vied with each other for supremacy. Other deities, as we shall see, were recognized also, but they occupied a distinctly subordinate place.

The solar faith

During the period of the Old Kingdom the solar faith, embodied in the worship of Re, was the dominant system of belief. It served as an official religion whose chief function was to give immortality to the state and to the people collectively. The pharaoh was the living representative of this faith on earth; through his rule the rule of the god was maintained. But Re was not only a guardian deity. He was in addition

Funerary Papyrus. The scene shows the heart of a princess of the XXIst Dynasty being weighed in a balance before the god Osiris. On the other side of the balance are the symbols for life and truth.

the god of righteousness, justice, and truth, and the upholder of the moral order of the universe. He offered no spiritual blessings or even material rewards to people as individuals. The solar faith was not a religion for the masses as such, except insofar as their welfare coincided with that of the state.

The cult of Osiris, as already observed, began its existence as a nature religion. The god personified the growth of vegetation and the life-giving powers of the Nile. The career of Osiris was wrapped about with an elaborate legend. In the remote past, according to belief, he had been a benevolent ruler, who taught his people agriculture and other practical arts and gave them laws. After a time he was treacherously slain by his wicked brother Set, and his body cut into pieces. His wife Isis, who was also his sister, went in search of the pieces, put them together, and miraculously restored his body to life. The risen god regained his kingdom and continued his beneficent rule for a time, but eventually descended to the nether world to serve as judge of the dead. Horus, his posthumous son, finally grew to manhood and avenged his father's death by killing Set.

The Osiris cult

Originally this legend seems to have been little more than a nature myth. The death and resurrection of Osiris symbolized the recession of the Nile in the autumn and the coming of the flood in the spring. But in time the Osiris legend began to take on a deeper significance. The human qualities of the deities concerned—the paternal solicitude

Significance of the Osiris legend

of Osiris for his subjects, the faithful devotion of his wife and son—appealed to the emotions of average Egyptians, who were now able to see their own tribulations and triumphs mirrored in the lives of the gods. More important still, the death and resurrection of Osiris came to be regarded as conveying a promise of personal immortality. As the god had triumphed over death and the grave, so might also the individual who followed him faithfully inherit everlasting life. Finally, the victory of Horus over Set appeared to foreshadow the ultimate ascendancy of good over evil.

Egyptian ideas of the hereafter

Egyptian ideas of the hereafter attained their full development in the later history of the Middle Kingdom. For this reason elaborate preparations had to be made to prevent the extinction of one's earthly remains. Not only were bodies mummified but wealthy men left munificent endowments to provide their mummies with food and other essentials. As the religion advanced toward maturity, however, a less naive conception of the afterlife was adopted. The dead were now believed to appear before Osiris to be judged according to their deeds on earth.

All of the departed who met the tests included in this system of judgment entered a celestial realm of physical delights and simple pleasures. Here in marshes of lilies and lotus-flowers they would hunt wild geese and quail with never-ending success. Or they might build houses in the midst of orchards with luscious fruits of unfailing yield. They would find lily-lakes on which to sail, pools of sparkling water in which to bathe, and shady groves inhabited by singing birds and every manner of gentle creature. The unfortunate victims whose hearts revealed their vicious lives were utterly destroyed.

The Egyptian religion attained its fullest development about the end of the Middle Kingdom. By this time the solar faith and the cult of Osiris had been merged in such a way as to preserve the best features of both. The province of Amon as the god of the living, as the champion of good in this world, was accorded almost equal importance with the functions of Osiris as the giver of personal immortality and the judge of the dead. The religion was now quite clearly an ethical one. People repeatedly avowed their desire to do justice because such conduct was pleasing to the great sun god.

Akhenaton. Above is a profile sketch, surviving from a sculptor's workshop; below, a full-sized weathered bust.

Soon after the establishment of the Empire the religion which has just been described underwent a serious debasement. Its ethical significance was largely destroyed, and superstition and magic gained the ascendancy. The chief cause seems to have been that the long and bitter war for the expulsion of the Hyksos fostered the growth of irrational attitudes and correspondingly depreciated the intellect. The result was a marked increase in the power of the priests, who preyed upon the fears of the masses to promote their own advantage. They inaugurated the practice of selling magical charms, which were supposed to have the effect of preventing the heart of the deceased from betraying his or her real character. They also sold formulas which, inscribed on rolls of

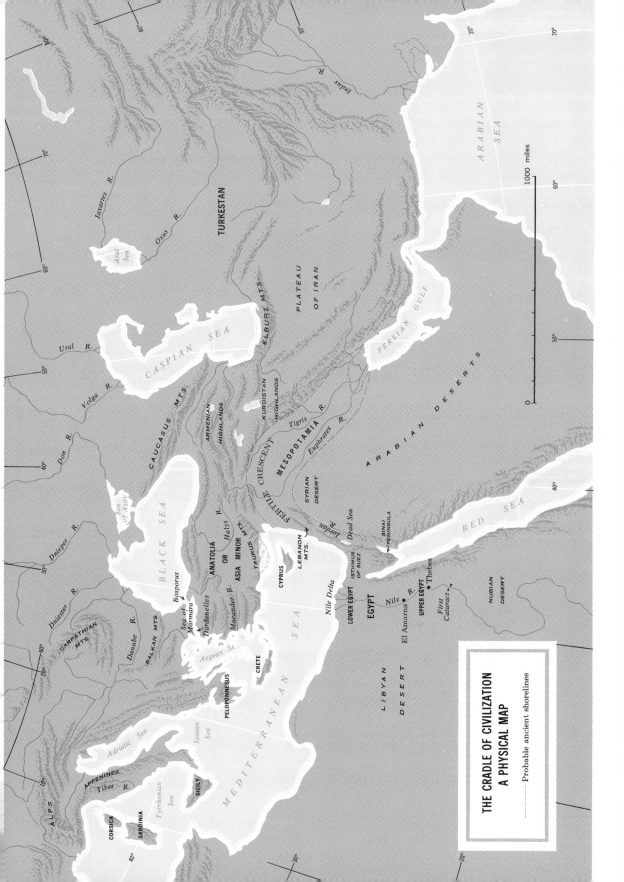

THE CRADLE OF CIVILIZATION
A PHYSICAL MAP

——— Probable ancient shorelines

1000 miles

ALPS

APPENINES

Tiber R.

CORSICA

SARDINIA

SICILY

Tyrrhenian
Sea

Adriatic Sea

Ionian
Sea

PELOPONNESUS

CRETE

MEDITERRANEAN SEA

CARPATHIAN
MTS.

BALKAN MTS.

Danube R.

Dniester R.

Dnieper R.

Don R.

Volga R.

Ural R.

BLACK SEA

Sea of Azov

Sea of
Marmara

Bosporus

Dardanelles

Aegean Se

Maeander R.

Halys R.

ANATOLIA
OR
ASIA MINOR

TAURUS MTS.

CYPRUS

LEBANON
MTS.

CAUCASUS MTS.

ARMENIAN
HIGHLANDS

KURDISTAN
HIGHLANDS

CASPIAN SEA

Aral
Sea

Jaxartes R.

Oxus R.

TURKESTAN

ELBURZ MTS.

PLATEAU
OF IRAN

FERTILE CRESCENT

MESOPOTAMIA

Tigris R.

Euphrates R.

SYRIAN
DESERT

Jordan R.

Dead Sea

SINAI
PENINSULA

ISTHMUS
OF SUEZ

Nile Delta

LOWER EGYPT

EGYPT

Nile R.

El Amarna

UPPER EGYPT

Thebes

First
Cataract

NUBIAN
DESERT

LIBYAN DESERT

ARABIAN DESERTS

PERSIAN GULF

RED SEA

ARABIAN
SEA

Indus R.

Gold and Inlay Pendant of Princess Sit Hat-Hor Yunet. Egyptian, Twelfth Dynasty.

Egyptian Pottery Jar, c. 3600 B.C. It was filled with food or water and placed in the tomb to provide for the afterlife. (MMA)

An Egyptian Official and His Son. Painted limestone, c. 2500 B.C.

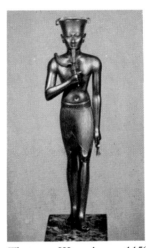

Farmhand Plowing. Egyptian tomb figures, c. 1900 B.C.

Thutmose III as Amon, 1450 B.C. The Pharaoh wears the crown and the beard of the god, and carries a scimitar and the symbol of "life."

Jeweled Headdress of Gold, Carnelian, and Glass. Egyptian, 1475 B.C.

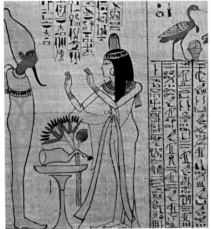

Part of the Egyptian "Book of the Dead." A collection of magic formulas to enable the deceased to gain admission to the realm of Osiris and to enjoy its eternal benefits.

Silversmiths Working on a Stand and a Jar. Egyptian, c. 1450 B.C.

A scribe writing on a papyrus roll. Egyptian, c. 1415 B.C.

Shawabty ("to answer") Figures, c. 1400 B.C. These were put in the tomb to do any degrading work the rich man might be called upon to do in the next world.

Stele or Grave Marker. It shows the deceased being presented to the Sun god on his throne. She is holding her heart in her hand.

Scarab or Beetle-Shaped Charm of a Pharaoh, c. 1395 B.C. The beetle was sacred in ancient Egypt.

Wall painting of an Egyptian house, c. 1400 B.C.

Painted limestone figures, c. 1300 B.C.

Head of Ramses II, 1324–1258 B.C.

Painted Wood Shrine Box for Shawabty Figures, c. 1200 B.C.

A hieroglyphic character for the idea "Millions of Years," 500–330 B.C.

A carved sandstone capital, c. 370 B.C., representing a bundle of papyrus reeds.

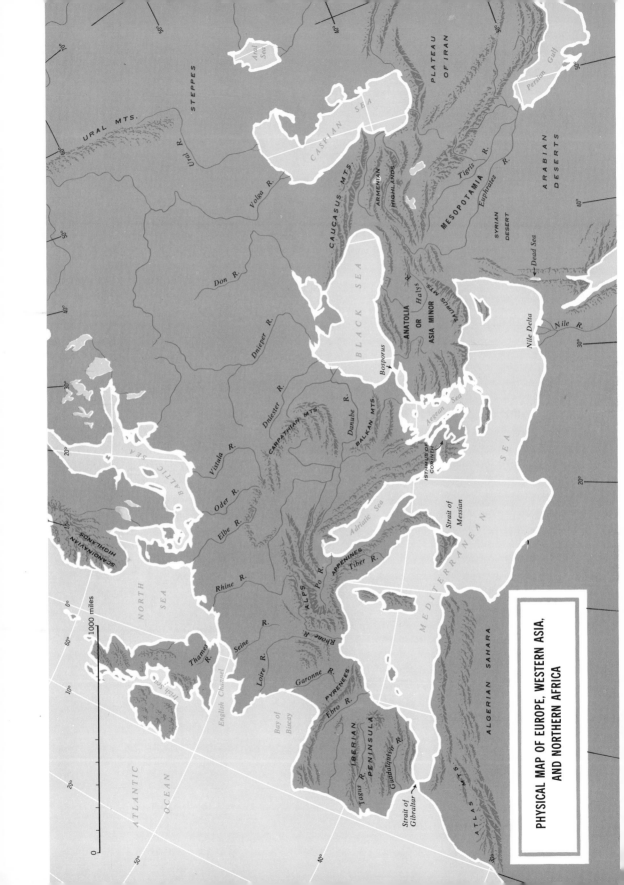

PHYSICAL MAP OF EUROPE, WESTERN ASIA,
AND NORTHERN AFRICA

papyrus and placed in the tomb, were alleged to be effective in facilitating the passage of the dead to the celestial realm. The aggregate of these formulas constituted what is referred to as the Book of the Dead. Contrary to the general impression, it was not an Egyptian Bible, but merely a collection of mortuary inscriptions.

This degradation of the religion at the hands of the priests into a system of magical practices finally resulted in a great religious upheaval. The leader of this movement was the Pharaoh Amenhotep IV, who began his reign about 1375 B.C. and died or was murdered about fifteen years later. After some fruitless attempts to correct the most flagrant abuses, he resolved to crush the system entirely. He drove the priests from the temples, hacked the names of the traditional deities from the public monuments, and initiated the worship of a new god whom he called "Aton," an ancient designation for the physical sun. He changed his own name from Amenhotep ("Amon rests") to Akhenaton, which meant "Aton is satisfied." His wife Nefertiti became Nefer-nefru-aton: "Beautiful is the beauty of Aton." In keeping with his desire to begin entirely anew, Akhenaton built a new capital, El-Amarna, which he dedicated to the worship of the new deity.

Akhenaton, His Wife Nefertiti, and Their Children. The god Aton is depicted here as a sun-disk, raining down his power on the royal family.

More important than these physical changes was the new set of doctrines enunciated by the reforming pharaoh. He taught first of all a religion of qualified monotheism. Aton and Akhenaton himself were the only gods in existence. Like none of the gods before him, Aton had no human or animal shape but was to be conceived in terms of the lifegiving, warming rays of the sun. He was the creator of all, and thus god not merely of Egypt but of the whole universe. Akhenaton deemed himself to be Aton's heir and co-regent; while the pharaoh and his wife worshiped Aton, others were to worship Akhenaton as a living deity. Aside from this important qualification Akhenaton restored the ethical quality of Egyptian religion at its best by insisting that Aton was the author of the moral order of the world and the rewarder of mankind for integrity and purity of heart. He envisaged the new god as the sustainer of all that is of benefit to humanity, and as a heavenly father who watches with benevolent care over all his creatures. Conceptions like these of the unity, righteousness, and benevolence of God were not attained again until the time of the Hebrew prophets some 600 years later.

Despite the energy with which Akhenaton pursued his religious revolution it was still a failure. The religion of Aton gained little popular following because the masses remained devoted to their old gods. The new religion was too strange for them and lacked the greatest attraction of the older faith: the promise of an afterlife. Moreover, the pharaohs who followed Akhenaton were allied with the priests of Amon and accordingly restored the older modes of worship. Akhenaton's successor, the pharaoh whom we refer to as "King Tut," changed his name from Tutankh*aton* to Tutankh*amen,* abandoned El-Amarna for the old capital of Thebes, and presided over a return to all

Tutankhamen or "King Tut." This solid-gold coffin weighs 2,500 pounds.

the old ways. His own burial was a lavish demonstration of commitment to the old rituals and belief in life after death. Thereafter Egyptian religion was characterized by growing faith in ritualism and magic. Priests sold formulas and charms which were supposed to trick the gods into granting salvation: thus even the cult of Osiris lost most of its elevated moral quality.

3. EGYPTIAN INTELLECTUAL ACHIEVEMENTS

The general character of Egyptian philosophy

The philosophy of ancient Egypt was chiefly ethical and political, although traces of broader philosophic conceptions are occasionally to be found. The idea that the universe is controlled by mind or intelligence, for example, is a notion that appeared from time to time in the writings of priests. Other philosophic ideas of the ancient Egyptians included the conception of an eternal universe, the notion of constantly recurring cycles of events, and the doctrine of natural cause and effect. No Egyptian writers could be classified as "pure" philosophers. They were concerned primarily with religion and with questions of individual conduct and social justice.

The earliest ethical philosophy

The earliest examples of Egyptian ethical philosophy were maxims similar to those of the Book of Proverbs in the Old Testament. They went little beyond practical wisdom, but occasionally they enjoined tolerance, moderation, and justice.

The Plea of the Eloquent Peasant

As political philosophers the Egyptians developed a concept of the state as a welfare institution presided over by a benevolent ruler. This concept was embodied especially in the *Plea of the Eloquent Peasant,* written about 2050 B.C. It sets forth the idea of a ruler committed to benevolence and justice for the good of his subjects. He is urged to act as the father of the orphan, the husband of the widow, and the brother of the forsaken. He is supposed to judge impartially and to execute punishment upon whom it is due; and to promote such an order of harmony and prosperity that no one will be deprived of basic human necessities.

Nature of Egyptian science

The branches of science which most absorbed the attention of the Egyptians were astronomy, mathematics, and medicine. All were developed for practical ends—astronomy primarily to compute the time of the Nile floods, mathematics for building purposes, and medicine for healing. By no means pure scientists, the Egyptians had little interest in the nature of the universe as such, a fact which probably accounts for their failure to advance very far in the science of astronomy. Nonetheless they did perfect a calendar based on the annual appearance of Sirius, the brightest star in the sky, whose yearly rising usually preceded the overflowing of the Nile. In addition they worked out a lunar calendar to mark the succession of religious rites.

Mathematics was more highly developed. The Egyptians laid the foundations for arithmetic and geometry. They devised the arithmetical operations of addition, subtraction, and division, but never discovered how to multiply except through a series of additions. They invented the decimal system, but had no symbol for zero. Fractions caused them some difficulty: all those with a numerator greater than one had to be broken down into a series, each with *one* as the numerator, before they could be used in mathematical calculations. The only exception was the fraction two-thirds, which the scribes had learned to use as it stood. The Egyptians also achieved a surprising degree of skill in the mathematics of measurement, computing with accuracy the areas of triangles, rectangles, and hexagons. The ratio of the circumference of a circle to its diameter they calculated to be 3.16, thereby coming very close to the modern calculation of 3.14. They learned how to compute the volume of the pyramid, the cylinder, and the hemisphere.

The Egyptians also did some remarkable work in medicine. Early medical practice was conservative and profusely corrupted by superstition, but a document dating from about 1700 B.C. reveals a fairly adequate conception of scientific diagnosis and treatment. Egyptian physicians were frequently specialists: some were oculists; others were dentists, surgeons, specialists in diseases of the stomach, and so on. In the course of their work they made many discoveries of lasting value. They recognized the importance of the heart and had some appreciation of the significance of the pulse. They acquired a degree of skill in the treatment of fractures and performed simple operations. Unlike some peoples of later date they ascribed disease to natural causes. They discovered the value of cathartics, noted the curative properties of numerous drugs, and compiled the first *materia medica,* or catalogue of medicines. Many of their remedies were later carried into Europe by the Greeks and are still employed by the peasantry of isolated regions.

In other scientific fields the Egyptians contributed less. Although they achieved great building feats, they possessed but the scantiest knowledge of physics. They knew the principle of the inclined plane, which they applied to the building of pyramids, but they were ignorant of the pulley. To their credit, on the other hand, must be assigned considerable progress in metallurgy, the invention of the sundial, and the making of papyrus and glass. With all their deficiencies as pure scientists, they equaled or surpassed in actual accomplishment most of the other peoples of the ancient Near East.

The Egyptians developed their first form of writing concurrently with the foundation of their first unified state around 3100 B.C. This system, known as the *hieroglyphic,* from the Greek words meaning sacred carving, was originally composed of pictographic signs denoting concrete objects. Gradually, certain of these signs were conventionalized and used to represent abstract concepts. Other characters were introduced to designate separate syllables which could be combined to form words. Finally, twenty-four symbols, each representing a single consonant sound of the human voice, were added early in the

Old Kingdom. Thus the hieroglyphic system of writing had come to include at an early date three separate types of characters, the pictographic, syllabic, and alphabetic.

The ultimate step in this evolution of writing would have been the complete separation of the alphabetic from the nonalphabetic characters and the exclusive use of the former in written communication. But the Egyptians, although they made frequent use of the consonant signs, did not commonly employ them as an independent system of writing. It was left for the Phoenicians to do this some 1,500 years later. Nevertheless, the Egyptians must be credited with the invention of the principle of the alphabet. It was they who first perceived the value of single symbols for the individual sounds of the human voice. The Phoenicians merely copied this principle, based their own system of writing on it, and diffused the idea among neighboring nations. In the final analysis it is therefore true that the Egyptian alphabet was the parent of every other that has ever been used in the Western world.

4. THE MEANING OF EGYPTIAN ART

No single interpretation will suffice to explain the meaning of Egyptian art. In general, it expressed the aspirations of a collectivized national life. It was not art for art's sake, nor did it serve to convey the individual's reactions to the problems of his or her personal world.

Yet there were times when the conventions of a communal society broke down, and the supremacy was accorded to a spontaneous individual art that expressed the beauty of a flower or caught the radiant idealism of a youthful face. Seldom was the Egyptian genius for

faithful reproduction of nature entirely suppressed. Even the rigid formalism of official architecture was commonly relieved by touches of naturalism—columns in imitation of palm trunks, lotus-blossom capitals, and occasional statues of pharaohs that were not stylized types but true individual portraits.

In most civilizations where the interests of society are exalted above those of individuals, architecture tends to be the most typical and the most highly developed of the arts. Egypt was no exception. Whether in the Old, Middle, or New Kingdom, it was the problems of building construction that most absorbed the talent of the artist. Although sculpture and painting were by no means primitive, they nevertheless had as their primary function the embellishment of temples. Only at times did they rise to the status of independent arts.

The characteristic examples of Old Kingdom architecture were the pyramids, the first of which was built as early as 2770 B.C. An amazing amount of labor and skill were expended in their construction. The Greek historian Herodotus estimated that 100,000 workers were employed for twenty years to complete the single pyramid of Khufu

The Pyramids of Gizeh with the Sphinx in the Foreground

(or Cheops) at Gizeh. Its height was 481 feet, and the more than 2 million limestone blocks it contains are fitted together with a precision which few modern masons could duplicate. Each of the blocks weighs between 2.5 and 15 tons. They were evidently hewn out of rock cliffs with drills and wedges and then dragged by gangs of workers without the aid of wheeled vehicles (as yet unknown) up earthen ramps and fitted into place.

Several theories have been advanced to explain the building of the pyramids. They may have been intended for the economic purpose of providing employment opportunities. This explanation would assume that the population had increased to overcrowding, and that the resources of agriculture, mining, industry, and commerce were no longer adequate to provide a livelihood for all the people. There may be some validity to this theory, but it is certain that the pyramids had primarily religious and political significance for those who ordered them built. The pyramids were unquestionably meant to be the tombs of the divine pharaohs: the mightier the pharaoh, the larger his resting place was supposed to be. And since the pharaoh stood for the state the pyramids certainly were also political statements. Not only did they glorify the rulers but they probably helped enhance the idea that the might of the Egyptian state was indestructible.

Later, when concern for personal salvation became predominant, the temple displaced the pyramid as the leading architectural form. The most noted examples were the great temples at Karnak and Luxor,

Significance of the pyramids

The temples

Egyptian sculpture

built during the period of the New Kingdom. Many of their gigantic, richly carved columns still stand as silent witness to a splendid architectural talent. Egyptian temples were characterized by massive size. The temple at Karnak, with a length of about 1,300 feet, covered the largest area of any religious edifice ever built. Its central hall alone could contain almost any of the Gothic cathedrals of Europe. The columns used in the temples had stupendous proportions. The largest of them were seventy feet high, with diameters in excess of twenty feet. It has been estimated that the capitals which surmounted them could furnish standing room for a hundred men.

As already mentioned, Egyptian sculpture and painting served primarily as adjuncts to architecture. The former was heavily laden with conventions that governed its style and meaning. Statues of pharaohs were commonly of colossal size. Those produced during the New Kingdom ranged in height from seventy-five to ninety feet. Some of them were colored to enhance the portrait, and the eyes were frequently inlaid with rock crystal. The figures were nearly always rigid, with the arms folded across the chest or fixed to the sides of the body and with the eyes staring straight ahead. Countenances were generally represented as impassive, utterly devoid of emotional expression. Anatomical distortion was frequently practiced: the natural length of the thighs might be increased, the squareness of the shoulders accentuated, or all of the fingers of the hand made equal in length. A familiar example of nonnaturalistic sculpture was the Sphinx, of which there were thousands in Egypt; the best-known example was the Great Sphinx at Gizeh. This represented the head of a pharaoh on the

The Temple at Karnak. Most of this building has collapsed or been carried away, but the huge pylons give an idea of the massiveness of Egyptian temples.

body of a lion. The purpose was probably to symbolize the notion that the pharaoh possessed the lion's qualities of strength and courage. The figures of sculpture in relief were even less in conformity with nature. The head was presented in profile, with the eye full-face; the torso was shown in the frontal position, while the legs were rendered in profile.

The meaning of Egyptian sculpture is not hard to perceive. The colossal size of the statues of pharaohs was doubtless intended to symbolize their power and the power of the state they represented. It is significant that the size of these statues increased as the empire expanded and the government became more absolute. The conventions of rigidity and impassiveness were meant to express the timelessness and stability of the national life. Here was a nation which, according to the ideal, was not to be torn loose from its moorings by the uncertain mutations of fortune but was to remain fixed and imperturbable. The portraits of its chief men consequently must betray no anxiety, fear, or triumph, but an unvarying calmness throughout the ages. In similar fashion, the anatomical distortion can probably be interpreted as a deliberate attempt to express some national ideal.

An intriguing exception to the mainstream of Egyptian artistic development is the art produced during the reign of Akhenaton. Because the pharaoh wished to break with all manifestations of the ancient Egyptian religion, including its artistic conventions, he presided over an artistic revolution. The new style he patronized was naturalistic because his new religion reverenced nature as the handiwork of Aton. Accordingly portrait busts of the pharaoh himself and his queen Nefertiti abandoned the earlier grandiloquent impassivity and distortion in favor of more realistic detail. A surviving bust of Nefertiti which reveals her slightly quizzical and haunting femininity is one of the greatest monuments in the history of art. For the same reasons painting under the patronage of Akhenaton also emerged as a highly expressive art form. Murals of this period display the world of experience above all in terms of movement. They catch the instant action of the wild bull leaping in the swamp, the headlong flight of the frightened stag, and the effortless swimming of ducks in a pond. But just as Akhenaton's religious reform was not lasting, neither was the more naturalistic art of his reign.

Pharaoh Mycerinus and His Queen. Sculpture from the IVth Dynasty, c. 2590 B.C.—an example of the impassive, grandiloquent style.

5. SOCIAL AND ECONOMIC LIFE

During the greater part of the history of Egypt the population was divided into five classes: the royal family; the priests; the nobles; the middle class of scribes, merchants, artisans, and wealthy farmers; and the peasants, who comprised by far the bulk of the population. During the New Kingdom a sixth class, the professional soldiers, was added, ranking immediately below the nobles. Thousands of slaves

Nefertiti. The famous portrait bust executed in Akhenaton's studios at El-Amarna.

Fishing and Fowling: Wall Painting, Thebes, XVIIIth Dynasty. Most of the women appear to belong to the prosperous classes, while the simple garb and insignificant size of the men indicates that they are probably slaves.

The principal classes of Egyptian society

were also captured in this period, and for a time these formed a seventh class. Despised by all, they were forced to labor in the government quarries and on the temple estates. Gradually, however, they were allowed to enlist in the army and even in the personal service of the pharaoh. With these developments they ceased to constitute a separate class. The position of the various ranks of society shifted from time to time. In the Old Kingdom the nobles and priests among all of the pharaoh's subjects held the supremacy. During the Middle Kingdom the classes of commoners came into their own. Merchants, artisans, and farmers gained concessions from the government. Particularly impressive is the dominant role played by the merchants and artisans in this period. The establishment of the Empire, accompanied as it was by the extension of government functions, resulted in the ascendancy of a new nobility, made up primarily of officials. The priests also gained more power with the growth of magic and ritualism.

The gulf between rich and poor

The gulf that separated the standards of living of the upper and lower classes of Egypt was perhaps even wider than it is today in Europe and America. The wealthy nobles lived in splendid villas that opened onto fragrant gardens and shady groves. Their food had all the richness and variety of sundry kinds of meat, poultry, cakes, fruit, wine, and sweets. They ate from vessels of alabaster, gold, and silver, and adorned themselves with expensive fabrics and costly jewels. By contrast, the life of the poor was wretched. The laborers in the towns inhabited congested quarters composed of mud-brick hovels whose only furnishings were stools, boxes, and a few crude pottery jars. The peasants on the great estates enjoyed a less crowded but no more abundant life.

Gold Shrine Depicting Akhenaton's Son, "King Tut," and His Queen. Note the more naturalistic style held over from Akhenaton's reign. As opposed to the rigid formality otherwise characteristic of Egyptian art, curved lines predominate and both figures seem completely at ease. The young king is pouring water for his bride, who cups it with her hand.

Although polygamy was permitted, normally the basic social unit was the monogamous family. Even the pharaoh, who could keep a harem of secondary wives and concubines, had a chief wife. Concubinage, however, was a socially reputable institution. Yet compared to women in most other ancient societies, Egyptian women were not entirely subordinated to men. Wives were not secluded; women could own and inherit property and engage in business. Almost alone among ancient peoples the Egyptians permitted women to succeed to the throne: Queen Sobeknofru reigned during the Twelfth Dynasty and Queen Hatshepsut during the Eighteenth.

Egyptian women

The Egyptian economic system rested primarily upon an agrarian basis. Agriculture was diversified and highly developed, and the soil yielded excellent crops of wheat, barley, millet, vegetables, fruits, flax, and cotton. Theoretically the land was the property of the pharaoh, but in the earlier periods he granted most of it to his subjects, so that in actual practice it was largely in the possession of individuals. Com-

Agriculture, trade, and industry

Sowing Seed and Working It into the Soil. From a bag which he wears over his left shoulder, the sower casts seed under the feet of cattle yoked to a plow. The plow is here used to harrow the soil. While one laborer guides the cows with a stick, another guides the plow straight and keeps the plowshare in the ground by bearing down on the handles. Sheep are then driven across the field to trample in the seed. From wall paintings at Sheikh Saîd, about 2700 B.C.

merce grew steadily after about 2000 B.C. to a position of first-rate importance. A flourishing trade was carried on with the island of Crete, with Phoenicia, Palestine, and Syria. Gold mines in Libya controlled by Egypt were an important source of wealth. The chief articles of export consisted of gold, wheat, and linen fabrics, with imports being confined primarily to silver, ivory, and lumber. Of no less significance than commerce was manufacturing. As early as 3000 B.C. large numbers of people were already engaged in artisanal crafts. In later times factories were established, employing twenty or more persons under one roof, and with some degree of division of labor. The leading industries were quarrying, shipbuilding, and the manufacture of pottery, glass, and textiles.

The development of instruments of business

From an early date the Egyptians made progress in the development of instruments of business. They knew the elements of accounting and bookkeeping. Their merchants issued orders and receipts for goods. They invented deeds for property, written contracts, and wills. While they had no system of coinage, they had nevertheless attained a money economy. Rings of copper or gold of definite weight circulated as media of exchange. This Egyptian ring-money is apparently the oldest currency in the history of civilizations. Probably it was not used except for larger transactions. The simple dealings of the peasants and poorer townsfolk doubtless continued on a basis of barter.

Economic collectivism

The Egyptian economic system was always collective. From the very beginning the energies of the people had been drawn into socialized channels. The interests of the individual and the interests of society were conceived as identical. The productive activities of the entire nation revolved around huge state enterprises, and the government remained by far the largest employer of labor. But this collectivism was not all-inclusive; a considerable sphere was left for private initia-

Sculptors at Work. From a tomb of the VIth Dynasty, c. 2300 B.C.

tive. Merchants conducted their own businesses; many of the craftsmen had their own shops; and as time went on, larger and larger numbers of peasants gained the status of independent farmers. The government continued to operate the quarries and mines, to build pyramids and temples, and to farm the royal estates.

The extreme development of state control came with the founding of the New Kingdom. The growth of a military absolutism and the increasing frequency of wars of conquest augmented the need for revenue and for unlimited production of goods. To fulfill this need the government extended its control over economic life. The services of craftsmen were conscripted for the erection of magnificent temples and for the manufacture of implements of war, while foreign trade became a state monopoly. As the New Kingdom staggered toward its downfall, the government absorbed more and more of the economic activities of the people.

The extreme development of state control under the New Kingdom

6. THE EGYPTIAN ACHIEVEMENT

Few civilizations of ancient times surpassed the Egyptian in impressive accomplishments. Important elements of mathematics and science had their beginnings in the Nile valley. The Egyptians also perfected techniques of irrigation, engineering, and the making of pottery and glass. They were one of the first peoples to have any clear conception of art for other than utilitarian purposes, and they originated architectural principles that were destined for extensive use in subsequent ages.

Egyptian contributions: (1) intellectual and artistic

Equally noteworthy were Egyptian religious and ethical ideas. Aside from the Persians, the dwellers on the banks of the Nile were the only peoples of the ancient world to build a national religion around the doctrine of personal immortality and the idea of rewards and punishments after death. Beyond that, Akhenaton's experiment in the cult of Aton was the first example in history of a religion of universal monotheism. Egyptian ethical prescriptions, moreover, were remarkably advanced in embracing not only the ordinary prohibitions of lying, theft, and murder, but in including exalted ideals of justice, benevolence, and equal rights. Egyptian thought had little direct influence on subsequent formulations because the Egyptian language and writing were hardly understood by others, but all told the Egyptian civilization stands as a remarkable and ever-fascinating monument of human accomplishments at the dawn of recorded time.

(2) religious and ethical

SELECTED READINGS

• *Items so designated are available in paperback editions.*
  Aldred, Cyril, *The Egyptians,* New York, 1963. A short but reliable account covering culture as well as political history.

Bibby, Geoffrey, *Four Thousand Years Ago,* Baltimore, 1961. Egyptian developments from 2000 to 1000 B.C. seen from the perspective of contemporary events elsewhere.

• Breasted, James H., *The Development of Religion and Thought in Ancient Egypt,* New York, 1912. Stimulating, but exaggerated in its claims for the work of Akhenaton; should be read in conjunction with Wilson.

————, *History of Egypt,* New York, 1912. The standard older work by America's first great Egyptologist. Full of valuable information but now regarded as being out of date in its extreme claims for Egyptian originality and influence.

• Childe, V. Gordon, *New Light on the Most Ancient East,* 4th ed., New York, 1957. Covers origins of civilization not just in Egypt but also in Mesopotamia and India.

Cottrell, Leonard, *Life under the Pharaohs,* New York, 1960. Fascinating account of life during the period of the Empire.

Desroches-Noblecourt, C., *Egyptian Wall Paintings,* New York, 1962.

• Edwards, I. E. S., *The Pyramids of Egypt,* Baltimore, 1961. Traces evolution of the form and speculates on the meaning of the pyramids.

Emery, Walter, *Archaic Egypt,* Baltimore, 1961. Controversial account of the earliest period.

• Frankfort, Henri, *Ancient Egyptian Religion: An Interpretation,* New York, 1948. A penetrating, profound study.

Hayes, William C., *The Sceptre of Egypt,* 2 vols., New York, 1953–1959. Written with special reference to the Egyptian holdings of the Metropolitan Museum of Art in New York.

• Mertz, B., *Temples, Tombs and Hieroglyphs,* New York, 1965. Intriguing approach by means of archeological discoveries.

• Smith, W. S., *Art and Architecture of Ancient Egypt,* Baltimore, 1958.

• Steindorff, G., and K. C. Seele, *When Egypt Ruled the East,* Chicago, 1963. Best account of political history of the Empire.

• Wilson, John H., *The Burden of Egypt,* Chicago, 1951. (Paperback edition under the title, *The Culture of Ancient Egypt.*) In a class by itself as the one book to read on Egypt if the student only wishes to read one book. Scintillating and masterful.

SOURCE MATERIALS

Grayson, A. Kirk, and D. B. Redford, eds., *Papyrus and Tablet,* Englewood Cliffs, N.J., 1973. Sources from both ancient Egypt and Mesopotamia. The best short collection for the beginner.

• Pritchard, James B., *The Ancient Near East: An Anthology of Texts and Pictures,* Princeton, N.J., 1965. Also covers both Egypt and Mesopotamia. An excellent selection.

Chapter 3

THE MESOPOTAMIAN AND PERSIAN CIVILIZATIONS

If a son strike his father, they shall cut off his hand.
If a man destroy the eye of an aristocrat, they shall destroy his eye.
If one break an aristocrat's bone, they shall break his bone.
If one destroy the eye of a commoner, or break the bone of a commoner,
  he shall pay one mina of silver.
If one destroy the eye of a slave, or break a bone of a slave, he shall pay
  one-half his price.

—The Code of Hammurabi, lines 195–199

The other of the most ancient civilizations was that which began in the Tigris-Euphrates valley at least as early as 3500 B.C. This civilization was formerly called the Babylonian or Babylonian-Assyrian civilization. It is now known, however, that the civilization was not founded by either the Babylonians or the Assyrians but by an earlier people called the Sumerians. It seems better, therefore, to use the geographical term "Mesopotamian" to cover the whole civilization.

Origin of the Mesopotamian civilization

The Mesopotamian civilization differed from the Egyptian in many fundamental respects. Because the Tigris and Euphrates rivers—unlike the Nile—flooded irregularly, and sometimes disastrously, the Mesopotamians, unlike the Egyptians, could not take nature for granted. Furthermore, the Mesopotamians were not naturally protected, as the Egyptians were, from foreign incursions. In general, therefore, life in the Tigris-Euphrates regions was far more of a struggle. The results of this can be seen in both political and cultural history. The political history of the Mesopotamian area was marked by much sharper interruptions than transpired in Egypt, as the dominance of one people succeeded that of another. Mesopotamian culture too was more warlike and far more gloomy and pessimistic than the Egyptian.

Comparisons with Egypt

Moreover, whereas the native of Egypt believed in immortality and dedicated a large part of his energy to preparing for the life to come, his Mesopotamian counterpart lived in the present and cherished few hopes regarding human fate beyond the grave. Further religious differences were that the Mesopotamians never advanced as far as the Egyptians did toward monotheism and conceived of their divinities more in terms of fear than of love. Finally, Mesopotamian art was fiercer and less personal than the Egyptian.

Similarities

But there were also important similarities between the two. Both civilizations made progress in ethical theory and in concepts of social justice. Both had their evils of slavery and imperialism, of oppressive kings and priests. Both had common problems of irrigation and land boundaries; and, as a result, both made notable progress in the sciences, especially in mathematics. Finally, rivalry among small states led eventually to consolidation and to the growth of mighty empires, especially in the case of Mesopotamia.

See color map facing page 65

1. FROM THE SUMERIAN TO THE PERSIAN CONQUEST

The Sumerians

The pioneers in the development of the Mesopotamian civilization were the people known as Sumerians, who settled in the lower Tigris-Euphrates valley around 3500 B.C. Their exact place of origin is obscure, but it seems likely that they came from the plateau of central Asia. They spoke a language unrelated to any now known, although their culture bore a certain resemblance to the earliest civilization of India. By a process of peaceful interaction they gradually began to guide the natives hitherto living in the lower valley, a mysterious people who were already advancing well beyond the Neolithic cultural stage. From around 2800 to 2340 B.C. a number of independent Sumerian city-states, the most important of which were Ur and Lagash, flourished in Lower Mesopotamia. Then, however, the period of Sumerian predominance was interrupted by a successful invasion from the north led by the mighty Sargon of Akkad (c. 2334–2279).[1] The Akkadians were Semites, a large grouping of peoples of the Near East who spoke related languages (the leading Semitic peoples today are Arabs and Jews). Under Sargon's leadership the Akkadians established the first extensive military empire in Mesopotamia, but this declined around 2200 B.C. and was supplanted by a Sumerian revival led by the city of Ur.

The period of Sumerian revival did not last long. Around 2000 B.C. the Amorites, another tribe of Semites, advanced from the west, conquered the Sumerian cities, and established a new empire in the Meso-

Hammurabi: King of Babylon and Law-Giver

[1] Here, and throughout, dates following a ruler's name refer to dates of reign.

potamian region. Since the Amorites made the village of Babylon the capital of their empire they are commonly called the Babylonians, or the Old Babylonians, to distinguish them from the Neo-Babylonians or Chaldeans, who occupied the Tigris-Euphrates valley much later. The rise of the Old Babylonians inaugurated the second important stage of Mesopotamian civilization after the Sumerian stage. Although most of the Sumerian culture survived, Sumerian dominance was now at an end. The Babylonians established an autocratic state and during the reign of their most famous king, Hammurabi (c. 1792–1750 B.C.), extended their dominion north to Assyria. But after his time their empire gradually declined until it was finally overthrown by the Kassites about 1550 B.C.

With the downfall of Old Babylonia a period of retrogression set in which lasted for 600 years, for the Kassites were barbarians with no interest in the cultural achievements of their predecessors. Indeed, the old culture probably would have died out entirely had it not been for its partial adoption by another Semitic people who, as early as 3000 B.C., had founded a tiny kingdom on the plateau of Assur some 500 miles up the Tigris River. These people came to be called the Assyrians, and their rise to power marked the beginning of the third stage in the development of the Mesopotamian civilization. They began to expand about 1300 B.C. and soon afterward made themselves masters of the whole northern valley. In the tenth century they overturned what was left of Kassite power in Babylonia. Their empire reached its height in the eighth and seventh centuries under Sargon II (722–705 B.C.) and Sennacherib (705–681), who built Nineveh, a magnificent new capital on the Tigris. The Assyrian Empire had now come to include nearly all of the Near East, since the Assyrians had conquered, one after another, Syria, Phoenicia, the Kingdom of Israel, and Egypt.

Brilliant though the successes of the Assyrians were, they did not endure. So rapidly were new territories annexed that the empire soon reached an unmanageable size. The Assyrians' ability at government was far inferior to their appetite for conquest. Subjugated nations chafed under the despotism that had been forced upon them and, as the empire gave signs of cracking from within, determined to regain their freedom. The death blow was delivered by the Chaldeans (pronounced Kaldeans), a nation of Semites who had settled southeast of the valley of the two rivers. Under the leadership of Nabopolassar, who had served the Assyrian emperors in the capacity of a provincial governor, they organized a revolt and finally captured Nineveh in 612 B.C. The most famous of the Chaldeans was Nebuchadnezzar (605–562 B.C.), who conquered Jerusalem and made his capital of Babylon the leading city of the Near East.

Assyrians Storming an Enemy City

In 539 B.C. the empire of the Chaldeans fell, after an existence of less than a century. It was overthrown by Cyrus the Persian, as he himself declared, "without a battle and without fighting." The easy victory appears to have been made possible by assistance from the Jews, who were being held captive in Babylon, and by a conspiracy of the priests of Babylon to deliver the city to Cyrus as an act of vengeance against the Chaldean king, whose policies they did not like. Members of other influential classes appear also to have looked upon the Persians as deliverers.

The Persians

Although the Persian state incorporated all of the territories that had once been embraced by the Mesopotamian empires, it included many other provinces besides. It was the vehicle, moreover, of a new and different culture. The downfall of Chaldea must therefore be taken as marking the end of Mesopotamian political history.

2. SUMERIAN ORIGINS OF MESOPOTAMIAN CIVILIZATION

Formative influence of the Sumerians

More than to any other people, the Mesopotamian civilization owed its character to the Sumerians. Much of what used to be ascribed to the Babylonians and Assyrians is now known to have been developed by the nation that preceded them. The system of writing was of Sumerian origin; likewise the religion, the laws, and a great deal of the science and commercial practice. Only in the evolution of government and military tactics and in the development of the arts was the originating talent of the later conquerors particularly manifest.

The Sumerian political system

Through the greater part of their history the Sumerians lived in a loose confederation of city-states, united only for military purposes. At the head of each was a *patesi,* who combined the functions of chief priest, commander of the army, and superintendent of the irrigation system. Occasionally one of the more ambitious of these rulers would extend his power over a number of cities and assume the title of king,

Diorama of a Part of Ur about 2000 B.C. A modern archeologist's conception. Walls are omitted to show interiors at left.

but no true empire was ever created like those of the Akkadians, or subsequent Babylonians, Assyrians, or Chaldeans.

The Sumerian economic pattern was relatively simple and permitted a wider scope for individual enterprise than was generally allowed in Egypt. The land was never the exclusive property of the ruler either in theory or in practice. Neither was trade or industry a monopoly of the government. The temples, however, seem to have fulfilled many of the functions of a collectivist state. They owned a large portion of the land and operated business enterprises. Because the priests alone had the technical knowledge to calculate the coming of the seasons and lay out canals, they controlled the irrigation system. The masses of the people had little they could call their own. Many of them were serfs, but even those who were technically free were little better off, forced as they were to pay high rents and to labor on public works. Slavery in the strict sense of the word was not an important institution. *The Sumerian economic pattern*

Agriculture was the chief economic pursuit of most of the citizens, and the Sumerians were excellent farmers. By virtue of their knowledge of irrigation they produced large crops of cereal grains and subtropical fruits. Since most of the land was divided into large estates held by the rulers, the priests, and the army officers, the average rural citizen was either a tenant farmer or a serf. Commerce was the second most important source of Sumerian wealth. A flourishing trade was established with all of the surrounding areas, revolving around the exchange of metals and timber from the north and west for agricultural products and handicrafted goods from the lower valley. Nearly all of the familiar adjuncts of business were highly developed; bills, receipts, notes, and letters of credit were regularly used. *Agriculture*

The most distinctive achievement of the Sumerians was their system of law. It was the product of a gradual evolution of local usage merging together with ideas absorbed from neighboring Semitic peoples. Only a few fragments of this law have survived in their original form, but the famous Code of Hammurabi, the Babylonian king, is now recognized to have been a variant of the code of the Sumerians. Ultimately this code became the basis of the laws of nearly all of the Semites—Babylonians, Assyrians, Chaldeans, and Hebrews. *Mesopotamian law*

The following may be regarded as the essential features of the Mesopotamian law:

(1) The *lex talionis,* or law of retaliation in kind—"an eye for an eye, a tooth for a tooth, a limb for a limb." This fundamental concept was one that the Sumerians learned from the Semites. *Essential features of Mesopotamian law*

(2) Semiprivate administration of justice. It was incumbent upon the victim or his family to bring the offender to justice. The court served principally as an umpire in the dispute between the plaintiff and defendant, not as an agency of the state to maintain public security, although constables attached to the court might assist in the execution of the sentence.

(3) Inequality before the law. Mesopotamian law divided the population into three classes: patricians or aristocrats; burghers or commoners; serfs and slaves. Penalties were graded according to the rank of the victim, but also in some cases according to the rank of the offender. The killing or maiming of a patrician was a much more serious offense than a similar crime committed against a burgher or a slave. On the other hand, when a patrician was the offender he was punished *more severely* than a person of inferior status would be for the same crime. The origin of this curious rule was probably to be found in considerations of military discipline. Since the patricians were army officers and therefore the chief defenders of the state, they could not be permitted to give vent to their passions or to indulge in riotous conduct.

(4) Inadequate distinction between accidental and intentional homicide. A person responsible for killing another accidentally did not escape penalty, as under modern law, but had to pay a fine to the family of the victim, apparently on the theory that children were the property of their fathers and wives the property of their husbands.

Quite as much as their law, the religion of the Sumerians illuminates their social attitudes and the character of their culture. They did not succeed in developing a very exalted religion; yet it occupied an important place in their lives. To begin with, it was polytheistic and anthropomorphic. They believed in a number of gods and goddesses, each a distinct personality with human attributes. The sun god, the lord of the rain and wind, the goddess of the generative powers of nature were only a few of them. All of these numerous deities were thought to be capable of performing both good and evil.

Sumerian religion

The Sumerian religion was a religion for this world exclusively; it offered no hope for a blissful, eternal afterlife. The afterlife was a mere temporary existence in a dreary, shadowy place which later came to be called Sheol. Here the ghosts of the dead lingered for a time, perhaps a generation or so, and then disappeared. No one could look forward to resurrection in another world and a joyous eternal existence as a recompense for the evils of this life; the victory of the grave was complete. In accordance with these beliefs the Sumerians bestowed only limited care upon the bodies of their dead. They practiced no mummification and built no elaborate tombs. Corpses were commonly interred beneath the floor of the house without a coffin and with comparatively few articles for the use of the ghost.

A religion neither ethical nor spiritual

There was little spiritual content in Sumerian religion. As we have seen, the gods were not spiritual beings but creatures cast in the human mold, with most of the weaknesses and passions of mortals. Nor were the purposes of the religion any more spiritual. It provided no blessings in the form of solace, uplift of the soul, or oneness with God. If it benefited humanity at all, it did so chiefly in the form of material gain—abundant harvests and prosperity in business. The re-

Sumerian Praying Figures. These statues dating from about 2700 B.C. show the immobile bodies and huge staring eyes characteristic of much of Mesopotamian art.

ligion did have some ethical content. All the major deities in the Sumerian pantheon were extolled in hymns as lovers of truth, goodness, and justice. The goddess Nanshe, for example, was said "to comfort the orphan, to make disappear the widow, to set up a place of destruction for the mighty." Yet the same deities who personified these noble ideals created such evils as falsehood and strife, and endowed every human being with a sinful nature. "Never," it was said, "has a sinless child been born to its mother."

In the field of intellectual endeavor the Sumerians achieved no small distinction. They produced a system of writing which was destined to be used for two thousand years after the downfall of their nation. This was the celebrated *cuneiform* writing, consisting of wedge-shaped characters (*cuneus* is Latin for wedge) imprinted on clay tablets with a square-tipped reed. At first a pictographic system, it was gradually transformed into an aggregate of syllabic and phonetic signs, some 350 in number. No alphabet was ever developed out of it, but cuneiform nonetheless became the standard medium for commercial transactions throughout most of the Near East (often including Egypt) from about 3000 to about 500 B.C. The Sumerians wrote nothing that could be called philosophy, but they did make some notable beginnings in science. In mathematics, for example, they surpassed the Egyptians in every field except geometry. They discovered the processes of multiplication and division and even the extraction of square and cube root. Their systems of numeration and of weights and measures were duodecimal, with the number sixty as the most common unit. They invented the water clock and the lunar calendar, the latter an inaccurate division of the year into months based upon cycles of the

The intellectual level of Sumerian culture

See color plates
following page 64

Two Portraits from Lugash. Although these Sumerian votive statues are separated by some seven centuries, dating from about 2700 B.C. and 2000 B.C. respectively, they show the barest minimum of artistic evolution.

moon. In order to bring it into harmony with the solar year, an extra month had to be added from time to time. The Sumerians were the first known peoples to believe in astrology—the belief that that human fates are determined by the courses of the stars—and this interest led them to pioneer in astronomical observations and predictions of planetary movements. Their medicine was a curious compound of herbalism and magic. The repertory of the physician consisted primarily of charms to exorcise the evil spirits which were believed to be the cause of the disease.

As artists, the Sumerians excelled in metalwork, gem carving, and sculpture. They produced some remarkable specimens of naturalistic art in their weapons, vessels, jewelry, and animal representations, which revealed alike a technical skill and a gift of imagination. Evidently religious conventions had not yet imposed any paralyzing influence, and consequently the artist was still free to follow his own impulses. Architecture, on the other hand, was distinctly inferior, probably because of the limitations enforced by the scarcity of good building materials. Since there was no stone in the valley, the architect had to depend upon sun-dried brick. The characteristic Sumerian edifice, extensively copied by their Semitic successors, was the *ziggurat,* a terraced tower set on a platform and surmounted by a shrine. Its construction was massive, its lines were monotonous, and little architectural ingenuity was exhibited in it. The royal tombs and private houses showed more originality. It was in them that the Sumerian inventions of the arch, the vault, and the dome were regularly employed, and the column was used occasionally.

3. OLD BABYLONIAN DEVELOPMENTS

Although the Old Babylonians were an alien nation, they had lived long enough in close contact with the Sumerians to be influenced profoundly by them. They had little culture of their own when they came into the valley, and in general they only appropriated and modified what the Sumerians had already developed. Thus the changes in Mesopotamian culture during the Old Babylonian period were essentially variations on Sumerian themes.

First among the alterations which the Old Babylonians made in their inheritance may be mentioned the political and legal. As military conquerors holding in subjection numerous vanquished nations, they found it necessary to establish a consolidated state. Vestiges of the old system of local autonomy were swept away, and the power of the king of Babylon was made supreme. Kings became gods, or at least claimed divine origin. A system of royal taxation was adopted as well as compulsory military service. The system of law was also changed to conform to the new condition of centralized despotism. The list of crimes against the state was enlarged, and the king's officers assumed a

The Great Ziggurat at Ur

more active role in apprehending and punishing offenders, although it was still impossible for any criminal to be pardoned without the consent of the victim or the victim's family. The severity of penalties was decidedly increased, particularly for crimes involving any suggestion of treason or sedition. Such apparently trivial offenses as "vagabondage" and "disorderly conduct at a tavern" were made punishable by death, probably on the assumption that they would be likely to foster disloyal activities. Whereas under the Sumerian law the harboring of fugitive slaves was punishable merely by a fine, the Babylonian law made it a capital crime. According to the Sumerian code, the slave who disputed his master's rights over him was to be sold; the Code of Hammurabi prescribed that he should have his ear cut off. Adultery was also made a capital offense, whereas under the Sumerian law it did not even necessarily result in divorce. In a few particulars the new system of law revealed some improvement. Wives and children sold for debt could not be held in bondage for longer than four years, and a female slave who had borne her master a child could not be sold at all.

The Old Babylonian laws also reflect a more extensive development of business than that which existed in the preceding culture. That an influential merchant class traded for profit and enjoyed a privileged position in society is evidenced by the fact that the commercial provisions of Hammurabi's code were based upon the principle of "Let the buyer beware." The Babylonian rulers did not believe in a regime of free competition, however. Trade and industry were subject to elaborate regulation by the state. There were laws regarding partnership, storage, and agency; laws respecting deeds, wills, and the taking of in-

Gold Jewelry from Ur, c. 3500–2800 B.C.

terest on money; and a host of others. For a deal to be negotiated without a written contract or without witnesses was punishable by death. Agriculture, which was still the occupation of a majority of the citizens, did not escape regulation. The code provided penalties for failure to cultivate a field and for neglect of dikes and canals. Both government ownership and private tenure of land were permitted; but, regardless of the status of the owner, the tenant farmer was required to pay two-thirds of all he produced as rent.

Religion under the Old Babylonians underwent only superficial changes. Deities that had been venerated by the Sumerians were now neglected and new ones exalted in their stead. Above all, a new god, Marduk, was imported to head the Mesopotamian pantheon. He and the other new deities carried no spiritual significance, however, conveying no promise of resurrection from the dead or of personal immortality. The Old Babylonians were no more otherworldly in their outlook than the Sumerians. The religions of both peoples were fundamentally materialistic.

Although there was some decline in artistic accomplishments during the period of Babylonian rule, this was by no means true of developments in literature. Building upon legends and myths already evolving under the Sumerians, the Babylonians contributed to world literature one of the greatest epics of all time, the epic of *Gilgamesh.* This long poem, comparable in sweep and power to the Greek *Iliad* and *Odyssey,* is a compilation of stories that were told and re-told over many generations. Its hero, Gilgamesh, is a Mesopotamian king who experiences many adventures. In one he seeks the secret of immortality from an old man and his wife who had been saved when the gods had decided to destroy the world by a flood. Many of the elements of this story are strikingly similar to the Old Testament story of Noah,

Scenes from the Epic of Gilgamash. A Sumerian inlaid shell panel.

Panel of Glazed Brick, Babylon, Sixth Century B.C. An ornamental relief on a background of earth brown. The lion is in blue, white, and yellow glazes.

including the details that the couple had survived the flood by floating
in an ark. But the message is rather different, for the Babylonian hero
learns only resignation from the old couple: the gods will preserve
those whom they please and there is nothing mankind can do to understand divine decisions. Gilgamesh does learn from the old pair of a
plant that will at least bring back his youth, but after gaining it with
great effort from the floor of the sea he leaves it unguarded while
asleep, and a snake eats it instead. According to the epic, this is why
snakes gain new life every year when they shed their skins. But the
human hero is finally forced to recognize that he himself can never
transcend old age and death. As the epic states in resigned summary:
"When the gods created man, they let death be his share, and life they
kept in their own hands."

Babylonian literature

4. THE METAMORPHOSIS UNDER ASSYRIA

Of all the peoples of the Mesopotamian area after the time of the
Sumerians, the Assyrians went through the most completely independent evolution. For several centuries they had lived a comparatively
isolated existence on top of their small plateau in the upper valley of
the Tigris. Eventually they came under the influence of the Babylonians, but not until after the course of their own history had been partially fixed. As a consequence, the period of Assyrian supremacy
(from about 1300 B.C. to 612 B.C.) had a more peculiar character than
any other era of Mesopotamian history.

*The evolution of Assyrian
supremacy*

The Assyrians were preeminently a nation of warriors because of
the special conditions of their own environment. The limited resources of their original home and the constant danger of attack from
hostile nations around them forced the development of warlike habits
and imperial ambitions. It is therefore not strange that their hunger for
territory should have known no limits. The more they conquered, the
more they felt they had to conquer, in order to protect what they had
already gained. Every success excited ambition and riveted the chains
of militarism more firmly than ever. Disaster was inevitable.

A nation of warriors

The exigencies of war determined the whole character of the Assyrian system. The state was a great military machine. The army commanders were at once the richest and the most powerful class in the
country. Not only did they share in the plunder of war, but they were
frequently granted huge estates as rewards for victory. At least one of
them, Sargon II, dared to usurp the throne. The military establishment itself represented the last word in preparedness. The standing
army greatly exceeded in size that of any other nation of the Near
East. New and improved armaments and techniques of fighting gave
to the Assyrian soldiers unparalleled advantages. Iron swords, heavy
bows, long lances, battering rams, fortresses on wheels, and metal
breastplates, shields, and helmets were only a few examples of their
superior equipment.

*Features of Assyrian
militarism*

Assyrian Winged Human-Headed Bull. This relief was found in the palace of King Sargon II (722–705 B.C.). It measures 16 feet wide by 16 feet high and weighs approximately 40 tons.

Frightfulness

But swords and spears and engines of war were not their only instruments of combat. As much as anything else the Assyrians depended upon frightfulness as a means of overcoming their enemies. Upon soldiers captured in battle, and sometimes upon noncombatants as well, they inflicted unspeakable cruelties—skinning them alive, impaling them on stakes, cutting off ears, noses, and sex organs, and then exhibiting the mutilated victims in cages for the benefit of cities that had not yet surrendered. Accounts of these cruelties are not taken from atrocity stories circulated by their enemies; they come from the records of the Assyrians themselves. Their chroniclers boasted of them as evidences of valor, and the people believed in them as guaranties of security and power. It is clear why the Assyrians were the most hated of all the nations of antiquity.

The tragedy of Assyrian militarism

Seldom has the decline of an empire been so complete as was that of Assyria. In spite of its magnificent armaments and its wholesale destruction of its foes, Assyria's period of imperial splendor lasted little more than a century. Nation after nation conspired against the Assyrians and finally accomplished their downfall. Their enemies took frightful vengeance. The whole land was so thoroughly sacked and the people so completely enslaved or exterminated that it has been difficult to trace any subsequent Assyrian influence upon history. The power and security which military strength was supposed to provide proved a mockery in the end. If Assyria had been utterly defenseless, its fate could hardly have been worse.

With so complete an absorption in military pursuits, it was inevitable that the Assyrians should have neglected in some measure the arts of peace. Industry and commerce appear to have declined under the regime of the Assyrians, for such pursuits were generally scorned as beneath the dignity of a soldierly people. The minimum of manufacturing and trade which had to be carried on was left quite largely to the Arameans, a people closely related to the Phoenicians and the Hebrews. The Assyrians themselves preferred to derive their living from agriculture. The land system included both public and private holdings. The temples held the largest share of the landed wealth. Although the estates of the crown were likewise extensive, they were constantly being diminished by grants to army officers.

An Assyrian King of the Ninth Century B.C.

Neither the economic nor the social order was sound. The frequent military campaigns depleted the energies and resources of the nation. In the course of time the army officers became a pampered aristocracy, delegating their duties to their subordinates and devoting themselves to luxurious pleasures. The stabilizing influence of a prosperous and intelligent merchant class was precluded by the rule that only foreigners and slaves could engage in commercial activities. Yet more serious was the treatment accorded to the lower classes, the serfs and the slaves. The former comprised the bulk of the rural population. Some of them cultivated definite portions of their master's estates and retained a part of what they produced for themselves. Others were "empty" men, without even a plot to cultivate and dependent on the need for seasonal labor to provide for their means of subsistence. All were extremely poor and were subject to the additional hardships of labor on public works and compulsory military service. The slaves, who were chiefly an urban working class, were of two different types: the domestic slaves, who performed household duties and sometimes engaged in business for their masters; and the war captives. The former were not numerous and were allowed a great deal of freedom, even to the extent of owning property. The latter suffered much greater miseries. Bound by heavy shackles, they were compelled to labor to the point of exhaustion in building roads, canals, and palaces.

*Defects in the economic
system*

Whether the Assyrians adopted the law of the Old Babylonians has never been settled. Undoubtedly they were influenced by it, but several of the features of Hammurabi's code are entirely absent. Notable among these are the *lex talionis* and the system of gradation of penalties according to the rank of the victim and the offender. Whereas the Babylonians prescribed the most drastic punishments for crimes suggestive of treason or sedition, the Assyrians reserved theirs for such offenses as abortion and homosexuality, probably for the military reason of preventing a decline in the birth rate. Another contrast is the more complete subjection of Assyrian women. Wives were treated as chattels of their husbands, polygamy was permitted, and the right of divorce was placed entirely in the hands of the male.

Assyrian law

That a military nation like the Assyrians should not have taken first rank in intellectual achievement is easily understandable. The atmo-

Scientific achievements

sphere of a military campaign is not favorable to reflection or disinterested research. Yet the demands of successful campaigning may lead to a certain accumulation of knowledge, for practical problems have to be solved. Under such circumstances the Assyrians accomplished some measure of scientific progress. They appear to have divided the circle into 360 degrees and to have estimated locations on the surface of the earth in something resembling latitude and longitude. They recognized and named five planets and achieved some success in predicting eclipses. Since the health of armies is important, medicine received considerable attention. More than five hundred drugs, both vegetable and mineral, were catalogued and their uses indicated. Symptoms of various diseases were described and were generally interpreted as due to natural causes, although incantations and the prescription of disgusting compounds to drive out demons were still commonly employed as methods of treatment.

The excellence of Assyrian art

See color plates following page 64

In the domain of art the Assyrians surpassed the Old Babylonians and at least equaled the work of the Sumerians, although in different form. Sculpture was the art most highly developed, particularly in the low reliefs. These portrayed dramatic incidents of war and the hunt with the utmost fidelity to nature and a vivid description of movement. The Assyrians delighted in depicting the cool bravery of the hunter in the face of terrific danger, the ferocity of lions at bay, and the death agonies of wounded beasts. Unfortunately this art was limited almost entirely to the two themes of war and sport. Its purpose was to glorify the exploits of the ruling class. Architecture ranked second to sculpture from the standpoint of artistic excellence. Assyrian palaces and temples were built of stone, obtained from the mountainous areas of the north, instead of the mud brick of former times. Their principal features were the arch and the dome. The column was also used but never very successfully. The chief demerit of this architecture was its hugeness, which the Assyrians appeared to regard as synonymous with beauty.

Assyrian Relief Sculpture. This panel depicts the Emperor Assurbanipal (668–626 B.C.) hunting lions.

5. THE CHALDEAN RENASCENCE

The Mesopotamian civilization entered its final stage with the overthrow of Assyria and the establishment of Chaldean supremacy. This stage is often called the Neo-Babylonian, because Nebuchadnezzar and his followers restored the capital at Babylon and attempted to revive the culture of Hammurabi's time. As might have been expected, their attempt was not wholly successful. The Assyrian metamorphosis had altered that culture in various profound and ineffaceable ways. Besides, the Chaldeans themselves had a history of their own which they could not entirely escape. Nevertheless, they did manage to revive certain of the old institutions and ideals. They restored the ancient law and literature, the essentials of the Old Babylonian form of government, and the economic system of earlier times with its dominance of industry and trade. Farther than this they were unable to go.

The Chaldean or final stage in Mesopotamian civilization

It was in religion that the failure of the Chaldean renascence was most conspicuous. Although Marduk was restored to his traditional place at the head of the pantheon, the system of belief was little more than superficially Babylonian. What the Chaldeans really did was to develop an astral religion. The gods were divested of their human qualities and exalted into transcendent, omnipotent beings. They were actually identified with the planets themselves. Though still not entirely aloof from humans, they certainly lost their character as beings who could be cajoled and threatened and coerced by magic. They ruled the universe almost mechanically. While their immediate intentions were sometimes discernible, their ultimate purposes were inscrutable.

The astral religion of the Chaldeans

Two significant results flowed from these conceptions. The first was an even greater attitude of fatalism than before. Since the ways of the gods were past comprehension, all that humans could do was to resign themselves to their fate. It behooved them therefore to submit absolutely to the gods, to trust in them implicitly, in the vague hope that the results in the end would be good. Thus arose for the first time in history the concept of piety as submission—a concept which was adopted in several other religions, as we shall see in succeeding chapters. For the Chaldeans it implied no otherwordly significance; one did not resign oneself to calamities in this life in order to be justified in the next. The Chaldeans had no interest in a life to come. Submission might bring certain earthly rewards, but in the main, as they conceived it, it was not a means to an end at all. It was rather the expression of an attitude of despair, of humility in the face of mysteries that could not be fathomed.

The growth of fatalism

The second great result which came from the growth of an astral religion was the development of a stronger spiritual consciousness.

This is revealed in the penitential hymns of unknown authors and in the prayers which were ascribed to Nebuchadnezzar and other kings as the spokesmen for the nation. In most of them the gods are addressed as exalted beings who are concerned with justice and righteous conduct on the part of humanity, although the distinction between ceremonial and genuine morality is not always sharply drawn. It has been asserted by one scholar that these hymns could have been used by the Hebrews with little modification except for the substitution of the name of Yahweh for that of the Chaldean god.

With the gods promoted to so lofty a plane, it was perhaps inevitable that human beings should have been abased. Mortal creatures could not be compared with the timeless beings who dwelt in the heavens and guided the destinies of the earth. Humans were lowly creatures, sunk in iniquity and vileness, and hardly worthy of approaching the gods. The consciousness of sin already present in the Babylonian and Assyrian religions now reached a stage of almost pathological intensity. Chaldean hymns compare people to prisoners, bound hand and foot, languishing in darkness, whose transgressions are "seven times seven." Their misery is increased by the fact that their evil nature has prompted them to sin unwittingly. Never before had humans been regarded as so hopelessly depraved.

Curiously enough, the pessimism of the Chaldeans does not appear to have affected their morality very much. So far as the evidence reveals, they indulged in no rigors of asceticism. Apparently they took it for granted that humans could not avoid sinning, no matter how hard they tried. They seem to have been just as deeply committed to enjoying creature comforts as any of the earlier nations. Occasional references were made in their hymns to reverence, kindness, and purity of heart as virtues, and to oppression, slander, and anger as vices, but these were intermingled with ritualistic conceptions of cleanness and uncleanness and with expressions of desire for physical satisfactions. When the Chaldeans prayed, it was not always that their gods would make them good, but more often that they would grant long life, abundant offspring, and material well-being.

Aside from religion, the Chaldean culture differed from that of the Sumerians, Babylonians, and Assyrians chiefly in regard to astronomical achievements. Without doubt the Chaldeans were the most capable astronomers in all of Mesopotamian history. They worked out the most elaborate system for recording the passage of time that had yet been devised, with their invention of the seven-day week and their division of the day into twelve double-hours of 120 minutes each. They kept accurate records of eclipses and other celestial occurrences for more than 350 years—until long after the downfall of their empire. The motivating force behind Chaldean astronomy was religion. The chief purpose of mapping the heavens and collecting celestial data was to discover the future the gods had prepared for mankind. Since the planets were gods themselves, that future could best be divined in the movements of the heavenly bodies. Astronomy was therefore primarily astrology.

Aside from astronomy, Chaldean culture showed little advance beyond the stage it had reached under the Assyrians. Art differed only in its greater magnificence. Literature, dominated by the antiquarian spirit, revealed a lack of originality. The writings of the Old Babylonians were extensively copied and reedited, but they were supplemented by little that was new.

Other aspects of Chaldean culture

6. THE PERSIAN EMPIRE AND ITS HISTORY

Comparatively little is known of the Persians before the sixth century B.C. Up to that time they appear to have led an obscure and peaceful existence on the eastern shore of the Persian Gulf. They were not Semites but spoke an Indo-European language, that is, one of a group that includes Sanskrit (the language of ancient India), Greek, Latin, and most of the modern European tongues. Their homeland afforded only modest advantages. On the east it was hemmed in by mountains, and its coastline lacked harbors. The fertile valleys of the interior, however, were capable of providing adequate subsistence for a limited population. Save for the development of an elaborate religion, the people had made little progress. At the dawn of their history they were not independent but were vassals of the Medes, a kindred people who ruled over a territory north and east of the Tigris.

The Persian background

In 559 B.C. a prince by the name of Cyrus became king of a southern Persian tribe. About five years later he made himself ruler of all the Persians, overthrew the domination of the Medes, and then began to conquer neighboring areas. As Cyrus the Great he has gone down in history as one of the most sensational conquerors of all time. Within the short space of twenty years he founded a vast empire, larger than any that had previously existed.

The rise of Cyrus

The first of the conquests of Cyrus was the kingdom of Lydia, which occupied the western half of Asia Minor and was separated from the lands of the Medes by the River Halys, in what is now northern Turkey. Perceiving the ambitions of the Persians, Croesus, the fabulously rich Lydian king, decided to wage a preventive war to preserve his own nation from conquest. According to the Greek historian Herodotus, Croesus consulted the oracle at Delphi as to the advisability of an immediate attack and gained the reply that if he would cross the Halys and assume the offensive he would destroy a great nation. He did, but that nation was his own. His forces were completely overwhelmed, and his prosperous realm was annexed as a province of the Persian state. Seven years later, in 539 B.C., Cyrus took advantage of discontent and conspiracies in the Chaldean Empire to capture the city of Babylon. His victory was easy, for he had the assistance of the Jews within the city and of the Chaldean priests, who were dissatisfied

The conquests of Cyrus

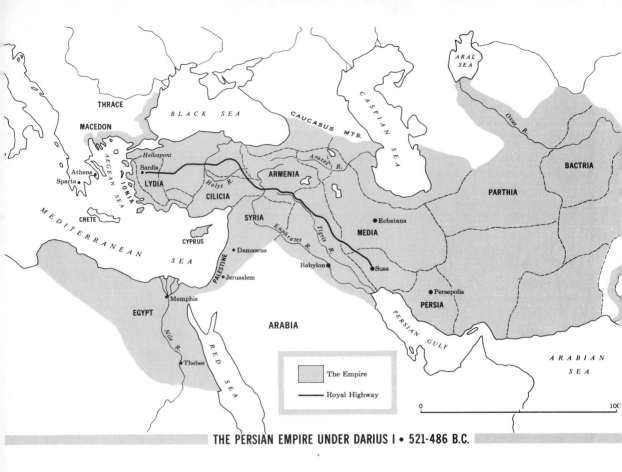

THE PERSIAN EMPIRE UNDER DARIUS I • 521-486 B.C.

with the policies of their king. The conquest of Babylon thereupon enabled Cyrus to gain control over the whole Chaldean Empire.

The successors of Cyrus

Cyrus the Great died in 529 B.C., as the result of wounds received in a war with barbarian tribes. Soon afterward a succession of troubles overtook the state he had founded. Like so many other empire-builders both before and since, he had devoted too much energy to conquest and not enough to internal development. He was succeeded by his son Cambyses, who conquered Egypt in 525 B.C. During the new king's absence revolt spread throughout his Asiatic possessions. Chaldeans and Medes strove to regain their independence. The chief minister of the realm, abetted by the priests, organized a movement to gain the throne for a pretender who was one of their puppets. Upon learning of conditions at home, Cambyses set out from Egypt with his most dependable troops, but he was murdered on the way. The most serious of the revolts was finally crushed by Darius, a powerful noble, who killed the pretender and seized the throne for himself.

Darius the Great

Darius I, or the Great, as he is often called, ruled the empire from 522 to 486 B.C. The early years of his reign were occupied in suppressing the revolts of subject peoples and in improving the administrative organization of the state. He completed the division of the empire into satrapies, or provinces, and fixed the annual tribute due from each province. He standardized the currency and weights and measures. He repaired and completed a primitive canal from the Nile to the Red Sea. He followed the example of Cyrus in tolerating and protecting the institutions of subject peoples. Not only did he restore ancient temples and foster local cults, but he ordered his satrap of Egypt to codify the Egyptian laws in consultation with the native priests. But in some of his military exploits Darius overreached himself. In order to check the incursions of the Scythians, who lived on the European shore of the Black Sea, he crossed the Hellespont and conquered a large part of the Thracian coast. In addition, he increased the oppression of the Greeks on the shore of Asia Minor, who had fallen under Persian domination with the conquest of Lydia. He collected heavier tribute from them, and forced them to serve in his armies. The immediate result was a revolt of the Greek cities with the assistance of Athens. And when Darius attempted to punish the Athenians for their part in the rebellion, he found that they offered stiff resistance.

Darius the Great died before the war with Athens and allied Greek cities had come to an end. The struggle was prosecuted vigorously but unsuccessfully by his successor, Xerxes I. By 479 B.C. the Persians *The end of the Persian* had been driven from all of Greece. Though they continued to hold *Empire* sway as a major power in Asia, their attempt to extend their dominion into Europe was thwarted. The last century and a half of the empire's existence was marked by frequent assassinations, revolts of provincial governors, and barbarian invasions, until finally, in 330 B.C., its independence was terminated by the armies of Alexander the Great.

Although the Persian government had its defects, it was certainly superior to most of the others that had existed in the Near East. The Persian rulers did not imitate the terrorism of the Assyrians. They *Persian government* levied tribute upon conquered peoples, but they generally allowed them to keep their own customs, religions, and laws. Indeed, the chief accomplishment of the Persian Empire lay in the fact that it achieved a synthesis of Near Eastern cultures, including those of Persia itself, Mesopotamia, Asia Minor, the Syria-Palestine coast, and Egypt.

The Persian rulers built excellent roads to help hold their empire together. Most famous was the Royal Road, some 1,600 miles in length. It extended from Susa near the Persian Gulf to Sardis near the *Persian roadways* western coast of Asia Minor. So well kept was this highway that royal messengers, traveling day and night, could cover all its length in less than a week. Other roads linked the various provinces with one or another of the four leading Persian cities: Susa, Persepolis, Babylon, and Ecbatana. Although they naturally contributed to ease of trade, the highways were built primarily to facilitate governmental control over the outlying sections of the empire.

7. PERSIAN CULTURE

The culture of the Persians, in the narrower sense of intellectual and artistic achievements, was largely derived from that of previous civili-

*The eclectic culture of
Persia*

*The eclectic character of
Persian architecture*

zations. Much of it came from Mesopotamia, but a great deal of it from Egypt, and some from Lydia and northern Palestine. Their system of writing was originally the cuneiform, but in time they devised an alphabet of thirty-nine letters, based upon the alphabet of the Arameans who traded within their borders. In science they accomplished nothing, except to adopt with some slight modifications the solar calendar of the Egyptians and to encourage exploration as an aid to commerce. They deserve credit also for diffusing a knowledge of the Lydian coinage throughout many parts of western Asia.

It was the architecture of the Persians which gave the most positive expression of the eclectic character of their culture. They copied the raised platform and the terraced building style that had been standard in Babylonia and Assyria. They imitated also the winged bulls, the brilliantly colored glazed bricks, and other decorative motifs of Mesopotamian architecture. But at least two of the leading features of Mesopotamian construction were not used by the Persians—the arch and the vault. In place of them they adopted the column and the colonnade from Egypt. In addition, interior arrangement and the use of palm and lotus designs at the base of columns also came from Egyptian influence. On the other hand, the fluting of the columns and the volutes or scrolls beneath the capitals were not Egyptian but Greek, adopted not from the mainland of Greece itself but from the Ionian cities of Asia Minor. If there was anything unique about Persian architecture, it was the fact that it was purely secular. The great Persian structures were not temples but palaces. They served to glorify not gods, but the "King of Kings." The most famous were the magnificent residences of Darius and Xerxes at Persepolis. The latter, built in imitation of the temple at Karnak, had an enormous central audience-hall containing a hundred columns and surrounded by innumerable

The Great Palace of Darius and Xerxes at Persepolis. Persian architecture made use of fluted columns, copied from the Greeks, and reliefs resembling those of the Assyrians.

Silver Figurine of a Kneeling Bull Holding a Vessel. Elamite, c. 3000 B.C.

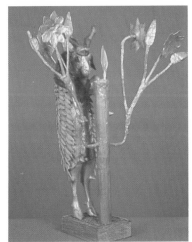

Gold, Silver, Shell, and Lapis Lazuli Statuette of a Ram in a Thicket. Sumerian, 2500 B.C.

Gold and Lapis Lazuli Lyre with Bull's Head. Sumerian, c. 2500 B.C.

Stone Head of Ur-Ningirsu, Son of Gudea of Lagash. Sumerian, c. 2100 B.C.

Gold Plaque with Animals and Stylized Trees in Relief. Persian, VII cent. B.C.

Bronze Bull, Symbol of Strength. Arabian, VI cent. B.C.

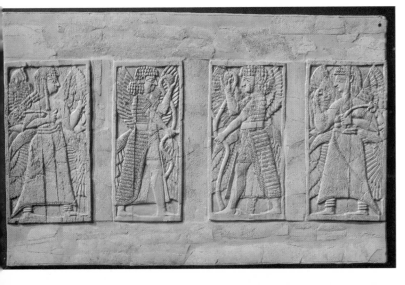

Ivory Screen of Four Winged Figures. Assyrian, VIII cent. B.C.

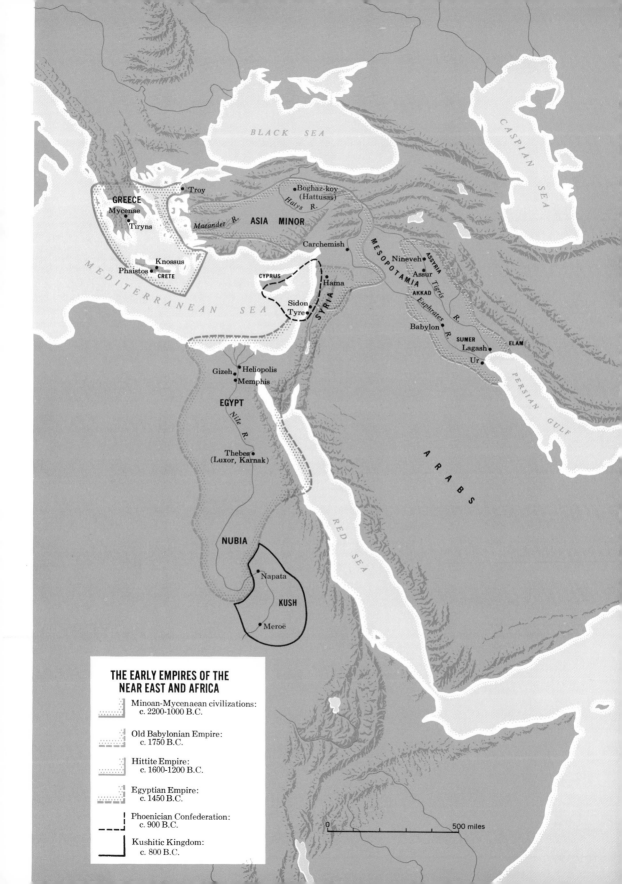

BLACK SEA

CASPIAN SEA

GREECE
Mycenae
Tiryns
Troy

Boghaz-koy
(Hattusas)
Halys R.

ASIA MINOR
Maeander R.

Carchemish

MESOPOTAMIA

Nineveh • *ASSYRIA*
Assur
Tigris R.

MEDITERRANEAN SEA

Knossus
Phaistos
CRETE

CYPRUS

Hama

SYRIA

Sidon
Tyre

Euphrates R.

AKKAD

Babylon

SUMER
Lagash

ELAM

Ur

PERSIAN GULF

Gizeh • Heliopolis
Memphis

EGYPT

Nile R.

A R A B S

Thebes
(Luxor, Karnak)

RED SEA

NUBIA

Napata

KUSH

Meroë

THE EARLY EMPIRES OF THE
NEAR EAST AND AFRICA

Minoan-Mycenaean civilizations:
c. 2200-1000 B.C.

Old Babylonian Empire:
c. 1750 B.C.

Hittite Empire:
c. 1600-1200 B.C.

Egyptian Empire:
c. 1450 B.C.

Phoenician Confederation:
c. 900 B.C.

Kushitic Kingdom:
c. 800 B.C.

0   500 miles

Two Reliefs from the Staircase of the Great Palace at Persepolis

rooms which served as offices and as quarters for the eunuchs and members of the royal harem.

8. THE ZOROASTRIAN RELIGION

By far the most enduring influence left by the ancient Persians was that of their religion. Their system of faith was of ancient origin. It was already highly developed when they began their conquests. So strong was its appeal, and so ripe were the conditions for its acceptance, that it spread through most of western Asia. Its doctrines turned other religions inside out, displacing beliefs which had been held for ages.

The religion of the Persians

Although the roots of this religion can be traced as far back as the fifteenth century B.C., its real founder was Zoroaster (the Greek form of the Persian name Zarathustra), who appears to have lived shortly before 600 B.C. From him the religion derives its name of Zoroastrianism. Zoroaster was probably the first real theologian in history, the first known person to devise a completely developed system of religious belief. He seems to have conceived it as his mission to purify the traditional customs of his people—to eradicate polytheism, animal sacrifice, and magic—and to establish their worship on a more spiritual and ethical plane. But in spite of his reforming efforts many of the old superstitions survived and were gradually fused with the new ideals.

The founding of Zoroastrianism

Zoroastrianism had a character unique among the religions of the world up to that time. It was dualistic—not monistic like the Sumerian and Babylonian religions, in which the same gods were capa-

Characteristics of Zoroastrianism: (1) dualism

ble of both good and evil; but it did not go as far in the direction of monotheism as did the religion of the Hebrews. According to Zoroaster, two spiritual principles ruled the universe: one, Ahura-Mazda, supremely good, embodied the principles of light, truth, and righteousness; the other, Ahriman, treacherous and malignant, presided over the forces of darkness and evil. The two were engaged in a desperate struggle for supremacy. Although they were about evenly matched in strength, the god of light would eventually triumph. On the last great day Ahura-Mazda would overpower Ahriman and cast him down into the abyss. The dead would then be raised from their graves to be judged according to their deserts. The righteous would enter into immediate bliss, while the wicked would be sentenced to the flames of hell. Ultimately, though, all would be saved; for the Persian hell, unlike the Christian, did not last forever.

(2) an ethical religion

The Zoroastrian religion was definitely an ethical one. Although it contained suggestions of predestination, of the election of some from all eternity to be saved, in the main it rested upon the assumption that humans possessed free will, that they were free to sin or not to sin, and that they would be rewarded or punished in the afterlife in accordance with their conduct on earth. Ahura-Mazda commanded that people should be truthful, that they should love and help one another to the best of their power, that they should befriend the poor and practice hospitality. The essence of these broader virtues was perhaps expressed in another of the god's decrees: "Whosoever shall give meat to one of the faithful . . . he shall go to Paradise." The forms of conduct forbidden were sufficiently numerous and varied to cover the whole list of sins of medieval Christianity and a great many more. Pride, gluttony, sloth, covetousness, wrathfulness, lust, adultery, abortion, slander, and waste were among the more typical. The taking of interest on loans to others of the same faith was described as the "worst of sins," and the accumulation of riches was condemned. The restraints which believers were to practice included also a kind of negative Golden Rule: "That nature alone is good which shall not do unto another whatever is not good for its own self."

9. THE MYSTICAL AND OTHERWORLDLY HERITAGE FROM PERSIA

The religion of the Persians as taught by Zoroaster did not long continue in its original state. It was corrupted, first of all, by the persistence of primitive superstitions, of magic and priestcraft. The farther the religion spread, the more of these relics of barbarism were engrafted upon it. As the years passed, additional modification resulted from the influence of alien faiths, particularly that of the Chaldeans. The outcome was the growth of a powerful synthesis in which the dualism of the Persians was combined with the pessimism and fatalism of the Chaldeans.

Out of this debased Zoroastrianism gradually emerged a profusion of cults, alike in their basic dogmas but according them different emphases. The oldest was Mithraism, deriving its name from Mithras, a lieutenant of Ahura-Mazda in the struggle against the powers of evil. At first only a minor deity in the religion of Zoroastrianism, Mithras finally won recognition by many of the Persians as the god most deserving of worship. The reason for this change was probably the emotional appeal made by the incidents of his career. He was believed to have lived an earthly existence involving great suffering and sacrifice. He performed miracles giving bread and wine to man and ending a drought and also a disastrous flood. Finally, he created much of the ritual of Zoroastrianism, proclaiming Sunday as the most sacred day of the week and the twenty-fifth of December as the most sacred day of the year. Since the sun was the giver of light and the faithful ally of Mithras, his day was naturally the most sacred. The twenty-fifth of December also possessed its solar significance: as the approximate date of the winter solstice it marked the return of the sun from its long journey south of the Equator. It was in a sense the "birthday" of the sun, since it connoted the revival of its life-giving powers for the benefit of humanity.

Exactly when Mithraism became an independent cult is unknown, but it was certainly not later than the fourth century B.C. Its spread thereafter was rapid. In the last century B.C. it was introduced into Rome, although it was of little importance in Italy itself until after 100 A.D. It drew its converts especially from the lower classes, from the ranks of soldiers, foreigners, and slaves. Ultimately it rose to the status of one of the most popular religions of the empire, the chief competitor of Christianity and of old Roman paganism. After 275, however, its strength rapidly waned. How much influence Mithraism exerted is impossible to say. Its superficial resemblance to Christianity is obvious, but this does not mean, of course, that the two were identical, or that one was an offshoot of the other. Nevertheless, it is probably true that Christianity as the younger of the two rivals borrowed some of its externals from Mithraism, at the same time preserving its own philosophy essentially untouched.

One of the principal successors of Mithraism in transmitting the legacy from Persia was Manicheism, founded around 250 A.D. by Mani, a high-born priest of Ecbatana. Like Zoroaster he became dedicated to reforming the prevailing religion, but he received scant sympathy in his own country and had to be content with missionary ventures in India and western China. About 276 A.D. he was condemned and executed by his Persian opponents. Following his death his teachings were carried by his disciples into practically every country of western Asia and finally into Italy about 330 A.D.

Of all the Zoroastrian teachings, the one that made the deepest impression upon the mind of Mani was dualism. But Mani gave to this doctrine a broader interpretation than it had ever received in the earlier religion. He conceived not merely of two deities engaged in a relentless struggle for supremacy, but of a whole universe divided into two kingdoms, each the antithesis of the other. The first was the kingdom of spirit ruled over by a God eternally good. The second was the kingdom of matter under the dominion of Satan. Only "spiritual" substances such as fire, light, and the souls of human beings were created by God. Darkness, sin, desire, and all things bodily and material owed their origin to Satan.

The moral implications of dualism

The moral implications of this rigorous dualism were profound. Since everything connected with sensation or desire was the work of Satan, humanity should strive to free itself as completely as possible from enslavement to physical needs. Humans should refrain from all forms of sensual enjoyment, the eating of meat, the drinking of wine, the gratification of sexual desire. Even marriage was prohibited, for this would result in the begetting of more physical bodies to people the kingdom of Satan. In addition, humans should subdue the flesh by prolonged fasting and infliction of pain. Recognizing that this program of austerities would be too difficult for ordinary mortals, Mani divided the human race into the "perfect" and the "hearers." Only the former would be obliged to adhere to the full program as the ideal of what all should hope to attain. To aid humanity in its struggle against the powers of darkness, God had sent prophets and redeemers from time to time to give comfort and inspiration. Noah, Abraham, Zoroaster, Jesus, and Paul were among these divine emissaries; but the last and greatest of them was Mani. Since Mani called himself "the apostle of Jesus Christ," many Manicheans in the West, including the great St. Augustine during his early career, considered themselves to be radical Christians. The faith had many followers in the Roman Empire around 400, but it died out thereafter as a result of persecution.

Gnosticism

The third most important cult which developed as an element in the Persian heritage was Gnosticism (from the Greek *gnosis,* meaning knowledge). It had no single founder but evolved out of Persian and Greek religious ideas and came to full fruition around the first century A.D., reaching the height of its popularity in the latter half of the second century. Although it gained some followers in Italy, it flourished primarily in the Near East. The feature which most sharply distinguished Gnosticism from the other cults was mysticism. The Gnostics denied that religious truths could be discovered by reason or could even be made intelligible. They regarded themselves as the exclusive possessors of a secret spiritual knowledge revealed to them directly by God. This knowledge was alone important as a guide to faith and conduct.

The combined influence of these several Persian-derived religions was enormous. Most of them were launched at a time when political and social conditions were particularly conducive to their spread. The breakup of Alexander the Great's empire about 300 B.C. inaugurated a peculiar period in the history of the ancient world. International barriers were broken down; there was an extensive migration and intermingling of peoples; and the collapse of the old social order gave rise to disillusionment with life on earth and a yearning for individual salvation. People's attentions were centered as never before upon compensations in a life to come. Under such circumstances religions of the kind described were bound to thrive. Otherworldly and mystical, they offered the very escape that people were seeking from a world of anxiety and confusion.

The combined influence of the several offshoots of Zoroastrianism

Although not exclusively religious, the heritage left by the Persians contained few elements of a secular nature. Their form of government was adopted by the later Roman monarchs, not in its purely political aspect, but in its character of a divine-right despotism. When such emperors as Diocletian and Constantine I invoked divine authority as a basis for their absolutism and required their subjects to prostrate themselves in their presence, they were really following patterns laid down by the Persians. At the same time the Romans were impressed by the Persian idea of a world empire. Darius and his successors conceived of themselves as the rulers of the whole civilized world, with a mission to reduce it to unity and, under Ahura-Mazda, to govern it justly. For this reason they generally conducted their wars with a minimum of savagery and treated conquered peoples humanely. Their ideal was a kind of prototype of the Roman peace. Traces of Persian influence upon certain Hellenistic philosophies are also discernible; but here again it was essentially religious, for it was confined almost entirely to spiritual and mystical theories.

Persian legacy

SELECTED READINGS

- *Items so designated are available in paperback editions.*
- Chiera, Edward, *They Wrote on Clay*, Chicago, 1956. An engrossing account of the discovery and decipherment of cuneiform tablets.
- Contenau, G., *Everyday Life in Babylonia and Assyria*, New York, 1954. Based on archeological evidence and well illustrated.
- Frankfort, H., *The Art and Architecture of the Ancient Orient*, rev. ed., Baltimore, 1971.
  ———, *The Birth of Civilization in the Near East*, Bloomington, Ind., 1951. Brief but useful.
  ———, et al., *The Intellectual Adventure of Ancient Man*, Chicago, 1946. Essays by leading experts on ancient myths; see that by T. Jakobsen on Mesopotamia.
  Frye, R. N., *The Heritage of Persia*, New York, 1963. A fascinating history of Persia from earliest times to the triumph of Islam in the seventh century A.D.
- Ghirshman, R., *Iran*, Baltimore, 1954.
- Hallo, W. W., and W. K. Simpson, *The Ancient Near East: A History*, New York, 1971. An authoritative survey.
  Kramer, S. N., *History Begins at Sumer*, New York, 1959.

• ———, *Sumerian Mythology*, New York, 1961. Develops different point of view about early myth than that found in Frankfort et al., *Intellectual Adventure*.

• ———, *The Sumerians: Their History, Culture, and Character*, Chicago, 1963. Best general treatment of Sumerian civilization.

Lloyd, Seton, *Foundations in the Dust*, Baltimore, 1955. Describes the development and accomplishments of Mesopotamian archeology.

Moscati, S., *The Face of the Ancient Orient*, New York, 1962. Deals with Assyrians and Chaldeans.

Neugebauer, Otto, *The Exact Sciences in Antiquity*, Princeton, N.J., 1952. Excellent on Mesopotamian mathematical accomplishments.

• Olmstead, A. T., *History of the Persian Empire*, Chicago, 1948. Detailed but somewhat uncritical.

• Oppenheim, A. Leo, *Ancient Mesopotamia*, Chicago, 1964. Concentrates on Babylonian and Assyrian culture.

• Roux, G., *Ancient Iraq*, London, 1964.

Russell, Jeffrey B., *The Devil: Perceptions of Evil from Antiquity to Primitive Christianity*, Ithaca, N.Y., 1977. Particularly strong on the religious revolution accomplished by Zoroaster.

• Saggs, H. W. F., *The Greatness That Was Babylon*, London, 1962.

Widengren, G., *Mani and Manicheism*, London, 1965.

• Woolley, C. L., *The Sumerians*, New York, 1928. A pioneer work, brief and interestingly written.

Zaehner, R. C., *The Dawn and Twilight of Zoroastrianism*, New York, 1961. The standard treatment.

SOURCE MATERIALS

• *Epic of Gilgamesh*, tr. N. Sandars, Baltimore, 1960.

Grayson, A. K., and D. B. Redford, *Papyrus and Tablet*, Englewood Cliffs, N.J., 1973.

Herodotus, *The Persian Wars*, tr. A. de Sélincourt, Baltimore, 1954.

Luckenbill, D. D., *Ancient Records of Assyria and Babylonia*, Chicago, 1926, 2 vols.

Pritchard, James B., *Ancient Near Eastern Texts Relating to the Old Testament*, rev. ed., Princeton, N.J., 1969.

Chapter 4

THE HEBREW CIVILIZATION

I am the Lord thy God, which brought thee out of the land of Egypt from
  the house of bondage.
Thou shalt have none other gods before me.
Thou shalt not make thee any graven image, or any likeness of any thing
  that is in heaven above, or that is in the earth beneath, or that is in the
  waters beneath the earth . . .
Thou shalt not take the name of the Lord thy God in vain.

—Deuteronomy 5:6–11

Of all the peoples of the ancient Near East, none has been of greater importance to the modern world than the Hebrews. It was the Hebrews, of course, who provided much of the background of the Christian religion—its view of the Creation, its Commandments, its concept of a single, transcendent God as lawgiver and judge, and more than two-thirds of its Bible. Hebrew conceptions of morality and political theory have also profoundly influenced modern nations. For these reasons we tend today to think of the Hebrew accomplishment as unique, and there is much truth in that assumption. But although Hebrew culture gradually came to differ greatly from that of neighboring Egypt and Mesopotamia it is necessary to remember that the Hebrews did not develop their culture in a vacuum. No more than any other people were they able to escape the influence of nations around them.

Importance of the Hebrew civilization

1. HEBREW ORIGINS AND RELATIONS WITH OTHER PEOPLES

The origin of the Hebrews is still a puzzling problem. Certainly they did not have any physical characteristics sufficient to distinguish them clearly from their neighbors, and their language belonged to the Near

Eastern Semitic family. Most scholars agree that the original home of the Hebrews was the Arabian Desert. The first definite appearance of the founders of the nation of Israel, however, was in northwestern Mesopotamia. Apparently as early as 1900 B.C. a group of Hebrews under the leadership of Abraham had settled there. Later Abraham's grandson Jacob led a migration westward and began the occupation of Palestine. It was from Jacob, subsequently called Israel, that the Israelites derived their name. Sometime before 1600 B.C. certain tribes of Israelites, together with other Hebrews, moved into Egypt to escape the consequences of famine. According to the biblical account they were gradually enslaved by the Egyptian government, although there is no record of this in the Egyptian evidence. At any rate, around 1300–1250 B.C. their descendants found a leader in the indomitable Moses, who led them to the Sinai peninsula and persuaded them to become worshipers of Yahweh, a god whose name was much later written erroneously as Jehovah. Hitherto Yahweh had been the deity of Hebrew shepherd folk in the Sinai area. Making use of a Yahwist cult as a nucleus, Moses welded the various tribes of his followers into a confederation, which thereupon occupied Palestine, or the land of Canaan.

With its scanty rainfall and rugged terrain, Palestine was a barren and inhospitable place. But compared with the arid wastes of Arabia it seemed a veritable paradise, and it is not surprising that the leaders should have pictured it as a "land flowing with milk and honey." Most of it was already occupied by the Canaanites, another Semitic people who had lived there for centuries. Through contact with the Babylonians, Hittites, and Egyptians they had built up a culture which was no longer primitive. They practiced agriculture and carried on trade. They knew the art of writing, and they had adapted the laws of Hammurabi's code to the needs of their simpler existence. Their religion, which was also derived in large part from Babylonia, was cruel and sensual, including human sacrifice and temple prostitution.

The Hebrew occupation of the land of Canaan was a slow and difficult process. Seldom did the tribes unite in a combined attack, and even when they did, the enemy cities were well enough fortified to resist capture. After several generations of sporadic fighting the Hebrews had succeeded in taking only the limestone hills and a few of the less fertile valleys. In the intervals between wars they mingled freely with the Canaanites and adopted no small amount of their culture. Before they had a chance to complete the conquest they found themselves confronted by a new and more formidable enemy, the Philistines, who appear to have entered Palestine from Asia Minor. Stronger than either the Hebrews or Canaanites, especially because they used iron weapons while the others used bronze, these invaders rapidly overran the country and forced the Hebrews to surrender much of the territory they had already gained. It is from the Philistines that Palestine derives its name.

2. THE RECORD OF POLITICAL HOPES AND FRUSTRATIONS

The crisis produced by the Philistine conquests served not to discourage the Hebrews but to unite them and to intensify their ardor for battle. Moreover, it led directly to the founding of the Hebrew monarchy about 1025 B.C. Up to this time the nation had been ruled by "judges," who possessed little more than the authority of religious leaders over twelve independent Hebrew tribes. But now with a greater need for organization and discipline, the people demanded a king to rule them and lead them in war. The man selected as the first incumbent of the office was Saul, a member of the tribe of Benjamin, who at first gained considerable success.

The founding of the Hebrew monarchy

But the reign of King Saul ultimately was not a happy one, either for the nation or for the ruler himself. Only a few suggestions of the reasons are given in the Old Testament account. Evidently Saul incurred the displeasure of Samuel, the last of the great judges, who had expected to remain the power behind the throne. Before long there appeared on the scene the ambitious David, who, with the encouragement of Samuel, carried on skillful maneuvers to draw popular support from the king. Waging his own military campaigns, he achieved one bloody triumph after another. By contrast, the armies of Saul met disastrous reverses. Finally the king, being critically wounded, requested his armor-bearer to kill him. When the latter would not, Saul drew his own sword, fell upon it, and died.

The reign of King Saul

David now became king and ruled for forty years. His reign was one of the most glorious periods in Hebrew history. He smote the Philistines hip and thigh and reduced their territory to a narrow strip of coast in the south. He united the twelve tribes into a consolidated state under an absolute monarch, and he began the construction of a magnificent capital at Jerusalem. But strong government, military glory, and material splendor were not unmixed blessings for the people. Their inevitable accompaniments were high taxation and conscription. As a consequence, before David died, rumblings of discontent were plainly to be heard in certain parts of his kingdom.

The mighty David

David was succeeded by his son Solomon, the last of the kings of the united monarchy. As a result of the nationalist aspirations of later times, Solomon has been pictured in Hebrew lore as one of the wisest and most enlightened rulers in all history. The facts of his career furnish little support for such a belief. About all that can be said in his favor is that he was a shrewd diplomat and an active patron of trade. Most of his policies were oppressive, although of course not deliberately so. Ambitious to copy the luxury and magnificence of other Oriental despots, he established a harem of 700 wives and 300 concubines and completed the construction of sumptuous palaces, stables for 4,000 horses, and a costly temple in Jerusalem. Since Palestine was

Solomon aspires to Oriental magnificence

Model of King Solomon's Temple. Significant details are: A, royal gates; B, treasury; C, royal palace; D, people's gate; E, western (wailing) wall; F, priests' quarters; G, courthouse; H, Solomon's porch.

The secession of the Ten Tribes

Roman Coin Celebrating the Destruction of Jerusalem. This coin, struck about 70 A.D., bears the inscription "IVDAEA CAPTA" (Captive Judea), and shows a female personification of the Jews propping her head in an attitude of dejection.

poor in resources, most of the materials for the building projects had to be imported. Gold, silver, bronze, and cedar were brought in in such quantities that the revenues from taxation and from the tolls levied upon trade were insufficient to pay for them. To make up the deficit Solomon ceded twenty towns and resorted to a system of conscripting labor. Every three months 30,000 Hebrews were drafted and sent into Phoenicia to work in the forests and mines of King Hiram of Tyre, from whom the most expensive materials had been purchased.

Solomon's extravagance and oppression produced acute discontent among his subjects. His death in 922 B.C. was the signal for open revolt. The ten northern tribes, refusing to submit to his son Rehoboam, seceded and set up their own kingdom. Sectional differences played their part also in the disruption of the nation. The northern Hebrews were sophisticated and accustomed to urban living. They benefited from their location at the crossroads of Near Eastern trade. While this factor increased their prosperity, it also caused them to be steeped in foreign influences. By contrast, the two southern tribes were composed very largely of pastoral and agricultural folk, loyal to the religion of their fathers, and hating the ways of the foreigner. Perhaps these differences alone would have been sufficient in time to have destroyed the Hebrews' national unity.

The northern kingdom came to be known as the Kingdom of Israel, having its capital in Samaria, while the two southern tribes comprised the Kingdom of Judah, which continued to have its capital in Jerusalem. For more than two centuries the two little states maintained their separate existences. But in 722 B.C. the Kingdom of Israel was conquered by the Assyrians. Its inhabitants were scattered throughout the vast empire of their conquerors and were eventually absorbed by the more numerous population around them. Ever since they have been referred to as the Ten Lost Tribes of Israel. The Kingdom of Judah managed to survive for more than a hundred years longer, successfully outlasting the Assyrian menace. But in 586 B.C. it was

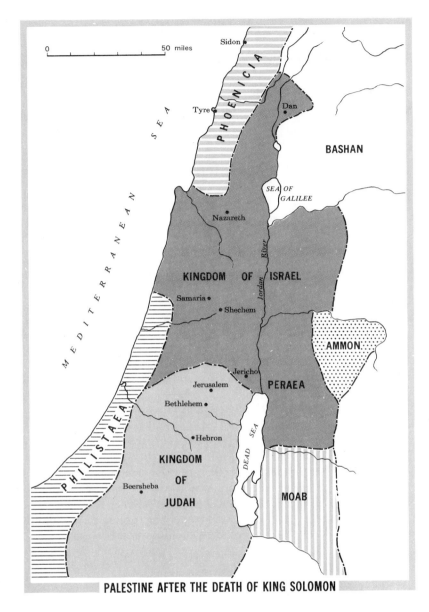

PALESTINE AFTER THE DEATH OF KING SOLOMON

overthrown by the Chaldeans under Nebuchadnezzar. Jerusalem was plundered and burned, and its leading citizens were carried off into captivity in Babylon. When Cyrus the Persian conquered the Chaldeans, he freed the Jews and permitted them to return to their native land. Few were willing to go, and considerable time elapsed before it was possible to rebuild the temple. From 539 to 332 B.C. Palestine was a vassal state of Persia. In 332 B.C. it was conquered by Alexander the Great and after his death was placed under the rule of Egypt. In 63 B.C. it became a Roman protectorate. Its political history as a Jewish commonwealth was ended in 70 A.D. after a desperate revolt which the

Masada. This ancient mountaintop fortress, which towers above the western shore of the Dead Sea in Israel, was the final outpost of the Jews in their war against Roman domination. The fortress, occupied by 1,000 men, women, and children, was besieged by the Roman army for two years before it fell in 73 A.D. Defiant to the end, almost all of the Jewish defenders killed themselves rather than be captured and enslaved by the Romans.

Romans punished by destroying Jerusalem and annexing the country as a province. The inhabitants were gradually diffused through other parts of the Roman Empire.

The Diaspora

The destruction of Jerusalem and annexation of the country by the Romans were the principal factors in the so-called Diaspora, or dispersion of the Jews from Palestine. Even earlier large number of them had fled into various parts of the Greco-Roman world on count of difficulties in their homeland. In their new environment they rapidly accepted foreign influences, a fact which was of tremendous importance in promoting a fusion of Greek and Oriental ideas. It was a Hellenized Jew, St. Paul, who was mainly responsible for remolding Christianity in accordance with Greek philosophical doctrines.

3. THE HEBREW RELIGIOUS EVOLUTION

Reasons for the varied evolution of Hebrew religion

Few peoples in history have gone through a religious evolution comparable to that of the Hebrews. Its cycle of development ranged all the way from the crudest superstitions to the loftiest spiritual and ethical conceptions. Part of the explanation lies in the peculiar geographic position occupied by the Hebrew people. Located as they were after their conquest of Canaan on the highroad between Egypt and the major civilizations of Asia, they were bound to be affected by an extraordinary variety of influences.

At least four different stages can be distinguished in the growth of the Hebrew religion. The first we can call the pre-Mosaic stage, from the earliest beginnings of the people to approximately 1250 B.C. This stage was characterized at first by animism, the worship of spirits that dwelt in trees, mountains, sacred wells and springs, and even in stones of peculiar shape. Diverse forms of magic were practiced also at this time—necromancy, imitative magic, and scapegoat sacrifices. Many traces of these early beliefs and rites are preserved in the Old Testament.

Gradually animism gave way to belief in anthropomorphic gods. How this transition occurred cannot be determined. Perhaps it was related to the fact that Hebrew society had become patriarchal, that is, the father exercised absolute authority over the family and descent was traced through the male line. The gods may have been thought to occupy a similar position in the clan or tribe. Apparently few of the new deities were as yet given names; each was usually referred to merely by the generic name of "El," that is, "god." They were guardians of particular places and probably of separate tribes. No *national* worship of Yahweh was known at this time.

The second stage, which lasted from the thirteenth century B.C. to the ninth, is frequently called the stage of national monolatry. The term may be defined as the exclusive worship of one god but without denial that other gods exist. Due chiefly to the influence of Moses, the Hebrews gradually adopted as their national deity during this period a god whose name appears to have been written "Yhwh." How it was pronounced no one knows, but scholars generally agree that it was probably uttered as if spelled "Yahweh." The meaning is also a mystery. When Moses inquired of Yahweh what he should tell the people when they demanded to know what god had sent him, Yahweh replied: "I AM THAT I AM: and he said, Thus shalt thou say unto the children of Israel, I AM hath sent me unto you" (Exodus 3:13–14).

During the time of Moses and for two or three centuries thereafter Yahweh was a somewhat peculiar deity. He was conceived almost exclusively in anthropomorphic terms. He possessed a physical body and the emotional qualities of men. He was capricious on occasions, and somewhat irascible—as capable of evil and wrathful judgments as he was of good. His decrees were often quite arbitrary, and he would punish someone who sinned unwittingly just about as readily as one whose guilt was real. By way of illustration, Yahweh reportedly struck Uzza dead merely because that unfortunate individual placed his hand upon the Ark of the Covenant to steady it while it was being transported to Jerusalem (I Chronicles 13:9–10). Yahweh was hardly omnipotent, for his power was limited to the territory occupied by the Hebrews. Nonetheless, some of the most important Hebrew contributions to subsequent Western thought were first formulated during this time. It was during this period that the Hebrews came to believe that God was not part of nature but entirely outside of it, and that humans, while part of nature, became the rulers of nature by divine dispensation. This "transcendent" theology meant that God

*The supremacy of law
and ritual*

*The stage of the prophetic
revolution*

could gradually be understood in purely intellectual or abstract terms, and that humanity could be regarded as having the potential for altering nature as it pleased.

The religion of this stage was neither primarily ethical nor profoundly spiritual. Yahweh was revered as a supreme law-giver and as the stern upholder of the moral order of the universe. According to the biblical account, he issued the Ten Commandments to Moses on top of Mount Sinai. Old Testament scholars, however, do not generally accept this tradition. They admit that a primitive set of commandments may have existed in Mosaic times, but they doubt that the Ten Commandments in the form in which they are preserved in the Book of Exodus go back any farther than the seventh century. In any event, it is clear that Moses's God was interested just about as much in sacrifice and in ritualistic observances as he was in good conduct or in purity of heart. Moreover, the religion was not vitally concerned with spiritual matters. It offered nothing but material rewards in this life and none at all in a life to come. Finally, the belief in monolatry was corrupted by certain elements of fetishism, magic, and even grosser superstitions that lingered from more primitive times or that were gradually acquired from neighboring peoples. These varied all the way from serpent worship to bloody sacrifices and fertility orgies.

The really important work of religious reform was accomplished by the great prophets—Amos, Hosea, Isaiah,[1] and Micah. And their achievements represented the third stage in the development of the Hebrew religion, the stage of the prophetic revolution, which occupied the eighth and seventh centuries B.C. The great prophets were men of broader vision than any of their forerunners. Three basic doctrines made up the substance of their teachings: (1) rudimentary monotheism—Yahweh is the ruler of the universe; He even makes use of nations other than the Hebrews to accomplish His purposes; the gods of other peoples are false gods and should not be worshiped for any reason; (2) Yahweh is a god of righteousness exclusively; He is not really omnipotent, but His power is limited by justice and goodness; the evil in the world comes from humanity not from God; (3) the purposes of religion are chiefly ethical; Yahweh cares nothing for ritual and sacrifice, but that His followers should "seek justice, relieve the oppressed, judge the fatherless, plead for the widow." Or as Micah expressed it: "What doth the Lord require of thee, but to do justly, and to love mercy, and to walk humbly with thy God?" (Micah 6:8).

Although these doctrines contradicted nearly everything the older religion had stood for, the prophets genuinely thought that they were

---

[1] Most Old Testament authorities consider the Book of Isaiah the work of three authors. They ascribe the first part to Isaiah, the second part from Chapters 40 to 55 to Deutero-Isaiah, or the second Isaiah, and the end to someone who wrote after the return to Jerusalem. The second Isaiah was more emphatic than the first in denying the existence of the gods of other peoples.

Remains of an Ancient Synagogue at Capernaum. Capernaum was supposed to have been the scene of many of the miracles attributed to Jesus. Here also he called out Peter, Andrew, and Matthew to be his disciples.

restoring Hebrew beliefs to their ancient purity, for they assumed that the crudities they opposed were foreign corruptions. Thus their actual accomplishments went so far beyond their conscious objectives that they amounted to a religious revolution. To a considerable extent this revolution also had its social and political aspects. Wealth had become concentrated in the hands of a few. Thousands of small farmers had lost their freedom to rich proprietors. If we can believe the testimony of Amos, bribery was so rife in the law courts that the plaintiff in a suit for debt had merely to give the judge a pair of shoes and the defendant would be handed over as a slave (Amos 2:6). Overshadowing all was the threat of Assyrian domination. To enable the Hebrews to cope with that threat, the prophets believed that social abuses should be stamped out and the people united under a religion purged of its alien corruptions.

Contrasts with the older religion; political and social aspects

The results of this revolution must not be misinterpreted. It did eradicate some of the most flagrant forms of oppression, and it rooted out permanently most of the barbarities that had crept into the religion from foreign sources. But the Hebrew faith did not yet bear much resemblance to modern Judaism. Instead of being otherworldly, it was oriented toward this life. Its purposes were social and ethical—to promote a just and harmonious society and to abate man's inhumanity to man—not to confer individual salvation in an afterlife. As yet there was no belief in heaven and hell or in Satan as a powerful opponent of God. The shades of the dead went down into Sheol to linger there for a time in the dust and gloom and then disappear.

The religion not yet otherworldly or mystical

The final significant stage in Hebrew religious evolution was the post-Exilic stage or the period of Persian influence. This may be considered to have covered the years from 539 to about 300 B.C. Perhaps enough has been said already to indicate the character of the influence from Persia. It will be recalled from the preceding chapter that

The post-Exilic stage

Zoroastrianism was a dualistic, messianic, and otherworldly religion. In the period following the exile in Babylon these influences gained wide acceptance among the Jews. They adopted a belief in Satan as the Great Adversary and the author of evil. They developed an eschatology (a set of doctrines concerning the end of the world) which included such notions as the coming of a spiritual savior, the resurrection of the dead, and a last judgment. They turned their attention to salvation in an afterworld as more important than enjoyment of this life. Last, they embraced the conception of a revealed religion, that is, they regarded the books of their Bible as having been directly inspired by God Himself.

4. HEBREW CULTURE

The limitations of the Hebrew accomplishment

In some respects Hebrew culture was inferior to that of other great nations of antiquity. In the first place, the Hebrews revealed no talent for science. Nor were they adept at appropriating the technological knowledge of others. They could not build a bridge or a tunnel except of the crudest sort. In the second place, they seem to have been almost entirely devoid of artistic skill. In part because of religious prohibitions concerning "graven images" they had no sculpture, but they also had no architecture or painting worthy of mention. The famous temple at Jerusalem was not a Hebrew building at all but a product of Phoenician skill, for Solomon imported artisans from Tyre to finish the more complicated tasks.

Hebrew law

It was rather in law, literature, and philosophy that the Hebrew genius was most perfectly expressed. Although all of these subjects were closely allied with religion, they did have their secular aspects. The foremost example of Jewish law was the Deuteronomic Code, which forms the core of the Book of Deuteronomy. Despite claims of its great antiquity, it was probably an outgrowth of the prophetic revolution. It was based in part upon an older Code of the Covenant, which was derived in considerable measure from the laws of the Canaanites and the Old Babylonians. In general, its provisions were more enlightened than those of Hammurabi's code. One of them enjoined liberality to the poor and to the stranger. Another commanded that the Hebrew slave who had served six years should be freed, and insisted that he must not be sent away empty. A third provided that judges and other officers should be chosen by the people and forbade them to accept gifts or to show partiality in any form. A fourth condemned witchcraft and divination. A fifth denounced the punishment of children for the guilt of their fathers and affirmed the principle of individual responsibility for sin. A sixth prohibited the taking of interest on any kind of loan made by one Jew to another. A seventh required that at the end of every seven years there should be a "release" of debts. "Every creditor that lendeth aught unto his neighbour shall release it; he shall not exact it of his neighbour, or of his brother . . . save when there shall be no poor among you" (Deuteronomy 15:1–4).

The literature of the Hebrews was the finest that the ancient Near East produced. Nearly all of it now extant is preserved in the Old Testament and in the books of the Apocrypha (ancient Hebrew works not recognized as scriptural because of doubtful religious authority). Except for a few fragments like the Song of Deborah in Judges 5, it is not really so old as is commonly supposed. Scholars now recognize that the Old Testament was built up through a series of collections and revisions in which old and new parts were merged and generally assigned to an ancient author—Moses, for example. But the oldest of these revisions was not prepared any earlier than 850 B.C. The majority of the books of the Old Testament were of still later origin, excepting some of the chronicles. Although the bulk of the Psalms were ascribed to King David, a good many of them refer to events of the Babylonian Captivity and it is certain that the collection of Psalms as a whole was the work of several centuries. Most recent of all were the books of Ecclesiastes, Esther, and Daniel, composed no earlier than the third century B.C. Likewise, the Apocryphal books did not see the light of day until Hebrew civilization was almost extinct. Some, like Maccabees I and II, relate events of the second century B.C. Others, including the Wisdom of Solomon and the Book of Enoch, were written under the influence of Greco-Oriental philosophy.

Hebrew literature

Granted that many parts of the Old Testament consist of dull, repetitious chronicles, many others, whether taking the form of battle song, prophecy, love lyric, or drama, are rich in rhythm, concrete images, and emotional vigor. Few passages in any language can surpass the scornful indictment of social abuses voiced by the prophet Amos:

Amos's indictment of social abuses

> Hear this, O ye that swallow up the needy, even to make the
>   poor of the land to fail,
> Saying, when will the new moon be gone, that we may sell
>   corn?
> And the sabbath that we may set forth wheat,
> Making the ephah small, and the shekel great,
> And falsifying the balances by deceit?
> That we may buy the poor for silver, and the need for a pair
>   of shoes;
> Yea, and sell the refuse of the wheat?

The most beautiful of Hebrew love lyrics is the Song of Songs, or Song of Solomon. Its theme was probably derived from an old Canaanite hymn of spring, celebrating the passionate affection of the Shulamith or fertility goddess for her lover, but it had long since lost its original meaning. The following verses are typical of its sensuous beauty:

The Song of Songs

King David as a Musician. A much later conception of David from the eighth century A.D. shows the Hebrew king playing his lyre and charming animals. According to tradition, David was the author of the Psalms, which he sung to his lyre (also known as a *psaltery*).

I am the rose of Sharon
and the lily of the valleys.
As the lily among thorns,
so is my love among the daughters.

. . . .

My beloved is white and ruddy,
the chiefest among ten thousand.
His head is as the most fine gold;
his locks are bushy and black as a raven:
His eyes are as the eyes of doves by the rivers of waters,
washed with milk and fitly set.
His cheeks are as a bed of spices, as sweet flowers;
his lips like lilies, dropping sweet smelling myrrh.

. . . . .

How beautiful are thy feet with shoes, O prince's daughter!
The joints of thy thighs are like jewels,
the work of the hands of a cunning workman.

The Book of Job

One other of the supreme Hebrew literary achievements is the Book of Job, written sometime between 500 and 300 B.C. In form the work is a drama of the tragic struggle between man and fate. Its central theme is the problem of evil: how it can be that the righteous suffer while the wicked prosper. The story was an old one, adapted very probably from an Old Babylonian writing of similar content. But the Hebrews introduced into it a much deeper realization of philosophical possibilities. The main character, Job, a man of unimpeachable virtue, is suddenly overtaken by a series of disasters: he is despoiled of his property, his children are killed, and his body is afflicted with a painful disease. His attitude at first is one of stoic resignation; the evil must be accepted along with the good. But as his sufferings increase he is plunged into despair. He curses the day of his birth and praises death, where "the wicked cease from troubling and the weary be at rest."

Then follows a lengthy debate between Job and his friends over the meaning of evil. The latter take the traditional Hebraic view that all suffering is a punishment for sin, and that those who repent are forgiven and strengthened in character. But Job is not satisfied with any of their arguments. Torn between hope and despair, he strives to review the problem from every angle. He even considers the possibility that death may not be the end, that there may be some adjustment of the balance hereafter. But the mood of despair returns, and he decides that God is an omnipotent demon, destroying without mercy wherever His caprice or anger directs. Finally, in his anguish he appeals to the Almighty to reveal Himself and make known His ways to him. God answers him out of the whirlwind with a magnificent exposition of the tremendous works of nature. Convinced of his own insignificance and of the unutterable majesty of God, Job despises himself and repents in dust and ashes. In the end no solution is given of the problem of individual suffering. No promise is made of recompense in a life hereafter, nor does God make any effort to refute the hopeless pessimism of Job. Humans must take comfort in the philosophic reflection that the universe is greater than themselves, and that God in the pursuit of His sublime purposes cannot really be limited by human standards of equity and goodness.

The problem of evil

As philosophers the Hebrews surpassed all other peoples before the Greeks. Although they were not brilliant metaphysicians and constructed no great theories of the universe, they did concern themselves with most of the problems relating to human life and destiny. Their thought was essentially personal rather than abstract. Probably the earliest of their writings of a distinctly philosophical character were the Book of Proverbs and the Book of Ecclesiasticus. In their final form both were of late composition, but much of the material they contain was doubtless quite ancient. These have as their basic teaching: be temperate, diligent, wise, and honest, and you will surely be rewarded with prosperity, long life, and a good reputation. Only in such isolated passages as the following is any recognition given to higher motives of sympathy or respect for the rights of others: "Whoso mocketh the poor reproacheth his Maker; and he that is glad at calamities shall not be unpunished" (Proverbs 17:5).

Hebrew philosophy: early examples

A much more profound and critical philosophy is contained in Ecclesiastes, an Old Testament book, not to be confused with the Ecclesiasticus mentioned above. The author of Ecclesiastes is unknown. In some way it came to be attributed to Solomon, but he certainly did not write it, for it includes doctrines and forms of expression unknown to the Hebrews for hundreds of years after his death. Scholars now date it no earlier than the third century B.C. The basic ideas of its philosophy may be summarized as follows:

(1) Mechanism. The universe is a machine that rolls on forever without evidence of any purpose or goal. Sunrise and sunset, birth and death are but phases of constantly recurring cycles and "there is nothing new under the sun."

(2) Fatalism. Humans are victims of the whims of fate. There is no necessary relation between effort and success. "The race is not to the swift, nor the battle to the strong, neither yet bread to the wise . . . but time and chance happeneth to them all."

(3) Pessimism. "All is vanity and vexation of spirit." Fame, riches, extravagant pleasure are snares and delusions in the end. Although wisdom is better than folly, even it is not a sure key to happiness, for an increase in knowledge brings a keener awareness of suffering.

(4) Moderation. Extremes of asceticism and extremes of indulgence are both to be avoided. "Be not righteous over much . . . be not over much wicked: why shouldest thou die before thy time?"

5. THE MAGNITUDE OF THE HEBREW INFLUENCE

The nature of the Hebrew influence

The influence of the Hebrews has been chiefly religious and ethical. While it is true that the Old Testament has served as a source of inspiration for some of the literature and art of medieval and early modern civilizations, this has resulted largely because the Bible was familiar material as a part of the religious heritage. The same explanation can be applied to the use of the Old Testament as a source of law and political theory by Protestants in the sixteenth century, and by many other Christians both before and since.

Hebrew foundations of Christianity: the beliefs of the Pharisees

But these facts do not mean that the Hebrew influence has been slight. On the contrary, the history of nearly every Western civilization during the past two thousand years would have been radically different without the heritage from Israel. For it must be remembered that the Hebrews developed the first sustained monotheism known to mankind and that Hebrew beliefs were among the principal foundations of Christianity. The relationship between the two religions is frequently misunderstood. The movement inaugurated by Jesus of Nazareth is commonly represented as a revolt against Judaism; but such was only partly the case. On the eve of the Christian era the Jewish nation had come to be divided into several different religious parties, including a majority group of Pharisees, and minority groups of Sadducees and Essenes. The Pharisees represented the middle classes and some of the better educated common folk. They believed in the resurrection, in rewards and punishments after death, and in the coming of a political messiah. Intensely nationalistic, they advocated participation in government and faithful observance of the ancient ritual. They regarded all parts of the law as of virtually equal importance, whether they applied to matters of ceremony or to obligations of social ethics. Their concern for the law was so great that they debated such questions as whether one could eat an egg laid on the Sabbath.

Representing altogether different strata of society, the minority parties disagreed with the Pharisees on both religious and political issues. The Sadducees, including the priests and the wealthier classes, were most famous for their denial of the resurrection and of rewards and punishments in an afterlife. Although they favored the temporary acceptance of Roman rule, their attitude toward the ancient law was even more inflexible than that of the Pharisees. The Essenes, who were not even a unified party but consisted of various similar but separate communities, drew their members from the lower classes, practiced asceticism, and preached otherworldliness as means of protest against the wealth and power of priests and rulers. They ate and drank only enough to keep themselves alive, held all their goods in common, and looked upon marriage as a necessary evil. Far from being fanatical patriots, they regarded government with indifference and refused to take oaths under any conditions. They emphasized the spiritual aspects of religion rather than the ceremonial, and stressed particularly the immortality of the soul, the coming of a religious messiah, and the early destruction of the world.

The Sadducees and the Essenes

Until recently scholars were dependent for their knowledge of the Essenes almost entirely upon secondary sources. But in 1947 an Arab shepherd unwittingly opened the way to a spectacular documentary discovery. Searching for a lost sheep on the shore of the Dead Sea, he threw a stone that entered a hole in the rocks and made such a strange noise that he ran away in fright. He returned, however, with a friend to investigate and discovered a cave in which were stored about fifty cylindrical earthen jars stuffed with writings on papyrus scrolls. Studied by scholars, the scrolls revealed the existence of a monastic community which flourished from about 130 B.C. to 67 A.D. Its members lived a life of self-denial, holding their goods in common, and devoting their time to prayer and sacraments and to studying and copying biblical texts. They looked forward confidently to the coming of a messiah, the overthrow of evil, and the establishment of God's kingdom on earth. That they belonged to the same general movement that fostered the growth of the Essenes seems beyond question.

The Dead Sea scrolls

All branches of Judaism except the Sadducees strongly influenced the development of Christianity. From Jewish sources Christianity obtained its cosmogony, or theory of the origin of the universe; the Ten Commandments; and a large portion of its theology, including the "transcendent" view of God as outside of nature and humanity as master of nature. Jesus himself, although he condemned the Pharisees for their legalism and hypocrisy, did not repudiate all of their tenets.

Hebrew influence upon Christianity

The Dead Sea Scrolls. Now on display in an underground vault at the Hebrew University in Jerusalem. The oldest extant examples of Hebrew religious literature, they furnish us with evidence of the activities of the Essenes and mystical and otherworldly sects about the beginning of the Christian era.

Instead of abolishing the ancient law, as he is popularly supposed to have done, he demanded its fulfillment, insisting, however, that it should not be made the essential part of religion. In the first flush of enthusiasm at the discovery of the Dead Sea Scrolls it seemed as if Christianity might have been most directly influenced by the Essenes. Scholars now, however, speak less of direct influences than of similarities, for early Christians, like the Essenes, practiced asceticism, regarded government with indifference and the Roman Empire with hostility, held their goods in common, and believed in the imminent end of the world. These parallels do not mean, of course, that Christianity was a mere adaptation of beliefs and practices emanating from Judaism. There was much in it that was unique; but that is a subject which will be discussed later on.[2]

Ethical and political influence of the Hebrews

The ethical and political influence of the Hebrews has also been substantial. Their moral conceptions have been a leading factor in the development of the negative approach toward ethics which has prevailed for so long in Western countries. For the early Hebrews, "righteousness" consisted primarily in the observance of taboos or prohibitions. "Thou shalt not . . ." is a major theme of many parts of the Old Testament. But a positive morality of charity and social justice made rapid headway during the time of the prophets and has had its great influence as well. With respect to political thought, Hebrew ideals of the

[2] See Chapter 9.

sovereignty of law, and regard for the dignity and worth of the individual have been among the major formative influences which have shaped the growth of modern democracy. It is now almost universally recognized that the traditions of Judaism contributed equally with the influence of Christianity and Stoic philosophy in fostering recognition of human rights and in promoting the development of free society.

SELECTED READINGS

• *Items so designated are available in paperback editions.*

• Albright, W. F., *From the Stone Age to Christianity,* New York, 1957. Emphasizes the development of Hebrew monotheism.

Anderson, Bernard, *Understanding the Old Testament,* 3rd ed., Englewood Cliffs, N.J., 1975.

Baron, Salo W., *A Social and Religious History of the Jews,* rev. ed., 17 vols., New York, 1952–1980. A modern classic: almost all work on Jewish history takes Baron as a point of departure.

• Bickermann, E., *From Ezra to the Last of the Maccabees: Foundations of Post-Biblical Judaism,* New York, 1962.

Bright, John, *A History of Israel,* 3rd ed., Philadelphia, 1981. A standard account.

Harrison, R. K., *The Dead Sea Scrolls: An Introduction,* New York, 1961. A valuable guide for the beginner.

Hermann, Siegfried, *A History of Israel in Old Testament Times,* London, 1975. Iconoclastic and challenging.

• Kaufmann, Yehezkel, *The Religion of Israel,* New York, 1972. Stresses the uniqueness of the Hebrew religious accomplishment.

• McCullough, W. S., *The History of the Palestinian Jews from Cyrus to Herod, 550 B.C. to 4 B.C.,* Toronto, 1976.

Noth, Martin, *The History of Israel,* 2nd ed., New York, 1960. A provocative reappraisal.

• Orlinsky, H. M., *Ancient Israel,* 2nd ed., Ithaca, N.Y., 1960. A good brief overview of ancient Hebrew history.

Rowley, H. H., *Growth of the Old Testament,* New York, 1963. A helpful survey of scholarly opinion concerning the circumstances of origin of the various Old Testament books.

• Schürer, E., *The History of the Jewish People in the Age of Jesus Christ (175 B.C.–A.D. 135),* rev. ed., 3 vols., Edinburgh, 1973–1983. A new edition of an irreplaceable nineteenth-century narrative.

• Vaux, Roland de, *Ancient Israel: Its Life and Institutions,* New York, 1962. Especially valuable for archeological data.

SOURCE MATERIALS

Baron, Salo W., and J. L. Blau, eds., *Judaism: Post-Biblical and Talmudic Periods,* New York, 1954.

Gaster, T. H., tr., *The Dead Sea Scriptures in English Translation,* New York, 1964.

The *Old Testament* and the *Apocrypha,* many editions.

Pritchard, J. B., ed., *Ancient Near Eastern Texts Relating to the Old Testament,* rev. ed., Princeton, N.J., 1969.

Chapter 5

THE HITTITE, MINOAN, MYCENAEAN, AND LESSER CIVILIZATIONS

But for them among these gods will be bled for annual food:
to the god Karnua one steer and one sheep;
to the goddess Kupapa one steer and one sheep;
to the divinity Sarku one sheep;
and a Kutupalis sheep to the male divinities.

> —Hittite sacrifice formula, translated
> from a hieroglyph by
> H. T. Bossert

A few other ancient civilizations require more than passing attention. Chief among them are the Hittite, the Minoan, the Mycenaean, the Lydian, and the Phoenician. The Hittites served primarily as intermediaries between East and West, linking the civilizations of Egypt and Mesopotamia with the region of the Aegean Sea. The Minoan and the Mycenaean civilizations were the oldest ones of Europe, significant above all for their remarkable achievements in the arts and as the starting points of Greek history. As for the Lydians, no one could overlook their importance as the originators of the first system of coinage. Finally, the Phoenicians were impressive traders who also invented an alphabet which lies behind all those used in the modern Western world.

Importance of these civilizations

1. THE HITTITES

Until about a century ago little was known of the Hittites except their name. They were commonly assumed to have played no role of any significance in the drama of history. The slighting references to them in the Bible give the impression that they were little more than a half-barbarian tribe. But in 1870 the discovery of some curiously inscribed

The discovery of remains of the Hittite civilization

stones found at Hama in Syria began an extensive inquiry which has continued with few interruptions to the present day. It was not long until scores of other monuments and clay tablets were discovered over most of Asia Minor and through the Near East as far as the Tigris-Euphrates valley. In 1907 some evidences of an ancient city were unearthed near the village of Boghaz-Koy in Turkey. Further excavation eventually revealed the ruins of a great fortified capital known as Hattusas or Hittite City, within whose walls were discovered more than 20,000 clay tablets.

The Hittite Empire

On the basis of these finds it has become clear that the Hittites were once the rulers of a mighty empire covering most of Asia Minor, extending to the upper reaches of the Euphrates, and, at its height, even including Syria and portions of Palestine. The Hittites reached the zenith of their power during the years from 1600 to 1200 B.C. In the last century of this period they waged a long war with Egypt, which probably contributed to the downfall of both empires. Neither was able to regain its strength. After 1200 B.C. Carchemish on the Euphrates for a time became the leading Hittite city, but as a commercial center rather than as the capital of a great unified state. Finally, after 717 B.C., all the remaining Hittite territories were conquered and absorbed by the Assyrians, Lydians, and Phrygians.

See color map facing
page 65

*The mystery of the race
and language of the
Hittites*

Where the Hittites came from and what their relationships were to other peoples are problems which still defy solution. Most modern scholars trace their place of origin to Turkestan and consider them related to the Greeks. Their language was Indo-European. Its secret was unlocked during World War I by the Czech scholar Bedrich Hrozny. Since then thousands of clay tablets making up the laws and official records of the emperors have been deciphered. They reveal a civilization resembling more closely the Old Babylonian than any other.

*The economic life of the
Hittites*

Insufficient evidence has yet been collected to make possible an accurate appraisal of Hittite civilization. Certainly, however, the Hittites had an extensive knowledge of agriculture and a highly developed economic life in general. They mined great quantities of silver, copper, and lead, which they sold to surrounding nations. They discovered the mining and use of iron and made that material available for the rest of the civilized world. Trade was also one of their principal pursuits. In fact, they seem to have depended almost as much upon commercial penetration as upon war for the expansion of their empire.

*The intellectual level of
Hittite culture*

The literature of the Hittites consisted chiefly of mythology, including adaptations of creation and flood legends from the Old Babylonians. They had nothing that could be described as philosophy, nor is there any evidence of scientific originality outside of the metallurgical arts. They evidently possessed some talent for the perfection of writing, for in addition to a modified cuneiform adapted from Mesopotamia they also developed a hieroglyphic system which was partly phonetic in character.

One of the most significant achievements of the Hittites was their system of law. Approximately two hundred separate paragraphs or decrees, covering a great variety of subjects, have been translated. They reflect a society comparatively urbane and sophisticated but subject to rigorous governmental control. The title to all land was vested in the king or in the governments of the cities. Grants were made to individuals only in return for military service and under the strict requirement that the land be cultivated. Prices were fixed in the laws themselves for an enormous number of commodities—not only for articles of luxury and the products of industry, but even for food and clothing. All wages and fees for services were likewise prescribed, with the pay of women fixed at less than half the rate for men.

Hittite law

On the whole, the Hittite law was more humane than that of the Old Babylonians. Death was the punishment for only eight offenses—such as witchcraft, and theft of property from the palace. Even premeditated murder was punishable only by a fine. Mutilation was not specified as a penalty at all except for arson or theft when committed by a slave. The contrast with the cruelties of Assyrian law was more striking. Not a single example is to be found in the Hittite decrees of such sadistic punishments as flaying, castration, and impalement, which the rulers at Nineveh seemed to think necessary for maintaining their authority.

Humane character of Hittite law

The art of the Hittites was not of outstanding excellence. So far as we know, it included only sculpture and architecture. The former was generally crude but not entirely lacking in freshness and vigor. Most of it was in the form of reliefs depicting scenes of war and mythology. Architecture was ponderous and huge. Temples and palaces were squat, unadorned structures with small, two-columned porches and great stone lions guarding the entrance.

The art of the Hittites

Not a great deal is known about the Hittite religion except that it had an elaborate mythology, innumerable deities, and forms of wor-

Hittite Sculpture. Perhaps the most highly conventionalized sculpture of the ancient world is found in Hittite reliefs.

ship of Mesopotamian origin. A sun god was worshiped, along with a host of other deities, some of whom appear to have had no particular function at all. The Hittites seem to have welcomed into the divine company practically all of the gods of the peoples they conquered and even of the nations that bought their wares. The practices of the religion included divination, sacrifice, and purification ceremonies. Nothing can be found in the records to indicate that the religion was in any sense ethical.

Hittite religion

The chief historical importance of the Hittites lies in the role which they played as intermediaries between the Tigris-Euphrates valley and the westernmost portions of the Near East. Doubtless in this way certain culture elements from Mesopotamia were transmitted to the Canaanites and to the peoples of the Aegean islands.

The importance of the
Hittites

2. THE MINOAN AND MYCENAEAN CIVILIZATIONS

By a strange coincidence the discovery of the existence of the Hittite, Minoan, and Mycenaean civilizations was made at just about the same time. Before 1870 scarcely anyone dreamed that great civilizations had flourished on the Aegean islands and on the shores of Asia Minor for hundreds of years prior to the rise of classical Greek civilization. Students of the *Iliad* knew, of course, of the references to a strange people who were supposed to have dwelt in Troy, to have kidnaped the fair Helen, and to have been punished by the Greeks for this act by the siege and destruction of their city. But it was commonly supposed that these accounts were mere figments of a poetical imagination. Today we are certain that Greek history, and thus European history, began over one thousand years before the Golden Age of Athens.

Long-forgotten
civilizations

The first discovery of a highly developed Aegean culture center was made not by a professional archeologist but by a retired German businessman, Heinrich Schliemann. Fascinated from early youth by the stories of the Homeric epics, he determined to dedicate his life to archeological research as soon as he had sufficient income to enable him to do so. Luckily for him and for the world he accumulated a fortune in Russian business ventures and then retired to spend both time and money in the pursuit of his boyhood dreams. In 1870 he began excavating at Troy. Within a few years he had uncovered portions of nine different cities, each built upon the ruins of its predecessor. The second of these cities he identified as the Troy of the *Iliad,* although it has been proved since then that Troy was the seventh city. After fulfilling his first great ambition, he started excavations on the mainland of Greece and eventually uncovered two other Aegean cities, Mycenae (pronounced My-sée-nee) and Tiryns. The work of Schliemann was soon followed by that of other investigators, notably the Englishman Sir Arthur Evans, who discovered Knossos, the resplendent capital of

The discoveries by
Schliemann and others

See color map facing
page 65

the Minoan kings of Crete. Up to the present time more than half of the ancient Aegean sites have been carefully searched, and a wealth of knowledge has been accumulated about various aspects of the culture.

The Minoan and Mycenaean civilizations originated on the island of Crete. (See the map on p. 122, below.) In few other cases in history does the geographic interpretation of culture origins fit so neatly. Crete has a benign and equable climate. While the soil is fertile, it is not of unlimited area; consequently, as the population increased, people were impelled to sharpen their wits and to contrive new means of earning a living. Some emigrated; others took to the sea; but a larger number remained at home and developed articles for export. The latter included wine and olive oil, pottery, gems and seals, knives and daggers, and objects of skilled craftsmanship. The chief imports were foodstuffs and metals. As a result of such trade, prosperity increased and extensive contacts were made with the surrounding civilized world. Added to these factors of a favorable environment were the beauties of nature which abounded almost everywhere, stimulating the development of a marvelous art.

*The favorable natural
environment of Crete*

The Minoan civilization, named after the legendary Cretan ruler Minos, was founded by peoples who emigrated from Asia Minor to Crete around 3000 B.C. In the millennium thereafter they made the transition from the Neolithic stage to the age of metals; by 2000 B.C. they had developed cities and an early form of writing. From then until about 1500 B.C. their civilization developed under the leadership of the cities of Knossos and Phaistos. Recently, evidence has been found of the existence of another great city, Kato Zakros, on the east coast of Crete. Here was a huge palace of 250 rooms, with a swimming pool, parquet floors, and thousands of decorated vases. Only severe earthquakes, which periodically shook the island, interrupted the serene existence of the sophisticated Cretans. These quakes caused much devastation, but after each one the inhabitants of the Cretan cit-

*Origins and flowering of
Minoan civilization*

Central Staircase of the Palace at Knossos

A Linear B Tablet from Knossos

ies set about the work of rebuilding and usually managed to construct even more splendid palaces than the ones which had been destroyed. So confident were the inhabitants of Knossos that they faced no threat of foreign invasion that they left their magnificent city without any protective walls.

Ultimately such confidence proved to be mistaken. While Cretan civilization was flourishing, a related one was emerging on the mainland of Greece. Around 1900 B.C. Indo-European peoples who spoke the earliest form of Greek invaded the Greek peninsula, and by 1600 B.C. they were beginning to form settled communities. After around 1600 they became greatly influenced in their cultural development by the neighboring civilization of Minoan Crete, with which they had been developing trading relations. The civilization that resulted from the fusion of Greek and Minoan elements is usually called *Mycenaean,* after Mycenae, the leading city of Greece from about 1600 to 1200 B.C. It was this civilization that became dominant in the Aegean world after about 1500 and even gained predominance on the island of Crete itself.

One of the greatest scholarly accomplishments of recent times has radically altered our understanding of Cretan and Greek history in the century between 1500 and 1400. It used to be thought that Greece throughout that time was still a semibarbarous economic colony of splendid Crete and that internal changes on Crete between 1500 and 1400 could be attributed to the rise of a "new dynasty." It was known that numerous specimens of the same linear script (called "Linear B") could be found on both Crete and the Greek mainland, but it was simply assumed that the script was Cretan in origin and spread from Crete to Greece. But in 1952 a brilliant young Englishman, Michael Ventris, who was then only thirty years old (and tragically died in an automobile accident four years later), succeeded in deciphering Linear B and demonstrating that it expressed an early form of Greek. Ventris's discovery revolutionized preclassical Greek studies by showing that the mainlanders dominated Crete in the late Minoan period and not vice versa.

The new scholarly consensus is that the Mycenaeans supplanted the Minoans as rulers of the Aegean world sometime shortly after 1500

Origin of the Mycenaean civilization

Linear B

B.C. Around 1500 a great earthquake on Crete probably brought about sufficient weakness to allow the mainlanders to take control of the island. These Mycenaean Greeks helped to rebuild Knossos and presided over roughly a century of continued prosperity and artistic accomplishment on Crete. Around 1400, however, another wave of Greek invaders crossed over to the island, destroyed Knossos entirely, and put a cataclysmic end to the Minoan civilization. Why this invasion was so destructive cannot be known, but it left mainland Greece unrivaled as the center of civilization in the Aegean world for about another 200 years. Around 1250 B.C. the Mycenaeans waged their successful war with the Trojans of western Asia Minor, but their own demise was now in the offing. In the course of the century between 1200 B.C. and 1100 B.C., the Mycenaeans, whose civilization seems to have been decaying from within, succumbed to the Dorians—barbaric northern Greeks who had iron weapons. (Iron weapons may not at first have been much superior to the bronze ones used by the Mycenaeans, but they were far cheaper, thereby allowing many more fighters to wield them.) Because the Dorians were primitive in all but their weaponry their ascendancy initiated a dark age in Greek history which lasted until about 800 B.C.

As can be seen from the foregoing account, the Minoan and Mycenaean civilizations were closely interrelated; even the greatest experts have difficulty in determining exactly where one left off and the other began. The problem is complicated by the fact that two forms of writing which predate Linear B and have been found on Crete alone have not yet been deciphered. (Anyone who wishes to become as famous as Schliemann, Evans, or Ventris may take the decipherment of Cretan writing as his or her goal.) Accordingly, discussions of Minoan civilization before about 1500 B.C. rely exclusively on visual and archeological evidence, leaving much to the realm of speculation. Such evidence, however, does suggest that Cretan civilization was one of the most progressive in all of early history.

The Minoan ruler was no bristling warlord like the Assyrian and Persian kings. He does seem to have commanded a large navy, but this was not for war but for the maintenance of trade. In fact, the king was the chief entrepreneur in the country. The workshops located near his palace turned out great quantities of fine pottery, textiles, and metal goods. Although private enterprise apparently was not prohibited it seems to have been heavily taxed. Nevertheless there were some privately owned workshops, especially in smaller towns, and much agriculture was also in private hands.

The Cretan state is probably best described as a bureaucratic monarchy. The ruler of each leading city and its surrounding territory appears to have been absolute, and toward the end of Minoan history (exactly when is hard to say) the ruler of Knossos appears to have taken over the entire island. The absolute Cretan ruler governed by means of a large administrative class. Scribes, who seem to have had a

Mycenaean Warrior Vase, c. 1250 B.C. Found in the ruins of Mycenae, this vase displays the warlike aspects of Mycenaean culture: the men might be marching off to the Trojan War.

Difficulty of distinguishing between early Minoan and Mycenaean characteristics

A Minoan Vase, c. 1400 B.C. The potter's wheel, probably invented by the Minoans, allowed a greater variety of shapes for vessels and encouraged Minoan artists to employ new styles and methods of decoration.

Scenes from the Bull Ring: Minoan Mural, c. 1500 B.C. Evident are the youth, skill, and agility of the Cretan athletes, the center one a male, the other two female. The body and horns of the bull are exaggerated, as are the slenderness of the athletes and their full-face eyes in profile heads. There is probably also some exaggeration in content: modern experts in bullfighting insist that it is impossible to somersault over the back of a charging bull.

monopoly of learning, kept close accounts of all aspects of economic life. All agricultural production and manufacturing was closely supervised for purposes of gathering or taxing whatever was owed to the king. Foreign trade too seems to have been closely supervised by the state; most likely the large Cretan ships that put into ports as far away as Syria and Egypt were owned or at least heavily taxed by the ruler and carefully watched over by the bureaucratic administration.

A bureaucratic monarchy

Despite such close supervision, the Cretan people of nearly all classes appear to have led fairly prosperous lives. Although there were great social and economic distinctions between the rulers and the ruled, there were apparently few gradations of wealth or status among the common people. If slavery existed at all, it certainly occupied an unimportant place. The dwellings in the poorest quarters of smaller towns such as Gournia were well built and commodious, often with as many as six or eight rooms, but we do not know how many families resided in them. Women seem to have enjoyed equality with men. Regardless of class there was no public activity from which they were debarred, and no occupation which they could not enter. In this the Minoans were the exception in the ancient world. Crete had female bullfighters and even female pugilists. Women of the upper strata devoted much time to fashion and other leisure activities.

Evidences of social equality

The natives of Crete delighted in games and sports of every description. Dancing, running matches, and boxing rivaled each other in their attraction for the people. The Cretans were the first to build stone theaters where processions and music entertained large audiences.

The love of sports and games

So far as we know, Minoan religion was a medley of strange characteristics. First of all it was apparently matriarchal. The chief deity was not a god but a goddess, who was the ruler of the entire universe—the sea and the sky as well as the earth. Originally no male deity appears to have been worshiped, but later a god was associated with the goddess as her son and consort. Although, like the divine sons in several other religions, he apparently died and rose from the dead, he was never regarded by the Cretans as of particular importance. In the second place, the Minoan religion was thoroughly monistic. The mother goddess was the source of evil as well as of good, but not in any morbid or terrifying sense. Though she brought the storm and spread destruction in her path, these served for the replenishment of nature. Death itself was interpreted as the prerequisite for life. Whether the religion had any body of ethical precepts is unknown.

Other features of the religion of the Minoans included the worship of animals and birds (the bull, the snake, and the dove); the worship of sacred trees; the veneration of sacred objects which were probably reproductive symbols (the double-axe, the pillar, and the cross); and, in accordance with the matriarchal nature of the belief system, the employment of priestesses instead of priests to administer sacred rites.

Since we cannot yet decipher the early Cretan scripts it is impossible to tell whether the Minoans had any literature or philosophy, although the existence of either seems extremely unlikely because there is none written in Linear B. The problem of scientific achievements is easier to solve, since we have material remains for our guidance. Archeological discoveries on the island of Crete indicate that the ancient inhabitants were gifted inventors and engineers. They built excellent stone roads about eleven feet wide. Nearly all the basic principles of modern sanitary engineering were known to the designers of the palace of Knossos, with the result that the royal family of Crete in the seventeenth century B.C. enjoyed comforts and conveniences, such as indoor running water, that were not available to the wealthiest rulers of Western countries in the seventeenth century A.D.

If any single achievement of the Minoans appears most to emphasize the vitality and freedom of their culture, it was their art. With the exception of the classical Greek, no other art of the ancient world was its equal. Its distinguishing features were delicacy, spontaneity, and naturalism. It served not to glorify the ambitions of an arrogant ruling class or to inculcate the doctrines of a religion, but to express the delight of the individual in the beauty and splendor of the Minoan world. As a result, it was remarkably free from the retarding influence of ancient tradition. It was unique, moreover, in the universality of its application, for it extended not merely to paintings and statues but even to the humblest objects of ordinary use.

Of the major arts, architecture was the least developed. The great palaces were not remarkably beautiful buildings but rambling struc-

Minoan Snake Goddess, Sixteenth Century B.C. A statuette made of ivory and gold.

Architecture

"La Parisienne"

Similarities between the Minoan and Mycenaean civilizations

tures designed primarily for capaciousness and comfort. As more and more functions were absorbed by the state, the palaces were enlarged to accommodate them. New quarters were annexed to those already built or piled on top of them without regard for order or symmetry. The interiors, however, were decorated with beautiful paintings and furnishings. The architecture of Crete may be said to have resembled the modern international style in its subordination of form to utility and in its emphasis upon a pleasing and livable interior as more important than external beauty.

Painting was the supreme Cretan art. Nearly all of it consisted of murals done in fresco, although painted reliefs were occasionally to be found. The murals in the palaces of Crete were by all odds the best that have survived from ancient times. They revealed almost perfectly the remarkable gifts of the Minoan artist—an instinct for the dramatic, a sense of rhythm, a feeling for nature in its most characteristic moods. So sophisticated and elegant was Cretan art that a Frenchman who was unearthing the remains of a fresco at Knossos could not help exclaiming when he saw a painting of a striking woman portrayed with curls, vivid eyes, and sensuous lips: "Mais, c'est la Parisienne!" ("Why, she's just like a woman from Paris!").

Sculpture and the ceramic and gem-carving arts were also developed to a high stage of perfection. The sculpture of the Cretans differed from that of any other people in the ancient Near East. It never relied upon size as a device to convey the idea of power. The Cretans produced no colossi like those of Egypt or reliefs like those of Babylonia depicting a king of gigantic proportions smiting his puny enemies. Instead, they preferred sculpture in miniature. Nearly all of the statues of human beings or of deities that the archeologists have found are smaller than life-size.

Mycenaean civilization appears to have been more warlike and less refined than the Minoan, but the most recent scholarship warns us to beware of exaggerating these differences. As on Crete, so on mainland Greece, the city was the center of civilization—the leading Mycenaean cities being Mycenae itself (according to Homer the home of the leading Greek king Agamemnon), Pylos (according to Homer the home of the wise Nestor), and Tiryns. Each city and its surrounding area was ruled over by a king called a *wanax,* who in many respects ruled like an Oriental despot. As on Crete, the Mycenaean state was a bureaucratic monarchy. We know for certain about some of the workings of this monarchy because of the decipherment of numerous Linear B tablets, all of which are records of a highly regulatory bureaucratic apparatus. Linear B tablets from Pylos report the minutest details of the economic lives of the king's subjects: the exact acreage of a given estate; the number of cooking utensils owned by so-and-so; the personal names given to somebody else's two oxen ("Glossy" and "Blackie"). Such detailed inventories show us that the state was highly centralized and that it was as supreme in its control over the economic activities of its citizens as any other in the Near East.

Although the bureaucratic monarchies of Crete and Mycenaean Greece were probably similar, there were still at least a few notable differences between the two related civilizations. One was that the Mycenaeans definitely had a slave system. Mycenaean society too was geared much more toward warfare. Because Mycenaean cities frequently fought with one another they were built on hilltops and were heavily fortified. In keeping with a somewhat more rugged and barbaric style of life than that of Crete, Mycenaean kings built themselves ostentatious graves in which they buried their best inlaid bronze daggers and other signs of their power and wealth.

It is also true that Mycenaean art is less elegant than Minoan. Without question the Mycenaeans never equaled the artistic delicacy and grace of their Minoan predecessors. Nevertheless, Mycenaean artwork done in Knossos between 1500 and 1400 B.C., while stiffer and more symmetrical in composition than earlier Minoan work, is by no means wholly different in kind. Moreover, the "Parisian woman" of Minoan Knossos has some very close stylistic relatives in a female procession fresco from about 1300 B.C. found in Mycenaean Tiryns. Nor should it be thought that all the best traits of Mycenaean art can merely be seen as debased borrowings from the Minoans: the superbly executed and exquisite Mycenaean inlaid daggers have no antecedents anywhere on Crete.

Detail from a Procession Fresco at Tiryns, c. 1300 B.C. Note the similarity of this Mycenaean female profile to the Minoan "La Parisienne" shown on p. 98.

The significance of the Minoan and the Mycenaean civilizations should not be estimated primarily in terms of subsequent influences. Minoan culture hardly influenced any peoples other than the Mycenaeans and it was then destroyed more or less without a trace after about 1400 B.C. The Mycenaeans left behind a few more traces, but still not very many. Later Greeks retained some Mycenaean gods and goddesses like Zeus, Hera, Hermes, and Poseidon, but they completely altered their role in the religious pantheon. It may also be that the later Greeks gained from the Mycenaeans their devotion to athletics and their system of weights and measures, but these connections remain uncertain. Homer definitely remembered the successful Mycenaean siege of Troy, but it is just as important to realize how much Homer forgot: writing in the eighth century B.C. Homer (actually several different writers who have come down to us under that name) entirely forgot the whole pattern of Mycenaean bureaucratic monarchy which we know from the Linear B tablets. It may well be that the break between the Mycenaeans and Homer was all for the good. Some historians maintain that the destruction of despotic Mycenae by the Dorians was a necessary prelude to the emergence of the freer and more enlightened later Greek outlook.

Influence of the Minoan and Mycenaean civilizations

Although the Minoan and Mycenaean civilizations had little subsequent influence, they are still noteworthy for at least four reasons. First of all, they were the earliest civilizations of Europe. Before the

Cretan accomplishments all civilizations had existed farther east, but afterward Europe was to witness the development of one highly impressive civilization after another. Second, in some respects the Minoans and the Mycenaeans seem to have looked forward to certain later European values and accomplishments even if they did not directly influence them. Minoan and Mycenaean political organization was similar to that of many Asian states but Minoan art in particular seems very different and more characteristic of later European patterns. Unlike most ancient Near Eastern artists, the Minoan gloried not in portraying the slaughter of armies or the sacking of cities but in picturing flowery landscapes, joyous festivals, thrilling exhibitions of athletic prowess, and similar scenes of a free and peaceful existence. Third, the Minoan civilization, and to a lesser degree also the Mycenaean one, is significant for its worldly and progressive outlook. This is exemplified in the devotion of the Aegean peoples to comfort and opulence, in their love of amusement, zest for life, and courage for experimentation. And finally, the Minoan civilization is particularly remarkable for having flourished for so long in peace. If there has never again been as peaceful a civilization as the Minoan then that is a fact we should not celebrate but deplore.

3. THE LYDIANS AND THE PHOENICIANS

After the last remnants of the Hittite Empire fell in the eighth century B.C., one of the successor states in Asia Minor was the Kingdom of Lydia. The Lydians established their rule in what is now the western part of Turkey. They quickly secured control of the Greek cities on the coast of Asia Minor and of the entire plateau west of the Halys River. But their power was short-lived. In 547 B.C. their king, Croesus, fancied he saw a good opportunity to add to his domain the territory of the Medes east of the Halys. The Median king had just been deposed by Cyrus the Great of Persia. Thinking this meant an easy triumph for his own armies, Croesus set out to capture the territory beyond the river. After an indecisive battle with Cyrus, he returned to his own capital (Sardis) for reinforcements. Here Cyrus caught him unprepared in a surprise attack and captured and burned the city. The Lydians never recovered from the blow, and soon afterward all of their territory, including the Greek cities on the coast, passed under the dominion of Cyrus.

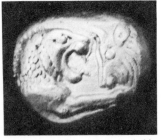

An Early Lydian Coin, Probably Struck during the Reign of Croesus

The Lydians, a people of Indo-European speech, were probably a mixture of native peoples of Asia Minor with migrant stocks from eastern Europe. Benefiting from the advantages of favorable location and abundance of resources, they enjoyed one of the highest standards of living of ancient times. They were famous for the splendor of their armored chariots and the quantities of gold and articles of luxury possessed by the citizens. The wealth of their kings was legendary, as shown by the simile "rich as Croesus." The chief sources of this prosperity were gold from the streams, wool from the thousands of sheep on the hills, and the profits of the extensive commerce which passed overland from the Tigris-Euphrates valley to the Aegean Sea. But with all their wealth and opportunities for leisure, they succeeded in making only one original contribution to civilization. This was the coinage of money from electrum or "white gold," a natural mixture of gold and silver found in the sands of one of their rivers. Hitherto all systems of money had consisted of weighed rings or bars of metal. The new coins, of varying sizes, were stamped with a definite value more or less arbitrarily given by the ruler who issued them.

The Lydian people and their culture

In contrast with the Lydians, who gained their ascendancy as a result of the downfall of the Hittites, were the Phoenicians, who benefited from the break-up of Aegean supremacy. But the Phoenicians were neither conquerors nor the builders of an empire. They exerted their influence through the arts of peace, especially through commerce. During most of their history their political system was a loose confederation of city-states, which frequently bought their security by paying tribute to foreign powers. The territory they occupied was the narrow strip north of Palestine between the Lebanon Mountains and the Mediterranean Sea and the islands off the coast. With good harbors and a central location, it was admirably situated for trade. The great centers of commerce included Tyre and Sidon. Under the leadership of Tyre, Phoenicia reached the zenith of its accomplishments from the tenth to the eighth century B.C. During the sixth century it passed under the domination of the Chaldeans and then of the Persians. In 332 B.C. Tyre was destroyed by Alexander the Great after a siege of seven months.

The Phoenician cities and confederation

See color map facing page 65

The Phoenicians were a Semitic people, closely related to the Canaanites. They displayed little creative genius, but were remarkable adapters of the achievements of others. They produced no original art worthy of the name, and they made but slight contributions to literature. Their religion, like that of the Canaanites, was characterized by human sacrifice to the god Moloch and by licentious fertility rites. They excelled, however, in specialized manufactures, in geography and navigation. They founded colonies at Carthage in North Africa, near modern-day Palermo on the island of Sicily, on the Balearic Islands, and at Cadiz and Malaga in Spain. They were renowned throughout the ancient world for their glass and metal industries and for their purple dye obtained from a mollusk in the adjacent seas. They developed the art of navigation to such a stage that they could sail by the stars at night. To less venturesome peoples, the North Star was known for some time as the Phoenicians' star. Phoenician ships and sailors were recruited by all the great powers. The most lasting achievement of the Phoenicians, however, was the invention and diffusion of an alphabet based upon principles set forth by the Egyptians.

Achievements of the Phoenicians

The Phoenician contribution was the adoption of a system of signs representing the sounds of the human voice, and the elimination of all pictographic and syllabic characters. This alphabet was taken up by the Greeks, who adapted it for their own language, and from the Greek alphabet was derived the modern Latin one, used throughout the West today.

4. LESSONS FROM THE HISTORY OF THE NEAR EASTERN STATES

Defects of the Near Eastern empires

Like most other periods in world history, the period of the states we have studied thus far was an era of contention and strife. Nearly all of the great empires, and the majority of the smaller states as well, devoted most of their energies to expansion and aggression. The only notable exceptions were the Minoan and Egyptian, but even the Egyptians in the later period of their history were imperialistic. The causes were largely geographic. Each nation grew accustomed to the pursuit of its own interests in some fertile river valley or on some easily defended plateau. Isolation bred fear of foreigners and an incapacity to think of one's own people as members of a common humanity. The feelings of insecurity that resulted seemed to justify aggressive foreign policies and the annexation of neighboring states to serve as buffers against a hostile world.

Results of Near Eastern imperialism

It seems possible to trace nearly all of the woes of the Near Eastern nations to wars of aggression. Arnold J. Toynbee has shown this in devastating fashion in the case of the Assyrians. He contends that it was no less true of such later peoples as the Spartans, the Carthaginians, the Macedonians, and the Ottoman Turks. Each made militarism and conquest its gods and wrought such destruction upon itself that when it made its last heroic stand against its enemies, it was a mere "corpse in armor." Not death by foreign conquest but national suicide was the fate which befell it.[1] The way of the warrior brought racism, a love of ease and luxury, crime, and crushing burdens of taxation. Expansion of empire promoted a fictitious prosperity, at least for the upper classes, and aroused enough envy among poorer nations to make them willing conspirators against a rich neighbor who could easily be portrayed as an oppressor. The use of hungry and discontented allies against powerful rivals is not new in history.

SELECTED READINGS

* *Items so designated are available in paperback editions.*
  Alsop, Joseph, *From the Silent Earth: A Report on the Greek Bronze Age,* New York, 1964. An enthusiastic account by a modern political reporter of

[1] D. C. Somervell (ed.), A. J. Toynbee's *A Study of History,* I, 338–43.

some of the most exciting recent discoveries and hypotheses. Favors the Mycenaeans in discussions of their relationships to the Minoans.

Blegen, C. W., *Troy and the Trojans*, New York, 1963. The most reliable archeological appraisal.

• Ceram, C. W., *The Secret of the Hittites*, New York, 1956. The best popular account.

• Chadwick, John, *The Decipherment of Linear B*, 2nd ed., New York, 1968. Chadwick was a research colleague of Michael Ventris and here gives the most accessible account of Ventris's brilliant work.

———, *The Mycenaean World*, New York, 1976. A lively account of the society based on the evidence of the Linear B tablets.

Finley, M. I., *Early Greece: The Bronze and Archaic Ages*, New York, 1970. An excellent survey that spans two different eras.

• Gordon, Cyrus H., *The Ancient Near East*, New York, 1965.

•———, *The Common Background of Greek and Hebrew Civilizations*, New York, 1965. Very controversial. Gordon believes that Greek culture was in its origins Semitic.

Gurney, O. R., *The Hittites*, Baltimore, 1961. More scholarly than Ceram.

Harden, Donald, *The Phoenicians*, New York, 1962. Best account of the Phoenicians at home and abroad.

• Higgins, Reynold, *Minoan and Mycenaean Art*, New York, 1967.

History of the Hellenic World, Vol. I, *Prehistory and Protohistory*, University Park, Pa., 1974.

Hutchinson, R. W., *Prehistoric Crete*, Baltimore, 1962.

Lloyd, Seton, *Early Anatolia*, Baltimore, 1956.

• MacDonald, William A., *Progress into the Past: The Rediscovery of Mycenaean Civilization*, New York, 1967.

Palmer, L. R., *Mycenaeans and Minoans*, New York, 1962. Includes bold statements on many debatable problems of interpretation.

Starr, C. G., *The Origins of Greek Civilization*, New York, 1961.

Trump, David, *The Prehistory of the Mediterranean*, New Haven, Conn., 1980. Treats the earliest European cultures from 5000 B.C. to 1000 B.C.

• Vermeule, Emily, *Greece in the Bronze Age*, Chicago, 1964. The best book on the subject.

Part Two

THE CLASSICAL CIVILIZATIONS OF GREECE AND ROME

After 600 B.C. the centers of civilization in the Western world were no longer mainly located in the Near East. By that time new cultures were already growing to maturity in Greece and in Italy. Both had started their evolution considerably earlier, but the civilization of Greece did not begin to ripen until about 600 B.C., while the Romans showed little promise of original achievement before 500. About 300 B.C. Greek civilization, properly speaking, came to an end and was superseded by a new culture representing a fusion of elements derived from Greece and the Near East. This was the Hellenistic civilization, which lasted until about the beginning of the Christian era and included not only the Greek peninsula but Egypt and most of Asia west of the Indus River. The outstanding characteristic which serves to distinguish these three civilizations from the ones that had gone before is secularism. No longer does religion absorb the interests of humans to the extent that it did in ancient Egypt or in the nations of Mesopotamia. The state is now above the church, and the power of the priests to determine the direction of cultural evolution has been greatly reduced. Furthermore, ideals of human freedom and an emphasis on the welfare of the individual have largely superseded the despotism and collectivism of the ancient Near East. Only late in Roman history, around the third century A.D., did Near Eastern despotism begin to reassert itself within the confines of imperial Rome. Around that time too, a new religion, Christianity, began to reshape the life of the West.

The Classical Civilizations of Greece and Rome

POLITICS	PHILOSOPHY AND SCIENCE

800 B.C.

Dark Ages of Greek history, 1100–800

Beginning of city-states in Greece, c. 800
Rome founded, c. 750

Thales of Miletus, c. 640–546
Pythagoras, c. 582–c. 507

Age of the tyrants in Greece, c. 650–c. 500
Reforms of Solon in Athens, 594
Tyranny of Peisistratus, 560
Reforms of Cleisthenes, 508

500 B.C.

Establishment of Roman Republic, c. 500
Greco-Persian War, 490–479

Protagoras, c. 490–c. 420
Socrates, 469–399

Delian League, 479–404
Perfection of Athenian democracy, 461–429
Law of the Twelve Tables, Rome, c. 450
Peloponnesian War, 431–404

Hippocrates, 460–c. 377
Democritus, c. 460–c. 362
The Sophists, c. 450–c. 400
Plato, 427–347

400 B.C.

Aristotle, 384–322

Theban supremacy in Greece, 371–362
Macedonian conquest of Greece, 338–337
Conquests of Alexander the Great, 336–323
Division of Alexander's empire, 323

Mencius, c. 373–288
Epicurus, 342–270
Zeno the Stoic, c. 320–c. 250
Euclid, c. 323–285

300 B.C.

Aristarchus, 310–230
Archimedes, c. 287–212
Eratosthenes, c. 276–c. 195

Herophilus, c. 220–c. 150
Polybius, c. 205–118

200 B.C.

The Skeptics, c. 200–c. 100

Punic Wars between Rome and Carthage, 264–146
Reforms of the Gracchi, 133–121
Dictatorship of Julius Caesar, 46–44
Principate of Augustus Caesar, 27 B.C.–14 A.D.

Introduction of Stoicism into Rome, c. 140
Cicero, 106–43

100 B.C.

Dictatorship of Julius Caesar, 46–44
Principate of Augustus Caesar, 27 B.C.–14 A.D.

Lucretius, 98–55

Seneca, 34 B.C.–65 A.D.

100 A.D.

"Five Good Emperors," 96–180
Completion of Roman jurisprudence by great
   jurists, c. 200

Marcus Aurelius, 121–180
Galen, 130–c. 200

200 A.D.

Civil war in Roman Empire, 235–284
Diocletian, 284–305

Plotinus, c. 204–270

300 A.D.

Constantine I, 306–337

400 A.D.

Theodosius I, 379–395
Visigoths sack Rome, 410
Deposition of last of Western Roman emperors, 476

500 A.D.

Theodoric the Ostrogoth king of Italy, 493–526
Justinian, 527–565
Corpus of Roman law, c. 550

Boethius, c. 480–524

ECONOMICS	RELIGION	ARTS AND LETTERS	
			800 B.C.
Economic revolution and colonization in Greece, c. 750–c. 600			
Rise of middle class in Greece, c. 750–c. 600		*Iliad* and *Odyssey*, c. 750	
		Doric architectural style, c. 650–c. 500	
	Orphic and Eleusinian mystery cults, c. 500–c. 100	Aeschylus, 525–456	**500** B.C.
		Phidias, c. 500–c. 432	
		Ionic architectural style, c. 500–c. 400	
		Sophocles, 496–406	
		Herodotus, c. 484–c. 420	
		Euripides, 480–406	
		Thucydides, c. 471–c. 400	
		The Parthenon, c. 460	**400** B.C.
		Aristophanes, c. 448–c. 380	
		Corinthian architectural style, c. 400–c. 300	
		Praxiteles, c. 370–c. 310	
Hellenistic international trade and growth of large cities, c. 300 B.C.–c. 100 A.D.			**300** B.C.
Growth of slavery, rise of middle class, decline of small farmer in Rome, c. 250–100	Oriental mystery cults in Rome, c. 250–50		
			200 B.C.
	Spread of Mithraism in Rome, 27 B.C.–270 A.D.	Virgil, 70–19	**100** B.C.
	The Crucifixion, c. 30 A.D.	Horace, 65–8	
Decline of slavery in Rome, c. 120–c. 476	St. Paul's missionary work, c. 35–c. 67	Livy, 59 B.C.–17 A.D.	
		Ovid, c. 43 B.C.–17 A.D.	
Growth of serfdom in Rome, c. 200–500		Tacitus, c. 55 A.D.–c. 117 A.D.	**100** A.D.
		The Colosseum, c. 80 A.D.	
Sharp economic contraction in Rome, c. 200–c. 300		The Pantheon, c. 120	**200** A.D.
	Beginning of toleration of Christians in the Roman Empire, 311	Height of Roman portrait statuary, c. 120–c. 250	
			300 A.D.
	St. Augustine, 354–430		
	Christianity made official Roman religion, 380		**400** A.D.
			500 A.D.
	Benedictine monastic rule, c. 520		

Chapter 6

GREEK CIVILIZATION

We love beauty without extravagance, and wisdom without weakness of will. Wealth we regard not as a means for private display but rather for public service; and poverty we consider no disgrace, although we think it is a disgrace not to try to overcome it. We believe a man should be concerned about public as well as private affairs, for we regard the person who takes no part in politics not as merely uninterested but as useless.

> —Pericles, *Funeral Oration,* on the ideals of Athens

Now, what is characteristic of any nature is that which is best for it and gives most joy. Such to man is the life according to reason, since it is this that makes him man.

> —Aristotle, *Nicomachean Ethics*

Among all the peoples of the ancient world, the one whose culture most clearly exemplified the spirit of Western society was the Greek or Hellenic. No one of these nations had so strong a devotion to liberty or so firm a belief in the nobility of human achievement. The Greeks glorified humanity as the most important creation in the universe and refused to submit to the dictation of priests or despots or even to humble themselves before their gods. Their attitude was essentially secular and rationalistic; they exalted the spirit of free inquiry and made knowledge supreme over faith. Largely for these reasons their culture advanced to the highest stage which the ancient world was destined to reach.

The character of Greek civilization

1. THE GREEK DARK AGES

The fall of the Mycenaean civilization was a major catastrophe for the Greek world. It ushered in a period usually called by historians the Dark Ages, which lasted from about 1100 to 800 B.C. Written records disappeared, except where accidentally preserved, and culture reverted to simpler forms than had been known for centuries. Toward

The Dark Ages

Greek Civilization

Bronze Centaur and Man. These figures date from about 750 B.C. They are no more than about five inches high.

Bronze Statuette. Perhaps representing Apollo, this work dates from about 750 B.C.

the end of the period some decorated pottery and skillfully designed metal objects began to appear on the islands of the Aegean Sea, but essentially the period was a long night. Aside from the development of writing at the very end, intellectual accomplishment was limited to ballads, and short epics sung and embellished by bards as they wandered from one village to another. A large part of this material was finally woven into a great epic cycle by one or more poets in the eighth century B.C. Though not all the poems of this cycle have come down to us, the two most important, the *Iliad* and the *Odyssey,* the so-called Homeric epics, provide us with a rich store of information about many of the customs and institutions of the Dark Ages.

The political institutions of the Dark Ages were exceedingly primitive. Each little community of villages was independent of external control, but political authority was so tenuous that it would not be too much to say that the state scarcely existed at all. The *basileus* or ruler was not much more than a tribal leader. He could not make or enforce laws or administer justice. He received no remuneration of any kind, and had to cultivate his farm for a living the same as any other citizen. Practically his only functions were military and priestly. He commanded the army in time of war and offered sacrifices to keep the gods on the good side of the community. Although each little community had its council of nobles and assembly of warriors, neither of these bodies had any definite membership or status as an organ of government. Almost without exception custom took the place of law, and the administration of justice was private. Even willful murder was punishable only by the family of the victim. While it is true that disputes were sometimes submitted to the ruler for settlement, he acted in such cases merely as an arbitrator, not as a judge. As a matter of fact, the political consciousness of the Greeks of this time was so poorly developed that they had no conception of government as an indispensable agency for the preservation of social order. When Odysseus, ruler of Ithaca, was absent for twenty years, no regent governed in his place and no session of the council or assembly was held. No one seemed to think that the complete suspension of government, even for so long a time, was a matter of critical importance.

The pattern of social and economic life was remarkably simple. Though the general tone of the society portrayed in the epics is aristocratic, no rigid stratification of classes existed. Manual labor was not looked upon as degrading, and there were apparently no idle rich. That there were dependent laborers who worked on the lands of the nobles and served them as faithful warriors seems clear from the Homeric epics, but they appear to have been serfs rather than slaves. The slaves were chiefly women, employed as servants, wool-processors, or concubines. Many were war captives, but they do not appear to have been badly treated. Agriculture and herding were the basic occupations of free men. Except for a few skilled crafts like those of wagonmaker, swordsmith, goldsmith, and potter, there was no specialization of labor. For the most part every household made its own tools, wove its own clothing, and raised its own food. So far were the Greeks of this time from being a trading people that they had no word in their language for "merchant," for barter was the only method of exchange.

To the Greeks of the Dark Ages religion meant chiefly a system for: (1) explaining the physical world in such a way as to remove its awesome mysteries and give people a feeling of intimate relationship with it; (2) accounting for the tempestuous passions that seized human nature; and (3) obtaining such tangible benefits as good fortune, long life, skill in craftsmanship, and abundant harvests. The Greeks did not expect that their religion would save them from sin or endow them with spiritual blessings. As they conceived it, piety was neither a matter of conduct nor of faith. Their religion, accordingly, had no commandments, dogmas, or sacraments. All were at liberty to believe what they pleased and to conduct their own lives as they chose without fear of divine wrath.

As is commonly known, the deities of the early Greek religion were merely human beings writ large. It was really necessary that this should be so if the Greeks were to feel at home in the world over which they ruled. Remote, omnipotent beings like the gods of most oriental religions would have inspired fear rather than a sense of security. What the Greeks wanted was not necessarily gods of great power, but deities who could be bargained with on equal terms. Consequently gods were endowed with attributes similar to human ones—with human bodies and human weaknesses and wants. The early Greeks imagined the great company of divinities as frequently quarreling with one another, mingling freely with mortals, and even occasionally procreating children by mortal women. They differed from humans only in the fact that they subsisted on ambrosia and nectar, which made them immortal. They dwelt not in the sky or in the stars but on the summit of Mount Olympus, a peak in northern Greece with an altitude of about 10,000 feet.

The religion was thoroughly polytheistic, with no one deity elevated very high above any of the others. Zeus, the sky god and wielder of the thunderbolt, who was sometimes referred to as the father of the gods and of men, frequently received less attention than did Poseidon, the sea god, Aphrodite, goddess of love, or Athena, variously considered goddess of wisdom and war and patroness of handicrafts. Since the Greeks had no Satan, their religion cannot be described as dualistic. All of the deities were deemed capable of malevolence as well as good.

Poseidon or Zeus. Detail from an Athenian statue of about 470 B.C., larger than life size.

The Greeks of the Dark Ages were almost completely indifferent to what happened to them after death. They did assume, however, that shades or ghosts survived for a time after the death of their bodies. All, with a few exceptions, went to the same abode—to the murky realm of Hades situated beneath the earth. This was neither a paradise

Indifference to life after death

nor a hell: no one was rewarded for good deeds, and no one was punished for sins. Each of the shades appeared to continue the same kind of life its human embodiment had lived on earth. The Homeric poems make casual mention of two other realms, the Elysian Plain and the realm of Tartarus, which seem at first glance to contradict the idea of no rewards and punishments in the hereafter. But the few individuals who enjoyed the ease and comfort of the Elysian Plain had done nothing to deserve such blessings: they were simply persons whom the gods had chosen to favor. The realm of Tartarus was not really an abode of the dead but a place of imprisonment for rebellious deities.

The external and mechanical character of worship

Worship in early Greek religion consisted primarily of sacrifice. The offerings were made, however, not as an atonement for sin, but chiefly in order to please the gods and induce them to grant favors. In other words, religious practice was external and mechanical and not far removed from magic. Reverence, humility, and purity of heart were not essentials in it. The worshiper just made the proper sacrifice and then hoped for the best. For a religion such as this no elaborate institutions were required. Even a professional priesthood was unnecessary. Since there were no mysteries and no sacraments, one man could perform the simple rites about as well as another. The Greek temple was not a church or place of religious assemblage, and no ceremonies were performed within it. Instead it was a shrine which the god might visit occasionally and use as a temporary house.

As intimated already, the morality of the Greeks in the Dark Ages had only the vaguest connection with their religion. While it is true that the gods were generally disposed to support the right, they did not consider it their duty to combat evil and make righteousness prevail. In meting out rewards to humans, they appear to have been influenced more by their own whims and by gratitude for sacrifices offered than by any consideration for moral character. The only crime they punished was perjury, and that none too consistently. Nearly all the virtues extolled in the epics were those which would make the individual a better soldier—bravery, self-control, patriotism, wisdom (in the sense of cunning), love of one's friends, and hatred of one's enemies. There was no conception of sin in the Christian sense of wrongful acts to be repented of or atoned for.

At the end of the Dark Ages the Greeks already had started along the road of social ideals that they would follow in later centuries. They were optimists, convinced that life was worth living for its own sake, and could see no reason for looking forward to death as a glad release. They were egotists striving for the fulfillment of self. As a consequence, they rejected mortification of the flesh and all forms of denial which implied the frustration of life. They could see no merit in humility or in turning the other cheek. Finally, they were humanists, who worshiped the finite and the natural rather than the otherworldly or sublime. For this reason they refused to invest their gods with awe-

Man Carrying a Calf for Sacrifice. A life-size Athenian sculpture from about 570 B.C.

Battle between the Gods and the Giants. This frieze dates from before 525 B.C. and is from the sanctuary of Apollo at Delphi.

inspiring qualities, or to invent any conception of humans as depraved and sinful creatures.

2. THE EVOLUTION OF THE CITY-STATES

About 800 B.C. the village communities which had been founded mainly upon tribal or clan organization, began to give way to larger political units. As trade and the need for defense increased, cities grew up around marketplaces and defensive fortifications as seats of government for whole communities. Thus emerged the city-state, the most famous unit of political society developed by the Greeks. Examples could be found in almost every section of the Hellenic world: Athens, Thebes, and Megara on the mainland; Sparta and Corinth on the Peloponnesus; Miletus on the shore of Asia Minor; and Mitylene and Samos on the islands of the Aegean Sea. They varied enormously in both area and population. Sparta with more than 3,000 square miles and Athens with 1,060 had by far the greatest extent; the others averaged less than 100. At the peak of their power Athens and Sparta, each with a population of about 400,000, had approximately three times the numerical strength of most of their neighboring states.

The origin and nature of the city-states

More important is the fact that the Greek city-states varied widely in cultural evolution. From 800 to 500 B.C., commonly called the Archaic period, the Peloponnesian cities of Corinth and Argos were leaders in the development of literature and the arts. In the seventh century Sparta outshone many of its rivals. Preeminent above all were the Greek-speaking cities on the coast of Asia Minor and the islands of the Aegean Sea. Foremost among them was Miletus, where a brilliant

Variations among the city-states

One of the Earliest Minted Greek Coins. Struck around 700 B.C. on the island of Aegina, near Athens, this coin shows a sea turtle, a symbol of the Greeks' ability to flourish by sea.

A Coin from Selinus, a Greek City in Sicily. Depicted is a sacrifice to Asclepius, god of healing, who is represented in the form of a cock.

See color map facing page 160

Internal development widely similar

flowering of philosophy and science occurred as early as the sixth century. Athens lagged behind until at least one hundred years later.

With a few exceptions the Greek city-states went through a similar political evolution. They began their histories as monarchies. During the eighth century they were changed into oligarchies. About a hundred years later, on the average, most of the oligarchies were overthrown by dictators, or "tyrants," as the Greeks called them, meaning usurpers who ruled without legal right whether oppressively or not. Finally, in the sixth and fifth centuries, democracies were set up, or in some cases "timocracies," that is, governments based upon a property qualification for the exercise of political rights.

On the whole, it is not difficult to determine the causes of this political evolution. The first change came about as a result of the concentration of landed wealth. As the owners of great estates gained ever-greater economic power, they determined to wrest political authority from the ruler, now commonly called king, and vest it in the council, which they generally controlled. In the end they abolished the kingship entirely. Then followed a period of sweeping economic changes and political turmoil.

These developments affected not only Greece itself but many other parts of the Mediterranean world. For they were accompanied and followed by a vast overseas expansion. The chief causes were an increasing scarcity of land, internal strife, and a general temper of restlessness and discontent. The Greeks rapidly learned of numerous areas, thinly populated, with climate and soil similar to those of the homelands. The parent states most active in the expansive movement were Corinth, Chalcis, and Miletus. Their citizens founded colonies along the Aegean shores and even in Italy and Sicily. Of the latter the best known were Taras (modern Taranto) and Syracuse. They also established trading centers on the coast of Egypt and as far east as Babylon. The results of this expansionist movement were momentous. Commerce and industry became leading pursuits and the urban population increased. Merchants and artisans now joined with dispossessed farmers in an attack upon the landholding oligarchy. The natural fruit of the bitter class conflicts that ensued was dictatorship. By encouraging extravagant hopes and promising relief from chaos, ambitious demagogues attracted enough popular support to ride into power in defiance of constitutions and laws. Ultimately, however, dissatisfaction with tyrannical rule and the increasing economic might and political consciousness of the common citizens led to the establishment of democracies or timocracies.

Unfortunately space does not permit an analysis of the political history of each of the Greek city-states. Except in the more backward sections of Thessaly and the Peloponnesus, it is safe to conclude that the internal development of all of them paralleled the account given above, although minor variations due to local conditions doubtless occurred. The two most important of the Hellenic states, Sparta and Athens, deserve more detailed study.

115

The Armed Camp of Sparta

3. THE ARMED CAMP OF SPARTA

The history of Sparta[1] was the great exception to the political evolution of the city-states. Despite the fact that its citizens sprang from the same origins as most of the other Greeks, Sparta failed to make any progress in the direction of democratic rule. Instead, its government gradually evolved into a form more closely resembling a modern elite dictatorship. Culturally, also, the nation stagnated after the sixth century. The causes were due partly to isolation. Hemmed in by mountains on the northeast and west and lacking good harbors, the Spartan people had little opportunity to profit from the advances made in the outside world. Besides, no middle class arose to aid the masses in the struggle for freedom.

The peculiar development of Sparta

The major explanation is to be found, however, in militarism. The Spartans were originally Dorians who had come into the eastern Peloponnesus as an invading army. Though by the end of the ninth century they had gained dominion over all of Laconia, they were not satisfied. West of the Taygetus Mountains lay the fertile plain of Messenia. The Spartans determined to conquer it. The venture was successful, and the Messenian territory was annexed to Laconia. About 640 B.C. the Messenians enlisted the aid of Argos and launched a revolt. The war that followed was desperately fought, Laconia itself was invaded, and only the death of the Argive commander and the patriotic pleas of the fire-eating poet Tyrtaeus saved the day for the Spartans. This time the victors took no chances. They confiscated the lands of the Messenians, murdered or expelled their leaders, and turned the masses into serfs called *helots*. Thereafter Spartan foreign policy was defensive. Following the Messenian wars the Spartans feared that further foreign warfare would provide the opportunities for a helot uprising; consequently Sparta devoted itself to keeping what it had already gained.

The Spartan desire for conquest

Almost all the major features of Spartan life resulted from their wars with the Messenians. In subduing and despoiling their enemies they unwittingly enslaved themselves, for they lived through the remaining centuries of their history in deadly fear of insurrections. This fear explains their conservatism, their stubborn resistance to change, lest any innovation result in a fatal weakening of the system. Their pro-

The results of Spartan militarism

---

[1]Sparata was the leading city of a district called Laconia or Lacedaemonia; sometimes the *state* was referred to by one or the other of these names. The people, also, were frequently called Laconians or Lacedaemonians. (The modern adjective "laconic" comes from the reputation of the ancient Spartans for being sparing with words.)

vincialism can also be attributed to the same cause. Frightened by the prospect that dangerous ideas might be brought into the country, they discouraged travel and prohibited trade with the outside world. The necessity of maintaining the absolute supremacy of the citizen class over an enormous population of serfs required an iron discipline and a strict subordination of the individual; hence the Spartan collectivism, which extended into every branch of the social and economic life. Finally, much of the cultural backwardness of Sparta grew out of the atmosphere of restraint which inevitably resulted from the bitter struggle to conquer the Messenians and hold them under stern repression.

The Spartan government

The Spartan constitution provided for a government preserving the forms of the old system of the Dark Ages. Instead of one king, however, there were two, representing separate families of exalted rank. The Spartan kings enjoyed but few powers and those were chiefly of a military and priestly character. A second branch of the government was the council, composed of the two kings and twenty-eight nobles sixty years of age and over. This body supervised the work of administration, prepared measures for submission to the assembly, and served as the highest court for criminal trials. The third organ of government, the assembly, composed of all adult male citizens, approved or rejected the proposals of the council and elected all public officials except the kings. But the highest authority under the Spartan constitution was vested in a board of five men known as the *ephorate*. The ephors virtually were the government. They presided over the council and the assembly, controlled the educational system and the distribution of property, censored the lives of the citizens, and exercised a veto power over all legislation. They had power also to determine the fate of newborn infants, to conduct prosecutions before the council, and even to depose the kings if the religious omens appeared unfavorable. The Spartan government dominated by the ephors was thus in effect an oligarchy.

The class system in Sparta

The population of Sparta was divided into three main classes. The ruling element was made up of the Spartiates, or descendants of the original conquerors. Though never exceeding one-twentieth of the total population, the Spartiates alone had political privileges. Next in order of rank were the *perioeci,* or "dwellers around." The origin of this class is uncertain, but it was probably composed of peoples that had at one time been allies of the Spartans or had submitted voluntarily to Spartan domination. In return for service as a buffer population between the ruling class and the helots, the perioeci were allowed to carry on trade and to engage in manufacturing. At the bottom of the scale were the helots, or serfs, bound to the soil.

Perioeci and helots

Among these classes only the perioeci enjoyed any appreciable measure of comfort and freedom. While it is true that the economic condition of the helots cannot be described in terms of absolute misery, since they were permitted to keep for themselves a good share of what they produced on the estates of their masters, they were personally subjected to such degrading treatment that they were constantly wretched and rebellious. To guard against rebellion young Spartiates were sometimes sent to live among the helots in disguise and act like a secret police with the power to murder whom they pleased. The brutalizing effects on both sides can be easily imagined.

Discipline for the benefit of the state

Those who were born into the Spartiate class were doomed to a respectable slavery for the major part of their lives. Forced to submit to the severest discipline and to sacrifice individual interests, they were little more than cogs in a vast machine. Spartan babies were examined for hardiness at birth and those who were thought to be potential weaklings were carried off to the hills to die of neglect. The education of Spartan males was limited almost entirely to military training, which began at the age of seven, supplemented by merciless floggings to harden the boys for the duties of war. Between the ages of twenty and sixty the men gave almost all their time to state service. Although marriage was practically compulsory there was little family life: young men had to live in barracks, and after the age of thirty they still had to eat in military messes. The husbands carried off their wives on their wedding nights by a show of force. Because they saw so little of them afterwards it sometimes happened that men "had children before they ever saw their wives' faces in daylight."[2] The production of vigorous offspring was the wives' main duty, but mothers had to accept the fact that children were virtually the property of the state. It may be doubted that the Spartiates resented these hardships and deprivations. Pride in their status as the ruling class probably compensated in their minds for harsh discipline and denial of privileges.

Economic regulations

The economic organization of Sparta was designed almost solely for the ends of military efficiency and the supremacy of the citizen class. The best land was owned by the state and was originally divided into equal plots which were assigned to the Spartiate class as inalienable estates. Later these holdings as well as the inferior lands were permitted to be sold and exchanged, with the result that some of the citizens became richer than others. The helots, who did all the work of cultivating the soil, also belonged to the state and were assigned to their masters along with the land. Their masters were forbidden to emancipate them or to sell them outside of the country. The labor of the helots provided for the support of the whole citizen class, whose members were not allowed to be associated with any economic enterprise other than agriculture. The minimal trade and industry of the Spartan state were reserved exclusively for the perioeci. Thus the Spartan economy was as static as Sparta's government was repressive.

[2] Plutarch, "Lycurgus," *Lives of Illustrious Men,* I, 81.

4. THE ATHENIAN TRIUMPH AND TRAGEDY

*Advantages enjoyed by
the Athenians*

Athens began its history under conditions quite different from those which prevailed in Sparta. The district of Attica in which Athens is situated had not been the scene of an armed invasion or of bitter conflict between opposing peoples. As a result, no military caste imposed its rule upon a vanquished nation. Furthermore, the wealth of Attica consisted of mineral deposits and splendid harbors in addition to agricultural resources. Athens, consequently, never remained a predominantly agrarian state but rapidly developed a prosperous trade and an essentially urban culture.

*From monarchy to
oligarchy in Athens*

Until the middle of the eighth century B.C. Athens, like the other Greek states, had a monarchical form of government. During the century that followed, the council of nobles, or Council of the Areopagus, as it came to be called, gradually divested the king of his powers. The transition to rule by the few was both the cause and the result of an increasing concentration of wealth. The introduction of vine and olive culture about this time led to the growth of agriculture as a large-scale enterprise. Since vineyards and olive orchards require considerable time to become profitable, only those farmers with abundant resources were able to survive in the business. Their poorer and less thrifty neighbors sank rapidly into debt, especially since grain was now coming to be imported at ruinous prices. The small farmer had no alternative but to mortgage his land, and then his family and himself, in the vain hope that some day a way of escape would be found. Ultimately many of this class became serfs when the mortgages could not be paid; those without land to mortgage were sold into slavery.

*Threats of revolution and
the reforms of Solon*

Bitter cries of distress now arose. The urban middle classes espoused the cause of the peasants in demanding liberalization of the government. Finally, in 594 B.C., all parties agreed upon the appointment of the aristocrat Solon as chief magistrate with absolute power to carry out reforms. The measures Solon enacted provided for both political and economic adjustments. The former included: (1) the establishment of a new council, the Council of Four Hundred, and the admission of the middle classes to membership in it; (2) the enfranchisement of the lower classes by making them eligible for service in the assembly; and (3) the organization of a final court of appeals in criminal cases, open to all citizens and elected by universal manhood suffrage. The economic reforms benefited the poor farmers by canceling existing mortgages, prohibiting enslavement for debt in the future, and limiting the amount of land any one individual could own. Nor did Solon neglect the middle classes. He introduced a new system of coinage designed to give Athens an advantage in foreign trade, imposed heavy penalties for idleness, ordered every man to teach his son a trade, and offered full privileges of citizenship to alien craftsmen who would become permanent residents of the country.

Significant though these reforms were, they did not allay the discontent. The nobles were disgruntled because some of their privileges had been taken away. The middle and lower classes were dissatisfied because they were still excluded from the offices of magistracy, and because the Council of the Areopagus was left with its powers intact. The chaos and disillusionment that followed paved the way in 560 B.C. for the triumph of Peisistratus, the first of the Athenian tyrants. Although he proved to be a benevolent despot who patronized culture, reduced the power of the aristocracy, and raised the standard of living of the average Athenian, his son Hippias, who succeeded him, was a ruthless and spiteful oppressor.

In 510 B.C. Hippias's tyranny was overthrown by a group of nobles with aid from Sparta. Factional conflict raged for another two years until Cleisthenes, an intelligent aristocrat, enlisted the support of the masses to eliminate his rivals from the scene. Having promised concessions to the people as a reward for their help, he proceeded to reform the government in so sweeping a fashion that he has since been known as the father of Athenian democracy. Cleisthenes, who dominated Athenian politics from 508 to 502, enlarged the citizen population by granting full rights to all free men who resided in the country at that time. He established a new council and made it the chief organ of government with power to prepare measures for submission to the assembly and with supreme control over executive and administrative functions. Members of this body were to be chosen by lot. Any male citizen over thirty years of age was eligible. Cleisthenes also expanded the authority of the assembly, giving it power to debate and pass or reject the measures submitted by the Council, to declare war, to appropriate money, and to audit the accounts of retiring magistrates.

Greeks at War. A battle scene from the interior of a drinking cup, done in Athens between about 530 and 500 B.C.

The Owl of Athens. An Athenian silver coin of around 470 B.C., showing the owl, thought to be sacred to Athens's protectress, the goddess Athena. The name Athens appears in the Greek letters ΑΘΕ.

The perfection of Athenian democracy

Athenian democracy compared with modern democracy

Lastly, not long after the time of Cleisthenes, in 487, the Athenians instituted the device of ostracism, whereby any citizen considered dangerous to the state could be sent into honorable exile for a ten-year period. The device was meant to eliminate men suspected of cherishing dictatorial ambitions, but too often its effect was to eliminate exceptional personalities and to allow mediocrity to flourish.

The Athenian democracy attained its full perfection in the Age of Pericles (461–429 B.C.). It was during this period that the assembly acquired the authority to initiate legislation in addition to its power to ratify or reject proposals of the council. During this time also the Board of Ten Generals rose to a position roughly comparable to that of the British cabinet. The generals were chosen by the assembly for one-year terms and were eligible for reelection indefinitely. Pericles held the position of chief strategus or president of the Board of Generals for more than thirty years. The generals were not simply commanders of the army but the chief legislative and executive officials in the state. Though wielding enormous power, they could not become tyrants, for their policies were subject to review by the assembly, and they could easily be recalled at the end of their one-year terms or indicted for malfeasance at any time. Finally, in the Age of Pericles the Athenian system of courts reached its completion. No longer was there merely a supreme court to hear appeals from the decisions of magistrates, but an array of popular courts were formed to try all kinds of cases. At the beginning of each year a list of 6,000 citizens was chosen by lot from the various sections of the country. From this list separate juries, varying in size from 201 to 1,001, were made up for particular trials. Each of these juries constituted a court with power to decide by majority vote every question involved in the case. Although one of the magistrates presided, he had none of the prerogatives of a judge; the jury itself was the judge, and from its decision there was no appeal.

The Athenian democracy differed from the modern form in various ways. First of all, it entirely excluded women. Even taking that into account, it did not extend to the whole population, but only to the citizen class. While it is true that in the time of Cleisthenes the citizens probably included a majority of the inhabitants because of his enfranchisement of resident aliens, in the Age of Pericles the citizens were distinctly a minority. It may be well to observe, however, that within its limits Athenian democracy was more thoroughly applied than is the modern form. The choice by lot of nearly all magistrates except the Ten Generals, the restriction of all terms of public officials to one year, and the uncompromising adherence to the principle of majority rule even in judicial trials were examples of a confidence in the political capacity of the citizen which few modern nations would be willing to accept. The democracy of Athens differed from the contemporary ideal also in the fact that it was direct, not representative. The Athenians were not interested in being governed by a few men of reputation and ability; what vitally concerned them was the assurance to every citizen of an actual voice in the control of all public affairs.

In the century of its greatest expansion and creativity, Athens fought two major wars. The first, the war with Persia, was an outgrowth of the expansion of that empire into the eastern Mediterranean area. The Athenians resented the oppression of the Greek-speaking cities in Asia Minor and aided them in their struggle for freedom. (These cities shared with Athens a common Greek dialect—Ionian—a fact which made the Athenians feel a particularly close kinship with them.) The Persians retaliated by sending a powerful army and fleet to attack the Greeks. Although all Greece was in danger of conquest, Athens bore the chief burden of repelling the invader. The war, which began in 490 B.C. and lasted with interludes of peace until 479, is commonly regarded as one of the most significant in the history of the world. The heroic victories of the Greeks in such battles as Marathon (490) and Salamis (480) put an end to the menace of Persian conquest and forestalled the submergence of Hellenic ideals of freedom in Near Eastern despotism. The war also strengthened democracy in Athens and made that state the leading power in Greece.

The other of the great struggles, the Peloponnesian War with Sparta, had results of a quite different character. Instead of being another milestone in the Athenian march to power, it ended in tragedy. The causes of this war are of particular interest to the student of the downfall of civilizations. First and most important was the growth of Athenian imperialism. In the last year of the war with Persia, Athens had joined with a number of other Greek states in the formation of an offensive and defensive alliance known as the Delian League. When peace was concluded the league was not dissolved, for many of the Greeks feared that the Persians might come back. As time went on, Athens gradually transformed the league into a naval empire for the advancement of its own interests. It used some of the funds in the common treasury for its own purposes. It tried to reduce all the other members to a condition of vassalage, and when one of them rebelled, Athens overwhelmed it by force, seized its navy, and imposed tribute upon it as if it were a conquered state. Such high-handed methods aroused the suspicions of the Spartans, who feared that an Athenian hegemony would soon be extended over all of Greece.

A second major cause was to be found in the social and cultural differences between Athens and Sparta. Athens was democratic, progressive, urban, imperialist, and intellectually and artistically advanced. Sparta was aristocratic, conservative, agrarian, provincial, and culturally backward. Where such sharply contrasting systems exist side by side, conflicts are almost bound to occur. The attitude of the Athenians and Spartans had been hostile for some time. The former looked upon the latter as uncouth barbarians. The Spartans accused the Athenians of attempting to gain control over the northern Peloponnesian states and of encouraging the helots to rebel. Economic fac-

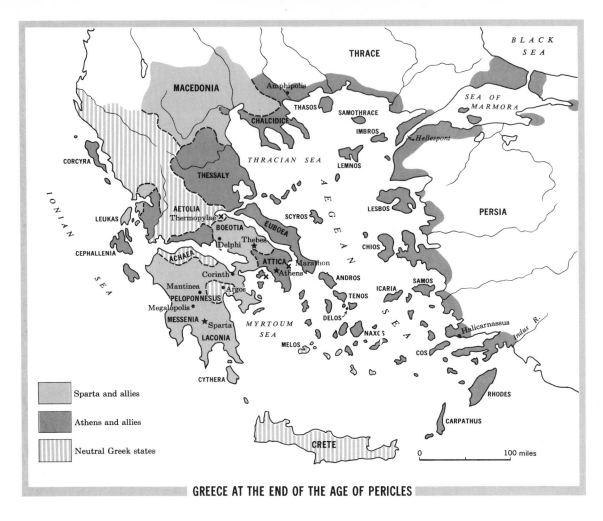

GREECE AT THE END OF THE AGE OF PERICLES

tors also played a large part in bringing the conflict to a head. Athens sought to dominate the Corinthian Gulf, the principal avenue of trade with Sicily and southern Italy. This made Athens the deadly enemy of Corinth, the chief ally of Sparta.

The defeat of Athens

The war, which broke out in 431 B.C. and lasted until 404, was a record of frightful calamities for Athens. Athenian trade was destroyed, its democracy overthrown, and the population decimated by a terrible pestilence. Quite as bad was the moral degradation which followed in the wake of the military reverses. Treason, corruption, and brutality were among the hastening ills of the last few years of the conflict. On one occasion the Athenians even slaughtered the whole male population of the island of Melos, and enslaved the women and children, for no other crime than refusing to abandon neutrality. Ultimately, deserted by all its allies except Samos and with its food supply cut off, Athens was left with no alternative but to surrender or starve. The terms imposed upon the Athenians were drastic enough: destruction of their fortifications, surrender of all foreign possessions and practically their entire navy, and submission to Sparta as a subject state. Though Athens recovered its leadership for a time in the fourth century, its period of glory was approaching its end.

5. POLITICAL DEBACLE—THE LAST DAYS

Not only did the Peloponnesian War put an end to the political supremacy of Athens, it annihilated freedom throughout the Greek world and sealed the doom of the Hellenic political genius. Following the war, Sparta asserted its power over all of Greece. Oligarchies supported by Spartan troops replaced democracies wherever they existed. Confiscation of property and assassination were the methods regularly employed to combat opposition. Although in Athens the tyrants were overthrown after a time and free government restored, Sparta was able to dominate the remainder of Greece for more than thirty years. In 371 B.C., however, Epaminondas of Thebes defeated the Spartan army at Leuctra and thereby inaugurated a period of Theban supremacy. Unfortunately Thebes showed little more wisdom and tolerance in governing than Sparta, and nine years later a combination was formed to free the Greek cities from their new oppressor. Failing to break up the alliance, the Thebans gave battle on the field of Mantinea. Both sides claimed the victory, but Epaminondas was slain, and his empire soon afterward collapsed.

Continuing conflict among the city-states

The long succession of wars had now brought the Greek states to the point of exhaustion. Though the glory of their culture was yet undimmed, politically they were prostrate and helpless. Their fate was soon decided for them by the rise of Philip of Macedon. Except for a thin veneer of Hellenic culture, the Macedonians were barbarians; but Philip, before becoming their king, had learned how to lead an army while a hostage at Thebes. Perceiving the weakness of the states to the south, he determined to conquer them. A series of early successes led to a decisive victory in 338 B.C. and soon afterward to dominion over all of Greece except Sparta. Two years later Philip was murdered as the sequel to a family brawl.

The Macedonian conquest

Rule over Greece now passed into the hands of his son Alexander, a youth of twenty years. After putting to death all possible aspirants to the throne and quelling some feeble revolts of the Greeks, Alexander, subsequently known as "the Great," conceived the grandiose scheme of conquering Persia. One victory followed another until, in the short space of twelve years, all the eastern territory from the Indus River to the Nile had been annexed to Greece as the personal domain of one man. Alexander did not live to enjoy it long. In 323 B.C. he fell ill of Babylonian swamp fever and died at the age of thirty-two.

Alexander the Great

It is difficult to gauge the significance of Alexander's career. Historians have differed widely in their interpretations. Some have seen him as one of the supreme galvanizing forces in history. Others would limit his genius to military strategy and organization and deny that he made a single major contribution of benefit to humanity. There can be no doubt that he was a master of the art of war (he never lost a battle), and that he was intelligent and endowed with charm and physical courage. Unquestionably, also, he was a man of vibrant energy and overpowering ambitions. Just what these ambitions were is not certain. Evidence eludes us that he aspired to conquer the world or to advance the Hellenic ideals of freedom and justice. It seems doubtful that he had much interest in lofty ideals or in using military force to extend them. His main goal was to enhance his own power and glory. The primary significance of his military accomplishment lay in the fact that he carried the Hellenic drive into Asia farther and faster than would otherwise have occurred. At the same time he appears to have placed too great a strain upon Hellenism with the result of encouraging a sweeping tide of Eastern influences into the West. Within a short period Hellenic and Eastern cultures interpenetrated to such an extent as to produce a new civilization. This was the Hellenistic civilization, to be discussed in the chapter that follows.

6. GREEK THOUGHT AND CULTURE

From what has been said in preceding chapters it should be clear that the popular notion that all philosophy originated with the Greeks is fallacious. Centuries earlier the Egyptians had given much thought to the nature of the universe and to the social and ethical problems of humanity. The achievement of the Greeks was rather the development of philosophy in a more inclusive manner than it had ever possessed before. They attempted to find answers to every conceivable question about the nature of the universe, the problem of truth, and the meaning and purpose of life. The magnitude of their accomplishment is attested by the fact that philosophy ever since has been largely a debate over the validity of their conclusions.

Greek philosophy had its origins in the sixth century B.C. in the work of the so-called Milesian school, whose members were natives of the commercial city of Miletus. Their philosophy was fundamentally scientific and materialistic. The problem which chiefly engaged them was to discover the nature of the physical world. They believed that all things could be reduced to some primary substance which was the source of worlds, stars, animals, plants, and humans, and to which all would ultimately return. Thales, the founder of the school, perceiving that all things contained moisture, taught that the primary substance is water. Anaximander insisted that it could not be any particular thing such as water or fire but something "uncreated and imperishable." He called this substance the Indefinite or the Boundless. A third Milesian, Anaximenes, declared that the original material of the universe is air. Air when rarefied becomes fire; when condensed it turns successively to wind, vapor, water, earth, and stone.

Although seemingly naive in its conclusions, the philosophy of the Milesian school was of real significance. It broke through the mythological beliefs of the Greeks about the origin of the world and substituted purely rational explanations. It expanded the Egyptian ideas of the eternity of the universe and the indestructibility of matter. It suggested very clearly, especially in the teachings of Anaximander, the concept of evolution in the sense of rhythmic change, of continuing creation and decay.

Before the end of the sixth century Greek philosophy developed a metaphysical turn; it ceased to be occupied solely with problems of the physical world and shifted its attention to abstruse questions about the nature of being, the meaning of truth, and the position of the divine in the scheme of things. First to exemplify the new tendency were the Pythagoreans, who interpreted philosophy largely in terms of religion. Little is known about them except that their leader, Pythagoras, migrated from Greece to southern Italy, where he founded a religious community at Croton in 530 B.C. He and his followers taught that the speculative life is the highest good, but that in order to pursue it, the individual must be purified of the evil desires of the flesh. They held that the essence of things is not a material substance but an abstract principle, number. Their chief significance lies in the sharp distinctions they drew between spirit and matter, harmony and discord, good and evil, which made them the founders of dualism in Greek thought.

A consequence of the work of the Pythagoreans was to intensify the debate over the nature of the universe. One of their contemporaries, Parmenides, argued that stability or permanence is the real nature of things; change and diversity are simply illusions of the senses. Directly opposed to this was the position taken by Heraclitus, who argued that permanence is an illusion, that change alone is real. The universe, he maintained, is in a condition of constant flux; therefore "it is impossible to step twice into the same stream." Creation and destruction, life and death, are but the obverse and reverse sides of the same picture. In other words, Heraclitus believed that the things we see, hear, and feel are all there is to reality. Evolution or constant change is the law of the universe. The tree or the stone that is here today is gone tomorrow; no underlying substance exists immutable through all eternity.

A final alternative to the question of the underlying character of the universe was provided by the atomists. The philosopher chiefly responsible for the development of the atomic theory was Democritus, who lived in Abdera on the Thracian coast in the second half of the fifth century. As their name implies, the atomists held that the ultimate constituents of the universe are atoms, infinite in number, indestructible, and indivisible. Although these differ in size and shape, they are exactly alike in composition. Because of the motion inherent in them, they are eternally uniting, separating, and reuniting in different arrangements. Every individual object or organism in the universe is thus the product of a fortuitous concourse of atoms. The only difference between a human and a tree is the difference in the number and arrangement of their atoms. This philosophy represented the final fruition of the materialistic tendencies of early Greek thought. Democritus denied the immortality of the soul and the existence of any spiritual world. Strange as it may appear to some people, he was a moral idealist, affirming that "good means not merely not to do wrong, but rather not to desire to do wrong."

About the middle of the fifth century B.C. an intellectual revolution began in Greece. It accompanied the high point of democracy in Athens. The rise in the power of the citizen, the growth of individualism, and the demand for the solution of practical problems produced a reaction against the old ways of thinking. As a result philosophers abandoned the study of the physical universe and turned to consideration of subjects more intimately related to the individual. The first exponents of the new intellectual trend were the Sophists. Originally the term meant "those who are wise," but later it came to be used in the derogatory sense of men who employ specious reasoning. Since most of our knowledge of the Sophists comes from Plato, one of their severest critics, they were commonly viewed as the enemies of all that was best in Hellenic culture. Modern research has rejected so extreme a conclusion, while conceding that some members of the group did lack a sense of social responsibility and were quite unscrupulous in "making the worse appear the better case."

One of the leading Sophists was Protagoras, a native of Abdera who did most of his teaching in Athens. His famous dictum, "Man is the measure of all things," contains the essence of the Sophist philosophy. By this he meant that goodness, truth, justice, and beauty are relative to the needs and interests of man. There are no absolute truths or eternal standards of right and justice. Since sense perception is the exclusive source of knowledge, there can be only particular truths valid for a given time and place. Morality likewise varies from one people to another, for there are no absolute canons of right and wrong eternally decreed in the heavens to fit all cases.

Some of the later Sophists went far beyond the teachings of Protagoras. The individualism implicit in the teachings of Protagoras was twisted by Thrasymachus into the doctrine that all laws and customs are merely expressions of the will of the strongest and shrewdest for their own advantage, and that therefore the wise man is the "perfectly unjust man" who is above the law and concerned with the gratification of his own desires. (It should also be mentioned that man, in the sense of the male, was the primary focus of this and all other Greek philosophy dealing with the individual.)

Yet there was much that was admirable in the teachings of the Sophists, even of those who were the most extreme. All of them condemned slavery and the racial exclusiveness of the Greeks. They were champions of liberty, the rights of the common man, and the practical and progressive point of view. They perceived the folly of war and ridiculed the chauvinism of many Athenian citizens. Perhaps most important, they broadened philosophy to include not only physics and metaphysics, but ethics and politics. As the Roman Cicero expressed it, they "brought philosophy down from heaven to the dwellings of men."

Inevitably the relativism, skepticism, and individualism of the Sophists aroused strenuous opposition. In the judgment of the more conservative Greeks these doctrines appeared to lead straight to atheism and anarchy. If there is no final truth, and if goodness and justice are merely relative to the whims of the individual, then neither religion, morality, the state, nor society itself can long be maintained. The result of this conviction was the growth of a new philosophic movement grounded upon the theory that truth is real and that absolute standards do exist. The leaders of this movement were perhaps the three most famous individuals in the history of thought—Socrates, Plato, and Aristotle.

Socrates was born in Athens in 469 B.C. of humble parentage; his father was a sculptor, his mother a midwife. How he obtained an education no one knows, but he was certainly familiar with the teachings of earlier Greek thinkers. The impression that he was a mere gabbler in the marketplace is quite unfounded. He became a philosopher on his own account chiefly to combat the doctrines of the Sophists. In 399 B.C. he was condemned to death on a charge of "corrupting the youth and introducing new gods." The real reason for the unjust sentence was the tragic outcome for Athens of the Peloponnesian War. Overwhelmed by resentment, the Athenian citizens turned against Socrates because of his associations with aristocrats, including the traitor Alcibiades, and because of his criticism of popular belief. There is also evidence that he disparaged democracy and contended that no government was worthy of the name except intellectual aristocracy.

Because Socrates wrote nothing himself, historians find it difficult to determine the exact scope of his teachings. He is generally regarded as primarily a teacher of ethics with no interest in abstract philosophy. Certain passages in Plato, however, raise the possibility that Plato's abstract doctrine of Ideas was ultimately of Socratic origin. At any rate we can be reasonably sure that Socrates believed in a stable and universally valid knowledge, which humans could possess if they pursued the right method. This would consist in the exchange and analysis of opinions, in the setting up and testing of provisional definitions, until finally an essence of truth recognizable by all could be distilled from them. Socrates argued that in similar fashion man could discover enduring principles of right and justice independent of the selfish desires of human beings. He believed, moreover, that the discovery of such rational principles of conduct would prove an infallible guide to virtuous living, for he denied that anyone who knows the good can choose the evil.

By far the most distinguished of Socrates's pupils was Plato, who

Socrates. According to Plato, Socrates looked like a goat-man but spoke like a god.

The philosophy of Socrates

Plato's philosophy of Ideas

Plato

Plato's ethical and religious philosophy

Plato as a political philosopher

was born in Athens around 429 B.C., the son of noble parents. At the age of twenty Plato joined the Socratic circle, remaining a member until the tragic death of his teacher. Unlike his great mentor, he was a prolific writer. The most noted of his works are such dialogues as the *Apology,* the *Phaedo,* the *Phaedrus,* the *Symposium,* and the *Republic.* He was engaged in the completion of the *Laws* when death overtook him in his eighty-first year.

Plato's objectives were similar to those of Socrates although somewhat broader: (1) to combat the theory of reality as a disordered flux and to substitute an interpretation of the universe as essentially spiritual and purposeful; (2) to refute the Sophist doctrines of relativism and skepticism; and (3) to provide a secure foundation for ethics. In order to realize these aims he developed his doctrine of Ideas. He admitted that relativity and change are characteristics of the world of physical things, of the world we perceive with our senses. But he denied that this world is the complete universe. A higher, spiritual realm exists, composed of eternal forms or Ideas which only the mind can conceive. These are not, however, mere abstractions invented by the mind, but spiritual things. Each is the pattern of some particular class of objects or relation between objects on earth. Thus there are Ideas of man, tree, shape, color, proportion, beauty, and justice. Highest of them all is the Idea of the Good, the active cause and guiding purpose of the universe. The things we perceive through our senses are merely imperfect copies of the supreme realities, Ideas.

Plato's ethical and religious philosophy was closely related to his doctrine of Ideas. Like Socrates he believed that true virtue has its basis in knowledge. But the knowledge derived from the senses is limited and variable; hence true virtue must consist in rational apprehension of the eternal Ideas of goodness and justice. By relegating the physical to an inferior place, he gave to his ethics an ascetic tinge. He regarded the body as a hindrance to the mind and taught that only the rational part of man's nature is noble and good. Yet in contrast with some of his later followers, he did not demand that appetites and emotions should be denied altogether, but urged that they should be strictly subordinated to reason. Plato never made his conception of God entirely clear, but it is certain that he conceived of the universe as spiritual in nature and governed by intelligent purpose. He rejected both materialism and mechanism. As for the soul, he regarded it not only as immortal but as preexisting through all eternity.

As a political philosopher Plato was motivated by the ideal of constructing a state which would be free from turbulence and self-seeking on the part of individuals and classes. Neither democracy nor liberty but harmony and efficiency were the ends he desired to achieve. Accordingly, he proposed in his *Republic* a famous plan for society which would have divided the population into three principal classes corresponding to the functions of the soul. The lowest class, representing the appetitive function, would include the farmers, artisans, and merchants. The second class, representing the spirited element or will, would consist of the soldiers. The highest class, representing the function of reason, would be composed of the intellectual aristocracy. Each of these classes would perform those tasks for which it was best fitted. The function of the lowest class would be the production and distribution of goods for the benefit of the whole community; that of the soldiers, defense; the aristocracy, by reason of special aptitude for philosophy, would enjoy a monopoly of political power. The division of the people into these several ranks would not be made on the basis of birth or wealth, but through a sifting process that would take into account the ability of each individual to profit from education. Thus the farmers, artisans, and merchants would be those who had shown the least intellectual capacity, whereas the philosopher-kings would be those who had shown the greatest.

The last of the great champions of the Socratic tradition was Aristotle, a native of Stagira, born in 384 B.C. At the age of seventeen he entered Plato's Academy,[3] continuing as student and teacher there for twenty years. In 343 he was invited by Philip of Macedon to serve as tutor to the young Alexander. History affords few more conspicuous examples of wasted effort, except for the fact that the young prince acquired an enthusiasm for science and for some other elements of Hellenic culture. Seven years later Aristotle returned to Athens, where he conducted a school of his own, known as the Lyceum, until his death in 322 B.C. Aristotle wrote even more voluminously than Plato and on a greater variety of subjects. His principal works include treatises on logic, metaphysics, rhetoric, ethics, natural sciences, and politics.

Aristotle

Though Aristotle was as much interested as Plato and Socrates in absolute knowledge and eternal standards, his philosophy differed from theirs in several outstanding respects. To begin with, he had a higher regard for the concrete and the practical. In contrast with Plato, the aesthete, and Socrates, who declared he could learn nothing from trees and stones, Aristotle was an empirical scientist with a compelling interest in biology, physics, and astronomy. Moreover, he was less inclined than his predecessors to a spiritual outlook. And last, he did not share their strong aristocratic sympathies.

Aristotle compared with Plato and Socrates

Aristotle agreed with Plato that universals, Ideas (or forms as he called them), are real, and that knowledge derived from the senses is limited and inaccurate. But he refused to go along with his teacher in ascribing an independent existence to universals and in reducing material things to pale reflections of their spiritual patterns. On the contrary, he asserted that form and matter are of equal importance; both are eternal, and neither can exist without the other. The union of these two gives the universe its character. Forms are the causes of all things;

Aristotle's conception of the universe

---

[3] So called from the grove of Academus, where Plato and his disciples met to discuss philosophic problems.

they are the purposive forces that shape the world of matter into the infinitely varied objects and organisms around us. All evolution, both cosmic and organic, results from the interaction of form and matter. Thus the presence of the form *man* in the human embryo molds and directs the development of the latter until it ultimately evolves as a human being. Aristotle's philosophy may be regarded as halfway between the spiritualism and transcendentalism of Plato on the one hand, and the mechanistic materialism of the atomists on the other. His conception of the universe was *teleological*—that is, governed by purpose; but he refused to regard the spiritual as overshadowing its material embodiment.

Aristotle's scientific attitude led him to conceive of God primarily as a First Cause. Aristotle's God was simply the Prime Mover, the original source of the purposive motion contained in the forms. In no sense was he a personal God, for his nature was pure intelligence, devoid of all feelings, will, or desire. Aristotle seems to have left no place for individual immortality: all the functions of the soul, except the creative reason which is not individual at all, depend upon the body and perish with it.

Aristotle's ethical philosophy was less ascetic than Plato's. He did not regard the body as the prison of the soul, nor did he believe that physical appetites are necessarily evil in themselves. He taught that the highest good consists in self-realization, that is, in the exercise of that part of man's nature which most truly distinguishes him as a human being. Self-realization would therefore be identical with the life of reason. But the life of reason is dependent upon the proper combination of physical and mental conditions. The body must be kept in good health and the emotions under adequate control. The solution is to be found in the *golden mean*, in preserving a balance between excessive indulgence on the one hand and ascetic denial on the other. This was simply a reaffirmation of the characteristic Greek ideal of *sophrosyne*, "nothing too much."

Although Aristotle included in his *Politics* much descriptive and analytical material on the structure and functions of government, he dealt primarily with the broader aspects of political theory. He considered the state as the supreme institution for the promotion of the good life, and he was therefore vitally interested in its origin and development and in the best forms it could be made to assume. Declaring that man is by nature a political animal, he denied that the state is an artificial product of the ambitions of the few or of the desires of the many. On the contrary, he asserted that it is rooted in the instincts of man himself, and that civilized life outside of its limits is impossible. He considered the best state to be neither a monarchy, an aristocracy, nor a democracy, but a *polity*—which he defined as a commonwealth intermediate between oligarchy and democracy. Essentially it would be a state under the control of the middle class, but Aristotle intended to make sure that the members of that class would be fairly numerous, for he advocated measures to prevent the concentration of wealth. He defended the institution of private property, but he opposed the heaping up of riches beyond what is necessary for intelligent living. He recommended that the government provide the poor with money to buy small farms or to "make a beginning in trade and husbandry" and thus promote their prosperity and self-respect.

Contrary to popular belief, the period of Greek civilization before the time of Alexander the Great was not a great age of science. The vast majority of the scientific achievements commonly thought of as Greek were made during the Hellenistic period, when the culture was no longer predominantly Greek but a mixture of Greek and Near Eastern. The interests of the Greeks in the Periclean Age and in the century that followed were chiefly speculative and artistic; they were not deeply concerned with material comforts or with mastery of the physical universe. Consequently, with the exception of some important developments in mathematics, biology, and medicine, scientific progress was relatively slight.

Greek thought not primarily scientific

The most significant Greek mathematical work was accomplished by the Pythagoreans. These followers of Pythagoras developed an elaborate theory of numbers, classifying them into various categories, such as odd, even, prime, composite, and perfect. They are also supposed to have discovered the theory of proportion and to have proved for the first time that the sum of the three angles of any triangle is equal to two right angles. But the most famous of their achievements was the discovery of the theorem attributed to Pythagoras himself: the square of the hypotenuse of any right-angled triangle is equal to the sum of the squares of the other two sides.

Pythagorean mathematics

The first of the Greeks to manifest an interest in biology was the philosopher Anaximander, who developed a crude theory of organic evolution based upon the principle of survival through progressive adaptations to the environment. The earliest ancestral animals, he asserted, lived in the sea, which originally covered the whole face of the earth. As the waters receded, some organisms were able to adjust themselves to their new environment and became land animals. The final product of this evolutionary process was man himself. The real founder of the science of biology, however, was Aristotle. Devoting many years of his life to painstaking study of the structure, habits, and growth of animals, he made many remarkable observations. The metamorphoses of various insects, the reproductive habits of the eel, the embryological development of the dog-fish—these are only samples of the wide extent of his knowledge. Unfortunately, however, Aristotle's biology was also heavily laden with misconceptions: he denied the sexuality of plants, for example, and he believed in the spontaneous generation of certain species of worms and insects.

Biology

Greek medicine also had its origin with the philosophers. A pioneer was Empedocles, exponent of the theory of the four elements (earth, air, fire, and water). He discovered that blood flows to and from the

Medicine

heart, and that the pores of the skin supplement the work of the respiratory passages in breathing. More important was the work of Hippocrates of Cos in the fifth and fourth centuries. By general consensus he is regarded as the father of medicine. He dinned into the ears of his pupils the doctrine that "Every disease has a natural cause, and without natural causes, nothing ever happens." In addition, by his methods of careful study and comparison of symptoms he laid the foundations for clinical medicine. He discovered the phenomenon of crisis in disease and improved the practice of surgery. Though he had a wide knowledge of drugs, his chief reliances in treatment were diet and rest. The main fact to his discredit was his development of the theory of the four humors—the notion that illness is due to excessive amounts of yellow bile, black bile, blood, and phlegm in the system. The practice of bleeding the patient was the regrettable outgrowth of this theory.

The Homeric epics

Generally the most common medium of literary expression in the formative age of a people is the epic of heroic deeds. The most famous of the Greek epics, the *Iliad* and the *Odyssey,* were put into written form at the end of the Dark Ages and commonly attributed to Homer. The first, which deals with the Trojan War, has its theme in the wrath of Achilles; the second describes the wanderings and return of Odysseus. Both have supreme literary merit in their carefully woven plots, in the realism of their character portrayals, and in their mastery of the full range of emotional intensity. They exerted an almost incalculable influence upon later writers. Their style and language inspired the fervid emotional poetry of the sixth century, and they were an unfailing source of plots and themes for the great tragedians of the Golden Age of the fifth century.

The three centuries which followed the Dark Ages were distinguished, as we have already seen, by tremendous social changes. The

Interior of a Greek Cup. Depicted is the friendship of leading characters from the *Iliad:* Patroklus and Achilles. Here Achilles is bandaging Patroklus's wounds.

rural pattern of life gave way to an urban society of steadily increasing complexity. The founding of colonies and the growth of commerce provided new interests and habits of living. Inevitably these changes were reflected in new forms of literature, especially of a more personal type. The first to be developed was the elegy, which was probably intended to be declaimed rather than sung to the accompaniment of music. Elegies varied in theme from individual reactions toward love to the idealism of patriots and reformers. Generally, however, they were devoted to melancholy reflection on the disillusionments of life or to bitter lament over the loss of prestige. Outstanding among the authors of elegiac verse was Solon the legislator.

Development of the elegy

In the sixth century and the early part of the fifth, the elegy was gradually displaced by the lyric, which derives its name from the fact that it was sung to the music of the lyre. The new type of poetry was particularly well adapted to the expression of passionate feelings, the violent loves and hates engendered by the strife of classes. It was employed for other purposes also. Both Alcaeus and Sappho, the latter a woman poet from the island of Lesbos, used it to describe the poignant beauty of love, the delicate grace of spring, and the starlit splendor of a summer night. Meanwhile other poets developed the choral lyric, intended to express the feelings of the community rather than the sentiments of any one individual. Greatest of all the writers of this group was Pindar of Thebes, who wrote during the first half of the fifth century. The lyrics of Pindar took the form of odes celebrating the victories of athletes and the glories of Greek civilization.

Lyric poetry

The supreme literary achievement of the Greeks was the tragic drama. Like so many of their other great works, it had its roots in religion. At the festivals dedicated to the worship of Dionysus, the god of spring and of wine, a chorus of men dressed as satyrs, or goat-men, sang and danced around an altar, enacting the various parts of a dithyramb or choral lyric that related the story of the god's career. In time a leader came to be separated from the chorus to recite the main parts of the story. The true drama was born about the beginning of the fifth century when Aeschylus introduced a second "actor" and relegated the chorus to the background. The name "tragedy," which came to be applied to this drama, was probably derived from the Greek word *tragos* meaning "goat."

The origins of tragic drama

Greek tragedy stands out in marked contrast to the tragedies of Shakespeare or modern playwrights. There was, first of all, little action presented on the stage; the main business of the actors was to recite the incidents of a plot which was already familiar to the audience, for the story was drawn from popular legends. Second, Greek tragedy devoted little attention to the study of complicated individual personality. There was no development of character as shaped by the vicissitudes of a long career. Those involved in the plot were scarcely individuals at all, but types. On the stage they wore masks to disguise any characteristics which might serve to distinguish them too sharply

Greek tragedy compared with modern tragedy

Greek Theater in Epidauros. The construction, to take advantage of the slope of the hill, and the arrangement of the stage are of particular interest. Greek dramas were invariably presented in the open air.

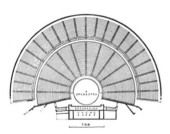

Epidauros Plan

Aeschylus and Sophocles

Euripides

from the rest of humanity. In addition, Greek tragedies differed from the modern variety in having as their theme the conflict between the individual and the universe, not the clash between personalities, or the internal conflicts of one person. The tragic fate that befell the main characters in these plays was external to individuals. It was brought on by the fact that someone had committed a crime against society, or against the gods, thereby violating the scheme of the universe. Punishment must follow in order to balance the scale of justice. Finally, the purpose of Greek tragedies was not merely to depict suffering and to interpret human actions, but to purify the emotions of the audience by representing the triumph of justice.

As already indicated, the first of the tragic dramatists was Aeschylus (525–456 B.C.). Though he is known to have written about eighty plays, only seven have survived in complete form, among them *Prometheus Bound* and a trilogy known as *The Oresteia.* Guilt and punishment is the recurrent theme of nearly all of them. The second of the leading tragedians, Sophocles (496–406), is often considered the greatest. His style was more polished and his philosophy more profound than that of his predecessor. He was the author of over a hundred plays. More than any other Greek writer he expressed the ideal of "nothing too much." His attitude was distinguished by love of harmony and peace, intelligent respect for democracy, and profound sympathy for human weakness. The most famous of his plays are *Oedipus Rex* and *Antigone.*

The work of the last of the great tragedians, Euripides (480–406), reflects a different spirit. He was a skeptic and individualist who took delight in ridiculing the ancient myths and the "sacred cows" of his time. An embittered pessimist who suffered from the barbs of his conservative critics, he loved to humble the proud in his plays and exalt the lowly. He was the first to give the ordinary man, even the beggar and the peasant, a place in the drama. Euripides is also noted for his sympathy for the slave, for his condemnation of war, and for his protests against the exclusion of women from social and intellectual life. Because of his humanism, his tendency to portray men as they actually were (or even a little worse), and his introduction of the love motif into drama, he is often considered a modernist. It must be remembered, however, that in other respects his plays were perfectly consistent with the Greek model. They did not exhibit the evolution of individual character or the conflict of egos to any greater extent than did the works of Sophocles or Aeschylus. Nevertheless, he has been called the most tragic of the Greek dramatists because he dealt with situations having analogues in real life. Among the best-known tragedies of Euripides are *Alcestis, Medea,* and *The Trojan Women.*

Greek comedy, in common with tragedy, appears to have grown out of the Dionysiac festivals, but it did not attain full development until late in the fifth century B.C. Its outstanding representative was Aristophanes (448?–380?), a somewhat coarse and belligerent aristocrat who lived in Athens. Most of his plays satirized the political and intellectual ideals of the radical democracy of his time. In *The Knights* he pilloried the incompetent and greedy politicians for their reckless adventures in imperialism. In *The Frogs* he lampooned Euripides's innovations in the drama. *The Clouds* he reserved for ridicule of the Sophists, ignorantly or maliciously classifying Socrates as one of them. While he was undoubtedly an imaginative and humorous writer, his ideas were founded largely upon prejudice. He deserves much credit, however, for his sharp criticisms of the policies of the warhawks of Athens during the struggle with Sparta. Though written as a farce, his *Lysistrata* cleverly pointed a way—however infeasible—to the termination of any war: in this play wives refuse to have sexual relations with their husbands until the latter agree to make peace with their foreign enemies.

No account of Greek literature would be complete without some mention of the two great historians of the Golden Age. Herodotus, the "father of history" (c. 484–c. 420), was a native of Halicarnassus in Asia Minor. He traveled extensively through the Persian empire, Egypt, Greece, and Italy, collecting a multitude of interesting data about various peoples. His famous account of the great war between the Greeks and the Persians included so much background that the work seems almost a history of the world. He regarded that war as an epic struggle between East and West, with Zeus giving victory to the Greeks against a mighty host of barbarians.

If Herodotus deserves to be called the father of history, much more does his younger contemporary, Thucydides (c. 460–c. 400), deserve to be considered the founder of scientific history. Influenced by the skepticism and practicality of the Sophists, Thucydides chose to work on the basis of carefully sifted evidence, rejecting legends and hearsay. The subject of his *History* was the war between Sparta and Athens, which he described scientifically and dispassionately, emphasizing the complexity of causes which led to the clash. His aim was to present an accurate record which could be studied with profit by statesmen and generals of all time, and it must be said that he was extremely successful. If there were any defects in his historical method, they consisted in overemphasizing political factors to the neglect of the social and economic and in failing to consider the importance of emotions in history.

7. THE MEANING OF GREEK ART

Greek art as an expression of the Greek spirit

Art as well as literature reflected the basic character of Hellenic civilization. The Greeks were essentially materialists who conceived of the world in physical terms. Plato and the followers of the mystic religions were exceptions, but few other Greeks believed in a universe of spiritual realities. It would be natural therefore to find that the material emblems of architecture and sculpture exemplified best the ideals the Greeks maintained.

The ideals embodied in Greek art

What did Greek art express? Above all, it symbolized humanism—the glorification of man as the most important creature in the universe. Though much of the sculpture depicted gods, and also goddesses, this did not detract in the slightest from its humanistic quality. The Greek deities existed for the benefit of man; in glorifying them he thus glorified himself. Both architecture and sculpture embodied the ideals of balance, harmony, order, and moderation. Anarchy and excess were abhorrent to the mind of the Greek, but so was absolute repression. Consequently, Greek art exhibited qualities of simplicity and dignified restraint—free from decorative extravagance on the one hand, and from restrictive conventions on the other. Moreover, Greek art was an expression of the national life. Its purpose was not merely

See color plates following page 160

aesthetic but political: to symbolize the pride of the people in their city and to enhance their consciousness of unity. The Parthenon at Athens, for example, was the temple of Athena, the protecting goddess who presided over the corporate life of the state. In providing her with a beautiful shrine which she might frequently visit, the Athenians were giving evidence of their love for their city and their hope for its continuing welfare.

Greek art compared with that of later peoples

The art of the Greeks differed from that of nearly every people since their time in a variety of ways. Like the tragedies of Aeschylus and Sophocles, it was universal. It included few portraits either in sculpture or in painting. (Most of the portrait busts commonly considered Greek really belong to the Hellenistic Age.) The human beings depicted were generally types, not individuals. Again, Greek art differed from

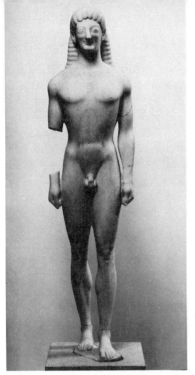  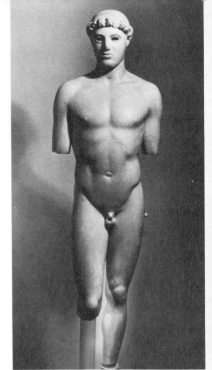

Apollo of Tenea; Apollo of Piombino; "The Critian Boy." These three statues, dating from about 560, 500, and 480 B.C. respectively, display the progressive "unfreezing" of Greek statuary art. The first stiff and symmetrical statue is imitative of Egyptian sculpture (see statue of the Pharoah Mycerinus, p. 39 above). Roughly half a century later it is succeeded by a figure which begins to display motion, as if awakening from a sleep of centuries in a fairy tale. The last figure introduces genuine naturalism in its delicate twists and depiction of the subject's weight resting on one leg.

that of most later peoples in its ethical purpose. It was not art for the sake of mere decoration or for the expression of the artist's own ideas, but a medium for the ennoblement of humanity. This does not mean that its merit depended upon the moral lesson it taught, but rather that it was supposed to exemplify qualities of living essentially artistic in themselves. The Athenian, at least, drew no sharp distinction between the ethical and aesthetic spheres; the beautiful and the good were really identical. True morality, therefore, consisted in rational living, in the avoidance of grossness, sensual excesses, and other forms of conduct aesthetically offensive. Finally, although the utmost attention was given to the depiction of beautiful bodies, this had little to do with fidelity to nature. The Greek was not interested in interpreting nature for its own sake, but in expressing *human* ideals.

The history of Greek art can be divided into three periods. The first covered the seventh and sixth centuries. During the greater part of this so-called archaic period sculpture was dominated by Egyptian influence, as can be seen in the frontality and rigidity of the statues, with their square shoulders and one foot slightly advanced. Toward

The three periods of Greek art

the end, however, these conventions were thrown aside. The chief architectural styles also had their origin in this period, and several crude temples were built. The second period, which occupied the fifth century, witnessed the full perfection of both architecture and sculpture. The art of this time was completely idealistic. During the fourth century, the last period of Greek art, architecture lost some of its balance and simplicity and sculpture assumed new characteristics. It came to reflect more clearly the reactions of the individual artist, to incorporate more realism, and to lose some of its quality as an expression of civic pride.

Greek architecture

For all its artistic excellence, Greek temple architecture was extremely simple. Greek temples consisted of only five elements: (1) the cella or nucleus of the building, which was a rectangular chamber to house the statue of the god; (2) the columns, which formed the porch and surrounded the cella; (3) the entablature, which rested upon the columns and supported the roof; (4) the gabled roof itself; and (5) the pediment or triangular section under the gable of the roof. Two different architectural styles were developed, representing modifications of certain of these elements. The more common was the Doric, which made use of a rather heavy, sharply fluted column surmounted by a plain capital. The other, the Ionic, had more slender and more graceful columns with flat flutings, a triple base, and a scroll or volute capital. The so-called Corinthian style, which was chiefly Hellenistic, differed from the Ionic primarily in being more ornate. The three styles differed also in their treatment of the entablature. In the Ionic style it was left almost plain. In the Doric and Corinthian styles it bore sculptured reliefs. The Parthenon, the best example of Greek architecture, was essentially a Doric building, but it reflected some of the grace and subtlety of Ionic influence.

Greek sculpture

According to the prevailing opinion among his contemporaries, Greek sculpture attained its height in the work of Phidias (c. 500–c. 432). His masterpieces were the statue of Athena in the Parthenon and the statue of Zeus in the Temple of Olympian Zeus. In addition, he

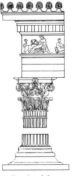

Corinthian

Ionic

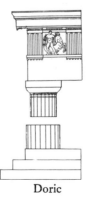
Doric

Details of the Three Orders of Greek Architecture

The Parthenon. The largest and most famous of Athenian temples, the Parthenon is considered the classic example of Doric architecture. Its columns were made more graceful by tapering them in a slight curve toward the top. Its friezes and pediments were decorated with lifelike sculptures of prancing horses (see above), fighting giants, and benign and confident deities.

designed the Parthenon reliefs. The main qualities of his work are grandeur of conception, patriotism, proportion, dignity, and restraint. Nearly all of his figures are idealized representations of deities and mythological creatures in human form. The second most renowned fifth-century sculptor was Myron, noted for his statue of the discus thrower and for his glorification of other athletic types. The names of three great sculptors in the fourth century have come down to us. The most gifted was Praxiteles, renowned for his portrayal of humanized deities with slender, graceful bodies and countenances of philosophic repose. His older contemporary, Scopas, gained distinction as an emotional sculptor. One of his most successful creations was the statue of a religious ecstatic, a worshiper of Dionysus, in a condition of mystic frenzy. At the end of the century Lysippus pioneered in sculptural realism and individualism. He was the first great master of the realistic portrait as a study of personal character.

Parthenon Frieze

8. ATHENIAN LIFE IN THE GOLDEN AGE

The population of Athens in the fifth and fourth centuries comprised three groups: the citizens, the metics, and the slaves. The citizens, who numbered at the most about 160,000, included only those males born of citizen parents, except for the few who were oc-

Athenian classes

Left: *The Discobolus or Discus Thrower of Myron.* The statue reflects the glorification of the human body characteristic of Athens in the Golden Age. Now in the Vatican Museum. Right: *Hermes with the Infant Dionysus, by Praxiteles, Fourth Century B.C.* Original in the Olympia Museum, Greece.

casionally enfranchised by special law. The metics, who probably did not exceed a total of 35,000, were resident aliens, chiefly non-Athenian Greeks. Save for the fact that they had no political privileges and generally were not permitted to own land, male metics had equal opportunities with citizens. They could engage in any occupation they desired and participate in any social or intellectual activities. Contrary to a popular tradition, the slaves in Athens were never a majority of the population. Their maximum number did not exceed 110,000. Urban slaves, at least, were very well treated and were sometimes rewarded for faithful service by being set free. The males could work for wages and own property, and some of them held responsible positions as minor public officials. The treatment of slaves who worked in the mines, however, was often cruel.

The amazing degree of social and economic equality.

Life in Athens stands out in sharp contrast to that in most other civilizations. One of its leading features was the great amount of social and economic equality that prevailed among all the inhabitants. Although there were many who were poor, there were few who were very rich. Nearly everyone, whether citizen, metic, or slave, ate the same kind of food, wore the same kind of clothing, and participated in the same kind of amusement. This substantial equality was enforced in part by the system of *liturgies,* which were services to the state rendered by wealthy men, chiefly in the form of contributions to support the drama, equip the navy, or provide for the poor.

A second outstanding characteristic of Athenian life was its lack of comforts and luxuries. Part of this was a result of the low income of the mass of the people. Teachers, sculptors, masons, carpenters, and common laborers all received the same low standard wage. Part of it may have been a consequence also of the mild climate, which allowed for a life of simplicity. But whatever the cause, the fact remains that, in comparison with modern standards, the Athenians made do with the barest essentials. They knew nothing of such commodities as clocks, soap, newspapers, cotton cloth, sugar, tea, or coffee. Their beds had no springs, their houses had no drains, and their food consisted chiefly of barley cakes, onions, and fish, washed down with diluted wine. From the standpoint of clothing they were no better off. A rectangular piece of cloth wrapped around the body and fastened with pins at the shoulders and with a rope around the waist served as the main garment. A larger piece was draped around the body as an extra garment for outdoor wear. No one wore either stockings or socks, and few had any footgear except sandals.

The poverty of Athenian life

But lack of luxury was a matter of little consequence to the Athenian citizen. Instead his aim was to live as interestingly and contentedly as possible without spending all his days working for the sake of a little more comfort for his family or of piling up riches as a source of power or prestige. What each citizen really wanted was a small farm or business that would provide him with a reasonable income and at the same time allow him an abundance of leisure for politics, for gossip in the marketplace, and for intellectual or artistic activities if he had the talent to enjoy them.

Indifference toward material comforts and wealth

In spite of the expansion of trade, Athenian economic organization never became very complex. Agriculture and commerce were by far

Young Men Baiting a Dog and Cat. This Athenian relief from about 510 B.C. depicts an odd form of leisure-time amusement.

the most important enterprises. Even in Pericles's day the majority of the citizens still lived in the country. Industry was not highly developed. Few examples of large-scale production are on record, and those chiefly in the manufacture of pottery and implements of war. The largest establishment that ever existed was apparently a shield factory owned by a metic and employing 120 slaves. No other was more than half as large. The enterprises which absorbed the most labor were the mines, but they were owned by the state and leased in sections to small contractors to be worked by slaves. The bulk of industry was carried on in shops owned by individual craftsmen who produced their wares directly to the order of the consumer.

Religion underwent some notable changes in the Golden Age of the fifth and fourth centuries. The polytheism and anthropomorphism of the Homeric myths were largely supplanted by a belief in one God as the creator and sustainer of the moral law. Other significant consequences flowed from the mystery cults. These new forms of religion first became popular in the sixth century because of the craving for an emotional faith to make up for the disappointments of life. One was the Orphic cult, which revolved around the myth of the death and resurrection of Dionysus. Another, the Eleusinian cult, had as its central theme the abduction of Persephone by Hades, god of the nether world, and her ultimate redemption by Demeter, the great Earth Mother. Both of these cults had as their original purpose worship of the life-giving powers of nature, but in time they came to express a much deeper significance. They communicated to their followers the ideas of vicarious atonement, salvation in an afterlife, and ecstatic union with the divine. Although entirely inconsistent with the spirit of the ancient religion, they made a powerful appeal to certain classes and were largely responsible for the spread of the belief in personal immortality. The more thoughtful Greeks, however, seem to have persisted in their adherence to the worldly, optimistic, and mechanical faith of their ancestors and to have shown little concern about sin or a desire for salvation in a life to come.

Head of Persephone. Obverse of a coin struck by the Greek city of Syracuse on the island of Sicily around 310 B.C.

It remains to consider briefly the position of the family in Athens in the fifth and fourth centuries. Though marriage was still an important institution for the procreation of children who would become citizens of the state, there is reason to believe that family life had declined. Men of the more prosperous classes, at least, now spent the greater part of their time away from their families. Wives were relegated to an inferior position and required to remain secluded in their homes. Their place as social and intellectual companions for their husbands was taken by alien women, the *hetaerae,* many of whom were highly cultured natives of the Ionian cities of Asia Minor. Marriage itself assumed the character of a political and economic arrangement devoid of romantic elements. Men married wives so as to ensure that at least some of their children would be legitimate and in order to obtain property in the form of a dowry. It was important also, of course, to have someone to care for the household. But husbands did not consider their wives as their equals and did not appear in public with them or encourage their participation in any form of social or intellectual activity.

9. THE GREEK ACHIEVEMENT AND ITS SIGNIFICANCE FOR US

No historian would deny that the achievement of the Greeks was one of the most remarkable in the history of the world. With no great expanse of fertile soil or abundance of mineral resources, they succeeded in developing a higher and more varied civilization than any of the most richly favored nations of the Near East. With only a limited cultural inheritance from the past to build upon, they produced intellectual and artistic achievements which have served ever since as models of perfection for the culture of the West. It may be argued as well that the Greeks achieved a more leisured and rational mode of living than most other peoples who strutted and fretted their hour upon this planet. The infrequency of brutal crimes and the contentment with simple amusements and modest wealth all point to a comparatively happy and satisfied existence.

The magnitude of the Greek achievement

It is necessary to be on guard, however, against uncritical adulation of the ancient Greeks. We must not assume that all of the natives of Hellas were as cultured, wise, and free as the citizens of Athens and of the Ionian states across the Aegean. The Spartans, the Arcadians, the Thessalians, and the majority of the Boeotians remained much less culturally advanced. Further, Athenian civilization itself was not without its defects. It permitted some exploitation of the weak, especially of the slaves who toiled in the mines. It was based upon a principle of racial exclusiveness which reckoned every man a foreigner whose parents were not both Athenians, and consequently denied political rights to the majority of the inhabitants. It was also characterized by the overt repression of the female members of the society. Its statecraft was not sufficiently enlightened to avoid the pitfalls of imperialism and aggressive war. Finally, the attitude of its citizens was not always tolerant and just. Socrates was put to death for his opinions, and two other philosophers, Anaxagoras and Protagoras, were forced to leave the city. It must be conceded, however, that the record of the Athenians for tolerance was better than that of most other nations, both ancient and modern. There was probably more freedom of expression in Athens during the war with Sparta than there was in the United States during World War I.

Undesirable features of Greek life

Nor is it true that the Greek influence has been as great as is often supposed. No well-informed student could accept the sentimental verdict of Shelley: "We are all Greeks; our laws, our literature, our religion, our arts have their roots in Greece." Our laws do not really have their roots in Greece but chiefly in Hellenistic and Roman sources. Much of our poetry is undoubtedly Greek in inspiration, but such is not the case with most of our prose literature. Our religion is no more than partly Greek; except as it was influenced by Plato and the Romans, it reflects primarily the spirit of the Near East. Even our arts derive from other sources almost as much as from Greece. Actually, modern civilization has been the result of the convergence of numerous influences coming from many different periods and places.

In spite of all this, the Hellenic adventure was of profound significance for the history of the world. For the Greeks were the founders of nearly all those ideals commonly thought of as peculiar to the West. The civilizations of the ancient Near East, with the exception, to a certain extent, of the Hebrew and Egyptian, were dominated by absolutism, supernaturalism, ecclesiasticism, the denial of both body and mind, and the subjection of the individual to the group. It is noteworthy that the Greek word for freedom—*eleutheria*—cannot be translated into any ancient Near Eastern language, not even Hebrew. The typical political regime of the Near East was that of an absolute monarch supported by a powerful priesthood. Culture in the Near Eastern empires served mainly as an instrument to magnify the power of the state and to enhance the prestige of rulers and priests.

In contrast, the civilization of Greece, notably in its Athenian form, was founded upon ideals of freedom, optimism, secularism, rationalism, the glorification of both body and mind, and a high regard for the dignity and worth of the individual. Insofar as anyone other than a slave was repressed, his subjection was to the rule of the majority. This, of course, was not always good, especially in times of crisis, when the majority might be swayed by prejudice. Religion was worldly and practical, serving the interests of human beings. Worship of the gods was a means for the ennoblement of man. As opposed to the ecclesiasticism of the Near East, the Greeks had no organized priesthood at all. They kept their priests in the background and refused to allow them to define dogma or to govern the realm of intellect. In addition, they excluded them from control over the sphere of moral-

The Acropolis Today. Occupying the commanding position is the Parthenon. To the left is the Erechtheum with its Porch of the Maidens facing the Parthenon.

ity. The culture of the Greeks was the first to be based upon the primacy of intellect—upon the supremacy of the spirit of free inquiry. There was no subject they feared to investigate, or any question they regarded as beyond the province of reason. To an extent never before realized, mind was supreme over faith, logic and science over superstition.

The supreme tragedy of the Greeks was, of course, their failure to solve the problem of political conflict. To a large degree, this conflict was the product of social and cultural dissimilarities. Because of different geographic and economic conditions the Greek city-states developed at an uneven pace. Some went forward rapidly to high levels of cultural superiority, while others lagged behind and made little or no intellectual progress. The consequences were discord and suspicion, which gave rise eventually to hatred and fear. Though some of the more advanced thinkers attempted to propagate the notion that the Hellenes were one people who should reserve their contempt for non-Hellenes, or "barbarians," the conception never became part of a national ethos. Athenians hated Spartans, and vice versa, almost as vehemently as they hated Persians. Not even the danger of Asian conquest sufficed to dispel the distrust and antagonism of Greeks for one another. Thus the war that finally broke out between Athens and Sparta sealed the doom of Hellenic civilization even though Greece remained undefeated by foreigners.

The tragedy of Hellenic history

SELECTED READINGS

• *Items so designated are available in paperback editions.*

• Andrewes, A., *The Greeks,* New York, 1967. An excellent, up-to-date account of archaic and classical Greek history from about 750 to 350 B.C.

Austin, M., and P. Vidal-Naquet, *The Economic and Social History of Ancient Greece,* Berkeley, Calif., 1977.

• Boardman, J., *Greek Art,* New York, 1964.

• ———, *The Greeks Overseas,* rev. ed., London, 1982. The standard treatment of Greek colonization.

Burn, A. R., *The Lyric Age of Greece,* New York, 1961. A lively introduction to the seventh and sixth centuries.

Davies, J. K., *Democracy and Classical Greece,* Glasgow, 1978.

• Dodds, E. R., *The Greeks and the Irrational,* Berkeley, Calif., 1963. A novel approach to classical Greek culture.

• Dover, K. J., *Greek Homosexuality,* Cambridge, Mass., 1978. A serious analysis of a basic aspect of classical Greek life.

• ———, et al., *Ancient Greek Literature,* Oxford, 1980.

• Ehrenberg, V., *From Solon to Socrates,* New York, 1967. An excellent treatment of early Athenian history by one of the twentieth century's leading authorities.

• Finley, M. I., *The Ancient Greeks: An Introduction to Their Life and Thought,* New York, 1963. An expert brief introduction to the Greeks.

• ———, *The World of Odysseus,* rev. ed., New York, 1978. Attempts to use the Homeric poems as a guide to Dark Ages Greece.

Forrest, W. G., *The Emergence of Greek Democracy,* London, 1966. An engaging account of the origins of democratic ideas and practices.

• ———, *A History of Sparta, 950–152 B.C.,* London, 1968.

• Guthrie, W. K. C., *The Greeks and Their Gods,* Boston, 1965.

Jones, A. H. M., *Athenian Democracy,* New York, 1957. Concentrates on actual political practice.

• Kitto, H. D. F., *The Greeks,* Baltimore, 1957. A delightfully written, highly personal interpretation.

• Lloyd, G. E. R., *Early Greek Science: Thales to Aristotle,* London, 1970.

• Marrou, H. I., *A History of Education in Antiquity,* New York, 1964. A modern classic that covers the entire ancient world.

• Meiggs, R., *The Athenian Empire,* Oxford, 1972. The major study of fifth-century Athenian imperialism; a monumental work.

Michell, H., *The Economics of Ancient Greece,* rev. ed., Cambridge, 1956.

Murray, D., *Early Greece,* Glasgow, 1980. An excellent analytical narrative of early Greek history before the fifth century.

Nilsson, M. P., *A History of Greek Religion,* New York, 1964.

• Pollitt, J. J., *Art and Experience in Classical Greece,* Cambridge, 1972. The best introduction to the social and intellectual forces behind Greek art.

• Pomeroy, Sarah B., *Goddesses, Whores, Wives, and Slaves: Women in Classical Antiquity,* New York, 1975. The best treatment of the role of women in Greece and Rome. Relies on a variety of source material and covers women of all classes.

Rose, H. J., *A Handbook of Greek Literature,* New York, 1960.

• ———, *A Handbook of Greek Mythology,* 6th ed., New York, 1960.

• Sealey, R., *A History of the Greek City States, ca. 700–338 B.C.,* Berkeley, Calif., 1977. A provocative account that reconsiders older assumptions about Greek political life.

Sinclair, T. A., *A History of Greek Political Thought,* London, 1951.

Snell, Bruno, *The Discovery of the Mind: The Greek Origins of European Thought,* Cambridge, Mass., 1953. Stimulating essays.

• Snodgrass, A. M., *Archaic Greece,* London, 1980.

• Starr, C. G., *The Economic and Social Growth of Early Greece: 800–500 B.C.,* New York, 1978. An excellent study of this difficult but important topic.

———, *The Origins of Greek Civilization, 1100–650 B.C.,* New York, 1961. The best detailed treatment of the early periods.

Zimmern, A. E., *The Greek Commonwealth,* 5th ed., New York, 1931. A classic study, perhaps too uncritical of the Athenians.

SOURCE MATERIALS

Most Greek authors have been translated in the appropriate volumes of the Loeb Classical Library, Harvard University Press.

In addition the following may be helpful:

Barnstone, Willis, tr., *Greek Lyric Poetry,* New York, 1962.

Kagan, Donald, *Sources in Greek Political Thought,* Glencoe, Ill., 1965.

Kirk, G. S., and J. E. Raven, *The Presocratic Philosophers,* Cambridge, 1957.

Lattimore, R., tr., *Greek Lyrics,* Chicago, 1960.

———, tr., *The Iliad,* Chicago, 1961.

———, tr., *The Odyssey,* New York, 1968.

Chapter 7

THE HELLENISTIC
CIVILIZATION

Beauty and virtue and the like are to be honored, if they give pleasure, but
if they do not give pleasure, we must bid them farewell.

> —Epicurus, "On the End of Life"

I agree that Alexander was carried away so far as to copy oriental luxury. I
hold that no mighty deeds, not even conquering the whole world, is of
any good unless the man has learned mastery of himself.

> —Arrian, *Anabasis of Alexander*

The death of Alexander the Great in 323 B.C. constituted a wa-
tershed in the development of world history. Greek civilization
as it had existed in its prime now came to an end. Of course, the
old institutions and ways of life did not suddenly disappear, but Alexander's career had cut so deeply into the old order that it could not be
restored intact. The fusion of cultures and intermingling of peoples
resulting from Alexander's conquests accomplished the overthrow of
many of the ideals developed in the Golden Age of the fifth and fourth
centuries. Gradually a new pattern of civilization emerged, based upon
a mixture of Greek and Eastern elements. To this new civilization,
which lasted until about the beginning of the Christian era, the name
Hellenistic is most commonly applied.

A new stage in world history

Although the break between the Hellenic and Hellenistic eras was
sharp, it would be a mistake to deny all continuity. The language of
the new cultured classes was predominantly Greek, and even the peoples whose heritage was non-Greek considered it desirable to have
some Hellenic culture. Hellenic achievements in science provided a
foundation for the great scientific advances of the Hellenistic Age.
Greek emphasis upon logic was likewise carried over into Hellenistic

Comparison of the Hellenistic Age with the Golden Age of Greece

philosophy, though the objectives of the latter were in many cases quite different. In the spheres of the political, social, and economic the resemblances were few indeed. The classical ideal of democracy was now superseded by despotism perhaps as rigorous as any that Egypt or Persia had ever produced. The Greek city-state survived in some parts of Greece itself, but elsewhere it was replaced by large-scale monarchy, and in the minds of some leaders by notions of a world state. The Hellenic devotion to simplicity and the golden mean gave way to extravagance in the arts and to a love of luxury. In the economic realm there was a growing stress on big business and vigorous competition for profits. In view of these changes it seems valid to conclude that the Hellenistic Age was sufficiently distinct from the Golden Age of Greece to justify its being considered the era of a new civilization.

1. POLITICAL HISTORY AND INSTITUTIONS

The Hellenistic states

When Alexander died in 323 B.C., he left no legitimate heir to succeed him save a feeble-minded half-brother. Tradition relates that when his friends requested him on his deathbed to designate a successor, he replied "To the strongest." After his death his highest-ranking generals proceeded to divide the empire among them. Some of the younger commanders contested this arrangement, and a series of wars followed which culminated in the decisive battle of Ipsus in 301 B.C. The

Alexander in Battle. A scene from a sarcophagus of about 300 B.C. Alexander is shown on horseback at the left.

result of this battle was a new division among the victors. Seleucus took possession of Persia, Mesopotamia, and Syria; Lysimachus assumed control over Asia Minor and Thrace; Cassander established himself in Macedonia; and Ptolemy added Phoenicia and Palestine to his original domain of Egypt. Twenty years later these four states were reduced to three when Seleucus defeated and killed Lysimachus in battle and appropriated his territory in Asia Minor. In the meantime most of the Greek states had revolted against the attempts of Macedon to extend its power over them. By banding together in defensive leagues several of them succeeded in maintaining their independence for nearly a century. Finally, between 146 and 30 B.C. nearly all of the Hellenistic territory passed under Roman rule.

Alexander the Great. Shown here is a silver coin struck in Thrace by King Lysimachus about 300 B.C.

The dominant form of government in the Hellenistic Age was the despotism of rulers who represented themselves as at least semi-divine. Alexander himself was recognized as a son of God in Egypt and was worshiped as a god in Greece. His most powerful successors, the Seleucid kings in western Asia and the Ptolemies in Egypt, made systematic attempts to deify themselves. A Seleucid monarch, Antiochus IV, adopted the title "Epiphanes" or "God Manifest." The later members of the dynasty of the Ptolemies signed their decrees "Theos" (God) and revived the practice of sister marriage which had been followed by the pharaohs as a means of preserving the divine blood of the royal family from contamination. Only in the kingdom of Macedonia was despotism tempered by a modicum of respect for the liberties of the citizens.

Two other political institutions developed as by-products of Hellenistic civilization: the Achaean and Aetolian Leagues. We have already seen that most of the Greek states rebelled against Macedonian rule following the division of Alexander's empire. The better to preserve their independence, several of these states formed alliances among themselves, which were gradually expanded to become confederate leagues. The organization of these leagues was essentially the same in all cases. Each had a federal council composed of representatives of the member cities with power to enact laws on subjects of general concern. An assembly which all of the citizens in the federated states could attend decided questions of war and peace and elected officials. Executive and military authority was vested in the hands of a general, elected for one year and eligible for reelection only in alternate years. Although these leagues are frequently described as federal states, they were scarcely more than confederacies, for the central authority depended upon the local governments for contributions of revenue and troops. Furthermore, the powers delegated to the central government were limited primarily to matters of war and peace, coinage, and weights and measures. The chief significance of these leagues lies in the fact that they constituted the nearest approach ever made in Greece to voluntary national union before modern times.

The Achaean and Aetolian Leagues

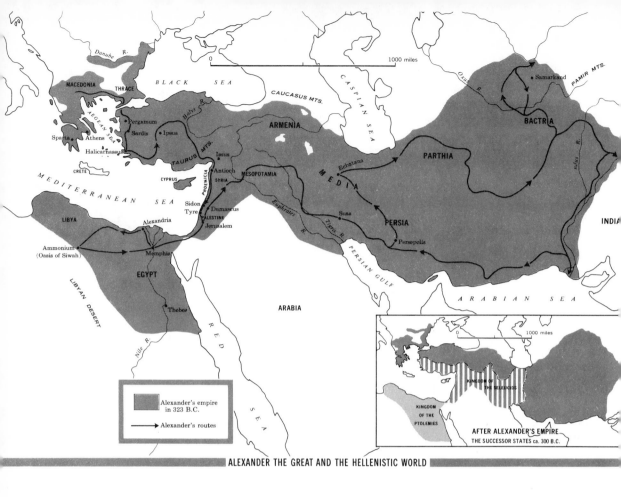

ALEXANDER THE GREAT AND THE HELLENISTIC WORLD

2. SIGNIFICANT ECONOMIC AND
SOCIAL DEVELOPMENTS

The economic revolution and its causes

Hellenistic civilization witnessed economic transformations second only in magnitude to the Industrial Revolution of the modern era. Several important causes can be distinguished: (1) the opening up of a vast area of trade from the Indus River to the Nile as a result of the Alexandrian conquests; (2) the rise in prices as a consequence of the release of an enormous Persian hoard of gold and silver into the channels of circulation, resulting in the growth of investment and speculation; and (3) the promotion of trade and industry by governments as a means of augmenting their revenues. The result was the growth of a system of large-scale production, trade, and finance, with the state as the principal entrepreneur.

The concentration of land ownership

Agriculture was as profoundly affected by the new developments as any other branch of economic life. The most dramatic changes were the concentration of landholdings and the degradation of the agricultural laborers. The successors of Alexander immediately confiscated the estates of the chief landowners and added them to their own domains. The lands thus acquired were then either granted to royal favorites or leased to tenants under an arrangement calculated to ensure an abundant income for the crown. The tenants were generally forbidden to leave the lands they cultivated until after the harvest and were not allowed to dispose of their grain until after the ruler had had a chance to sell the share he received as rent at the highest price the market would bring. When some of the tenants went on strike or attempted to run away, they were all bound to the soil as hereditary serfs. Many of the small independent farmers also became serfs when they got into debt as a result of inability to compete with large-scale production.

In an effort to make all of the resources of the state contribute to the profit of the government, the rulers of Egypt and the Seleucid Empire promoted and regulated industry and trade. The Ptolemies established factories and shops in nearly every village and town to be owned and operated by the government for its own financial benefit. In addition, they assumed control over all privately owned enterprises, fixing the prices the owners could charge and manipulating markets to the advantage of the crown. A similar plan of regimentation for industry, although not on quite so ambitious a scale, was enforced by the Seleucid rulers of western Asia. Trade was left by both of these governments very largely in private hands, but it was heavily taxed and regulated in such a way as to make sure that an ample share of the profits went to the ruler. Every facility was provided by the government for the encouragement of new trading ventures. Harbors were improved, warships were sent out to police the seas, and roads and canals were built. Moreover, the Ptolemies employed famous geographers to discover new routes to distant lands and thereby open up valuable markets. As a result of such methods Egypt developed a flourishing commerce in the widest variety of products. Into the port of Alexandria came spices from Arabia, copper from Cyprus, gold from Ethiopia and India, tin from Britain, elephants and ivory from Nubia, silver from the northern Aegean and Spain, fine carpets from Asia Minor, and even silk from China. Profits for the government and for some of the merchants were often as high as 20 or 30 percent.

*State regimentation of
industry and trade*

Further evidence of the significant economic development of the Hellenistic Age is to be found in the growth of finance. An international money economy, based upon gold and silver coins, now became general throughout the Near East. Banks, usually owned by the government, developed as the chief institutions of credit for business ventures of every description. Speculation, cornering of markets, intense competition, the growth of large business houses, and the development of insurance and advertising were other significant phenomena of this remarkable age.

The growth of finance

According to the available evidence, the Hellenistic Age was a period of prosperity. Although serious crises frequently followed the collapse of speculative booms, they appear to have been of short duration. But

Hellenistic Coins. Obverse and reverse sides of the silver tetradrachma of Macedon, 336–323 B.C. Objects of common use from this period often show as much beauty of design as formal works of art.

The disparity between rich and poor

the prosperity that existed seems to have been limited chiefly to the rulers, the upper classes, and the merchants. It certainly did not extend to the peasants or even to the workers in the towns. The daily wages of both skilled and unskilled workers in Athens in the third century had dropped to less than half of what they had been in the Age of Pericles. The cost of living, on the other hand, had risen considerably. To make matters worse, unemployment in the large cities posed so serious a problem that the government had to provide free grain for many of the poor. Slavery declined in the Hellenistic world, partly because of the influence of the Stoic philosophy, but mainly for the reason that wages had fallen so low that it was cheaper to hire a free laborer than to purchase and maintain a slave.

The growth of large cities

A primary result of social and economic conditions in the Hellenistic Age was the growth of large cities. Despite the fact that most people still lived in the country, urbanization increased because of the expansion of industry and commerce, the enlargement of governmental functions, and the desire of former independent farmers to escape the hardships of serfdom. Cities multiplied and grew in the Hellenistic empires almost as rapidly as in nineteenth- and twentieth-century America. The population of Antioch in Syria quadrupled during a single century. Seleucia on the Tigris grew from nothing to a metropolis of several hundred thousand in less than two centuries. The largest and most famous of all the Hellenistic cities was Alexandria in Egypt, with over 500,000 inhabitants and possibly as many as 1,000,000. No other city in ancient times before imperial Rome surpassed it in size or in magnificence. Its streets were well paved and laid out in regular order. It had splendid public buildings and parks, a museum, and a library of 700,000 scrolls. It was the most brilliant center of Hellenistic cultural achievement, especially in the field of scientific research. The masses of its people, however, had no share in the brilliant and luxurious life around them, although it was paid for in part out of the fruits of their labor.

3. HELLENISTIC CULTURE: PHILOSOPHY, LITERATURE, AND ART

Hellenistic philosophy exhibited two trends that ran almost parallel throughout the civilization. The major trend, exemplified by Stoicism and Epicureanism, showed a fundamental regard for reason as the key to the solution of human problems. This trend was a manifestation of Greek influence, though philosophy and science, as combined in Aristotle, had now come to a parting of the ways. The minor trend, exemplified by the Cynics, Skeptics, and various Asian cults, tended to reject reason, to deny the possibility of attaining truth, and in some cases to turn toward mysticism and a reliance upon faith. Despite the differences in their teachings, the philosophers of the Hellenistic Age generally agreed upon one thing: the necessity of finding some release from the hardships and evils of human existence.

Trends in philosophy

The first of the Hellenistic philosophers were the Cynics, who arose about 350 B.C. Their foremost leader, Diogenes, won fame by his ceaseless quest for an "honest" man. The Cynics argued for the adoption of the "natural" life and the repudiation of everything conventional and artificial. Their principal goal was the cultivation of "self-sufficiency": everyone should cultivate within himself the ability to satisfy his own needs. Obviously the Cynics bore some resemblance to other movements that have cropped up through the ages—the hippie movement of the 1960s, for example. There were notable differences, however. The Cynics spurned music and art as manifestations of artificiality, and they were not representative of a youth generation. But all such movements seem to reflect a sense of frustration and hopeless conflict in society. According to one story, Alexander the Great once asked Diogenes's disciple Crates whether the city of Thebes, recently destroyed in war, should be rebuilt: "Why?" replied the Cynic, "Another Alexander will surely tear it down again."

The Cynics

Epicureanism and Stoicism both originated about 300 B.C. The founders were, respectively, Epicurus (c. 342–270) and Zeno (fl. after 300), who were residents of Athens. Epicureanism and Stoicism had several features in common. Both were individualistic, concerned not with the welfare of society but with the good of the individual. Both were materialistic, denying categorically the existence of any spiritual substances; even divine beings and the soul were declared to be formed of matter. Moreover, Stoicism and Epicureanism alike contained elements of universalism, since both taught that people are the same the world over and recognized no distinctions between Greeks and "barbarians."

Epicureanism and Stoicism

But in many ways the two systems were quite different. Zeno and his disciples taught that the cosmos is an ordered whole in which all contradictions are resolved for ultimate good. Evil is, therefore, relative; the particular misfortunes which befall human beings are but necessary incidents to the final perfection of the universe. Everything that

*The Stoics' pursuit of
tranquility of mind through
fatalism*

happens is rigidly determined in accordance with rational purpose. No individual is master of his fate; human destiny is a link in an unbroken chain. People are free only in the sense that they can accept their fate or rebel against it. But whether they accept or rebel, they cannot overcome it. Their supreme duty is to submit to the order of the universe in the knowledge that that order is good; in other words, to resign themselves as graciously as possible to their fate. Through such an act of resignation the highest happiness will be attained, which consists in tranquility of mind. The individual who is most truly happy is therefore the one who by the assertion of his rational nature has accomplished a perfect adjustment of his life to the cosmic purpose and has purged his soul of all bitterness and whining protest against evil turns of fortune.

The Stoics developed an ethical and social theory that accorded well with their general philosophy. Believing that the highest good consists in serenity of mind, they naturally emphasized duty and self-discipline as cardinal virtues. Recognizing the prevalence of particular evil, they taught tolerance for and forgiveness of one another. Unlike the Cynics, they did not recommend withdrawal from society but urged participation in public affairs as a duty for the citizen of rational mind. They condemned slavery and war, but it was far from their purpose to preach any crusade against these evils. They believed that the results that might arise from violent measures of social change would be worse than the diseases they were meant to cure. Besides, what difference did it make if the body were in bondage so long as the mind was free? Despite its negative character, the Stoic philosophy was the noblest product of the Hellenistic Age. Its equalitarianism, pacifism, and humanitarianism were important factors in mitigating the harshness not only of that time but of later centuries as well.

The Epicureans derived their metaphysics chiefly from Democritus. Epicurus taught that the basic ingredients of all things are minute, indivisible atoms, and that change and growth are the results of the combination and separation of these particles. Nevertheless, while accepting the materialism of the atomists, Epicurus rejected their absolute mechanism. He denied that an automatic, mechanical motion of the atoms can be the cause of all things in the universe. Though he taught that the atoms move downward in perpendicular lines because of their weight, he insisted upon endowing them with a spontaneous ability to swerve from the perpendicular and thereby to combine with one another. This modification of the atomic theory made possible a belief in human freedom. If the atoms were capable only of mechanical motion, then a human being, also made up of atoms, would be reduced to the status of an automaton, and fatalism would be the law of the universe. In this repudiation of the mechanistic interpretation of life, Epicurus was probably closer to the Hellenic spirit than either Democritus or the Stoics.

The ethical philosophy of the Epicureans was based upon the doctrine that the highest good is pleasure. But they did not include all forms of indulgence in the category of genuine pleasure. The so-called pleasures of the flesh should be avoided, since every excess of carnality must be balanced by its portion of pain. On the other hand, a moderate satisfaction of bodily appetites is permissible and may be regarded as a good in itself. Better than this is mental pleasure, sober contemplation of the reasons for the choice of some things and the avoidance of others, and mature reflection upon satisfactions previously enjoyed. The highest of all pleasures, however, consists in serenity of soul, in the complete absence of both mental and physical pain. This end can be best achieved through the elimination of fear, especially fear of the supernatural, since that is the sovereign source of mental pain. The individual must recognize from the study of philosophy that the soul is material and therefore cannot survive the body, that the universe operates of itself, and that the gods do not intervene in human affairs. The gods live remote from the world and are too intent upon their own happiness to bother about what takes place on earth. Since they do not reward or punish mortals either in this life or in a life to come there is no reason why they should be feared. The Epicureans thus came by a different route to the same general conclusion as the Stoics—the supreme good is tranquillity of mind.

The Epicurean pursuit of tranquility of mind through overcoming fear of the supernatural

The ethics of the Epicureans as well as their political theory rested squarely upon a utilitarian basis. In contrast with the Stoics, they did not insist upon virtue as an end in itself but taught that the only reason why one should be good is to increase his own happiness. In like manner, they denied that there is any such thing as absolute justice: laws and institutions are just only insofar as they contribute to the welfare of the individual. Certain rules have been found necessary in every complex society for the maintenance of security and order. These rules are obeyed solely because it is to each individual's advantage to do so. Epicurus held no high regard for either political or social life. He considered the state as a mere convenience and taught that the wise man should take no active part in politics. Unlike the Cynics, he did not propose that civilization should be abandoned; yet his conception of the happiest life was essentially passive and defeatist. Epicurus taught that the thinking person will recognize that evils in the world cannot be eradicated by human effort; the individual will therefore withdraw to study philosophy and enjoy the fellowship of a few congenial friends.

The ethical and political theories of the Epicureans

A more radically defeatist philosophy was that propounded by the Skeptics. Skepticism reached the zenith of its popularity about 200 B.C. under the influence of Carneades. The chief source of its inspiration was the Sophist teaching that all knowledge is derived from sense perception and therefore must be limited and relative. From this was deduced the conclusion that we cannot prove anything. Since the im-

The defeatist philosophy of the Skeptics

pressions of our senses deceive us, no truth can be certain. All we can say is that things *appear* to be such and such; we do not know what they really *are*. We have no definite knowledge of the supernatural, of the meaning of life, or even of right and wrong. It follows that the sensible course to pursue is suspension of judgment: this alone can lead to happiness. If we will abandon the fruitless quest for absolute truth and cease worrying about good and evil, we will attain that equanimity of mind which is the highest satisfaction that life affords. The Skeptics were even less concerned than the Epicureans with political and social problems. Their ideal was the typically Hellenistic one of escape for the individual from a world neither understandable nor capable of reform.

The new religious philosophies

The nonrational trend in Hellenistic thought reached its farthest extreme in the philosophies of Philo Judaeus and the Neo-Pythagoreans in the last century B.C. and the first century A.D. The proponents of the two systems generally agreed in their basic teachings. They believed in a transcendent God so far removed from the world as to be utterly unknowable to mortal minds. They conceived of the universe as being sharply divided between spirit and matter. They considered everything physical and material as evil; the soul is imprisoned in the body, from which an escape can be effected only through rigorous denial and mortification of the flesh. Their attitude was mystical and nonintellectual: truth comes neither from science nor from reason but from revelation. Philo, a Jew who lived in Alexandria, maintained that the books of the Old Testament were of absolute divine authority and contained all truth; the ultimate aim in life is to accomplish a mystic union with God, to lose one's self in the divine. Both Philo and the Neo-Pythagoreans influenced the development of Christian theology—Philo, in particular, with his dualism of matter and spirit and his doctrine of the Logos, the word, or highest intermediary between God and the universe.

The profusion of ephemeral literature

Hellenistic literature is significant mainly for the light it throws upon the character of the civilization. Most of the writings showed little originality or depth of thought. But they poured forth from the hands of the copyists in a profusion that is almost incredible when we consider that the art of printing by movable type was unknown. We know the names of at least 1,100 authors. Much of what they wrote was trash, comparable to some of the cheap novels of our own day. Nevertheless, there were several works of more than mediocre quality and a few which met the highest standards ever set by the Greeks.

Hellenistic poetry

Among the leading types of Hellenistic literature were the drama and the pastoral. Drama was almost exclusively comedy, represented mainly by the plays of Menander. His plays were very different from the comedy of Aristophanes. They were distinguished by naturalism rather than by satire, by preoccupation with the seamy side of life rather than with political or intellectual issues. Their dominant theme was romantic love, with its pains and pleasures, its intrigues and seductions, and its culmination in happy marriage. The greatest author of pastorals was Theocritus of Syracuse, who wrote in the first half of the third century B.C. His pastorals, as the name implies, celebrate the charm of life in the country and idealize the simple pleasures of rustic folk. Theocritus later found greater imitators in the Roman poet Virgil and the Elizabethan poet Edmund Spenser.

The field of prose literature was dominated by the historians, the biographers, and the authors of utopias. By far the ablest of the writers of history was Polybius of Megalopolis, who lived during the second century B.C. From the standpoint of his scientific approach and his zeal for truth, he probably deserves to be ranked second only to Thucydides among all the historians in ancient times; but he excelled Thucydides in his grasp of the importance of social and economic forces. Although most of the biographies were of a light and gossipy character, their tremendous popularity bears eloquent testimony to the literary tastes of the time. Even more significant was the popularity of the utopias, or descriptive accounts of ideal states. Virtually all of them depicted a life of social and economic equality, free from greed, oppression, and strife, on an imaginary island or in some distant, unfamiliar region. Generally in these paradises money was considered to be unknown, trade was prohibited, all property was held in common, and all were required to work with their hands in producing the necessities of life. We are probably justified in assuming that the profusion of this utopian literature was a direct result of the evils and injustices of Hellenistic society and a consciousness of the need for reform.

Hellenistic art did not preserve all of the characteristic qualities of

The Dying Gaul. A good example of Hellenistic realism in sculpture, which often reflected a preoccupation with the morbid and sensational. Every detail of the warrior's agony is dramatically portrayed. Now in the Capitoline Museum, Rome.

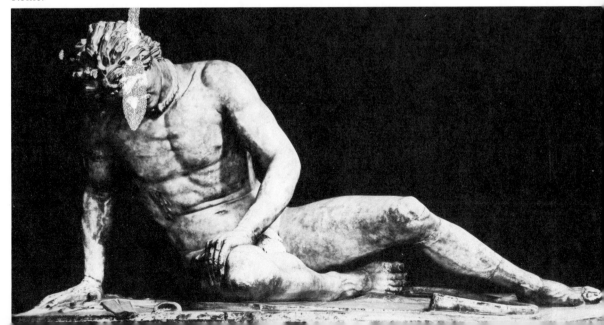

Left: *The Winged Victory of Samothrace*. In this figure, done around 200 B.C., a Hellenistic sculptor preserved some of the calmness and devotion to grace and proportion characteristic of Hellenic art in the Golden Age. Right: *Laocoön*. In sharp contrast to the serenity of the Winged Victory is this famous sculpture group from the late second century B.C., depicting the death of Laocoön. According to legend, Laocoön warned the Trojans not to touch the wooden horse sent by the Greeks and was punished by Poseidon, who sent two serpents to kill him and his sons. The intense emotionalism of this work later had a great influence on western European art from Michelangelo onward. See, for example, the painting by El Greco on page 535.

Hellenistic art

the art of the Greeks. In place of the humanism, balance, and restraint which had distinguished the architecture and sculpture of the Golden Age, qualities of exaggerated realism, sensationalism, and voluptuousness now became dominant. The simple and dignified Doric and Ionic temples gave way to luxurious palaces, costly mansions, and elaborate public buildings and monuments symbolic of power and wealth. A typical example was the great lighthouse of Alexandria, which rose to a height of nearly four hundred feet, with three diminishing stories and eight columns to support the light at the top. Sculpture likewise exhibited extravagant and sentimental tendencies. Many of the statues and figures in relief were huge and some of them almost grotesque. Violent emotionalism and exaggerated realism were features common to the majority. But by no means all of Hellenistic sculpture was overwrought. Some of it was distinguished by a calmness and compassion for human suffering reminiscent of the best work of the great fourth-century artists. Statues which exemplify these superior qualities include the *Aphrodite of Melos* (*Venus de Milo*) and the *Winged Victory of Samothrace*.

4. THE FIRST GREAT AGE OF SCIENCE

The most brilliant age in the history of science prior to the seventeenth century A.D. was the period of the Hellenistic civilization. Indeed, many modern scientific achievements would scarcely have been possible without the discoveries of the scientists of Alexandria, Syracuse, Pergamum, and other great Hellenistic cities. The reasons for the impressive development of science in the centuries after the downfall of Alexander's empire are manifold. Alexander himself had given some financial encouragement to scientific research. More important was the stimulus provided for intellectual inquiry by the fusion of Chaldean and Egyptian science with the learning of the Greeks. Possibly a third factor was the new interest in material comfort and a fourth the demand for practical knowledge that would enable the scientific thinker to solve the problems of a disordered and unsatisfying existence.

Factors responsible for the remarkable progress of science

The major Hellenistic sciences were astronomy, mathematics, geography, medicine, and physics. Chemistry, aside from metallurgy, was practically unknown. Except for the work of Theophrastus, who was the first to recognize the sexuality of plants, biology was also largely neglected. Neither chemistry nor biology bore any definite relationship to trade or to the forms of industry then in existence and hence were not regarded as having much practical value.

The most popular sciences

The most renowned of the earlier Hellenistic astronomers was Aristarchus of Samos (310–230 B.C.), sometimes called the "Hellenistic Copernicus." His chief accomplishment was his deduction that the earth and the other planets revolve around the sun. Unfortunately this view was not accepted by his successors because it conflicted with the teachings of Aristotle and with the conviction of the Greeks that man, and therefore the earth, must be at the center of the universe. Another important Hellenistic astronomer was Hipparchus, who flourished in Alexandria in the latter half of the second century B.C. His chief contributions were the invention of the astrolabe and the approximately correct calculation of the diameter of the moon and its distance from the earth. His fame was eventually overshadowed, however, by the reputation of Ptolemy of Alexandria (second century A.D.). Although Ptolemy made few original discoveries, he systematized the work of others. His principal writing, the *Almagest,* based upon the geocentric theory (the view that all heavenly bodies revolve around the earth), was handed down to medieval Europe as the classic summary of ancient astronomy. Ptolemy's geography too had a considerable influence on medieval and Renaissance thought.

Astronomy

Closely allied with astronomy were two other sciences, mathemat-

Mathematics and geography

ics and geography. The Hellenistic mathematician of greatest renown was Euclid (c. 323–c. 285 B.C.), the master of geometry. Until the middle of the nineteenth century his *Elements of Geometry* remained the accepted basis for the study of that branch of mathematics. Much of the material in this work was not original but was a synthesis of the discoveries of others. The most original of the Hellenistic mathematicians was probably Hipparchus, who laid the foundations of both plane and spherical trigonometry. Hellenistic geography owed most of its development to Eratosthenes (c. 276–c. 196 B.C.), astronomer, poet, and librarian of Alexandria. By means of sundials placed some hundreds of miles apart, he calculated the circumference of the earth with an error of less than 200 miles. He produced the most accurate map that had yet been devised, with the surface of the earth divided into degrees of latitude and longitude. He propounded the theory that all of the oceans are really one, and he was the first to suggest the possibility of reaching India by sailing west. One of his successors divided the earth into the five climatic zones which are still recognized, and explained the ebb and flow of the tides as due to the influence of the moon.

Medicine: the development of anatomy

Perhaps none of the Hellenistic advances in science surpassed in importance the progress in medicine. Especially significant was the work of Herophilus of Chalcedon, who conducted his researches in Alexandria about the beginning of the second century. Without question he was the greatest anatomist of antiquity and probably the first to practice human dissection. Among his most important achievements were a detailed description of the brain, with an attempt to distinguish between the functions of its various parts; the discovery of the significance of the pulse and its use in diagnosing illness; and the discovery that the arteries contain blood alone, not a mixture of blood and air as Aristotle had taught, and that their function is to carry blood from the heart to all parts of the body.

Physiology

The ablest of the colleagues of Herophilus was Erasistratus, who flourished in Alexandria about the middle of the third century. He is considered the founder of physiology as a separate science. Not only did he practice dissection, but he is believed to have gained a great deal of his knowledge of bodily functions from vivisection. He discovered the valves of the heart, distinguished between motor and sensory nerves, and taught that the ultimate branches of the arteries and veins are connected. He was the first to reject absolutely the humoral theory of disease and to condemn excessive blood-letting as a method of cure. Unfortunately this theory was revived by Galen, the great encyclopedist of medicine who lived in the Roman Empire in the second century A.D.

Physics

Prior to the third century B.C. physics had been a branch of philosophy. It was made a separate experimental science by Archimedes of Syracuse (c. 287–212 B.C.). Archimedes discovered the law of floating bodies, or specific gravity, and formulated with scientific exactness

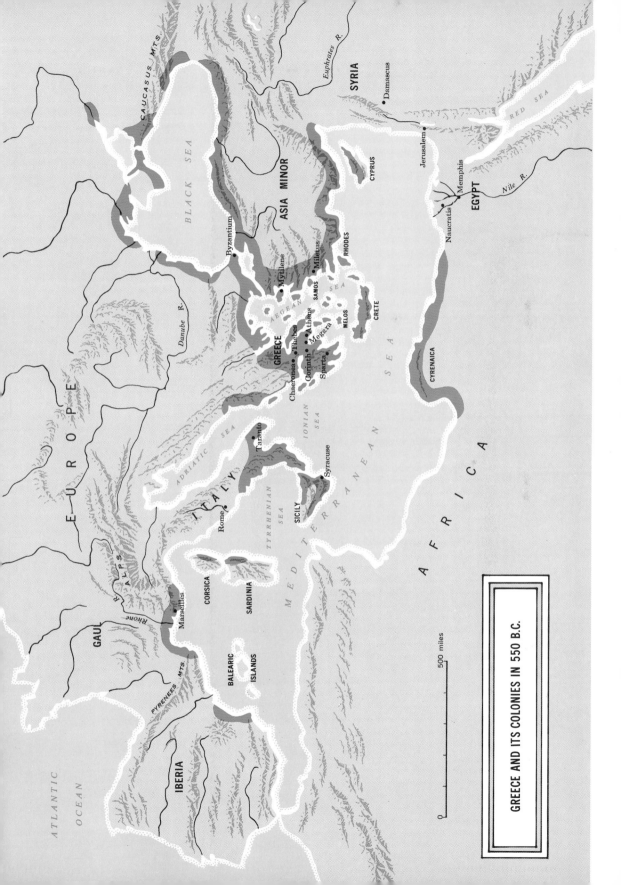

GREECE AND ITS COLONIES IN 550 B.C.

Geometric Horse, VIII cent. B.C. Greek art of this early period was angular, formal, and conventionalized.

Geometric Jar, VIII cent. B.C. Another example of the stylized decorative patterns of early Greek art.

Sphinx, c. 540–530 B.C. Though doubtless of Oriental derivation, Greek sphinxes had a softer and more human aspect than the Oriental.

Statue of an Amazon, one of the fabled tribe of women warriors, V cent. B.C. *(Roman copy)*

Departure of a Warrior. Gravestone, c. 530 B.C., a period when naturalism was the dominant note of Greek art.

Athena, c. 460 B.C. The young, graceful patron-goddess of Athens is about to send forth an owl as a sign of victory.

Jar, 500–490 B.C. The figures depicted in a fine black glaze on the natural red clay show athletes in the Panathenaic games.

Chorus of Satyrs, c. 420 B.C. The background is black with the figures in red clay. The satyrs, dressed in fleecy white, with flowing tails, are the chorus of a play.

Toilet Box, 465–460 B.C. This scene shows the judgment of Paris, an event which touched off the Trojan War.

Bronze Mirror Case, V cent. B.C. Greek articles of everyday use were commonly finished with the same delicacy and precision as major works of art.

Diadoumenos, after Polykleitos, V cent. B.C. An idealized statue of a Greek athlete tying the "diadem," or band of victory, around his head.

Bracelet Pendant, IV–III cent. B.C. This tiny figure of the god Pan is a masterpiece of detail and expression.

Woman Arranging Her Hair, 400–300 B.C. Sculptors of antiquity took pride in these statuettes of ordinary people in ordinary activities, which were usually made of terracotta painted soft blue, pink, or yellow.

Head of an Athlete, c. 440–420 B.C. The sculptor aimed to express manly beauty in perfect harmony with physical and intellectual excellence.

Statuette of Hermarchos, III cent. B.C. An example of the realism of Hellenistic sculpture.

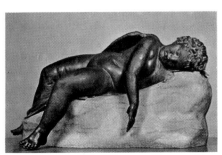

Sleeping Eros, 250–150 B.C. Along with a penchant for realism, Hellenistic sculptors were fond of portraying serenity or repose.

Comic Actor, 200–100 B.C. Hellenistic realism often included portrayal of ugly and even deformed individuals.

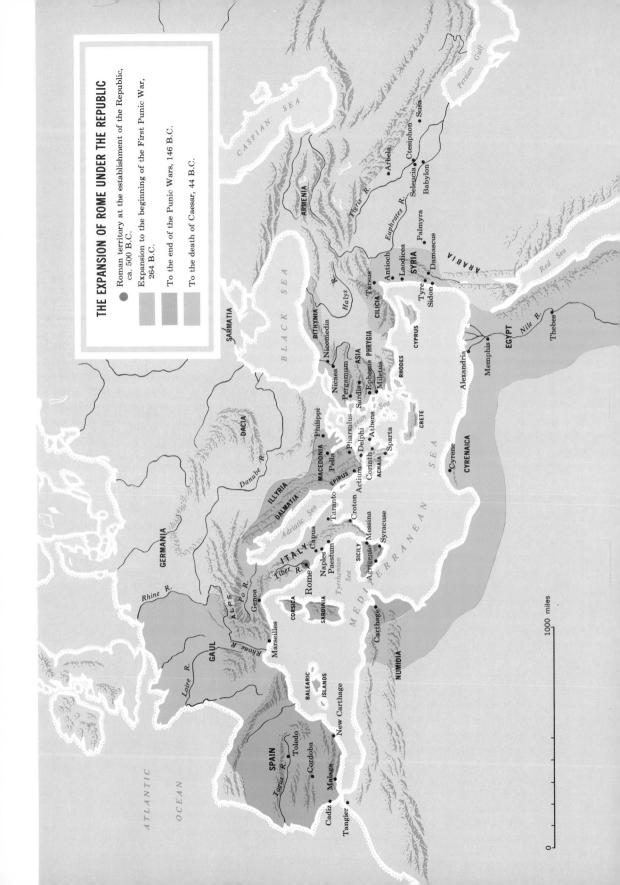

THE EXPANSION OF ROME UNDER THE REPUBLIC

- Roman territory at the establishment of the Republic, ca. 500 B.C.
- Expansion to the beginning of the First Punic War, 264 B.C.
- To the end of the Punic Wars, 146 B.C.
- To the death of Caesar, 44 B.C.

1000 miles

ATLANTIC OCEAN

SPAIN
Toledo
Cordoba
Malaga
Cadiz
Tangier
Tagus R.
New Carthage
BALEARIC ISLANDS

GAUL
Rhone R.
Loire R.
Rhine R.
Marseilles
Genoa
ALPS
Po R.
CORSICA
SARDINIA

GERMANIA

ITALY
Rome
Tiber R.
Naples
Paestum
Capua
Taranto
Croton
SICILY
Agrigento
Messina
Syracuse
Carthage
NUMIDIA
Tyrrhenian Sea

ILLYRIA
DALMATIA
Adriatic Sea

DACIA
Danube R.

SARMATIA

BLACK SEA

MACEDONIA
Pella
Philippi
EPIRUS
Pharsalus
Actium
Delphi
Corinth
Athens
ACHAIA
Sparta
Aegean Sea
CRETE

MEDITERRANEAN SEA

CYRENAICA
Cyrene

EGYPT
Alexandria
Memphis
Thebes
Nile R.

BITHYNIA
Nicomedia
Nicaea
Pergamum
ASIA
Sardis
Ephesus
Miletus
PHRYGIA
RHODES
CYPRUS

Halys R.
ARMENIA
Tigris R.
Euphrates R.
CILICIA
Tarsus
Antioch
Laodicea
SYRIA
Palmyra
Damascus
Tyre
Sidon
ARABIA
Red Sea

Seleucia
Ctesiphon
Babylon
Arbela
Susa
Persian Gulf

CASPIAN SEA

the principles of the lever, the pulley, and the screw. Among his memorable inventions were the compound pulley, the tubular screw for pumping water, the screw propeller for ships, and the burning lens. Although he has been called the "technical Yankee of antiquity," there is evidence that he set no high value upon his ingenious mechanical contraptions and preferred to devote his time to pure scientific research.

Certain other individuals in the Hellenistic Age also devoted themselves to applied science. Preeminent among them was Hero of Alexandria, who lived in the last century B.C. The record of inventions credited to him almost passes belief. The list includes a fire engine, a siphon, a jet engine, a hydraulic organ, a slot machine, and a catapult operated by compressed air. How many of these inventions were really his own is impossible to say, but there appears to be no question that such contrivances were actually in existence in his time or soon thereafter. Nevertheless, the total progress in applied science was comparatively slight, probably for the reason that human labor continued to be so abundant and cheap that it was not worthwhile to substitute the work of machines.

Applied science

5. RELIGION IN THE HELLENISTIC AGE

If there was one aspect of the Hellenistic civilization which served more than others to accent the contrast with Hellenic culture, it was the new trend in religion. The civic religion of the Greeks as it was in the age of the city-states had now almost entirely disappeared. For the majority of the intellectuals its place was taken by the philosophies of Stoicism, Epicureanism, and Skepticism. Some who were less philosophically inclined turned to the worship of Fortune.

The new trend in religion

Among the common people a tendency to embrace emotional religions was even more dominant. The Orphic and Eleusinian mystery cults attracted more votaries than ever before. The worship of the Egyptian mother-goddess, Isis, threatened for a time to predominate throughout the Near East. The astral religion of the Chaldeans likewise spread rapidly, with the result that its chief product, astrology, was received with intense enthusiasm throughout the Hellenistic world. But the most powerful influence of all came from the offshoots of Zoroastrianism, especially from Mithraism and Gnosticism. While all of the cults of Oriental origin resembled each other in their promises of salvation in a life to come, Mithraism and Gnosticism had a more ethically exalted mythology, a deeper contempt for this world, and a more clearly defined doctrine of redemption through a personal savior. These were the ideas which satisfied the emotional cravings of the common people, convinced as they were of the worthlessness of this life and ready to be lured by extravagant promises of better things in a world to come.

The popularity of mystical religions

A factor by no means unimportant in the religious developments of the Hellenistic Age was the dispersion of the Jews. As a result of Alexander's conquest of Palestine in 332 B.C. and the Roman conquest about three centuries later, thousands of Jews migrated to various sections of the Mediterranean world. It has been estimated that 1,000,000 of them lived in Egypt in the first century A.D. and 200,000 in Asia Minor. They mingled freely with other peoples, adopting the Greek language and no small amount of the Hellenic culture which still survived from earlier days. At the same time they played a major part in the diffusion of Eastern beliefs. Some of the Hellenistic Jews eventually became converts to Christianity and were instrumental in the spread of that religion outside of Palestine. A notable example was Saul of Tarsus, known in Christian history as St. Paul.

6. A FORETASTE OF MODERNITY?

With the possible exception of the Roman, no great culture of ancient times resembles the modern age quite so much as does the Hellenistic civilization. Here, as in the twentieth century, were to be found a considerable variety of forms of government, the growth of militarism, and a trend in the direction of authoritarian rule. Many of the characteristic economic and social developments of the Hellenistic Age are equally suggestive of contemporary experience: the growth of big business, the expansion of trade, the zeal for exploration and discovery, the interest in technology, the devotion to material prosperity, the growth of cities with congested slums, and the widening gulf between rich and poor. In the realms of intellect and art the Hellenistic civilization also had a distinctly modern flavor. This was exemplified by the emphasis upon science, the narrow specialization of learning, the penchant for realism and naturalism, the vast production of mediocre literature, and the popularity of mysticism side by side with extreme skepticism and dogmatic unbelief.

Because of these resemblances there has been a tendency among certain writers to regard our own civilization as decadent. But this is based partly upon a false conception of Hellenistic culture as merely a degenerate phase of Greek civilization. Instead, it was a new social and cultural organism born of a fusion of Greek and Near Eastern elements. Moreover, the differences between the Hellenistic civilization and that of the contemporary world ultimately outweigh the resemblances. The Hellenistic political outlook was essentially cosmopolitan; nothing comparable to the national patriotism of modern times really prevailed. Despite the remarkable expansion of trade in the Hellenistic Age, no industrial revolution ever took place. Finally, Hellenistic science was more limited than that of the present day. Modern pure science is to a very large extent a species of philosophy—

Statue of an Old Market Woman. In the Hellenic Age the idealism and restraint of Hellenic art were succeeded by a tendency to portray the humble aspects of life and to express compassion for human suffering. Original in the Metropolitan Museum of Art, New York.

an adventure of the mind in the realm of the unknown. Notwithstanding frequent assertions to the contrary, much of it is gloriously impractical and will probably remain so.

SELECTED READINGS

• *Items so designated are available in paperback editions.*

Cary, Max, *The Legacy of Alexander: A History of the Greek World from 323 to 146 B.C.,* New York, 1932. A firm guide to the complicated political history of the period.

Clagett, M., *Greek Science in Antiquity,* New York, 1963. A solid and dependable introduction.

Festugière, A. J., *Epicurus and His Gods,* Cambridge, Mass., 1956.

• Finley, M. I., *The Ancient Economy,* Berkeley, Calif., 1973. A fundamental topical treatment by a brilliant scholar.

Grant, F. C., *Hellenistic Religions,* New York, 1963. A standard work.

Hamilton, J. R., *Alexander the Great,* London, 1973. The best concise scholarly biography currently available.

Lane Fox, R., *Alexander the Great,* London, 1973. Longer and more interpretative than Hamilton but highly recommended.

Larsen, J. A. O., *Greek Federal States,* Oxford, 1968.

Rostovtzeff, M., *The Social and Economic History of the Hellenistic World,* 3 vols., Oxford, 1941. An authoritative mine of information.

• Tarn, W. W., *Alexander the Great,* Cambridge, 1948. Tarn was the leading English expert on Hellenistic history of the earlier part of this century.

———, and G. T. Griffith, *Hellenistic Civilization,* 3rd ed., London, 1952. Still indispensible.

Walbank, F. W., *The Hellenistic World,* Cambridge, Mass., 1982. An excellent college-level survey by one of the world's most prominent experts.

• Wilcken, U., *Alexander the Great,* New York, 1932. A fundamental older interpretation, translated from the German.

SOURCE MATERIALS

Greek source materials for the Hellenistic period are available in the appropriate volumes of the Loeb Classical Library, Harvard University Press.

Chapter 8

ROMAN CIVILIZATION

My city and country, so far as I am Antoninus, is Rome, but so far as I am
a man, it is the world.

—Marcus Aurelius Antoninus, *Meditations*

For the categories into which you divide the world are not Hellenes and
Barbarians. . . . The division which you substituted is one into Romans
and non-Romans. To such a degree have you expanded the name of your
city.

—Aelius Aristides, *Oration to Rome*

Well before the glory that was Greece had begun to fade,
another civilization, ultimately much influenced by Greek
culture, had started its growth in the West on the banks of
the Tiber. Around the time of Alexander's conquests the new civilization of Rome was already a dominant force on the Italian peninsula.
For five centuries thereafter Rome's power increased. By the end of
the first century B.C. it had imposed its rule over the entire Hellenistic
world as well as over most of western Europe. By conquering the old
Hellenistic states and destroying the North African civilization of Carthage, Rome was able to make the Mediterranean a "Roman lake." In
so doing it brought Greek institutions and ideas to the western half of
the Mediterranean world. And by pushing northward to the Rhine
and Danube rivers it brought Mediterranean urban culture to lands
still sunk in the Iron Age. Rome, then, was the builder of a great
historical bridge between East and West.

The rise of Rome

Of course Rome would not have been able to play this role had it
not followed its own peculiar course of development. This was
marked by the tension between two different cultural outlooks. On
the one hand Romans throughout most of their history tended to be
conservative: they revered their old agricultural traditions, household
gods, and ruggedly warlike ways. But they also strove to be builders
and could not resist the attractions of Greek culture. For a few centu-

The Roman synthesis

ries their greatness was based on a synthesis of these different traits: respect for tradition, order, and military prowess, together with Greek urbanization and cultivation of the mind. The synthesis could not last forever, but as long as it did the glory that was Greece was replaced by the grandeur that was Rome.

1. EARLY ITALY AND THE ROMAN MONARCHY

The impact of geography on Roman history

The geographical character of the Italian peninsula contributed significantly to the course of Roman history. Except for some excellent marble and small quantities of tin, copper, iron, and gold, Italy has no mineral resources. The extensive coastline is broken by few good harbors. On the other hand, the amount of fertile land is greater than that of Greece. As a result, the Romans remained a predominantly agrarian people through the greater part of their history. They seldom enjoyed the intellectual stimulus which comes from extensive trading with other areas. In addition, the Italian peninsula was more open to invasion than was Greece. The Alps posed no effective barrier to the influx of peoples from central Europe, and the low-lying coast in many places invited conquest by sea. Domination of the territory by force was therefore more common than peaceful intermingling of immigrants with original settlers. The Romans became absorbed in military pursuits almost from the moment of their settlement on Italian soil, for they were forced to defend their own conquests against other invaders.

An Etruscan Musician. This well-coordinated flutist appears in an Etruscan wall painting dating from about 480 B.C.

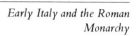

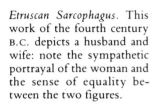

Etruscan Sarcophagus. This work of the fourth century B.C. depicts a husband and wife: note the sympathetic portrayal of the woman and the sense of equality between the two figures.

Archeological evidence indicates that Italy was inhabited at least as far back as the later Paleolithic Age. At this time the territory was occupied by a people closely related to the Cro-Magnons of southern France. In the Neolithic period people of Mediterranean stock entered the land, some coming in from northern Africa and others from Spain and Gaul. The beginning of the Bronze Age witnessed several new incursions. From north of the Alps came the first of the immigrants of the Indo-European language group. They were herdsmen and farmers, who brought the horse and the wheeled cart into Italy. Their culture was based upon the use of bronze, although after about 900 B.C. they appear to have acquired a knowledge of iron. These Indo-Europeans seem to have been the ancestors of most of the so-called Italic peoples, including the Romans, and they were probably related to the Hellenic invaders of Greece.

The earliest inhabitants of Italy

Probably during the eighth century B.C. two other nations of immigrants occupied different portions of the Italian peninsula: the Etruscans and the Greeks. Where the Etruscans came from is a question which has never been satisfactorily answered, although it is certain that they were not Indo-Europeans. Most authorities believe that they were natives of Asia Minor. Whatever their origins, by the sixth century B.C. they had established a great federation of cities that stretched over most of northern and central Italy. Although their writing has never been completely deciphered, enough materials survive to indicate the nature of their culture. They had an alphabet based upon the Greek, a high degree of skill in metalwork, great artistic talents, a flourishing trade with the East, and a religion based upon the worship of gods in human form. They bequeathed to the Romans a knowledge of the arch and the vault, the cruel amusement of gladiatorial combats, and the practice of foretelling the future by supernatural means such as studying the entrails of animals or the flight of

The Etruscans and the Greeks

birds. One of their most distinctive traits was the comparatively great respect they showed for women. Etruscan wives, unlike those in other contemporary societies, ate with their husbands, and some Etruscan families listed descent through the maternal line.

The Greeks settled mainly along the southern and southwestern shores of Italy and the island of Sicily, as well as along the southern coast of Gaul. Their most important settlements were Taranto, Naples, and Syracuse, each of which was an independent city-state. Greek civilization in Italy and Sicily was as advanced as in Greece itself. Such famous Greeks as Pythagoras, Archimedes, and even Plato for a time, lived in the Italian West. From the Greeks the Romans derived their alphabet, a number of their religious concepts, and much of their art and mythology.

The founders of Rome itself were Italic peoples who lived in the area south of the Tiber River. Though the exact year of the founding of the city is unknown, recent archeological research places the event quite near the traditional date of 753 B.C. By reason of its strategic location, Rome came to exercise an effective suzerainty over several of the most important neighboring cities. One conquest followed another until, by the sixth century B.C., Rome came to dominate most of the surrounding area. But just then Etruscans took over power in Rome.

At first Roman government aimed far more at establishing stability than at creating liberty. The original Roman state was essentially an application of the idea of the patriarchal family to the whole community, with the king exercising a jurisdiction over his subjects comparable to that of the head of the family over the members of his household. But just as the authority of the father was limited by custom and by the requirement that he respect the wishes of his adult sons, the authority of the king was limited by the ancient constitution, which he was powerless to change without the consent of the chief men of the realm. His prerogatives were not primarily legislative but executive, priestly, military, and judicial. He judged all civil and criminal cases, but he had no authority to pardon without the consent of the assembly. Although his accession to office had to be confirmed by the people, he could not be deposed, and there was no one who could really challenge the exercise of his powers.

In addition to the kingship, the Roman government of this time included an assembly and a Senate. The former was composed of all the male citizens of military age. As one of the chief sources of sovereign power, according to the theory, this body could veto any proposal for a change in the law which the king might make. Moreover, it determined whether pardons should be granted and whether aggressive war should be declared. But it was essentially a ratifying body with no right to initiate legislation or recommend changes of policy. The Senate, or council of elders, comprised in its membership the heads of the various clans which formed the community. Even more than the common citizens, the rulers of the clans embodied the sovereign power of the state. The king was only one of their number to whom they had delegated the active exercise of their authority. When the royal office became vacant, the powers of the king immediately reverted to the Senate until the succession of a new monarch had been confirmed by the people. In ordinary times the chief function of the Senate was to examine proposals of the king which had been ratified by the assembly and to veto them if they violated rights established by ancient custom. It was thus almost impossible for fundamental changes to be made in the law even when the majority of the citizens were ready to sanction them. This extremely conservative attitude of the ruling classes persisted until the end of Roman history.

Toward the end of the sixth century (the date traditionally given is 509 B.C.) the monarchy was overthrown and replaced by a republic. Legend has it that this revolution was provoked by the crimes of the Tarquins, an Etruscan family that had taken over the kingship in Rome around the middle of the century. After suffering numerous indignities, the last and worst of which was the rape and subsequent suicide of a virtuous Roman matron, Lucretia, by a lustful Tarquin prince, the native Romans could stand no more and rose up to expel their alien oppressors. In fact the story of the rape of Lucretia is fictional but the change in government was probably in part a native uprising against foreigners, as well as a successful movement of the Roman senatorial aristocracy to gain full power for itself. The result was the beginning of Etruscan decline in Italy, as well as a lasting conviction among Romans that kingship was evil.

End of the monarchy

2. THE EARLY REPUBLIC

The history of the Roman Republic for more than two centuries after its establishment was one of almost constant warfare. Many of the most familiar Roman legends, such as that of the brave Horatio, who with only two friends held off an entire army in front of a bridge, date from this period. At first the Romans were on the defensive. The overthrow of the Tarquins resulted in acts of reprisal by their allies in neighboring regions, and other peoples on the borders took advantage of the confusion accompanying the change of regime to slice off portions of Roman territory. After Rome managed to ward off these attacks it began to expand in order to gain more land and satisfy a rapidly growing population. As time went on Rome steadily conquered all the Etruscan territories and then took over all the Greek cities in the southernmost portion of the Italian mainland. Not only did the latter add to the Roman domain, they also brought the Romans into fruitful contact with Greek culture. The Romans were then frequently confronted with revolts of peoples previously conquered. The suppression of these revolts awakened the suspicions of surrounding states

Early Roman expansion

See color map facing page 161

Roman Battle Sarcophagus. This relief displays the glories of war and expresses the Roman military ideal.

and sharpened the appetite of the victors for further triumphs. New wars followed each other in what seemed an unending succession, until by 265 B.C. Rome had conquered the entire Italian peninsula.

Effects of the early military conflicts

This long series of military conflicts had profound social, economic, and cultural effects upon the subsequent history of Rome. It affected adversely the interests of the poorer citizens and furthered the concentration of land in the possession of wealthy proprietors. Long service in the army forced the ordinary farmers to neglect the cultivation of the soil, with the result that they fell into debt and frequently lost their farms. Many took refuge in the city, until they were settled later as tenants on great estates in the conquered territories. The wars had the effect also of confirming the agrarian character of the Roman nation. The repeated acquisition of new lands made it possible to absorb the entire population into agricultural pursuits. As a consequence Romans saw no need for the development of industry and commerce. Last, the continual warfare of this formative period served to develop among the Romans a strong military ideal: along with Horatio, another of Rome's great early legendary heroes was Cincinnatus, who supposedly left his farm at a moment's notice for the battlefield.

Political changes following the overthrow of the monarchy

During this same period of the early Republic, Rome underwent some significant political changes. These were not products so much of the revolution of the sixth century as of the developments of later years. The revolution which overthrew the monarchy was about as conservative as it is possible for a revolution to be. Its chief effect was to substitute two elected officials called consuls for the king and to exalt the position of the Senate by granting it control over the public funds and a veto on all actions of the assembly. The consuls themselves were usually senators and acted as the agents of their class. They did not rule jointly, but each was supposed to possess the full executive and judicial authority which had previously been wielded by the king. If a conflict arose between them, the Senate might be called upon to decide; or, in time of grave emergency, a dictator might be appointed for a term not greater than six months. In other respects the government remained the same as in the days of the monarchy.

Not long after the establishment of the Republic a struggle for power began among factions of the common citizens. Before the end of the monarchy the Roman population had come to be divided into two great classes—the patricians and the plebeians. The former were the aristocracy, wealthy landowners who monopolized the seats in the Senate and the offices of magistracy. Among the plebeians were some wealthy families who were barred from the patriciate because they were of recent foreign origin, but most plebeians were common people—small farmers, craftsmen, and tradesmen. Many were clients or dependents of the patricians, obliged to fight for them, to render them political support, and to cultivate their estates in return for protection. The grievances of the plebeians were numerous. Compelled to pay heavy taxes and forced to serve in the army in time of war, they were nevertheless excluded from all part in the government except membership in the assembly. Moreover, they felt themselves the victims of discriminatory decisions in judicial trials. They did not even know what legal rights they were supposed to enjoy, for the laws were unwritten, and no one but the consuls had the power to interpret them. In suits for debt the creditor was frequently allowed to sell the debtor into slavery.

In order to obtain a redress of these grievances the plebeians rebelled soon after the beginning of the fifth century B.C. They gained their first victory about 494 B.C., when they forced the patricians to agree to the election of a number of officers known as tribunes with power to protect the citizens by means of a veto over unlawful acts of the magistrates. This victory was followed by a successful demand for codification of the laws about 450 B.C. The result was the publication of the famous Law of the Twelve Tables, so called because it was written on tablets of wood. Although the Twelve Tables came to be revered by the Romans of later times as a kind of charter of the people's liberties, they were really nothing of the sort. For the most part they merely perpetuated ancient custom without even abolishing enslavement for debt. They did, however, enable the people to know where they stood in relation to the law, and they permitted an appeal to the assembly against a magistrate's sentence of capital punishment. About a generation later the plebeians won eligibility to positions as lesser magistrates, and about 367 B.C. the first plebeian consul was elected. Since ancient custom provided that, upon completing their term of office, consuls should automatically enter the Senate, the patrician monopoly of seats in that body was broken. The final plebeian victory came in 287 B.C. with the passage of a law which provided that measures enacted by the assembly should become binding upon the state whether the Senate approved them or not.

The significance of these changes must not be misinterpreted. They did not constitute a revolution to gain more liberty for the individual but merely to curb the power of the magistrates and to win for the plebeians a larger share in government. The state as a whole remained as despotic as ever, for its authority over the citizens was not even challenged. Indeed, the Romans of the early Republic "never really abandoned the principle that the people were not to govern but to be governed."[1] Because of this attitude the grant of full legislative powers to the assembly seems to have meant little more than a formality; the Senate continued to rule as before. Nor did the admission of plebeians to membership in the Senate have any effect in liberalizing that body. So high was its prestige and so deep was the veneration of the Roman for authority, that the new members were soon swallowed up in the conservatism of the old. Moreover, the fact that the magistrates received no salaries prevented most of the poorer citizens from seeking public office.

Intellectually and culturally the Romans developed very slowly. Life in Rome was still harsh and crude. Though writing had been adopted as early as the sixth century, little use was made of it except for the copying of laws, treaties, and funerary inscriptions. Inasmuch as education was limited to instruction imparted by the father in manly sports, practical arts, and soldierly virtues, the great majority of the people were still illiterate. War and agriculture continued as the chief occupations for the bulk of the citizens. A few craftsmen were to be found in the cities, and a minor development of trade had occurred. But the fact that the country had no standard system of coinage until 269 B.C. clearly demonstrates the comparative insignificance of Roman commerce at this time.

During the period of the early Republic Roman religion assumed the character it retained through the greater part of Roman history. In several ways this religion resembled that of the Greeks, partly for the reason that the Etruscan religion was deeply indebted to the Greek, and the Romans, in turn, were influenced by the Etruscans. Both the Greek and Roman religions emphasized the performances of rites in order to gain benefits from the gods or keep them from anger. The deities in both religions performed similar functions: Jupiter corresponded to Zeus as god of the sky, Minerva to Athena as goddess of wisdom and patroness of crafts, Venus to Aphrodite as goddess of love, Neptune to Poseidon as god of the sea, and so on. The Roman religion, like the Greek, had no dogmas or sacraments or belief in rewards and punishments in an afterlife.

But there were significant differences also. The Roman religion was distinctly more political and less humanist in purpose. It served not to glorify humanity or establish a comfortable relationship between human beings and their world but to protect the state from its enemies

[1] Theodor Mommsen, *The History of Rome*, I, 313.

Intervention of Jupiter. This scene from the first century A.D. depicts Jupiter, god of the sky, supporting the Romans in a battle against Germanic barbarians.

and to augment its power and prosperity. The gods were less human; indeed, it was only as a result of Greek and Etruscan influences that they were made personal deities at all, having previously been worshiped as animistic spirits. The Romans never conceived of their deities as quarreling among themselves or mingling with human beings after the fashion of the Homeric divinities. Finally, the Roman religion contained a much stronger element of priestliness than the Greek. The priests, or pontiffs as they were called, formed an organized class, a branch of the government itself. They not only supervised the offering of sacrifices, they were also guardians of an elaborate body of sacred traditions and laws which they alone could interpret. It must be understood, however, that these pontiffs were not priests in the sense of intermediaries between the individual Roman and the gods; they heard no confessions, forgave no sins, and administered no sacraments.

The morality of the Romans in this as in later periods had almost no connection with religion. The Romans did not ask their gods to make them good, but to bestow upon the community and upon their families material blessings. Morality was a matter of patriotism and of respect for authority and tradition. The chief virtues were bravery, honor, self-discipline, reverence for the gods and for one's ancestors, and duty to country and family. Loyalty to Rome took precedence over everything else. For the good of the state the citizen had to be ready to sacrifice not only his own life but, if necessary, the lives of his family and friends. The courage of certain consuls who dutifully put their sons to death for breaches of military discipline was a subject of

Morality in the Early Republic

profound admiration. Few peoples in European history with the exception of the Spartans and modern totalitarians have ever taken the problems of national interest so seriously or subordinated the individual so completely to the welfare of the state.

3. THE FATEFUL WARS WITH CARTHAGE

The beginning of imperialism on a major scale

By 265 B.C. Rome had conquered and annexed almost the entire Italian mainland. Proud and confident of its strength, it was almost certain to strike out into new fields of empire. The prosperous island of Sicily was not yet within its grasp, nor could it regard with indifference the situation in other parts of the Mediterranean world. Rome was now prone to interpret almost any change in the status quo as a threat to its own power and security. It was for such reasons that Rome soon became involved in a series of wars with other great nations which decidedly altered the course of its history.

Carthage

The first and most important of these wars was the struggle with Carthage, a great maritime empire that stretched along the northern coast of Africa from modern-day Tunisia to the Strait of Gibraltar. Carthage had originally been founded about 800 B.C. as a Phoenician colony. In the sixth century it severed its ties with the homeland and gradually developed into a rich and powerful state. The prosperity of its upper classes was founded upon commerce and upon exploitation of the silver and tin resources of Spain and the tropical products of north central Africa. Carthaginian government was oligarchic. The real rulers were thirty merchant princes who constituted an inner council of the Senate. These men controlled elections and dominated every other branch of the government. The remaining 270 members of the Senate appear to have been summoned to meet only on special occasions. In spite of these political deficiencies and a cruel religion that demanded blood sacrifices, Carthage had a civilization superior in luxury and scientific attainment to that of Rome when the struggle between the two states began.

Causes of the First Punic War

The initial clash with Carthage started in 264 B.C.[2] The primary cause was Roman jealousy over Carthaginian expansion in Sicily. Carthage already controlled the western portion of the island and was threatening the Greek cities of Syracuse and Messina on the eastern coast. If these cities were captured, all chances of Roman occupation of Sicily would be lost. Faced with this danger, Rome declared war upon Carthage with the hope of forcing it back into its African domain. Twenty-three years of fighting finally brought victory to the Roman generals. Carthage was compelled to surrender its possessions in Sicily and to pay a very large indemnity.

---

[2] The wars with Carthage are known as the Punic Wars. The Romans called the Carthaginians *Poeni,* i.e., Phoenicians, whence is derived the adjective "Punic."

But the Romans had exerted such heroic efforts to defeat Carthage that when victory was finally secured it made them more arrogant and acquisitive than ever. As a result, the struggle with Carthage was renewed on two subsequent occasions. In 218 B.C., the Romans interpreted the Carthaginian attempt to rebuild an empire in Spain as a threat to their interests and responded with a declaration of war. This struggle raged through a period of sixteen years. Italy was ravaged by the armies of Hannibal, the famous Carthaginian commander, who crossed the Alps with sixty elephants, and whose tactics have been copied by military experts to the present day. Rome escaped defeat by the narrowest of margins. Only the durability of its system of alliances in Italy saved the day. As long as these alliances held, Hannibal dared not besiege the city of Rome itself for fear of being attacked from the rear. In the end Carthage was more completely humbled than before, being compelled to abandon all its possessions except the capital city and its surrounding territory in Africa, and to pay an indemnity three times greater than that paid at the end of the First Punic War.

Roman vindictiveness reached its peak about the middle of the second century B.C. By this time Carthage had recovered a modicum of its former prosperity—enough to excite the displeasure of its conquerors. Nothing would now satisfy the senatorial magnates but the complete destruction of Carthage and the expropriation of its land. In 149 B.C. the Senate dispatched an ultimatum demanding that the Carthaginians abandon their city and settle at least ten miles from the coast. Since this demand was tantamount to a death sentence for a nation dependent upon commerce, it was refused—as the Romans probably hoped it would be. The result was the Third Punic War, a brutal conflict which was fought between 149 and 146 B.C. The final Roman assault upon the city was carried into the houses of the inhabitants and a frightful butchery took place. When the victorious Roman general saw Carthage going up in flames he said: "It is a glorious moment, but I have a strange feeling that some day the same fate will befall my own homeland." With the resistance of the Carthaginians finally broken, the few citizens left to surrender were sold into slavery, their once magnificent city was razed, and the ground was plowed over with salt. Carthaginian territory was then organized into a Roman province, with the best areas parceled out as senatorial estates.

The wars with Carthage had momentous effects on Rome. First, victory in the Second Punic War led to Roman occupation of Spain. This not only brought great new wealth—above all from Spanish silver—but was the beginning of a policy of westward expansion that proved to be one of the great formative influences on the history of Europe. Then too the wars brought Rome into conflict with eastern Mediterranean powers and thereby paved the way for still greater dominion. During the Second Punic War, Philip V of Macedon had entered into an alliance with Carthage and had plotted with the king of Syria to divide Egypt between them. In order to forestall the execu-

The Second Punic War

Hannibal. A coin from Carthage representing Hannibal as a victorious general, with an elephant on the reverse.

The Third Punic War and the destruction of Carthage

See color map facing page 161

Results of the wars with Carthage: (1) *conquest of Spain and the Hellenistic East*

tion of Philip's plans, Rome sent an army into the East. The result was the conquest of Greece and Asia Minor and the establishment of a protectorate over Egypt. Thus before the end of the second century B.C. virtually the entire Mediterranean area had been brought under Roman control. The conquest of the Hellenistic East led to the introduction of Greek ideas and customs into Rome. Despite formidable resistance, these novelties exerted considerable influence in changing some aspects of social and cultural life.

(2) a social and economic revolution

Still another effect of the Punic Wars was a great social and economic revolution that swept over Rome in the third and second centuries B.C. The changes wrought by this revolution may be enumerated as follows: (1) a marked increase in slavery due to the capture and sale of prisoners of war; (2) the decline of the small farmer as a result of the establishment of the plantation system in conquered areas and the influx of cheap grain from the provinces; (3) the growth of a disgruntled urban element composed of impoverished farmers and workers displaced by slave labor; (4) the appearance of a middle class comprising merchants, moneylenders, and men who held government contracts to operate mines, build roads, or collect taxes; and (5) an increase in luxury and vulgar display, particularly among the newly rich who fattened themselves on the profits of war.

Cato's attempt to prevent the transformation of Roman society

As a consequence of this social and economic revolution, Rome was changed from a republic of yeoman farmers into a complex society with new habits of luxury and indulgence. Though property had never been evenly distributed, the gulf which separated rich and poor now yawned more widely than before. The old-fashioned ideals of discipline and devotion to the service of the state were weakened, and people began to live more for pleasure. A few members of the senatorial aristocracy exerted efforts to check these tendencies and to restore the simple virtues of the past. The leader of this movement was the dour Cato the Elder, who inveighed against the new rich for their soft living and strove to set an example to his countrymen by performing hard labor on his farm and dwelling in a house with a dirt floor and no plaster on the walls. In addition he was a prude who showed contempt for women and boasted that his wife never came into his arms except during great thunder. Cato also strove, often cantankerously, to prevent the influx of Greek intellectual influences. But his efforts on all fronts had no lasting effect because the clock could not be turned back.

4. THE SOCIAL STRUGGLES OF THE LATE REPUBLIC

The new period of turbulence

The period from the end of the Punic Wars in 146 B.C. to about 30 B.C. was one of the most turbulent in the history of Rome. It was between these years that the nation reaped the full harvest of the seeds of violence sown during the wars of conquest. Bitter class conflicts, assassinations, desperate struggles between rival dictators, wars, and insurrections were the all too common occurrences of this time. Even the slaves contributed to the general disorder: first, in 104 B.C. when they ravaged Sicily; and again in 73 B.C. when 70,000 of them under the leadership of a slave named Spartacus held the consuls at bay for more than a year. Spartacus was finally slain in battle and 6,000 of his followers were captured and left crucified along the length of a long road to provide a warning for others.

The first stage in the conflict between classes of citizens began with the revolt of the Gracchi brothers. The Gracchi were leaders of the liberal, pro-Greek elements in Rome and had the support of the middle classes and a number of influential senators as well. Though of aristocratic lineage themselves, they strove for a program of reforms to alleviate the country's ills. They considered these to be a result of the decline of the free peasantry, and proposed the simple remedy of dividing state lands among the landless. The first of the brothers to take up the cause of reform was Tiberius. Elected tribune in 133 B.C., he proposed a law that restricted the current renters or holders of state lands to a maximum of 640 acres. The excess was to be confiscated by the government and given to the poor in small plots. Conservative aristocrats bitterly opposed this proposal and brought about its veto by Tiberius's colleague in the tribunate, Octavius. Tiberius removed Octavius from office, and when his own term expired attempted to stand for reelection. Both of these moves were unconstitutional and gave the conservative senators an excuse for violence. Armed with clubs, they went on a rampage during the elections and murdered Tiberius and 300 of his followers.

The revolt of the Gracchi: the land program of Tiberius

Nine years later Gaius Gracchus, the younger brother of Tiberius, renewed the struggle for reform. Though Tiberius's land law had finally been enacted by the Senate, Gaius believed that the campaign had to go further. Elected tribune in 123 B.C., and reelected in 122, he procured the enactment of various laws for the benefit of the less privileged. The first provided for stabilizing the price of grain in Rome. For this purpose great public granaries were built along the Tiber. A second law proposed to extend the franchise to Roman allies, giving them the rights of Latin citizens. Still a third gave the middle class the right to make up the juries that tried governors accused of exploiting the provinces. These and similar measures provoked so much anger and contention among the classes that civil war broke out. Gaius was proclaimed an enemy of the state, and the Senate authorized the consuls to take all necessary steps for the defense of the Republic. In the ensuing conflict Gaius committed suicide and about 3,000 of his followers were killed.

Gaius Gracchus and the renewed fight for reform

The Gracchan revolt had a broad significance. It demonstrated, first of all, that the Roman Republic had outgrown its constitution. Over the years the assembly had gained powers almost equal to those of the Senate. Instead of working out a peaceful accommodation to these changes, both sides resorted to violence. By so doing they set a prece-

Significance of the Gracchan revolt

Pompey

Julius Caesar

Pompey and Julius Caesar

See color map facing page 161

dent for the unbridled use of force by any politician ambitious for supreme power and thereby paved the way for the destruction of the Republic. The Romans had shown a remarkable capacity for organizing an empire and for adapting the Greek idea of a city-state to a large territory, but the narrow conservatism of their upper classes was a fatal hindrance to the health of the state. Regarding all reform as evil, they failed to understand the reasons for internal discord and seemed to think that repression was its only remedy.

After the downfall of the Gracchi, two military leaders who had won fame in foreign wars successively made themselves rulers of the state. The first was Marius, who was elevated to the consulship by the masses in 107 B.C. and reelected six times thereafter. Unfortunately, Marius was no statesman and accomplished nothing for his followers beyond demonstrating the ease with which a general with an army at his back could override opposition. Following his death in 86 B.C. the aristocrats took a turn at government by force. Their champion was Sulla, another victorious commander. Appointed dictator in 82 B.C. for an unlimited term, Sulla ruthlessly proceeded to exterminate his opponents and to restore to the Senate its original powers. Even the senatorial veto over acts of the assembly was revived, and the authority of the tribunes was sharply curtailed. After three years of rule Sulla decided to exchange the pomp of power for the pleasures of the senses and retired to a life of luxury and ease on his country estate.

It was not to be expected that the "reforms" of Sulla would stand unchallenged after he had relinquished his office, for the effect of his decrees was to give control to a selfish aristocracy. Several new leaders now emerged to espouse the cause of the people. The most famous of them were Pompey (106–48 B.C.) and Julius Caesar (100–44 B.C.). For a time they pooled their energies and resources in a plot to gain control of the government, but later they became rivals and sought to outdo each other in bids for popular support. Pompey won fame as the conqueror of Syria and Palestine, while Caesar devoted his talents to a series of brilliant forays against the Gauls, adding to the Roman state the territory of modern Belgium, Germany west of the Rhine, and France. In 52 B.C., after a series of mob disorders in Rome, the Senate turned to Pompey and caused his election as sole consul. Caesar, stationed in Gaul, was eventually branded an enemy of the state, and Pompey conspired with the senatorial faction to deprive him of political power. The result was a deadly war between the two men. In 49 B.C. Caesar crossed the Rubicon River into Italy (ever since then an image for a fateful decision) and marched on Rome. Pompey fled to the East in the hope of gathering an army large enough to regain control of Italy. In 48 B.C. the forces of the two rivals met at Pharsalus in Greece. Pompey was defeated and soon afterward was murdered by agents of the ruler of Egypt.

Caesar then intervened in Egyptian politics at the court of Cleopatra (whom he left pregnant). Then he conducted another military campaign in Asia Minor in which victory was so swift that he could report "I came, I saw, I conquered" (*veni, vidi, vici*). After that Caesar returned to Rome. There was now no one who dared to challenge his power. With the aid of his veterans he cowed the Senate into granting his every desire. In 46 B.C. he became dictator for ten years, and two years later for life. In addition, he assumed nearly every other title that could augment his power. He obtained from the Senate full authority to make war and peace and to control the revenues of the state. For all practical purposes he was above the law, and the other agents of the government were merely his servants. Unquestionably he had little respect for the constitution, and rumors spread that he intended to make himself king. At any rate, it was on such a charge that he was assassinated on the Ides of March in 44 B.C. by a group of conspirators, under the leadership of Brutus and Cassius, who hoped to rid Rome of the dictatorship.

Although Caesar used to be revered by historians as a superhuman hero, it is now customary to dismiss him as insignificant. But both extremes of interpretation should be avoided. Certainly he did not "save Rome" and was not the greatest statesman of all time, for he treated the Republic with contempt and made the problem of governing more difficult for those who came after him. Yet some of the measures he took as dictator did have lasting effects. With the aid of a Greek astronomer he revised the calendar so as to make a year last for 365 days (with an extra day added every fourth year). This "Julian" calendar—subject to adjustments made by Pope Gregory XIII in 1582—is still with us. It is thus only proper that the seventh month is named after Julius as "July." By conferring citizenship upon thousands of Spaniards and Gauls, Caesar took an important step toward eliminating the distinction between Italians and provincials. He also helped relieve economic inequities by settling many of his veterans and some of the urban poor on unused lands. Vastly more important than these reforms, however, was Caesar's far-sighted resolve, made before he seized power, to invest his efforts in the West. While Pompey, and before him Alexander, went to the East to gain fame and fortune, Caesar was the first great leader to recognize the potential significance of northwestern Europe. By incorporating Gaul into the Roman world he brought Rome great agricultural wealth and helped bring urban life and culture to what was then the wild West. Western European civilization, later to be anchored in just those regions that Caesar conquered, might not have been the same without him.

Ides of March Coin. This coin was struck by Brutus to commemorate the assassination of Julius Caesar. Brutus is depicted on the obverse; on the reverse is a liberty cap between two daggers and the Latin abbreviation for the Ides of March.

5. ROME BECOMES SOPHISTICATED

The culture that Rome brought to Gaul was itself taken from the Greek East. During the last two centuries of republican history Rome came under the influence of Hellenistic civilization. The result was a flowering of intellectual activity and a further impetus to social change beyond what the Punic Wars had produced. The fact must be noted, however, that several of the components of the Hellenistic pattern of culture were never adopted by the Romans. The science of the Hellenistic Age, for example, was largely ignored, and the same was true of some of its art.

Roman Epicureanism: Lucretius

One of the most notable effects of Hellenistic influence was the adoption of Epicureanism and, above all, Stoicism by numerous Romans of the upper classes. The most renowned of the Roman exponents of Epicureanism was Lucretius (98–55 B.C.), author of a book-length philosophical poem entitled *On the Nature of Things*. In writing this work Lucretius was moved to explain the universe in such a way as to remove all fear of the supernatural, which he regarded as the chief obstacle to peace of mind. Worlds and all things in them, he taught, are the results of fortuitous combinations of atoms. Though he admitted the existence of the gods, he conceived of them as living in eternal peace, neither creating nor governing the universe. Everything is a product of mechanical evolution, including human beings, and their habits, institutions, and beliefs. Since mind is indissolubly linked with matter, death means utter extinction; consequently, no part of the human personality can survive to be rewarded or punished in an afterlife. Lucretius's conception of the good life was simple: what one needs, he asserted, is not enjoyment but "peace and a pure heart." Whether one agrees with Lucretius's philosophy or not, there is no doubt that he was an extraordinarily fine poet. In fact his musical cadences, sustained majesty of expression, and infectious enthusiasm earn him a rank among the greatest poets who ever lived.

The Stoic philosophy of Cicero

Stoicism was introduced into Rome about 140 B.C. and soon came to include among its converts numerous influential leaders of public life. The greatest of these was Cicero (106–43 B.C.), the "father of Roman eloquence." Although Cicero adopted doctrines from a number of philosophers, including both Plato and Aristotle, he derived more of his ideas from the Stoics than from any other source. Cicero's ethical philosophy was based on the Stoic premises that virtue is sufficient for happiness and that tranquility of mind is the highest good. He conceived of the ideal human being as one who has been guided by reason to an indifference toward sorrow and pain. Where Cicero diverged from the Greek Stoics was in his greater approval of the active, political life. To this degree he still spoke for the older Roman tradition of service to the state. Cicero never claimed to be an original philosopher but rather conceived his goal to be that of bringing the best of Greek philosophy to the West. In this he was remarkably successful, for he wrote in a rich and elegant Latin prose style that has never been surpassed. Cicero's prose immediately became a standard for composition and has remained so until the present century. Thus even though not a truly great thinker Cicero was the most influential Latin transmitter of ancient thought to the medieval and modern western European worlds.

Lucretius and Cicero were the two leading exponents of Greek thought but not the only two fine writers of the later Roman Republic. It now became the fashion among the upper classes to learn Greek and to strive to reproduce in Latin some of the more popular forms of Greek literature. Some results of enduring literary merit were the ribald comedies of Plautus (257?–184 B.C.), the passionate love poems of Catullus (84?–54? B.C.), and the crisp military memoirs of Julius Caesar, the opening of which all beginning students of Latin used to know as well as the pledge of allegiance.

The conquest of the Hellenistic world accelerated the process of social change which the Punic Wars had begun. The effects were most clearly evident in the growth of luxury, in a widened cleavage between classes, and in a further increase in slavery. The Italian people, numbering about eight million at the end of the Republic, had come to be divided into four main castes: the aristocracy, the equestrians, the common citizens, and the slaves. The aristocracy included the senatorial class with a total membership of 300 citizens and their families. The majority of them inherited their status, although occasionally a plebeian would gain admission to the Senate through serving a term as consul. Most of the aristocrats gained their living as office-holders and as owners of great landed estates. The equestrian order was made up of government contractors, bankers, and the wealthier merchants. Originally this class had been composed of those citizens with incomes sufficient to enable them to serve in the cavalry at their own ex-

Roman literary achievements

Social conditions in the late Republic

Left: *Atrium of an Upper-class House in Pompeii, Seen from the Interior.* Around the atrium or central court were grouped suites of living rooms. The marble columns and decorated walls still give an idea of the luxury and refinement enjoyed by the privileged minority. Right: *Orpheus Floor Mosaic.* This luxurious adornment to an upper-class Roman dwelling, in what is today Arles in southern France, represents the inspired musician soothing lions and tigers as well as numerous other representatives of the animal kingdom.

pense, but the term equestrian had now come to be applied to all outside of the senatorial class who possessed property in substantial amount. The equestrians were the chief offenders in the indulgence of vulgar tastes and in the exploitation of the poor and the provincials. As bankers they regularly charged exorbitant interest rates whenever they could get them. By far the largest number of the citizens were mere commoners or plebeians. Some of these were independent farmers, a few were industrial workers, but the majority were members of the city mob. When Julius Caesar became dictator, 320,000 citizens were receiving free grain from the state.

The status of the slaves

The Roman slaves were scarcely considered people at all but instruments of production like cattle or horses to be worked for the profit of their masters. Notwithstanding the fact that some of them were cultivated foreigners taken as prisoners of war, they had none of the privileges granted to slaves in Athens. The policy of many of their owners was to get as much work out of them as possible during their prime and then to turn them loose to be fed by the state when they became old and useless. Of course, there were exceptions, especially as a result of the civilizing effects of Stoicism. Cicero, for example, reported himself very fond of his slaves. It is, nevertheless, a sad commentary on Roman civilization that nearly all of the productive labor in the country was done by slaves. They produced practically all of the nation's food supply, for the amount contributed by the few surviving independent farmers was quite insignificant. At least 80 percent of the workers employed in shops were slaves or former slaves. But many of the members of the servile population were engaged in nonproductive activities. A lucrative form of investment for the business classes was ownership of slaves trained as gladiators, who could be rented to the government or to aspiring politicians for the amusement of the people. The growth of luxury also required the employment of thousands of slaves in domestic service. The man of great wealth must have his doorkeepers, his litter-bearers, his couriers (for the government of the Republic had no postal service), his valets, and his tutors for his children. In some great households there were special servants with no other duties than to rub the master down after his bath or to care for his sandals.

Changes in religion

The religious beliefs of the Romans were altered in various ways in the last two centuries of the Republic—again mainly because of the extension of Roman power over most of the Hellenistic states. First of all, the upper classes tended to abandon the traditional religion for the philosophies of Stoicism and, to a lesser degree, Epicureanism. But many of the common people also found worship of the ancient gods no longer satisfying because it was too formal and mechanical and demanded too much in the way of duty and self-sacrifice to meet their needs. Furthermore, Italy had attracted a stream of immigrants from the East, most of whom had a religious background totally different from that of the Romans. The result was the spread of Eastern mystery cults, which satisfied the craving for a more emotional religion and offered the reward of immortality to the wretched and downtrodden of the earth. From Egypt came the cult of Osiris (or Serapis, as the god was now more commonly called), while from Phrygia in Asia Minor was introduced the worship of the Great Mother, with her eunuch priests and wild, symbolic orgies. So strong was the appeal of these cults that the decrees of the Senate against them proved almost impossible to enforce. In the last century B.C. the Persian cult of Mithraism, which came to surpass all the others in popularity, gained a foothold in Italy.

6. THE PRINCIPATE OR EARLY EMPIRE (27 B.C.–180 A.D.)

Shortly before his death in 44 B.C., Julius Caesar had adopted as his sole heir his grandnephew Octavian (63 B.C.–14 A.D.), then a young man of eighteen quietly pursuing his studies in Illyria across the Adriatic Sea. Upon learning of his uncle's death, Octavian hastened to Rome to take control of the government. He soon found that he had to share his ambition with two of Caesar's powerful friends, Mark Antony and Lepidus. The following year the three men formed an alliance for the purpose of crushing the power of the aristocratic group responsible for Caesar's murder. The methods employed were not to the new leaders' credit. Prominent members of the aristocracy were hunted down and slain and their property confiscated. The most noted of the victims was Cicero, brutally slain by Mark Antony's thugs though he had taken no part in the conspiracy against Caesar's life. The real murderers, Brutus and Cassius, escaped and organized an army, but were finally defeated by Octavian and his colleagues near Philippi in 42 B.C.

An alliance to avenge Caesar's death

Thereafter a quarrel developed between the members of the alliance, inspired primarily by Antony's jealousy of Octavian. The subsequent struggle became a contest between East and West. Antony went to the East and made an alliance with Cleopatra that was dedicated to introducing principles of Oriental despotism into Roman rule. Octavian consolidated the forces of the West and came forward as the champion of Greek cultural traditions. As in the earlier contest between Caesar and Pompey the victory again went to the West. In the naval battle of Actium (31 B.C.) Octavian's forces defeated those of Antony and Cleopatra, both of whom soon afterward committed suicide. It was now clear that Rome would not be swallowed up by the East. Actium guaranteed that there would be several more centuries for the consolidation of Greek ideals and urban life, a development important above all for the future of western Europe.

Enchained Crocodile. This bizarre coin from the Roman city of Nîmes in southern France symbolizes Augustus's victory at Actium. The crocodile stands for Egyptian prisoners whom Augustus sent as colonists to Nîmes.

The victory of Octavian ushered in a new period in Roman history, the most glorious and the most prosperous that the nation experienced. Although problems of peace and order were still far from being completely solved, the deadly civil strife was over, and the people now had their first opportunity to show what their talents could achieve. Octavian was determined to preserve the forms if not the substance of constitutional government. He accepted the titles of Augustus and emperor (which then only meant "victorious general") conferred upon him by the Senate and the army. He held the authority of proconsul and tribune permanently; but he refused to make himself dictator or even consul for life, despite the pleas of the populace that he do so. In his view the Senate and the people were the supreme sovereigns, as they had been under the early Republic. The title by which he preferred to have his authority designated was princeps, or first citizen of the state. For this reason the period of his rule and that of his successors is properly called the Principate, or early Empire, to distinguish it from the periods of the Republic (sixth century B.C. to 27 B.C.), the time of upheavals (180 A.D. to 284 A.D.), and the period of the late Empire (284 A.D. to 610 A.D.).

Octavian, or Augustus as he was now more commonly called, ruled over Italy and the provinces for forty-four years (31 B.C.–14 A.D.). At the beginning of the period he governed by military power and by common consent, but in 27 B.C. the Senate bestowed upon him the series of offices and titles described above. His work as a statesman at least equaled in importance that of Julius Caesar. Among the reforms of Augustus were the establishment of a new coinage system, the creation of a centralized system of courts under his own supervision, and the bestowal of a large measure of local self-government upon cities and provinces. He insisted upon experience and intelligence as qualifi-

The Emperor Augustus Receiving the Submission of German Barbarians. A drinking cup of the first century A.D.

cations for appointment to administrative office. By virtue of his proconsular authority he assumed direct control over the provincial governors and punished them severely for graft and extortion. He abolished the old system of farming out the collection of taxes in the provinces, which had led to great abuses, and appointed his own personal representatives as collectors at regular salaries. But he did not stop with political reforms. He enacted laws designed to check the more glaring social and moral evils of the time. By his own example of temperate living he sought to discourage luxurious habits and to set the precedent for a return to the ancient virtues.

After the death of Augustus in 14 A.D. until almost the end of the century Rome had no really capable rulers, with the single exception of Claudius (41–54). Several of Augustus's successors, most infamously Caligula (37–41) and Nero (54–68), were brutal tyrants who squandered the resources of the state and kept the city of Rome in an uproar by their deeds of bloody violence. But starting in 96 A.D., a period of strong and stable government returned with the advent of "five good emperors": Nerva (96–98), Trajan (98–117), Hadrian (117–138), Antoninus Pius (138–161), and Marcus Aurelius (161–180). These five ruled in harmony with the Senate, displayed great gifts as administrators, and, each in their turn, were able to bequeath a well-ordered and united realm to their designated successors.

Trajan

From the time of Augustus until that of Trajan, the Roman Empire continued to expand. Augustus gained more land for Rome than did any other Roman ruler. His generals advanced into central Europe, conquering the territories known today as Switzerland, Austria, and Bulgaria. Only in modern-day central Germany did Roman troops meet defeat, a setback which convinced Augustus to hold the Roman borders at the Rhine and Danube. Subsequently, in 43 A.D., the Emperor Claudius began the conquest of Britain, and at the beginning of the next century Trajan pushed beyond the Danube to add Dacia (now Rumania) to the Roman realms. Trajan also conquered territories in Mesopotamia but thereby incurred the enmity of the Persians, causing his successor Hadrian to embark on a defensive policy. The Roman Empire had now reached its ultimate territorial limits; in the third century these limits would begin to recede.

Augustus

Rome's peaceful sway over a vast empire for about two centuries from the time of Augustus to that of Marcus Aurelius was certainly one of its most impressive accomplishments. As the historian Gibbon said, "the Empire of Rome comprehended the fairest part of the earth and the most civilized portion of mankind." The celebrated *Pax Romana,* or Roman peace, was unprecedented. The Mediterranean was now under the control of one power (as it has never been before or since) and experienced the passage of centuries without a single naval battle. On land one rule held without contention from the borders of Scotland to those of Persia. A contemporary orator justly boasted that "the whole civilized world lays down the arms which were its ancient

The Pax Romana

load, as if on holiday . . . all places are full of gymnasia, fountains, monumental approaches, temples, workshops, schools; one can say that the civilized world, which had been sick from the beginning . . . , has been brought by the right knowledge to a state of health." But much of this health, as we will see, proved illusory.

7. CULTURE AND LIFE IN THE PERIOD OF THE PRINCIPATE

Cultural progress under the Principate

From the standpoint of variety of intellectual and artistic interests the period of the Principate outshone all other ages in the history of Rome. From 27 B.C. to about 200 A.D. Roman philosophy attained its most characteristic form. The same period also witnessed the production of outstanding literary works, the growth of a distinctive architecture and art, and the greatest triumphs of Roman engineering.

Roman Stoicism

The form of philosophy that appealed most strongly to the Romans was Stoicism. The reasons for Stoicism's popularity are easy to discover. With its emphasis upon duty, self-discipline, and subjection to the natural order of things, it accorded well with the ancient virtues of the Romans and with their habits of conservatism. Moreover, its insistence upon civic obligations and its doctrine of cosmopolitanism appealed to the Roman political-mindedness and pride in world empire. It is necessary to observe, however, that the Stoicism developed in the days of the Principate was somewhat different from that of Zeno and his school. The old physical theories borrowed from Heraclitus were now discarded and replaced by a broader interest in politics and ethics. Roman Stoicism also tended to assume a more distinctly religious tone than that which had characterized the original philosophy.

See color map facing page 193

Three eminent apostles of Stoicism lived and taught in Rome in the

Marcus Aurelius. The mounted figure of the emperor-philosopher, now standing on the Piazza del Campidoglio in Rome, is the only full-sized equestrian statue surviving from the ancient world. The Christians destroyed other such statues because they seemed to stand for ruler worship, but they saved this one on the mistaken assumption that it represented Constantine, the first Christian Roman emperor.

two centuries that followed the rule of Augustus: Seneca (4 B.C.–65 A.D.), millionaire adviser for a time to Nero; Epictetus, the slave (60?–120 A.D.); and the Emperor Marcus Aurelius (121–180 A.D.). All of them agreed that inner serenity is the ultimate goal to be sought, that true happiness can be found only in surrender to the benevolent order of the universe. They preached the ideal of virtue for virtue's sake, deplored the sinfulness of human nature, and urged obedience to conscience as the voice of duty. Seneca and Epictetus adulterated their philosophy with such deep mystical yearnings as to make it almost a religion. They worshiped the cosmos as divine, governed by an all-powerful Providence who ordains all that happens for ultimate good. The last of the Roman Stoics, Marcus Aurelius, was more fatalistic and less hopeful. Although he did not reject the conception of an ordered and rational universe, he shared neither the faith nor the dogmatism of the earlier Stoics. He was confident of no blessed immortality to balance the sufferings of one's earthly career and was inclined to think of humans as creatures buffeted by evil fortune for which no distant perfection of the whole could fully atone. He urged, nevertheless, that people should continue to live nobly, that they should neither abandon themselves to gross indulgence nor break down in angry protest, but that they should derive what contentment they could from dignified resignation to suffering and tranquil submission to death.

Seneca, Epictetus, and Marcus Aurelius

The literary achievements of the Romans bore a definite relation to their philosophy. This was especially true of the works of the most distinguished writers of the Augustan Age. Horace (65–8 B.C.), for example, in his famous *Odes* drew copiously from the teachings of both Epicureans and Stoics. He confined his attention, however, to their doctrines of a way of life, for like most of the Romans he had little curiosity about the workings of the universe. He developed a philosophy which combined the Epicurean justification of pleasure with the Stoic bravery in the face of trouble. While he never reduced pleasure to the mere absence of pain, he was sophisticated enough to know that the highest enjoyment is possible only through the exercise of rational control.

Roman literature: Horace

Virgil (70–19 B.C.) likewise reflects a measure of the philosophical temper of his age. Though his *Eclogues* convey something of the Epicurean ideal of quiet pleasure, Virgil was much more of a Stoic. His utopian vision of an age of peace and abundance, his brooding sense of the tragedy of human fate, and his idealization of a life in harmony with nature indicate an intellectual heritage similar to that of Seneca and Epictetus. Virgil's most noted work, the *Aeneid,* like several of the *Odes* of Horace glorified Roman imperialism. The *Aeneid* in fact was an epic of empire recounting the toils and triumphs of the founding of the state, its glorious traditions, and its magnificent destiny. Other major writers of the Augustan Age were Ovid (43 B.C.?–17 A.D.) and Livy (59 B.C.–17 A.D.). The former was the chief represen-

Virgil, Ovid, and Livy

tative of the cynical and individualist tendencies of his day. His brilliant and witty writings often reflected the dissolute tastes of the time. The chief claim of Livy to fame rests upon his skill as a prose stylist. As a historian he was woefully deficient. His main work, a history of Rome, is replete with dramatic and picturesque narrative, designed to appeal to the patriotic emotions rather than to present an accurate record of events.

Petronius, Apuleius, Martial, Juvenal, and Tacitus

The literature of the period which followed the death of Augustus also exemplified conflicting social and intellectual tendencies. The tales of Petronius and Apuleius and the epigrams of Martial describe the more exotic and sometimes sordid aspects of Roman life. The aim of the authors is not to instruct or uplift but chiefly to tell an entertaining story or turn a witty phrase. An entirely different viewpoint is presented in the works of the other most important writers of this age: Juvenal, the satirist (60?–140 A.D.), and Tacitus, the historian (55?–117? A.D.). Juvenal wrote under the influence of the Stoics but with narrow vision. Convinced that the troubles of the nation were due to moral degeneracy, he censured the vices of his countrymen with the fury of an evangelist. A somewhat similar attitude characterized the writing of his younger contemporary, Tacitus. The best-known of Roman historians, Tacitus described the events of his age not with a view to dispassionate analysis but largely for the purpose of moral indictment. His description of the customs of the ancient Germans in his *Germania* served to heighten the contrast between the manly virtues of an unspoiled race and the effeminate vices of the decadent Romans. Whatever his failings as a historian, he was a master of ironic wit and brilliant aphorism. Referring to the boasted *Pax Romana*, he makes a barbarian chieftain say: "They create a wilderness and call it peace."

Achievements in art

Roman art first assumed its distinctive character during the period of the Principate. Before this time what passed for an art of Rome was really an importation from the Hellenistic East. Conquering armies brought back to Italy wagonloads of statues, reliefs, and marble columns as part of the plunder from Greece and Asia Minor. These became the property of wealthy businessmen and were used to embellish their sumptuous mansions. As the demand increased, hundreds of copies were made, with the result that Rome came to have by the end of the Republic a profusion of objects of art which had no more cultural significance than the Picassos in the home of some modern stockbroker. The aura of national glory which surrounded the early Principate stimulated the growth of an art that was more indigenous.

See color plates following page 192

Augustus himself boasted that he found Rome a city of brick and left it a city of marble. Nevertheless, much of the old Hellenistic influence remained until the talent of the Romans themselves was exhausted.

The arts most truly expressive of the Roman character were architecture and sculpture. Architecture was monumental, designed to symbolize power and grandeur. It contained as its leading elements

The Pantheon in Rome. Built by the Emperor Hadrian it boasted the largest dome without interior supports of the ancient world. The dome forms a perfect sphere, exactly as high as it is wide.

the round arch, the vault, and the dome, although at times the Corinthian column was employed, especially in the construction of temples. The materials most commonly used were brick, squared stone blocks, and concrete, the last a Roman invention. As a further adornment of public buildings, sculptured entablatures and facades, built up of tiers of colonnades or arcades, were frequently added. Roman architecture was devoted primarily to utilitarian purposes. The foremost examples were government buildings, amphitheaters, baths, race courses, and private houses. Nearly all were of massive proportions and solid construction. Among the largest and most noted were the Pantheon, with its dome having a diameter of 142 feet, and the Colosseum, which could accommodate 65,000 spectators at the gladiatorial combats. Roman sculpture included as its main forms triumphal arches and columns, narrative reliefs, altars, and portrait busts and statues. Its distinguishing characteristics were individuality and naturalism. Sometimes Roman statues and busts served only to express the vanity of the aris-

The Baths of Caracalla, Rome. The gigantic scale is typical of late empire buildings. Elaborate and luxurious public baths like these were often presented to the public by the emperor or rich citizens. The floor plan above indicates the separate chambers for hot tub baths.

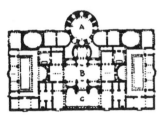

Floor Plan of the Baths of Caracalla

Pliny

tocracy, but the best Roman sculptured portraiture succeeded in conveying qualities of simple human dignity similar to those espoused in the philosophy of the Stoics.

Closely related to their achievements in architecture were Roman triumphs in engineering and public services. The imperial Romans built marvelous roads and bridges, many of which still survive. In the time of Trajan eleven aqueducts brought water into Rome from the nearby hills and provided the city with 300 million gallons daily for drinking and bathing as well as for flushing a well-designed sewage system. Water was cleverly funneled into the homes of the rich for their private gardens, fountains, and pools. Romans also established the first hospitals in the Western world and the first system of state medicine for the benefit of the poor.

For all their achievements in engineering, the Romans accomplished little in science. They excelled, as has been jokingly but not inaccurately said, in drains, not brains. Scarcely an original discovery of fundamental importance was made by anyone of Latin nationality. This fact seems strange when we consider that the Romans had the advantage of Hellenistic science as a foundation upon which to build. But they neglected their opportunity almost completely because they had no vigorous curiosity about the natural world in which they lived. Roman writers on scientific subjects were hopelessly devoid of critical intelligence. The most renowned and typical of them was Pliny the Elder (23–79 A.D.), who completed about 77 A.D. a voluminous encyclopedia of "science" which he called *Natural History*. The subjects discussed varied from cosmology to economics. Despite the wealth of material it contains, Pliny's work is of limited value, for he was totally unable to distinguish between fact and fable.

The only real scientific advance made during the period of the Principate was the work of Hellenistic scientists who lived in Italy or in the provinces. One of these was the astronomer Ptolemy, who flourished in Alexandria around the middle of the second century (see above, p. 159). Another was the physician Galen, active in Rome at various times during the latter half of the second century. While Galen's fame rests primarily on his medical encyclopedia, systematizing the learning of others, he deserves more credit for his own experiments which brought him close to a discovery of the circulation of the blood. He not only taught but proved that the arteries carry blood, and that severance of even a small one is sufficient to drain away all of the blood of the body in little more than half an hour.

Roman society exhibited the same general tendencies under the Principate as in the last days of the Republic. One of the least attractive of its traits was the low status it accorded to women. The historian M. I. Finley has remarked that the two most famous women in Roman history were Cleopatra, who was not even a Roman, and the fictional Lucretia, who earned her fame by being raped and killing herself. Seldom have women been so confined to domesticity and obscurity. Roman women did not even really have their own names but were given family names with feminine endings—for example, Julia from Julius, Claudia from Claudius, and Livia from Livius. When there were two daughters in a family they would be distinguished only as "Julia the elder" and "Julia the younger," and when several as "Julia the first," "second," and "third." Women were expected to be subservient to their fathers and husbands, were valued to the degree they produced progeny, and were expected to stay at home. A typical tomb epitaph might say: "She loved her husband . . . she bore two sons . . . she was pleasant to talk with . . . she kept the house and

Galen

Roman women

Roman Aqueduct at Segovia, Spain. Aqueducts conveyed water from mountains to the larger cities.

Gladiatorial combat

worked in wool. That is all." During the Principate Roman women from imperial families not surprisingly tried to escape these limitations by taking a backstage and often literally murderous role in politics. Less highly placed women sought outlets in the excitement of gladiatorial shows—making gladiators the equivalent of modern rock-and-roll stars—or in the ceremonies of religious cults.

Along with the confinement of women, the most serious indictment which can be brought against the age was the further growth of the passion for cruelty. Whereas the Greeks entertained themselves with theater, the Romans more and more preferred "circuses," which were really exhibitions of human slaughter. In the period of the Principate the great games and spectacles became bloodier than ever. The Romans could no longer obtain a sufficient thrill from mere exhibitions of athletic prowess: pugilists were now required to have their hands wrapped with thongs of leather loaded with iron or lead. The most popular amusement of all was watching the gladiatorial combats in the Colosseum or in other amphitheaters capable of accommodating thousands of spectators. Fights between gladiators were nothing new, but they were now presented on a much more elaborate scale. Not only the common people attended them, but wealthy aristocrats also, and frequently the head of the government himself. The

The Colosseum. Built by the Roman emperors between 75 and 80 A.D. as a place of entertainment, it was the scene of gladiatorial combats. The most common form of Greek secular architecture was the theater (see p. 134), but the most common Roman form was the amphitheater.

Unidentified Man, I cent. B.C. The Romans excelled in portraits of sharp individuality.

Augustus, Reigned 31 B.C.–A.D. 14. This portrait suggests the contradictory nature of the genius who gave Rome peace after years of strife.

Constantine, Reigned A.D. 306–337. The head is from a statue sixteen feet in height.

Mummy Portrait, II cent. A.D. A Roman woman buried in Egypt.

Mosaic, I cent. A.D. A floor design composed of small pieces of colored marble fitted together to form a picture.

Wall Painting of a Satyr Mask, I cent. B.C. The belief in satyrs, thought to inhabit forests and pastures, was taken over from the Greeks.

Architectural Wall Painting from a Pompeiian Villa, I cent. B.C. Such paintings suggest the Greek origin of Roman forms of architecture.

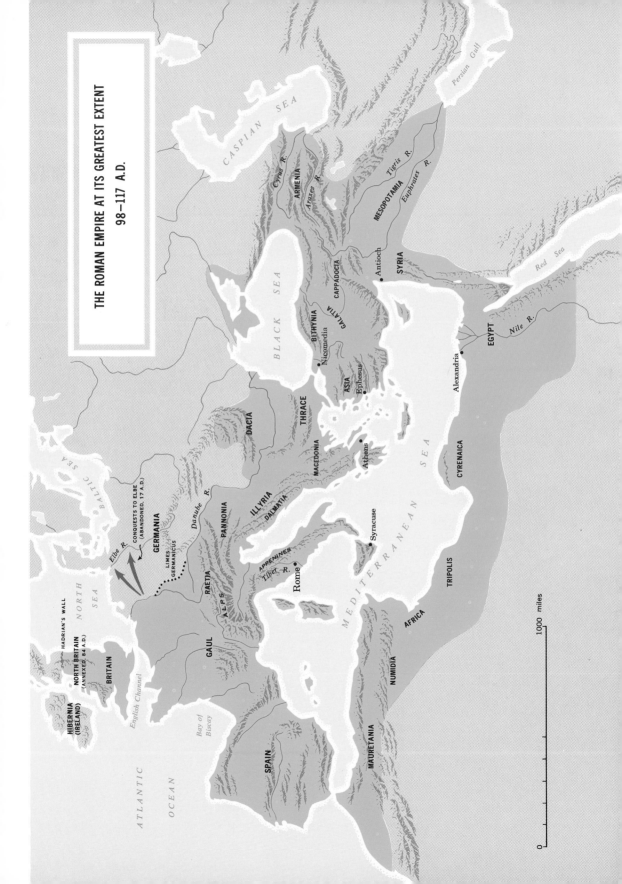

THE ROMAN EMPIRE AT ITS GREATEST EXTENT
98–117 A.D.

Persian Gulf

CASPIAN SEA

Cyrus R.

ARMENIA

Araxes R.

Tigris R.

MESOPOTAMIA

Euphrates R.

CAPPADOCIA

GALATIA

Antioch

SYRIA

Red Sea

BITHYNIA

Nicomedia

ASIA

Ephesus

BLACK SEA

Nile R.

EGYPT

Alexandria

THRACE

Athens

MACEDONIA

DACIA

CYRENAICA

MEDITERRANEAN SEA

Danube R.

PANNONIA

ILLYRIA

DALMATIA

Elbe R.

CONQUESTS TO ELBE
(ABANDONED, 17 A.D.)

GERMANIA

LIMES
GERMANICUS

RAETIA

ALPS

APPENINES

Syracuse

Tiber R.

Rome

TRIPOLIS

HADRIAN'S WALL

NORTH SEA

BALTIC SEA

AFRICA

GAUL

English Channel

NUMIDIA

NORTH BRITAIN
(ANNEXED 84 A.D.)

BRITAIN

HIBERNIA
(IRELAND)

Bay of
Biscay

SPAIN

MAURETANIA

ATLANTIC

OCEAN

1000 miles

0

The Maison Carrée at Nîmes, France. The most perfect example of a Roman temple extant. Reflecting possible Etruscan influence, it was built on a high base or podium with great steps leading to the entrance. It dates from the beginning of the Christian era.

gladiators fought to the accompaniment of savage cries and curses from the audience. When one went down with a disabling wound, the crowd was asked to decide whether his life should be spared or whether the weapon of his opponent should be plunged into his heart. One contest after another, often featuring the sacrifice of men to wild animals, was staged in the course of a single exhibition. Should the arena become too sodden with blood, it was covered over with a fresh layer of sand, and the revolting performance went on. Most of the gladiators were condemned criminals or slaves, but some were volunteers even from the respectable classes. Commodus, the worthless son of Marcus Aurelius, entered the arena several times for the sake of the plaudits of the mob: this was his idea of a Roman holiday.

Notwithstanding its low moral tone, the age of the Principate was characterized by an even deeper interest in salvationist religions than that which had prevailed under the Republic. Mithraism now gained adherents by the thousands, absorbing many of the followers of the cults of the Great Mother and of Serapis. About 40 A.D. the first Christians appeared in Rome. The new sect grew steadily and eventually succeeded in displacing Mithraism as the most popular of the salvationist faiths. More will be said about its nature and success in the next chapter.

The spread of Mithraism and Christianity

The establishment of stable government by Augustus ushered in a

Portrait Bust of a Roman Lady.
The ostentatiousness of upper-
class culture during the period
of the Principate is well displayed by this sculpture, done
around 90 A.D.

period of prosperity for Italy which lasted for more than two centuries. Trade was now extended to all parts of the known world, even
to Arabia, India, and China. Manufacturing increased somewhat, especially in the production of pottery, textiles, and articles of metal and
glass. In spite of all this, the economic order was far from healthy.
Prosperity was not evenly distributed but was confined primarily to
the upper classes. Since the stigma attached to manual labor persisted
as strongly as ever, production was bound to decline as the supply of
slaves diminished. Perhaps worse was the fact that Italy had a decidedly unfavorable balance of trade. The meager industrial development was by no means sufficient to provide enough articles of export
to meet the demand for luxuries imported from the provinces and
from the outside world. As a consequence, Italy was gradually drained
of its supply of precious metals. By the third century the Western
Roman economy began to collapse.

8. ROMAN LAW

There is general agreement that one of the most important legacies
which the Romans left to succeeding cultures was their system of law.
This resulted from a gradual evolution which began roughly with the
publication of the Twelve Tables about 450 B.C. In the later centuries
of the Republic the law of the Twelve Tables was modified and practically superseded by the growth of new precedents and principles.
These emanated from different sources: from changes in custom, from
the teachings of the Stoics, from the decisions of judges, but especially
from the edicts of the *praetors*. The Roman praetors were magistrates
who had authority to define and interpret the law in a particular suit
and issue instructions to the jury for the decision of the case. The jury
merely decided questions of fact; all issues of law were settled by the
praetor, and generally his interpretations became precedents for the
decision of similar cases in the future.

It was under the Principate, however, that the Roman law attained
its highest stage of development. This later progress was the result in
part of the extension of the law over a wider field of jurisdiction, over
the lives and properties of aliens in strange environments as well as
over the citizens of Italy. But the major reason was the fact that
Augustus and his successors gave to certain eminent jurists the right to
deliver opinions on the legal issues of cases under trial in the courts.
The most prominent of the men thus designated from time to time
were Gaius, Ulpian, Papinian, and Paulus. Although most of them
held high judicial office, they had gained their reputations primarily as
lawyers and writers on legal subjects. The responses of these jurists
came to embody a science and philosophy of law and were accepted as
the basis of Roman jurisprudence.

The Roman law as it was developed under the influence of the jurists comprised three great branches or divisions: the civil law, the law of peoples, and the natural law. The civil law was the law of Rome and its citizens. As such it existed in both written and unwritten forms. It included the statutes of the Senate, the decrees of the princeps, the edicts of the praetors, and also certain ancient customs operating with the force of law. The law of peoples was the law held to be common to all people regardless of nationality. This law authorized the institutions of slavery and private ownership of property and defined the principles of purchase and sale, partnership, and contract. It was not superior to the civil law but supplemented it as especially applicable to the alien inhabitants of the empire.

The most interesting and in many ways the most important branch of the Roman law was the natural law, a product not of judicial practice, but of philosophy. The Stoics had developed the idea of a rational order of nature which is the embodiment of justice and right. They had affirmed that all men are by nature equal, and that they are entitled to certain basic rights which governments have no authority to transgress. The father of the law of nature as a legal principle, however, was not one of the Hellenistic Stoics, but Cicero. "True law," he declared, "is right reason consonant with nature, diffused among all men, constant, eternal. To make enactments infringing this law, religion forbids, neither may it be repealed even in part, nor have we power through Senate or people to free ourselves from it." This law is prior to the state itself, and any ruler who defies it automatically becomes a tyrant. Most of the great jurists subscribed to conceptions of the law of nature very similar to those of the philosophers. Although the jurists did not regard this law as an automatic limitation upon the civil law, they thought of it nevertheless as a great ideal to which the statutes and decrees of men ought to conform. This development of the concept of abstract justice as a legal principle was one of the noblest achievements of the Roman civilization.

The three divisions of
Roman law

The natural law

9. THE CRISIS OF THE THIRD CENTURY (180–284 A.D.)

With the death of Marcus Aurelius in 180 A.D. the period of beneficent imperial rule came to an end. One reason for the success of the "five good emperors" was that the first four designated particularly promising young men, rather than sons or close relatives, for the succession. But Marcus Aurelius broke this pattern with results that were to prove fateful. Although he was one of the most philosophic and thoughtful rulers who ever reigned, he was not wise enough to recognize that his son Commodus was a vicious incompetent. Made emperor by his father's wishes, Commodus indulged his taste for perversities, showed

Commodus. The self-deluded ruler encouraged artists to portray him as the equal of the superhuman Hercules.

open contempt for the Senate, and ruled so brutally that a palace clique finally had him murdered by strangling in 192. Matters thereafter became worse. With the lack of an obvious successor to Commodus, the armies of the provinces raised their own candidates and civil war ensued. Although a provincial general, Septimius Severus (193–211), emerged victorious, it now became clear that provincial armies could interfere in imperial politics at will. Severus and some of his successors aggravated the problem by eliminating even the theoretical rights of the Senate and ruling frankly as military dictators. Once the role of brute force was openly revealed any aspiring general could try his luck at seizing power. Hence civil war became endemic. From 235 to 284 there were no less than twenty-six "barracks emperors," of whom only one managed to escape a violent death.

Consequences of civil war

The half-century between 235 and 284 was certainly the worst for Rome since its rise to world power. In addition to political chaos, a number of other factors combined to bring the empire to the brink of ruin. One was that civil war had disastrous economic effects. Not only did constant warfare interfere with agriculture and trade, but the rivalry of aspirants to rule led them to drain the wealth of their territories in order to gain favor with their armies. Following the maxim of "enriching the soldiers and scorning the rest," they could only raise funds by debasing the coinage and by nearly confiscatory taxation of civilians. Landlords, small tenants, and manufacturers thus had little motive to produce at a time when production was most necessary. In human terms the poorest, as is usual in times of economic contraction, suffered the most. Often they were driven to the most abject destitution. In the wake of war and hunger, disease then became rampant.

Arch of Septimius Severus. This monument to the feats of Septimius Severus was constructed about 200 A.D.

Already in the reign of Marcus Aurelius a terrible plague had swept through the empire, decimating the army and the population at large. In the middle of the third century pestilence returned and struck at the population with its fearful scythe for fifteen years.

The resulting strain on human resources came at a time when Rome could least afford it, for still another threat to the empire in the middle of the third century was the advance of Rome's external enemies. With Roman ranks thinned by disease and Roman armies fighting each other, Germans in the West and Persians in the East broke through the old Roman defense lines. In 251 the Goths defeated and slew the Emperor Decius, crossed the Danube, and marauded at will in the Balkans. A more humiliating disaster came in 260 when the Emperor Valerian was captured in battle by the Persians and made to kneel as a footstool for their ruler. When he died his body was stuffed and hung on exhibition. Clearly the days of Caesar and Augustus were very far off.

Understandably enough the culture of the third century was marked by pervasive anxiety. One can even see expressions of worry in the surviving statuary, as in the bust of the Emperor Philip (244–249) who appears almost to realize that he would soon be killed in battle. Suiting the spirit of the age, the Neoplatonic philosophy of otherworldlyism came to the fore. Neoplatonism (meaning "New Platonism") drew the spiritualist tendency of Plato's thought to extremes. The first of its basic teachings was emanationism: everything that exists proceeds from God in a continuing stream of emanations. The initial stage in the process is the emanation of the world-soul. From this come the divine Ideas or spiritual patterns, and then the souls of particular things. The final emanation is matter. But matter has no form or quality of its own; it is simply the privation of spirit, the residue which is left after the spiritual rays from God have burned themselves out. It follows that matter is to be despised as the symbol of evil and darkness. The second major doctrine was mysticism. The human soul was originally a part of God, but it has become separated from its divine source through its union with matter. The highest goal of life should be mystic reunion with the divine, which can be accomplished through contemplation and through emancipation of the soul from bondage to matter. Human beings should be ashamed of the fact that they possess a physical body and should seek to subjugate it in every way possible. Asceticism was therefore the third main teaching of this philosophy.

The real founder of Neoplatonism was Plotinus, who was born in Egypt about 204 A.D. In the later years of his life he taught in Rome and won many followers among the upper classes before he died in 270. His principal successors diluted the philosophy with more and more bizarre superstitions. In spite of its antirational viewpoint and its utter indifference to the state, Neoplatonism became so popular in Rome in the third and fourth centuries A.D. that it almost completely

The Emperor Decius. The extreme naturalism and furrowed brow is typical of the portraits of this period.

The Emperor Philip the Arab. An artistic legacy of the Roman "age of anxiety."

Plotinus

supplanted Stoicism. No fact could have expressed more eloquently the turn of Rome away from the realities of the here and now.

10. CAUSES FOR ROME'S DECLINE

As Rome was not built in a day, so it was not lost in one. As we will see in the next chapter, strong rule returned in 284. Thereafter the Roman Empire endured in the West for two hundred years more and in the East for a millennium. But the restored Roman state differed greatly from the old one—so much so that it is proper to end the story of characteristically Roman civilization here and review the reasons for Rome's decline.

More has been written on the fall of Rome than on the death of any other civilization. The theories offered to account for the decline have been many and varied. A popular recent one is that Rome fell from the effects of lead poisoning, but this cannot be accepted for many reasons, one of which is that most Roman pipes were not made of lead but of terracotta. Moralists have found the explanation for Rome's fall in the descriptions of lechery and gluttony presented in the writings of such authors as Juvenal and Petronius. Such an approach, however, overlooks the facts that much of this evidence is patently overdrawn, and that nearly all of it comes from the period of the early Principate: in the later centuries, when the empire was more obviously collapsing, morality became more austere through the influence of ascetic religions. One of the simplest explanations is that Rome fell only because of the severity of German attacks. But barbarians had always stood ready to attack Rome throughout its long history: German pressures indeed mounted at certain times but German invasions would never have succeeded had they not come at moments when Rome was already weakened internally.

It is best then, to concentrate on Rome's most serious internal problems. Some of these were political. The most obvious political failing of the Roman constitution under the Principate was the lack of a clear law of succession. Especially when a ruler died suddenly there was no certainty about who was to follow him. In modern America the deaths of a Lincoln or Kennedy might shock the nation, but people at least knew what would happen next; in imperial Rome no one knew and civil war was generally the result. From 235 to 284 such warfare fed upon itself. Civil war was also nurtured by the lack of constitutional means for reform. If regimes became unpopular, as most did after 180, the only means to alter them was to overthrow them. But the resort to violence always bred more violence. In addition to those problems, imperial Rome's greatest political weakness may ultimately have been that it did not involve enough people in the work of government. The vast majority of the empire's inhabitants were subjects who did not participate in the government in any way. Hence they

Slaves Towing a Barge. This relief shows very graphically how heavily Roman civilizations relied on slave labor.

looked on the empire at best with indifference and often with hostility, especially when tax-collectors appeared. Loyalty to Rome was needed to keep the empire going, but when the tests came such loyalty was lacking.

Even without political problems the Roman Empire would probably have been fated to extinction for economic reasons. Rome's worst economic problems derived from its slave system and from manpower shortages. Roman civilization was based on cities, and Roman cities existed largely by virtue of an agricultural surplus produced by slaves. Slaves were worked so hard that they did not normally reproduce to fill their own ranks. Until the time of Trajan Roman victories in war and fresh conquests provided fresh supplies of slaves to keep the system going, but thereafter the economy began to run out of human fuel. Landlords could no longer be so profligate of human life, barracks slavery came to an end, and the countryside produced less of a surplus to feed the towns. The fact that no technological advance took up the slack may also be attributed to slavery. Later in Western history agricultural surpluses were produced by technological revolutions, but Roman landlords were indifferent to technology because interest in it was thought to be demeaning. As long as slaves were present to do the work there was no interest in labor-saving devices, and attention to any sort of machinery was deemed a sign of slavishness. Landlords proved their nobility by their interest in "higher things," but while they were contemplating these heights their agricultural surpluses gradually became depleted.

Economic causes

Manpower shortages greatly aggravated Rome's economic problems. With the end of foreign conquests and the decline of slavery there was a pressing need for people to stay on the farm, but because of constant barbarian pressures there was also a steady need for men to serve in the army. The plagues of the second and third centuries

Inadequate manpower

sharply reduced the population just at the worst time. It has been estimated that between the reign of Marcus Aurelius and the restoration of strong rule in 284 the population of the Roman Empire was reduced by one third. (Demoralization seems also to have lowered the birthrate.) The result was that there were neither sufficient forces to work the land nor men to fight Rome's enemies. No wonder Rome began to lose battles as it had seldom lost them before.

Lack of civic ideals

Enormous dedication and exertion on the part of large numbers might just possibly have saved Rome, but few were willing to work hard for the public good. For this cultural explanations may be posited. Most simply stated the Roman Empire of the third century could not draw upon commonly shared civic ideals. By then the old republican and senatorial traditions had been rendered manifestly obsolete. Worse, provincials could hardly be expected to fight or work hard for Roman ideals of any sort, especially when the Roman state no longer stood for beneficent peace but only brought recurrent war and oppressive taxation. Regional differences, the lack of public education, and social stratification were further barriers to the development of any unifying public spirit. As the empire foundered new ideals indeed emerged, but these were religious, otherworldly ones. Ultimately, then, the decline of Rome was accompanied by disinterest, and the Roman world slowly came to an end not so much with a bang as with a whimper.

11. THE ROMAN HERITAGE

Comparison of Rome with the modern world

It is tempting to believe that we today have many similarities to the Romans: first of all, because Rome is nearer to us in time than any of the other civilizations of antiquity; and second, because Rome seems to bear such a close kinship to the modern temper. The resemblances between Roman history and the history of Great Britain or the United States in the nineteenth and twentieth centuries have often been noted. The Roman economic evolution progressed all the way from a simple agrarianism to a complex urban system with problems of unemployment, gross disparities of wealth, and financial crises. The Roman Empire, in common with the British, was founded upon conquest. It must not be forgotten, however, that the heritage of Rome was an ancient heritage and that consequently, the similarities between the Roman and modern civilizations are not so important as they seem.

As noted already, the Romans disdained industrial activities, and they were not interested in science. Neither did they have any idea of the modern national state; the provinces were really colonies, not integral parts of a body politic. The Romans also never developed an adequate system of representative government. Finally, the Roman conception of religion was vastly different from our own. Their system of wor-

The Forum, the Civic Center of Ancient Rome. In addition to public squares, the Forum included triumphal arches, magnificent temples, and government buildings. In the foreground is the Temple of Saturn. Behind it is the Temple of Antoninus and Faustina. The three columns at the extreme right are what is left of the Temple of Castor and Pollux, and in the farthest background is the arch of Titus.

ship, like that of the Greeks, was external and mechanical, not inward or spiritual. What Christians consider the highest ideal of piety—an emotional attitude of love for the divine—the Romans regarded as gross superstition.

Nevertheless, the civilization of Rome exerted a great influence upon later cultures. The form, if not the spirit, of Roman architecture was preserved in the ecclesiastical architecture of the Middle Ages and survives to this day in the design of many of our government buildings. The sculpture of the Augustan Age also lives on in the equestrian statues, the memorial arches and columns, and in the portraits in stone of statesmen and generals that adorn our streets and parks. Although subjected to new interpretations, the law of the great jurists became an important part of the Code of Justinian and was thus handed down to the Middle Ages and modern times. American judges frequently cite maxims originally invented by Gaius or Ulpian. Further, the legal systems of nearly all continental European countries today incorporate much of the Roman law. This law was one of the grandest of the Romans' achievements and reflected their genius for governing a vast and diverse empire. It should not be forgotten either that Roman liter-

The influence of Roman civilization

ary achievements furnished much of the inspiration for the revival of learning that spread over Europe in the twelfth century and reached its zenith in the Renaissance. Perhaps not so well known is the fact that the organization of the Catholic Church, to say nothing of part of its ritual, was adapted from the structure of the Roman state and the complex of the Roman religion. For example, the pope still bears the title of supreme pontiff (*pontifex maximus*), which was used to designate the authority of the emperor as head of the civic religion.

Rome's role as conveyor of Greek civilization

Most important of all Rome's contributions to the future was the transmission of Greek civilization to the European West. The development in Italy of a culture that was highly suffused by Greek ideals from the second century B.C. onward was in itself an important counterweight to the earlier predominance of Greek-oriented civilization in the East. Then, following the path of Julius Caesar, this culture advanced still further West. Before the coming of Rome the culture of northwestern Europe (modern France, the Benelux countries, western and southern Germany, and England) was tribal. Rome brought cities and Greek ideas, above all conceptions of human freedom and individual autonomy that went along with the development of highly differentiated urban life. It is true that ideals of freedom were often ignored in practice—they did not temper Roman dependence on slavery and subjugation of women, or prevent Roman rule in conquered territories from being exploitive and sometimes oppressive. Nonetheless, Roman history is the real beginning of Western history as we now know it. Greek civilization brought to the East by Alexander was not enduring, but the same civilization brought West by the work of such men as Caesar, Cicero, and Augustus was the starting point for many of the subsequent accomplishments of western Europe. As we will see, the development was not continuous and there were many other ingredients to later European success, but the influence of Rome was no less profound.

SELECTED READINGS

• *Items so designated are available in paperback editions.*

POLITICAL HISTORY

• Adcock, F. E., *Roman Political Ideas and Practice,* Ann Arbor, Mich., 1964.
  Bloch, Raymond, *The Origins of Rome,* New York, 1960.
  Cary, M., and H. H. Scullard, *A History of Rome,* 3rd ed., New York, 1975.
    A basic college-level textbook.
• Chambers, M., ed., *The Fall of Rome,* New York, 1970. A collection of
    readings on this perennially fascinating subject.
  Cowell, F. R., *Cicero and the Roman Republic,* New York, 1948.
  Grant, M., *The Etruscans,* New York, 1980.

Gruen, E. S., *The Last Generation of the Roman Republic*, Berkeley, Calif., 1964.

Haywood, R. M., *The Myth of Rome's Fall*, New York, 1962.

Mommsen, Theodor, *The History of Rome*, Chicago, 1957. An abridged reissue of one of the greatest historical works of the nineteenth century. Emphasizes personalities, especially that of Julius Caesar.

Ogilvie, R. M., *Early Rome and the Etruscans*, Atlantic Highlands, N.J., 1976. Now the best specialized review of the earliest period.

• Scullard, H. H., *From the Gracchi to Nero*, New York, 1959. Good survey of events in this central period.

Sinnigen, W., and A. E. R. Boak, *A History of Rome to A.D. 565*, 6th ed., New York, 1977. A good alternative to Cary and Scullard as a basic textbook.

• Starr, C. G., *The Emergence of Rome*, Ithaca, N.Y., 1953. A brief elementary introduction.

• Syme, Ronald, *The Roman Revolution*, New York, 1939. A pathfinding work on the late Republic and early empire that stresses power politics and the role of factions rather than the clash of institutional principles. Also extremely well written.

• Taylor, Lily Ross, *Party Politics in the Age of Caesar*, Berkeley, Calif., 1949. Still the best introduction to society and politics in the late republican period.

Warmington, B. H., *Carthage*, Baltimore, 1965.

CULTURAL AND SOCIAL HISTORY

Africa, T., *Rome of the Caesars*, New York, 1965. An entertaining approach to the history of imperial Rome by means of short biographies.

Arnold, E. V., *Roman Stoicism*, New York, 1911.

• Badian, Ernst, *Roman Imperialism in the Late Republic*, Oxford, 1967. Very sophisticated analysis.

Bailey, Cyril, ed., *The Legacy of Rome*, New York, 1924. An older collection of readings on different aspects of the Roman legacy to later times.

Balston, J. P. V. D., *Life and Leisure in Ancient Rome*, New York, 1969.

• Brunt, P. A., *Social Conflicts in the Roman Republic*, London, 1971.

• Carcopino, Jerome, *Daily Life in Ancient Rome*, New Haven, Conn., 1960.

Dill, Samuel, *Roman Society from Nero to Marcus Aurelius*, New York, 1905.

Duff, J. W., *A Literary History of Rome in the Golden Age*, New York, 1964.

——, *A Literary History of Rome in the Silver Age*, New York, 1960.

Earl, Donald, *The Moral and Political Tradition of Rome*, Ithaca, N.Y., 1967.

Frank, Tenney, *Economic History of Rome*, Baltimore, 1927. Still valuable.

Grant, M., *Roman Literature*, New York, 1954.

Laistner, M. L. W., *The Greater Roman Historians*, Berkeley, Calif., 1947.

McMullen, R., *Enemies of the Roman Order*, Cambridge, Mass., 1966.

• ——, *Roman Social Relations, 50 B.C. to A.D. 284*, New Haven, Conn., 1974.

Rostovtzeff, M. I., *Social and Economic History of the Roman Empire*, 2nd ed., 2 vols., New York, 1957. By one of the greatest historians of the early twentieth century. Important both for its interpretations and the wealth of information it contains.

• Sandbach, F. H., *The Stoics*, London, 1975.

Scullard, H. H., *The Etruscan Cities and Rome,* Ithaca, N.Y., 1967.
- Starr, C. G., *Civilization and the Caesars,* Ithaca, N.Y., 1954. Surveys Roman intellectual developments in the four centuries after Cicero.
Toynbee, A. J., *Hannibal's Legacy,* 2 vols., London, 1965.
Westermann, W. L., *The Slave Systems of Greek and Roman Antiquity,* Philadelphia, 1955. The best overview of this basic subject.
- Wheeler, Mortimer, *The Art of Rome,* New York, 1964.
Yavetz, Z., *Plebs and Princeps,* London, 1969.

SOURCE MATERIALS

Translations of Roman authors are available in the appropriate volumes of the Loeb Classical Library, Harvard University Press.

See also:

- Lewis, Naphtali, and M. Reinhold, *Roman Civilization,* 2 vols., New York, 1955.
MacKendrick, P., *The Roman Mind at Work,* Princeton, N.J., 1958.

Chapter 9

CHRISTIANITY AND THE TRANSFORMATION OF THE ROMAN WORLD

Who will hereafter credit the fact . . . that Rome has to fight within her own borders not for glory but for bare life? . . . The poet Lucan describing the power of the city in a glowing passage says: "If Rome be weak, where shall we look for strength?" We may vary his words and say: "If Rome be lost, where shall we look for help?"

For mortals this life is a race: we run it on earth that we may receive our crown elsewhere. No man can walk secure amid serpents and scorpions.

—St. Jerome, *Letters*

The Roman Empire declined after 180 A.D., but it did not collapse. In 284 the vigorous soldier-emperor Diocletian began a reorganization of the empire which gave it a new lease on life. Thereafter, throughout the fourth century the Roman state continued to surround the Mediterranean. In the fifth century the western half of the empire did fall to invading Germans, but even then Roman institutions were not entirely destroyed, and in the sixth century the eastern half of the empire managed to reconquer a good part of the western Mediterranean shoreline. Only in the seventh century did it become fully evident that the Roman Empire could only hope to survive by turning away from the West and consolidating its strength in the East. When that happened antiquity clearly came to an end.

The protracted decline of the Roman Empire

Historians used to underestimate the longevity of Roman institutions and begin their discussions of medieval history in the third, fourth, or fifth century. Since historical periodization is always approximate and depends largely on which aspects of development a historian wishes to emphasize, this approach cannot be dismissed. Certainly the transition from the ancient to the medieval world was gradual and many "medieval" ways were slowly emerging in the West

The age of late antiquity (284–610)

*Christianity and the
Transformation of the
Roman World*

as early as the third century. But it is now more customary to conceive of ancient history as continuing after 284 and lasting until the Roman Empire lost control over the Mediterranean in the seventh century. The period from 284 to about 610, although transitional (as, of course, all ages are), has certain themes of its own and is perhaps best described as neither Roman nor medieval but as the age of late antiquity.

*Rise of Christianity and
decline of urban life*

The major cultural trend of late-antique history was the spread and triumph of Christianity throughout the Roman world. At first Christianity was just one of several varieties of otherworldlyism which appealed to increasing numbers of persons during the later empire. But in the fourth century it was adopted as the Roman state religion and thereafter became one of the greatest shaping forces in the development of the West. While Christianity was spreading, the Roman Empire was indubitably declining. Central to this decline was a contraction of the urban life on which the empire had been based. As the empire began to experience severe pressures, urban contraction was most pronounced in the European northwest because city civilization there was least deeply rooted and most distant from the empire's major trade and communications lifelines on the Mediterranean. Contraction was also felt in parts of the West that were closer to the Mediterranean because western cities depended far more on declining agricultural production than eastern ones, which relied more on trade in luxury goods and industry. Consequently the entire period saw a steady shift in the weight of civilization and imperial government from West to East. The most visible manifestations of this shift were the German successes of the fifth century. These surely helped open a new chapter in Western political history, but their immediate impact should not be exaggerated. Even with the influx of Germans, Roman institutions continued to decline gradually. Particularly in areas that were on or close to the Mediterranean, Roman city life persisted, albeit with steadily declining vigor, until the Mediterranean was no longer a Roman lake.

1. THE REORGANIZED EMPIRE

The reforms of Diocletian

Before we examine the emergence and triumph of Christianity, it is best to survey the nature of the government and society in which the new religion became a dominant force. The fifty years of chaos that threatened to destroy Rome in the third century were ended by the energetic work of a remarkable soldier named Diocletian, who ruled as emperor from 284 to 305. Conscious of some of the more obvious problems that had undone his predecessors, Diocletian embarked on a number of fundamental political and economic reforms. Recognizing that the dominance of the army in the life of the state had hitherto been too great, he introduced measures to separate military from civilian administrative chains of command. Aware that new pressures, both external and internal, had made it nearly impossible for one man to govern the entire Roman Empire, he divided his realm in half, granting the western part to a trusted colleague, Maximian, who recognized Diocletian as the senior ruler. The two then chose lieutenants, called *caesars,* to govern large subsections of their territories. This system was also meant to provide for an orderly succession, for the caesars were supposed to inherit the major rule of either East or West and then appoint new caesars in their stead. In the economic sphere Diocletian stabilized the badly debased currency, introduced a new system of taxation, and issued legislation designed to keep agricultural workers and town-dwellers at their jobs so that the basic work necessary to support the empire would continue to be done.

Although Diocletian's program of reorganization was remarkably successful in restoring an empire that had been on the verge of expiring, it also transformed the empire by "orientalizing" it in three primary and lasting ways. Most literally, Diocletian began a geographical orientalization of the empire by shifting its administrative weight toward the East. Since he was a "Roman" emperor we might assume that he ruled from Rome, but in fact between 284 and 303 he was never there, ruling instead from Nicomedia, a city in modern-day Turkey. This he did in tacit recognition of the fact that the wealthier and more vital part of the empire was clearly in the East. Second, as befitting one who turned his back on Rome, Diocletian adopted the titles and ceremonies of an Oriental potentate. Probably he did this less because he had Eastern tastes than because he wished to avoid the fate of his predecessors who were insufficiently respected. Most likely he thought that if he were feared and worshiped he would stand a greater chance of dying in bed. Accordingly, Diocletian completely abandoned Augustus's policy of appearing to be a constitutional ruler and came forward as an undisguised autocrat. He took the title not of *princeps,* or first citizen, but of *dominus,* or lord, and he introduced Oriental ceremony into his court. He wore a diadem and a purple gown of silk interwoven with gold. Those who gained an audience had to prostrate themselves before him; a privileged few were allowed to kiss his robe.

The third aspect of orientalization in Diocletian's policy was his growing reliance on an imperial bureaucracy. By separating civilian from military commands and legislating on a wide variety of economic and social matters, Diocletian created the need for many new officials. Not surprisingly, by the end of his reign subjects were complaining that "there were more tax-collectors than taxpayers." The officials did keep the empire going, but the new bureaucracy was prone—as all are—to graft and corruption; worse, the growth of officialdom called for reservoirs of manpower and wealth at a time when the Roman Empire no longer had large supplies of either. Taken together, the various aspects of Diocletian's easternizing made him

Diocletian. His short hair is in the Roman military style.

Diocletian's easternizing policy

The growth of imperial bureaucracy

208

*Christianity and the
Transformation of the
Roman World*

The Emperor Honorius. An example of the impassive portrait sculpture brought in by the age of Diocletian. Compare the lack of individuality of this bust to the portraits of Decius and Philip the Arab, above, p. 197.

The reign of Constantine

seem more like a pharaoh than a Roman ruler: it was almost as if the defeat of Antony and Cleopatra at Actium was now being avenged.

The new coercive regime of Diocletian left no room for the cultivation of individual spontaneity or freedom. The results can be seen most clearly in the architecture and art of the age. Diocletian himself preferred a colossal bombastic style of building that was meant to emphasize his own power. The baths he had constructed in Rome, when he finally arrived there in 303, were the largest yet known, encompassing about thirty acres. When he retired in 305 Diocletian built a palace for himself in what is now Split (Yugoslavia) that was laid out along a rectilinear grid like an army camp. A plan of this palace shows clearly how Diocletian favored regimentation in everything.

Also in the age of Diocletian, Roman portrait statuary, which had hitherto featured striking naturalism and individuality, became impersonal. Human faces became impassive and symmetrical rather than reflecting a free play of emotions. Porphyry, a particularly hard and dark stone that had to be imported from Egypt—itself a sign of easternization—often replaced marble for imperial busts. Porphyry groups of Diocletian, Maximian, and their two caesars show the new hardness and symmetry at their fullest, for the figures were made to look so similar that they are indistinguishable from each other.

In 305 Diocletian decided to abdicate to raise cabbages—an unprecedented achievement for a late-Roman ruler. At the same time he obliged his colleague Maximian to retire as well, and their two caesars moved peacefully up the ladders of succession. Such concord, however, could not last. Soon civil war broke out among Diocletian's successors and continued until Constantine, the son of one of the original caesars, emerged victorious. From 312 until 324 Constantine ruled only in the West, but from the latter year until his death in 337 he did away with the sharing of powers and ruled over a reunited empire. Except for the fact that he favored Christianity, an epoch-making decision to be examined in the next section, Constantine otherwise con-

Diocletian's Palace in Split. An artistic reconstruction.

Left: *Porphyry Sculptures of Diocletian and His Colleagues in Rule.* Every effort is made to make the two senior rulers and their two junior colleagues look identical by means of stylization. Note also the emphasis on military strength. Right: *Colossal Head of Constantine.* In the head of Constantine the eyes are enlarged as if to emphasize the ruler's spiritual vision. The head is approximately ten times larger than life.

tinued to govern along the lines laid down by Diocletian. Bureaucracy proliferated and the state became so vigilant in keeping town-dwellers and agricultural laborers at their posts that society began to harden into a caste system. Although Constantine was a Christian, he never thought for a moment of acting with any Christlike humility: on the contrary, he made court ceremonials more elaborate and generally behaved as if he were a god. In keeping with this he built a new capital in 330 and named it Constantinople, after himself. Although he declared that he moved his government from Rome to Constantinople in order to demonstrate his abandonment of paganism, self-esteem was no doubt a major factor, and the shift was the most visible manifestation of the continued move of Roman civilization to the East. Situated on the border of Europe and Asia, Constantinople had commanding advantages as a center for Eastern-oriented communications, trade, and defense. Surrounded on three sides by water and protected on land by walls, it was to prove nearly impregnable and would remain the center of "Roman" government for as long as the Roman Empire was to endure.

Constantine also made the succession hereditary. By so doing he brought Rome back to the principle of dynastic monarchy that it had thrown off about eight hundred years earlier. But Constantine, who treated the empire as if it were his private property, did not pass on

Two Contemporary Representations of Theodosius. Above is a detail from a silver plate. Theodosius is shown here with an orb in his hand, symbolizing his worldly power, and a halo, symbolizing his supernatural strength. In both the plate and the coin shown below the emperor is depicted in military garb.

united rule to one son. Instead he divided his realm among three of them. Not surprisingly his three sons started fighting each other upon their father's death, a conflict exacerbated by religious differences. The warfare and succeeding dynastic squabbles that continued on and off for most of the fourth century need not detain us here. Suffice it to say that they were not as serious as the civil wars of the third century, and that from time to time one or another contestant was able to reunite the empire for a period of years. The last to do so was Theodosius I (379–395), who butchered thousands of innocent citizens of Thessalonica in retribution for the death of one of his officers, but whose energies in preserving the empire by holding off Germanic barbarians still gave him some claim to his surname "the Great."

The period between Constantine and Theodosius saw the steady development of earlier tendencies. With Constantinople now the leading city of the empire, the center of commerce and administration was located clearly in the East. Regionalism too grew more pronounced: the Latin-speaking West was losing a sense of rapport and contact with the Greek-speaking East, and in both West and East local differences were becoming accentuated. In economic life the hallmark of the age was the growing gap between rich and poor. In the West large landowners were able to consolidate their holdings, and in the East some individuals became prosperous by rising through the bureaucracy and enriching themselves with graft, or by trading in luxury goods. But the taxation system initiated by Diocletian and maintained throughout the fourth century weighed down heavily on the poor, forcing them to carry the burden of supporting the bureaucracy, the army, and the lavish imperial court or courts. The poor, moreover, had no chance to escape their poverty, for legislation demanded that they and their heirs stay at their unrewarding and heavily taxed jobs. Since most people in the fourth century were poor, most people lived in desperate and unrelenting poverty against a backdrop of ostentatious wealth. The Roman Empire may have been restored in the years from 284 to 395, but it was nonetheless a fertile breeding-ground for a new religion of otherworldly salvation.

2. THE EMERGENCE AND TRIUMPH OF CHRISTIANITY

The origins and spread of Christianity

Christian beginnings of course go back several centuries before Constantine to the time of Jesus. Christianity was formed primarily by Jesus and St. Paul and gained converts steadily thereafter. But the new religion only became widespread during the chaos of the third century and only triumphed in the Roman Empire during the demoralization of the fourth. At the time of its humble beginnings nobody could have known that Christianity would be decreed the sole religion of the Roman Empire by the year 380.

Jesus of Nazareth was born in Bethlehem, a small town of Judea, sometime near the beginning of the Christian era (but not exactly in the "year one"—we owe this mistake in our dating system to a sixth-century monk). While Jesus was growing up Judea was under Roman rule. The atmosphere of the country was charged with religious emotionalism and political discontent. Some of the people, notably the Pharisees, concentrated on preserving the Jewish law and looked forward to the coming of a political messiah who would rescue the country from Rome. Most extreme of those who sought hope in politics were the "Zealots," who wished to overthrow the Romans by means of armed force. Some groups, on the other hand, were not interested in politics at all. Typical of these were the Essenes, who hoped for spiritual deliverance through asceticism, repentance, and mystical union with God. The ministry of Jesus was clearly more allied to this pacific orientation.

When Jesus was about thirty years old, he was acclaimed by an ascetic evangelist, John the Baptist, as one "mightier than I, whose shoes I am not worthy to bear." Thenceforth for about three years his career, according to the New Testament accounts, was a continuous course of preaching and teaching and of healing the sick, "casting out devils," restoring sight to the blind, and raising the dead. He not only denounced shame, greed, and licentious living but set the example himself by a life of humility and self-denial. Though the conception he held of himself is somewhat obscure, he apparently believed that he had a mission to save humanity from error and sin. His preaching and other activities eventually aroused the antagonism of some of the chief priests and conservative rabbis. They disliked his caustic references to the legalism of the Pharisees, his contempt for form and ceremony, and his scorn for pomp and luxury. They feared also that his active leadership would cause trouble with the Romans. Accordingly, they brought him into the highest court in Jerusalem, where he was solemnly condemned for blasphemy and for setting himself up as "king of the Jews" and turned over to Pontius Pilate, the Roman governor, for execution of the sentence. After hours of agony he died on the cross between two thieves on the hill of Golgotha outside Jerusalem.

The crucifixion of Jesus marked a great climax in Christian history. At first his death was viewed by his followers as the end of their hopes. Their despair soon vanished, however, for rumors began to spread that the Master was alive and had been seen by some of his faithful disciples. The remainder of his followers were quickly convinced that he had risen from the dead and that he was truly a divine being. With their courage restored, they organized their little band and began preaching and testifying in the name of their martyred leader. Thus one of the world's great religions was launched on a course that would ultimately convert an empire no less mighty than Rome.

Jesus Christ. An artist's conception from a sixth-century mosaic in Ravenna.

Christianity and the
Transformation of the
Roman World

A Carved Tablet, c. 400 A.D., Depicting Christ's Tomb and Ascension into Heaven

St. Paul. From a Ravenna mosaic.

There has never been complete agreement among Christians as to the precise teachings of Jesus of Nazareth. The only dependable records are the four Gospels, but the earliest of these was not written until at least a generation after Jesus's death. According to the beliefs of his orthodox followers, the founder of Christianity revealed himself as the Christ, the divine Son of God, who was sent on this earth to suffer and die for the sins of humanity. They were convinced that after three days in the tomb, he had risen from the dead and ascended into heaven, whence he would come again to judge the world. The Gospels at least make it clear that he included the following among his basic teachings: (1) the fatherhood of God and the brotherhood of humanity; (2) the Golden Rule; (3) forgiveness and love of one's enemies; (4) repayment of evil with good; (5) self-denial; (6) condemnation of hypocrisy and greed; (7) opposition to ceremonialism as the essence of religion; (8) the imminent approach of the end of the world; and (9) the resurrection of the dead and the establishment of the kingdom of heaven. Recent research has tended to emphasize the last two of these points as being at the center of Jesus's mission.

Christianity was broadened and invested with a more elaborate theology by some of the successors of Jesus, above all the Apostle Paul, originally known as Saul of Tarsus (10?–67?A.D.). Paul was not a native of Palestine but a Jew born in the city of Tarsus in southeastern Asia Minor. Originally a persecutor of Christians, he later converted to Christianity and devoted his limitless energy to propagating that faith throughout the Near East. It would be almost impossible to overestimate the significance of his work. Denying that Jesus was sent merely as the redeemer of the Jews, Paul proclaimed Christianity to be a universal religion. Furthermore, he placed major emphasis on the idea of Jesus as the Christ, as the anointed God-man whose death on the cross was an atonement for the sins of humanity. Not only did he reject the works of the Law (i.e., Jewish ritualism) as of primary importance in religion, but he declared them to be utterly worthless in procuring salvation. Sinners by nature, human beings can be saved only by faith and by the grace of God "through the redemption that is in Christ Jesus." It follows, according to Paul, that human fate in the life to come is almost entirely dependent upon the will of God; for "Hath not the potter power over the clay, of the same lump to make one vessel unto honor, and another unto dishonor?" (Romans 9:21). God has mercy "on whom He will have mercy, and whom He will He hardeneth" (Romans 9:18).

Although it may be something of a simplification, it seems basically true to say that whereas Jesus proclaimed the imminent coming of the kingdom of God, Paul laid the basis for a religion of personal salvation through Christ and the ministry of the Church. Therefore, after Paul Christianity developed both ceremonies, or sacraments, to bring the believer closer to Christ and an organization of priests to administer those sacraments. In teaching that priests who administered sacraments were endowed with supernatural powers, Christianity gradually posited a distinction between clergy and laity much sharper than that which had existed in most earlier religions. This would become the basis of subsequent Western controversies and divisions between "Church" and "State." In the meantime, Christianity's emphasis on otherworldly salvation ministered by a worldly priestly organization helped it greatly to grow and ultimately to flourish.

Christianity grew steadily in the first two centuries after Christ but only really began to flourish in the third. To understand this we must recall that the third century in Roman history was an "age of anxiety." At a time of extreme political turbulence and economic hardship people understandably began to treat life on earth as an illusion and place their hopes in the beyond. The human body and the material world were more and more regarded as either evil or basically unreal. As the Neoplatonic philosopher and leading thinker of that age, Plotinus, wrote, "when I come to myself, I wonder how it is that I have a body . . . by what deterioration did this happen?" Plotinus devised a whole philosophical system to answer this question, but this system was far too abstruse to have much meaning for large numbers of people. Instead, several religions that emphasized the dominance in this world of spiritual forces and the absolute preeminence of otherworldly salvation gained hold as never before.

At first Christianity was just another of these religions; Mithraism, Gnosticism, and the cults of Isis and Serapis were others. It is natural to ask, therefore, why Christianity gained converts in the third century at the expense of its rivals. A number of answers may be posited. One of the simplest, but not the least important, is that even though Christianity borrowed elements from older religions—above all Judaism and Gnosticism—it was new and hence possessed a sense of dynamism lacking among the salvationist religions which had existed for centuries. (It is noteworthy in this regard that one of Christianity's most serious rivals in the period from 276 to about 400 was Manicheanism, which was even newer than the Christian faith.) Christianity's dynamism was also enhanced by its rigorous exclusiveness. Hitherto people had adopted religions as people today take on insurance policies, piling one on another in order to feel more secure. The fact that Christianity prohibited this, demanding that the Christian God be worshiped alone, made the new religion most appealing at a time when people were searching desperately for absolutes. Similarly, Christianity alone among its rivals (with the later exception of Manicheanism) had an all-embracing theory to explain evil on earth, namely as the work of demons governed by the devil. When Christian missionaries sought converts they successfully emphasized the new faith's ability to combat these demons by reputed miracles.

An Early-Christian Woman. A wall-painting from the catacomb of Priscilla, Rome, third century A.D.

Although Christianity's novelty, exclusiveness, and theory of evil help greatly to explain its success, probably the greatest attractions of the religion had to do with three other traits: its view of salvation, its social dimensions, and its organizational structure. Exorcism of demons might help to make life more tolerable on earth, but ultimately people in the later Roman Empire were most concerned with other-worldly salvation. Rival religions also promised an afterlife, but Christianity's doctrine on this subject was the most far-reaching. Christian preachers who warned that nonbelievers would "liquefy in fierce fires" for eternity and that believers would enjoy eternal blessedness understandably made many converts in an age of fears. They made converts too among all classes because Christianity had from its origins been a religion of the humble—carpenters, fishermen, and tent-makers—which promised the exaltation of the lowly. As the religion grew it gained a few wealthy patrons, but it continued to find its greatest strength among the lower and middle classes who comprised the greatest numbers in the Roman Empire. Moreover, while Christianity forbade women to become priests or discuss the faith and, as we will see, adopted many attitudes hostile to women, it at least accorded women some rights of participation in worship and equal hope for salvation. This fact gave it an advantage over Mithraism, which excluded women from its cult entirely. In addition to all these considerations, a final reason for Christianity's success lay in its organization. Unlike the rival mystery religions, it had by the third century developed an organized hierarchy of priests to direct the life of the faith. More than that, Christian congregations were tightly knit communities that provided services to their members—such as nursing, support of the unprotected, and burial—that went beyond strictly religious concerns. Those who became Christians found human contacts and a sense of mission while the rest of the world seemed to be collapsing about them.

Jonah under the Gourd. A Christian marble statue done around the time of Constantine's conversion. Jonah resting after leaving the whale's belly was a symbol for the risen Christ.

Christianity was never as brutally persecuted by the Roman state as used to be thought. In fact the attitude of Rome was usually one of indifference: Christians were customarily tolerated unless certain magistrates decided to prosecute them for refusing to worship the official state gods. From time to time there were more concerted persecutions, but these were too intermittent and short-lived to do irreparable damage: on the contrary, they served to give Christianity some helpful publicity. To this degree the blood of martyrs really was the seed of the Church, but only because the blood did not flow too freely. One last great persecution took place toward the end of the reign of Diocletian and was continued by one of his immediate successors, a particularly bitter enemy of Christianity named Galerius. But by then the religion was far too strong to be wiped out by persecution, a fact that Galerius finally recognized by issuing an edict of toleration right before his death in 311. Thereafter Christianity was to be supported by the Roman state rather than persecuted by it.

*Roman persecution of
Christians relatively
moderate*

The adoption of Christianity by the Roman Empire was initiated by Constantine and completed by Theodosius. Constantine did not yet make Christianity the official religion of the empire, but he clearly favored it. Probably he did so both because he associated his own conversion to the faith (around the year 312) with a rise of his political fortunes, and because he hoped that Christianity might bring a spiritual unity to an empire that had been badly demoralized and religiously divided. Some of his successors, who were brought up in the Christian religion, pursued this end by ordering the persecution of pagans even more ruthlessly than some pagan emperors had formerly persecuted Christians. Christianity probably would have triumphed merely with official support because aspiring functionaries were usually quick to accept the religion of their rulers. The masses too were easily converted to the faith once it was supported by the state because, even though the fourth century was politically more stable than the third, the reorganization of the empire weighed most heavily on the lower classes and made them as desperate for otherworldly salvation as they had been in the century before. Substantial numbers, too, simply followed the lead of authority. Christians probably comprised no more than a fifth of the population of the Roman Empire at the time of the conversion of Constantine; with state support they quickly became an overwhelming majority. When Theodosius the Great forbade the worship of all religions other than Christianity by an edict of 380, paganism, already disappearing, was soon wiped out in all but the most rural backlands of the Roman realms.

*The triumph of
Christianity*

3. THE NEW CONTOURS OF CHRISTIANITY

Once the new faith became dominant within the Roman Empire it underwent some major changes in forms of thought, organization, and

*Christianity and the
Transformation of the
Roman World*

conduct. These changes all bore relationships to earlier tendencies, but the triumph of the faith greatly accelerated certain trends and altered the course of others. The result was that in many respects the Christianity of the late fourth century was a very different religion from the one persecuted by Diocletian and Galerius.

One consequence of Christianity's triumph was the flaring up of bitter doctrinal disputes. These brought great turmoil to the Church but resulted in the hammering out of dogma and discipline. Before the conversion of Constantine there had of course been disagreements among Christians about doctrinal matters, but as long as Christianity was a minority religion it managed to control its internal divisions in order to present a united front against hostile outsiders. Hardly had the new faith emerged victorious, however, than sharp splits developed within its own ranks. These were due partly to the fact that there had always been a tension between the intellectual and emotional tendencies within the religion which could now come more fully into the open, and partly to the fact that different regions of the empire tried to preserve a sense of their separate identities by preferring different theological formulas.

Controversy over doctrinal matters

The first of the bitter disputes was between the Arians and Athanasians over the nature of the Trinity. The Arians—not to be confused with Aryans (a racial term)—were followers of a priest named Arius and were the more intellectual group. Under the influence of Greek philosophy they rejected the idea that Christ could be equal with God. Instead they maintained that the Son was created by the Father and therefore was not co-eternal with Him or formed of the same substance. The followers of St. Athanasius, indifferent to human logic, held that even though Christ was the Son he was fully God: that Father, Son, and Holy Ghost were all absolutely equal and composed of an identical substance. After protracted struggles Athanasius's side won out and the Athanasian doctrine became the Christian dogma of the Trinity, as it remains today.

Division between the Arians and Athanasians

The struggle between the Arians and Athanasians was followed by numerous other doctrinal quarrels during the next few centuries. The issues at stake were generally too abstruse to warrant explaining here, but the results were momentous. One was that the dogmas of the Catholic faith gradually became fixed. It should be emphasized that this was a slow development and that many basic tenets of Catholicism were only defined much later (for example, the theory of the Mass was not formally promulgated until 1215; the doctrine of the Immaculate Conception of the Virgin Mary until 1854; and that of the Bodily Assumption of the Virgin until 1950). Nonetheless, the faith was beginning to take on a sharply defined form unprecedented in the history of earlier religions. Above all, this meant that any who differed from a certain formulation would be excluded from the community and often persecuted as a heretic. In the subsequent history of Christianity this concern for doctrinal uniformity was to result in both strengths and weaknesses for the Church.

Consequences of successive doctrinal disputes

A second result of the doctrinal quarrels was that they aggravated regional hostilities. In the fourth century differences among Christians increased alienation between West and East and also aggravated hostilities among regions within the East. Although the Roman Empire was evolving toward regionalism for many different reasons, including economic and administrative ones, and although regionalism was partly a cause of religious differences, the sharper and more frequent doctrinal quarrels became, the more they served to intensify regional hostilities.

Finally, the doctrinal quarrels provoked the interference of the Roman state in the governance of the Church. The same Constantine who favored Christianity as a unifying force was horrified by the prompt emergence of the Arian conflict and intervened in it by calling the Council of Nicea (325), which condemned Arius. It is noteworthy that this council—the first general council of the Church—was convened by a Roman emperor and that Constantine served during its meetings as a presiding officer. Thereafter secular interference in Church matters continued, above all in the East. There were two major reasons for this. First, religious disputes were more prevalent in the East than the West and quarreling parties often appealed to the emperor for support. Second, the weight of imperial government was generally heavier in the East, and after 476 there were no Roman emperors in the West at all. When Eastern emperors were not appealed to by quarreling parties they interfered in religious disputes themselves, as Constantine had done before them, in order to preserve unity. The result was that in the East the emperor assumed great religious authority and control, while in the West the future of relations between State and Church was more open.

*Imperial involvement in
religious conflicts*

Even while emperors were interfering in religious matters, however, the Church's own internal organization was becoming more complex and articulated. We have seen that a clear distinction between clergy and laity was already a hallmark of the early Christian religion after the time of St. Paul. The next step was the development of a hierarchical organization within the ranks of the clergy. The superiority of bishops over priests was recognized before Christianity's triumph. Christian organization was centered in cities and one bishop in each important city became the authority to which all the clergy in the surrounding vicinity answered. This organization was sufficient for a minority religion, but as the number of congregations multiplied and as the influence of the Church increased due to the adoption of Christianity as the official religion of Rome, distinctions of rank among the bishops themselves began to appear. Those who had their headquarters in the larger cities came to be called metropolitans (today known in the West as archbishops), with authority over the clergy of an entire province. In the fourth century the still higher rank of patriarch was established to designate those bishops who ruled over the oldest and largest of Christian communities—such cities as Rome, Jerusalem, Constantinople, Antioch, and Alexandria, and their sur-

*The organization
of the clergy*

218

*Christianity and the
Transformation of the
Roman World*

The rise of the papacy

rounding districts. Thus the Christian clergy by 400 A.D. had come to embrace a definite hierarchy of patriarchs, metropolitans, bishops, and priests.

The climax of all this development—still largely in the future—was the growth of the primacy of the bishop of Rome, or in other words the rise of the papacy. For several reasons the bishop of Rome enjoyed a preeminence over the other patriarchs of the Church. The city in which he ruled was venerated by the faithful as a scene of the missionary activities of the Apostles Peter and Paul. The tradition was widely accepted that Peter had founded the bishopric of Rome and that therefore all of his successors were heirs of his authority and prestige. This tradition was supplemented by the theory that Peter had been commissioned by Christ as his vicar on earth and had been given the keys of the kingdom of heaven with power to punish people for their sins and even to absolve them from guilt (Matthew 16:18–19). This theory, known as the doctrine of the Petrine Succession, has been used by popes ever since as a basis for their claims to authority over the Church. The bishops of Rome had an advantage also in the fact that after the transfer of the imperial capital to Constantinople there was seldom any emperor with effective sovereignty in the West. Finally, in 445 the Emperor Valentinian III issued a decree commanding all western bishops to submit to the jurisdiction of the pope. It must not be supposed, however, that the Church was by any means yet under a monarchical form of government. The patriarchs in the East regarded the extreme assertions of papal claims as brazen effrontery, and even many bishops in the West continued to ignore them for some time. The clearest example of the papacy's early weakness is the fact that the popes did not even attend the first eight general councils of the Church (from 325 to 869), although later they were to convene and preside over all the others.

*Effects of the
rationalization of
ecclesiastical
administration*

The growth of ecclesiastical organization helped the Church to conquer the Roman world in the fourth century and to minister to the needs of the faithful thereafter. The existence of an episcopal administrative structure was particularly influential in the West as the Roman Empire decayed and finally collapsed in the fifth century. Since every city had a bishop trained to some degree in the arts of administration, the Church in the West took over many of the functions of government and helped to preserve order amid the deepening chaos. But the new emphasis on administration also had its inevitably deleterious effects: as the Church developed its own rationalized administrative structure it inevitably became more worldly and distant in spirit from the simple faith of Jesus and the Apostles.

The rise of monasticism

The clearest reaction to this trend was expressed in the spread of monasticism. Today we are accustomed to thinking of monks as groups of priests who live communally in order to dedicate themselves primarily to lives of contemplation and prayer. In their origins, however, monks were not priests but laymen who almost always lived alone and who sought extremes of self-torture rather than ordered lives of spirituality. Monasticism began to emerge in the third century as a response to the anxieties of that age, but it only became a dominant movement within Christianity in the fourth century. Two obvious reasons for this fact stand out. First of all, the choice of extreme hermitlike asceticism was a substitute for martyrdom. With the conversion of Constantine and the abandonment of persecution, most chances of winning a crown of glory in heaven by undergoing death for the faith were eliminated. But the desire to prove one's religious ardor by self-abasement and suffering was still present. Second, as the fourth century progressed the priesthood became more and more immersed in worldly concerns. Those who wished to avoid secular temptations fled to the deserts and woods to practice an asceticism that priests and bishops were forgetting. (Monks customarily became priests only later during the Middle Ages.) In this way even while Christianity was accommodating itself to practical needs, monasticism satisfied the inclinations of ascetic extremists who otherwise might have become Gnostics or Manicheans and who looked forward to lives of torture and deprivation that far outstripped those of Christ and the Apostles.

Monasticism first emerged in the East, where for about one hundred years after Constantine's conversion it spread like a mania. Hermit monks of Egypt and Syria vied with each other in their pursuit of the most inhuman and humiliating excesses. Some grazed in the fields after the manner of cows, others penned themselves into small cages, and others hung heavy weights around their necks. A monk named Cyriacus stood for hours on one leg like a crane until he could bear it no more. The most extravagant of these monastic ascetics was St. Simeon Stylites, who performed self-punishing exercises—such as touching his feet with his head 1,244 times in succession—on top of a high pillar for thirty-seven years, while crowds gathered below to worship "the worms that dropped from his body."

*The extremes of
monastic asceticism*

In time such ascetic hysteria subsided and it became recognized that monasticism would be more enduring if monks lived in a community and did not concentrate on self-torture. The most successful architect of communal monasticism in the East was St. Basil (330?–379), who started his monastic career as a hermit and ascetic extremist but came to prefer communal and more moderate forms of life. Basil expressed this preference in writings for monks that laid down the basic guidelines for eastern monasticism down to the present. Rather than encouraging extremes of self-torture, Basil encouraged monks to discipline themselves by useful labor. Although his teachings were still extremely severe by modern standards, he prohibited monks from engaging in prolonged fasts or lacerating their flesh. Instead he urged them to submit to obligations of poverty and humility, and to spend many hours of the day in silent religious meditation. With the triumph of St. Basil's ideas, eastern monasticism became more organized and subdued, but even so Basilian monks preferred to live as far away

*The communal
monasticism of St. Basil*

220

*Christianity and the
Transformation of the
Roman World*

The rule of St. Benedict

from the "world" as they could and never had the same civilizing influence on external society as did their brothers in western Europe.

Monasticism did not at first spread so quickly in the West as it did in the East because the appeal of asceticism was much weaker there. This situation changed only in the sixth century when St. Benedict (480?–547?) drafted his famous Latin rule which ultimately became the guide for nearly all the monks in the West. Recent research has shown that Benedict copied much of his rule from an earlier Latin text, but he still produced a document notable for its brevity, flexibility, and moderation. The Benedictine rule imposed obligations similar to those laid down by St. Basil: poverty, obedience, labor, and religious devotion. Yet Benedict prescribed less austerity than Basil did: the monks were granted a sufficiency of simple food, clothing, and enough sleep; they were even allowed to drink a small amount of wine, although meat was only granted to the sick. The abbot's authority was absolute and the abbot was allowed to flog monks for disobedience, yet Benedict urged him to try "to be loved rather than feared," and ordained that the abbot take counsel before making decisions "because the Lord often reveals to a younger member what is best." For such reasons the Benedictine monastery became a center of deep religious enrichment rather than a school for punishment.

*The significance of
Benedictine monasticism:
(1) missionary activities;
(2) attitude toward manual
labor*

We will have occasion for continuing the story of Benedictine monasticism later on, but here we may point in advance to some of its greatest contributions to the development of Western civilization. One was that Benedictine monks were committed from an early date to missionary work: they were primarily responsible for the conversion of England and later most of Germany. Such activities not only helped to spread the faith but also served to create a sense of cultural unity for western Europe. Another positive contribution lay in the at-

A Monastery of the Basilian Order on Mt. Athos. The asceticism of the Basilian monks caused them to build their monasteries in almost inaccessible places on lofty crags or on the steep sides of rugged mountains.

St. Benedict Offering His Rule to Grateful Monks. A late-medieval conception from an Austrian manuscript of about 1355.

titude of the Benedictines toward work. Whereas the highest goal for ancient philosophers and aristocrats was to have enough leisure time for unimpeded contemplation, St. Benedict wanted his monks always to keep busy, for he believed that "idleness is an enemy of the soul." Therefore he prescribed that they should be occupied at certain times in manual labor, a prescription that would have horrified most thinkers of earlier times. Accordingly, early Benedictines worked hard themselves and spread the idea of the dignity of labor to others. With Benedictine support, this idea would become one of the most distinctive traits of Western culture. We read of Benedictines who gladly milked cows, threshed, plowed, and hammered: in so doing they increased the prosperity of their own monasteries and provided good examples for others. Benedictine monasteries became particularly successful in farming and later in estate-managing. Thus they often helped to advance the level of the western European economy and sometimes even to provide wealth that could be drawn upon by emerging western European states.

The fact that Benedictine monasteries were often islands of culture when literacy and learning were all but forgotten in the secular world is better known. St. Benedict himself was no admirer of classical culture. Quite to the contrary, he wanted his monks to serve only Christ— not literature or philosophy. But he did assume that monks would have to read well enough to say their prayers. That meant that some teaching in the monasteries was necessary because it was seldom available outside, and because boys were often given over from birth to the monastic profession. Once there was teaching there would obviously be at least a few writing implements and books. This explains why Benedictines always maintained some literacy but not why some of them became devoted to perpetuating classical culture. The impetus

(3) the preservation of classical culture; Cassiodorus

behind the latter development was the work of a monastic thinker named Cassiodorus (477?–570?). Inspired by St. Augustine, whom we will treat in more detail later, Cassiodorus believed that some basic classical learning was necessary for the proper understanding of the Bible; this justified the study of the classics by monks. Furthermore, Cassiodorus recognized that copying manuscripts was in itself "manual labor" (literally work with the hands) and might be even more appropriate for monks than hard work in the fields. As Benedictines began to subscribe to these ideas, Benedictine monasteries became centers for learning and transcribing that were without rival for centuries. No work of classical Latin literature, including such "licentious" writings as the poems of Catullus and Ovid, would survive today had they not been copied and preserved during the early Middle Ages by Benedictine monks.

Love of women was of course, however, not a Benedictine preference. Returning to our original subject—the changes that took place in Christian institutions and attitudes during the fourth century—a final fateful trend was the development of a negative attitude toward the role of women in human life. Compared to most other religions, Christianity was favorable to women. Female souls were regarded as equal to male ones in the eyes of God, and human nature was deemed to be complete only in both sexes. St. Paul even went so far as to say that after baptism "there is neither male nor female" (Galatians 3:28), a spiritual equalitarianism which meant that women could be saved as fully as men. But Christians from earliest times shared the view of their contemporaries that in everyday life and in marriage women were to be strictly subject to men. Not only did early Christians believe, with all male supremacists of the ancient world, that women should be excluded from positions of leadership or decision-making, meaning that they should be "silent in Church" (I Corinthians 14:34–35) and could never be priests, but they added to this the view that women were more "fleshly" than men and therefore should be subjected to men as the flesh is subjected to the spirit (Ephesians 5:21–33).

Monks Chopping Down Trees (above) *and Harvesting Grain* (below). From a twelfth-century French manuscript.

With the growth of the ascetic movement in the third and fourth centuries, the denigration of women as dangerously "fleshly" creatures became more and more pronounced. Since sexual abstinence lay at the heart of asceticism, the most perfect men were expected to shun women. Monks, of course, shunned women the most. This was a primary reason why they fled to deserts and forests. One eastern ascetic was struck by the need for virginity in the midst of his marriage ceremony, ran off to a hermit's cell, and blocked the entrance; another monk who was forced to carry his aged mother across a stream swaddled her up as thoroughly as he could so that he would not catch any "fire" and no thoughts of other women attack him. With monks taking such an uncompromising attitude, the call for continence was extended to the priesthood. Originally priests could be married; it seems that even some of the Apostles had wives (I Corinthians 9:5). But

223

*The Germanic Invasions and the
Fall of the Roman Empire in the
West*

in the course of the fourth century the doctrine spread that priests could not be married after ordination, and that those already married were obliged to live continently with their wives afterward.

Once virginity was accepted as the highest standard, marriage was taken to be only second-best. St. Jerome expressed this view most earthily when he said that virginity was wheat, marriage barley, and fornication cow-dung: since people should not eat cow-dung he would permit them barley. The major purposes of marriage were to keep men from "burning" and to propagate the species. (St. Jerome went so far as to praise marriage above all because it brought more virgins into the world!) Thus Christianity reinforced the ancient view that woman's major earthly purpose was to serve as mother. Men and women were warned not to take pleasure even in marital intercourse but to indulge in it only for the purpose of procreation. Women were to be "saved in childbearing" (I Timothy 2:15). Since they could not become priests and only a very few could become nuns (female monasticism was regarded as a very expensive luxury in the premodern world), almost all women were expected to become submissive wives and mothers. As wives they were not expected to have their own careers and were not meant to be educated or even literate. Hence even though they had full hopes for salvation, they were treated as inferiors in the everyday affairs of the world, a treatment that would endure until modern times.

4. THE GERMANIC INVASIONS AND THE FALL OF THE ROMAN EMPIRE IN THE WEST

While Christianity was conquering the Roman Empire from within, another force, that of the Germanic barbarians, was threatening it from without. The Germans, who had already almost brought Rome to its knees in the third century, were held off from the time of Diocletian until shortly before the reign of Theodosius the Great. But thereafter they demolished Western Roman resistance and, by the end of the fifth century, succeeded in conquering all of the Roman West. Germanic kingdoms then became the new form of government in territories once ruled over by Caesar and Augustus.

It is customary to think, perhaps with the encouragement of grade-B movies, that the Germans who destroyed the Western Roman Empire were fierce and thoroughly uncouth savages. But that is a misunderstanding. The Germans were barbarians in the sense that they did not live in cities and were customarily illiterate, but they were not therefore savages. On the contrary, they often practiced settled agriculture—although they preferred hunting and grazing—and were adept at making iron tools and weapons as well as jewelry and pottery. Physically they looked enough like Romans to intermarry without causing much comment, and their Indo-European language was related

*Christianity and the
Transformation of the
Roman World*

to Latin and Greek. Prolonged interaction with the Romans had a decisive civilizing influence on the Germans before they started their final conquests. Germans and Romans who shared common borders along the Rhine and Danube had steady trading relations with each other. Even during times of war Romans were often allied with some German tribes while they fought others. By the fourth century, moreover, German tribes often served as auxiliaries of depleted Roman armies and were sometimes allowed to settle on borderlands of the empire where Roman farmers had given up trying to cultivate the land. Finally, many German tribes had been converted to Christianity in the fourth century, although the Christianity they accepted was of the heretical Arian version. All these interactions made the "barbarians" very familiar with Roman civilization and substantially favorable to it.

The Germans began their final push not to destroy Rome but to find more and better land. The first breakthrough occurred in 378 when one tribe, the Visigoths, who had recently settled on some Roman lands in the Danube region, revolted against mistreatment by Roman officials and then decisively defeated a punitive Roman army in the Battle of Adrianople. The Visigoths did not immediately follow up this victory because they were cleverly bought off and made allies of the empire by Theodosius the Great. But when Theodosius died in 395 he divided his realm between his two sons, neither of whom was as competent as he, and both halves of the empire were weakened by political intrigues. The Visigoths under their leader Alaric took advantage of this situation to wander through Roman realms almost at will, looking for the best land and provisions. In 410 they sacked Rome itself—a great shock to some contemporaries—and in the following years marched into southern Gaul. Meanwhile, in December of 406, a group of allied Germanic tribes led by the Vandals crossed the frozen Rhine and capitalized on Roman preoccupation with the Visigoths by streaming through Gaul into Spain. Later they were able to cross the straits into northwest Africa, then one of the richest agricultural regions of the empire. From Africa they took control of the central Mediterranean, even sacking Rome from the sea in 455. By 476 the entirely ineffectual Western Roman emperor, a mere boy derisively nicknamed Augustulus ("little Augustus"), was easily deposed by a leader of a mixed band of Germans who then assumed the title of king of Rome. Accordingly, 476 is conventionally given as the date for the end of the Western Roman Empire. But it must be remembered that a Roman emperor, who maintained some claims to authority in the West, continued to rule in Constantinople.

*The Visigoths and the
Vandals*

Two questions that historians of the German invasions customarily ask are: How did the Germans manage to triumph so easily? Why was it that they were particularly successful in the West rather than the East? The ease of the German victories appears particularly striking when it is recognized that the German armies were remarkably small:

*Reasons for the German
success*

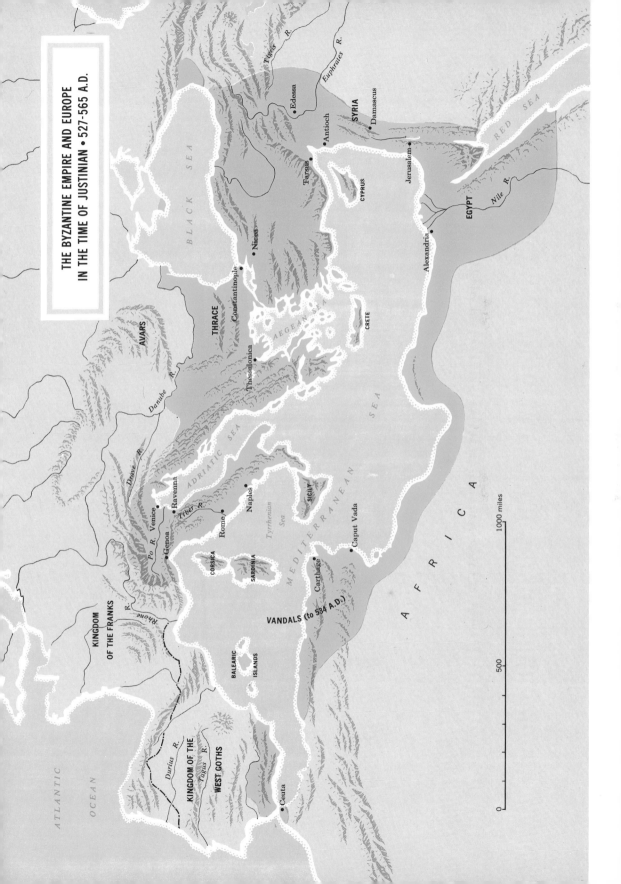

THE BYZANTINE EMPIRE AND EUROPE
IN THE TIME OF JUSTINIAN · 527-565 A.D.

ATLANTIC
OCEAN

KINGDOM
OF THE FRANKS

KINGDOM OF THE

WEST GOTHS

Durius R.

Tagus R.

Rhone R.

BALEARIC
ISLANDS

Ceuta

VANDALS (to 534 A.D.)

CORSICA

SARDINIA

Carthage

A F R I C A

AVARS

Danube R.

Drave R.

Po R.

Venice

Genoa

Ravenna

Tiber R.

Rome

Naples

SICILY

Tyrrhenian
Sea

Caput Vada

M E D I T E R R A N E A N   S E A

ADRIATIC SEA

THRACE

Thessalonica

Constantinople

Nicæa

AEGEAN SEA

B L A C K   S E A

CRETE

CYPRUS

Tigris R.

Euphrates R.

Edessa

Antioch

Tarsus

SYRIA

Damascus

Jerusalem

EGYPT

Alexandria

Nile R.

R E D
S E A

0   500   1000 miles

Byzantine Gold Cup, VI–IX cent.
The relief shows Constantinople
personified as a queen holding the
sceptre of imperial rule. (MMA)

Merovingian Fibula or Brooch, VII cent. A
fabulous gold-plated animal set with
garnets and colored paste. (MMA)

*Sienese Madonna and Child, Byzantine School,
XIII cent.* The painters of Siena in Italy imitated the opulent style of Byzantine art. Their
madonnas were not earthly mothers, but
celestial queens reigning in dignified splendor. (National Gallery)

Saint John Writing His Gospel. From a Carolingian illuminated manuscript, c. 850. The monastic artist was
indifferent to perspective, but excelled in coloring and
conveying a sense of vitality and energy. (Morgan
Library)

the Goths who won at Adrianople numbered no more than 10,000 men, and the total number of the Vandal "hordes" (including women and children) was about 80,000—a population about the same as that of an average-sized American suburb. But the Roman armies themselves were depleted because of declining population and the need for manpower in other occupations, above all in the new bureaucracies. More than that, German armies often won by default (Adrianople was one of the few pitched battles in the history of their advance) because the Romans were no longer zealous about defending themselves. Germans were seldom regarded with horror—many German soldiers had even risen to positions of leadership within Roman ranks—and the coercive regime begun by Diocletian was not deemed to be worth fighting for.

The reasons why the Germans fared best in the West are complex—some having to do with personalities and mistakes of the moment, and others with geographical considerations. But the primary explanation why the Eastern Roman Empire survived while the Western did not is that the East was simply richer. By the fifth century most Western Roman cities had shrunk in terms of both population and space to a small fraction of their earlier size and were often little more than empty administrative shells or fortifications. The economy of the West was becoming more and more strictly agricultural, and agricultural produce served only to feed farm laborers and keep rich landlords in luxuries. In the East, on the other hand, cities like Constantinople, Antioch, and Alexandria were still teeming metropolises because of their trade and industry. Because the eastern state had greater reserves of wealth to tax, it was more vigorous. It could also afford to buy off the barbarians with tribute money, which it did with increasing regularity. So Constantinople was able to stay afloat while Rome floundered and then sank.

Why the Eastern Roman Empire survived and the Western collapsed

The effects of the Germanic conquests in the West were not cataclysmic. The greatest difference between the Germans and the Romans had been that the former did not live in cities, but since the Western Roman cities were already in a state of decline, the invasions only served at most to accelerate the progress of urban decay. On the land Germans replaced Roman landlords without interrupting basic Roman agricultural patterns. Moreover, since the Germans never comprised very large numbers, they usually never took over more than a part of Roman lands. Germans also tried to avail themselves of Roman administrative apparatuses, but these tended to diminish gradually because of the diminishing of wealth and literacy. Thus the only major German innovation was to create separate tribal kingdoms in the West in place of a united empire.

Consequences of the Germanic invasions

The map of western Europe around the year 500 reveals the following major political divisions. Germanic tribes of Anglo-Saxons, who had crossed the English Channel in the middle of the fifth century, were extending their rule on the island of Britain. In the northern part

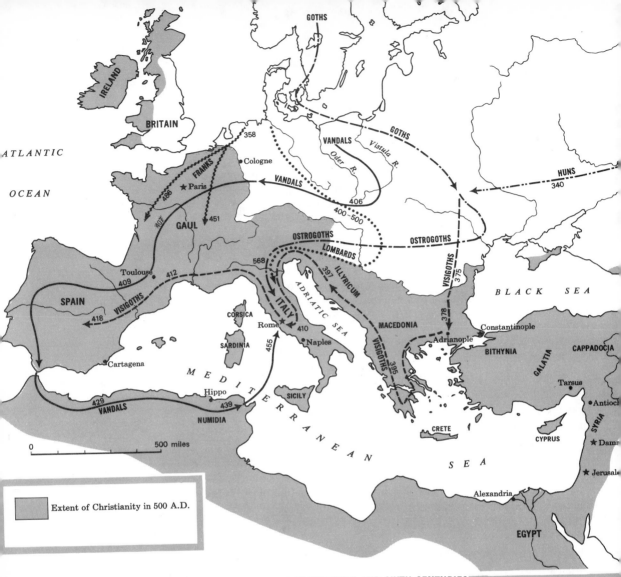

THE BARBARIAN INVASIONS IN THE FIFTH AND SIXTH CENTURIES

Germanic kingdoms in the year 500

of Gaul, around Paris and east to the Rhine, the growing kingdom of the Franks was ruled by a crafty warrior named Clovis. South of the Franks stood the Visigoths, who ruled the southern half of Gaul and most of Spain. South of them were the Vandals, who ruled throughout previously Roman northwest Africa. In all of Italy the Ostrogoths, eastern relatives of the Visigoths, held sway under their impressive King Theodoric. Of these kingdoms the Frankish would be the most promising for the future (for that reason it will be taken up in the next chapter) and the seemingly strongest for the present was that of the Ostrogoths.

Theodoric the Ostrogoth, who ruled in Italy from 493 to 526, was a great admirer of Roman civilization; this he tried to preserve as best he could. He fostered agriculture and commerce, repaired public buildings and roads, patronized learning, and maintained a policy of religious toleration. In short he gave Italy a more enlightened rule than it had known under most of its earlier emperors. But since Theodoric and his sparsely numbered Ostrogoths were Arian Christians while the local bishops and native population were Catholics, his rule, no matter how tolerant and benign, was viewed with some hostility. The "Roman" rulers in Constantinople were also hostile to Theodoric because he was an Arian and because they had not given up hopes of reconquering Italy themselves. All these circumstances led to the demise of Theodoric's Ostrogothic kingdom not long after his death. In fact, none of the continental barbarian kingdoms would last long except for that of the Franks.

Theodoric the Ostrogoth. The barbarian ruler is shown here in Roman dress, with an ornate Roman hairstyle and a Roman symbol of victory in his hand. The inscription reads REX THEODERICVS PIVS PRINCIS, Latin for King Theodoric, pious prince.

5. THE SHAPING OF WESTERN CHRISTIAN THOUGHT

The period of the decline and fall of the Roman Empire in the West was also the time when a few Western Christian thinkers formulated an approach to the world and to God that was to guide the thought of the West for roughly the next 800 years. This concurrence of political decline and theological advance was not coincidental. With the empire falling and being replaced by barbarian kingdoms, it seemed clearer than ever to thinking Christians both that the classical inheritance had to be reexamined and that God had not intended the world to be anything more than a transitory testing place. The consequences of these assumptions accordingly became urgent questions. Between about 380 and 525 answers were worked out by Western Christian thinkers whose accomplishments were intimately interrelated. The towering figure among them was St. Augustine, but some others had great influence as well.

Three contemporaries who knew and influenced each other—St. Jerome (340?–420), St. Ambrose (340?–397), and St. Augustine (354–430)—count as three of the four greatest "fathers" of the Western, Latin Church. (The fourth, St. Gregory the Great, came later and will be discussed in the next chapter.) St. Jerome's greatest single contribution to the future was his translation of the Bible from Hebrew and Greek into Latin. His version, known as the "Vulgate" (or "common" version), became the standard Latin Bible used throughout the Middle Ages; with minor variations it continued to be used long afterward by the Roman Catholic Church. Fortunately Jerome was one of the best writers of his day, and he endowed his translation with vigorous, often colloquial prose and, occasionally, fine poetry. Since the Vulgate was the most widely read work in Latin for centuries, Jerome's writing had as much influence on Latin style and thought as the

St. Jerome

Mosaic of Theodoric's Palace at Ravenna. At the right is a stylized conception of the ruler's palace, with the Latin inscription PALA TIVM; to the left of it is a row of saints, who would be indistinguishable were it not for the initials on their clothing: for early Christian artists, supernatural merits rather than individual personality traits were of the essence.

King James Bible has had on English literature. Jerome, who was the least original thinker of the great Latin fathers, also influenced the Western Christian future by his contentious but eloquent formulations of contemporary views. Among the most important of these were the beliefs that much of the Bible was to be understood allegorically rather than literally, that classical learning could be valid for Christians if it was thoroughly subordinated to Christian aims, and that the most perfect Christians were rigorous ascetics. In keeping with the last position Jerome avidly supported monasticism. He also taught that women should not take baths so that they would not see their own bodies naked.

Unlike Jerome, who was primarily a scholar, St. Ambrose was most active in the concerns of the world. As archbishop of Milan, Ambrose was the most influential Church official in the West—more so even than the pope. Guided by practical concerns, he wrote an ethical work, *On the Duties of Ministers,* which followed closely upon Cicero's *On Duties* in title and form, and also drew heavily on Cicero's Stoic ethics. But Ambrose differed from Cicero and most of traditional classical thought on two major points. One was that the beginning and end of human conduct should be the reverence and search for God rather than any self-concern or interest in social adjustment. The other—Ambrose's most original contribution—was that God helps some Christians but not others in this pursuit by the gift of grace, a point that was to be greatly refined and amplified by St. Augustine. Ambrose put his concern for proper conduct into action by his most famous act, his confrontation with the Emperor Theodosius the Great for massacring innocent civilians. Ambrose argued that by violating di-

St. Ambrose

vine commandments Theodosius had made himself subject to Church discipline. Remarkably the archbishop succeeded in forcing the sovereign emperor to do penance. This was the first time that a churchman had subordinated the Roman secular power in matters of morality. Consequently it symbolized the Church's claim to preeminence in this sphere, and particularly the *Western* Church's developing sense of autonomy and moral superiority that would subsequently make it so much more independent and influential on the secular world than the Eastern Church.

St. Ambrose's disciple, St. Augustine, was the greatest of all the Latin fathers; indeed he was one of the most powerful Christian intellects of all time. Augustine's influence on subsequent medieval thought was incalculable. Even after the Middle Ages his theology had a profound influence on the development of Protestantism; in the twentieth century many leading Christian thinkers have called themselves Neo-Augustinians. It may be that one reason why Augustine's Christianity was so searching was because he began his career by searching for it. Nominally a Christian from birth, he hesitated until the age of thirty-three to be baptized, passing from one system of thought to another without being able to find intellectual or spiritual satisfaction in any. Only increasing doubts about all other alternatives, the appeals of St. Ambrose's teachings, and a mystical experience movingly described in his *Confessions* led Augustine to embrace the faith wholeheartedly in 387. Thereafter he advanced rapidly in ecclesiastical positions, becoming bishop of the North African city of Hippo in 395. Although he led a most active life in this office, he still found time to write a large number of profound, complex, and powerful treatises in which he set forth his convictions concerning the most fundamental problems of Christian thought and action.

St. Augustine's theology revolved around the principles of divine omnipotence and the profound sinfulness of humanity. Ever since Adam and Eve turned away from God in the Garden of Eden humans have remained basically sinful. One of Augustine's most vivid illustrations of human depravity appears in the *Confessions,* where he tells how he and some other boys once were driven to steal pears from a neighbor's garden, not because they were hungry or because the pears were beautiful, but for the sake of the evil itself. God would be purely just if He condemned all human beings to hell, but since He is also merciful He has elected to save a few. Ultimately human will has nothing to do with this choice: although one has the power to choose between good and evil, one does not have the power to decide whether he will be saved. God alone, from eternity, predestined a portion of the human race to be saved and sentenced the rest to be damned. In other words, God fixed for all time the number of human inhabitants of heaven. If any mere mortals were to respond that this seems unfair, the answer is first that strict "fairness" would confine all to perdition,

St. Augustine

Augustine's theology

*Christianity and the
Transformation of the
Roman World*

*The doctrine of
predestination*

On the City of God

*Augustine's view of
classical learning*

and second that the basis for God's choice is a mystery shrouded in
His omnipotence—far beyond the realm of human comprehension.

Even though it might seem to us that the practical consequences of
this rigorous doctrine of predestination would be lethargy and fatalism, Augustine and subsequent medieval Christians did not see it
that way at all. Humans themselves must do good, and if they are
"chosen" they usually will do good; since no one knows who is chosen and who is not, all should try to do good in the hope that they are
among the chosen. For Augustine the central guide to doing good was
the doctrine of "charity," which meant leading a life devoted to loving
God and loving one's neighbor for the sake of God. Seen from the
opposite, humans should avoid "cupidity," or loving earthly things
for their own sake. Put in other terms, Augustine taught that humans
should behave on earth as if they were travelers or "pilgrims," keeping their eyes at all times on their heavenly home and avoiding all
materialistic concerns.

Augustine built an interpretation of history on this view in one of
his major works, *On the City of God*. In this, he argued that the entire
human race from the Creation until the Last Judgment was and will be
composed of two warring societies, those who "live according to
man" and love themselves, and those who "live according to God."
The former belong to the "City of Earth" and will be damned, while
the blessed few who compose the "City of God" will on Judgment
Day put on the garment of immortality. This reading of history subsequently went unquestioned throughout the Middle Ages.

Although Augustine worked out for the first time major new
aspects of Christian theology, he believed that he was only putting
together truths found in the Bible. Indeed, he was convinced that
the Bible alone contained all the wisdom worth knowing. But he also
believed that much of the Bible was expressed obscurely, and that it
was therefore necessary to have a certain amount of education in order
to understand it thoroughly. This conviction led him to a modified
acceptance of classical learning. The ancient world had already worked
out an educational system based on the "liberal arts," or those subjects
necessary for the worldly success and intellectual growth of free men.
Augustine argued that privileged Christians could learn the fundamentals of these subjects, but only in a limited way and for a completely different end—study of the Bible. Since nonreligious schools
existed in his day which taught these subjects, he permitted a Christian elite to attend them; later, when such schools died out, their place
was taken by schools in monasteries and cathedrals. Thus Augustine's
teaching laid the groundwork for some continuity of educational
practice as well as for the theory behind the preservation of some classical treatises. But we must qualify this by remarking that Augustine
intended liberal education only for an elite; all others were simply to
be catechized, or drilled, in the faith. He also thought it far worse
that anyone should become engaged in classical thought for its own

sake than that someone might not know any classical thought at all. The true wisdom of mortals, he insisted, was piety.

Augustine had many followers, of whom the most interesting and influential was Boethius, a Roman aristocrat who lived from about 480 to 524. To say that Boethius was a follower of St. Augustine might until recently have been regarded as controversial because some of his works make no explicit mention of Christianity. Indeed, since Boethius was indisputably interested in ancient philosophy, wrote in a polished, almost Ciceronian style, and came from a noble Roman family, it has been customary to view him as the "last of the Romans." But in fact he intended the classics to serve Christian purposes, just as Augustine had prescribed, and his own teachings were basically Augustinian.

Because Boethius lived a century after Augustine he could see far more clearly that the ancient world was coming to an end. Therefore he made it his first goal to preserve as much of the best ancient learning as possible by a series of handbooks, translations, and commentaries. Accepting a contemporary division of the liberal arts into seven subjects—grammar, rhetoric, logic, arithmetic, geometry, astronomy, and music—he wrote handbooks on two: arithmetic and music. These summaries were meant to convey all the basic aspects of the subject matter that a Christian might need to know. Had Boethius lived longer he probably would have written similar treatments of the other liberal arts, but as it was he concentrated his efforts on his favorite subject: logic. In order to preserve the best of classical logic, he translated from Greek into Latin some of Aristotle's logical treatises as well as an introductory work on logic by Porphyry (another ancient philosopher). He also wrote his own explanatory commentaries on these works in order to help beginners. Since Latin writers had never been interested in logic, even in the most flourishing periods of Roman culture, Boethius's translations and commentaries became a crucial link between the Greeks and the Middle Ages. Boethius helped endow the Latin language with a logical vocabulary, and when interest in logic was revived in the twelfth-century West it rested first on a Boethian basis.

Although Boethius was an exponent of Aristotle's logic, his worldview was not Aristotelian but Augustinian. This can be seen both in his several orthodox treatises on Christian theology and above all in his masterpiece, *The Consolation of Philosophy*. Boethius wrote the *Consolation* at the end of his life, after he had been condemned to death for treason by Theodoric the Ostrogoth, whom he had served as an official. (Historians are unsure about the justice of the charges.) In it Boethius asks the age-old question of what is human happiness and concludes that it is not found in earthly rewards such as riches or fame but only in the "highest good," which is God. Human life, then, should be spent in pursuit of God. Since Boethius speaks in the *Consolation* as a philosopher rather than a theologian, he does not refer to

Boethius

Boethius's intellectual contributions

Boethius. A twelfth-century artist's conception of Boethius as a musician, a reputation he earned because of his treatise on music.

*Christianity and the
Transformation of the
Roman World*

*The Consolation of
Philosophy*

*The myth of Orpheus as
a symbol for Christian
truths*

*Boethius's execution a
turning point*

The Emperor Justinian

Christian revelation or to the role of divine grace in salvation. But his basically Augustinian message is unmistakable. *The Consolation of Philosophy* became one of the most popular books of the Middle Ages because it was extremely well written, because it showed how classical expression and some classical ideas could be appropriated and subordinated into a clearly Christian framework, and most of all, because it seemed to offer a real meaning to life. In times when all earthly things really did seem crude or fleeting it was genuinely consoling to be told eloquently and "philosophically" that life has purpose if led for the sake of God.

At a climactic moment in the *Consolation* Boethius retold in verse the myth of Orpheus in a way that might stand for the common position of the four writers just discussed; i.e., how Christian thinkers were willing to accept and maintain some continuity with the classical tradition. But Boethius also made new sense of the story. According to Boethius Orpheus's wife, Eurydice, symbolized hell; since Orpheus could not refrain from looking at her he was forced to die and was condemned to hell himself. In other words, Orpheus was too worldly and material; he should not have loved a woman but should have sought God. True Christians, on the other hand, know that "happy is he who can look into the shining spring of good [i.e., the divine vision]; happy is he who can break the heavy chains of earth."

6. EASTERN ROME AND THE WEST

Boethius's execution by Theodoric the Ostrogoth in 524 was in many ways an important historical turning point. For one, Boethius was both the last noteworthy philosopher and last writer of cultivated Latin prose the West was to have for many hundreds of years. Then too Boethius was a layman, and for hundreds of years afterward almost all western European writers would be priests or monks. In the political sphere Boethius's execution was symptomatic as well because it was the harbinger of the collapse of the Ostrogothic kingdom in Italy. Whether or not he was justly condemned, Boethius's execution showed that the Arian Ostrogoths could not live in perfect harmony with Catholic Christians such as himself. Soon afterward, therefore, the Ostrogoths were overthrown by the Eastern Roman Empire. That event in turn was to be a major factor in the ultimate divorce between East and West and the consequent final disintegration of the old Roman World.

The conquest of the Ostrogoths was part of a larger plan for Roman revival conceived and directed by the Eastern Roman Emperor Justinian (527–565). Eastern Rome, with its capital at Constantinople, had faced many external pressures from barbarians and internal religious dissensions since the time of Theodosius. But throughout the fifth century it had managed to weather these, and by the time of Justinian's accession had regained much of its strength. Although the Eastern Roman Empire—which then encompassed the modern-day territories of Greece, Turkey, most of the Middle East, and Egypt—was largely Greek- and Syriac-speaking, Justinian himself came from a westernmost province (modern-day Yugoslavia) and spoke Latin. Not surprisingly, therefore, he concentrated his interests on the West. He saw himself as the heir of imperial Rome, whose ancient power and western territory he was resolved to restore. Aided by his astute and determined wife Theodora, who, unlike earlier imperial Roman consorts, played an influential role in his reign, Justinian took great strides toward this goal. But ultimately his policy of recovering the West proved unrealistic.

One of Justinian's most impressive and lasting accomplishments was his codification of Roman law. This project was part of his attempt to emphasize continuities with earlier imperial Rome and was also meant to enhance his own prestige and absolute power. Codification of the law was necessary because between the third and sixth centuries the volume of statutes had continued to grow, with the result that the vast body of enactments contained many contradictory or obsolete elements. Moreover, conditions had changed so radically that many of the old legal principles could no longer be applied, due to the establishment of an Oriental despotism and the adoption of Christianity as the official religion. When Justinian came to the throne in 527, he immediately decided upon a revision and codification of the existing law to bring it into harmony with the new conditions and to establish it as an authoritative basis of his rule. To carry out the actual work he appointed a commission of lawyers under the supervision of his minister, Tribonian. Within two years the commission published the first result of its labors. This was the Code, a systematic revision of all of the statutory laws which had been issued from the reign of Hadrian to the reign of Justinian. The Code was later supplemented by the Novels, which contained the legislation of Justinian and his immediate successors. By 532 the commission had completed the Digest, a summary of all of the writings of the great jurists. The final product of the work of revision was the Institutes, a textbook of the legal principles reflected in both the Digest and the Code. The combination of all four of these results of the program of revision constitutes the *Corpus Juris Civilis,* or the body of the civil law.

Justinian's *Corpus* was a brilliant achievement in its own terms: the Digest alone has been justly called "the most remarkable and important lawbook that the world has ever seen." In addition, the *Corpus* had an extraordinarily great influence on subsequent legal and governmental history. Revived and restudied in western Europe from the eleventh century on, Justinian's *Corpus* became the basis of all the law

Codification and revision of Roman law; the Corpus Juris Civilis

General significance of Justinian's Corpus

Justinian and Theodora. Sixth-century mosaics from the church of San Vitale, Ravenna. The emperor and empress are conceived here to have supernatural, almost priestly powers: they are advancing toward the altar, bringing the communion dish and chalice respectively. Both rulers are set off from their

and jurisprudence of European states, exclusive of England (which followed its own "common law"). The nineteenth-century Napoleonic Code, which provided the basis for the laws of modern European countries and also of Latin America, is fundamentally the Institutes of Justinian in modern dress.

Only a few of the more specific influences of Justinian's legal work can be enumerated here. One is that in its basic governmental theory it *Other influences* was a bastion of absolutism. Starting from the maxim that "what pleases the prince has the force of law," it granted untrammeled powers to the imperial sovereign and therefore was adopted with alacrity by later European monarchs and autocrats. But the *Corpus* also provided some theoretical support for constitutionalism because it maintained that the sovereign originally obtained his powers from the people rather than from God. Since government came from the people it could in theory be given back to them. Perhaps most important and influential was the *Corpus*'s view of the state as an abstract public and secular entity. In the Middle Ages rival views of the state as the private property of the ruler or as a supernatural creation meant to control sin often predominated. The modern conception of the state as a public entity concerned not with the future life but with everyday affairs gained strength toward the end of the Middle Ages largely because of the revival of assumptions found in Justinian's legal compilations.

Justinian aimed to be a full Roman emperor in geographical practice as well as in legal theory. To this end he sent out armies to reconquer

retinues by their haloes. The observant viewer is also meant to note the representation of the "three wise kings from the East" at the hem of Theodora's gown: just as the "three magi" once had supernatural knowledge of Christ, so now do their counterparts, Justinian and Theodora.

the West. At first they were quickly successful. In 533 Justinian's brilliant general Belisarius conquered the Vandal kingdom in northwest Africa, and in 536 Belisarius seemed to have won all Italy, where he was welcomed by the Catholic subjects of the Ostrogoths. But the first victories of the Italian campaign were illusory. After their initial defeats the Ostrogoths put up stubborn resistance and the war dragged on for decades until the exhausted Eastern Romans finally reduced the last Gothic outposts in 563. Shortly before he died Justinian became master of all Italy as well as northwest Africa and coastal parts of Spain that his troops had also managed to recapture. The Mediterranean was once more briefly a "Roman" lake. But the cost of the endeavor was soon going to call the very existence of the Eastern Roman Empire into question.

Justinian's policy of reconquest in the West

There were two major reasons why Justinian's Western campaigns were ill-advised. One was that his realm really could not afford them. Belisarius seldom had enough troops to do his job properly: he began his Italian campaign with only 8,000 men. Later, when Justinian did grant his generals enough troops, it was only at the cost of oppressive taxation. But additional troops would probably have been insufficient to hold the new lines in the West because the empire had greater interests, as well as enemies, to the East. While the Eastern Roman Empire was exhausting itself in Italy the Persians were gathering strength. Justinian's successors had to pull away from the West in order to meet the threat of a revived Persia, but even so, by the beginning of the seventh

The Western campaigns unwise

century, it seemed as if the Persians would be able to march all the way to the waters that faced Constantinople. Only a heroic reorganization of the empire after 610 saved the day, but it was one that helped withdraw Eastern Rome from the West and helped the West begin to lead a life of its own.

In the meantime Justinian's wars had left most of Italy in a shambles. In the course of the protracted fighting much devastation had been wrought. Around Rome aqueducts were cut and the countryside returned to marshes that would not be drained until the time of Mussolini. In 568, only three years after Justinian's death, another Germanic tribe, the Lombards, invaded the country and took much of it away from the Eastern Romans. They met little resistance because the latter were now properly paying more attention to the East, but the Lombards were still too weak to conquer the whole Italian peninsula. Instead, Italy became divided between Lombard, Eastern Roman, and papal territories. At the same time Slavs took advantage of Eastern Roman weakness to sweep into the Balkans. Farther west the Franks in Gaul were fighting among themselves, and it would be only a matter of time before northwest Africa and most of Spain would fall to Arabs. So the Roman unity had finally come to an end. The future in this decentralized world may have looked bleak, but new forces in the separate areas would soon be gathering strength.

SELECTED READINGS

• *Items so designated are available in paperback editions.*
Anderson, Hugh, *Jesus,* Englewood Cliffs, N.J., 1967. An excellent collection of readings displaying many different scholarly points of view.
Bonner, Gerald, *St. Augustine of Hippo,* London, 1963. The best biography for beginners.
Brown, Peter, *Augustine of Hippo,* Berkeley, Calif., 1967. An extremely subtle study.
———, *The World of Late Antiquity,* New York, 1971. A survey that approaches the period in its own terms rather than as a prelude to the Middle Ages.
• Bultmann, Rudolf, *Primitive Christianity in Its Contemporary Setting,* New York, 1956. Summarizes the ideas of one of our century's most important biblical scholars.
• Bury, J. B., *The Invasion of Europe by the Barbarians,* London, 1928. A straightforward narrative.
• Chadwick, Henry, *The Early Church,* Baltimore, 1967.
• Cochrane, C. N., *Christianity and Classical Culture,* Oxford, 1940. Difficult but fundamental.
Daniélou, J., and H. I. Marrou, *The Christian Centuries; I: The First Six Hundred Years,* London, 1964. A survey from the Roman Catholic perspective.
Dill, Samuel, *Roman Society in the Last Century of the Western Empire,* London, 1921.

• Dodds, E. R., *Pagan and Christian in an Age of Anxiety,* Cambridge, 1965. A short but brilliant study of what pagans and Christians had in common as well as what made Christianity ultimately successful.

• Enslin, M. S., *The Prophet from Nazareth,* New York, 1961.

• Jones, A. H. M., *The Decline of the Ancient World,* New York, 1966. A survey that emphasizes economic and social factors.

• Katz, Solomon, *The Decline of Rome,* Ithaca, N.Y., 1955. The best brief introduction.

• Knowles, David, *Christian Monasticism,* New York, 1969.

• Latourette, K. S., *A History of Christianity,* New York, 1953.

• L'Orange, H. P., *Art Forms and Civic Life in the Late Roman Empire,* Princeton, N.J., 1965. An imaginative and stimulating essay displaying how developments in art reflected developments in political and social life.

Lot, Ferdinand, *The End of the Ancient World,* New York, 1931. The best detailed treatment of the political history of the period.

• Lyon, Bryce, *The Origins of the Middle Ages,* New York, 1971.

MacMullen, Ramsay, *Constantine,* New York, 1969. A good popular biography.

Markus, R. A., *Christianity in the Roman World,* New York, 1974.

• Mattingly, Harold, *Christianity in the Roman Empire,* New York, 1967.

Momigliano, A., *The Conflict between Paganism and Christianity,* New York, 1963.

Pelikan, J., *The Christian Tradition; I: The Emergence of the Catholic Tradition,* Chicago, 1971. An advanced survey of doctrine.

• Rand, E. K., *Founders of the Middle Ages,* Cambridge, Mass., 1928. A thoroughly engaging account of the early Christian reactions to the classics.

• Riché, Pierre, *Education and Culture in the Barbarian West,* Columbia, S.C., 1976. A magisterial survey of learning in the Christian West from the fall of Rome to about 800.

• White, Lynn T., Jr., *The Transformation of the Roman World,* Berkeley, Calif., 1966. Stimulating essays.

Workman, H. B., *The Evolution of the Monastic Ideal,* London, 1913. Highly interpretative but still one of the best works on the subject.

SOURCE MATERIALS

• St. Augustine, *City of God,* tr. H. Bettenson, Baltimore, 1972.

• ———, *Confessions,* tr. R. S. Pine-Coffin, Baltimore, 1961.

• ———, *The Enchiridion on Faith, Hope and Love,* ed. H. Paolucci, Chicago, 1961.

• ———, *On Christian Doctrine,* tr. D. W. Robertson, Jr., New York, 1958.

• Boethius, *The Consolation of Philosophy,* tr. R. Green, Indianapolis, 1962.

• Cassiodorus, *An Introduction to Divine and Human Readings,* tr. L. W. Jones, New York, 1946.

• *Early Christian Writings: The Apostolic Fathers,* tr. M. Staniforth, Baltimore, 1968.

• Eusebius, *The History of the Church,* tr. G. A. Williamson, Baltimore, 1965.

Procopius, *The Secret History,* tr. G. A. Williamson, Baltimore, 1966.

Part Three

THE MIDDLE AGES

The term "Middle Ages" was coined by Europeans in the seventeenth century to express their view that a long and dismal period of interruption extended between the glorious accomplishments of classical Greece and Rome and their own "modern age." Because the term became so widespread, it is now an ineradicable part of our historical vocabulary; but no serious scholar uses it with the sense of contempt it once had. Between about 600 and 1500—the rough opening and closing dates of the Middle Ages—too many different things happened to be characterized in any single way. In the eastern parts of the old Roman Empire two new civilizations emerged, the Byzantine and the Islamic, which must rank among the most impressive civilizations of all time. Although the Byzantine civilization came to an end in 1453, the Islamic one has continued to exist without major interruption right up to the present. Seen from an Islamic perspective, therefore, the "Middle Ages" was not a middle period at all but a marvelous time of birth and vigorous early youth. The history of western Europe in the Middle Ages is conventionally divided into three parts: the early Middle Ages; the High Middle Ages; and the later Middle Ages. Throughout the early, High, and later Middle Ages the Christian religion played an extraordinarily important role in human life, but otherwise there are few common denominators. The early Middle Ages, from about 600 to about 1050, came closest to appearing like an interval of darkness, for the level of material and intellectual accomplishment was, in fact, very low. Nonetheless, even during the early Middle Ages important foundations were being laid for the future: above all, western Europe was beginning to develop its own distinct sense of cultural identity. The High Middle Ages, from about 1050 to 1300, was one of the most creative epochs in the history of human endeavor. Europeans greatly improved their standard of living, established enduring national states, developed new institutions of learning and modes of thought, and created magnificent works of literature and art. During the later Middle Ages, from about 1300 to 1500, the survival of many high-medieval accomplishments was threatened by numerous disasters, particularly profound economic depression and lethal plague. But people in the later Middle Ages rose above adversity, tenaciously held on to what was most valuable in their inheritance, and, where necessary, created new institutions and thought-patterns to fit their altered circumstances. The Middle Ages thus were really many hundred years of enormous diversity. They may be studied profitably both for their own intrinsic interest and for the fundamental contributions they made to the development of the modern world.

The Middle Ages

POLITICS	PHILOSOPHY AND SCIENCE	
Byzantine Emperor Heraclius, 610–641		**600**
Muhammad enters Mecca in triumph, 630		
Muslims conquer Syria, Persia, and Egypt, 636–651		
Muslims conquer Spain, 711		
Muslim attack on Constantinople repulsed, 717		**700**
Charles Martel defeats Muslims at Poitiers, 732		
Abbasid dynasty in Islam, 750–1258		
Pepin the Short anointed king of the Franks, 751		
Charlemagne, 768–814		
Charlemagne crowned emperor, 800		**800**
Carolingian Empire disintegrates, c. 850–911		
Alfred the Great of England, 871–899		
High point of Viking raids in Europe, c. 880–911	Al-Farabi, d. 950	
Otto the Great of Germany, 936–973	Avicenna, d. 1037	**900**
Foundation of Kievan state in Russia, c. 950	Peter Abelard, 1079–1142	**1000**
Norman Conquest of England, 1066		
Seljuk Turks defeat Byzantines at Manzikert, 1071		
Penance of Henry IV at Canossa, 1077		
Henry I of England, 1100–1135	Origins of universities in the West, c. 1100–c. 1300	**1100**
Louis VI of France, 1108–1137	Translation of Aristotle's works into Latin, c. 1140–c. 1260	
Frederick I (Barbarossa) of Germany, 1152–1190	Peter Lombard's *Sentences,* c. 1155	
Henry II of England, 1154–1189	Robert Grosseteste, c. 1168–1253	
Philip Augustus of France, 1180–1223	Windmill invented, c. 1180	
	Averroës, d. 1198	
Crusaders take Constantinople (Fourth Crusade), 1204	Maimonides, d. 1204	**1200**
Spanish victory over Muslims at Las Navas de Tolosa, 1212		
Frederick II of Germany and Sicily, 1212–1250	Roger Bacon, c. 1214–1294	
	St. Thomas Aquinas, 1225–1274	
Magna Carta, 1215	Height of Scholasticism, c. 1250–c. 1277	
Louis IX (St. Louis) of France, 1226–1270	William of Ockham, c. 1285–1349	
	Mechanical clock invented, c. 1290	
Edward I of England, 1272–1307		
Philip IV (the Fair) of France, 1285–1314	Master Eckhart, active c. 1300–c. 1327	**1300**
Hundred Years' War, 1337–1453	Height of nominalism, c. 1320–c. 1500	
Political chaos in Germany, c. 1350–c. 1450		
Appearance of Joan of Arc, 1429–1431		**1400**
Reassertion of royal power in France, c. 1143–c. 1513	Printing with movable type, c. 1450	
Rise of princes in Germany, c. 1450–c. 1500	Heavy artillery helps Turks capture Constantinople and French end Hundred Years' War, 1453	
Capture of Constantinople by Ottoman Turks, 1453		
Wars of the Roses in England, 1455–1485		
Peace among northern Italian states, 1454–1485		
Marriage of Ferdinand and Isabella, 1469		
Ivan III lays groundwork for Russian Empire, 1462–1505		
Strong Tudor dynasty in England, 1485–1603		

The Middle Ages (continued)

	ECONOMICS	RELIGION	ARTS AND LETTERS
600	Decline of towns and trade in the West, c. 500–c. 700	Muhammad, c. 570–632 Pope Gregory I, 590–604 Muhammad's *Hijrah,* 622	Byzantine church of Santa Sophia, 532–537
700	Height of Islamic commerce and industry, c. 700–c. 1300 Predominantly agrarian economy in the West, c. 700–c. 1050	Split in Islam between Shiites and Sunnites, c. 656 Missionary work of St. Boniface in Germany, c. 715–754 Iconoclasm in Byzantine Empire, 726–843	The Venerable Bede, d. 735 *Beowulf,* c. 750 Irish "Book of Kells," c. 750
800	Height of Byzantine commerce and industry, c. 800–c. 1000	Foundation of Cluny, 910	Carolingian Renaissance, c. 800–c. 850
900		Byzantine conversion of Russia, c. 988	
1000	Destruction of Byzantine free peasantry, c. 1025–c. 1100 Agricultural advance, revival of towns and trade in the West, c. 1050– c. 1300	Beginning of Reform Papacy, 1046 Schism between Roman and Eastern Orthodox Churches, 1054 Pope Gregory VII, 1073–1085 St. Bernard of Clairvaux, 1090–1153 First Crusade, 1095–1099	Romanesque style in architecture and art, c. 1000–c. 1200
1100		Height of Cistercian monasticism, c. 1115–c. 1153 Concordat of Worms ends investiture struggle, 1122 Crusaders lose Jerusalem to Saladin, 1187 Pope Innocent III, 1198–1216	*Song of Roland,* c. 1095 Troubadour poetry, c. 1100–c. 1220 *Rubaiyat* of Umar Khayyam, c. 1120 Anna Comnena's biography of Alexius, 1148 Gothic style in architecture and art, c. 1150–c. 1500 Poetry of Chretien de Troyes, c. 1165–c. 1190
1200		Albigensian Crusade, 1208–1213 Founding of Franciscan Order, 1210 Fourth Lateran Council, 1215 Founding of Dominican Order, 1216 Fall of last Christian outposts in Holy Land, 1291	Development of polyphony in Paris, c. 1170 Wolfram von Eschenbach, c. 1200 Gottfried von Strassburg, c. 1210
1300	European economic depression, c. 1300–c. 1450	Pope Boniface VIII, 1294–1303 Babylonian Captivity of papacy, 1305–1378 John Wyclif, c. 1330–1384	Persian poetry of Sadi, c. 1250 *Romance of the Rose,* c. 1270 Paintings of Giotto, c. 1305–1337 Dante's *Divine Comedy,* c. 1310 Boccaccio's *Decameron,* c. 1350
1400	Floods through western Europe, 1315 Black Death, 1347–1350 Height of Hanseatic League, c. 1350–c. 1450 English Peasants' Revolt, 1381 Medici Bank, 1397–1494	Great Schism of papacy, 1378–1417 John Hus preaches in Bohemia, c. 1408–1415 Council of Constance, 1414–1417 Hussite Revolt, 1420–1434 *Imitation of Christ,* c. 1427 Council of Basel, defeat of conciliarism, 1431–1449	Persian poetry of Hafiz, c. 1370 Chaucer's *Canterbury Tales,* c. 1390 Paintings of Jan van Eyck, c. 1400–c. 1441

Chapter 10

ROME'S THREE HEIRS: THE BYZANTINE, ISLAMIC, AND EARLY-MEDIEVAL WESTERN WORLDS

Constantinople is a bustling city, and merchants come to it from all over, by sea or land, and there is none like it in the world except Baghdad, the great city of Islam. In Constantinople is the church of Santa Sophia, and the seat of the Pope of the Greeks, since the Greeks do not obey the Pope of Rome. There are also as many churches as there are days of the year. A quantity of wealth is brought to them from the islands, and the like of this wealth is not to be found in any other church in the world.

—Benjamin of Tudela, *Travels*

You have become the best community ever raised up for mankind, enjoining the right and forbidding the wrong, and having faith in God.

—The Koran, III, 110

He who ordains the fate of kingdoms and the march of events, the almighty Disposer, having destroyed one extraordinary image, that of the Romans, which had feet of iron, or even feet of clay, then raised up among the Franks the golden head of a second image, just as remarkable, in the person of the glorious Charlemagne.

—A monk of St. Gall

A new period in the history of Western civilizations began in the seventh century, when it became clear that there would no longer be a single empire ruling over all the territories bordering on the Mediterranean. By about 700 A.D., in place of a united Rome, there were three successor civilizations that stood as rivals on different Mediterranean shores: the Byzantine, the Islamic, and the Western Christian. Each of these had its own language and distinctive forms of life. The Byzantine civilization, which descended directly from the Eastern Roman Empire, was Greek-speaking and dedicated to combining Roman governmental traditions with intense pursuit of

The successors of Rome

the Christian faith. The Islamic civilization was based on Arabic and inspired in government as well as culture by the idealism of a dynamic new religion. Western Christian civilization in comparison to the others was a laggard. It was the least economically advanced and faced organizational weaknesses in both government and religion. But it did have some base of unity in Christianity and the Latin language, and would soon begin to find greater political and religious cohesiveness.

Reappraisal of the Byzantine and Islamic civilizations

Because the Western Christian civilization ultimately outstripped its rivals, Western writers until recently have tended to denigrate the Byzantine and Islamic civilizations as backward and even irrational. Of the three, however, the Western Christian was certainly the most backward from about the seventh to the eleventh centuries. For some four or five hundred years the West lived in the shadow of Constantinople and Mecca. Scholars are only now beginning to recognize the full measure of Byzantine and Islamic accomplishments. These greatly merit our attention both for their own sakes and because they influenced western European development in many direct and indirect ways.

1. THE BYZANTINE EMPIRE AND ITS CULTURE

The Byzantine achievement impressive despite weaknesses

Once dismissed by the historian Gibbon as "a tedious and uniform tale of weakness and misery," the story of Byzantine civilization is today recognized as a most interesting and impressive one. It is true that the Byzantine Empire was in many respects not very innovative; it was also continually beset by grave external threats and internal weaknesses. Nonetheless it managed to survive for a millennium. In fact the empire did not just survive, it frequently prospered and greatly influenced the world around it. Among many other achievements, it helped preserve ancient Greek thought, created magnificent works of art, and brought Christian culture to pagan peoples, above all the Slavs. Simply stated it was one of the most enduring and influential empires the world has ever known.

Problems of periodization in Byzantine history

It is impossible to date the beginning of Byzantine history with any precision because the Byzantine Empire was the uninterrupted successor of the Roman state. For this reason different historians prefer different beginnings. Some argue that "Byzantine" characteristics already emerged in Roman history as a result of the easternizing policy of Diocletian, and others that Byzantine history began when Constantine moved his capital from Rome to Constantinople, the city which subsequently became the center of the Byzantine world. (The old name for the site on which Constantinople was built was Byzantium, from which we get the adjective Byzantine; it would be more accurate but cumbersome to say Constantinopolitine.) Diocletian and Constantine, however, continued to rule a united Roman Empire. As we have seen, as late as the sixth century, after the western part of the empire had fallen to the Germans, the Eastern Roman Emperor Justinian thought of himself as an heir to Augustus and fought hard to win back the West. Justinian's reign was clearly an important turning point in the direction of Byzantine civilization because it saw the crystallization of new forms of thought and art that can be considered more "Byzantine" than "Roman." But this still remains a matter of subjective emphasis: some scholars emphasize these newer forms, while others respond that Justinian continued to speak Latin and dreamed of restoring old Rome. Only after 610 did a new dynasty emerge that came from the East, spoke Greek, and maintained a fully Eastern or properly "Byzantine" policy. Hence although good arguments can be made for beginning Byzantine history with Diocletian, Constantine, or Justinian, we will begin here with the accession in 610 of the Emperor Heraclius.

It is also convenient to begin in 610 because from then until 1071 the main lines of Byzantine military and political history were determined by resistance against successive waves of invasions from the East. When Heraclius came to the throne the very existence of the Byzantine Empire was being challenged by the Persians, who had conquered almost all of the empire's Asian territories. As a symbol of their triumph the Persians in 614 even carried off the relic believed to be part of the original cross from Jerusalem. By enormous effort Heraclius rallied Byzantine strength and turned the tide, routing the Persians and retrieving the cross in 627. Persia was then reduced to subordination and Heraclius reigned in glory until 641. But in his last years new armies began to invade Byzantine territory, swarming out of hitherto placid Arabia. Inspired by the new religion of Islam and profiting from Byzantine exhaustion after the struggle with Persia, the Arabs made astonishingly rapid gains. By 650 they had taken most of the Byzantine territories the Persians had occupied briefly in the early seventh century, had conquered all of Persia itself, and were making their way westward across North Africa. Having become a Mediterranean power, the Arabs also took to the sea. In 677 they tried to conquer Constantinople with a fleet. Failing that, they attempted to take the city again in 717 by means of a concerted land and sea operation.

The Arab threat to Constantinople in 717 was a new low in Byzantine fortunes, but the threat was countered by the Emperor Leo the Isaurian (717–741) with as much resolution as Heraclius had met the Persian threat a century before. With the help of a secret incendiary device known as "Greek fire"[1] and great military ability, Leo was able

The reign of Heraclius; the rise of Islam

The Byzantine Emperor Heraclius, Shown Together with His Son. Comparison to coins of Trajan and Theodosius (above, pp. 185, 210) shows at a glance that a new style of civilization has emerged with much less attachment to naturalistic portraiture.

---

[1] This is believed to have been a mixture of sulfur, naphtha, and quicklime. Bronze tubes placed on the prows of ships, and also on the walls of Constantinople, released this liquid fire at the enemy.

Ἡ πυρφόρων. Ἡρῶν δὲ καὶ πλοῖον κατὰ ἐπρωτολῶντι πυρί

φύλαξ πυρπολ... πυρ πολ... τὸν τῶν Ῥωμαίων πλοῖον.

Greek Fire

Byzantine revival prior to the Battle of Manzikert

to defeat the Arab forces on sea and land. Leo's relief of Constantinople in 717 was one of the most significant battles in European history, not just because it allowed the Byzantine Empire to endure for centuries more, but also because it helped to save the West: had the Islamic armies taken Constantinople there would have been little to stop them from sweeping through the rest of Europe. Over the next few decades the Byzantines were able to reconquer most of Asia Minor. This territory, together with Greece, became the heartland of their empire for the next three hundred years. Thereafter the Byzantines achieved a stalemate with Islam until they were able to take the offensive against a decaying Islamic power in the second half of the tenth century. In that period—the greatest in Byzantine history—Byzantine troops reconquered most of Syria. But in the eleventh century a different Islamic people, the Seljuk Turks, cancelled out all the prior Byzantine gains. In 1071 the Seljuks annihilated a Byzantine army at Manzikert in Asia Minor, a stunning victory which allowed them to overrun the remaining Byzantine eastern provinces. Constantinople was now thrown back upon itself more or less as it had been in the days of Heraclius and Leo.

The end of the Byzantine Empire

After Manzikert the Byzantine Empire managed to survive, but never regained its earlier vigor. One major reason for this was the fact that, from 1071 until the final destruction of the empire in 1453, Byzantine fortunes were greatly complicated by the rise of western Europe. Hitherto the West had been far too weak to present any major challenge to Byzantium, but that situation changed entirely in the course of the eleventh century. In 1071, the same year that saw the victory of the Seljuks over the Byzantines in Asia Minor, westerners known as Normans expelled the Byzantines from their last holdings in southern Italy. Despite this clear sign of Western enmity, in 1095 a Byzantine emperor named Alexius Comnenus issued a call for Western help against the Turks. He could hardly have made a worse mistake: his call helped inspire the Crusades, and the Crusades became a major cause for the fall of the Byzantine state. Westerners on the First Crusade did help the Byzantines win back Asia Minor but they also carved out territories for themselves in Syria, which the Byzantines considered to be their own. As time went on frictions mounted and the westerners, now militarily superior, looked more and more upon Constantinople as a fruit ripe for the picking. In 1204 they finally picked it: Crusaders who should have been intent on conquering Jerusalem conquered Constantinople instead and sacked the city with ruthless ferocity. A greatly reduced Byzantine government was able to survive nearby and return to Constantinople in 1261, but thereafter the Byzantine state was an "empire" in name and recollection of past glories only. After 1261 it eked out a reduced existence in parts of Greece until 1453, when powerful Turkish successors to the Seljuks, the Ottomans, completed the Crusaders' work of destruction by conquering the last vestiges of the empire and taking Constantinople. Turks rule in Constantinople—now Istanbul—even today.

That Constantinople was finally taken was no surprise. What *is* a cause for wonder is that the Byzantine state survived for so many centuries in the face of so many different hostile forces. This wonder becomes all the greater when it is recognized that the internal political history of the empire was exceedingly tumultuous. Because Byzantine rulers followed their late-Roman predecessors in claiming the powers of divinely appointed absolute monarchs, there was no way of opposing them ·other than by intrigue and violence. Hence Byzantine history was marked by repeated palace revolts; mutilations, murders, and blindings were almost commonplace. Byzantine politics became so famous for their behind-the-scenes complexity that we still use the word "Byzantine" to refer to highly complex and devious backstage machinations. Fortunately for the empire some very able rulers did emerge from time to time to wield their untrammeled powers with efficiency, and, even more fortunately, a bureaucratic machinery always kept running during times of palace upheaval.

Factors of the stability of the Byzantine Empire: (1) occasional able rulers

Efficient bureaucratic government indeed was one of the major elements of Byzantine success and longevity. The Byzantines could count on having an adequate supply of manpower for their bureaucracy because Byzantine civilization preserved and encouraged the practice of education for the laity. This was one of the major differences between the Byzantine East and the early Latin West: from about 600 to about 1200 there was practically no literate laity in Western Christendom, while lay literacy in the Byzantine East was the basis of governmental accomplishment. Byzantine officialdom regulated many aspects of life, far more than we would think proper

(2) efficient bureaucratic administration

today. Bureaucrats helped supervise education and religion and presided over all forms of economic endeavor. Urban officials in Constantinople, for example, regulated prices and wages, maintained systems of licensing, controlled exports, and enforced the observance of the Sabbath. What is more, they usually did this with comparative efficiency and did not stifle business initiative. Bureaucratic methods too helped regulate the army and navy, the courts, and the diplomatic service, endowing them with organizational strengths incomparable for their age.

(3) firm economic base

Another explanation for Byzantine endurance was the comparatively sound economic base of the state until the eleventh century. As the historian Sir Steven Runciman has said, "if Byzantium owed her strength and security to the efficiency of her Services, it was her trade that enabled her to pay for them." While long-distance trade and urban life all but disappeared in the West for hundreds of years, commerce and cities continued to flourish in the Byzantine East. Above all, in the ninth and tenth centuries Constantinople was a vital trade emporium for Far Eastern luxury goods and Western raw materials. The empire also nurtured and protected its own industries, most notably that of silk-making, and it was renowned until the eleventh century for its stable gold and silver coinage. Among its great urban centers was not only Constantinople, which at times may have had a population of close to a million, but also in certain periods Antioch, and up until the end of Byzantine history the bustling cities of Thessalonica and Trebizond.

The significance of Byzantine agricultural history

Historians emphasize Byzantine trade and industry because these were so advanced for the time and provided most of the surplus wealth which supported the state. But agriculture was really at the heart of the Byzantine economy as it was of all premodern ones. The story of Byzantine agricultural history is mainly one of a struggle of small peasants to stay free of the encroachments of large estates owned by wealthy aristocrats and monasteries. Until the eleventh century the free peasantry just managed to maintain its existence with the help of state legislation, but after 1025 the aristocracy gained power in the government and began to transform the peasants into impoverished tenants. This had many unfortunate results, not the least of which was that the peasants became less interested in resisting the enemy. The defeat at Manzikert was the inevitable result. The destruction of the free peasantry was accompanied and followed in the last centuries of Byzantine history by foreign domination of Byzantine trade. Primarily the Italian cities of Venice and Genoa established trading outposts and privileges within Byzantine realms after 1204, which channeled off much of the wealth on which the state had previously relied. In this way the empire was defeated by the Venetians from within before it was destroyed by the Turks from without.

So far we have spoken about military campaigns, government, and economics as if they were at the center of Byzantine survival. Seen from hindsight they were, but what the Byzantines themselves cared about most was usually religion. Remarkable as it might seem, Byzantines fought over abstruse religious questions as vehemently as we today might argue about politics and sports—indeed more vehemently because the Byzantines were often willing to fight and even die over some words in a religious creed. The intense preoccupation with questions of doctrine is well illustrated by the report of an early Byzantine writer who said that when he asked a baker for the price of bread, the answer came back, "the Father is greater than the Son," and when he asked whether his bath was ready, was told that "the Son proceeds from nothing." Understandably such zealousness could harm the state greatly during times of religious dissension but endow it with a powerful sense of confidence and mission during times of religious concord.

Byzantine religious dissensions were greatly complicated by the fact that the emperors took an active role in them. Because the emperors carried great power in the life of the Church—emperors were sometimes deemed by churchmen to be "similar to God"—they exerted great influence in religious debates. Nonetheless, especially in the face of provincial separatism, rulers could never force all their subjects to believe what they did. Only after the loss of many eastern provinces and the refinement of doctrinal formulae did religious peace seem near in the eighth century. But then it was shattered for still another century by what is known as the Iconoclastic Controversy.

The Iconoclasts were those who wished to prohibit the worship of icons—that is, images of Christ and the saints. Since the Iconoclastic movement was initiated by the Emperor Leo the Isaurian, and subsequently directed with even greater energy by his son Constantine V (740–775), historians have discerned in it different motives. One was certainly theological. The worship of images seemed to the Iconoclasts to smack of paganism. They believed that nothing made by human beings should be worshiped by them, that Christ was so divine that he could not be conceived of in terms of human art, and that the prohibition of worshiping "graven images" in the Ten Commandments (Exodus 20:4) placed the matter beyond dispute.

Iconoclasts' Cross. The Iconoclasts covered over beautiful apse mosaics with unadorned crosses. This example survives in St. Irene's church, Greece.

In addition to these theological points, there were probably other considerations. Since Leo the Isaurian was the emperor who saved Constantinople from the onslaught of Islam, and since Muslims zealously shunned images on the grounds that they were "the work of Satan" (Koran, V. 92), it has been argued that Leo's Inconoclastic policy was an attempt to answer one of Islam's greatest criticisms of Christianity and thereby deprive Islam of some of its appeal. There may also have been certain internal political and financial motives. By proclaiming a radical new religious movement the emperors may have wished to reassert their control over the Church and combat the

Christ as Ruler of the Universe. A twelfth-century Byzantine mosaic from the cathedral of Cefalù in Sicily. Although the Byzantines did not rule in Sicily in the twelfth century, the Norman rulers employed Byzantine workmen. Note the use of Greek—the Byzantine language—on the left-handed Bible page and Latin—the Norman language—on the right.

growing strength of monasteries. In the event, the monasteries did rally behind the cause of images and as a result were bitterly persecuted by Constantine V, who took the opportunity to appropriate much monastic wealth.

The Iconoclastic Controversy was resolved in the ninth century by a return to the status quo, namely the worship of images, but the century of turmoil over the issue had some profound results. One was the destruction by imperial order of a large amount of religious art. Pre–eighth-century Byzantine religious art that survives today comes mostly from places like Italy or Palestine, which were beyond the easy reach of the Iconoclastic emperors. When we see how great this art is we can only lament the destruction of the rest. A second consequence of the controversy was the opening of a serious religious breach between East and West. The pope, who until the eighth century had usually been a close ally of the Byzantines, could not accept Iconoclasm for many reasons. The most important of these was that extreme Iconoclasm tended to question the cult of saints, and the claims of papal primacy were based on an assumed descent from St. Peter. Accordingly, the eighth-century popes combated Byzantine Iconoclasm and turned to the Frankish kings for support. This "about-face of the papacy" was both a major step in the worsening of East–West relations and a landmark in the history of western Europe.

Those were some consequences of Iconoclasm's temporary victory; a major consequence of its defeat was the reassertion of some major traits of Byzantine religiosity, which from the ninth century until the end of Byzantine history remained predominant. One of these was the reemphasis of a faith in traditionalism. Even when Byzantines were experimenting in religious matters they consistently stated that they were only restating or developing the implications of tradition. Now, after centuries of turmoil, they abandoned experiment almost entirely and reaffirmed tradition more than ever. As one opponent of Iconoclasm said: "If an angel or an emperor announces to you a gospel other than the one you have received, close your ears." This view gave strength to Byzantine religion internally by ending controversy and heresy, and helped it gain new adherents in the ninth and tenth centuries. But it also inhibited free speculation not just in religion but also in related intellectual matters.

Allied to this development was the triumph of Byzantine contemplative piety. Supporters defended the use of icons not on the grounds that they were meant to be worshiped for themselves but because they helped lead the mind from the material to the immaterial. The emphasis on contemplation as a road to religious enlightenment thereafter became the hallmark of Byzantine spirituality. While westerners did not by any means reject such a path, the typical Western saint was an activist who saw sin as a vice and sought salvation through good works. Byzantine theologians on the other hand saw sin more as ignorance and believed that salvation was to be found in illumination. This led to a certain religious passivity and mysticism in Eastern Christianity which makes it seem different from Western varieties up to the present time.

Since religion was so dominant in Byzantine life, certain secular aspects of Byzantine civilization often go unnoticed, but there are good reasons why some of these should not be forgotten. One is Byzantine cultivation of the classics. Commitment to Christianity by no means inhibited the Byzantines from revering their ancient Greek inheritance. Byzantine schools based their instruction on classical Greek literature to the degree that educated people could quote Homer more extensively than we today can quote Shakespeare. Byzantine scholars studied and commented on the philosophy of Plato and Aristotle, and Byzantine writers imitated the prose of Thucydides. Such dedicated classicism both enriched Byzantine intellectual and literary life, which is too often dismissed entirely by moderns because it generally lacked originality, and helped preserve the Greek classics for later ages. The bulk of classical Greek literature that we have today survives only because it was copied by Byzantine scribes.

Byzantine classicism was a product of an educational system for the laity which extended to the education of women as well as men. Given attitudes and practices in the contemporary Christian West and Islam, Byzantine commitment to female education was truly unusual. Girls from aristocratic or prosperous families did not go to schools but were relatively well educated at home by private tutors. We are told, for example, of one Byzantine woman who could discourse like Plato or Pythagoras. The most famous Byzantine female intellectual was the Princess Anna Comnena, who described the deeds of her father Alexius in an urbane biography in which she freely cited Homer and the ancient tragedians. In addition to such literary figures there were

Santa Sophia. The greatest monument of Byzantine architecture. The four minarets were added after the fall of the Byzantine Empire, when the Turks turned the church into a mosque. As the diagram shows, the central dome rests on four massive arches.

women doctors in the Byzantine Empire, a fact which may serve to remind us that there have hardly been any in America almost to the present day.

Byzantine achievements in the realms of architecture and art are more familiar. The finest example of Byzantine architecture was the Church of Santa Sophia (Holy Wisdom), built at enormous cost in the sixth century. Although built before the date taken here as the beginning of Byzantine history, it was typically Byzantine in both its style and subsequent influence. Though designed by architects of Hellenic descent, it was vastly different from any Greek temple. Its purpose was not to express human pride in the power of the individual, but to symbolize the inward and spiritual character of the Christian religion. For this reason the architects gave little attention to the external appearance of the building. Nothing but plain brick covered with plaster was used for the exterior walls; there were no marble facings, graceful columns, or sculptured entablatures. The interior, however, was decorated with richly colored mosaics, gold leaf, colored marble columns, and bits of tinted glass set on edge to refract the rays of sunlight after the fashion of sparkling gems. To emphasize a sense of the miraculous, the building was constructed in such a way that no light appeared to come from the outside at all but to be manufactured within.

The structural design of Santa Sophia was something altogether new in the history of architecture. Its central feature was the application of the principle of the dome to a building of square shape. The church was designed, first of all, in the form of a cross, and then over the central square was to be erected a magnificent dome, which would dominate the entire structure. The main problem was how to fit the round circumference of the dome to the square area it was supposed to cover. The solution consisted in having four great arches spring from

Byzantine architecture; the Church of Santa Sophia

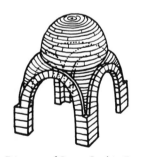

Diagram of Santa Sophia Dome

Novel structural design

pillars at the four corners of the central square. The rim of the dome was then made to rest on the keystones of the arches, with the curved triangular spaces between the arches filled in with masonry. The result was an architectural framework of marvelous strength, which at the same time made possible a style of imposing grandeur and even some delicacy of treatment. The great dome of Santa Sophia has a diameter of 107 feet and rises to a height of nearly 180 feet from the floor. So many windows are placed around its rim that the dome appears to have no support at all but to be suspended in mid-air.

As in architecture, so in art the Byzantines profoundly altered the earlier Greek classical style. Byzantines excelled in ivory-carving, manuscript illumination, jewelry-making, and, above all, the creation of mosaics—that is, designs of pictures produced by fitting together small pieces of colored glass or stone. Human figures in these mosaics were usually distorted and elongated in a very unclassical fashion to create the impression of intense piety or extreme majesty. Most Byzantine art is marked by highly abstract, formal, and jewel-like qualities. For this reason many consider Byzantine artistic culture to be a model of timeless perfection. The modern poet W. B. Yeats expressed this point of view most eloquently when he wrote in his "Sailing to Byzantium" of artificial birds made by Byzantine goldsmiths ". . . to sing / To lords and ladies of Byzantium / Of what is past, or passing, or to come."

See color plates facing page 225

Probably the single greatest testimony to the vitality of Byzantine civilization at its height was the conversion of many Slavic peoples, especially those of Russia. According to the legend, which has a basic kernel of fact, a Russian ruler named Vladimir decided around 988 to abandon the paganism of his ancestors. Accordingly, he sent emissaries to report on the religious practices of Islam, Roman Catholicism, and Byzantine Christianity. When they returned to tell him that only among the Byzantines did God seem to "dwell among men," he promptly agreed to be baptized by a Byzantine missionary. The event was momentous because Russia thereupon became a cultural province of Byzantium. From then until the twentieth century Russia remained a bastion of the Eastern Orthodox religion.

After Constantinople fell in 1453 Russians began to feel that they were chosen to carry on both the faith and the imperial mission of the fallen Byzantine Empire. Thus their ruler took the title of tsar—which simply means caesar—and Russians asserted that Moscow was "the third Rome": "Two Romes have fallen," said a Russian spokesman, "the third is still standing, and a fourth there shall not be." Such ideology helps explain in part the later growth of Russian imperialism. Byzantine traditions also may help explain the dominance of the ruler in the Russian state. Without question Byzantine stylistic principles influenced Russian religious art, and Byzantine ideas influenced the thought of modern Russia's greatest writers, Dostoevsky and Tolstoy.

Byzantine Metalwork. **This dish,** from about 620, represents literally David and Goliath, and figuratively the New Dispensation (David was the ancestor of Christ) overcoming the Old. The New, Christian, Dispensation is also symbolized by the sun, and the Old by a crescent moon.

Russian Icon. This early–seventeenth-century Russian painting depicts an angel in a distinctly Byzantine style.

Unfortunately, just at the time when relations between Constantinople and Russia were solidifying, relations with the West were deteriorating to a point of no return. After the skirmishes of the Iconoclastic period relations between Eastern and Western Christians remained tense, partly because Constantinople resented Western claims (initiated by Charlemagne in 800) of creating a rival empire, but most of all because cultural and religious differences between the two were growing. From the Byzantine point of view westerners were uncouth and ignorant, while to western European eyes Byzantines were effeminate and prone to heresy. Once the West started to revive, it began to take the offensive against a weakened East in theory and practice. In 1054 extreme papal claims of primacy over the Eastern Church provoked a religious schism which since then has never been healed. Thereafter the Crusades drove home the dividing wedge.

After the sack of Constantinople in 1204 Byzantine hatred of westerners became understandably intense. "Between us and them," one Byzantine wrote, "there is now a deep chasm: we do not have a single thought in common." Westerners called easterners "the dregs of the dregs . . . unworthy of the sun's light," while easterners called westerners the children of darkness, alluding to the fact that the sun sets in the West. The beneficiaries of this hatred were the Turks, who not only conquered Constantinople in 1453, but soon after conquered most of southeastern Europe up to Vienna.

St. Mark's Church, Venice. The most splendid example of Byzantine architecture in Italy.

The Interior of St. Mark's, Venice

In view of this sad history of hostility it is best to end our treatment of Byzantine civilization by recalling how much we owe to it. In simple physical terms the Byzantine Empire acted as a bulwark against Islam from the seventh to the eleventh centuries, thus helping to preserve an independent West. If the Byzantines had not prospered and defended Europe, Western Christian civilization might well have been snuffed out. Then too we owe an enormous amount in cultural terms to Byzantine scholars who helped preserve classical Greek learning. The most famous moment of communication between Byzantine and western European scholars came during the Italian Renaissance, when Byzantines helped introduce Italian humanists to the works of Plato. But westerners were already learning from Byzantines before then, and they continued to gain riches from Byzantine manuscripts until the sixteenth century. Similarly, Byzantine art exerted a great influence on the art of western Europe over a long period of time. To take only some of the most famous examples, St. Mark's basilica in Venice was built in close imitation of the Byzantine style, and the art of such great Western painters as Giotto and El Greco owes much in different ways to Byzantine influences. Nor should we stop at listing influences because the great surviving monuments of Byzantine culture retain their imposing appeal in and of themselves. Travelers who view Byzantine mosaics in such cities as Ravenna and Palermo are continually awe-struck; others who make their way to Istanbul still find Santa Sophia to be a marvel. In such jeweled beauty, then, the light from the Byzantine East, which once glowed so brightly, continues to shimmer.

The Byzantine contribution to Western civilization

2. THE FLOWERING OF ISLAM

In contrast to Byzantine history, which has no clearly datable beginning but a definite end in 1453, the history of Islamic civilization has a clear point of origin, beginning with the career of Muhammad in the seventh century, but no end since Islam, Muhammad's religion, is still a major force in the modern world. Believers in Islam, known as Muslims, currently comprise about one-seventh of the global population: in their greatest concentrations they extend from Africa through the Middle East and the Soviet Union to India, Bangladesh, and Indonesia. All these Muslims subscribe both to a common religion and a common way of life, for Islam has always demanded from its followers not just adherence to certain forms of worship but also adherence to set social and cultural norms. Indeed, more than Judaism or Christianity, Islam has been a great experiment in trying to build a worldwide society based on the fullest harmony between religious requirements and precepts for everyday existence. In practice, of course, that experiment has differed in its success and quality according to time and place, but it is still being tested, and it accounts for the fact that there remains an extraordinary sense of community between all Muslims regardless of race, language, and geographical distribution. In this section we will trace the early history of the Islamic experiment with primary emphasis on its orientation toward the West. But it must always be remembered that Islam expanded in many directions and that it ultimately had as much influence on the history of Africa and India as it did on that of Europe or western Asia.

Although Islam spread to many lands it was born in Arabia, so the story of its history must begin there. Arabia, a peninsula of deserts, had been so backward before the founding of Islam that the two dominant neighboring empires, the Roman and the Persian, had not deemed it worthwhile to extend their rule over Arabian territories. Most Arabs were Bedouins, wandering camel herdsmen who lived off the milk of their animals and the produce, such as dates, that was grown in desert oases. In the second half of the sixth century there was a quickening of economic life owing to a shift in long-distance trade routes. The protracted wars between the Byzantine and Persian Empires made Arabia a safer transit route for caravans going between Africa and Asia than were other areas, and some towns grew to direct and take advantage of this growth of trade. Most prominent of these was Mecca, which not only lay on the junction of major trade routes, but also had long been a local religious center. In Mecca was located the Kabah, a pilgrimage shrine which served as a central place of worship for many different Arabian clans and tribes. (Within the Kabah was the Black Stone, a meteorite worshiped as a miraculous relic by adherents of many different divinities.) The men who controlled this shrine and also directed the economic life of the Meccan area belonged to the tribe of Quraish, an aristocracy of traders and entrepreneurs who provided the area with whatever little government it knew.

Muhammad, the founder of Islam, was born in Mecca to a family of the Quraish about 570. Orphaned early in life, he entered the service of a rich widow whom he later married, thereby attaining financial security. Until middle age he lived as a prosperous trader, behaving little differently from his fellow townsmen, but around 610 he underwent a religious experience which changed the course of his life and ultimately that of a good part of the world. Although most Arabs until then had been polytheists who recognized at most the vague superiority of a more powerful god they called Allah, Muhammad in 610 believed he heard a voice from heaven tell him that there was no god but Allah alone. In other words, as the result of a conversion experience he became an uncompromising monotheist. Thereafter he received further messages which served as the basis for a new religion and which commanded him to accept the calling of "Prophet" to proclaim the monotheistic faith to the Quraish. At first he was not very successful in gaining converts beyond a limited circle, perhaps because the leading Quraish tribesmen believed that establishment of a new religion would deprive the Kabah, and therewith Mecca, of its central place in local worship. The town of Yathrib to the north, however, had no such concerns, and its representatives invited Muhammad to emigrate there so that he could serve as a neutral arbiter of local rivalries. In 622 Muhammad and his followers accepted the invitation. Because their migration—called in Arabic the *Hijrah* (or Hegira)—saw the beginning of an advance in Muhammad's fortunes, it is considered by Muslims to mark the beginning of their era: as Christians begin their era with the birth of Christ so Muslims begin their dating system with the *Hijrah* of 622.

Muhammad changed the name of Yathrib to Medina (the "city of the Prophet") and quickly succeeded in establishing himself as ruler of the town. In the course of doing this he consciously began to organize his converts into a political as well as religious community. But he still needed to find some means of support for his original Meccan fol-

The consolidation of Muhammad's religion

The Kabah. It contains the black stone which was supposed to have been miraculously sent down from heaven, and rests in the courtyard of the great mosque in Mecca.

lowers, and he also desired to wreak vengeance on the Quraish for not heeding his calls for conversion. Accordingly, he started leading his followers in raids on Quraish caravans traveling beyond Mecca. The Quraish endeavored to defend themselves, but after a few years Muhammad's band, fired by religious enthusiasm, succeeded in defeating them. In 630, after several desert battles, Muhammad entered Mecca in triumph. The Quraish thereupon submitted to the new faith and the Kabah was not only preserved but made the main shrine of Islam, as it remains today. With the taking of Mecca other tribes throughout Arabia in turn accepted the new faith. Thus, although Muhammad died in 632, he lived long enough to see the religion he had founded become a success.

The doctrines of Islam

The doctrines of Islam are very simple. The word *islam* itself means submission, and the faith of Islam called for absolute submission to God. Although the Arabic name for the one God is Allah, it is mistaken to believe that Muslims worship a god like Zeus or Jupiter who is merely the first among many: Allah for Muslims means the Creator God Almighty—the same omnipotent deity worshiped by Christians and Jews. Instead of saying, then, that Muslims believe "there is no god but Allah," it is more correct to say they believe that "there is no divinity but God." In keeping with this, Muslims believe that Muhammad himself was God's last and greatest prophet, but not that he was God himself. In addition to strict monotheism Muhammad taught above all that men and women must surrender themselves entirely to God because divine judgment was imminent. Mortals must make a fundamental choice about whether to begin a new life of divine service: if they decide in favor of this, God will guide them to blessedness, but if they do not, God will turn away from them and they will become irredeemably wicked. On judgment day the pious will be granted eternal life in a fleshly paradise of delights, but the damned will be sent to a realm of eternal fire and torture. The practical steps the believer can take are found in the Koran, the compilation of the revelations purportedly sent by God to Muhammad, and hence the definitive Islamic scripture. These steps include thorough dedication to moral rectitude and compassion, and fidelity to set religious observances: i.e., a regimen of prayers and fasts, pilgrimage to Mecca, and frequent recitation of parts of the Koran.

Judeo-Christian influence on Islam

The fact that much in the religion of Islam resembles Judaism and Christianity is not just coincidental; Muhammad was definitely influenced by the two earlier religions. (There were many Jews in Mecca and Medina; Christian thought was also known to Muhammad, although more indirectly.) Islam most resembles the two earlier religions in its strict monotheism, its stress on personal morality and compassion, and its reliance on written, revealed scripture. Muhammad proclaimed the Koran as the ultimate source of religious authority but accepted both the Old and New Testaments as divinely inspired. From Christianity Muhammad seems to have derived his doctrines of

The Archangel Gabriel Brings Revelation to Muhammad. A much later Persian conception.

the last judgment, the resurrection of the body with subsequent rewards and punishments, and his belief in angels (he thought that God's first message to him had been sent by the angel Gabriel). But although Muhammad accepted Jesus Christ as one of the greatest of a long line of prophets, he did not believe in Christ's divinity and himself laid claim to no miracles other than the writing of the Koran. He also ignored the Christian doctrine of sacrificial love, and most important, preached a religion without sacraments or priests. For Muslims every believer has direct responsibility for living the life of the faith without intermediaries; instead of priests there are only religious scholars who may comment on problems of Islamic faith and law. Muslims are expected to pray together in mosques, but there is nothing like a Muslim mass. The absence of clergy makes Islam more like Judaism, a similarity which is enhanced by Islamic stress on the inextricable connection between the religious and sociopolitical life of the divinely inspired community. But, unlike Judaism, Islam laid claim to universalism and a unique role in uniting the world as it started to spread far beyond the confines of Arabia.

This move toward world influence began immediately upon Muhammad's death. Since he had made no provision for the future, and since the Arabs had no clear concept of political succession, it was unclear whether Muhammad's community would survive at all. But his closest followers, led by his father-in-law Abu-Bakr and a zealous early convert named Umar, quickly took the initiative by naming Abu-Bakr *caliph* meaning "deputy of the Prophet." Thereafter, for about three hundred years, the caliph was to serve as the supreme religious and political leader of all Muslims. Immediately after becoming caliph Abu-Bakr began a military campaign to subdue various Arabian tribes which had followed Muhammad but were not willing to accept his

The unification of Arabia after Muhammad: the caliphs

Two Views of the Dome of the Rock, Jerusalem. According to Muslim tradition, Muhammad made a miraculous journey to Jerusalem before his death and left a footprint in a rock. The mosque which was erected over the site in the seventh century is, after the Kabah, Islam's second-holiest shrine.

successor's authority. In the course of this thoroughly successful military action Abu-Bakr's forces began to spill northward over the borders of Arabia. Probably to their surprise they found that they met minimal resistance from Byzantine and Persian forces.

Arab expansion and conquests

Abu-Bakr died two years after his accession but was succeeded as caliph by Umar, who continued to direct the Arabian invasions of the neighboring empires. In the following years triumph was virtually uninterrupted. In 636 the Arabs routed a Byzantine army in Syria and then quickly swept over the entire area, occupying the leading cities of Antioch, Damascus, and Jerusalem; in 637 they destroyed the main army of the Persians and marched into the Persian capital of Ctesiphon. Once the Persian administrative center was taken, the Persian Empire offered scarcely any more resistance: by 651 the Arabian conquest of the entire Persian realm was complete. Since Byzantium was centered around distant Constantinople, the Arabs were not similarly able to stop its imperial heart from beating. But they did quickly manage to deprive the Byzantine Empire of Egypt by 646 and then swept west across North Africa. In 711 they crossed from there into Spain and quickly took almost all of that area too. Thus within less than a century Islam had conquered all of ancient Persia and much of the old Roman world.

How can we explain this prodigious expansion? The best approach is to see first what impelled the conquerors and then to see what circumstances helped to ease their way. Contrary to widespread belief the early spread of Islam was not achieved through a religious crusade. At first the Arabs were not at all interested in converting other peoples: to the contrary, they hoped that conquered populations would not convert so that they could maintain their own identity as a community of rulers and tax-gatherers. But although their motives for expansion were not religious, religious enthusiasm played a crucial role in making the hitherto unruly Arabs take orders from the caliph and in instilling a sense that they were carrying out the will of God. What really moved the Arabs out of the desert was the search for richer territory and booty, and what kept them moving ever farther was the ease of acquiring new wealth as they progressed. Fortunately for the Arabs their inspiration by Islam came just at the right time in terms of the weakness of their enemies. The Byzantines and Persians had become so exhausted by their long wars that they could hardly rally for a new effort. Moreover, Persian and Byzantine local populations were hostile to the financial demands made by their bureaucratic empires; also, in the Byzantine lands of Syria and Egypt "heretical" Christians were at odds with the persecuting orthodoxy of Constantinople. Because the Arabs did not demand conversion and exacted fewer taxes than the Byzantines and Persians, they were often welcomed as preferable to the old rulers. One Christian writer in Syria went so far as to say "the God of vengeance delivered us out of the hands of the Romans [i.e., the Byzantine Empire] by means of the Arabs." For all these reasons Islam quickly spread over the vast extent of territory between Egypt and Iran, and has been rooted there ever since.

While the Arabs were extending their conquests they ran into their first serious political divisions. In 644 the Caliph Umar died; he was replaced by one Uthman, a weak ruler who had the added drawback for many of belonging to the Umayyad family, a wealthy clan from Mecca which had not at first accepted Muhammad's call. Those dissatisfied with Uthman rallied around the Prophet's cousin and son-in-law Ali, whose blood, background, and warrior spirit made him seem a more appropriate leader of the cause. When Uthman was murdered in 656 by mutineers, Ali's partisans raised him up as caliph. But Uthman's powerful family and supporters were unwilling to accept Ali. In subsequent disturbances Ali was murdered and Uthman's party emerged triumphant. In 661 a member of the Umayyad family took over as caliph and that house ruled Islam until 750. Even then, however, Ali's followers did not accept defeat. As time went on they hardened into a minority religious party known as Shiites; this group insisted that only descendants of Ali could be caliphs or have any authority over the Muslim community. Those who stood instead for the actual historical development of the caliphate and became committed to its customs were called Sunnites. The cleft between the two parties has been a lasting one in Islamic history. Often persecuted, Shiites developed great militancy and a deep sense of being the only true

Reasons for the spread of Islam

Division between Shiites and Sunnites

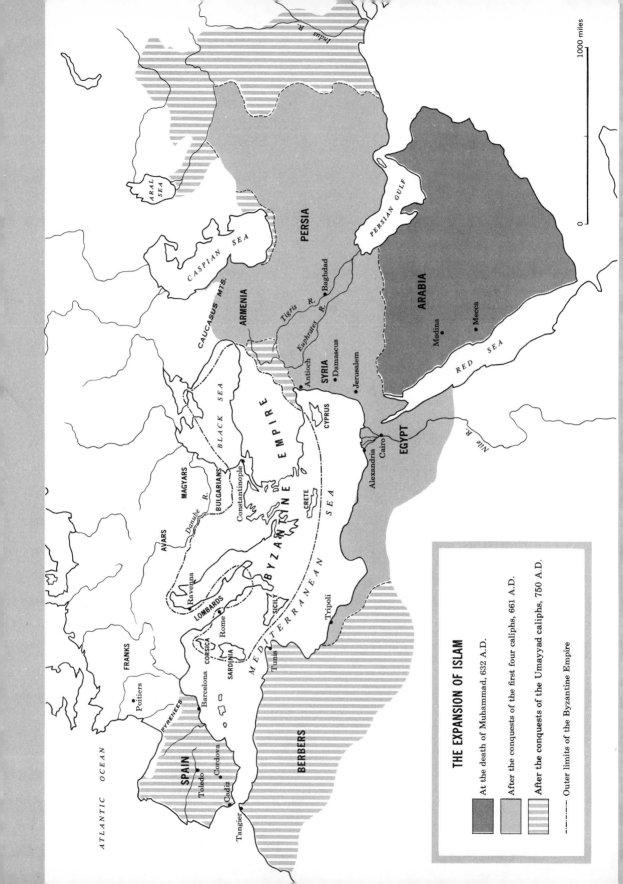

THE EXPANSION OF ISLAM

At the death of Muhammad, 632 A.D.

After the conquests of the first four caliphs, 661 A.D.

After the conquests of the Umayyad caliphs, 750 A.D.

Outer limits of the Byzantine Empire

1000 miles

ATLANTIC OCEAN

FRANKS

Poitiers

SPAIN
Toledo
Cordova
Cadiz
Tangier

PYRENEES
Barcelona

CORSICA
SARDINIA

BERBERS

Tunis

Rome
Ravenna
LOMBARDS
SICILY

MEDITERRANEAN SEA

CRETE

Tripoli

AVARS
MAGYARS
BULGARIANS

Danube R.

Constantinople

BYZANTINE EMPIRE

BLACK SEA

CYPRUS

Antioch
SYRIA
Damascus
Jerusalem

Alexandria
Cairo

EGYPT

Nile R.

RED SEA

Medina
Mecca

ARABIA

PERSIAN GULF

CASPIAN SEA

ARMENIA
CAUCASUS MTS.

Baghdad
Tigris R.
Euphrates R.

PERSIA

ARAL SEA

Indus R.

preservers of the faith. From time to time they were able to seize power in one or another area, but they never succeeded in converting the majority of Muslims. Today they rule in Iran and are very numerous in Iraq but comprise only about one-tenth of the worldwide population of Islam.

The triumph of the Umayyads in 661 began a more settled period in the history of the caliphate, lasting until 945. During that time there were two major governing orientations: that represented by the rule of the Umayyads, and that represented by their successors, the Abbasids. The Umayyads centered their strength in the old Byzantine territories in Syria and continued to use local officials who were not Muslims for their administration. For these reasons the Umayyad caliphate appears to some extent like a Byzantine successor state. With their more Western orientation the Umayyads concentrated their energies on dominating the Mediterranean and conquering Constantinople. When their most massive attack on the Byzantine capital failed in 717, Umayyad strength was seriously weakened; it was only a matter of time before a new orientation would develop.

The Umayyads

This was represented by the takeover of a new family, the Abbasids, in 750. Their rule may be said to have stressed Persian more than Byzantine elements. Characteristic of this change was a shift in capitals, for the second Abbasid caliph built his new capital of Baghdad in Iraq near the ruins of the old Persian capital and even appropriated stones from the ruins. The Abbasids developed their own Muslim administration and imitated Persian absolutism. Abbasid caliphs ruthlessly cut down their enemies, surrounded themselves with elaborate court ceremonies, and lavishly patronized sophisticated literature. This is the world described in the *Arabian Nights,* a collection of stories of dazzling Oriental splendor written in Baghdad under the Abbasids. The dominating presence in those stories, Harun al-Rashid, actually reigned as caliph from 786 to 809 and behaved as extravagantly as he was described, tossing coins in the streets, passing out sumptuous gifts to his favorites and severe punishments to his enemies. From a Western point of view the Abbasid caliphate was of significance not just in creating legends and literature but also because its Eastern orientation took much pressure off the Mediterranean. The Byzantine state, accordingly, was able to revive, and the Franks in the far West began to develop some strength of their own. (The greatest Frankish ruler, Charlemagne, maintained diplomatic relations with the caliphate of Harun al-Rashid, who patronizingly sent the much poorer westerner a gift of an elephant.)

The Abbasids

When Abbasid power began to decline in the tenth century there followed an extended period of decentralization. The major cause for growing Abbasid weakness was the gradual impoverishment of their primary economic base, the agricultural wealth of the Tigris-Euphrates basin. Their decline was further accelerated by the later Abbasids' practice of surrounding themselves with Turkish soldiers, who

Islamic political history after the fall of the Abbasid Empire

soon realized that they could take over actual power in the state. In 945 the Abbasid Empire fell apart when a Shiite tribe seized Baghdad. Thereafter the Abbasids became powerless figureheads until their caliphate was completely destroyed with the destruction of Baghdad by the Mongols in 1258. From 945 until the sixteenth century Islamic political life was marked by localism, with different petty rulers, most often Turkish, taking command in different areas. It used to be thought that this decentralization also meant decay, but in fact Islamic civilization greatly prospered in the "middle period," above all from about 900 to about 1250, a time also when Islamic rule expanded into modern-day Turkey and India. Later, new Islamic empires developed, the leading one in the West being that of the Ottoman Turks, who controlled much of eastern Europe and the Near East from the fifteenth century until 1918. It is therefore entirely false to believe that Islamic history descended upon an ever-downward course sometime shortly after the reign of Harun al-Rashid.

The character of Islamic culture and society

For those who approach Islamic civilization with modern preconceptions, the greatest surprise is to realize that from the time of Muhammad until at least about 1500 Islamic culture and society was extraordinarily cosmopolitan and dynamic. Muhammad himself was not a desert Arab but a town-dweller and trader imbued with advanced ideals. Subsequently, Muslim culture became highly cosmopolitan for several reasons: it inherited the sophistication of Byzantium and Persia; it remained centered at the crossroads of long-distance trade between the Far East and West; and the prosperous town life in most Muslim territories counterbalanced agriculture. Because of the importance of trade there was much geographical mobility. Muhammad's teachings furthermore encouraged social mobility because the Koran stressed the equality of all Muslims. The result was that at the court of Baghdad, and later at those of the decentralized Muslim states, careers were open to those with talent. Since literacy was remarkably widespread—a rough estimate for around the year 1000 is 20 percent of all Muslim males—many could rise through education. Offices were seldom regarded as being hereditary and "new men" could arrive at the top by enterprise and skill. Muslims were also remarkably tolerant of other religions. As stated above, they rarely sought forced conversions, and they generally allowed a place within their own states for Jews and Christians, whom they accepted as "people of the book" because the Bible was seen as a precursor of the Koran. In keeping with this attitude of toleration an early caliph employed a Christian as his chief secretary, the Umayyads patronized a Christian who wrote poetry in Arabic, and Muslim Spain saw the greatest flowering of Jewish culture between ancient and modern times. The greatest fruit of this Jewish flowering was the work of Moses Maimonides (1135–1204), a profound religious thinker, sometimes called "the second Moses," who wrote both in Hebrew and Arabic.

There was one major exception to this rule of Muslim equalitarianism and tolerance: the treatment of women. Perhaps because social status was so fluid, successful men were extremely anxious to preserve and enhance their positions and their "honor." They could accomplish this by maintaining and/or expanding their worldly possessions, which category included women. For a man's females to be most "valuable" to his status, their inviolability had to be assured. The Koran allowed a man to marry four wives, so women were at a premium, and married ones were segregated from other males. A prominent man would also have a number of female servants and concubines, and he kept all these women in a part of his residence called the harem, where they were guarded by eunuchs, i.e., castrated men. Within these enclaves women vied with each other for preeminence and engaged in intrigues to advance the fortunes of their children. Although large harems could be kept only by the wealthy, the system was imitated as far as possible by all classes. Based on the principle that women were chattel, these practices did much to debase women and to emphasize attitudes of domination in sexual life. Male homosexual relations were tolerated in upper-class society, yet they too were based on patterns of domination, usually that of a powerful adult over an adolescent.

There were two major Islamic avenues for devotion to the particularly religious life. One was that of the *ulama,* learned men who came closest to being like priests. Their job was to study and offer advice on all aspects of religion and religious law. Not surprisingly they usually stood for tradition and rigorous maintenance of the faith; most often they exerted great influence on the conduct of public life. But complementary to them were the *sufis,* religious mystics who might be equated with Christian monks were it not for the fact that they were not committed to celibacy and seldom withdrew from the life of the community. Sufis stressed contemplation and ecstasy as the ulama stressed religious law: they had no common program and in practice behaved very differently. Some sufis were "whirling dervishes," so known in the West because of their dances; others were *faqirs,* associated in the West with snake-charming in marketplaces; and others were quiet meditative men who practiced no exotic rites. Sufis were usually organized into "brotherhoods," which did much to convert outlying areas such as Africa and India. Throughout the Islamic world sufism provided a channel for the most intense religious impulses. The ability of the ulama and sufis to coexist is in itself a remarkable index of Islamic cultural pluralism.

More remarkable still is the fact that these two groups often coexisted with representatives of yet another worldview, students and practitioners of philosophy and science. Islamic philosophers were actually called *faylasufs* in Arabic because they were dedicated to the cultivation of what the Greeks had called *philosophia.* Islamic philosophy was based on the study of earlier Greek thought, above all the Aristotelian and Neoplatonic strains. Around the time when the philosophical schools were closed in Athens by order of the Emperor Justinian, Greek philosophers migrated east, and the works of Aristotle and others were translated into Syriac, a Semitic dialect. From that point of transmission Greek philosophy gradually entered the life of Islam and became cultivated by the class of faylasufs, who believed that the universe is rational and that a philosophical approach to life was the highest god-given calling. The faylasufs' profound knowledge of Aristotle can be seen, for example, in the fact that Avicenna (d. 1037), one of the greatest of them, read practically all of Aristotle's works in the Far Eastern town of Bukhara before he reached the age of eighteen.

The problem of reconciling Greek ideas with Islamic religion

The most serious problem faced by the faylasufs was that of reconciling Greek philosophy with Islamic religion because they followed their Greek sources in believing—in opposition to Islamic doctrine—that the world is eternal and that there is no immortality for the individual soul. Different faylasufs reacted to this problem in different ways. Of the three greatest, Al-Farabi (d. 950), who lived mainly in Baghdad, was least concerned by it; he taught that an enlightened elite could philosophize without being distracted by the binding common beliefs of the masses. Even so, he never attacked these beliefs, considering them necessary to hold society together.

Avicenna and Averroës

Unlike Al-Farabi, Avicenna, who was active farther east, taught a less rationalistic philosophy that came close in many points to sufi mysticism. (A later story held that Avicenna said of a sufi "all I know, he sees," while the sufi replied "all I see, he knows.") Finally, Averroës (1126–98) of Cordova, in Spain, was a thoroughgoing Aristotelian who led two lives, one in private as an extreme rationalist and the other in public as a believer in the official faith, indeed even as an official censor. Averroës was the last really important Islamic philosopher: after him rationalism either blended into sufism, the direction pointed to by Avicenna, or became too constrained by religious orthodoxy to lead an independent existence. But in its heyday between about 850 and 1200 Islamic philosophy was far more advanced and sophisticated than anything found in either the Byzantine or Western Christian realms.

Islamic science; the practice of astrology

Before their decline Islamic faylasufs were as distinguished in studying natural science as they were in philosophical speculation. Usually the same men were both philosophers and scientists because they could not make a living by commenting on Aristotle (there were no universities in which to teach) but could rise to positions of wealth and power by practicing astrology and medicine. Astrology sounds to us today less like science than superstition, but among the Muslims it was an "applied science" intimately related to accurate astronomical observation: after an Islamic astrologer carefully studied and foretold the courses of the heavenly bodies, he would endeavor to apply his knowledge to the course of human events, particularly the fortunes of

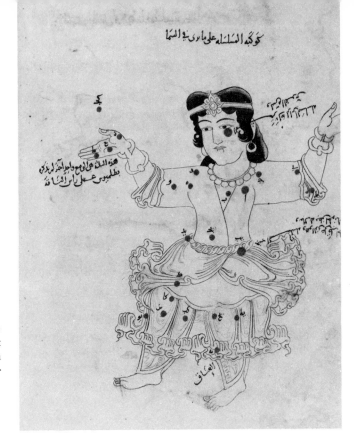

The Planetary Constellation of Andromeda as Visualized by the Muslims. This manuscript illumination executed in western Iran in 1009 A.D. shows clearly how Muslim culture reconceived Greek learning.

wealthy patrons. In order to account most simply for heavenly motions, some Muslims considered the possibilities that the earth rotates on its axis and revolves around the sun, but these theories were not accepted because they did not fit in with ancient preconceptions such as the assumption of circular planetary orbits. It was therefore not in these suggestions that Muslim astrologers later influenced the West, but rather in their extremely advanced observations and predictive tables that often went beyond the most careful work of the Greeks.

Islamic accomplishments in medicine were equally remarkable. Faylasufs serving as physicians appropriated the knowledge contained in the medical writings of the Hellenistic Age but were rarely content with that. Avicenna discovered the contagious nature of tuberculosis, described pleurisy and several varieties of nervous ailments, and pointed out that disease can be spread through contamination of water and soil. His chief medical writing, the *Canon,* was accepted in Europe as authoritative until late in the seventeenth century. Avicenna's older contemporary, Rhazes (865–925), was the greatest clinical physician of the medieval world. His major achievement was the discovery of the difference between measles and smallpox. Other Islamic physicians discovered the value of cauterization and of styptic agents, diagnosed cancer of the stomach, prescribed antidotes for cases of poisoning, and made notable progress in treating diseases of the eyes. In addition,

Islamic contributions to medicine

they recognized the infectious character of bubonic plague, pointing out that it could be transmitted by clothes. Finally, the Muslims excelled all other medieval peoples in the organization of hospitals and in the control of medical practice. There were at least thirty-four great hospitals located in the principal cities of Persia, Syria, and Egypt, which appear to have been organized in a strikingly modern fashion. Each had wards for particular cases, a dispensary, and a library. The chief physicians and surgeons lectured to the students and graduates, examined them, and issued licenses to practice. Even the owners of leeches, who in most cases were also barbers, had to submit them for inspection at regular intervals.

Optics, chemistry, and mathematics

Other great Islamic scientific achievements were in optics, chemistry, and mathematics. Islamic physicists founded the science of optics and drew a number of significant conclusions regarding the theory of magnifying lenses and the velocity, transmission, and refraction of light. Islamic chemistry was an outgrowth of alchemy, an invention of the Hellenistic Greeks, the system of belief that was based upon the principle that all metals were the same in essence, and that baser metals could therefore be transmuted into gold if only the right instrument, the philosopher's stone, could be found. But the efforts of scientists in this field were by no means confined to this fruitless quest; some even denied the whole theory of transmutation of metals. As a result of experiments by Muslim scientists, various new substances and compounds were discovered, among them carbonate of soda, alum, borax, nitrate of silver, saltpeter, and nitric and sulphuric acids. In addition, Islamic scientists were the first to describe the chemical processes of distillation, filtration, and sublimation. In mathematics Islam's greatest accomplishment was to unite the geometry of the Greeks with the number science of the Hindus. Borrowing what westerners know as "Arabic numerals," including the zero, from the Hindus, Islamic mathematicians were able to develop an arithmetic based on the decimal system and also make advances in algebra (itself an Arabic word). Building upon Greek geometry with reference to heavenly motions, they made great progress in spherical trigonometry. Thus they brought together and advanced all the areas of mathematical knowledge which would later be further developed in the Christian West.

In addition to its philosophers and scientists Islam had its poets too. The primitive Arabs themselves had excelled in writing poetry, and literary accomplishment became recognized as a way to distinguish oneself at court. Probably the greatest of Islamic poets were the Persians (who wrote in their own language), the best known of whom in the West is Umar Khayyam (d. 1123) because his *Rubaiyat* was turned into a popular English poem by the Victorian Edward Fitzgerald. Although Fitzgerald's translation distorts much, Umar's hedonism ("a jug of wine, a loaf of bread—and thou") shows us that all Muslims were by no means dour puritans. Actually Umar's poetry was excelled by the works of Sadi (1193–1292) and Hafiz (d. 1389). And far

The Great Mosque, Qayrawan, Tunisia. This ninth-century minaret, from which the criers call the faithful to prayer, is a leading monument of the North African Islamic architectural style.

The Court of the Lions in the Alhambra, Granada, Spain. The palace-fortress of the Alhambra is one of the finest monuments of the Islamic architectural style. Notable are the graceful columns, the horseshoe arches, and the delicate tracery in stone that surmounts the arches.

from Persia lush poetry was cultivated as well in the courts of Muslim Spain. This poetry too was by no means inhibited, as can be seen from lines like "such was my kissing, such my sucking of his mouth / that he was almost made toothless."

In their artistic endeavors Muslims were highly eclectic. Their main source of inspiration came from the art of Byzantium and Persia. The former contributed many of the structural features of Islamic architecture, especially the dome, the column, and the arch. Persian influence was probably responsible for the intricate, nonnaturalistic designs which were used as decorative motifs in practically all of the arts. From both Persia and Byzantium came the tendency to subordinate form to rich and sensuous color. Architecture was the most important of the Islamic arts; the development of both painting and sculpture was inhibited by religious prejudice against representation of the human form. By no means all of the examples of this architecture were mosques; many were palaces, schools, libraries, private dwellings, and hospitals. Indeed, Islamic architecture had a much more decidedly secular character than any in medieval Europe. Among its principal elements were bulbous domes, minarets, horseshoe arches, and twisted columns, together with the use of tracery in stone, alternating stripes of black and white, mosaics, and Arabic script as decorative devices. As in the Byzantine style, comparatively little attention was given to exterior ornamentation. The so-called minor arts of the Muslims included the weaving of gorgeous pile carpets and rugs, magnificent leather tooling, and the making of brocaded silks and tapestries, inlaid metalwork, enameled glassware, and painted pottery. Most of the products of these arts were embellished with compli-

The eclectic art of the Muslims

cated patterns of interlacing geometric designs, plants and fruits and flowers, Arabic script, and fantastic animal figures. In general, art laid particular emphasis on pure visual design. Separated from any role in religious teaching, it became highly abstract and nonrepresentational. For these reasons Islamic art often seems more secular and "modern" than any other art of premodern times.

The economic development of the Islamic Empire: (1) commerce

The economic life of the Islamic world varied greatly according to time and place, but underdevelopment was certainly not one of its primary characteristics. On the contrary, in the central areas of Islamic civilization from the first Arab conquests until about the fourteenth century mercantile life was extraordinarily advanced. The principal reason for this was that the Arabs inherited in Syria and Persia an area that was already marked by an enterprising urban culture and that was at the crossroads of the world, lying athwart the major trade routes between Africa, Europe, India, and China. Islamic traders and entrepreneurs built venturesomely on these earlier foundations. Muslim merchants penetrated into southern Russia and even into the equatorial regions of Africa, while caravans of thousands of camels traveled to the gates of India and China. (The Muslims used camels as pack animals instead of building roads and drawing wheeled carts.) Ships from Islam established new routes across the Indian Ocean, the Persian Gulf, and the Caspian Sea. For periods of time Islamic ships also dominated parts of the Mediterranean. Indeed, one reason for subsequent Islamic decline was that the Western Christians took hold of the Mediterranean in the eleventh and twelfth centuries and wrested control of the Indian Ocean in the sixteenth century.

The great Islamic expansion of commerce would scarcely have been possible without a corresponding development of industry. It was the

Interior of the Great Mosque at Cordova, Spain. This splendid specimen of Moorish architecture gives an excellent view of the cusped arches and alternating stripes of black and white so commonly used by Islamic architects.

ability of the people of one region to turn their natural resources into finished products for sale to other regions which provided a basis for a large part of the trade. Nearly every one of the great cities specialized in some particular variety of manufactures. Mosul, in Syria, was a center of the manufacture of cotton cloth; Baghdad specialized in glassware, jewelry, pottery, and silks; Damascus was famous for its fine steel and for its "damask" or woven figured silk; Morocco was noted for the manufacture of leather; and Toledo, in Spain, for its excellent swords. The products of these cities did not exhaust the list of manufactures. Drugs, perfumes, carpets, tapestries, brocades, woolens, satins, metal products, and a host of others were turned out by the craftsmen of many cities. From the Chinese the Muslims learned the art of papermaking, and the products of that industry were in great demand, not only within the empire itself but in Europe as well.

In all the areas we have reviewed Islamic civilization so over-shadowed that of the Christian West until about the twelfth century that there can be no comparison. When the West did move forward it was able to do so partly because of what it learned from Islam. In the economic sphere westerners profited from absorbing many accomplishments of Islamic technology, such as irrigation techniques, the raising of new crops, papermaking, and the distillation of alcohol. The extent of our debt to Islamic economic influence is well mirrored in the large number of common English words which were originally of Arabic or Persian origin. Among these are traffic, tariff, magazine, alcohol, muslin, orange, lemon, alfalfa, saffron, sugar, syrup, and musk. (Our word admiral also comes from the Arabic—in this case deriving from the title of emir.)

The West was as much indebted to Islam in intellectual and scientific as in economic life. In those areas, too, borrowed words tell some of the story: algebra, cipher, zero, nadir, amalgam, alembic, alchemy, alkali, soda, almanac, and names of many stars such as Aldebaran and Betelgeuse. Islamic civilization both preserved and expanded Greek philosophical and scientific knowledge when such knowledge was almost entirely forgotten in the West. All the important Greek scientific works surviving from ancient times were translated into Arabic and most of these in turn were translated in the medieval West from Arabic into Latin. Above all, the preservation and interpretation of the works of Aristotle was one of Islam's most enduring accomplishments. Not only was Aristotle first reacquired in the West by means of the Arabic translations, but Aristotle was interpreted with Islamic help, above all that of Averroës, whose prestige was so great that he was simply called "the Commentator" by medieval Western writers. Of course Arabic numerals, too, rank as a tremendously important intellectual legacy, as anyone will discover by trying to balance a checkbook with Roman ones.

Aside from all these specific contributions, the civilization of Islam probably had its greatest influence on the West merely by standing as a powerful rival and spur to the imagination. Byzantine civilization was at once too closely related to the Christian West and too weak to serve this function. Westerners usually, for right or wrong, looked down on the Byzantine Greeks, but they more often respected and feared the Muslims. And right they were as well, for Islamic civilization at its zenith (to use another Arabic word) was surely one of the world's greatest. Though loosely organized, it united peoples as diverse as Arabs, Persians, Turks, various African tribes, and Hindus by means of a great religion and common institutions. Unity within multiplicity was an Islamic hallmark, which created both a splendid diverse society and a splendid legacy of original discoveries and achievements.

3. WESTERN CHRISTIAN CIVILIZATION IN THE EARLY MIDDLE AGES

*The shaping of a cultural
unity in the early-
medieval West*

Western Europeans in the early Middle Ages (the period between about 600 and 1050) were so backward in comparison to their Byzantine and Islamic neighbors that a tenth-century Arabic geographer could write of them that "they have large bodies, gross natures, harsh manners, and dull intellects . . . those who live farthest north are particularly stupid, gross, and brutish." Material conditions throughout this period were so primitive that one can almost speak of five centuries of camping-out. Yet new and promising patterns were definitely taking shape. Above all, a new center of civilization was emerging in the North Atlantic regions. Around 800 the Frankish monarchy, based in agriculturally rich northwestern Europe, managed to create a western European empire in alliance with the Western Christian Church. Although this empire did not last long, it still managed to hew out a new Western cultural unity that was to be an important building block for the future.

Once the Eastern Romans under Justinian had destroyed the Ostrogothic and Vandal kingdoms in Italy and Africa, and the Arabs had eliminated the Visigothic kingdom in Spain, the Frankish rulers in Gaul remained as the major surviving barbarian power in western Europe. But it took about two centuries before they began to exercise their full hegemony. The founder of the Frankish state was the brutal and wily chieftain Clovis, who conquered most of modern-day France and Belgium around 500 and cleverly converted to western Catholic Christianity, the religion of the local bishops and indigenous population. Clovis founded the Merovingian dynasty (so called from Merovech, the founder of the family to which he belonged). He did not, however, pass on a united realm but followed the typical barbarian custom of dividing up his kingdom among his sons. More or less without interruption for the next two hundred years sons fought sons for a larger share of the Merovingian inheritance. Toward the end of that period the line also began to degenerate, and numerous so-called do-nothing kings left their government and fighting to their chief ministers, known as "mayors of the palace." Throughout this era, one of the darkest in the recorded history of Europe, trade contracted, towns declined, literacy was almost forgotten, and violence was endemic. Minimal agricultural self-sufficiency coexisted with the rule of the battle-axe.

Largely unnoticed, however, some hope for the future was coalescing around the institutions of the Roman papacy and Benedictine monasticism. The architect of a new western European religious policy that was based on an alliance between these two institutions was Pope Gregory I (reigned 590–604), known as St. Gregory the Great. Until his time the Roman popes were generally subordinate to the emperors in Constantinople and to the greater religious prestige of the Christian East, but Gregory sought to counteract this situation by creating a more autonomous western-oriented Latin Church. This he tried to do in many ways. As a theologian—the fourth great "Latin father" of the Church—he built upon the work of his three predecessors, Jerome, Ambrose, and especially Augustine, in articulating a theology that had its own distinct characteristics. Among these were emphasis on the idea of penance and the concept of purgatory as a place for purification before admission into heaven. (Western belief in purgatory was thereafter to become one of the major differences in the dogmas of the Eastern and Western Churches.) In addition to his theological work, Gregory pioneered in the writing of a simplified unadorned Latin prose that corresponded to the actual spoken language of his contemporaries, and presided over the creation of a powerful Latin liturgy. If Gregory did not actually invent the "Gregorian chant," it was under his impetus that this new plainsong—forever after a central part of the Roman Catholic ritual—developed. All of these innovations helped to make the Christian West religiously and culturally more independent of the Greek-speaking East than it had ever been before.

Gregory the Great was as much a statesman as he was a theologian and shaper of Latin. Within Italy he assured the physical survival of the papacy in the face of the barbarian Lombard threat of his day by clever diplomacy and expert management of papal landed estates. He also began to reemphasize earlier claims of papal primacy, especially over Western bishops, that were in danger of being forgotten. Above all, he patronized the order of Benedictine monks and used them to help evangelize new Western territories. Gregory himself had been a Benedictine—perhaps the first Benedictine monk to become pope—and he wrote the standard life of St. Benedict. Because the Benedictine order was still very young and the times were turbulent, Gregory's patronage helped the order to survive and later to become for centuries the only monastic order in the West. In return the pope could profit from using the Benedictines to carry out special projects. The

Pope Gregory the Great. In this tenth-century German ivory panel the pope is receiving inspiration from the Holy Spirit in the form of a dove.

Gregory's religious policies

most significant of these was the conversion of Anglo-Saxon England to Christianity. This was a long-term project which took about a century to complete, but its great result was that it left a Christian outpost to the far northwest that was thoroughly loyal to the papacy and that would soon help to bring together the papacy and the Frankish state. Gregory the Great himself did not live to see that union, but it was his policy of invigorating the Western Church that most helped to bring it about.

Around 700, when the Benedictines were completing their conversion of England, the outlook for Frankish Gaul was becoming somewhat brighter. The most profound reason for this was that the long, troubled period of transition between the ancient and medieval worlds was finally coming to an end. The ancient Roman civilization of cities and Mediterranean trade was in its last gasps in Gaul in the time after Clovis. Then, when the Arabs conquered the southern Mediterranean shore and took to the sea in the seventh century, northwestern Europe was finally thrown back upon itself and forced to look away from the Mediterranean. In fact the lands of the north—modern-day northern France, the Low Countries, Germany, and England—were extremely fertile: with adequate farming implements they could yield great natural wealth. Given the proper circumstances, a new power could emerge in the north to make the most of a new pattern of life based predominantly on agrarianism instead of urban commerce and Mediterranean trade. Around 700 that is exactly what happened in Merovingian Gaul.

The proper circumstances were the triumph of a succession of able rulers and their alliance with the Church. In 687 an energetic Merovingian mayor of the palace, Pepin of Heristal, managed to unite all the Frankish lands under his rule and build a new power base for his own family in the region of Belgium and the Rhine. He was succeeded by his aggressive son, Charles Martel ("the Hammer"), who is sometimes considered a second founder of the Frankish state. Charles's claim to this title is twofold. First, in 732 he turned back a Muslim force from Spain at the Battle of Poitiers, some 150 miles from Paris. Although the Muslim contingent was not a real army but merely a marauding band, the incursion was the high-water mark of their progress toward the northwest and Charles's victory won him great prestige. Equally important, around the end of his reign Charles began to develop an alliance with the Church, particularly with the Benedictines of England. Having finished most of their conversion work on their island, the Benedictines, under their idealistic leader St. Boniface, were moving across the English Channel in an attempt to convert central Germany. Charles Martel realized that he and they had common interests, for after he had guarded his southern flank against the Muslims he was seeking to direct Frankish expansion eastward in the direction of Germany. Missionary work and Frankish expansion could go hand in hand, so Charles offered St. Boniface and his Benedictines material aid in return for their support of his territorial aims.

Once allied with the Franks, St. Boniface provided further service in the next reign in helping to contribute to one of the most momentous events in Western history. Charles Martel had never assumed the royal title, but his son, Pepin the Short, wished to take it. Even though Pepin and not the reigning "do-nothing king" was the real power, Pepin needed the prestige of the Church for supporting a change in dynasties. Fortunately for him the times were highly propitious for obtaining Church support. St. Boniface supported Pepin because the young ruler continued his father's policy of collaborating with the Benedictines in Germany. And Boniface had great influence in Rome because the Anglo-Saxon Benedictines had remained in the closest touch with the papacy since the time of Gregory the Great.

The papacy was now fully prepared to cast its own lots with a strong Frankish ruler because it was in the midst of a bitter fight with the Byzantine emperors over Iconoclasm. The Byzantines until then had offered papal territories in Italy some protection against the Lombards, but the increasingly powerful Franks were now fully able to take over that role. The papacy accordingly made an epochal about-face, turning once and for all to the West. In 750 the pope encouraged Pepin to depose the Merovingian figurehead, and in 751 St. Boniface, acting as papal emissary, anointed Pepin as a divinely sanctioned king. Thus the Frankish monarchy attained a spiritual mandate and was fully integrated into the papal-Benedictine orbit. Shortly afterward Pepin paid his debt to the pope by conquering the Lombards in Italy. The West was now achieving its own unity based on the Frankish state and the Latin church, not coincidentally just at the time when the Abbasid caliphate was being founded in the East and the Byzantines were going their own fully Greek way.

The ultimate consolidation of the new pattern took place in the reign of Pepin's son, Carolus Magnus or Charlemagne (768–814), from whom the new dynasty takes its name of "Carolingian." Without question Charlemagne ranks as one of the most important rulers of the whole medieval period. Had it been possible to ask him what his greatest accomplishment was, he almost certainly would have replied that it lay in greatly increasing the Frankish realm. Except for the English, there was scarcely a people of western Europe against whom he did not fight. Most of his campaigns were successful; he annexed the greater part of central Europe and northern and central Italy to the Frankish domain. To rule this vast area he bestowed all the powers of local government upon his own appointees, called counts, and tried to remain in control of them by sending representatives of the court to observe them. Among the counts' many duties were the administration of justice and the raising of armies. Although Charlemagne's system in practice was far from perfect, it led to the best government that

Solidification of the alliance in the time of Pepin the Short

The "about-face" of the papacy

Charlemagne. A silver penny struck between 804 and 814 in Mainz (as indicated by the letter M at the bottom) showing Charlemagne in a highly stylized fashion as emperor with Roman military cloak and laurel. The inscription reads KAROLVS IMP AVG (Charles, Emperor, Augustus). See p. 185, above, for the variety of late-Roman coin portraiture that must have served as the Carolingian minter's model.

*The Carolingian
Renaissance*

Europe had seen since the Romans. Because of the military triumphs and internal peace of his reign, Charlemagne was long remembered and revered as a western European folk hero.

Primarily to aid his territorial expansion and help administer his realm Charlemagne presided over a revival of learning known as the "Carolingian Renaissance." Charlemagne extended his rule into Germany in the name of Christianity, but in order to proselytize he needed educated monks and priests. More than that, in order to administer his far-flung territories he needed at least a few people who could read and write. Amazing as it may seem to us, at first hardly any people in his entire realm were literate, so thoroughly had the rudiments of learning been forgotten since the decay of Roman city life. Only in Anglo-Saxon England had literacy been cultivated by the Benedictine monks. The reason for this was that the Anglo-Saxons spoke a form of German but the monks needed to learn Latin in order to say their offices and study the Bible. Since they knew no Latin to begin with they had to go about learning it by a very self-conscious program of studies. The greatest Anglo-Saxon Benedictine scholar before Charlemagne's time was the Venerable Bede (d. 735), whose *History of the English Church and People,* written in Latin, was one of the best historical writings of the early-medieval period and can still be read with pleasure. When Charlemagne came to the throne he invited the Anglo-Saxon Benedictine Alcuin—a student of one of Bede's students—to direct a revival of studies on the continent. With Charlemagne's active support Alcuin helped establish new schools to teach reading, directed the copying and correcting of important Latin works, including many Roman classics, and inspired the formulation of a new clear handwriting that is the ancestor of our modern "Roman" print. These were the greatest achievements of the Carolingian Renaissance, which stressed practicality rather than original literary or intellectual endeavors. Thoroughly unpretentious as they were, they

Carolingian Handwriting. Even the untrained reader has little difficulty in reading this excerpt from a Carolingian manuscript.

established a bridgehead for literacy on the Continent which thereafter would never be completely lost. They also helped to preserve Latin literature, and they made the Latin language the language of state and diplomacy for all of western Europe, as it remained until comparatively recent times.

The climax of Charlemagne's career came in the year 800 when he **was crowned emperor on Christmas Day in Rome by the pope.** Historians continue to debate whether this was Charlemagne's or the pope's idea, but there is no doubt that the pope did not gain any immediate power from it. Once the Franks ruled Italy they came to dominate the papacy, and indeed the whole Church, to such a degree that by 800 the pope was very close to being Charlemagne's puppet. Charlemagne did not gain any actual new power by taking the imperial title either, but the significance of the event is nonetheless great. Up until 800 the only emperor ruled in Constantinople and could lay claim to being the direct heir of Augustus. Although the Byzantines had lost most of their interest in the West, they still continued to regard it vaguely as an outlying province and were actively opposed to any westerner calling himself emperor. Charlemagne's assumption of the title was virtually a declaration of Western self-confidence and independence. Since Charlemagne's vast realm was fully as large as that of the Byzantines, had great reserves of agricultural wealth, and was defining its own culture based on Western Christianity and the Latin linguistic tradition, the claim to empire was largely justified. More than that, it was never forgotten. Both for its symbolism and for its contribution toward giving westerners a sense of unity and purpose it was a major landmark on the road to the making of a great western Europe.

Charlemagne's coronation as emperor

Although the claim to empire was bold and memorable, Charlemagne's actual empire disintegrated quickly after his death for many reasons. The simplest was that hardly any of his successors were as competent and decisive as he was. In order to rule an empire in those still extremely primitive times, one had to have enormous reserves of strength and energy—one had to travel on horseback over enormous distances, fight and win battles at the head of unruly armies, and know how to delegate power to others yet guard against its abuse. Unfortunately for western Europe few of Charlemagne's heirs had such combinations of energy and talent. To make matters worse, Charlemagne's sole surviving son, Louis the Pious, who inherited the Frankish realm intact, divided his inheritance among his own three sons, thereby bringing civil war back to Frankish Europe. And to make matters worst of all, new waves of invasions began just as Charlemagne's grandsons and great-grandsons started fighting each other: from the north came the Scandinavian Vikings; from the east came the Asiatic Magyars (or Hungarians); and from the south came new attacks by marauding Muslims, attacking now from the sea. Under these pressures the Carolingian Empire completely fell apart and a new political map of Europe was drawn in the tenth century.

Viking Dragon Head. Wooden carvings like these on the stemposts of Viking ships were calculated to inspire terror.

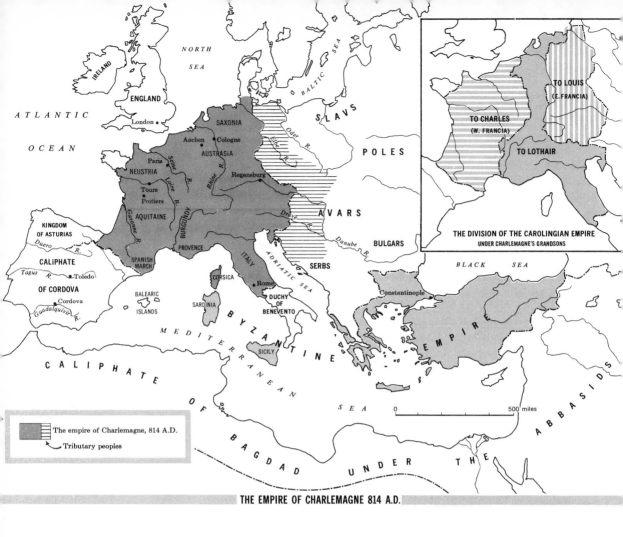

THE EMPIRE OF CHARLEMAGNE 814 A.D.

Within the map:

NORTH SEA
ATLANTIC OCEAN
BALTIC SEA
IRELAND
ENGLAND
London
SAXONIA
Aachen · Cologne
AUSTRASIA
Paris
NEUSTRIA
Regensburg
Tours
Poitiers
AQUITAINE
BURGUNDY
PROVENCE
SPANISH MARCH
KINGDOM OF ASTURIAS
Duero R.
CALIPHATE
Tagus R. · Toledo
OF CORDOVA
Cordova
Guadalquivir R.
BALEARIC ISLANDS
SARDINIA
CORSICA
ITALY
Rome
DUCHY OF BENEVENTO
SICILY
Seine R.
Loire R.
Garonne R.
Rhine R.
Elbe R.
Oder R.
Drave R.
Danube R.
SLAVS
POLES
AVARS
BULGARS
SERBS
BYZANTINE EMPIRE
Constantinople
BLACK SEA
ADRIATIC SEA
MEDITERRANEAN SEA
CALIPHATE OF BAGDAD UNDER THE ABBASIDS

0   500 miles

Inset map:
THE DIVISION OF THE CAROLINGIAN EMPIRE
UNDER CHARLEMAGNE'S GRANDSONS
TO LOUIS (E. FRANCIA)
TO CHARLES (W. FRANCIA)
TO LOTHAIR

Legend:
The empire of Charlemagne, 814 A.D.
Tributary peoples

As the Carolingian period was crucial for marking the beginnings of a common North Atlantic western European civilization, so the tenth century was crucial for marking the beginnings of the major modern European political entities. England, which never had been part of Charlemagne's empire, and which hitherto had been divided among smaller warring Anglo-Saxon states, became unified in the late ninth and the tenth century owing to the work of King Alfred the Great (871–899) and his direct successors. Alfred and his heirs reorganized the army, infused new vigor into local government, and codified the English laws. In addition, Alfred founded schools and fostered an interest in Anglo-Saxon writing and other elements of a national culture.

England in the time of Alfred the Great

Across the Channel, France (now the name for the main part of Roman Gaul because it was the original seat of the Frankish monarchy) was most devastated by the invasions of Vikings, who had sailed up the French rivers. For that reason France broke up into small principalities rather than developing a strong national monarchy on the

Political conditions in France and Germany

pattern of England. Nonetheless there was a king in France, who, however weak, was recognized as the ruler of the western part of Charlemagne's former territories. Directly to the east, the kings of Germany were the strongest continental monarchs of the tenth century, ruling over an essentially united realm. In addition to Germany, their lands encompassed most of the Low Countries and a good part of modern eastern France.

The most important German ruler of the period was Otto the Great. He became king in 936, resoundingly defeated the Hungarians in 955—thereby relieving Germany of its greatest foreign threat—and took the title of emperor in Rome in 962. By this last act Otto strengthened his claim to being the greatest continental monarch since Charlemagne. Otto and his successors, who continued to call themselves emperors, tried to rule over Italy but barely succeeded in doing so. Instead, Italy in the tenth century saw the greatest western European development of urban life, a pattern on which the Italians would subsequently build.

*Otto the Great of
Germany*

Although Italy did develop some city life in the tenth century, this was by no means typical of the early-medieval period in western Europe as a whole. Quite to the contrary, from the eighth to the eleventh century the European economy was based almost entirely on agriculture and very limited local trade. Roads deteriorated and barter widely replaced the use of money. Whatever cities survived from Roman days were usually empty shells that served at most as administrative centers for bishops and fortified places in case of common danger. The main economic unit throughout the period was the self-supporting large landed estate, usually owned by kings, warrior aristocrats, or large-scale monasteries. Although the northern European soil was rich, farming tools in most places were still too primitive to bring in a fully adequate return on the enormous investment of effort expended by the laboring masses. Agricultural yields in all but the most fertile Carolingian heartlands (and often even in them) were pitifully low, and Europeans, except the rulers and the higher clergy, lived on the edge of subsistence. It is true that some increase in agricultural income had underpinned the Carolingian successes and some progress in farming might have continued had the peace of Charlemagne's reign endured. But the subsequent invasions of the ninth and tenth centuries set agricultural life back and new beginnings would have to be made in the years thereafter.

*The economy of western
Europe in the early
Middle Ages*

Given the low level of early-medieval economic life, it is not surprising that the age was not a prosperous time for learning or the arts: with scarcely enough wealth to keep most people alive, there is not going to be much to support schools or major artistic projects. Throughout the period, even in the best of years, learning was a privilege for the few: the masses received no formal education, and even most members of the secular aristocracy were illiterate. Learning also consisted mostly of memorization, without regard for criticism or

*The low level of
intellectual life*

refutation. We have seen that there was some revival of learning under Charlemagne that may be called a "renaissance" but that it did not issue into any real intellectual creativity. Its major accomplishment was the founding of enough schools to educate the clergy in the rudiments of reading and the training of enough monastic scribes to recopy and preserve some major works of Roman literature. Even this accomplishment was jeopardized in the period of invasions that accompanied the fall of the Carolingian Empire. Fortunately just enough schools and manuscripts survived to become the basis for another—far greater—revival of learning that began in the eleventh and twelfth centuries.

Literature

In the realm of literature the early Middle Ages had an extremely meager production. This was because few Christians could write and those who could were usually monks and priests, who were not supposed to engage in purely literary endeavors. There was some impressive writing of history in Latin, most notably that of Bede and Charlemagne's eloquent biographer, Einhard, but otherwise Latin composition was little cultivated. Toward the close of the period, however, the vernacular languages, which were either Germanic or based on different regional dialects of Latin (the "Romance" languages, so-called because they were based on "Roman" speech) began to be employed for crude poetic expression, usually first by oral transmission.

Beowulf

The best-known example of this literature in the vernacular is the Anglo-Saxon epic poem *Beowulf.* First put into written form about the eighth century, this poem incorporates ancient legends of the Germanic peoples of northwestern Europe. It is a story of fighting and seafaring and of heroic adventure against deadly dragons and the forces of nature. The background of the epic is pre-Christian, but the author of the work introduced into it some qualities of Christian idealism. *Beowulf* is important not only as one of the earliest specimens of Anglo-Saxon or Old English poetry, but also for the picture it gives of the society of the English and their ancestors in the early Middle Ages.

The artistic history of the early Middle Ages was a story of isolated and interrupted accomplishments because artistic life relied most of all on brief moments of local peace or royal patronage. The earliest enduring monuments of early-medieval art were those created by monks in Ireland—which had its own unique culture—between the sixth and the eighth centuries. Above all in manuscript illumination (i.e., painted illustrations) the Irish monks developed a thoroughly anticlassical and almost surrealistic style, whose origins are most difficult to account for. The greatest surviving product from this school is the stunning "Book of Kells," an illuminated Gospel book that has been called "the most sophisticated work of decorative art in the history of painting." The Irish school declined without subsequent influence and was followed by artistic products of the Carolingian Renaissance.

The art of Charlemagne's period returned for much of its inspira-

Irish Art. The opening of a gospel page that shows the Irish style at its most surrealistic.

Carolingian Art. The fountain of life: an illuminated manuscript page from Gottschalk's Evangeliary (book with four gospels), dating from 781.

tion to classical models, yet it also retained some of the spontaneous vitality of barbarian decoration. When Charlemagne's empire declined and disintegrated there was a corresponding decline and then interruption in the history of Western art. In the tenth century, however, new regional schools emerged. The greatest of these were the English, which emphasized restless fluency in manuscript illumination; the German, which was more grave but still managed to communicate extreme religious ecstasy; and the northern Spanish, which, though Christian, created a rather strange and independent style mostly influenced by the decorative style of Islamic art.

Regional variations in early-medieval art

See color plates facing page 225

Undoubtedly, there is no single, obvious terminal date for early-medieval history as a whole. The date 1000 is sometimes given because it is a convenient round number, but even as late as 1050 Europe had not changed on the surface very much from the way it had been since the end of the Carolingian period. Indeed, looking at Europe as late as 1050 it would at first seem that not much progress had been made over the entire course of the early-medieval centuries. Except for Germany there was hardly any centralized government because by 1050 the Anglo-Saxon English state created by King Alfred and his successors was falling apart. Throughout Europe, all but the most privileged individuals continued to live on the brink of starvation and cultural attainments were minimal and sparse. But actually much had been accomplished. By shifting its main weight to the Atlantic northwest, European civilization became centered in lands that would soon harvest great agricultural wealth. By preserving some of the traditions developed by Gregory the Great, St. Boniface, Pepin, and Charle-

A distinct western European civilization evident in 1050

Left: *Utrecht Psalter.* This Carolingian manuscript of the Psalms from about 820 later provided the basis for the "nervous expressiveness" of the tenth-century English regional school. Right: *Bamberg Apocalypse.* In this manuscript illumination from about 1000 A.D. the fall of Babylon in the Book of Revelation (18: 1–20) is displayed by depicting the city upside down. An example of the grave regional German style.

magne, European civilization had also developed an enduring sense of cultural unity based on Western Christianity and the Latin inheritance. And in the tenth century the beginnings of the future European kingdoms and city-states started to coalesce. Western European civilization was thus for the first time becoming autonomous and distinctive. From then on it would become a leading force in the history of the world.

SELECTED READINGS

• *Items so designated are available in paperback editions.*

BYZANTINE CIVILIZATION

Beckwith, John, *The Art of Constantinople,* 2nd ed., London, 1968. A standard account.

• Diehl, Charles, *Byzantium: Greatness and Decline,* New Brunswick, N.J., 1957. Evaluates strengths and weaknesses of Byzantine civilization.

Hussey, J. M., *The Byzantine World,* London, 1957. Half-narrative, half-topical; a useful short introduction.

• Krautheimer, R., *Early Christian and Byzantine Architecture,* Baltimore, 1970.

Magoulias, H. J., *Byzantine Christianity: Emperor, Church and the West*, Chicago, 1970. Limited to three themes mentioned in title.

Miller, D. A., *The Byzantine Tradition*, New York, 1966. The briefest introduction.

Ostrogorsky, George, *History of the Byzantine State*, New Brunswick, N.J., 1957. The most authoritative longer account of political developments; very scholarly.

• Pelikan, J., *The Christian Tradition; II: The Spirit of Eastern Christendom*, Chicago, 1974. An advanced treatment of religious doctrines.

Runciman, S., *Byzantine Civilization*, New York, 1933. A topical approach; well written but in parts outdated.

———, *Byzantine Style and Civilization*, Baltimore, 1975. A fine study of Byzantine art.

• Vasiliev, A. A., *History of the Byzantine Empire*, 2 vols., Madison, Wisc., 1928. Supplements Ostrogorsky; valuable for its detail on social and intellectual as well as political history.

Vryonis, S., *Byzantium and Europe*, New York, 1967. Noteworthy for its illustrations.

ISLAMIC CIVILIZATION

Arnold, Thomas, and A. Guillaume, *The Legacy of Islam*, New York, 1931.

Gabrieli, F., *Muhammad and the Conquests of Islam*, New York, 1968.

Gibb, H. A. R., *Arabic Literature: An Introduction*, 2nd ed., Oxford, 1963. An excellent survey.

———, *Mohammedanism: An Historical Survey*, 2nd ed., Oxford, 1953. The best brief interpretation of Islamic religion.

• Goitein, S. D., *Jews and Arabs, Their Contacts through the Ages*, New York, 1955.

Grube, E. J., *The World of Islam*, New York, 1966.

• Hodgson, M., *The Venture of Islam*, 3 vols., Chicago, 1974. A masterwork. One of the greatest works of history written by a modern American. Advanced and sometimes difficult, but always rewarding.

Kennedy, Hugh, *The Early Abbasid Caliphate: A Political History*, Totowa, N.J., 1981.

• Lewis, Bernard, *The Arabs in History*, rev. ed., New York, 1966. The best short survey of the conquests and political fortunes of the Arabs.

Lombard, Maurice, *The Golden Age of Islam*, New York, 1975.

Peters, F. E., *Aristotle and the Arabs*, New York, 1968. A well-written and engaging account.

Watt, W. Montgomery, *Islamic Philosophy and Theology*, Edinburgh, 1962.

• ———, *Muhammad: Prophet and Statesman*, Oxford, 1961. A good short biography.

Watt, W. M., and P. Cachia, *A History of Islamic Spain*, Edinburgh, 1965. Briefly covers an undeservedly neglected subject.

EARLY–MEDIEVAL WESTERN CHRISTIAN CIVILIZATION

• Barraclough, G., *The Crucible of Europe: The Ninth and Tenth Centuries in European History*, Berkeley, Calif., 1976. A controversial and sometimes wrongheaded but clear and stimulating interpretation of political developments.

- Dawson, Christopher, *The Making of Europe,* London, 1932. A brilliant interpretation that emphasizes cultural and religious developments by one of this century's most eminent Catholic historians.
- Duby, G., *The Early Growth of the European Economy,* Ithaca, N.Y., 1974. Emphasizes role of lords and peasants; very sophisticated economic history.

  Fichtenau, H., *The Carolingian Empire,* Oxford, 1957. A highly interpretative account that aims to whittle its subject down to size.
- Ganshof, F. L., *Frankish Institutions under Charlemagne,* Providence, 1958. A straightforward technical exposition.

  Halphen, L., *Charlemagne and the Carolingian Empire,* New York, 1977. An older French survey recently translated into English.
- Kitzinger, Ernst, *Early Medieval Art,* London, 1940. A very short but masterful introduction.
- Laistner, M. L. W., *Thought and Letters in Western Europe, A. D. 500–900,* rev. ed., Ithaca, N.Y., 1957. An old-fashioned but standard account; should be supplemented by Wolff.
- Pirenne, Henri, *Mohammed and Charlemagne,* New York, 1939. A bold interpretation, now no longer widely accepted but still thought-provoking.

  Stenton, Frank, *Anglo-Saxon England,* 3rd ed., Oxford, 1971. A standard work.
- Sullivan, Richard E., *Heirs of the Roman Empire,* Ithaca, N.Y., 1960. An elementary introduction.
- Wallace-Hadrill, J. M., *The Barbarian West, A. D. 400–1000,* 2nd ed., London, 1962. A sophisticated short account that emphasizes analysis of the historical sources and questions earlier scholarly assumptions.

  Wemple, S. F., *Women in Frankish Society: Marriage and the Cloister, 500–900,* Philadelphia, 1981. Describes changing attitudes toward marriage among the early Franks.

  Wolff, Philippe, *The Awakening of Europe,* Baltimore, 1968. The "new intellectual history": emphasizes interrelations between the development of thought and material foundations. Masterfully written and organized.

SOURCE MATERIALS

- Arberry, A. J., *The Koran Interpreted,* 2 vols., London, 1955.
- Bede, *A History of the English Church and People,* tr. L. Sherley-Price, Baltimore, 1955.

  Brand, Charles M., ed., *Icon and Minaret: Sources of Byzantine and Islamic Civilization,* Englewood Cliffs, N.J., 1969.
- Brentano, Robert, ed., *The Early Middle Ages: 500–1000,* New York, 1964. The best shorter anthology of the Western Christian sources, enlivened by the editor's subjective commentary.
- Einhard and Notker the Stammerer, *Two Lives of Charlemagne,* tr. L. Thorpe, Baltimore, 1969.
- Gregory Bishop of Tours, *History of the Franks,* tr. E. Brehaut, New York, 1965.

Chapter 11

THE HIGH MIDDLE AGES
(1050–1300): ECONOMIC, SOCIAL,
AND POLITICAL INSTITUTIONS

I judge those who write at this time to be in a certain measure happy. For, after the turbulence of the past, an unprecedented brightness of peace has dawned again.

—The historian Otto of
Freising, writing around 1158

The period between about 1050 and 1300, termed by historians the High Middle Ages, was the time when western Europe first clearly emerged from backwardness to become one of the greatest powers on the globe. Around 1050 the West was still less developed in most respects than the Byzantine Empire or the Islamic world, but by 1300 it had forged ahead of these two rivals. From a global perspective, only China was its equal in economic, political, and cultural prosperity. Given the sorry state of western Europe around 1050, this startling leap forward was certainly one of the most impressive achievements of human history. Those who think that the entire Middle Ages were times of stagnation could not be more wrong.

Western Europe emerges from backwardness

The reasons for Europe's enormous progress in the High Middle Ages are predictably complex, yet medieval historians agree upon certain broad lines of interpretation. One is that Europe between 900 and 1050 was already poised for growth and could finally begin to live up to its potential once the devastating invasions of Vikings, Hungarians, and Muslims had ceased. Most of these invasions had tapered off by around 1000, but in the eleventh century England was still troubled by the Danes: the year 1066, more famous as the year of the Norman Conquest, was also the year of the last Viking invasion of England.

Reasons for the "great leap forward"

Once foreign invasions were no longer imminent, western Europeans could concentrate on developing their economic life with much less fear of interruption than before. Because of the relative continuity allowed by this change, extraordinarily important technological breakthroughs were made, above all those that contributed to the first great western European "agricultural revolution." The revolution in agriculture made food more bountiful and provided a solid basis for economic development and diversification in other spheres. Population grew rapidly, and towns and cities grew to such a degree that we can speak also of an "urban revolution," even though western Europe remained predominantly agrarian. At the same time political life in the West became more stable. In the course of the High Middle Ages strong new secular governments began to provide more and more internal peace for their subjects and became the foundations of our modern nation-states. In addition to all these advances, there were also striking new religious and intellectual developments, to be treated in the next chapter, which helped give the West a new sense of mission and self-confidence. Although in this chapter we will treat only the economic, social, and political accomplishments of the High Middle Ages, it is well to bear in mind that religion played a pervasive role in all of medieval life, and that all aspects of the high-medieval "great leap forward" were inextricably interrelated.

1. THE FIRST AGRICULTURAL REVOLUTION

*The state of agriculture
before 1050*

The agricultural worker, the "Man with the Hoe," supported European civilization materially by his labors more than anyone else until the industrialization of modern times. Yet, amazing as it seems, until about 1050 he had hardly so much as a hoe. Inventories of farm implements from the Carolingian period reveal that metal tools on the wealthiest rural estates were extremely rare, and even wooden implements were so few in number that many laborers must have had to grapple with nature quite literally with only their bare hands. Between about 1050 and 1250 all that changed. In roughly those two centuries an agricultural revolution took place which entirely altered the nature and vastly increased the output of western European farming.

*Prerequisities for the
medieval agricultural
revolution: (1) shift in
area of cultivation*

Many of the prerequisites for the medieval agricultural revolution had been present before the middle of the eleventh century. The most important was the shift in the weight of European civilization from the Mediterranean to the North Atlantic regions. Most of northern Europe from southern England to the Urals is a vast, wet, and highly fertile alluvial plain. The Romans had hardly begun to cultivate this area because they only ruled part of it, because it lay too far away from the center of their civilization, and because they did not have the proper tools and systems to work the soil. Starting around the time of the Carolingians much more attention was paid to colonizing and cultivating the great alluvial plain. The Carolingians opened up all of western and central Germany to agricultural settlement and started experimenting with new tools and methods that would be most appropriate for cultivating the newly settled lands. The results helped support other Carolingian achievements, but the Carolingian peace, as we have seen, was too brief to allow for any cumulative development. After the invasions of the tenth century, it was necessary to start again in a systematic attempt to exploit the potential wealth of the north. As long as Western civilization was centered in England, northern France, the Low Countries, and Germany, however, the rich lands remained available for cultivation.

Another prerequisite for agricultural development was improved climate. We know far less about European climatic patterns in past centuries than we would like to, but historians of climate are reasonably certain that there was an "optimum," or period of improved climate for western Europe, lasting from about 700 to 1200. This meant not only that during those centuries the temperature on the average was somewhat warmer than it had been before (at most only a rise of about 1° Centigrade), but also that the weather was somewhat drier. Dryness was of primary advantage to northern Europe, where lands were, if anything, usually too wet for good farming, whereas it was disadvantageous to the Mediterranean south, which was already dry enough. Among other things, the occurrence of this optimum helps explain why there was more agricultural cultivation in northern climes such as Iceland than there has been since then. (Also, with fewer icebergs in the northern seas, Norsemen were able to reach Greenland and Newfoundland, and Greenland then was probably indeed more green than white.) Although the optimum began around 700 and continued through the ninth and tenth centuries, it could not by itself counteract the deleterious effects of the tenth-century invasions. Fortunately the weather stayed propitious when Europeans again were able to take advantage of it.

(2) improved climate

Similar remarks apply to the fact that the Carolingians knew about many of the technological devices to be discussed presently that later helped western Europeans accomplish their first agricultural revolution. Although the most basic new devices were known before 1050, all came into widespread use and were brought to greatest perfection between then and about 1200 because only then was there a conjunction of the most favorable circumstances. Not only did the invasions end and good climate continue, but better government gradually provided the more lasting peace necessary for agricultural expansion. Landlords too became more interested in profit-making than mere consumption. Above all, from about 1050 to 1200 there was a greater consolidation of wealth for further investment as one advance helped support another; quite simply, technological devices could now be afforded.

*(3) technology in
conjunction with favorable
circumstances*

One of the first and most important breakthroughs in agriculture

Light Plow and Heavy Plow. Note that the peasant using the light plow had to press his foot on it to give it added weight. The major innovation of the heavy plow (often wheeled, as shown here) was the long moldboard, which turned

Technological innovations: (1) the heavy plow

was the use of the heavy plow. The plow itself, of course, is an ancient tool, but the Romans knew only a light "scratch plow" that broke up the surface of the ground without fully turning it over. This implement was sufficient for the light soil of the Mediterranean regions but was virtually useless with the much heavier, wetter soil of the European north. During the course of the early Middle Ages a much heavier and more efficient plow was developed that could cultivate the northern lands. Not only could this heavier plow deal with heavier soils, but it was fitted with new parts that enabled it to turn over furrows and fully aerate the ground. The benefits were immeasurable. In addition to the fact that the plow allowed for the cultivation of hitherto unworkable lands, the furrows it made provided excellent drainage systems for water-logged territories. It also saved labor: whereas the Roman scratch plow had to be dragged over the fields twice in two different directions, the heavy plow did more thorough work in one operation. In short, the opening up of northern Europe for intensive agriculture and everything that followed would have been inconceivable without the heavy plow.

(2) the three-field system

Closely allied to the use of the heavy plow was the introduction of the three-field system of crop rotation. Before modern times, farmers always let a large part of their arable land lie fallow for a year to avoid exhaustion of the soil because there was not enough fertilizer to support more intensive agriculture, and nitrogen-fixing crops such as clover and alfalfa were almost unknown. But the Romans represented an unproductive extreme in their inability to cultivate any more than half of their arable land in any year. The medieval innovation was to reduce the fallow to one-third by introducing a three-field system. In a given year one third of the land would lie fallow, one third would be

over the ground after the plowshare cut into it. The picture on the right depicts a second crucial medieval invention as well—the padded horse collar which allowed horses to throw their full weight into pulling.

given to cereal that was sown in the fall and harvested in early summer, and one third to a new crop—oats, barley, or legumes—that would be planted in the late spring and harvested in August or September. The fields were then rotated over a three-year cycle. The major innovation was the planting of the new crop which grew over the summer. The Romans could not have supported this system because their lands were poorer and especially because the Mediterranean area is too dry to support much summer growth at all. In this respect the wetter north obviously had a great advantage. The benefits of the new crop were that it did not deplete the soil as much as cereal like wheat and rye (in fact, it restored nitrogen taken from the soil by these crops); that it provided some insurance against loss from natural disasters by diversifying the growth of the fields; and that it produced new types of food. If the third field was planted with oats, the crop could be consumed by both humans and horses; if planted with legumes, it helped to balance the human diet by providing a source of protein to balance the major intake of cereal carbohydrates. Since the new system also helped to diversify labor over the course of the year and raised production from one-half to two-thirds, it was nothing short of an agricultural miracle.

A third major innovation was the use of mills. The Romans had known about water mills but hardly used them, partly because they had enough slaves to be indifferent to labor-saving devices and partly because most Roman territories were not richly endowed with swiftly flowing streams. Starting around 1050, however, there was a veritable craze in northern Europe for building increasingly efficient water mills. One French area saw a growth from 14 water mills in the eleventh century to 60 in the twelfth; in another part of France about 40

(3) *use of mills*

mills were built between 850 and 1080, 40 more between 1080 and 1125, and 245 between 1125 and 1175. Once Europeans had mastered the complex technology of building water mills, they turned their attention to harnessing the power of wind: around 1170 they constructed the first European windmills. Thereafter, in flat lands like Holland that had no swiftly flowing streams, windmills proliferated as rapidly as water-powered ones had spread elsewhere. Although the major use of mills was to grind grain, they were soon adapted for a variety of other important functions: for example, they were employed to drive saws, process cloth, press oil, brew beer, provide power for iron forges, and crush pulp for manufacturing paper. Paper had been made in China and the Islamic world before this but never with the aid of paper mills, which is evidence of the technological sophistication the West was achieving in comparison to other advanced civilizations.

*(4) other technological
developments*

Other important technological breakthroughs that gathered force around 1050 should be mentioned. Several related to providing the means for using horses as farm animals. Around 800 a padded collar was first introduced into Europe; this allowed the horse to put his full weight into pulling without choking himself. Roughly a century later iron horseshoes were first used to protect hooves, and perhaps around 1050 tandem harnessing was developed to allow horses to pull behind each other. With these advances and the greater abundance of oats due to the three-field system, horses replaced oxen as farm animals in some parts of Europe and brought with them the advantages of working more quickly and working longer hours. Further inventions were the wheelbarrow and the harrow, a tool drawn over the field after the plow to level the earth and mix in the seed. Important for most of these inventions was the greater use of iron in the High Middle Ages to reinforce all sorts of agricultural implements, most crucially the parts of the heavy plow that came into contact with the soil.

Peasants Bringing Grain to Windmills. Shown here are two different kinds of mills: those set to operate by prevailing winds (at left) and those that are pivoted to face into chance winds (middle and right).

So far we have been speaking of technological developments as if they alone account for the high-medieval agricultural revolution. But that is by no means the case. Along with improved technology came a great extension in the amount of land made arable and more intensive cultivation of the land already cleared. Although the Carolingians had begun to open the rich plain of northwestern Europe to tillage, they had only chosen to clear the most easily workable patches: a map of Carolingian agricultural settlements would show numerous tiny islands of cultivated lands surrounded by vast stretches of forests, swamps, and wastes. Starting around 1050, and greatly accelerating in the twelfth century, movements of land-clearing entirely changed the topography of northern Europe. First, greater peace and stability allowed farm workers in northern France and western Germany to begin pushing beyond the islands of settlement, clearing little bits of land at a time. At first they did this surreptitiously because they were poaching on territories that were actually owned by aristocratic lords. In time the aristocratic landowners gave their support to the clearing activities because they demanded their own profits from them. When that happened the work of clearing forests and draining swamps was carried on more swiftly. Thus, as the twelfth century progressed the isolated arable islands of Carolingian times expanded to meet each other. While this was going on, and continuing somewhat later, entirely new areas were colonized and opened to cultivation, for example, in northern England, Holland, and above all the eastern parts of Germany. Finally, in the twelfth and thirteenth centuries, peasants began working all the lands they had cleared more efficiently and intensively in order to gain more income for themselves. They harrowed after plowing, hoed frequently to keep down weeds, and added extra plowings to their yearly cycle, thereby greatly helping to renew the fertility of the soil.

The result of all these changes was an enormous increase in agricultural production. With more land opened for cultivation obviously more crops were raised, but the increase was magnified by the introduction of more efficient farming methods. Thus, average yields from grains of seed sown increased from at best twofold in Carolingian times to three- or fourfold by around 1300. And all the additional grain could be ground far more rapidly than before because a mill could grind grain in the same time that it would have taken forty men to do the same job. Europeans, therefore, could for the first time begin to rely on a regular and stable food supply.

That fact in turn had the profoundest consequences for the further development of European history. To begin with, it meant that more land could be given over to uses other than raising grain. Accordingly, as the High Middle Ages progressed, there was greater agricultural diversification and specialization. Large areas were turned over to sheep-raising, others to viniculture, and others to raising cotton and dyestuffs. Many of the products of these new enterprises were con-

Extension and intense cultivation of arable land

Enormous increase in agricultural productivity

Consequences of the agricultural revolution

sumed locally, but many were also traded over long distances or used to provide the raw materials for new industries—above all those of cloth-making. The growth of this trade and manufacturing helped initiate and support, as we will see, the growth of towns. The agricultural boom also helped sustain the growth of towns in another way: by supporting a great spurt in population. With more food and a better diet (above all the increase in proteins) life expectancy increased from perhaps as low as an average of thirty years for the poor of Carolingian Europe to between forty and fifty years in the High Middle Ages. Healthier people also increased their birthrate. For these reasons the population of the West grew about threefold between about 1050 and 1300. More people and more labor-saving devices meant that not everybody had to stay on the farm: some could migrate to new towns and cities where they found a new way of life.

Other results

Still other results of the agricultural revolution were that it raised the incomes of lords, thereby underpinning a great increase in the sophistication of aristocratic life, and raised the incomes of monarchs, underpinning the growth of states. European-wide prosperity also helped support the growth of the Church and paid the way for the burgeoning of schools and intellectual enterprises. One final, more intangible, result was that Europeans apparently became more optimistic, more energetic, and more willing to experiment and take risks than any of their rivals on the world scene.

2. LORD AND SERF: SOCIAL CONDITIONS AND QUALITY OF LIFE IN THE MANORIAL REGIME

The meaning of the term
manorialism

While agriculture was being transformed, social and economic conditions began to change for both landowners and agricultural laborers. Since for much of the High Middle Ages, however, rural life revolved around the institution of the manor owned by lords and worked by serfs, it is best to describe this manorial regime in its most typical form before describing basic changes. In reading the following it should be understood that the term manorialism is not synonymous with feudalism: manorialism was an economic system in which large agricultural estates were worked by serfs, whereas feudalism, in the sense the word is used by most medieval historians, was a political system in which government was greatly decentralized (see the fourth section of this chapter). It should also be borne in mind that when scholars talk about manorialism based on a "typical manor" they are resorting to a historical approximation: no two manors were ever exactly alike; indeed many differed enormously in size and basic characteristics. Moreover, in those parts of Europe farthest away from the original centers of Carolingian settlement between the Seine and the Rhine, there were few, if any, manors at all. In Italy there was still much agriculture based on slavery, and in central and eastern Germany there were many smaller farms worked by free peasants.

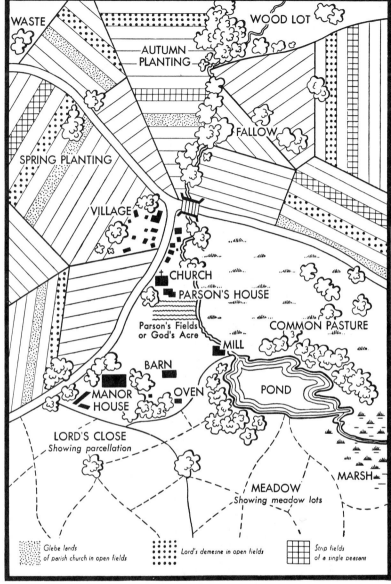

Within the diagram:

WASTE

WOOD LOT

AUTUMN PLANTING

FALLOW

SPRING PLANTING

VILLAGE

CHURCH

PARSON'S HOUSE

Parson's Fields or God's Acre

COMMON PASTURE

MILL

BARN

OVEN

POND

MANOR HOUSE

LORD'S CLOSE
Showing parcellation

MEADOW
Showing meadow lots

MARSH

Glebe lands of parish church in open fields

Lord's demesne in open fields

Strip fields of a single peasant

Diagram of a Manor

   The manor first clearly emerged in Carolingian times and continued
to be the dominant form of agrarian social and economic organization
in most of northwestern Europe until about the thirteenth century. It
descended from the large Roman landed estate, but, unlike the Roman
estate, the manor was worked by serfs (sometimes called villeins) and
not slaves. Serfs were definitely not free in the modern sense: above all,
they could not leave their lands, were forced to work for their lords
regularly without pay, and were subject to numerous humiliating dues
and to the jurisdiction of the lord's court. But they were much better
off than slaves insofar as they were allocated land which they culti-

The manor; serfs

vated to support themselves and which normally could not be taken away from them. Thus, when agricultural improvements took place the serfs themselves could hope to profit at least a little from them. More than that, although the lord theoretically had the right to levy dues at will, in practice obligations tended to remain fixed. Although the lot of the serfs was surely terribly hard, they were seldom entirely at their lord's whim.

*The manorial system of
agriculture*

The lands of the manor, which might run from several hundred to several thousand acres, were divided into those that belonged to the lord and those that were allocated to the serfs. The former, called the lord's *demesne* (pronounced demean), usually comprised between a third and a half of the arable land. It was worked by the serfs on certain days, perhaps three days a week. The demesne did not consist of big parcels but was made up of narrow strips alternating with strips belonging to different peasants (and sometimes also strips set aside for the Church). All these strips were long and narrow because a heavy plow drawn by a yoke of horses or oxen could not be turned around easily. Because all the strips were generally separated only by a narrow band of unplowed turf, the whole regime is sometimes called the *open-field system*. Even when the serfs tilled their own lands they almost always worked together because they usually owned farm animals and implements in common. For the same reason, grazing lands were called "commons" because the commonly owned herds grazed there together. In addition to cultivated fields and pastures, the serfs usually had their own small gardens. Most manors also had forests set aside primarily for the lord's hunting which were also useful for the foraging of pigs and the gathering of firewood. Insofar as serfs were allowed

Sowing Seed. When the peasant sows his seed broadcast, the crows are not far off to help themselves. Here, one is bold enough to peck at the sack while another is momentarily chased off by a dog.

Medieval Peasants Slaughtering a Pig. Deep in winter, probably around Christmas, it is finally time to slaughter the household pig. But nothing can be wasted, so even the blood is caught in a pan to make blood pudding.

to take advantage of such opportunities they did that too in common: indeed, the entire manorial system emphasized communal enterprise and solidarity.

Communalism must have helped make a barely endurable life seem slightly more bearable. Even though the lot of the medieval serf was surely far superior to that of the Roman slave, and even though it improved from around 1050 to 1300, it was still primitive and pitiful beyond modern comprehension. Dwellings were usually miserable hovels constructed of wattle—braided twigs—smeared over with mud. As late as the thirteenth century an English peasant was convicted of destroying his neighbor's house simply by sawing apart one central beam. The floors of most huts were usually no more than the bare earth, often cold or damp. For beds there was seldom more than bracken, and beyond that there was hardly any furniture. Not entirely jokingly it may be said that a good meal often consisted of two courses: one a porridge very much like gruel and the other a gruel very much like porridge. Fruit was almost unheard of, and meager vegetables were limited to such fare as onions, leeks, turnips, and cabbages—all boiled to make a thin soup. Meat came at most a few times a year, either on holidays or deep in winter, when all the fodder for a scrawny ox or pig had run out. Cooking utensils were never cleaned, so as to make sure that there was never any waste. In addition, there was always the possibility of crop failures, which affected the serfs far more than their lords, since the lords demanded the same income as always. At such times the serfs were forced to surrender whatever grain they had and watched their children die slowly of starvation. It is particularly heart-rending to realize that children might be dying

Improvements in the
condition of serfs

while there was still a bit of grain in the granaries: but that grain could not be touched because it was set aside as next year's seed, and without that there would be no future at all.

To counterbalance this grim picture we may now turn to patterns of change and improvement. One, as we have already seen, was dietary. In the High Middle Ages famines were actually far rarer than before and people grew stronger because some protein, mostly in the form of legumes, was added to their fare. There was also a widespread enfranchisement (i.e., freeing) of serfs for many reasons. Once landlords started opening up new lands, they could only attract laborers by guaranteeing their freedom. New centers of free labor usually attracted runaway serfs and became models of a new system whereby landlords asked for fixed rents rather than demanding services. Then, even on the old manors, lords began to realize that they might be able to raise profits by demanding rents instead of duties. Alternatively, by selling their excess produce at free markets serfs might become sufficiently rich to buy their freedom.

The decline of serfdom

In these different ways serfdom gradually came to an end throughout most of Europe in the course of the thirteenth century. The process, however, moved more or less swiftly in different areas—it was somewhat delayed in England and was seldom so complete that former serfs did not owe some remnant of labor service and dues to powerful local lords. In France some of these obligations continued to exist as nagging indignities right down to the French Revolution in 1789. Serfs who became enfranchised often continued to work communally, but they were now free peasants who produced more for the open market than for their own subsistence.

Benefits of the agricultural
revolution for lords

The lords profited even more than their serfs from the agricultural revolution for several reasons. One was that whenever lords enfranchised serfs they obtained large sums of cash, usually about all the wealth that the serfs had hitherto amassed. Afterward the lords lived mainly on their rents. Since some of these were levied on lands that the lords had once owned but had never been cultivated, noble income rose greatly. Even more than that, once the lords began to prefer rents to services, they found that rents were easier to increase. In their capacity as rent-collectors the lords did not personally supervise their lands as much as before but traveled more freely, sometimes going off crusading and sometimes living at royal courts. Consequently, added wealth allowed them to live better, and greater mobility gave them new ideas for improving their style of life.

The medieval nobility;
the rise of chivalry

Increased sophistication of the nobility was much enhanced by the fact that in the High Middle Ages there was less tumultuous local warfare than before. Until around 1100 the typical European noble was a crude and brutal warrior who spent most of his time engaging in combat with his neighbors and pillaging the defenseless. Much of this violence slackened off in the twelfth century as a result of ecclesiastical constraints, because emerging states were more effectively enforcing

Jousting in a Tournament

local peace, and because the nobles themselves were beginning to enjoy a more settled existence. Nobles continued to go on crusades and to fight in national wars, but they engaged in petty quarrels with each other less frequently. Apparently as an unconscious surrogate for the old fighting spirit the code of *chivalry* was developed. This channeled martial conduct into relatively benign activities. Chivalry literally means "horsemanship," and the chivalrous noble was expected to be thoroughly adept at the equestrian arts. Chivalry also imposed the obligation of fighting in defense of honorable causes; if none was to be found there were opportunities for combat in tournaments, mock battles that at first were quite savage but later became elaborate ceremonial affairs. Above all, the chivalric lord—typically a "knight" who owned less land than the upper aristocracy—was expected to be not only brave and loyal but generous, truthful, reverent, kind to the poor, and disdainful of unfair advantage or sordid gain.

By-products of the increase in noble wealth and the rise of chivalry were improvements in the quality of living conditions and the treatment of women. Until around 1100 most noble dwellings were made of wood, and burned down frequently because of primitive heating and cooking methods. With increasing wealth and more advanced technology, castles after 1100 were usually built of stone and were thus far less flammable. Moreover, they were now equipped with chimneys and mantled fireplaces, both medieval inventions, which meant that instead of having one large fire in a central great hall, indi-

Improvements in the quality of noble life

Aristocratic Table Manners. There are knives but no forks or napkins on the table. The large stars mark these nobles as members of a chivalric order.

vidual rooms could be heated and individuals gained some privacy. Nobles customarily ate fewer vegetables than peasants, but their diet was laden with meat; increased luxury trade also brought costly exotic spices like pepper and saffron to their tables. Although table manners were still atrocious—all used only knives and spoons but no forks and blew their noses on their sleeves—nobles tried to show their superiority to others by dressing elegantly, indeed ostentatiously. During this period snug-fitting clothing also became available because both knitting and the button and buttonhole had just been invented.

Changes in noble attitudes toward women

The history of noble attitudes toward women in the High Middle Ages is somewhat controversial for two reasons. One is that most of our evidence comes from literature, and historians differ as to what degree literature actually reflects life. The other is that according to some scholars women were at best put on a pedestal, whereas modern women rightly prefer to move "up from the pedestal." Nonetheless, there can be no question that as the material quality of noble life improved it did so for women as well as men. More than that, there definitely was a revolution in some verbalized attitudes toward the female sex. Until the twelfth century, aside from a few female saints, women were virtually ignored in literature: the typical French epic told of bloody warlike deeds that either made no mention of women or portrayed them only in passing as being totally subservient. But within a few decades after 1100 noblewomen were suddenly turned into objects of veneration by lyric poets and writers of romances (see the following chapter). A typical troubadour poet could write of his lady that "all I do that is fitting I infer from her beautiful body," and that "she is the tree and the branch where joy's fruit ripens."

Changes in the status of noblewomen

Although the new "courtly" literature was extremely idealistic and somewhat artificial, it surely expressed the values of a gentler culture wherein upper-class women were in practice more respected than before. Moreover, there is no question that certain royal women in the twelfth and thirteenth centuries actually did rule their states on various occasions when their husbands or sons were dead or unable to do so.

The indomitable Eleanor of Aquitaine, wife of Henry II, for example, helped rule England even though she was over seventy years old when her son Richard I went on a crusade from 1190 to 1194, and the strong-willed Blanche of Castile ruled France extremely well twice in the thirteenth century, once during the minority of her son Louis IX and again when he was off crusading. No doubt from a modern perspective high-medieval women were still very constrained, but from the point of view of the past the High Middle Ages was a time of progress for the women of the upper classes. The most striking symbol comes from the history of the game of chess: before the twelfth century chess was played in Eastern countries, but there the equivalent of the queen was a male figure, the king's chief minister, who could only move diagonally one square at a time; in twelfth-century western Europe, however, this piece was turned into a queen, and sometime before the end of the Middle Ages she began to move all over the board.

3. THE REVIVAL OF TRADE AND THE URBAN REVOLUTION

Patterns of trade

Inseparable from the agricultural revolution, the enfranchisement of serfs, and the growing sophistication of noble life was the revival of trade and the burgeoning of towns. Reviving trade was of many different sorts. Most fundamental was the mundane trade at local markets, where serfs or free peasants sold their excess grain or perhaps a few dozen eggs. But with growing specialization, produce like wine or cotton might be shipped over longer distances. River and sea routes were used wherever possible, but land transport was also necessary, and this was aided by improvements in road-building, the introduction of packhorses and mules, and the building of bridges. Whereas the Romans were really only interested in land *communications,* medieval people, starting in the eleventh century, concentrated on land *transport* to the degree that they were much better able to maintain a vigorous land-based trade. And that is not to say that they ignored Mediterranean communications either. On the contrary, starting again in the eleventh century they began to make the former Roman "lake" the intermediary for an extensive seaborne trade that stretched over shorter and longer distances. Between 1050 and 1300 the Italian city-states of Genoa, Pisa, and Venice freed much of the Mediterranean from Muslim control, started monopolizing trade on formerly Byzantine waters, and began to establish in eastern Mediterranean outposts a flourishing commerce with the Orient. As a result, luxury goods such as spices, gems, perfumes, and fine cloths began to appear in Western markets and stimulated economic life by inspiring nobles to accelerate the agricultural revolution in order to pay for them.

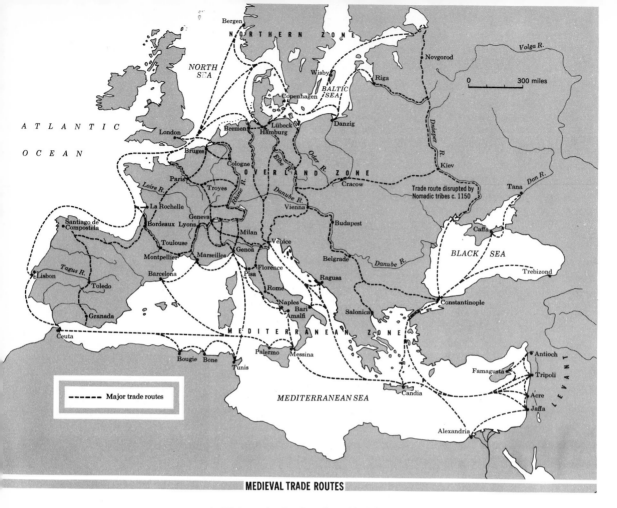

MEDIEVAL TRADE ROUTES

The revival of a money economy

This revival of trade called for new patterns of payment and the development of new commercial techniques. Most significantly, western Europe returned to a money economy after about four centuries when coined money was hardly used as a medium of exchange. The traditional manor had been almost self-sufficient and the few external items needed could be bartered for. But with the growth of markets coins became indispensable. At first these were coins of only the smallest denominations, but as luxury trade grew in the West the denominations increased apace; by the thirteenth century gold coins were minted by Italian states such as Florence and Venice.

Long-distance trade and new commercial techniques

In a similar pattern of development, long-distance traders were first itinerant merchants, often not unlike peddlers, but gradually they found it best to exhibit and sell their wares at international trade fairs. The most prosperous of these fairs were held in the French province of Champagne, where, for example, cloths from Flanders and spices brought by Italians from the East were exhibited and sold. Later, by around 1300, trade fairs declined because prosperous merchants were now sending out whole fleets from Italy to the North Atlantic and staying at home themselves. To facilitate this more sedentary pattern of business life, merchants perfected modern techniques of business partnerships, letters of credit, and accounting. Because such entrepreneurs invested in trade intentionally for profit and devised and used sophisticated credit mechanisms, most modern historians agree in calling them the first Western commercial capitalists.

In addition to the expansion of money and credit, trade was vastly facilitated by the rapid growth of towns. If we could imagine an aerial view of twelfth-century Europe, the mushrooming of towns would be the most strikingly visible phenomenon after the clearing of forests and wastes. Some historians misleadingly include under the heading of towns the numerous new agricultural village communities of peasants that were established in clearings. These, however, were not really urban in any sense. Putting them aside, many urban agglomerations were built from the ground up in the High Middle Ages, and existing towns that had barely survived from the Roman period grew enormously in size. To take some examples, in central and eastern Germany, which had not been part of the old Roman area of settlement, new towns such as Freiburg, Lübeck, Munich, and Berlin were founded in the twelfth century. Farther west, where old Roman towns had become little more than episcopal residences or stockades, formerly insignificant towns like Paris, London, and Cologne roughly doubled in size between 1100 and 1200 and doubled again in the next century. Urban life was above all concentrated in Italy, which encompassed most of Europe's largest cities: Venice, Genoa, Milan, Bologna, Palermo, Florence, and Naples. In the thirteenth century the population of the largest of these—Venice, Genoa, and Milan—was in the range of 100,000. We lack accurate growth figures for other Italian cities, but it seems likely that many at least trebled in population between about 1150 and 1300 because we do know that the smaller Italian town of Imola, near Bologna, grew from some 4,200 in 1210 to 11,500 in 1312. Considering that town life had come very close to disappearing in most of Europe between 750 and 1050, it is warranted to speak of a high-medieval urban revolution. Moreover, from the High Middle Ages until now a vigorous urban life has been a major characteristic of western European and subsequently modern world civilization.

It used to be thought that the primary cause of the medieval urban revolution was the revival of long-distance trade. Theoretically, itinerant peddlers, who had no secure place in the dominantly agrarian society of Europe, gradually settled together in towns in order to offer each other much-needed protection and establish markets to sell their wares. In fact, the picture is far more complicated than that. While some towns did receive great stimulus from long-distance trade, and the growth of a major city such as Venice would have been unthinkable without it, most towns relied for their origin and early economic vitality far more on the wealth of their surrounding areas. These brought them surplus agricultural goods, raw materials for manufac-

Growth of towns

Venetian Coin. Minted between 1280 and 1289 this obverse depicts the patron saint of Venice, Saint Mark, granting a banner symbolizing worldly rule to the Venetian doge.

Causes of the urban revolution

View of Paris. The city looked this way at the end of the Middle Ages, around 1480. Note the prominence of the cathedral of Notre Dame in the center and the large number of other church spires; note, too, how closely all the buildings are packed behind the walls.

Old Houses in Strassburg. In the Middle Ages food was stored in attics, with special openings for ventilation, as insurance against famine. Of course there was still much spoilage.

ture, and an influx of population. In other words, the quickening of economic life in general was the major cause of urban growth: towns existed in a symbiotic relationship with the countryside by providing markets and also wares made by artisans, while they lived off the rural food surplus and grew with the migration of surplus serfs or peasants who were seeking a better life. (Escaped serfs were guaranteed their freedom if they stayed in a town a year and a day.) Once towns started to flourish, many of them began to specialize in certain enterprises. Paris and Bologna gained considerable wealth by becoming the homes of leading universities; Venice, Genoa, Cologne, and London became centers of long-distance trade; and Milan, Ghent, and Bruges specialized in manufactures. The most important urban industries were those devoted to cloth-making. Cloth manufacturers sometimes developed techniques of large-scale production and investment that are ancestors of the modern factory system and industrial capitalism. But it must be emphasized that large industrial enterprises were atypical of medieval economic life as a whole.

Medieval cities and towns were not smaller scale facsimiles of modern ones; to our own eyes they would still have seemed half-rural and uncivilized. Streets were often unpaved, houses had gardens for raising vegetables, and cows and pigs were kept in stables and pigsties. Passing along the streets of a major metropolis one might be stopped by a flock of bleating sheep or a crowd of honking geese. Sanitary conditions were often very poor and the air must often have reeked of excrement—both animal and human. Town-dwellers were cursed by the frequency of fires that swept quickly through closely settled wooden or straw quarters and went unstopped by the lack of fire stations. People were also highly susceptible to contagious diseases bred by unsanitary conditions and crowding. Still another problem was that economic tensions and family rivalries could lead to bloody riots. Yet for all this, urban folk took great pride in their new cities and ways of life. A famous paean to London, for example, written by a twelfth-century denizen of that city, boasted of its prosperity, piety, and perfect climate (!), and claimed that except for frequent fires, London's only nuisance was "the immoderate drinking of fools."

The most distinctive form of economic and social organization in the medieval towns was the guild. This was, roughly speaking, a professional association organized to protect and promote special interests. The main types were merchant guilds and craft guilds. The primary functions of the merchant guild were to maintain a monopoly of the local market for its members and to preserve a stable economic system. To accomplish these ends the merchant guild severely restricted trading by foreigners in the city, guaranteed to its members the right to participate in sales offered by other members, enforced uniform pricing, and did everything possible to ensure that no individual would corner the market for goods produced by its members.

Craft guilds similarly regulated the affairs of artisans. Usually their only full-fledged voting members were so-called master craftsmen, who were experts at their trades and ran their own shops. Hence if these guilds were anything like modern trade unions, they were unions of bosses. Second-class members of craft guilds were journeymen, who had learned their trades but still worked for the masters (*journeyman* is from the French *journée,* meaning "day," or by extension "day's work"), and apprentices. Terms of apprenticeship were carefully regulated: if an apprentice wished to become a master he often had to produce a "masterpiece" for judging by the masters of the guild. Craft guilds, like merchant guilds, sought to preserve monopo-

A Medieval Shoemaker

The Great Crane at Bruges. A pulley device operated by human energy. Animals wander through the narrow street in the background.

A Medieval Weaver

*Medieval attitudes toward
merchants*

lies and to limit competition. Thus they established uniformity of prices and wages, prohibited working after hours, and formulated detailed regulations governing methods of production and quality of materials. In addition to all their economic functions, both kinds of guilds served important social ones. Often they acted in the capacity of religious associations, benevolent societies, and social clubs. Wherever possible guilds tried to minister to the human needs of their members. Thus in some cities they came close to becoming miniature governments.

Town merchants and artisans were particularly concerned to protect themselves because they had no accepted role in the older medieval scheme of things. Usually merchants were disdained by the landed aristocracy because they could claim no ancient lineages and were not versed in the ways of chivalry. Worst of all, they were too obviously concerned with pecuniary gain. Although nobles too were gradually becoming interested in making profits, they displayed this less openly: they paid little attention in their daily lives to accounts and made much of their free-spending largesse. Still another reason why medieval merchants were on the defensive was that the Church, opposed to illicit gain, taught a doctrine of the "just price" that was often at variance with what the merchants thought they deserved. Clergymen too condemned usury—i.e., the lending of money for interest—even though it was often essential for doing business. A decree of the Second Lateran Council of 1139, to take one example, excoriated the "detestable, shameful, and insatiable rapacity of moneylenders." As time went on, however, attitudes slowly changed. In Italy it often became hard to tell merchants from aristocrats because the latter customarily lived in towns and often engaged in trade themselves. In the rest of Europe, the most prosperous town-dwellers, called patricians, developed their own sense of pride verging on that of the nobility. The medieval Church never abandoned its prohibition of usury, but it did

*Medieval Walled City of
Carcassonne, France.
These walls date from
1240 to 1285.*

come to approve making profits on commercial risks, which was often close to the same thing. Moreover, starting around the thirteenth century leading churchmen came to speak more favorably of merchants. St. Bonaventure, a leading thirteenth-century churchman, argued that God showed special favors to shepherds like David in the time of the Old Testament, to fishers like Peter in the time of the New, and to merchants like St. Francis in the thirteenth century.

All in all, the importance of the high-medieval urban revolution can scarcely be overestimated. The fact that the new towns were the vital pumps of the high-medieval economy has already been sufficiently emphasized: in providing markets and producing wares they kept the entire economic system thriving. In addition, cities and towns made important contributions to the development of government because in many areas they gained their own independence and ruled themselves as city-states. Primarily in Italy, where urban life was by far the most advanced, city governments experimented with new systems of tax-collecting, record-keeping, and public participation in decision-making. Italian city-states were particularly advanced in their administrative techniques and thereby helped influence a general European-wide growth in governmental sophistication.

Significance of the urban revolution: (1) development of the economy and government

Finally, the rise of towns contributed greatly to the quickening of intellectual life in the West. New schools were invariably located in towns because towns afforded domiciles and legal protection for scholars. At first, students and teachers were always clerics, but by the thirteenth century the needs of merchants to be trained in reading and accounting led to the foundation of numerous lay primary schools. Equally momentous for the future was the fact that the stimulating urban environment helped make advanced schools more open to intellectual experimentation than any in the West since those of the Greeks. Not coincidentally, Greek intellectual life too was based on thriving cities. Thus it seems that without commerce in goods there can be little exciting commerce in ideas.

(2) towns as a foundation for intellectual life

4. FEUDALISM AND THE RISE OF THE NATIONAL MONARCHIES

If any western European city of around 1200 epitomized Europe's greatest new accomplishments it was Paris: that city was not only a bustling commercial center and an important center of learning, it was also the capital of what was becoming Europe's most powerful government. France, like England and the new Christian kingdoms of the Iberian peninsula, was taking shape in the twelfth and thirteenth centuries as a *national monarchy,* a new form of government which was to dominate Europe's political future. Because the developing national monarchies were the most successful and promising European governments we must concentrate on them. But before we do it is well

A Medieval Tailor

*The political decline of
medieval Germany an
intriguing historical
problem*

*The German monarchy in
the tenth and eleventh
centuries*

*The struggle between
Henry IV and Gregory
VII*

to see what was happening from the political point of view in Germany and Italy.

Around 1050 Germany was unquestionably the most centralized and best-ruled territory in Europe, but by 1300 it had fallen into a congeries of warring petty states. Since most other areas of Europe were gaining stronger rule in the very same period, the political decline of Germany becomes an intriguing historical problem. It is also a problem of fundamental importance because from a political point of view Germany only caught up with the rest of Europe in the nineteenth century and its belated efforts to gain its full place in the European political system created difficulties that have just come to be resolved in our own age.

The major sources of Germany's strength from the reign of Otto the Great in the middle of the tenth century until the latter part of the eleventh century were its succession of strong rulers, its resistance to political fragmentation, and the close alliance of its crown with the Church. By resoundingly defeating the Hungarians and taking the title of emperor, Otto kept the country from falling prey to further invasions and won great prestige for the monarchy. For over a century afterward there was a nearly uninterrupted succession of rulers as able and vigorous as Otto. Their nearest political rivals were the dukes, military leaders of five large German territories (Lorraine, Saxony, Franconia, Swabia, and Bavaria), but throughout most of this period the dukes were overawed by the emperors' greater power. The latter, in order to rule their wide territories—which included Switzerland, eastern France, and most of the Low Countries, as well as claims to northern Italy—relied heavily on cooperation with the Church. The leading royal administrators were archbishops and bishops whom the emperors appointed without interference from the pope and who often came from their own families. The German emperors were so strong that, when they chose to do so, they could come down to Italy and name their own popes. The archbishops and bishops ran the German government fairly well for the times without any elaborate administrative machinery, and they counterbalanced the strength of the dukes. In the course of the eleventh century the emperors were starting tentatively to develop their own secular administration. Had they been allowed to continue this policy, it might have provided a really solid governmental foundation for the future. But just then the whole system shaped by Otto the Great and his successors was dramatically challenged by a revolution within the Church.

The challenge to the German government came in the reign of Henry IV (1056–1106) and was directed by Pope Gregory VII (1073–1085). For reasons that will be discussed in the next chapter, Gregory wished to free the Church from secular control and launched a struggle to achieve this aim against Henry IV. Gregory immediately placed Henry on the defensive by forging an alliance with the dukes and other German princes, who only needed a sufficient pretext to rise up against their ruler. When the princes threatened to depose Henry because of his disobedience to the pope, the hitherto mighty ruler was forced to seek absolution from Gregory VII in one of the most melodramatic scenes of the Middle Ages. In the depths of winter in 1077 Henry hurried over the Alps to abase himself before the pope in the north Italian castle of Canossa. As Gregory described the scene in a letter to the princes: "There on three successive days, standing before the castle gate, laying aside all royal insignia, barefooted and in coarse attire, Henry ceased not with many tears to beseech the apostolic help and comfort." No German ruler had ever been so humiliated. Although the events at Canossa forestalled Henry's deposition, they robbed him of his great prestige. By the time his struggle with the papacy, continued by his son, was over, the princes had won far more practical independence from the crown than they had ever had. More than that, in 1125 they made good their claims to be able to elect a new ruler regardless of hereditary succession—a principle that would thereafter often lead them to choose the weakest successors or to embroil the country in civil war. Meanwhile, the crown had lost much of its control of the Church and thus in effect had its administrative rug pulled out from under it. While France and England were gradually consolidating their centralized governmental apparatuses, Germany was losing its own.

A major attempt to stem the tide running against the German monarchy was made in the twelfth century by Frederick I (1152–1190), who came from the family of Hohenstaufen. Frederick, called "Barbarossa" (meaning "red beard"), tried to reassert his imperial dignity by calling his realm the "Holy Roman Empire," on the theory that it was a universal empire descending from Rome and blessed by God. Laying claim to Roman descent, he promulgated old Roman imperial laws—preserved in the Code of Justinian—that gave him much theoretical power. But he could not hope to enforce such laws unless he had his own material base of support. Therefore the major policy of his reign was to balance the power of the princes by carving out his own geographical domain from which he might draw wealth and strength.

Unfortunately for Frederick, his ancestral lands were located in Swabia, a poorer part of Germany that even today still consists of relatively unproductive hill country and the Black Forest. So Frederick decided to make northern Italy his power base in addition to Swabia. In this he could hardly have made a worse decision. Northern Italy was certainly wealthy, but it was also fiercely independent. Its rich towns and cities, led by Milan, offered stiff resistance. They were further lent helpful moral support by the papacy, which had no wish to see a strong German emperor ruling powerfully in Italy. Frederick came very close to overpowering the urban-papal alliance but ultimately the Alps proved to be too great a barrier to allow him to enforce his will in Italy and hope to rule in Germany as well. Whenever

Frederick Barbarossa. A stylized contemporary representation.

Frederick's Italian policy

he subdued the towns he would shortly afterward have to leave for home, and the towns, with papal encouragement, would then rise up again. Finally, in 1176, insufficient German imperial forces were resoundingly defeated by the troops of a north Italian urban coalition at Legnano, and Barbarossa was forced to concede the area's de facto independence. In the meantime, the princes in Germany were continuing to gather strength, especially by colonizing the rich agricultural lands east of the Elbe where Frederick really should have busied himself, and the emperor's struggle with the popes further alienated elements within the German church. Because Barbarossa was a dashing figure he was well remembered by Germans, but his reign virtually made it certain that the German empire would not rise again during the medieval period.

Frederick II; his personality and policies

The reign of Barbarossa's equally famous grandson, Frederick II (1212–1250), was merely a playing out of Germany's fate. In terms of his personality Frederick was probably the most fascinating of all medieval rulers. Because his father, Henry VI, had inherited through marriage the kingdom of southern Italy and Sicily (later called the Kingdom of the Two Sicilies), Frederick grew up in Palermo, where he absorbed elements of Islamic culture. (Arabs had ruled in Sicily for two and a half centuries, from 831 to 1071.) Frederick II spoke five or six languages, was a patron of learning, and wrote his own book on falconry, which takes an honored place in the early history of Western observational science. He also performed bizarre and brutal "experiments," such as disemboweling men to observe the comparative effects of rest and exercise upon digestion. Such practices corresponded to Frederick's overall policy of trying to rule like an Oriental despot. In his autonomous kingdom of southern Italy he introduced Eastern forms of absolutist and bureaucratic government. He established a professional army, levied direct taxation, and promulgated uniform Roman law. Typically, Frederick tried to create a ruler cult and decreed it an act of sacrilege even to discuss his statutes or judgments. For a while these policies seemed successful in ruling southern Italy, but Frederick's power base in Italy led to renewed conflicts with the papacy and the north Italian cities. These dragged on indecisively until his death, but thereafter the papacy was resolved to see no further Hohenstaufens ruling in Italy and proceeded to eliminate the remaining contenders from the line by calling crusades against them. Overtaxed by Frederick's ruthlessness and subsequent wars, southern Italy gradually sank into the backwardness from which it is only barely emerging today. And Frederick's reign was as damaging to Germany as well. Bent on pursuing his Italian policies without hindrance, Frederick formally wrote Germany off to the princes by granting them large areas of sovereignty. Although titular "emperors" afterward continued to be elected, the princes were the real rulers of the country. Yet they fought with each other so much that peace was rare, and they subdivided their lands among their heirs to such an extent that the

The Emperor Frederick II. He is shown holding a *fleur de lis,* as a symbol of rule, with a falcon, his favorite bird, at his side.

map of Germany began to look like a jig-saw puzzle. As the French philosopher Voltaire later said, the German "Holy Roman Empire" had become neither holy, nor Roman, nor an empire.

The story of high-medieval Italian politics may be told more quickly. Southern Italy and Sicily had been welded together into a strong monarchical state in the twelfth century by Norman-French descendants of the Vikings. But then, as we have seen, the area went to the Hohenstaufens and was subsequently brought to ruin. Central Italy was largely ruled by the papacy in the High Middle Ages, but the popes were seldom strong enough to create a really well-governed state, partly because they were at constant loggerheads with the German emperors. Farthest north were the rich commercial and manufacturing cities which had successfully fought off Barbarossa. These were usually organized politically in the form of republics or "communes." They offered much participation in governmental life to their more prosperous inhabitants. But because of diverse economic interests and family antagonisms, the Italian cities were usually riven with internal strife. Moreover, although they could unite in leagues against foreign threats such as those represented by Barbarossa or Frederick II, the cities often fought each other when foreign threats were absent. The result was that although economic and cultural life was very far advanced in the Italian cities, and although the cities made important experiments in administrative techniques, political stability was widely lacking in northern Italy throughout most of the high-medieval period.

If one looks for the centers of growing political stability in Europe, then one has to seek them in high-medieval France and England. Ironically, some of the most basic foundations for future political achievement in France were established without any planning just when that area was most politically unstable. These foundations were aspects of a level of political decentralization often referred to by historians as the system of "feudalism." The use of this word is controversial because ever since Marx some historians prefer to use it as a term to describe an agrarian economic and social system wherein large estates are worked by a dependent peasantry. The difficulty with this usage is that it is too imprecise, for such large estates existed in many times and places beyond the European Middle Ages and the medieval agrarian system can best be called manorialism. Some historians on the other extreme argue that even if the word feudalism is used to describe a medieval political system, medieval realities were so diverse that no one definition of feudalism can accurately or even usefully be extended to cover more than a single case. Nonetheless, for convenience we can retain the use of the word here and apply it to a specific point in medieval political development so long as we bear in mind that, like manorialism, it is only meant to serve as an approximation and that other historians may use it as a term for economic or sociological analysis.

GERMAN EMPIRE c. 1200 A.D.

Political feudalism

Political feudalism was essentially a system of extreme political decentralization wherein what we today would call public power was widely vested in private hands. From a historical perspective it was most fully experienced in France during the tenth century when the Carolingian empire had disintegrated and the area was being buffeted by devastating Viking invasions. The Carolingians had maintained a modicum of public authority, but they proved to be no help whatsoever in warding off the invasions. So local landlords had to fend for themselves. In the end, the landlords turned out to offer the best defense against the Vikings and accordingly were able to acquire practically all the old governmental powers. They raised their own small armies, dispensed their own crude justice, and occasionally issued their own primitive coins. Despite such decentralization, however, it was never forgotten that there once had been higher and larger units of government. Above all, no matter how weak the king was (and he was indeed usually very weak), there always remained a king in France who descended directly or indirectly from the western branch of the Carolingians. There also were scattered remaining dukes or counts, who in theory were supposed to have more power and authority than petty landlords or knights. So, by a complicated and hard-to-trace process of rationalization, a vague theory was worked out in the course of the tenth and eleventh centuries that tried to establish some order within feudalism. According to this, minor feudal lords did not hold their powers outright but only held them as so-called *fiefs* (rhymes with reefs), which could be revoked upon noncompliance with certain obligations. In theory—and much of this theory was ignored in practice for long periods of time—the king or higher lords granted fiefs, that is, governmental rights over various lands, to lesser lords in return for a stipulated amount of military service. In turn, the lesser lords could grant some of those fiefs to still lesser lords for military services until the chain stopped at the lowest level of knights. The holder of a fief was called a *vassal* of the granter, but this term had none of the demeaning connotations that it has gained today. Vassalage—much unlike serfdom—was a purely honorable status and all fief-holders were "noble."

Since feudalism was originally a form of decentralization, it once was considered by historians to have been a corrosive or divisive historical force; in common speech today many use the word feudal as a synonym for backward. But scholars more recently have come to the conclusion that feudalism was a force for progress and a fundamental point of departure for the growth of the modern state. They note that in areas such as Germany and Italy, where there was hardly any feudalism, political stabilization and unification came only in later times, whereas in the areas of France and England, which saw full feudalization, stabilization and governmental centralization came rapidly afterward. Scholars now posit several reasons for this. Because feudalism was originally spontaneous and makeshift, it was highly flexible. Local lords, instead of being bound by anachronistic, procrustean principles, could rule as seemed best at the moment, or could bend to the dictates of particular local customs. Thus their governments, however crude, worked the best for their times and could be used for building an even stronger government as time went on. A second reason for the effectiveness of feudalism was that it drew more people into direct contact with the actual workings of political life than had the old Roman or Carolingian systems. Government on the most local level could most easily be seen or experienced; as it became

*Feudalism as a cause of
political progress*

tangible people began to appreciate and identify with it far more than they had appreciated empires. The result was that feudalism inculcated growing governmental loyalty, and once that loyalty was developed it could be drawn upon by still larger units. Third, feudalism helped lead to certain more modern institutions by its emphasis on courts. As the feudal system became more regularized, it became customary for vassals to appear at the court of their overlords at least once a year. There they were expected to "pay court," i.e., show certain ceremonial signs of loyalty, and also to serve on "courts" in the sense of participating in trials and offering counsel. Thus they became more and more accustomed to performing governmental business and began to behave more like courtiers or politicians. As the monarchical states of France and England themselves developed, kings saw how useful the feudal court was and made it the administrative kernel of their expanding governmental systems. A final reason why feudalism led to political progress is not really intrinsic to the system itself. Because the theory of larger units was never forgotten, it could be drawn upon by greater lords and kings when the right time came to reacquire their rights.

The Norman Conquest

The greatest possibilities for the use of feudalism were first demonstrated in England after the Norman Conquest of 1066. We have seen that England became unified and enjoyed strong kingship under the Saxon Alfred and his successors in the late ninth and tenth centuries. But then the Saxon kingship began to weaken, primarily as the result of renewed Viking invasions and poor leadership. In 1066 William, the duke of Normandy (in western France), laid claim to the English crown and crossed the Channel to conquer what he had claimed. Fortunately for him the newly installed English king, Harold, had just warded off a Viking attack in the north and thus could not offer resistance at full strength. At the Battle of Hastings Harold and his Saxon troops fought bravely, but ultimately could not withstand the on-

Battle of Hastings. A scene from the Bayeux tapestry, embroidered shortly after William the Conqueror's victory. The inscription reads in translation: "Here the English and French have fallen together in battle."

slaught of the fresher Norman troops. As the day waned Harold fell, mortally wounded by a random arrow, his forces dispersed, and the Normans took the field and with it, England. Duke William now became King William, the Conqueror, and proceeded to rule his new prize as he wished.

With hindsight we can say that the Norman Conquest came at just the right time to preserve and enhance political stability. Before 1066 England was threatened with disintegration under warrior aristocrats called earls, but William destroyed their power entirely. In its place he substituted the feudal system, whereby all the land in England was newly granted in the form of fiefs held directly or indirectly from the king. Fief-holders had most of the governmental rights they had obtained less formally on the Continent, but William retained the prerogatives of coining money, collecting a land tax, and supervising justice in major criminal cases. He also retained the Anglo-Saxon officer of local government, known as the sheriff, to help him administer and enforce these rights. In order to make sure that none of his barons (the English term for major fief-holders) became too powerful, William was careful to scatter the fiefs granted to them throughout various parts of the country. In these ways William used feudal practices to help govern England when there were not yet enough trained administrators to allow any real governmental professionalization. But he also retained much royal power and kept the country thoroughly unified under the crown.

The feudal system in Norman England

The history of English government in the two centuries after William is primarily a story of kings tightening up the feudal system to their advantage until they superseded it and created a strong national monarchy. The first to take steps in this direction was the Conqueror's energetic son Henry I (1100–1135). One of his most important accomplishments was to start a process of specialization at the royal court whereby certain officials began to take full professional responsibility for supervising financial accounts; these officials became known as clerks of the *Exchequer*. Another accomplishment was to institute a system of traveling circuit-judges to administer justice as direct royal representatives in various parts of the realm.

The growth of national monarchy in England; the reign of Henry I

After an intervening period of civil war Henry I was succeeded by his grandson Henry II (1154–1189), who was very much in his grandfather's activist mold. Henry II's reign was certainly one of the most momentous in all of English history. One reason for this was that it saw a great struggle between the king and the flamboyant archbishop of Canterbury, Thomas Becket, over the status of Church courts and Church law. In Henry's time priests and other clerics were tried for any crimes in Church courts under the rules of canon law. Punishment in these courts was notoriously lax. Even murderers were seldom sentenced to more than penance and loss of their clerical status. Also, decisions handed down in English Church courts could be appealed to the papal *curia* in Rome. Henry, who wished to have royal law prevail

The struggle between Henry II and Thomas Becket

Martyrdom of Thomas Becket. From a thirteenth-century English Psalter. One of the knights has struck Becket so mightily that he has broken his sword.

as far as possible and maintain judicial standards for all subjects in his realm, tried to limit these practices by the Constitutions of Clarendon of 1164. On the matter of clerics accused of crime he was willing to compromise by allowing them to be judged in Church courts but then have them sentenced in royal ones. Becket, however, resisted all attempts at change with great determination. The quarrel between king and archbishop was made more bitter by the fact that the two had earlier been close friends. It reached a tragic climax when Becket was murdered in Canterbury Cathedral by four of Henry's knights, after the king, in an outburst of anger, had rebuked them for doing nothing to rid him of his antagonist. The crime so shocked the English public that Becket was quickly revered as a martyr and became the most famous English saint. More important for the history of government, Henry had to abandon most of his program of bringing the Church courts under royal control, and his aims were only fulfilled in the sixteenth century with the coming of the English Reformation.

Despite this major setback, Henry II made enormous governmental gains in other areas, so much so that some historians maintain that Henry was the greatest king that England has ever known. His most important contributions were judicial. He greatly expanded the use of the itinerant judges instituted by Henry I and began the practice of commanding sheriffs to bring before these judges groups of men who were familiar with local conditions. These were then required to report under oath every case of murder, arson, robbery, or other major

The judicial reforms of Henry II

crimes known to them to have occurred since the judges' last visit. This was the origin of the grand jury. Henry also for the first time allowed parties in civil disputes to obtain royal justice. In the most prevalent type of case, someone who claimed to have been recently dispossessed of his land could obtain a writ from the crown, which would order the sheriff to bring twelve men who were assumed to know the facts before a judge. The twelve were then asked under oath if the plaintiff's claim was true, and the judge rendered his decision in accordance with their answers. Out of such practices grew the institution of the trial jury, although the trial jury was not used in criminal cases until the thirteenth century.

Henry II's legal innovations benefited both the crown and the country in several ways. Most obviously, they made justice more uniform and equitable throughout the realm. They also thereby made royal justice sought after and popular. Particularly in disputes over land—the most important and frequent disputes of the day—the weaker party was no longer at the mercy of a strong-arming neighbor. Usually the weaker parties were knights, with whom the crown before then had not been in close touch. In helping defend their rights Henry gained valuable allies in his policy of keeping the stronger barons in tow. Finally, the widespread use of juries in Henry's reign brought more and more people into actual participation in royal government. In so doing it got them more interested in government and more loyal to government. Since these people served without pay, Henry brilliantly managed to expand the competence and popularity of his government at very little cost.

The benefits of Henry's legal work

The most concrete proof of Henry II's success is that after his death his government worked so well that it more or less ran on its own. Henry's son, the swashbuckling Richard I, the "Lionhearted," ruled for ten years, from 1189 to 1199, but in that time he only stayed in England for six months because he was otherwise engaged in crusading or defending his possessions on the Continent. Throughout the time of Richard's absence governmental administration actually became more efficient, owing to the work of capable ministers. The country also raised two huge sums for Richard by taxation: one to pay for his crusade to the Holy Land and the other to buy his ransom when he was captured by an enemy on his return. But later when a new king needed still more money, most Englishmen were disinclined to pay it.

The new king was Richard's brother, John (1199–1216), who has the reputation of being a villain but was more a victim of circumstances. Ever since the time of William the Conqueror, English kings had continued to rule in large portions of modern-day France, but by John's reign the kings of France were becoming strong enough to take back much of these territories. John had the great misfortune of facing the able French King Philip Augustus, who won back Normandy and neighboring lands by force of arms in 1204 and reinsured this victory by military successes in 1214. John needed money both to govern Eng-

King John. An effigy in Worcester cathedral.

*The reign of John;
Magna Carta*

land and to fight in France, but his defeats made his subjects disinclined to give it to him. The barons particularly resented John's financial exigencies and in 1215 they made him renounce these in the subsequently famous Magna Carta (Great Charter), a document which was also designed to redress all the other abuses the barons could think of. Most common conceptions of Magna Carta are erroneous. It was not intended to be a bill of rights or a charter of liberties for the common man. On the contrary, it was basically a feudal document in which the king as overlord pledged to respect the traditional rights of his vassals. Nonetheless, it did enunciate in writing the important principles that large sums of money could not be raised by the crown without consent given by the barons in a common council, and that no free man could be punished by the crown without judgment by his equals and by the law of the land. Above all, Magna Carta was important as an expression of the principle of limited government and of the idea that the king is bound by the law.

*The progress of
centralized government in
the reign of Henry III*

As the contemporary American medievalist J. R. Strayer has said, "Magna Carta made arbitrary government difficult, but it did not make centralized government impossible." In the century following its issuance, the progress of centralized government continued apace. In the reign of John's son, Henry III (1216–1277), the barons vied with the weak king for control of the government but did so on the assumption that centralized government itself was a good thing. Throughout that period administrators continued to perfect more efficient legal and administrative institutions. Whereas in the reign of Henry I financial administration began to become a specialized bureau of the royal court, in the reign of Henry III this became true of legal administration (the creation of permanent High Courts) and administration of foreign correspondence (the so-called Chancery). English central government was now fully developing a trained officialdom.

*Origins of the English
Parliament*

The last and most famous branch of the medieval English governmental system was Parliament. This gradually emerged as a separate branch of government in the decades before and after 1300, above all owing to the wishes of Henry III's son, Edward I (1272–1307). Although Parliament later became a check against royal absolutism, nothing could be further from the truth than to think that its first meetings were "demanded by the people." In its origins Parliament actually had little to do with popular representation, but was rather the king's feudal court in its largest gathering. Edward I was a strong king who called Parliaments frequently to raise money as quickly and efficiently as possible in order to help finance his foreign wars. Those present at Parliaments were not only expected to give their consent to taxation—in fact, it was virtually inconceivable for them to refuse—but while they were there they were told why taxes were necessary so that they would pay them less grudgingly. They could also agree upon details of collection and payment. At the same meetings Edward could take advice about pressing concerns, have justice done for exceptional cases, review local administration, and promulgate new laws. Probably the most unusual trait of Edward's Parliaments in comparison to similar assemblies on the Continent was that they began to include representatives from the counties and towns in addition to the higher nobility. These representatives, however, scarcely spoke for "the people" because most of the people of England were unfranchised serfs and peasants—not to mention women, who were never consulted in any way. Most likely, Edward had predominantly financial motives for calling representatives from the "commons." He probably also realized the propaganda value of overawing local representatives with royal grandeur at impressive parliamentary meetings so that they would then spread a favorable impression of the monarchy back home. As time went on, commoners were called to Parliament so often that they became a recognized part of its organization: by the middle of the fourteenth century they sat regularly in their own "house." But they still represented only the prosperous people of countryside and towns and were usually manipulated by the crown or the nobles.

Edward I's reign also saw the culmination of the development of a strong national monarchy in other aspects. By force of arms Edward nearly unified the entire island of Britain, conquering Wales and almost subduing Scotland (which, however, was to rise up again soon after his death). Edward began the practice of regularly issuing statute law, that is, original public legislation designed to apply indefinitely to the entire realm. Because of his role as a law-giver, Edward is sometimes referred to as the "English Justinian." Most important, Edward also curtailed the feudal powers of his barons by limiting their rights to hold private courts and to grant their own lands as fiefs. Thus, by the end of his reign much of the independent power once consciously vested with the barons by William the Conqueror was being taken away from them. The explanation for this is that in the intervening high-medieval centuries the king was developing his own royal institutions of government to the degree that old-fashioned feudalism was now no longer of any real service. Because Edward pressed his strong government and financial demands somewhat excessively for the spirit of the age, there was an antimonarchical reaction after his death. But it is striking that after Edward's time whenever there were baronial rebellions they were always made on the assumption that England would remain a unified country, governed by the basic high-medieval monarchical institutions. England was unified around the crown in the High Middle Ages and would remain a basically well-governed and unified country right up to modern times.

While the process of governmental centralization was making impressive strides in England, it developed more slowly in France. But by around 1300 it had come close to reaching the same point of completion. French governmental unification proceeded more slowly because France in the eleventh century was more decentralized than England

The English monarchy under Edward I

The process of political centralization in France

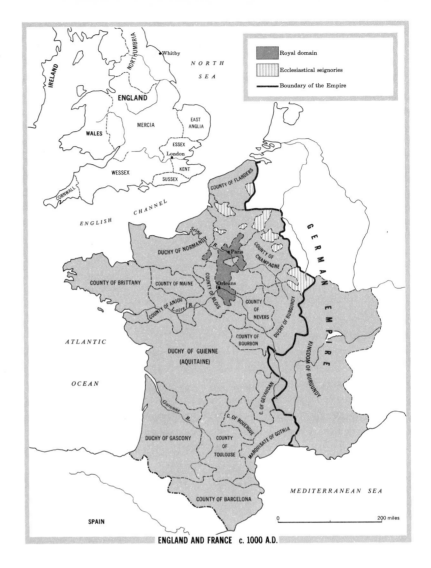

ENGLAND AND FRANCE c. 1000 A.D.

and faced greater problems. The last of the weak Carolingian monarchs was replaced in 987 by Hugh Capet, the count of Paris, but the
new Capetian dynasty—which was to rule without interruption until
1328—was at first no stronger than the old Carolingian one. Even
through most of the twelfth century the kings of France ruled directly
only in a small area around Paris known as the Ile-de-France, roughly
the size of Vermont. Beyond that territory the kings had shadowy
claims to being the feudal overlords of numerous counts and dukes
throughout much of the area of modern France, but for practical purposes those counts and dukes were almost entirely independent. It was
said that when the king of France demanded homage from the first
duke of Normandy, the duke had one of his warriors pretend to kiss
the king's foot but then seize the royal leg and pull the king over
backwards, to the mockery of all those present. While the French king-

ship was so weak, the various parts of France were developing their own distinct local traditions and dialects. Thus, whereas William the Conqueror inherited in England a country that had already been unified and was just on the verge of falling apart, the French kings of the High Middle Ages had to unify their country from scratch, with only a vague reminiscence of Carolingian unity to build upon.

*Factors facilitating the
growth of the French
monarchy*

In many respects, however, luck was on their side. First of all, they were fortunate for hundreds of years in having direct male heirs to succeed them. Consequently, there were no deadly quarrels over the right of succession. In the second place, most of the French kings lived to an advanced age, the average period of rule being about thirty years. That meant that sons were already mature men when they came to the throne and there were few regencies to squander the royal power during the minority of a prince. More than that, the kings of France were always highly visible, if sometimes not very imposing, when there were power struggles elsewhere, so people in neighboring areas became accustomed to thinking of the kingship as a force for stability in an unstable world. A third favorable circumstance for the French kings was the growth of agricultural prosperity and trade in their home region; this provided them with important sources of revenue. A fourth fortuitous development was that the kings were able to gain the support of the popes because the latter usually needed allies in their incessant struggles with the German emperors. The popes lent the French kings prestige, as they earlier had done for the Carolingians, and they also allowed them much direct power over the local Church, thereby bringing the kings further income and influence from patronage. A fifth factor in the French king's favor was the growth in the twelfth and thirteenth centuries of the University of Paris as the leading European center of studies. As foreigners came flocking to the university, they learned of the French king's growing authority and spread their impressions when they returned home. Finally, and by no means least of all, great credit must be given to the shrewdness and vigor of several of the French kings themselves.

*Foundations of the French
monarchy; Louis VI and
Philip Augustus*

The first noteworthy Capetian king was Louis VI, "the Fat" (1108–1137). While accomplishing nothing startling, Louis at least managed to pacify his home base, the Ile-de-France, by driving out or subduing its turbulent "robber barons." Once this was accomplished, agriculture and trade could prosper and the intellectual life of Paris could start to flourish. Thereafter, the French kings had a geographical source of power of exactly the kind that the German ruler Barbarossa sought but never found. The really startling additions to the realm were made by Louis's grandson, Philip Augustus (1180–1223). Philip was wily enough to know how to take advantage of certain feudal rights in order to win large amounts of western French territory from the English King John. He was also decisive enough to know how to defend his gains in battle. Most impressive of all, Philip worked out an excellent formula for governing his new acquisitions. Since these in-

A Seal Depicting Philip Augustus

St. Louis

King Philip the Fair of France

creased his original lands close to fourfold, and since each new area had its own highly distinct local customs, it would have been hopeless to try to enforce strict governmental standardization by means of what was then a very rudimentary administrative system. Instead, Philip allowed his new provinces to maintain most of their indigenous governmental practices but superimposed on them new royal officials known as *baillis*. These officials were entirely loyal to Philip because they never came from the regions in which they served and were paid impressive salaries for the day. They had full judicial, administrative, and military authority in their bailiwicks: on royal orders they tolerated regional diversities but guided them to the king's advantage. Thus there were no revolts in the conquered territories and royal power was enhanced. This pattern of local diversity balanced against bureaucratic centralization was to remain the basic pattern of French government. Thus Philip Augustus can be seen as an important founder of the modern French state.

In the brief reign of Philip's son, Louis VIII (1223–1226), almost all of southern France was added to the crown in the name of intervention against religious heresy. Once incorporated, this territory was governed largely on the same principles laid down by Philip. The next king, Louis IX (1226–1270), was so pious that he was later canonized by the Church and is commonly referred to as St. Louis. He ruled strongly and justly (except for great intolerance of Jews and heretics), decreed a standardized coinage for the country, perfected the judicial system, and brought France a long, golden period of internal peace. Because he was so well-loved, the monarchy lived off his prestige for many years afterward.

That prestige, however, came close to being squandered by St. Louis's more ruthless grandson, Philip IV, "the Fair" (1285–1314). Philip fought many battles at once, seeking to round out French territories in the northeast and southwest and to gain full control over the French Church instead of sharing it with the pope in Rome. All these activities forced him to accelerate the process of governmental centralization, especially with the aim of trying to raise money. Thus his reign saw the quick formulation of many administrative institutions that came close to completing the development of medieval French government, as the contemporary reign of Edward I did in England. Philip's reign also saw the calling of assemblies that were roughly equivalent to the English Parliaments, but these—later called "Estates General"—never played a central role in the French governmental system. Philip the Fair was successful in most of his ventures; above all, as we will later see, in reducing the pope to the level of a virtual French figurehead. After his death there would be an antimonarchical reaction, as there was at the same time in England, but by his reign France was unquestionably the strongest power in Europe. With only a sixteenth-century interruption, it would remain so until the nineteenth century.

While England and France followed certain similar processes of monarchical centralization and nation-building, they were also marked by basic differences that are worth describing because they were to typify differences in development for centuries after. England, a far smaller country than France, was much better unified. Aside from Wales and Scotland, there were no regions in Britain that had such different languages or traditions that they thought of themselves as separate territories. Correspondingly, there were no aristocrats who could move toward separatism by drawing on regional resentments. This meant that England never really had to face the threat of internal division and could develop strong institutions of united national government such as Parliament. It also meant that the English kings, starting primarily with Henry II, could rely on numerous local dignitaries, above all, the knights, to do much work of local government without pay. The obvious advantage was that local government was cheap, but the hidden implication of the system was that government also had to be popular, or else much of the voluntary work would grind to a halt. This doubtless was the main reason why English kings went out of their way to seek formal consent for their actions. When they did not they could barely rule, so wise kings learned the lesson and as time went on England became most clearly a limited monarchy. The French kings, much to the contrary, ruled a richer and larger country, which gave them—at least in times of peace—sufficient wealth to pay for a more bureaucratic, salaried administration at both the central and local levels. French kings therefore could rule more absolutely. But they were continually faced with serious threats of regional separatism. Different regions continued to cherish their own traditions and often supported centrifugalism in league with the upper aristocracy. So French kings often had to struggle with attempts at regional breakaways and take various measures to subdue their aristocrats. Up to around 1700 the monarchy had to fight a steady battle against regionalism, but it had the resources to win consistently and thereby managed to grow from strength to strength.

The only continental state that would rival France until the rise of Germany in the nineteenth century was Spain. The foundations of Spain's greatness were also laid in the High Middle Ages on the principle of national monarchy, but in the Middle Ages there was not yet one monarchy that ruled through most of the Iberian peninsula. After the Christians started pushing back the forces of Islam around 1100 there were four Spanish Christian kingdoms: the tiny northern mountain state of Navarre, which would always remain comparatively insignificant; Portugal in the west; Aragon in the northeast; and Castile in the center. The main Spanish occupation in the High Middle Ages was the *Reconquista,* i.e., the reconquest of the peninsula for Christianity. This reached its culmination in the year 1212 in a major victory of a combined Aragonese-Castilian army over the Muslims at Las Navas de Tolosa. The rest was mostly mopping up. By the end of the thirteenth century all that remained of earlier Muslim domination

Comparison of England and France

Medieval Spain

Bullfighting in a Thirteenth-Century Spanish Arena. Times do not seem to have changed much, although here the spectators are taking a rather unsporting part in the action.

was the small state of Granada in the extreme south, and Granada existed largely because it was willing to pay tribute to the Christians. Because Castile had the largest open frontier, it became by far the largest Spanish kingdom, but it was balanced in wealth by the more urban and trade-oriented Aragon. Both kingdoms developed institutions in the thirteenth century that roughly paralleled those of France. But until the union of Aragon and Castile under King Ferdinand and Queen Isabella in the fifteenth century, the Iberian states individually could not hope to be as strong as the much richer and more populous France.

Before concluding this chapter it is best to assess the general significance of the rise of the national monarchies in high-medieval western Europe. Until their emergence there had been two basic patterns of government in Europe: city-states and empires. City-states had the advantage of drawing heavily upon citizen participation and loyalty and thus were able to make highly efficient use of their human potential. But they were often divided by economic rivalries and they were not sufficiently large or militarily strong to defend themselves against imperial forces. The empires, on the other hand, could win battles and often had the resources to support an efficient bureaucratic administrative apparatus, but they drew on little voluntary participation and were too far-flung or rapacious to inspire any deep loyalties. The new national monarchies were to prove the "golden mean" between these extremes. They were large enough to have adequate military strength and they developed administrative techniques that would rival and eventually surpass those of the Roman or Byzantine Empires. More than that, building at first upon the bases of feudalism,

Historical role of the national monarchies

they drew upon sufficient citizen participation and loyalty to help support them in times of stress when empires would have foundered. By about 1300 the monarchies of England, France, and the Iberian peninsula had gained the primary loyalties of their subjects, superseding loyalties to communities, regions, or to the government of the Church. For all these reasons they brought much internal peace and stability to large parts of Europe where there had been little stability before. Thus they contributed greatly to making life fruitful. The medieval national monarchies were also the ancestors of the modern nation-states—the most effective and equitable governments of our day (the current Soviet Union being something more like an empire). In short, they were one of the Middle Ages' most beneficial bequests to modern times.

SELECTED READINGS

• *Items so designated are available in paperback editions.*

GENERAL STUDIES

• Bloch, Marc, *Feudal Society*, Chicago, 1961. A modern classic, first published in France in 1940. Full of valuable insights but outdated in some respects.
• Heer, Friedrich, *The Medieval World*, London, 1961. A controversial interpretation that opposes an "open" twelfth century to a "closed" thirteenth century. Very detailed.
• Southern, R. W., *The Making of the Middle Ages*, New Haven, Conn., 1953. A subtle and brilliant reading of eleventh- and twelfth-century developments. Difficult but most rewarding.
• Strayer, J. R., *Western Europe in the Middle Ages*, 3rd ed., Glenview, Ill., 1982. In a class by itself as the best short introduction to medieval political and cultural history.
 Wood, Charles T., *The Age of Chivalry* (also published as *The Quest for Eternity*), London, 1970. A lively work for the beginner that supplements Strayer in its emphasis on economic and social history.

ECONOMIC AND SOCIAL CONDITIONS

• Barber, Richard, *The Knight and Chivalry*, 2nd ed., London, 1974.
 Bautier, R. H., *The Economic Development of Medieval Europe*, London, 1971.
• Duby, G., *Rural Economy and Country Life in the Medieval West*, London, 1968. The best work on agrarian history. Highly recommended as an example of recent French historiography at its highest level.
 Ennen, E., *The Medieval Town*, New York, 1979. Complements Duby on urban development.
• Gies, J. and F., *Life in a Medieval City*, New York, 1973. An engaging popular account concentrating on life in thirteenth-century Troyes.
 Labarge, M. W., *A Baronial Household of the Thirteenth Century*, New York, 1965. Particularly valuable for its emphasis on the career of a woman.
• Lopez, Robert S., *The Commercial Revolution of the Middle Ages*, Englewood Cliffs, N.J., 1971.

• Pirenne, H., *Economic and Social History of Medieval Europe*, London, 1936. Many of Pirenne's ideas are no longer accepted but this is still an extremely useful brief account.

Postan, M. M., *The Medieval Economy and Society: An Economic History of Britain, 1100–1500*, Berkeley, Calif., 1972.

• Power, Eileen, *Medieval Women*, Cambridge, 1975. Very brief but informative.

• White, Lynn, Jr., *Medieval Technology and Social Change*, Oxford, 1962. Controversial but excellently written and thought-provoking.

POLITICAL DEVELOPMENTS

• Barraclough, G., *The Origins of Modern Germany*, 2nd ed., Oxford, 1947. Highly interpretative, should be read in conjunction with Hampe.

Douglas, David, *The Norman Achievement, 1050–1100*, Berkeley, Calif., 1969.

———, *The Norman Fate, 1100–1154*, Berkeley, Calif., 1976.

• Fawtier, R., *The Capetian Kings of France*, London, 1962. The best single volume on medieval French politics.

Hampe, K., *Germany under the Salian and Hohenstaufen Emperors*, Totowa, N.J., 1973. An older, reliable German work recently translated.

Hyde, J. K., *Society and Politics in Medieval Italy*, New York, 1973. An excellent survey that integrates political and social history.

Loyn, H. R., *The Norman Conquest*, London, 1965.

O'Callaghan, Joseph F., *A History of Medieval Spain*, Ithaca, N.Y., 1975.

Petit-Dutaillis, Charles, *The Feudal Monarchy in France and England*, London, 1936. An excellent essay in comparative history.

Poole, Austin L., *From Domesday Book to Magna Carta, 1087–1216*, 2nd ed., Oxford, 1955. Very detailed yet clear.

• Sayles, G. O., *The King's Parliament of England*, New York, 1974. Emphasizes the role of the crown and downplays the importance of the commons.

———, *The Medieval Foundations of England*, London, 1952. An excellent interpretation of medieval English political developments.

• Stephenson, Carl, *Mediaeval Feudalism*, Ithaca, N.Y., 1942. Very elementary.

• Strayer, J. R., *On the Medieval Origins of the Modern State*, Princeton, N.J., 1970. A distillation of the ideas of one of America's greatest medievalists.

SOURCE MATERIALS

Herlihy, David, ed., *The History of Feudalism*, New York, 1970.

• Lopez, Robert S., and I. W. Raymond, eds., *Medieval Trade in the Mediterranean World*, New York, 1955.

• Lyon, Bryce, ed., *The High Middle Ages*, New York, 1964.

• Otto of Freising, *The Deeds of Frederick Barbarossa*, tr. C. C. Mierow, New York, 1953. A contemporary chronicle that is interesting enough to read from start to finish.

Strayer, J. R., ed., *Feudalism*, Princeton, N.J., 1965.

Chapter 12

THE HIGH MIDDLE AGES (1050–1300): RELIGIOUS AND INTELLECTUAL DEVELOPMENTS

You would see men and women dragging carts through marshes . . . everywhere miracles daily occurring, jubilant songs rendered to God. . . . You would say that the prophecy was fulfilled, "The Spirit of Life was in the wheels."

—Abbot Robert of Torigni,
on the building of the cathedral
of Chartres, 1145

The religious and intellectual changes that transpired in the West between 1050 and 1300 were as important as the economic, social, and political ones. In the sphere of religion, the most fundamental organizational development was the triumph of the *papal monarchy*. Before the middle of the eleventh century certain popes had laid claim to primacy within the Church, but very few were able to come close to making good on such claims. Indeed, most popes before about 1050 were hardly able to rule effectively as bishops of Rome. But then, most dramatically, the popes emerged as the supreme religious leaders of Western Christendom. They centralized the government of the Church, challenged the sway of emperors and kings, and called forth the crusading movement. By 1300 the temporal success of the papacy had proven to be its own nemesis, but the popes still ruled the Church internally, as they continue to rule the Roman Catholic Church today.

Religious changes

While the papacy was assuming power, a new vitality infused the Christian religion itself, enabling Christianity to capture the human imagination as never before. At the same time too there was a remarkable revival of intellectual and cultural life. In education, thought, and

Intellectual changes

the arts, as in economics and politics, the West before 1050 had been a backwater. Thereafter it emerged swiftly from backwardness to become an intellectual and artistic leader of the globe. Westerners boasted that learning and the arts had moved northwest to them from Egypt, Greece, and Rome—a boast that was largely true. In the High Middle Ages Europeans first started building on ancient intellectual foundations and also contributed major intellectual and artistic innovations of their own.

1. THE CONSOLIDATION OF THE PAPAL MONARCHY

The sorry state of religious life in the tenth and early eleventh centuries

To understand the origins and appreciate the significance of the western European religious revival of the High Middle Ages it is necessary to have some idea of the level to which religion had sunk in the tenth and early eleventh centuries. Around 800 the Emperor Charlemagne had made some valiant attempts to enhance the religious authority of bishops, introduce the parish system into rural regions where there had hardly been any priests before, and provide for the literacy of the clergy. But with the collapse of the Carolingian Empire, religious decentralization and ensuing corruption prevailed throughout most of Europe. Most churches and monasteries became the private property of strong local lords. The latter disposed of Church offices under their control as they wished, often by selling them or by granting them to close relatives. Obviously this was not the best way to find the most worthy candidates, and many priests were quite unqualified for their jobs. They were almost always illiterate, and often they lived openly with concubines. When archbishops or bishops were able to control appointments the results were not much better because such officials were usually close relatives of secular lords who followed their practices of financial or family aggrandizement. As for the popes, they were usually incompetent or corrupt, the sons or tools of powerful families who lived in or around the city of Rome. Some were astonishingly debauched. John XII may have been the worst of them. He was made pope at the age of eighteen in 955 because of the strength of his family. It is certain that he ruled for nine years as a thorough profligate, but there is some uncertainty about the cause of his death: either he was caught *in flagrante delicto* by a jealous husband and murdered on the spot, or else he died in the midst of a carnal act from sheer amorous exertion.

*Religious revival: (1)
Cluny and monastic
reform*

Once Europe began to catch its breath from the wave of external invasions that peaked in the tenth century, the wide extent of religious corruption or indifference was bound to call forth some reaction. The first successful measures of reform were taken in the monasteries because the work of a bishop was limited to what he could do in his lifetime, and even more because most archbishops and bishops were unable to disentangle themselves from the political affairs of their day. Monasteries could be somewhat more independent and could count more on the support of their reforms by lay lords, insofar as lords feared for the health of their souls if monks did not serve their proper function in saying offices (i.e., prayers). The movement for monastic reform began with the foundation of the monastery of Cluny in Burgundy in 910 by a pious nobleman. Cluny was a Benedictine house but it introduced two constitutional innovations. One was that, in order to remain free from domination by either local secular or ecclesiastical powers, it was made directly subject to the pope. The other was that it undertook the reform or foundation of numerous "daughter monasteries": whereas formerly all Benedictine houses had been independent and equal, Cluny founded a monastic "family," whose members were subordinate to it. Owing to the succession of a few extremely pious, active, and long-lived abbots, the congregation of Cluniac houses grew so rapidly that there were sixty-seven by 1049. In all of them dedicated priors were chosen who followed the dictates of the abbot of Cluny rather than being responsible to local potentates. Cluniac monks accordingly became famous for their industry in the saying of offices. And Cluny was only the most famous of the new congregations. Other similar ones spread just as rapidly in the years around 1000 and succeeded in making the reformed monasteries vital centers of religious life and prayer.

Around the middle of the eleventh century, after so many monasteries had been taken out of the control of secular authorities, the leaders of the monastic reform movement started to lobby for the reform of the clerical hierarchy as well. They centered their attacks upon *simony*—i.e., the buying and selling of positions in the Church— and they also demanded celibacy for all levels of clergy. Their entire program was directed toward depriving secular powers of their ability to dictate appointments of bishops, abbots, and priests, and toward making the clerical estate as "pure" and as distinct from the secular one as possible. Once this reform program was appropriated by the papacy, it would begin to change the face of the entire Church.

(2) reform of the secular clergy

Considering that the reformers were greatly opposed to lay interference, it is ironic that their party was first installed in the papacy by a German emperor, namely Henry III. In 1046 this ruler came to Italy, deposed three rival Italian claimants to the papal title, and named as pope a German reformer from his own retinue. Henry III's act brought in a series of reforming popes, who started to promulgate decrees against simony, clerical marriage, and immorality of all sorts throughout the Church. These popes also insisted upon their own role as primates and universal spiritual leaders in order to give strength to their actions. One of the most important steps they took was the issuance in 1059 of a decree on papal elections. This vested the right of naming a new pope solely with the cardinals, thereby depriving the

Emperor Henry III and reform of the papacy

Roman aristocracy or the German emperor of the chance to interfere in the matter. The decree preserved the independence of papal elections thereafter. In granting the right of election to cardinals the decree also became a milestone in the evolution of a special body within the Church. Ever since the tenth century a number of bishops and clerics, known as cardinals, from sees in and near Rome had taken on an important role as advisors and administrative assistants of the popes, but the election decree of 1059 first gave them their clearest powers. Thereafter the "college of cardinals" took on more and more administrative duties and helped create continuity in papal policy, especially when there was a quick succession of pontiffs. The cardinals still elect the pope today.

The ideals of Pope Gregory VII

A new and most momentous phase in the history of the reform movement was initiated during the pontificate of Gregory VII (1073–1085). Scholars disagree about how much Gregory was indebted to the ideas and policies of his predecessors in the reform movement and how much he departed from them. The answer seems to be that Gregory supported reform as much as others, indeed he explicitly renewed his predecessors' decrees against simony and clerical marriage. Yet he was not only more zealous in trying to enforce these decrees—a contemporary even called him a "Holy Satan"—but he brought with him a basically new conception of the role of the Church in human life. Whereas the older Christian ideal had been that of withdrawal, and the perfect "athlete of Christ" had been a passive contemplative, or ascetic monk, Gregory VII conceived of Christianity as being much more activist and believed that the Church was responsible for creating "right order in the world." To this end he demanded absolute obedience and strenuous chastity from his clergy: some of his clerical opponents complained that he wanted clerics to live like angels. Equally important, he thought of kings and emperors as his inferiors, who would carry out his commands obediently and help him reform and evangelize the world. Gregory allowed that secular princes would continue to rule directly and make their own decisions in purely secular matters, but he expected them to accept ultimate papal overlordship. Put in other terms, in contrast to his predecessors who had sought merely a duality of ecclesiastical and secular authority, Gregory VII wanted to create a papal monarchy over both. When told that his ideas were novel, he and his immediate followers replied: "The Lord did not say 'I am custom'; the Lord said 'I am truth.' " Since no pope had spoken like this before, it is proper to accept the judgment of a modern historian who called Gregory "the great innovator, who stood quite alone."

The investiture struggle

Gregory's actual conduct as pope was nothing short of revolutionary. From the start he was determined to enforce a decree against "lay investiture," the practice whereby secular rulers ceremonially granted clerics the symbols of their office. The German Emperor

Henry IV was bound to resist this because the ceremony was a manifestation of his long-accepted rights to appoint and control churchmen: without these his own authority would be greatly weakened. The ensuing fight is often called "the investiture struggle" because the problem of investitures was a central one, but the struggle was really about the relative obedience and strength of pope and emperor. The larger issue was immediately joined when Henry IV flouted Gregory's injunctions against appointing prelates. Whereas earlier popes might have tried to deal with such insubordination diplomatically, Gregory rapidly took the entirely unprecedented step of excommunicating the emperor and suspending him from all his powers as an earthly ruler. This bold act amazed all who learned of it. Between 955 and 1057 German emperors had deposed five and named twelve out of twenty-five popes; now a pope dared to dismiss an emperor! We have seen in the previous chapter that in 1077 Henry IV abased himself before the pope in order to forestall a formal deposition: that act amazed contemporaries even more. Thereafter Henry was able to rally some support and sympathy for himself and a terrible war of words ensued, while on the actual battlefield the emperor was able to place troops supporting the pope on the defensive. In 1085 Gregory died, seemingly defeated. But Gregory's successors continued the struggle with Henry IV and later with his son, Henry V.

The long and bitter contest on investiture only came to an end with the Concordat of Worms (a city in Germany) of 1122. Under this compromise the German emperor was forbidden to invest prelates with the religious symbols of their office but was allowed to invest them with the symbols of their rights as temporal rulers because the emperor was recognized as their temporal overlord. That settlement was ultimately less significant than the fact that the struggle had lastingly impaired the prestige of the emperors and raised that of the popes. In addition, the dramatic struggle helped rally the Western clergy behind the pope and galvanized the attentions of all onlookers. As one contemporary reported, nothing else was talked about "even in the women's spinning-rooms and the artisans' workshops." This meant that people who had earlier been largely indifferent to or excluded from religious issues became much more absorbed by them. *Results of the conflict*

Gregory VII's successors and most of the popes of the twelfth century were fully committed to the goal of papal monarchy. But they were far less impetuous than Gregory had been and were more interested in the everyday administration of the Church. They apparently recognized that there was no point in claiming to rule as papal monarchs unless they could avail themselves of a governmental apparatus to support their claims. To this end they presided over an impressive growth of law and administration. Under papal guidance the twelfth century saw the basic formulation of the canon law of the Church. Canon law claimed ecclesiastical jurisdiction for all sorts of cases per- *The growth of papal
monarchy*

Pope Innocent III. A mosaic dating from the thirteenth century.

Innocent's policies in action

taining not only to the clergy but also to problems of marriage, inheritance, and rights of widows and orphans. Most of these cases were supposed to originate in the courts of bishops, but the popes insisted that they alone could issue dispensations from the strict letter of the law and that the papal *consistory*—comprised of the pope and cardinals—should serve as a final court of appeals. As the power of the papacy and the prestige of the Church mounted, cases in canon law courts and appeals to Rome rapidly increased; after the middle of the twelfth century legal expertise became so important for exercising the papal office that most popes were trained canon lawyers, whereas previously they had usually been monks. Concurrent with this growth of legalism was the growth of an administrative apparatus to keep records and collect income. As the century wore on, the papacy developed a bureaucratic government that was far in advance of most of the secular governments of the day. This allowed it to become richer, more efficient, and ever stronger. Finally, the popes asserted their powers within the Church by gaining greater control over the election of bishops and by calling general councils in Rome to promulgate laws and demonstrate their leadership.

By common consent the most capable and successful of all high-medieval popes was Innocent III (1198–1216). Innocent, who was elected at the age of thirty-seven, was one of the youngest and most vigorous individuals ever to be raised to the papacy; more than that, he was expertly trained in theology and had also studied canon law. His major goal was to unify all Christendom under papal hegemony and to bring in the "right order in the world" so fervently desired by Gregory VII. He never questioned the right of kings and princes to rule directly in the secular sphere but believed that he could step in and discipline kings whenever they "sinned," a wide opening for interference. Beyond that, he saw himself as the ultimate overlord of all. In his own words he said that "as every knee is bowed to Jesus . . . so all men should obey His Vicar [i.e., the pope]."

Innocent sought to implement his goals in many different ways. In order to give the papacy a solid territorial base of support, like the one drawn upon by the French kings, he tried to initiate strong rule in the papal territories around Rome by consolidating them where possible and providing for efficient and vigilant administration. For this reason Innocent is often considered to be the real founder of the Papal States. But because some urban communities tenaciously sought to maintain their independence, he never came close to dominating the papal lands in Italy so completely as the French kings controlled the Ile-de-France. In other projects he was more completely successful. He intervened in German politics assertively enough to engineer the triumph of his own candidate for the imperial office, the Hohenstaufen Frederick II. He disciplined the French King Philip Augustus for his marital misconduct and forced John of England to accept an unwanted candidate as archbishop of Canterbury. To demonstrate his superiority and also gain income, Innocent forced John to grant England to the papacy as a fief, and he similarly gained the feudal overlordship of Aragon, Sicily, and Hungary. When southern France was threatened by the spread of the Albigensian heresy (to be discussed later) the pope effectively called a crusade that would extinguish it by force. He also levied the first income tax on the clergy to support a crusade to the Holy Land. The crown of Innocent's religious achievement was the calling of the Fourth Lateran Council in Rome in 1215. This defined central dogmas of the faith and made the leadership of the papacy within Christendom more apparent than ever. The pope was now clearly both disciplining kings and ruling over the Church without hindrance.

Innocent's reign was certainly the zenith of the papal monarchy, but it also sowed some of the seeds of future ruin. Innocent himself could administer the Papal States and seek new sources of income without seeming to compromise the spiritual dignity of his office. But future popes who followed his policies had less of his stature and thus began to appear more like ordinary acquisitive rulers. Moreover, because the Papal States bordered on the Kingdom of Sicily, Innocent's successors quickly came into conflict with the neighboring ruler, who was none other than Innocent's protégé Frederick II. Although Innocent had raised up Frederick, he never dreamed that Frederick would later become an inveterate opponent of papal power in Italy.

*Problems for Innocent's
successors*

At first these and other problems were not fully apparent. The popes of the thirteenth century continued to enhance their powers and centralize the government of the Church. They gradually asserted the right to name candidates for ecclesiastical benefices, both high and low, and they asserted control over the curriculum and doctrine taught at the University of Paris. But they also became involved in a protracted political struggle which led to their own demise as temporal powers. This struggle began with the attempt of the popes to destroy Frederick II. To some degree they were acting in self-defense because Frederick threatened their own rule in central Italy. But in combating him they overemployed their spiritual weapons. Instead of merely excommunicating and deposing Frederick, they also called a crusade against him—the first time a crusade was called on a large scale for blatantly political purposes.

*The papacy's struggle
with Frederick II and his
heirs; political crusades*

After Frederick's death in 1250 a succession of popes made a still worse mistake by renewing and maintaining their crusade against all of the emperor's heirs, whom they called the "viper brood." In order to implement this crusade they became preoccupied with raising funds, and they sought and won as their military champion a younger son from the French royal house, Charles of Anjou. But the latter only helped the popes for the purely political motive of winning the Kingdom of Sicily for himself. Charles in fact won Sicily in 1268 by defeating the last of Frederick II's male heirs. But he then taxed the realm so excessively that the Sicilians revolted in the "Sicilian Vespers" of 1282 and offered their crown to the king of Aragon, who had married Fred-

*The effects of the
political crusades*

Pope Boniface VIII. From a portrait by Giotto.

erick II's granddaughter. The king of Aragon accordingly entered the Italian arena and came close to winning Frederick's former kingdom for himself. To prevent this Charles of Anjou and the reigning pope prevailed upon the king of France—then Philip III (1270–1285)—to embark on a crusade against Aragon. This crusade was a terrible failure and Philip III died on it. In the wake of these events Philip's son, Philip IV, resolved to alter the traditional French pro-papal policy. By that time France had become so strong that such a decision was fateful. More than that, by misusing the institution of the crusade and trying to raise increasingly large sums of money to support it, the popes had lost much of their prestige. The denouement would be played out at the very beginning of the next century.

The temporal might of the papacy was toppled almost melodramatically in the reign of Boniface VIII (1294–1303). Many of Boniface's troubles were not of his own making. His greatest obstacle was that the national monarchies had gained more of their subjects' loyalties than the papacy could draw upon because of the steady growth of royal power and erosion of papal prestige. Boniface also had the misfortune to succeed a particularly pious, although inept, pope who resigned his office within a year. Since Boniface was entirely lacking in conventional piety or humility, the contrast turned many Christian observers against him. Some even maintained—incorrectly—that Boniface had convinced his predecessor to resign and had murdered him shortly afterward. Boniface ruled assertively and presided over the first papal "jubilee" in Rome in 1300. This was an apparent, but, as events would show, hollow demonstration of papal might.

Two disputes with the kings of England and France proved to be Boniface's undoing. The first concerned the clerical taxation that had

*Two crucial disputes: (1)
the issue of clerical
taxation*

been initiated by Innocent III. Although Innocent had levied this tax to support a crusade and had collected it himself, in the course of the thirteenth century the kings of England and France had begun to levy and collect clerical taxes on the pretext that they would use them to help the popes on future crusades to the Holy Land or aid in papal crusades against the Hohenstaufens. Then, at the end of the century, the kings started to levy their own war taxes on the clergy without any pretexts at all. Boniface understandably tried to prohibit this step, but quickly found that he had lost the support of the English and French clergy. Thus when the kings offered resistance he had to back down.

*(2) quarrel with the king
of France*

Boniface's second dispute was with the king of France alone. Specifically it concerned Philip IV's determination to try a French bishop for treason. As in the earlier struggle between Gregory VII and Henry IV of Germany, the real issue was the comparative strength of papal and secular power, but this time the papacy was decisively defeated. As before, there was a bitter propaganda war, but now hardly anyone listened to the pope. The king instead pressed absurd charges of heresy against Boniface and sent his minions to arrest the pope to stand trial. At the papal residence of Anagni in 1303 Boniface, who was in his eighties, was captured and mistreated before he was released by the local citizens. These events exhausted the old man's strength and he died a month later. Immediately thereupon it was said that he had entered the papacy like a fox, reigned like a lion, but died like a dog.

After Boniface VIII's death the papacy became virtually a pawn of French temporal authority for most of the fourteenth century. But the emergence and success of the papal monarchy in the High Middle Ages had several beneficial effects during the course of that period. One was that the international rule of the papacy over the Church enhanced international communications and uniformity of religious practices. Another was that the papal cultivation of canon law aided a growing respect for law of all sorts and often helped protect the causes of otherwise defenseless subjects, like widows and orphans. The popes also managed to advance very far in their campaigns to eliminate the sale of Church offices and to raise the morals of the clergy. By centralizing appointments they made it easier for worthy candidates who had no locally influential relatives to gain advancement. There was of course corruption in the papal government too, but in an age of entrenched localism the triumph of an international force was mainly beneficial. Finally, as we will see later, the growth of the papal monarchy helped bring vitality to popular religion and helped support the revival of learning.

Beneficial effects of the papal monarchy

2. THE CRUSADES

The rise and fall of the crusading movement was closely related to the fortunes of the high-medieval papal monarchy. The First Crusade was initiated by the papacy, and its success a great early victory for the papal monarchy. But the later decline of the crusading movement helped undermine the pope's temporal authority. Thus the Crusades can be seen as part of a chapter in papal and religious history. In addition, the Crusades opened the first chapter in the history of Western colonialism.

Two themes of the crusading movement

The immediate cause of the First Crusade was an appeal for aid in 1095 by the Byzantine Emperor Alexius Comnenus. Alexius hoped to reconquer Byzantine territory in Asia Minor which had recently been lost to the Turks. Since he had already become accustomed to using Western mercenaries as auxiliary troops, he asked the pope to help rally some Western military support. But the emperor soon found, no doubt to his great surprise, that he was receiving not just simple aid but a *crusade*. In other words, instead of a band of mercenaries to fight in Asia Minor, the West sent forth an enormous army of volunteers whose goal was to wrest Jerusalem away from Islam. Since the decision to turn Alexius's call for aid into a crusade was made by the pope, it is well to examine the latter's motives.

The direct cause of the First Crusade

The Roman pope in 1095 was Urban II, an extremely competent

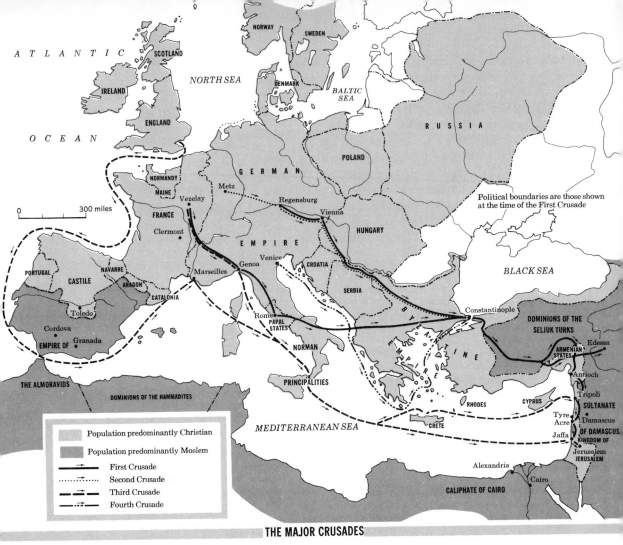

THE MAJOR CRUSADES

The Gregorian theory of Christian Warfare

disciple of Gregory VII. Without question, Urban called the First Crusade to help further the policies of the Gregorian papacy. Urban's very patronage of Christian warfare was Gregorian. Early Christianity had been pacifistic: St. Martin, for example, a revered Christian saint of the fourth century, gave up his career as a soldier when he converted with the statement "I am Christ's soldier; I cannot fight." The Latin fathers St. Augustine and St. Gregory worked out theories to justify Christian warfare but only in the eleventh century, with the triumph of the Gregorian movement, were these put into practice. Gregory VII engineered papal support for the Norman Conquest even before he became pope, and he, or popes under his influence, blessed Christian campaigns against Muslims in Spain, Greeks in Italy, and Slavs in the German east. All these campaigns were considered by Gregory VII and his followers to be steps toward gaining "right order in the world."

Following in Gregory VII's footsteps, Urban II probably conceived of a great crusade to the Holy Land as a means for achieving at least four ends. One was to bring the Greek Orthodox Church back into the fold. By sending a mighty volunteer army to the East, Urban might overawe the Byzantines with Western strength and convince them to reaccept Roman primacy. If he was successful in that, he would gain a great victory for the Gregorian program of papal monarchy. A second motive was to embarrass the pope's greatest enemy, the German emperor. In 1095 Henry IV had become so militarily strong that Urban had been forced to flee Italy for France. By calling a mighty crusade of all westerners but Germans, Urban might hope to show up the emperor as a narrow-minded, un-Christian persecutor, and demonstrate his own ability to be the spiritual leader of the West. Third, by sending off a large contingent of fighters Urban might help to achieve peace at home. Earlier, the local French Church had supported a "peace movement" which prohibited attacks on noncombatants (the "Peace of God") and then prohibited fighting on certain holy days (the "Truce of God"). Right before he called the First Crusade Urban promulgated the first full papal approval and extension of this peace movement. Clearly the crusade was linked to the call for peace: in effect, Urban told unruly warriors that if they really wished to fight they could do so justly for a Christian cause overseas. Finally, the goal of Jerusalem itself must have genuinely inspired Urban. Jerusalem was thought to be the center of the earth and was the most sacred shrine of the Christian religion. It must have seemed only proper that pilgrimages to Jerusalem should not be impeded and that Christians should rule the city directly. "Right order in the world" could scarcely mean less.

Urban II's motives

When Urban called his crusade at a Church council in the French town of Clermont in 1095, the response was more enthusiastic than he could possibly have expected. Many in the crowd interrupted the pope's speech with spontaneous cries of "God wills it," and many impetuously rushed off to the East shortly thereafter. All told, there were probably about a hundred thousand men in the main crusading army, an enormous number for the day. Accordingly, the question arises as to why Urban's appeal was so remarkably successful. Certainly there were economic and political reasons. Many of the poorer people who went crusading came from areas that by 1095 were already becoming overpopulated: these crusaders may have hoped to do better for themselves in the East than they could on their crowded lands. Similarly, some lords were feeling the pressures of growing political stability and a growing acceptance of *primogeniture* (inheritance limited to the eldest male heir). Hitherto younger sons might have hoped to make their own fortune in endemic warfare, or at least inherit a small piece of territory for themselves, but now there were more and longer-lived siblings, warfare was becoming limited, and only the eldest son in-

Economic and political causes of the First Crusade

Religion the dominant motive: crusades as armed pilgrimages

herited his father's lands. Clearly, leaving for the East was an attractive alternative to chafing at home.

But the dominant motive for going on the First Crusade was definitely religious. Nobody could have gone crusading out of purely calculating motives because nobody could have predicted for certain that new lands would be won. Indeed, any rational caculation would have predicted at best an unremunerative return trip, or, more likely, death at the hands of the Muslims. But the journey offered great solace for the Christian soul. For centuries pilgrimages had been the most popular type of Christian penance, and the pilgrimage to Jerusalem was considered to be the most sacred and efficacious one of all. Obviously the greatest of all spiritual rewards would come from going on an armed pilgrimage to Jerusalem in order to win back the holiest of sacred places for Christianity. To make this point explicit, Urban II at Clermont promised that Crusaders would be freed from all other penances imposed by the Church. Immediately afterward some Crusade preachers went even further by promising, without Urban's authorization, what became known as a *plenary indulgence*. This was the promise that all Crusaders would be entirely freed from otherworldly punishments in purgatory and that their souls would go straight to heaven if they died on the Crusade. The plenary indulgence was a truly extraordinary offer and crowds streamed in to take advantage of it. As they flocked together they were further whipped up by preachers into a religious frenzy that approached mass hysteria. They were convinced that they had been chosen to cleanse the world of unbelievers. One terrible consequence was that even before they had fully set out for the East they started slaughtering European Jews in the first really virulent outbreak of Western anti-Semitism.

Burning of Jews. From a late-medieval German manuscript. After the persecutions of the First Crusade, treatment of Jews in western Europe became worse and worse. These Jews were set upon by the populace because they were suspected of poisoning wells.

King Louis VII of France and His Queen, Eleanor of Aquitaine, Embarking for the Second Crusade. This late-medieval conception is idealized inasmuch as Louis did not travel to the Holy Land by sea but took a land route.

Against great odds the First Crusade was a thorough success. In 1098 the Crusaders captured Antioch and with it most of Syria; in 1099 they took Jerusalem. Their success came mainly from the facts that their Muslim opponents just at that time were internally divided and that the appearance of the strange, uncouth, and terribly savage westerners took the Muslims by surprise. From the start the Crusaders in the Holy Land acted like imperialists. As soon as they conquered new territories they claimed them as property for themselves, carving out their acquisitions into four different principalities. They also exulted in their own ferocity. When they captured Antioch, instead of taking prisoners they killed all the Turks they laid their hands on. Similarly, when they conquered Jerusalem they ignored Christ's own pacifistic precepts, mercilessly slaughtering all the Muslim inhabitants of the city. Some Crusaders actually boasted in a joint letter home that "in Solomon's Porch and in his temple our men rode in the blood of the Saracens up to the knees of their horses." Those Crusaders who stayed on in the Holy Land gradually became more civilized and tolerant, but new waves of armed pilgrims from the West continued to act brutally. Moreover, even the settled Crusaders never became fully integrated with the local population but remained a separate, exploiting foreign element in the heart of the Islamic world.

Given the fact that the Christian states comprised only an underpopulated, narrow strip of colonies along the coastline of Syria and Palestine, it was only a matter of time before they would be won back for Islam. By 1144 the northernmost principality fell. When Christian warriors led by the king of France and emperor of Germany came East in the Second Crusade to recoup the losses, they were too internally

The brutal conduct of the Crusaders

Failure of subsequent crusades; the triumph of Frederick II's diplomacy

divided to win any victories. Not long afterward the Islamic lands of the region were united from Egypt by the Sultan Saladin, who recaptured Jerusalem in 1187. Again a force from the West tried to repair the damages: this was the Third Crusade, led by the German Emperor Frederick Barbarossa, the French King Philip Augustus, and the English King Richard the Lionhearted. Even this glorious host, however, could not triumph, above all because rival leaders again quarreled among themselves. When Innocent III became pope his main ambition was to win back Jerusalem. He called the Fourth Crusade to that end, but that Crusade was an unprecedented disaster from the point of view of a united Christendom. The pope could not control its direction and the Crusaders in 1204 wound up seizing Orthodox Christian Constantinople instead of marching on the Holy Land. As we have seen, the ultimate result of this act was to help destroy the Byzantine Empire and open up eastern Europe to the Ottoman Turks. Innocent convened the Fourth Lateran Council in 1215 partially to prepare for yet another crusade that would be more directly under papal guidance. That crusade, the fifth, was launched from the sea against Egypt in order to penetrate Muslim power at its base, but after a promising start it too was a failure. Only the Sixth Crusade, led from 1228 to 1229 by the Emperor Frederick II, was a success; this, however, was not for any military reasons. Frederick, who knew Arabic and could communicate easily with the Egyptian sultan, did not fight but skillfully negotiated a treaty whereby Jerusalem and a narrow access route were restored to the Christians. Thus diplomacy triumphed where warfare had failed. But the Christians could not hold on to their gains and Jerusalem fell again in 1244, never to be recaptured by the West until 1917. The Christian "states" were now only a small enclave around the Palestinian city of Acre.

The papacy's sacrifice of the crusading ideal to political interests

While Frederick II was negotiating for Jerusalem, he was under excommunication by the pope; therefore, when he entered the city, he had to crown himself king of Jerusalem in the Church of the Holy Sepulcher with his own hands. This was indicative of the fact that by then the papacy was becoming more intent on advancing European political aims than on reconquering the Holy Land. The victory of the First Crusade had greatly enhanced the prestige and strength of the papal monarchy, but the subsequent failures were increasingly calling into question the papal ability to unite the West for a great enterprise. The Albigensian Crusade, called by Innocent III in 1208, established the crucial precedent that a believer could receive the same spiritual rewards by crusading within Europe as by going on a much longer and more risky crusade to the East. The Albigensian Crusade did not damage the papacy's religious image, however, because the Albigensian heretics (whose beliefs will be discussed later) were a clear religious threat to the Church. Once the papacy launched its crusade against Frederick II and his heirs, however, it fully sacrificed the crusading ideal to political interests.

It was then that the decline of the crusading movement and the decline of the papacy became most closely interrelated. In the crusades against Frederick and his successors, and later against the king of Aragon, the popes offered the same plenary indulgence that was by then officially offered to all Crusaders against Islam. Worse, they granted the same indulgence to anyone who simply contributed enough money to arm a Crusader for the enterprise. This created a great inflation in indulgences. By 1291 the last Christian outposts in the Holy Land had fallen without any Western help while the papacy was still trying to salvage its losing crusade against Aragon. Boniface VIII's papal jubilee of 1300, which offered a plenary indulgence to all those who made a pilgrimage to Rome, was a tacit recognition that the Eternal City and not the Holy Land would henceforth have to be the central goal of Christian pilgrimage. Boniface fell from power three years later for many reasons, but one was certainly that the prestige of the papacy had become irreparably damaged by the misuses and failures of crusading.

The decline of the crusading movement and the decline of the papacy interrelated

So, while the crusading idea helped build up the papal monarchy, it also helped destroy it. Other than that, what practical significance did the Crusades have? On the credit side, the almost incredible success of the First Crusade greatly helped raise the self-confidence of the medieval West. For centuries western Europe had been on the defensive against Islam; now a Western army could march into a center of Islamic power and take a coveted prize seemingly at will. This dramatic victory contributed to making the twelfth century an age of extraordinary buoyancy and optimism. To Western Christians it must have seemed as if God was on their side and that they could accomplish almost anything they wished. The Crusades also helped broaden Western horizons. Few westerners in the Holy Land ever bothered to learn Arabic or profit from specific Islamic institutions or ideas—the most profitable cultural communications between Christians and Muslims took place in Spain and Sicily—but Crusaders who traveled long dis-

Positive effects of the Crusades

Krak des Chevaliers. This Crusader castle in northern Syria is one of the best preserved fortresses of the Middle Ages. The word *krak* comes from the Arabic *karak,* meaning strong fort.

tances through foreign lands were bound to become somewhat more sophisticated. The Crusades certainly stimulated interest in hitherto unknown luxury goods and presented a wealth of subjects for literature and fable.

Commerce and taxation

From an economic point of view, the success of the First Crusade helped open up the eastern Mediterranean to Western commerce. The Italian cities of Venice and Genoa particularly began to dominate trade in that area, thereby helping to enhance Western prosperity as a whole. The need to transfer money over long distances also stimulated early experiments in banking techniques. Politically, the precedent of taxing the clergy for financing crusades was not only quickly turned to the advantage of the Western monarchies, it also stimulated the development of various forms of national taxation. More than that, the very act of organizing a country to help support a royal crusade by raising funds and provisions was an important stimulus to the development of efficient administrative institutions in the emerging nation-states.

Negative consequences

But there was a debit as well as a credit side to the crusading balance sheet. There is no excusing the Crusaders' savage butchery—of Jews at home and of Muslims abroad. As we have seen too in Chapter 10, the Crusades greatly accelerated the deterioration of Western relations with the Byzantine Empire and contributed fundamentally to the destruction of that realm, with all the disastrous consequences that followed. And Western colonialism in the Holy Land was only the beginning of a long history of colonialism that has continued until modern times.

3. THE OUTBURST OF RELIGIOUS VITALITY

The awakening of religious interest

The First Crusade would never have succeeded if westerners had not become enthusiastic about religion. The growth of that enthusiasm itself was a most remarkable development. Had the First Crusade been called about fifty years earlier it is doubtful that many people would have joined it. But the eleventh-century reform movement and the pontificate of Gregory VII awakened interest in religion in all quarters. Thereafter the entire high-medieval period was to be marked by extraordinary religious vitality.

The impact of the Gregorian reform movement on religious revival

The reformers and Gregory VII stimulated a European religious revival for two reasons. One was that the campaign to cleanse the Church actually achieved a large measure of success: the laity could now respect the clergy more and increasingly large numbers of people were inspired to join the clergy themselves. According to a reliable estimate, the number of people who joined monastic orders in England increased tenfold between 1066 and 1200, a statistic that does not include the increase in priests. The other reason why the work of Gregory VII in particular helped inspire a revival was that Gregory explicitly called upon the laity to help discipline their priests. In letters of great propagandistic power he denounced the sins of "fornicating priests" (by which he really meant just married ones) and urged the laity to drive them from their pulpits or boycott their services. Not surprisingly, this touched off something close to a vigilante movement in many parts of Europe. This excitement, taken together with the fact that the papal struggle with Henry IV was really the first European event of universal interest, increased religious commitment immensely. Until about 1050 most western Europeans were Christians in name, but religiosity seems to have been lukewarm and attendance at church services quite rare; after the Gregorian period Christianity was becoming an ideal and practice which really began to direct human lives.

One of the most visible manifestations of the new religiosity was the spread of the Cistercian movement in the twelfth century. By around 1100 the Cluniac monks had begun to sink into the same morass of worldliness and corruption that had engulfed their older Benedictine brothers whom they had set about to reform. The result was the founding of new orders to provide for the fullest expression of monastic idealism. One was the Carthusian order, whose monks were required to live in separate cells, abstain from meat, and fast three days each week on bread, water, and salt. The Carthusians never sought to attract great numbers and therefore remained a small group. But the same was by no means true of the Cistercians. The latter were monks who were first organized around 1100 and who sought to follow the Benedictine Rule in the purest and most austere way possible. In order

The new religiosity: the Carthusian and Cistercian orders; St. Bernard of Clairvaux

St. Bernard of Clairvaux. Here the saint, in the white habit of the Cistercians, has a miraculous vision of Christ during Mass. From a manuscript of about 1290.

to avoid the worldly temptations to which the Cluniacs had succumbed, they founded new monasteries in forests and wastelands as far away from civilization as possible. They shunned all unnecessary church decoration and ostentatious utensils, abandoned the Cluniac stress on an elaborate liturgy in favor of more contemplation and private prayer, and seriously committed themselves to hard manual labor. Under the charismatic leadership of St. Bernard of Clairvaux (1090–1153), a spellbinding preacher, brilliant writer, and the most influential European religious personality of his age, the Cistercian order grew exponentially. There were only 5 houses in 1115 but no less than 343 on St. Bernard's death in 1153. This growth not only meant that many more men were becoming monks—the older houses did not disappear—but that many pious laymen were donating funds and lands to support the new monasteries.

New forms of religious belief and practice

As more people were entering or patronizing new monasteries, the very nature of religious belief and devotion was changing. One of many examples was a shift away from the cult of saints to emphasis on the worship of Jesus and veneration of the Virgin Mary. Older Benedictine monasteries encouraged the veneration of the relics of local saints that they housed in order to attract pilgrims and donations. But the Cluniac and Cistercian orders were both centralized congregations that allowed only one saintly patron for all their houses: respectively, St. Peter (to honor the founder of the papacy) and the Virgin. Since these monasteries contained few relics (the Virgin was thought to have been taken bodily into heaven, so there were no corporeal relics for her at all) they deemphasized their cult. The veneration of relics was replaced by a concentration on the Eucharist, or the sacrament of the Lord's Supper. Of course celebration of the Eucharist had always been an important part of the Christian faith, but only in the twelfth century was it made really central, for only then did theologians fully work out the doctrine of *transubstantiation*. According to this the priest during mass cooperates with God in the performance of a miracle whereby the bread and wine on the altar are changed or "transubstantiated" into the body and blood of Christ. Popular reverence for the Eucharist became so great in the twelfth century that for the first time the practice of elevating the consecrated host was initiated so that the whole congregation could see it. The new theology of the Eucharist greatly enhanced the dignity of the priest and also encouraged the faithful to meditate on the Passion of Christ. As a result many developed an intense sense of identification with Christ and tried to imitate his life in different ways.

The cult of the Virgin Mary

Coming a very close second to the renewed worship of Christ in the twelfth century was veneration of the Virgin Mary. This development was more unprecedented because until then the Virgin had been only negligibly honored in the Western Church. Exactly why veneration of the Virgin became so pronounced in the twelfth century is not fully clear, but, whatever the explanation, there is no doubt that in the

Christ Blessing the Coronation of His Mother, the Virgin Mary. A relief from the cathedral of Notre Dame, Paris.

twelfth century the cult of Mary blossomed throughout all of western Europe. The Cistercians made her their patron saint, St. Bernard constantly taught about her life and virtues, and practically all the magnificent new cathedrals of the age were dedicated to her: there was Notre Dame ("Our Lady") of Paris, and also a "Notre Dame" of Chartres, Rheims, Amiens, Rouen, Laon, and many other places. Theologically, Mary's role was that of intercessor with her son for the salvation of human souls. It was held that Mary was the mother of all, an infinite repository of mercy who urged the salvation even of sinners so long as they were loving and ultimately contrite. Numerous stories circulated about seeming reprobates who were saved because they venerated Mary and because she then spoke for them at the hour of death.

The significance of the new cult was manifold. For the first time a woman was given a central and honored place in the Christian religion. Theologians still taught that sin had entered the world through the woman, but they now counterbalanced this by explaining how the triumph over sin transpired with the help of Mary. Moreover, this emphasis on Mary gave women a religious figure with whom they could identify, thereby enhancing their own religiosity. A third result was that artists and writers who portrayed Mary were able to concentrate on femininity and scenes of human tenderness and family life. This contributed greatly to a general softening of artistic and literary style. But perhaps most important of all, the rise of the cult of Mary was closely associated with a general rise of hopefulness and optimism in the twelfth-century West.

Significance of the cult

The Virgin in Majesty. A representation from a stained-glass window in the cathedral of Chartres.

Innocent III's response to heresy

Sometimes the great religious enthusiasm of the twelfth century went beyond the bounds approved by the Church. After Gregory VII had called upon the laity to help discipline their clergy it was difficult to control lay enthusiasm. As the twelfth century progressed and the papal monarchy concentrated on strengthening its legal and financial administration, some lay people began to wonder whether the Church, which had once been so inspiring, had not begun to lose sight of its idealistic goals. Another difficulty was that the growing emphasis on the miraculous powers of priests tended to inhibit the religious role of the laity and place it in a distinct position of spiritual inferiority. The result was that in the second half of the twelfth century large-scale movements of popular heresy swept over western Europe for the first time in its history. The two major twelfth-century heresies were Albigensianism and Waldensianism. The former, which had its greatest strength in Italy and southern France, was a recrudescence of Eastern dualism. Like the Zoroastrians, Gnostics, and Manicheans before them, the Albigensians believed that all matter was created by an evil principle and that therefore the flesh should be thoroughly mortified. This teaching was completely at variance with Christianity, but it seems that most Albigensians believed themselves to be Christians and subscribed to the heresy mainly because it challenged the authority of insufficiently zealous Catholic priests and provided an outlet for intense lay spirituality. More typical of twelfth-century mainstream religious protest was Waldensianism, a heresy that originated in southern France and spread throughout most of Europe. Waldensians wished to imitate the life of Christ and the Apostles to the fullest possible extent. Therefore, they translated and studied the Gospels, and dedicated themselves to lives of poverty and preaching. Since the Waldensians did not attack any actual doctrines or practices of the Church, the ecclesiastical hierarchy did not at first interfere with them. But it was soon recognized that they were becoming too independent and that their simple piety could prove an embarrassing contrast to the life of worldly prelates. So the papacy forbade them to preach without authorization; when they refused to accept this they were condemned for heresy. This only made them more radical, and they began to teach that people could be saved by living the simple apostolic life without any need for the sacraments administered by priests.

When Innocent III became pope in 1198 he was faced with a very serious challenge from growing heresies. His response was characteristically decisive and fateful for the future of the Church. Simply stated it was two-pronged. On the one hand, Innocent resolved to crush all disobedience to papal authority, but on the other, he decided to patronize whatever idealistic religious groups he could find that were willing to acknowledge obedience. Papal monarchy could thus be protected without frustrating all dynamic spirituality within the Church. Innocent not only launched a full-scale crusade against the Albigensians, he also encouraged the use against heresy of judicial procedures that included ruthless techniques of religious "inquisition." In 1252 the papacy first approved the use of torture in inquisitorial trials, and burning at the stake became the prevalent punishment for religious disobedience. Neither the crusade nor the inquisitorial procedures were fully successful in uprooting the Albigensian heresy in Innocent's own lifetime, but the extension of such measures did result in destroying the heresy by fire and sword after about the middle of the thirteenth century. Waldensians, like Albigensians, were hunted down by inquisitors and their numbers reduced, but scattered Waldensian groups did manage to survive until modern times.

Another aspect of Innocent's program was to pronounce formally the new religious doctrines that enhanced the special status of priests and the ecclesiastical hierarchy. Thus at the Fourth Lateran Council of 1215 he reaffirmed the doctrine that the sacraments administered by the Church were the indispensable means of procuring God's grace, and that no one could be saved without them. The decrees of the Lateran Council emphasized two sacraments: the Eucharist and penance. The doctrine of transubstantiation was formally defined and it was made a requirement—as it remains today—that all Catholics confess their sins to a priest at least once a year. The council also promulgated other doctrinal definitions and disciplinary measures which served both to oppose heresy and to assert the unique dignity of the clergy.

Innocent III's emphasis on the sacraments

As stated above, the other side of Innocent's policy was to support obedient idealistic movements within the Church. The most important of these were the new orders of *friars*—the Dominicans and the Franciscans. Friars resembled monks in vowing to follow a rule, but they differed greatly from monks in their actual conduct. Above all, they did not retreat from society into monasteries. Assuming that the way of life originally followed by Christ and the Apostles was the most holy, they wandered through the countryside and especially the towns ministering to the sick and poor, preaching, and teaching. In imitation of Christ they also resolved to wed themselves to poverty. In many respects they resembled the Waldensian heretics, but they professed absolute obedience to the pope and sought to fight heresy themselves.

The new orders of friars

The Dominican order, founded by St. Dominic in 1216 with Innocent III's approval, was particularly dedicated to the fight against heresy and also to the conversion of Jews and Muslims. At first the Dominicans hoped to achieve these ends by preaching and public debate. Hence they became intellectually oriented. Many members of the order gained teaching positions in the infant European universities and contributed much to the development of philosophy and theology. The most influential thinker of the thirteenth century, St. Thomas Aquinas, was a Dominican who addressed one of his major theological works to converting the "gentiles" (i.e., all non-Christians). The Dominicans always retained their reputation for learning, but they

The Dominican order

St. Francis of Assisi. By the great Italian painter of the late thirteenth century, Cimabue.

The working relationship between the papal monarchy and the friars

The age of faith

also came to believe that stubborn heretics were best controlled by legal procedures. Accordingly, they became the leading medieval administrators of inquisitorial trials.

The Franciscan order was in many respects quite different and more radical. Its founder, St. Francis of Assisi (1182–1226), behaved at first remarkably like a social rebel and heretic. The son of a rich Italian merchant, he became dissatisfied with the values of his father and determined to become a servant of the poor. Giving away all of his property, he threw off all of his clothes in public, donned the simple garb of a beggar, and began to preach salvation and minister to outcasts in the darkest corners of Italian cities. He rigorously imitated the life of Christ and displayed indifference to doctrine, form, and ceremony. But he did wish to gain the support of the pope. One day in 1210 he appeared in Rome with a small ragged band to request that Innocent III approve a primitive "rule" that was little more than a collection of Gospel precepts. Some other pope might have rejected the layman Francis as a hopelessly unworldly, perhaps even demented, religious anarchist. But Francis was thoroughly willing to profess obedience, and Innocent had the genius to approve Francis's rule and give him permission to preach. With papal support the Franciscan movement spread rapidly. Thus Innocent managed to harness a vital new force that would help maintain a sense of religious enthusiasm within the Church.

Until the end of the thirteenth century both the Franciscans and Dominicans worked closely together with the papal monarchy in a mutually supportive relationship. The popes helped the friars establish themselves throughout Europe and often allowed them to infringe on the duties of parish priests. On their side the friars combated heresy, helped preach papal crusades, were active in missionary work, and otherwise undertook special missions for the popes. Above all, by the power of their examples and by their vigorous preaching the friars helped maintain religious intensity throughout the thirteenth century.

The entire period from 1050 to 1300 was hence unquestionably a great "age of faith." The products of this faith were both tangible and intangible. We will examine the tangible products—works of theology, literature, art, and architecture—presently. Great as these were, the intangible products were equally important. Until the Christian religion became deeply felt in the High Middle Ages hardly any common ideals inspired average men and women. Life in the Middle Ages was extraordinarily hard, and until about 1050 there was not much to give it meaning. Then, when people began to take Christianity more seriously, an impetus was provided for performing hard work of all sorts. As we have seen in the last chapter, Europeans after 1050 literally had better food than before, and now we have seen that they were better fed figuratively as well. With more spiritual as well as material nourishment they accomplished great feats in all forms of human endeavor.

The major intellectual accomplishments of the High Middle Ages were of four related but different sorts: the spread of primary education and literacy; the origin and spread of universities; the acquisition of classical and Islamic knowledge; and the actual progress in thought made by westerners. Any one of these accomplishments would have earned the High Middle Ages a signal place in the history of Western learning; taken together they began the era of Western intellectual predominance which became a hallmark of modern times.

Four major intellectual accomplishments

Around 800 Charlemagne ordered that primary schools be established in every bishopic and monastery in his realm. Although it is doubtful that this command was carried out to the letter, many schools were certainly founded during the Carolingian period. But their continued existence was later endangered by the Viking invasions. Primary education in some monasteries and cathedral towns managed to survive, but until around 1050 the extent and quality of basic education in the European West were meager. Thereafter, however, there was a blossoming that paralleled the efflorescence we have seen in other human activities. Even contemporaries were struck by the rapidity with which schools sprang up all over Europe. One French monk writing in 1115 stated that when he was growing up around 1075 there was "such a scarcity of teachers that there were almost none in the villages and hardly any in the cities," but that by his maturity there was "a great number of schools," and the study of grammar was "flourishing far and wide." Similarly, a Flemish chronicle referred to an extraordinary new passion for the study and practice of rhetoric around 1120. Clearly, the economic revival, the growth of towns, and the emergence of strong government allowed Europeans to dedicate themselves to basic education as never before.

The spread of primary education

The high-medieval educational boom was more than merely a growth of schools, for the nature of the schools changed, and as time went on so did the curriculum and the clientele. The first basic mutation was that monasteries in the twelfth century abandoned their practice of educating outsiders. Earlier, monasteries had taught a few privileged nonmonastic students how to read because there were no other schools for such pupils. But by the twelfth century sufficient alternatives existed. The main centers of European education became the cathedral schools located in the growing towns. The papal monarchy energetically supported this development by ordering in 1179 that all cathedrals should set aside income for one schoolteacher, who could then instruct all who wished, rich or poor, without fee. The papacy believed correctly that this measure would enlarge the number of well-trained clerics and potential administrators.

Changes in medieval education: (1) the development of cathedral schools

At first the cathedral schools existed almost exclusively for the basic training of priests, with a curriculum designed to teach only such literacy necessary for reading the Church offices. But soon after 1100

Two Medieval Advertisements for Elementary Education. On the left an illumination from a twelfth-century Austrian manuscript depicts a kneeling student saying "I wish to study, dear master," which is perhaps not too surprising given the fact that his teacher seems to be threatening to beat and kick him. Grammar school education is advertised more gently on the right, a late-medieval scene in which a woman personifying the alphabet leads a willing boy into a palace of learning wherein the stories ascend from grammar through logic and rhetoric to the heights of theology.

(2) the broadening of the curriculum

the curriculum was broadened, for the growth of both ecclesiastical and secular governments created a growing demand for trained officials who had to know more than how to read a few prayers. The revived reliance on law especially made it imperative to improve the quality of primary education in order to train future lawyers. Above all, a thorough knowledge of Latin grammar and composition began to be inculcated, often by studying some of the Roman classics such as the works of Cicero and Virgil. The revived interest in these texts, and attempts to imitate them, have led scholars to refer to a "Renaissance of the Twelfth Century."

(3) the growth of lay education

Until about 1200 the students in the urban schools remained predominantly clerical. Even those who hoped to become lawyers or administrators rather than mere priests usually found it advantageous to take Church orders. But afterward more pupils entered schools who were not in the clergy and never intended to be. Some were children of the upper classes who began to regard literacy as a badge of status. Others were future notaries (i.e., men who drew up official documents) or merchants who needed some literacy and/or computational skills to advance their own careers. Customarily, the latter groups would not go to cathedral schools but to alternate ones which were more practically oriented. Such schools grew rapidly in the course of the thirteenth century and became completely independent of ecclesiastical control. Not only were their students recruited from the laity, their teachers were usually laymen as well. As time went on instruction ceased being in Latin, as had hitherto been the case, and was offered in the European vernacular languages instead.

The rise of lay education was an enormously important development in western European history for two related reasons. The first was that the Church lost its monopoly over education for the first time in almost a millennium. Learning and resultant attitudes could now become more secular, and they did just that increasingly over the course of time. Laymen could not only evaluate and criticize the ideas of priests, they could also pursue entirely secular lines of inquiry. Western culture therefore ultimately became more independent of religion, and much of the traditionalism associated with religion, than any other culture in the world. Second, the growth of lay schools, taken together with the growth of church schools which trained the laity, led to an enormous growth of lay literacy: by 1340 roughly 40 percent of the Florentine population could read; by the later fifteenth century about 40 percent of the total population of England was literate as well. (These figures include women, who were usually taught to read by paid tutors or male family members at home rather than in schools.) When one considers that literacy around 1050 was almost entirely limited to the clergy and that the literate comprised less than 1 percent of the population of western Europe, it can be appreciated that an astonishing revolution had taken place. Without it, many of Europe's other accomplishments would have been inconceivable.

*Significance of the rise of
lay education*

The emergence of universities was part of the same high-medieval educational boom. Originally, universities were institutions that gave specialized instruction in advanced studies which could not be pursued in average cathedral schools. In Italy the earliest universities took shape in the eleventh and twelfth centuries: those of Salerno, which specialized in medicine, and Bologna, which specialized in law—both Roman law and the canon law of the Church. North of the Alps the earliest and for a long time the most prominent university was that of Paris. The University of Paris started out as a cathedral school like many others, but in the twelfth century it began to become a recognized center of northern intellectual life. One reason for this was that scholars there found necessary conditions of peace and stability provided by the increasingly strong French kingship; another was that food was plentiful because the area was rich in agricultural produce; and another was that the cathedral school of Paris in the first half of the twelfth century boasted the most charismatic and controversial teacher of the day, Peter Abelard (1079–1142). Abelard, whose intel-

The origins of universities

See color map facing
page 353

lectual accomplishments we will discuss later, attracted students from all over Europe in droves. According to an apocryphal story that was told at the time, he was such an exciting teacher that when he was forbidden to teach in French lands, because of his controversial views, he climbed a tree and students flocked under it to hear him lecture; when he was then forbidden to teach from the air he started lecturing from a boat and students massed to hear him from the banks. As a result of his reputation many other teachers settled in Paris and began to offer much more varied and advanced instruction than anything offered in other French cathedral schools. By 1200 Paris was evolving into a university that specialized in liberal arts and theology. Around then Innocent III, who had studied in Paris himself, called the school "the oven that bakes the bread for the entire world."

Nature of the medieval university

It should be emphasized that the institution of the university was really a medieval invention. Of course advanced schools existed in the ancient world, but they did not have fixed curricula or organized faculties, and they did not award degrees. At first, medieval universities themselves were not so much places as groups of scholars. The term university originally meant a corporation or guild. In fact, all of the medieval universities were corporations, either of teachers or students, organized like other guilds to protect their interests and rights. But gradually the word university came to mean an educational institution with a school of liberal arts and one or more faculties in the professional subjects of law, medicine, and theology. Salerno never became more than a medical school, but Bologna and Paris after about 1200 were regarded as the prototypic universities. During the thirteenth century such famous institutions as Oxford, Cambridge, Montpellier, Salamanca, and Naples were founded or granted formal recognition. In Germany there were no universities until the fourteenth century—a reflection of the disorganized condition of that area—but in 1385 Heidelberg, the first university on German soil, was founded and many others quickly followed.

Organization of universities

Every university in medieval Europe was patterned after one or the other of two different models. Throughout Italy, Spain, and southern France the standard was generally the University of Bologna, in which the students themselves constituted the corporation. They hired the teachers, paid their salaries, and fined or discharged them for neglect of duty or inefficient instruction. The universities of northern Europe were modeled after Paris, which was not a guild of students but of teachers. It included four faculties—arts, theology, law, and medicine—each headed by a dean. In the great majority of the northern universities arts and theology were the leading branches of study. Before the end of the thirteenth century separate colleges came to be established within the University of Paris. The original college was nothing more than an endowed home for poor students, but eventually the colleges become centers of instruction as well as residences. While most of these colleges have disappeared from the Continent, the

A Lecture Class in a Medieval University. Some interesting similarities and contrasts may be observed between this scene and a modern classroom.

universities of Oxford and Cambridge still retain the pattern of federal organization copied from Paris. The colleges of which they are composed are semi-independent educational units.

Most of our modern degrees as well as our modern university organization derive from the medieval system, but actual courses of study have been greatly altered. No curriculum in the Middle Ages included history or anything like the modern social sciences. The medieval student was assumed to know Latin grammar thoroughly before entrance into a university—this he learned in the primary, or "grammar," schools. Upon admission, limited to males, he was required to spend about four years studying the basic liberal arts, which meant doing advanced work in Latin grammar and rhetoric, and mastering the rules of logic. If he passed his examinations he received the preliminary degree of bachelor of arts (the prototype of our B.A.), which conferred no unusual distinction. To assure himself a place in professional life he then usually had to devote additional years to the pursuit of an advanced degree, such as master of arts (M.A.), or doctor of laws, medicine, or theology. For the M.A. degree three or four years had to be given to the study of mathematics, natural science, and philosophy. This was accomplished by reading and commenting on standard ancient works, such as those of Euclid and especially Aristotle. Abstract analysis was emphasized and there was no such thing as laboratory science. The requirements for the doctors' degrees included more specialized training. Those for the doctorate in theology were particularly arduous: by the end of the Middle Ages the course for the doctorate in theology at the University of Paris had been extended to twelve or thirteen years after the roughly eight years taken for the M.A.! Continuous residence was not required and it was accordingly

The courses of study

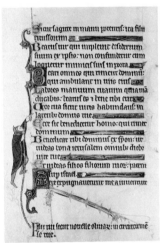

A Scribe with a Sense of Humor. An English scribe of around 1300, having noticed that he left out a whole line in a luxurious prayerbook, devised this ingenious way to rectify the error.

Acquisition of Greek and Arabic knowledge

rare to become a doctor of theology before the age of forty; statutes in fact forbade awarding the degree to anyone under thirty-five. Strictly speaking, doctor's degrees, including even the one in medicine, only conferred the right to teach. But in practice university degrees of all grades were recognized as standards of attainment and became pathways to nonacademic careers.

Student life in medieval universities was often very rowdy. Many students were very immature because it was customary to begin university studies between the ages of twelve and fifteen. Moreover, all university students believed that they comprised an independent and privileged community, set aside from that of the local townspeople. Since the latter tried to reap financial profits from the students and the students were naturally boisterous, there were frequent riots and sometimes pitched battles between "town" and "gown." But actual study was very intense. Because the greatest emphasis was placed on the value of authority and also because books were prohibitively expensive (they were handwritten and made from rare parchment), there was an enormous amount of rote memorization. As students advanced in their disciplines they were also expected to develop their own skills in formal, public disputations. Advanced disputations could become extremely complex and abstract; sometimes they might also last for days. The most important fact pertaining to medieval university students was that, after about 1250, there were so many of them. The University of Paris in the thirteenth century numbered about seven thousand students and Oxford somewhere around two thousand in any given year. This means that a relatively appreciable proportion of male Europeans who were more than peasants or artisans were gaining at least some education at the higher levels.

As the numbers of those educated at all levels vastly increased during the High Middle Ages, so did the quality of learning. This was owing first and foremost to the reacquisition of Greek knowledge and to the absorption of intellectual advances made by the Muslims. Since practically no western Europeans knew Greek or Arabic, works in those languages had to be transmitted by means of Latin translations. But there were very few of these before about 1140: of all the many works of Aristotle only a few logical treatises were available in Latin translations before the middle of the twelfth century. But then, suddenly, an enormous burst of translating activity made almost all of ancient Greek and Arabic scientific knowledge accessible to western Europeans. This activity transpired in Spain and Sicily because Christians there lived in close proximity with Arabic speakers, or Jews who knew Latin and Arabic, either of whom could aid them in their tasks. Greek works were first translated into Latin from earlier Arabic translations; then many were retranslated directly from the Greek by a few westerners who had managed to learn that language, usually by traveling in Greek-speaking territories. The result was that by about 1260

Ivory Plaque, German, X cent. The plaque shows Otto the Great presenting a church to Christ while St. Peter watches, a reference to Otto's building an empire by cooperating with the Church. (MMA)

Aquamanile, German, XII–XIII cent. Aquamaniles were water jugs used for handwashing during Church ritual, or at mealtimes. (MMA)

Chalice, German, XIII cent. A beautifully embellished cup used to hold the wine in the sacrament of the Eucharist. (MMA)

Kings in Battle, French, c. 1250. A scene depicting Joshua's fight against the five kings of Canaan. In the center Joshua raises his hand, commanding the sun and moon to stand still to enable him to complete his victory. Since the artist was oblivious to the concept of anachronism all these Old Testament figures are shown in contemporary medieval armor. (Morgan Library)

The French King, Louis IX, XIII cent. Although Louis was later recognized as a saint, the artist here depicts him as a young and earthly ruler. (Morgan Library)

THE RISE OF THE MEDIEVAL UNIVERSITY

△ Founded in the 12th century

■ Founded in the 13th century

● Founded in the 14th century   Boundaries ca. 1500 A.D.

△ Founded in the 15th century

almost the entire Aristotelian corpus that is known today was made available in Latin. So also were basic works of such important Greek scientific thinkers as Euclid, Galen, and Ptolemy. Only the milestones of Greek literature and the works of Plato were not yet translated because they had not been made available to the Arabs; they existed only in inaccessible Byzantine manuscripts. But in addition to the thought of the Greeks, Western scholars became familiar with the accomplishments of all the major Islamic philosophers and scientists such as Avicenna and Averroës.

Having acquired the best of Greek and Arabic scientific and speculative thought, the West was able to build on it and make its own advances. This progress transpired in different ways. When it came to natural science, westerners were able to start building on the acquired learning without much difficulty because it seldom conflicted with the principles of Christianity. But when it came to philosophy, the basic question arose as to how thoroughly Greek and Arabic thought was compatible with the Christian faith. The most advanced thirteenth-century scientist was the Englishman Robert Grosseteste (c. 1168–1253), who was not only a great thinker but was also very active in public life as bishop of Lincoln. Grosseteste became so proficient at Greek that he translated all of Aristotle's *Ethics*. More important, he made very significant theoretical advances in mathematics, astronomy, and optics. He formulated a sophisticated scientific explanation of the rainbow, and he posited the use of lenses for magnification. Grosseteste's leading disciple was Roger Bacon (c. 1214–1294), who is today more famous than his teacher because he seems to have predicted automobiles and flying machines. Bacon in fact had no real interest in machinery, but he did follow up on Grosseteste's work in optics, discussing, for example, further properties of lenses, the rapid speed of light, and the nature of human vision. Grosseteste, Bacon, and some of their followers at the University of Oxford argued that natural knowledge was more certain when it was based on sensory evidence than when it rested on abstract reason. To this degree they can be seen as early forerunners of modern science. But the important qualification remains that they did not perform any real laboratory experiments.

The growth of western scientific and speculative thought; Robert Grosseteste and Roger Bacon

The story of the high-medieval encounter between Greek and Arabic philosophy and Christian faith is basically the story of the emergence of Scholasticism. This word can be, and has been, defined in many ways. In its root meaning Scholasticism was simply the method of teaching and learning followed in the medieval schools. That meant that it was highly systematic and also that it was highly respectful of authority. Yet Scholasticism was not only a method of study: it was a worldview. As such, it taught that there was a fundamental compatability between the knowledge humans can obtain naturally, i.e., by experience or reason, and the teachings imparted by

The meaning of Scholasticism

Peter Abelard

Abelard. A late-medieval conception.

Abelard's autobiography

Sic et Non *and the
Scholastic method*

Divine Revelation. Since medieval scholars believed that the Greeks were the masters of natural knowledge and that all revelation was in the Bible, Scholasticism consequently was the theory and practice of reconciling classical philosophy with Christian faith.

One of the most important thinkers who paved the way for Scholasticism without yet being fully a Scholastic himself was the stormy petrel Peter Abelard. As a student Abelard was so adept in logic and theology that he publicly humiliated his teachers in and around Paris in debate. Such arrogant conduct made him many enemies. These engineered his first conviction for heresy in 1121. To complicate matters, Abelard entered upon an affair with a young woman, Heloise, herself a scholar, without marrying her. Abelard had been hired to be Heloise's tutor by her uncle, Fulbert, canon of Notre Dame of Paris. A child was the result of the affair, and Heloise's uncle took revenge upon Abelard by having him castrated. Heloise became a nun and Abelard a monk, but Abelard was too restless and cantankerous a personality to find real peace in a monastery. After quarreling and breaking with the monks of two different communities, he set himself up as a teacher in Paris from about 1132 until 1141. This was the peak of his career. In 1141, however, he was again charged with heresy, this time by the highly influential St. Bernard, and condemned by a Church council. Not long afterward the persecuted thinker abjured, and in 1142 he died in retirement.

Abelard recounted many of these trials in a letter called *The Story of My Calamities,* one of the first autobiographical accounts written in the West since St. Augustine's *Confessions.* On first reading, this work appears "modern" because Abelard seems to revel in himself and boast a great deal. But actually he did not write about his calamities in order to boast. Rather, his main intention was to moralize about how he had been appropriately punished for his intellectual pride by his first condemnation and for his "lechery" by the loss of those parts which had "offended." Abelard certainly represents a reawakening interest in personal introspection, but in this he did not differ much from St. Augustine. More important is the fact that he was the first westerner who sought to make a full profession out of the life of the mind.

Abelard's greatest contributions to the subsequent development of Scholasticism were made in his *Sic et Non* (Yes and No) and in a number of original theological works. In the *Sic et Non* Abelard prepared the way for the Scholastic method by gathering a collection of statements from the church fathers that spoke for both sides of 150 theological questions. It used to be thought that the brash Abelard did this in order to embarrass authority, but the contrary is true. What Abelard really hoped to do was begin a process of careful study whereby it could be shown that the highest authority of the Bible was infallible and that the best authorities, despite any appearances to the contrary, really agreed with each other. Later Scholastics would follow his method of studying theology by raising fundamental questions and arraying the answers that had been put forth in authoritative texts. Abelard did not propose any solutions of his own in the *Sic et Non,* but he did start to do this in his original theological writings. In these he proposed to treat theology like a science, by studying it as comprehensively as possible and by applying to it the tools of logic, of which he was a master. He did not even shrink from applying logic to the mystery of the Trinity, one of the excesses for which he was condemned. Thus he was one of the first to try to harmonize religion with rationalism and was in this capacity a herald of the Scholastic outlook.

Immediately after Abelard's death two further steps were taken to prepare for mature Scholasticism. One was the writing of the *Book of Sentences* between 1155 and 1157 by Abelard's student Peter Lombard. This raised all the most fundamental theological questions in rigorously consequential order, adduced answers from the Bible and Christian authorities on both sides of each question, and then proposed a judgment on every case. By the thirteenth century Peter Lombard's work became a standard text. Once formal schools of theology were established in the universities, all aspirants to the doctorate were required to study and comment upon it; not surprisingly, theologians also followed its organizational procedures in their own writings. Thus the full Scholastic method was born.

The other basic step in the development of Scholasticism, as mentioned above, was the reacquisition of classical philosophy that occurred after about 1140. Abelard would probably have been glad to have drawn upon the thought of the Greeks, but he could not because few Greek works were yet available in translation. Later theologians, however, could avail themselves fully of the new knowledge, above all, the works of Aristotle and his Arabic commentators. By around 1250 Aristotle's authority in purely philosophical matters became so great that he was referred to as "the Philosopher" pure and simple. Scholastics of the mid–thirteenth century accordingly adhered to Peter Lombard's organizational method, but added the consideration of Greek and Arabic philosophical authorities to that of purely Christian theological ones. In doing this they tried to construct systems of understanding the entire universe that most fully harmonized the earlier separate realms of faith and natural knowledge.

Peter Lombard

Influence of Aristotle

By far the greatest accomplishments in this endeavor were made by St. Thomas Aquinas (1225–1274), the leading Scholastic theologian of the University of Paris. As a member of the Dominican order, St. Thomas was committed to the principle that faith could be defended by reason. More important, he believed that natural knowledge and the study of the created universe were legitimate ways of approaching theological wisdom because "nature" complements "grace." By this he meant to say that because God created the natural world He can be

St. Thomas Aquinas

St. Thomas Aquinas. A fifteenth-century painting by Justus of Ghent, after an earlier copy.

approached through its terms even though ultimate certainty about the highest truths can only be obtained through the supernatural revelation of the Bible. Imbued with a deep confidence in the value of human reason and human experience, as well as in his own ability to harmonize Greek philosophy with Christian theology, Thomas was the most serene of saints. In a long career of teaching at the University of Paris and elsewhere he indulged in few controversies and worked quietly on his two great *Summaries* of theology: the *Summa contra Gentiles* and the much larger *Summa Theologica*. In these he hoped to set down all that could be said about the faith on the firmest of foundations.

Most experts think that St. Thomas came extremely close to fulfilling this extraordinarily ambitious goal. His vast *Summaries* are awesome for their rigorous orderliness and intellectual penetration. He admits in them that there are certain "mysteries of the faith," such as the doctrines of the Trinity and the Incarnation, that cannot be approached by the unaided human intellect; otherwise, he subjects all theological questions to philosophical inquiry. In this, St. Thomas relied heavily on the work of Aristotle, but he is by no means merely "Aristotle baptized." Instead, he fully subordinated Aristotelianism to basic Christian principles and thereby created his own original philosophical and theological system. Scholars disagree about how far this system diverges from the earlier Christian thought of St. Augustine, but there seems little doubt that Aquinas placed a higher value on human reason, on human life in this world, and on the abilities of humans to participate in their own salvation. Not long after his death St. Thomas was canonized, for his intellectual accomplishments seemed like miracles. His influence lives on today insofar as he helped to revive confidence in rationalism and human experience. More directly, philosophy in the modern Roman Catholic Church is supposed to be taught according to the Thomistic method, doctrine, and principles.

The achievements of the thirteenth century

With the achievements of St. Thomas Aquinas in the middle of the thirteenth century, Western medieval thought reached its pinnacle. Not coincidentally, other aspects of medieval civilization were reaching their pinnacles at the same time. France was enjoying its ripest period of peace and prosperity under the rule of St. Louis, the University of Paris was defining its basic organizational forms, and the greatest French Gothic cathedrals were being built. Some ardent admirers of medieval culture have fixed on these accomplishments to call the thirteenth the "greatest of centuries." Such a judgment, of course, is a matter of taste, and many might respond that life was still too harsh and requirements for religious orthodoxy too great to justify this extreme celebration of the lost past. Whatever our individual judgments, it seems wise to end this section by correcting some false impressions about medieval intellectual life.

It is often thought that medieval thinkers were excessively conservative, but in fact the greatest thinkers of the High Middle Ages were astonishingly receptive to new ideas. As committed Christians they could not allow doubts to be cast upon the principles of their faith, but otherwise they were glad to accept whatever they could from the Greeks and Arabs. Considering that Aristotelian thought differed radically from anything accepted earlier in its emphasis on rationalism and the fundamental goodness and purposefulness of nature, its rapid acceptance by the Scholastics was a philosophical revolution. Another false impression is that Scholastic thinkers were greatly constrained by authority. Certainly they revered authority more than we do today, but Scholastics like St. Thomas did not regard the mere citation of texts—except biblical revelation concerning the mysteries of the faith—as being sufficient to clinch an argument. Rather, the authorities were brought forth to outline the possibilities, but reason and experience then demonstrated the truth. Finally, it is often believed that Scholastic thinkers were "antihumanistic," but modern scholars are coming to the opposite conclusion. Scholastics unquestionably gave primacy to the soul over the body and to the otherworldly salvation over life in the here and now. But they also exalted the dignity of human nature because they viewed it as a glorious divine creation, and they believed in the possibility of a working alliance between themselves and God. Moreover, they had extraordinary faith in the powers of human reason—probably more than we do today.

5. THE BLOSSOMING OF LITERATURE, ART, AND MUSIC

The literature of the High Middle Ages was as varied, lively, and impressive as that produced in any other period in Western history. The revival of grammatical studies in the cathedral schools and universities led to the production of some excellent Latin poetry. The best examples were secular lyrics, especially those written in the twelfth century by a group of poets known as the Goliards. How these poets got their name is uncertain, but it possibly meant followers of the devil. That would have been appropriate because the Goliards were riotous poets who wrote parodies of the liturgy and burlesques of the Gospels. Their lyrics celebrated the beauties of the changing seasons, the carefree life of the open road, the pleasures of drinking and sporting, and especially the joys of love. The authors of these rollicking and satirical songs were mainly wandering students, although some were men in more advanced years. The names of most are unknown. Their poetry is particularly significant both for its robust vitality and for being the first clear counterstatement to the ascetic ideal of Christianity.

Charlemagne Weeping for His Knights. A scene from the *Song of Roland.*

The growth of vernacular literature; the epic

In addition to the use of Latin, the vernacular languages of French, German, Spanish, and Italian became increasingly popular as media of literary expression. At first, most of the literature in the vernacular languages was written in the form of the heroic epic. Among the leading examples were the French *Song of Roland,* the Norse eddas and sagas, the German *Song of the Nibelungs,* and the Spanish *Poem of the Cid.* Practically all of these works were originally composed between 1050 and 1150, although some were first set down in writing afterward. These epics portrayed a virile but unpolished warrior society. Blood flowed freely, skulls were cleaved by battleaxes, and heroic warfare, honor, and loyalty were the major themes. If women were mentioned at all, they were subordinate to men. Brides were expected to die for their betrotheds, but husbands were free to beat their wives. In one French epic a queen who tried to influence her husband met with a blow to the nose; even though blood flowed she replied: "Many thanks, when it pleases you, you may do it again." Despite the repugnance we find in such passages, the best of the vernacular epics have much unpretentious literary power. Above all, the *Song of Roland,* though crude, is like an uncut gem.

In comparison to the epics, an enormous change in both subject matter and style was introduced in twelfth-century France by the troubadour poets and the writers of courtly romances. The dramatic nature of this change represents further proof that high-medieval culture was not at all conservative. The troubadours were courtier poets who came from southern France and wrote in a language related to French known as Provençal. The origin of their inspiration is debated, but there can be no doubt that they initiated a movement of profound importance for all subsequent Western literature. Their style was far

The love songs of the troubadours

more finely wrought and sophisticated than that of the epic poets, and the most eloquent of their lyrics, which were meant to be sung to music, originated the theme of romantic love. The troubadours idealized women as marvelous beings who could grant intense spiritual and sensual gratification. Whatever greatness the poets found in themselves they usually attributed to the inspiration they found in love. But they also assumed that their love would lose its magic if it were too easily or frequently gratified. Therefore, they wrote more often of longing than of romantic fulfillment.

In addition to their love lyrics, the troubadours wrote several other kinds of short poems. Some were simply bawdy. In these, love is not mentioned at all, but the poet revels in thoughts of carnality, comparing, for example, the riding of his horse to the "riding" of his mistress. Other troubadour poems treat of feats of arms, others comment on contemporary political events, and a few even meditate on matters of religion. But whatever the subject matter, the best troubadour poems were always cleverly and innovatively expressed. The literary tradition originated by the southern French troubadours was continued by the *trouvères* in northern France and by the *minnesingers* in Germany. Thereafter many of their innovations were developed by later lyric poets in all Western languages. Some of their poetic devices were consciously revived in the twentieth century by such "modernists" as Ezra Pound.

Other troubadour poems

An equally important twelfth-century French innovation was the composition of longer narrative poems known as romances. These were the first clear ancestors of the modern novel: they told engaging stories, they often excelled in portraying character, and their subject matter was usually love and adventure. Some romances elaborated on classical Greek themes, but the most famous and best were "Arthurian." These took their material from the legendary exploits of the Celtic hero King Arthur and his many chivalrous knights. The first great writer of Arthurian romances was the northern Frenchman Chrétien de Troyes, who was active between about 1165 and 1190. Chrétien did much to help create and shape the new form, and he also introduced innovations in subject matter and attitudes. Whereas the troubadours exalted unrequited, extramarital love, Chrétien was the first to hold forth the ideal of romantic love within marriage. He also described not only the deeds but the thoughts and emotions of his characters.

The Arthurian romances; Chrétien de Troyes

A generation later, Chrétien's work was continued by the great German poets Wolfram von Eschenbach and Gottfried von Strassburg. These are recognized as the greatest writers in the German language before the eighteenth century. Wolfram's *Parzival,* a story of love and the search for the Holy Grail, is more subtle, complex, and greater in scope than any other high-medieval literary work except Dante's *Divine Comedy.* Like Chrétien, Wolfram believed that true love could only be fulfilled in marriage, and in *Parzival,* for the first time in West-

A Thirteenth-Century Miniature. From a manuscript of Wolfram von Eschenbach's *Parzival.*

*Wolfram von Eschenbach
and Gottfried von
Strassburg*

ern literature since the Greeks, one can see a full psychological development of the hero. Gottfried von Strassburg's *Tristan* is a more somber work, which tells of the hopeless adulterous love of Tristan and Isolde. Indeed, it might almost be regarded as the prototype of modern tragic romanticism. Gottfried was one of the first to develop fully the idea of individual suffering as a literary theme and to point out the indistinct line which separates pleasure from pain. For him, to love is to yearn, and suffering and unfulfilled gratification are integral chapters of the book of life. Unlike the troubadours, he could only see complete fulfillment of love in death. *Parzival* and *Tristan* have become most famous today in the form of their operatic reconceptions by the nineteenth-century German composer Richard Wagner.

The fabliaux

Not all high-medieval narratives were so elevated as the romances in either form or substance. A very different new narrative form was the *fabliau,* or verse fable. Although *fabliaux* derived from the moral animal tales of Aesop, they quickly evolved into short stories that were written less to edify or instruct than to amuse. Often they were very coarse, and sometimes they dealt with sexual relations in a broadly humorous and thoroughly unromantic manner. Many were also strongly anticlerical, making monks and priests the butts of their jokes. Because the *fabliaux* are so "uncourtly" it used to be thought that they were written solely for the new urban classes. But there is now little doubt that they were addressed at least equally to the "refined" aristocracy who liked to have their laughs too. They are significant as expressions of growing worldliness and as the first manifestations of the robust realism which was later to be perfected by Boccaccio and Chaucer.

Completely different in form but similar as an illustration of growing worldliness was the sprawling *Romance of the Rose.* As its title indicates, this was begun as a romance, specifically around 1230 by the courtly Frenchman William of Lorris. But William left his rather flowery, romantic work unfinished, and it was completed around 1270 by another Frenchman, John of Meun. The latter changed its nature greatly. He inserted long, biting digressions in which he skewered religious hypocrisy, and made his major theme the need for procreation. Not love, but the service of "Dame Nature" in sexual fecundity is urged in numerous witty but extremely earthy images and metaphors. At the climax the originally dreamy hero seizes his mistress, who is allegorically depicted as a rose, and rapes her. Since the work became enormously popular, it seems fair to conclude that tastes, then as now, were very diverse.

Nature Perpetuates the Species. A miniature from a manuscript of the *Romance of the Rose.*

In a class by itself as the greatest work of medieval literature is Dante's *Divine Comedy.* Not much is known about the life of Dante Alighieri (1265–1321), except that he was active during the early part of his career in the political affairs of his native city of Florence. Despite his engagement in politics and the fact that he was a layman, he managed to acquire an awesome mastery of the religious, philosophic, and literary knowledge of his time. He not only knew the Bible and the church fathers, but—most unusual for a layman—he also absorbed the most recent Scholastic theology. In addition, he was thoroughly familiar with Virgil, Cicero, Boethius, and numerous other classical writers, and was fully conversant with the poems of the troubadours and the Italian poetry of his own day. In 1302 he was expelled from Florence after a political upheaval and was forced to live the rest of his life in exile. The *Divine Comedy,* his major work, was written during this final period.

Dante's *Divine Comedy* is a monumental narrative in powerful rhyming Italian verse, which describes the poet's journey through hell, purgatory, and paradise. At the start Dante tells of how he once found himself in a "dark wood," his metaphor for a deep personal mid-life crisis. He is led out of this forest of despair by the Roman Virgil, who stands for the heights of classical reason and philosophy. Virgil guides Dante on a trip through hell and purgatory, and afterward Dante's deceased beloved, Beatrice, who stands for Christian wisdom and blessedness, takes over and guides him through paradise. In the course of this progress Dante meets both historical beings and the poet's contemporaries, all of whom have already been assigned places in the afterlife, and he is instructed by them and his guides as to why they met their several fates. As the poem progresses the poet himself leaves the condition of despair to grow in wisdom and ultimately to reach assurance of his own salvation.

Every reader finds a different combination of wonder and satisfaction in Dante's magnificent work. Some—especially those who know Italian—marvel at the vigor and inventiveness of Dante's language and images. Others are awed by his subtle complexity and poetic symmetry; others by his array of learning; others by the vitality of his characters and individual stories; and still others by his soaring imagination. The historian finds it particularly remarkable that Dante could sum up the best of medieval learning in such an artistically satisfying manner. Dante stressed the precedence of salvation, but he viewed the earth as existing for human benefit. He allowed humans free will to choose good and avoid evil, and accepted Greek philosophy as authoritative in its own sphere; for example, he called Aristotle "the master of them that know." Above all, his sense of hope and his ultimate faith in humanity—remarkable for a defeated exile—most powerfully expresses the dominant mood of the High Middle Ages and makes Dante one of the two or three most stirringly affirmative writers who ever lived.

The closest architectural equivalents of the *Divine Comedy* are the great high-medieval Gothic cathedrals, for they too have qualities of vast scope, balance of intricate detail with careful symmetry, soaring height, and affirmative religious grandeur. But before we approach the Gothic style, it is best to introduce it by means of its high-medieval predecessor, the style of architecture and art known as the Roman-

The Divine Comedy

Quarter Barrel Vaults, Typical of Romanesque Architecture. St. Etienne, Nevers.

Medieval architecture: (1) the Romanesque style

Romanesque Sculpture. Shown here is Jesus with two of his Apostles. The elongation and distortion is typical. From a church in Spain.

esque. This style had its origins in the tenth century, but became fully formed in the eleventh and first half of the twelfth centuries, when the religious reform movement led to the building of many new monasteries and large churches. The Romanesque was primarily a building style: it aimed to manifest the glory of God in ecclesiastical construction by rigorously subordinating all architectural details to a uniform system. In this it was very severe: we may think of it as the architectural analogue of the unadorned hymn. Aside from its primary stress on systematic construction, the essential features of the Romanesque style were the rounded arch, massive stone walls, enormous piers, small windows, and the predominance of horizontal lines. The plainness of interiors was sometimes relieved by mosaics or frescoes in bright colors, and, a very important innovation for Christian art, the introduction of sculptural decoration, both within and without. For the first time, full-length human figures appeared on facades. These are usually grave and elongated far beyond natural dimensions, but they have much evocative power and represent the first manifestations of a revived interest in sculpting the human form.

In the course of the twelfth and thirteenth centuries the Romanesque style was supplanted throughout most of Europe by the Gothic. Although trained art historians can see how certain traits of the one style led to the development of the other, the actual appearance of the two styles is enormously different. In fact, the two seem as different as the epic is different from the romance, an appropriate analogy because the Gothic style emerged in France in the mid–twelfth century exactly when the romance did, and because it was far more sophisticated,

Worms Cathedral, Eleventh-Century Romanesque

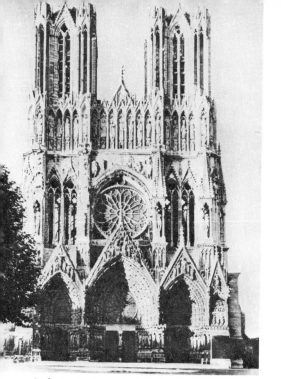

Left: *Rheims Cathedral*. Built between 1220 and 1299, this High Gothic cathedral places great stress on the vertical elements. The gabled portals, the windows above the doorways, the gallery of royal statues, and the multitude of pinnacles all accentuate the height of the structue. Right: *The High Chapel of La Sainte-Chapelle, Paris*. High Gothic is here carried to its logical extreme. Slender columns, tracery, and stained-glass windows take the place of walls.

graceful, and elegant than its predecessor, in the same way that the romance compared with the epic. The rapid development and acceptance of the Gothic shows for a last time—if any more proof be needed—that the twelfth century was experimental and dynamic, arguably at least as much as the twentieth. When the abbey church of St. Denis, venerated as the shrine of the French patron saint and burial place of French kings, was torn down in 1144 in order to make room for a much larger one in the strikingly new Gothic style, it was as if the president of the United States were to tear down the White House and replace it with a Mies van der Rohe or Frank Lloyd Wright edifice. Such an act today would be highly improbable, or at least would create an enormous uproar. But in the twelfth century the equivalent actually happened and was taken in stride.

(2) the development of the Gothic style

Gothic architecture was one of the most intricate of building styles. Its basic elements were the pointed arch, groined and ribbed vaulting, and the flying buttress. These devices made possible a much lighter and loftier construction than could ever have been achieved with the round arch and the engaged pier of the Romanesque. In fact, the Gothic cathedral could be described as a skeletal framework of stone enclosed by enormous windows. Other features included lofty spires,

Elements of the Gothic style

Gothic Sculpture. The three kings bearing gifts, from the thirteenth-century cathedral of Amiens. Note the greater naturalism in comparison to the Romanesque sculpture shown on p. 362.

rose windows, delicate tracery in stone, elaborately sculptured facades, multiple columns, and the use of gargoyles, or representations of mythical monsters, as decorative devices. Ornamentation in the best of the cathedrals was generally concentrated on the exterior. Except for the stained-glass windows and the intricate carving on woodwork and altars, interiors were kept rather simple and occasionally almost severe. But the inside of the Gothic cathedral was never somber or gloomy. The stained-glass windows served not to exclude the light but to glorify it, to catch the rays of sunlight and suffuse them with a richness and warmth of color which nature itself could hardly duplicate even in its happiest moods.

The significance of Gothic architecture

See color plates facing page 352

Many people still think of the Gothic cathedral as the expression of purely ascetic otherworldliness, but this estimation is highly inaccurate. Certainly all churches are dedicated to the glory of God and hope for life everlasting, but Gothic ones sometimes included stained-glass scenes of daily life that had no overt religious significance at all. More important, Gothic sculpture of religious figures such as Jesus, the Virgin, and the saints was becoming far more naturalistic than anything hitherto created in the medieval West. So also was the sculptural representation of plant and animal life, for interest in the human person and in the world of natural beauty was no longer considered sinful. Moreover, Gothic architecture was also an expression of the medieval intellectual genius. Each cathedral, with its mass of symbolic figures, was a kind of encyclopedia of medieval knowledge carved in stone for those who could not read. Finally, Gothic cathedrals were manifestations of urban pride. Always located in the growing medieval cities, they were meant to be both centers of community life and expressions of a town's greatness. When a new cathedral went up the people of the entire community participated in erecting it, and rightfully regarded it as almost their own property. Many of the Gothic cathedrals were the products of urban rivalries. Each city or town sought to overawe its neighbor with ever bigger or taller buildings, to the degree that ambitions sometimes got out of bounds and many of the cathedrals were left unfinished. But most of the finished ones are still vast enough. Built to last into eternity, they provide the most striking visual manifestation of the soaring exuberance of their age.

Surveys of high-medieval accomplishments often omit drama and music, but such oversights are unfortunate. Our own modern drama descends at least as much from the medieval form as from the classical one. Throughout the medieval period some Latin classical plays were known in manuscript but were never performed. Instead drama was born all over again within the Church. In the early Middle Ages certain passages in the liturgy began to be acted out. Then, in the twelfth century, primarily in Paris, these were superseded by short religious plays in Latin, performed inside the Church. Rapidly thereafter, and still in twelfth-century Paris, the Latin plays were supplemented or supplanted by ones in the vernacular so that the whole congregation could understand them. Then, around 1200, these started to be performed outside, in front of the Church, so that they would not take time away from the services. As soon as that happened, drama entered the everyday world: nonreligious stories were introduced, character portrayal was expanded, and the way was fully prepared for the Elizabethans and Shakespeare.

As the drama grew out of developments within the liturgy and then moved far beyond them, so did characteristically Western music. Until the High Middle Ages Western music was *homophonic,* as is most non-Western music even today. That is, it developed only one melody at a time without any harmonic background. The great high-medieval invention was *polyphony,* or the playing of two or more harmonious melodies together. Some experiments along these lines may have been made in the West as early as the tenth century, but the most fundamental breakthrough was achieved in the cathedral of Paris around 1170, when the Mass was first sung by two voices weaving together two different melodies in "counterpoint." Roughly concurrently, systems of musical notation were invented and perfected so that performance no longer had to rely on memory and could become more complex. All the greatness of Western music followed from these first steps.

It may have been noticed that many of the same people who made such important contributions to learning, thought, literature, architecture, drama, and music, must have intermingled with each other in

The revival of drama

Medieval music: polyphony

*The enduring
achievements of the High
Middle Ages*

the Paris of the High Middle Ages. Some of them no doubt prayed together in the cathedral of Notre Dame. The names of the leading scholars are remembered, but the names of most of the others are forgotten. Yet taken together they did as much for civilization and created as many enduring monuments as their counterparts in ancient Athens. If their names are forgotten, their achievements in many different ways live on still.

SELECTED READINGS

• Items so designated are available in paperback editions.

RELIGION AND THE CRUSADES

• Barraclough, G., *The Medieval Papacy*, New York, 1968. A forcefully argued analytical treatment. Noteworthy too for its illustrations.

Daniel-Rops, H., *Cathedral and Crusade*, 2 vols., New York, 1963. The best survey from a Roman Catholic perspective.

Erdmann, Carl, *The Origin of the Idea of Crusade*, Princeton, N.J., 1978. A brilliant advanced work on the background to the First Crusade.

Lambert, Malcolm, *Medieval Heresy*, London, 1977. A masterful synthesis.

Leclercq, Jean, *Bernard of Clairvaux and the Cistercian Spirit*, Kalamazoo, Mich., 1976.

• Mayer, Hans Eberhard, *The Crusades*, New York, 1972. The best one-volume survey.

Moorman, J. R. H., *A History of the Franciscan Order from its Origins to the Year 1517*, Oxford, 1968. Exhaustive.

Runciman, S., *A History of the Crusades*, 3 vols., Cambridge, 1951–54. Colorful and engrossing.

Southern, R. W., *Western Society and the Church in the Middle Ages*, Baltimore, 1970. An extremely insightful and well-written interpretation of the interplay between society and religion.

Tellenbach, G., *Church, State and Christian Society at the Time of the Investiture Contest*, Oxford, 1940. Stresses revolutionary aspects of Gregory VII's thought and career.

Ullmann, Walter, *A Short History of the Papacy in the Middle Ages*, 2nd ed., London, 1974.

THOUGHT, LETTERS, AND THE ARTS

• Baldwin, John W., *The Scholastic Culture of the Middle Ages*, Lexington, Mass., 1971. A fine introduction.

Bergin, T. G., *Dante*, New York, 1965.

Chenu, M. D., *Toward Understanding St. Thomas*, Chicago, 1964. An excellent approach to St. Thomas's work by a contemporary Dominican.

Cobban, Alan B., *The Medieval Universities*, London, 1975. The best shorter treatment in English.

Curtius, E. R., *European Literature and the Latin Middle Ages*, New York, 1953. An exhaustive treatment of medieval Latin literature in terms of its classical background and influence on later times.

Frankl, P., *Gothic Architecture*, Baltimore, 1962.

• Gilson, E., *Reason and Revelation in the Middle Ages*, New York, 1938. A brief but illuminating treatment by the greatest modern student of Scholasticism.

• Haskins, C. H., *The Renaissance of the Twelfth Century*, Cambridge, Mass., 1927. Treats Latin writings in many different genres.

• Henderson, George, *Gothic*, Baltimore, 1967.

Holmes, Urban T., *A History of Old French Literature*, 2nd ed., London, 1948.

Hoppin, Richard H., *Medieval Music*, New York, 1978.

• Knowles, David, *The Evolution of Medieval Thought*, New York, 1962. A very authoritative and well-written but often difficult survey.

Leclercq, Jean, *The Love of Learning and the Desire for God*, New York, 1961. About monastic culture, with special reference to St. Bernard.

Leff, G., *Paris and Oxford Universities in the Thirteenth and Fourteenth Centuries*, New York, 1968. Covers both thought and institutions of learning.

• Lewis, C. S., *The Discarded Image*, Cambridge, 1964.

• Lindberg, David C., ed., *Science in the Middle Ages*, Chicago, 1978. A collection of introductory essays by leading authorities in their respective fields.

• Mâle, E., *The Gothic Image*, New York, 1913.

• Morris, Colin, *The Discovery of the Individual*, London, 1972. A provocative interpretation which sees "individualism" as a twelfth-century discovery.

Southern, R. W., *Medieval Humanism*, New York, 1970. A collection of essays, almost all of which are exciting. Most exciting is the title piece.

Ullmann, W., *Medieval Political Thought*, rev. ed., Baltimore, 1976. The best short survey.

Van Steenberghen, F., *Aristotle in the West*, New York, 1970. A short account of the recovery of Aristotelian thought in the High Middle Ages.

• Von Simson, O., *The Gothic Cathedral*, New York, 1956. A controversial argument that Gothic architecture was meant to be "scientific."

SOURCE MATERIALS

• *An Aquinas Reader*, ed. Mary T. Clark, New York, 1972.

• Chrétien de Troyes, *Arthurian Romances*, tr. W. W. Comfort, New York, 1914.

• Dante, *The Divine Comedy*, tr. J. Ciardi, New York, 1977.

• Goldin, F., ed., *Lyrics of the Troubadours and Trouvères*, New York, 1973.

• Gottfried von Strassburg, *Tristan*, tr. A. T. Hatto, Baltimore, 1960.

• Joinville and Villehardouin, *Chronicles of the Crusades*, tr. M. R. B. Shaw, Baltimore, 1963.

• *The Letters of Abelard and Heloise* (includes Abelard's *Story of My Calamities*), tr. B. Radice, Baltimore, 1974.

• Peters, Edward, ed., *The First Crusade: The Chronicle of Fulcher of Chartres and Other Source Materials*, Philadelphia, 1971.

The Romance of the Rose, tr. Harry W. Robbins, New York, 1962.

- *The Song of Roland,* tr. F. Goldin, New York, 1978.
- Thorndike, Lynn, ed., *University Records and Life in the Middle Ages,* New York, 1944.
- Tierney, Brian, ed., *The Crisis of Church and State, 1050–1300,* Englewood Cliffs, N.J., 1964. An excellent anthology of readings introduced and connected by masterful commentary.
- Wolfram von Eschenbach, *Parzival,* tr. H. M. Mustard and C. E. Passage, New York, 1961.

Chapter 13

THE LATER MIDDLE AGES
(1300–1500)

My lot has been to live amidst a storm
Of varying disturbing circumstances.
For you . . . a better age awaits.
Our descendants—the darkness once dispersed—
Can come again to the old radiance.

—The poet Petrarch,
writing in the 1340s

I f the High Middle Ages were "times of feasts," then the late Middle Ages were "times of famine." From about 1300 until the middle or latter part of the fifteenth century calamities struck throughout western Europe with appalling severity and dismaying persistence. Famine first prevailed because agriculture was impeded by soil exhaustion, colder weather, and torrential rainfalls. Then, on top of those "acts of God," came the most terrible natural disaster of all: the dreadful plague known as the "Black Death," which cut broad swaths of mortality throughout western Europe. As if all that were not enough, incessant warfare continually brought hardship and desolation. Common people suffered most because they were most exposed to raping, stabbing, looting, and burning by soldiers and organized bands of freebooters. After an army passed through a region one might see miles of smoldering ruins littered with putrefying corpses; in many places the desolation was so great that wolves roamed the countryside and even entered the outskirts of the cities. In short, if the serene Virgin symbolized the High Middle Ages, the grinning death's-head symbolized the succeeding period. For these reasons we should not look to the later Middle Ages for the dramatic progress we saw transpiring earlier; but this is not to say that there was no progress at all. In the last two centuries of the Middle Ages Europeans dis-

The later Middle Ages:
catastrophe and adaptation

played a tenacious perseverance in the face of adversity. Instead of abandoning themselves to apathy, they resolutely sought to adjust themselves to changed circumstances. Thus there was no collapse of civilization as there was with the fall of the Roman Empire, but rather a period of transition that resulted in preserving and building upon what was most solid in Europe's earlier legacy.

1. ECONOMIC DEPRESSION AND THE EMERGENCE OF A NEW EQUILIBRIUM

Economic crisis

By around 1300 the agricultural expansion of the High Middle Ages had reached its limits. Thereafter yields and areas under cultivation began to decline, causing a decline in the whole European economy that was accelerated by the disruptive effects of war. Accordingly, the first half of the fourteenth century was a time of growing economic depression. The coming of the Black Death in 1347 made this depression particularly acute because it completely disrupted the affairs of daily life. Subsequent recurrences of the plague and protracted warfare continued to depress most of the European economy until deep into the fifteenth century. But between roughly 1350 and 1450 Europeans learned how to adjust to the new economic circumstances and succeeded in placing their economy on a sounder basis. This became most evident after around 1450, when the tapering off of disease and warfare permitted a slow, but steady economic recovery. All told, therefore, despite a prolonged depression of roughly 150 years, Europe emerged in the later fifteenth century with a healthier economy than it had known earlier.

Agricultural adversity

The limits to agricultural expansion reached around 1300 were natural ones. There was a limit to the amount of land that could be cleared and a limit to the amount of crops that could be raised without the introduction of scientific farming. In fact, Europeans had gone further in clearing and cultivating than they should have: in the enthusiasm of the high-medieval colonization movement, marginal lands had been cleared that were not rich enough to sustain intense cultivation. In addition, even the best plots were becoming overworked. To make matters worse, after around 1300 the weather deteriorated. Whereas western Europe had been favored with a drying and warming trend in the eleventh and twelfth centuries, in the fourteenth century the climate became colder and wetter. Although the average decline in temperature over the course of the century was only at most 1° Centigrade, this was sufficient to curtail viticulture in many northern areas such as England. Cereal farming too became increasingly impractical in far northern regions because the growing season became too short: in Greenland and parts of Scandinavia agricultural settlements were abandoned entirely. Increased rainfall also took its toll.

Terrible floods that deluged all of northwestern Europe in 1315 ruined crops and caused a prolonged, deadly famine. For three years peasants were so driven by hunger that they ate their seed grain, ruining their chances for a full recovery in the following season. In desperation they also ate cats, dogs, and rats. Many peasants were so exposed to unsanitary conditions and weakened by malnutrition that they became highly susceptible to disease. Thus there was an appalling death rate. In one Flemish city a tenth of the population was buried within a six-month period of 1316 alone. Relatively settled farming conditions returned after 1318, but in many parts of Europe heavy rains or other climatic disasters came again. In Italy floods swept away Florentine bridges in 1333 and a tidal wave destroyed the port of Amalfi in 1343. With nature so recurrently capricious economic life could only suffer.

Although ruinous wars combined with famine to kill off many, Europe remained overpopulated until the middle of the fourteenth century. The reason for this was that population growth was still outstripping food supply. Since people continued to multiply while cereal production declined, there was just not enough food to go around. Accordingly, grain prices soared and the poor throughout Europe paid the penalty in hunger. And then a disaster struck which was so appalling that it seemed to many to presage the end of the world.

*The pressure of
population*

This was the Black Death, a combined onslaught of bubonic and pneumonic plague which first swept through Europe from 1347 to 1350, and returned at periodic intervals for roughly the next hundred years. This calamity was fully comparable—in terms of the death, dislocation, and horror it wrought—to the two world wars of the twentieth century. The clinical effects of the plague were hideous. Once infected with bubonic plague by a flea-bite, the diseased person would develop enormous swellings in the groin or armpits; black spots might appear on the arms and legs, diarrhea would ensue, and the victim would die between the third and fifth day. If the infection came in the pneumonic form, i.e., caused by inhalation, there would be coughing of blood instead of swellings, and death would follow within three days. Some people went to bed healthy and were dead the next morning after a night of agony; ships with dead crews floated aimlessly on the seas. Although the successive epidemics left a few localities unscathed, the overall demographic effects of the plague were devastating. To take just a few examples: the population of Toulouse declined from roughly 30,000 in 1335, to 26,000 in 1385, to 8,000 in 1430; the total population of eastern Normandy fell by 30 percent between 1347 and 1357, and again by 30 percent before 1380; in the rural area around Pistoia a population depletion of about 60 percent occurred between 1340 and 1404. Altogether, the combined effects of famine, war, and, above all, plague reduced the total population of western Europe by at least one half and probably more like two-thirds between 1300 and 1450.

The Black Death

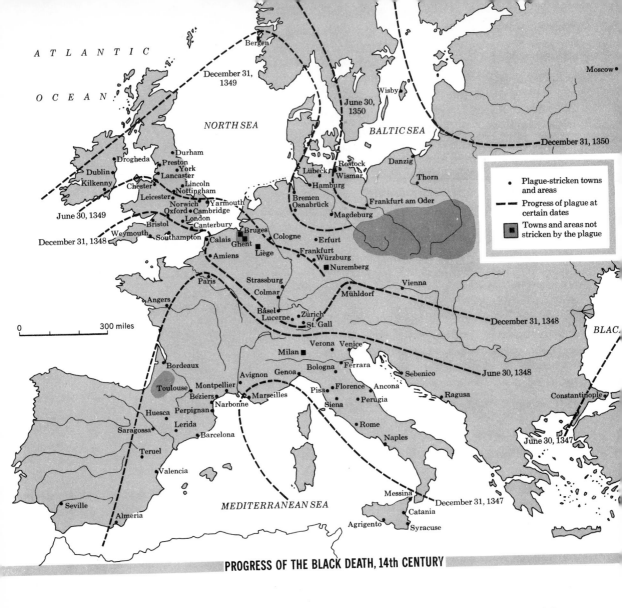

PROGRESS OF THE BLACK DEATH, 14th CENTURY

The Black Death disrupts society and economy

At first, the Black Death caused great hardships for most of the survivors. Since panic-stricken people wished to avoid contagion, many fled from their jobs to seek isolation. Town-dwellers fled to the country and country-dwellers fled from each other. Even the pope retreated to the interior of his palace and allowed no one entrance. With large numbers dead and others away from their posts, harvests were left rotting, manufacturing was disrupted, and conveyance systems were abandoned. Hence basic commodities became scarcer and prices rose. For these reasons the onslaught of the plague greatly intensified Europe's economic crisis.

But after around 1400 the new demographic realities began to turn prices around and alter basic economic patterns. Particularly, the prices of staple foodstuffs began to decline because production gradually returned to normal and there were fewer mouths to feed. Recurrent reappearances of the plague or natural disasters sometimes caused prices to fluctuate greatly in certain years, but overall prices of basic commodities throughout most of the fifteenth century went down or remained stable. This trend led to new agricultural specialization. Since cereals were cheaper, people could afford to spend a greater percentage of their income on comparative luxuries such as dairy products, meat, and wine. Hitherto farmers all over Europe had concentrated on cereals because bread was the staff of life, but now it was wisest, particularly in areas of poorer soil or unpropitious climate, to shift to specialized production. Depending upon whatever seemed most feasible, land might be used for the raising of livestock for milk, grapes for wine, or malt for beer. Specialized regional economies resulted: parts of England were given over to sheep-raising or beer production, parts of France concentrated on wine, and Sweden traded butter for cheap German grain. Most areas of Europe turned to what they could do best, and reciprocal trade of basic commodities over long distances created a sound new commercial equilibrium.

Another economic result of the Black Death was an increase in the relative importance of towns and cities. Urban manufacturers usually could respond more flexibly than landlords to drastically changed economic conditions because their production capabilities were more elastic. When markets shrank, manufacturers could cut back supply more easily to match demand; they could also raise production more easily when circumstances warranted. Thus urban entrepreneurs bounced back from disaster more quickly than landowners. Often they took advantage of their greater strength to attract rural labor by

Economic consequences of the Black Death: (1) agricultural specialization

(2) the growth in importance of urban centers

A Late-Medieval Funeral Scene

means of higher salaries. Thereby the population balance between countryside and town was shifted slightly in favor of the latter.

Certain urban centers, especially those in northern Germany and northern Italy, profited the most from the new circumstances. In Germany a group of cities and towns under the leadership of Lübeck and Bremen allied in the so-called Hanseatic League to control long-distance trade in the Baltic and North Seas. Their fleets transported German grain to Scandinavia and brought back dairy products, fish, and furs. The enhanced European per capita ability to buy luxury goods brought new wealth to the northern Italian trading cities of Genoa and, especially, Venice because these cities controlled the importation of spices from the East. Greater expenditures on luxury also aided the economies of Florence, Venice, Milan, and other neighboring cities because those cities concentrated on the manufacture of silks and linens, light woolens, and other fine cloths. Milan, in addition, prospered from its armaments industry, which kept the warring European states supplied with armor and weapons. Because of varying local conditions, some cities and towns, above all those of Flanders, became economically depressed, but altogether European urban centers profited remarkably well from the new economic circumstances and emphasis on specialization.

The changed circumstances also helped stimulate the development of sophisticated business, accounting, and banking techniques. Because sharp fluctuations in prices made investments precarious, new forms of partnerships were created to minimize risks. Insurance contracts were also invented to take some of the risk out of shipping. Europe's most useful accounting invention, double-entry bookkeeping, was first put into use in Italy in the mid–fourteenth century and spread rapidly thereafter north of the Alps. This allowed for quick discovery of computational errors and easy overview of profits and losses, credits and debits. Large-scale banking had already become common after the middle of the thirteenth century, but the economic crises of the later Middle Ages encouraged banks to alter some of their ways of doing business. Most important was the development of prudent branch-banking techniques, especially by the Florentine house of the Medici. Earlier banks had built branches, but the Medici bank, which flourished from 1397 to 1494, organized theirs along the lines of a modern holding company. The Medici branches, located in London, Bruges, and Avignon, as well as several Italian cities, were dominated by senior partners from the Medici family who followed common policies. Formally, however, each branch was a separate partnership which did not carry any other branch down with it if it collapsed. Other Italian banks experimented with advanced credit techniques. Some even allowed their clients to transfer funds between each other without any real money changing hands. Such "book transfers" were at first executed only by oral command, but around 1400 they started to be carried out by written orders. These were the earliest ancestors of the modern check.

The towns of northern Germany and northern Italy

The growth of advanced business and financial techniques

An Artisan Making Chain Mail. One can easily see why late-medieval knightly armor was terribly expensive.

In surveying the two centuries of late-medieval economic history, both the role of nature and that of human beings must be emphasized. The premodern history of all parts of the globe tends to show that whenever population becomes excessive natural controls manage to reduce it. Bad weather and disease may come at any time, but when humans are already suffering from hunger and conditions of over-crowding, the results of natural disasters will be particularly devastating. That certainly is what happened in the fourteenth century. Nature intervened cruelly in human affairs, but no matter how cruel the im-mediate effects, the results were ultimately beneficial. By 1450 a far smaller population had a higher average standard of living than the population of 1300. In this result humans too played their part. Because people were determined to make the best of the new circumstances and avoid a recurrence of economic depression, they managed to reor-ganize their economic life and place it on a sounder footing. The gross European product of about 1450 was probably smaller than it was in 1300, but this is not surprising given the much smaller population. In fact, per capita output had risen with per capita income, and the Euro-pean economy was ready to move on to new conquests.

The interaction of man and nature in late-medieval economic history

2. SOCIAL AND EMOTIONAL DISLOCATION

Before the healthy new equilibrium was reached, the economic crises of the later Middle Ages contributed from about 1300 to 1450 to pro-voking a rash of lower-class rural and urban insurrections more nu-merous than Europe had ever known before or has ever known since. It used to be thought that these were all caused by extreme depriva-tion, but as we will see, that was not always the case.

Social crisis: lower-class revolts

The one large-scale rural uprising that was most clearly caused by extreme poverty was the northern French "Jacquerie" of 1358. This took its name from the prototypical French peasant, "Jacques Bon-homme," who had finally suffered more than he could endure. In 1348 and 1349 the Black Death had brought its terror and wreaked havoc with the economy and with people's lives. Then a flare-up of war between England and France had spread great desolation over the countryside. The peasants, as usual in late-medieval warfare, suffered most from the pillaging and burning carried out by the rapacious sol-diers. To make matters even less endurable, after the English deci-sively defeated the French in 1356 at the Battle of Poitiers the French king, John II, and numerous aristocrats had to be ransomed. As always in such cases, the peasants were asked to bear the heaviest share of the burden, but by 1358 they had had enough and rose up with astound-ing ferocity. Without any clear program they burned down castles, murdered their lords, and raped their lords' wives. Undoubtedly their intense (and justified) economic resentments were the major cause for the uprising, but it should be said too that 1358 was a year of deep po-litical uncertainty for northern France, thus making an uprising of

Rural insurrections: the Jacquerie

peasants possible. While the king was in captivity in England, groups of townsmen were trying to reform the governmental system by limiting monarchical powers, and certain aristocrats were plotting to seize power. In the meantime, John II's son, Charles, was trying both to raise a large ransom for his father and subdue the crown's enemies. Although we can never be certain, it seems unlikely that the peasants would have revolted had they not sensed an opportunity to take advantage of France's political confusion. But in fact the opportunity was not as great as they may have thought: within a month the privileged powers closed ranks, massacred the rebels, and quickly restored order.

Background of the English Peasants' Revolt

The English Peasants' Revolt of 1381—the most serious lower-class rebellion in English history—is frequently bracketed with the Jacquerie, but its causes were very different. Instead of being a revolt of abject desperation, it was one of frustrated rising expectations. By 1381 the effects of the Black Death should have been working in favor of the peasants. Above all, a shortage of labor should have placed their services in demand. In fact, the incidence of the plague did help to increase manumissions (i.e., freeings) of serfs and raise salaries or lower rents of free farm laborers. But aristocratic landlords fought back to preserve their own incomes. They succeeded in passing legislation that aimed to keep wages at pre-plague levels and force landless laborers to work at the lower rates. Aristocrats furthermore often tried to exact all their old dues and unpaid services. Because the peasants were unwilling to be pushed down into their previous poverty and subservience, a collision was inevitable.

The course of the revolt

The spark that ignited the great revolt of 1381 was an attempt to collect a national tax levied equally on every head instead of being made proportional to wealth. This was an unprecedented development in English tax-collecting that the peasants understandably found unfair. Two head-taxes were levied without resistance in 1377 and 1379, but when agents tried to collect a third in 1381 the peasantry rose up to resist and seek redress of all their grievances. First they burned local records and sacked the dwellings of those they considered their exploiters; then they marched on London, where they executed the lord chancellor and treasurer of England. Recognizing the gravity of the situation, the fifteen-year-old king, Richard II, went out to meet the peasants and won their confidence by promising to abolish serfdom and keep rents low; meanwhile, during negotiations, the peasant leader, Wat Tyler, was murdered in a squabble with the king's escort. Lacking leadership, the peasants, who mistakenly thought they had achieved their aims, rapidly dispersed. But once the boy-king was no longer in danger of his life he kept none of his promises. Instead, the scattered peasant forces were quickly hunted down and a few alleged trouble-makers were executed without any mass reprisals. The revolt itself therefore accomplished nothing, but within a few decades the natural play of economic forces caused serfdom to disappear and considerably improved the lot of the rural wage laborer.

Other rural revolts took place in other parts of Europe, but we may now look at some urban ones. Conventionally, the urban revolts of the later Middle Ages are viewed as uprisings of exploited proletarians who were more oppressed than ever because of the effects of economic depression. But this is probably too great a simplification because each case differed and complex forces were always at work. For example, an uprising in the north German town of Brunswick in 1374 was much less a movement of the poor against the rich than a political upheaval in which one political alliance replaced another. A different north German uprising, in Lübeck in 1408, has been aptly described as a "taxpayer's" revolt. This again was less a confrontation of the poor versus the rich than an attempt of a faction that was out of power to initiate less costly government.

The nearest thing to a real proletarian revolt was the uprising in 1378 of the Florentine *Ciompi* (pronounced "cheeompi"). The Ciompi were wool-combers who had the misfortune to be engaged in an industry that had become particularly depressed. Some of them had lost their jobs and others were frequently cheated or underpaid by the masters of the woolen industry. The latter wielded great political power in Florence, and thus could pass economic legislation in their own favor. This fact in itself meant that if there were to be economic reforms, they would have to go together with political changes. As events transpired it was a political crisis that called the Ciompi into direct action. In 1378 Florence had become exhausted by three years of war with the papacy. Certain patrician leaders overthrew the old regime to alter the war policy and gain their own political advantage. Circumstances led them to seek the support of the lower classes and, once stirred up, the Ciompi became emboldened after a few months to launch their own far more radical rebellion. This was inspired primarily by economic hardship and grievances, but personal hatreds also played a role. The Ciompi gained power for six weeks, during which they tried to institute tax relief, fuller employment, and representation of themselves and other proletarian groups in the Florentine government. But they could not maintain their hold on power and a new oligarchical government revoked all their reforms.

If we try to draw any general conclusions about these various uprisings, we can certainly say that few if any of them would have occurred had there not been an economic crisis. But political considerations always had some influence, and the rebels in some uprisings were more prosperous than in others. It is noteworthy that all the genuinely lower-class uprisings of economically desperate groups quickly failed. This was certainly because the upper classes were more accustomed to wielding power and giving orders; even more important, they had access to the money and troops necessary to quell revolts. Sometimes

Tombstone of a Leader of a Fourteenth-Century German Peasant Uprising. In 1336 a petty knight from Franconia (central Germany) marched at the head of impoverished peasants who vented their resentments by robbing and murdering all the Jews they could find in the nearby towns. After several months of leading this rampage the knight was finally apprehended and executed by governing authorities. His tombstone shows him with bound hands at the moment of his beheading, but the inscription calls him "blessed," a sign that some wished to view him as a martyred saint.

General observations on the nature of popular uprisings

elements within the lower classes might fight among themselves, whereas the privileged always managed to rally into a united front when faced by a lower-class threat to their domination. In addition, lower-class rebels were usually more intent on redressing immediate grievances than on developing fully coherent long-term governmental programs; inspiring ideals for cohesive action were generally lacking. The case of the Hussite Revolution in Bohemia—to be treated later—shows that religion in the later Middle Ages was a more effective rallying ground for large numbers of people than political, economic, and social demands.

The crisis of the late-medieval aristocracy

Although the upper classes succeeded in overcoming popular uprisings, they perceived the economic and emotional insecurities of the later Middle Ages and the possibility of revolt as a constant threat, and became obsessed with maintaining their privileged social status. Late-medieval aristocrats were in a precarious economic position because they gained most of their income from land. In times when grain prices and rents were falling and wages rising, landowners were obviously in economic trouble. Some aristocrats probably also felt threatened by the rapid rise of merchants and financiers who could make quick killings because of sharp market fluctuations. In practice, really wealthy merchants bought land and were absorbed into the aristocracy. Moreover, most landowning aristocrats were able to stave off economic threats by expert estate management; in fact, many of them actually became richer than ever. But most still felt more exposed to social and economic insecurities than before. The result was that they tried to set up artificial barriers behind which they separated themselves from other classes.

A Party of Late-Medieval Aristocrats. Notice the pointed shoes and the women's pointed hats, twice as high as their heads.

Two of the most striking examples of this separation were the aristocratic emphasis on luxury and the formation of exclusive chivalric orders. The late Middle Ages was the period par excellence of aristocratic ostentation. While famine or disease raged, aristocrats regaled themselves with lavish banquets and magnificent pageants. At one feast in Flanders in 1468 a table decoration was forty-six feet high. Aristocratic clothing too was extremely ostentatious: men wore long, pointed shoes, and women ornately festooned headdresses. Throughout history rich people have always enjoyed dressing up, but the aristocrats of the later Middle Ages seem to have done so obsessively to comfort themselves and convey the message that they were entirely different from others. The insistence on maintaining a sharply defined social hierarchy also accounts for the late-medieval proliferation of chivalric orders, such as those of the Knights of the Garter or the Golden Fleece. By joining together in exclusive orders which prescribed special conduct and boasted special insignia of membership, aristocrats who felt threatened by social pressures again tried to set themselves off from others, in effect, by putting up a sign that read "for members only."

Duke Philip the Good of Burgundy. The duke proudly wears the emblem of the Order of the Golden Fleece around his neck.

Another explanation for the exorbitant stress on luxury is that it was a form of escapism. Aristocrats who were continually exposed to the sight and smell of death must have found it emotionally comforting to retreat into a dream-world of elegant manners, splendid feasts, and multicolored clothes. In a parallel fashion, nonaristocrats who could not afford such luxuries often sought relief from the vision of death in crude public entertainments: for example, crowds would watch blind beggars try to catch a squealing pig but beat each other with clubs instead, or they would cheer on boys to clamber up greasy poles in order to win prizes of geese.

Tears and sorrow

It must not be thought, however, that late-medieval Europeans gave themselves over to riotous living without interruption. In fact, the same people who sought elegant or boisterous diversions just as often went to the other emotional extreme when faced by the psychic stress caused by the troubles of the age, and abandoned themselves to sorrow. Throughout the period grown men and women shed tears in abundance. The queen mother of France wept in public when she first viewed her grandson; the great preacher Vincent Ferrer had to interrupt his sermons on Christ's Passion and the Last Judgment because he and his audience were sobbing too convulsively; and the English king, Edward II, supposedly wept so much when imprisoned that he gushed forth enough hot water for his own shave. The last story taxes the imagination, but it does illustrate well what contemporaries thought was possible. We know for certain that the Church encouraged crying because of the survival of moving statuettes of weeping St. Johns, which were obviously designed to call forth tears from their viewers.

People also were encouraged by preachers to brood on the Passion of Christ and on their own mortality. Fearsome crucifixes abounded,

A Late-Medieval Crucifixion Scene. The Virgin has to be held up to keep from swooning, and the angels are weeping.

and the figure of the Virgin Mary was less a smiling madonna than a sorrowing mother: now she was most frequently depicted slumping with grief at the foot of the cross, or holding the dead Christ in her lap. The late-medieval obsession with mortality can also still be seen in sculptures, frescoes, and book illustrations that reminded viewers of the brevity of life and the torments of hell. The characteristic tombs of the High Middle Ages were mounted with sculptures that either showed the deceased in some action that had been typical of his or her accomplishments in life, or else in a state of repose that showed death to be nothing more than peaceful sleep. But in the late fourteenth century, tombs appeared that displayed the physical ravages of death in the most gruesome ways imaginable: emaciated corpses were displayed with protruding intestines or covered with snakes or toads. Some tombs bore inscriptions stating that the viewer would soon be "a fetid cadaver, food for worms"; some warned chillingly: "What you are, I was; what I am, you will be." Omnipresent illustrations displayed figures of grinning Death, with his scythe, carrying off elegant and healthy men and women, or sadistic devils roasting pain-wracked humans in hell. Because people who painted or brooded on such pictures might the next day indulge in excessive revels, late-medieval culture often

Left: *A Dead Man Before His Judge.* A late-medieval reminder of human mortality. Right: *Tomb of François de la Sarra.* This late–fourteenth-century Swiss nobleman is shown with snakes around his arms and toads littering his face.

seems to border on the manic-depressive. But apparently such extreme reactions were necessary to help people cope with their fears.

3. TRIALS FOR THE CHURCH AND HUNGER FOR THE DIVINE

The intense concentration on the meaning of death was also a manifestation of a very deep and pervasive religiosity. The religious enthusiasm of the High Middle Ages by no means flagged after 1300; if anything, it became more intense. But religious enthusiasm took on new forms of expression because of the institutional difficulties of the Church and the turmoils of the age.

After the humiliation and death of Pope Boniface VIII in 1303, the Church experienced a period of institutional crisis that was as severe and prolonged as the contemporary economic crisis. We may distinguish three phases: the so-called Babylonian Captivity of the papacy, 1305–1378; the Great Schism, 1378–1417; and the period of the Italian territorial papacy, 1417–1517. During the Babylonian Captivity the papacy was located in Avignon instead of Rome and was generally subservient to the interests of the French crown. There were several reasons for this: the most obvious was that since the test of strength between Philip the Fair and Boniface VIII had resulted in a clear victory for the French king, subsequent popes were unwilling to risk French royal ire. In fact, once the popes recognized that they could not give orders to the French kings, they found that they could gain certain advantages from currying their favor. One was a safe home in southern France, away from the tumult of Italy. Central Italy and the city of Rome in the fourteenth century had become so politically turbulent and rebellious that the pope could not even count on finding personal safety there, let alone sufficiently peaceful conditions to maintain orderly ecclesiastical administration. But no such danger existed in Avignon. Even though Avignon was not then part of the French kingdom—it was the major city of a small papal territory—French military might was close enough to guarantee the pope his much-needed security. Another advantage of papal subservience to French power was help from the French in pursuing mutually advantageous policies in Germany and southern Italy. Perhaps most important was a working agreement whereby the French king would propose his own candidates to become bishops and the pope would then name them, thereby gaining sizable monetary payments. After 1305 the pro-French system became so entrenched that a majority of cardinals and all the popes until 1378 were themselves French.

At Avignon the popes were more successful than ever in pursuing their policy of centralizing the government of the Church. For the first time they worked out a really sound system of papal finance, based on the systematization of dues collected from the clergy throughout

The Prince of the World. A stone figure from the church of St. Sebald, Nuremberg, from about 1330. From the front the man is smiling and master of all he surveys; from the rear he is crawling with vermin.

Europe. The papacy also succeeded in appointing more candidates to vacant benefices than before (in practice often naming candidates proposed by the French and English kings), and they proceeded against heresy with great determination, indeed with ruthlessness. But whatever the popes achieved in power they lost in respect and loyalty. The clergy became alienated as a result of being asked to pay so much money, and much of the laity was horrified by the corruption and unbridled luxury displayed at the papal court: there the cardinals lived more splendidly than lords, dining off peacocks, pheasants, grouse, and swans, and drinking from elaborately sculptured fountains that spouted the finest wines. Most of the Avignonese popes themselves were personally upright and abstemious, but one, Clement VI (1342–1352), was worse than his cardinals. Clement was ready to offer any spiritual benefit for money, boasted that he would appoint even a jackass as bishop if political circumstances warranted, and defended his incessant sexual transgressions by insisting that he fornicated on doctors' orders.

As time went on the pressures of informed public opinion forced the popes to promise that they would return to Rome. After one abortive attempt by Urban V in 1367, Pope Gregory XI finally did return to the Holy City in 1377. But he died a year later and then disaster struck. The college of cardinals, surrounded in Rome by clamoring Italians, yielded to local sentiment by naming an Italian as pope, who took the title of Urban VI. But most of the cardinals were Frenchmen and quickly regretted their decision, especially because Urban VI immediately began quarreling with them and revealing what were probably paranoid tendencies. Therefore, after only a few months, the French cardinals met again, declared the previous election void, and replaced Urban with one of their own number, who called himself Clement VII.

Unfortunately, however, Urban VI did not meekly resign. On the contrary, he named an entirely new Italian college of cardinals and remained entrenched in Rome. Clement VII quickly retreated with his own party to Avignon and the so-called Great Schism ensued. France and other countries in the French political orbit—such as Scotland, Castile, and Aragon—recognized Clement, while the rest of Europe recognized Urban as the true pope. For three decades Christians looked on helplessly while the rival pontiffs hurled curses at each other and the international monastic orders became divided into Roman and Avignonese camps. The death of one or the other pope did not end the schism; each camp had its own set of cardinals which promptly named either a French or Italian successor. The desperateness of the situation led a council of prelates from both camps to meet in Pisa in 1409 to depose both popes and name a new one instead. But neither the Italian nor the French pope accepted the council's decision and both had enough political support to retain some obedience. So after 1409 there were three rival claimants hurling curses instead of two.

The Great Schism was finally ended in 1417 by the Council of Constance, the largest ecclesiastical gathering in medieval history. This time the assembled prelates made certain to gain the crucial support of secular powers and also to eliminate the prior claimants before naming a new pope. After the council's election of Martin V in 1417, European ecclesiastical unity was thus fully restored. But a struggle over the nature of Church government followed immediately. The members of the Council of Constance challenged the prevailing medieval theory of papal monarchy by calling for balanced, "conciliar," government. In two momentous decrees they stated that a general council of prelates was superior in authority to the pope, and that such councils should meet regularly to govern the Church. Not surprisingly, subsequent popes—who had now returned to Rome—sought to nullify these decrees. When a new council met in Basel in 1431, in accordance with the principles laid down at Constance, the reigning pope did all he could to sabotage its activities. Ultimately he was successful: after a protracted struggle the Council of Basel dissolved in 1449 in abject failure, and the attempt to institute constitutional government in the Church was completely defeated. But the papacy only won this victory over conciliarism by gaining the support of the rulers of the European states. In separate concordats with kings and princes the popes granted the secular rulers much authority over the various local churches. The popes thus became assured of theoretical supremacy at the cost of surrendering much real power. To compensate for this they concentrated on consolidating their own direct rule in central Italy. Most of the fifteenth-century popes ruled very much like any other princes, leading armies, jockeying for alliances, and building magnificent palaces. Hence, although they did succeed for the first time in creating a viable political state, their reputation for disinterested piety remained low.

While the papacy was undergoing these vicissitudes, the local clergy throughout Europe was undergoing a loss of prestige for several reasons. One was that the pope's greater financial demands forced the clergy to demand more from the laity, but such demands were bitterly resented, especially during times of prevailing economic crisis. Then too during outbreaks of plague the clergy sometimes fled their posts just like everyone else, but in so doing they lost whatever claim they had for being morally superior. Probably the single greatest reason for growing dissatisfaction with the clergy was the increase in lay literacy. The continued proliferation of schools and the decline in the cost of books—a subject we will treat later—made it possible for large numbers of lay people to learn how to read. Once that happened, the laity could start reading parts of the Bible, or, more frequently, popular religious primers. These made it clear that their local priests were not living according to the standards set by Jesus and the Apostles. In the meantime, the upheavals and horrors of the age drove people to seek religious solace more than ever. Finding the conventional channels of church attendance, confession, and submission to clerical au-

*The end of the Schism;
conciliarism*

*The decline of clerical
prestige*

A German Flagellant Procession. These penitents hoped they could ward off the Black Death by their mutually inflicted tortures.

thority insufficient, the laity sought supplementary or alternate routes to piety. These differed greatly from each other, but they all aimed to satisfy an immense hunger for the divine.

The growth of lay piety: (1) devotional practices

The most widely-traveled route was that of performing repeated acts of external devotion in the hope that they would gain the devotee divine favor on earth and salvation in the hereafter. People flocked to go on pilgrimages as never before and participated regularly in bare-footed religious processions: the latter were often held twice a month and occasionally as often as once a week. Men and women also eagerly paid for thousands of masses to be said by full-time "mass priests" for the souls of their dead relatives and left legacies for the reading of numerous requiem masses to save their own souls after death. Obsession with repeating prayers reached a peak when some pious individuals tried to compute the number of drops of blood that Christ shed on the cross so that they could say the same number of Our Fathers. The most excessive and repugnant form of religious ritual in the later Middle Ages was flagellation. Some women who lived in communal houses beat themselves with the roughest animal hides, chains, and knotted thongs. A young girl who entered such a community in Poland in 1331 suffered extreme internal injuries and became completely disfigured within eleven months. Flailings were not usually performed in public, but during the first onslaught of the Black Death in 1348 and 1349, whole bands of lay people marched through northern Europe chanting and beating each other with metal-tipped scourges in the hope of appeasing the apparent divine wrath.

Building Operations. From a French picture Bible, c. 1250. Note the treadmill, with wheel, ropes, and pulley, by means of which a basket of stones is brought to the construction level. (Morgan Library)

Siege of a City, c. 1470. The use of cannon would soon put an end to traditional medieval fortifications. (Morgan Library)

Stained Glass, German, c. 1300. One of the kings from the House of David, Christ's royal ancestry. (MMA)

The Virgin and Chancellor Rolin, Jan van Eyck (1390–1444). The early Flemish painters loved to present scenes of piety in the sumptuous surroundings of wealthy burghers. (Louvre)

Vespers of the Holy Ghost, with a View of Paris, Jean Fouquet. From the *Book of Hours* of Etienne Chevalier, 1461. Demons in the sky are sent flying by the divine light from heaven. The cathedral is Notre Dame. (Robert Lehman)

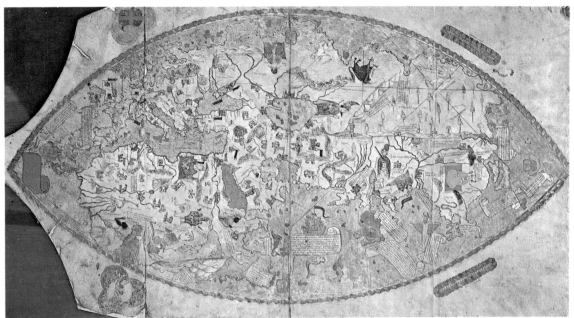

A Fifteenth-Century Map of the World. The European continent is in the upper left, China and Japan are at the far right, and a western hemisphere is lacking. (Scala)

An opposite route to godliness was the inward path of mysticism. Throughout the European continent, but particularly in Germany and England, male and female mystics, both clerical and lay, sought union with God by means of "detachment," contemplation, or spiritual exercises. The most original and eloquent late-medieval mystical theorist was the German Dominican, Master Eckhart (c. 1260–1327), who taught that there was a power or "spark" deep within every human soul that was really the dwelling-place of God. By renouncing all sense of selfhood one could retreat into one's innermost recesses and there find divinity. Eckhart did not recommend ceasing attendance at church—he hardly could have because he preached in churches—but he made it clear that outward rituals were of comparatively little importance in reaching God. He also gave the impression to his lay audiences that they might attain godliness largely on their own volition. Thus ecclesiastical authorities charged him with inciting "ignorant and undisciplined people to wild and dangerous excesses." Although Eckhart pleaded his own doctrinal orthodoxy, some of his teachings were condemned by the papacy.

(2) mysticism

That Eckhart's critics were not entirely mistaken in their worries is shown by the fact that some lay people in Germany who were influenced by him did fall into the heresy of believing that they could become fully united with God on earth without any priestly intermediaries. But these so-called heretics of the Free Spirit were few in number. Much more numerous were later orthodox mystics, sometimes influenced by Eckhart and sometimes not, who placed greater emphasis on the divine initiative in the meeting of the soul with God and made certain to insist that the ministrations of the Church were a necessary contribution to the mystic way. Even they, however, believed that "churches make no man holy, but men make churches holy." Most of the great teachers and practitioners of mysticism in the fourteenth century were clerics, nuns, or hermits, but in the fifteenth century a modified form of mystical belief spread among lay people. This "practical mysticism" did not aim for full ecstatic union with God, but rather for an ongoing sense of some divine presence during the conduct of daily life. The most popular manual that pointed the way to this goal was the Latin *Imitation of Christ,* written around 1427, probably by the north German canon Thomas à Kempis. Because this was written in a simple but forceful style and taught how to be a pious Christian while still living actively in the world, it was particularly attractive to lay readers. Thus it quickly became translated into the leading European vernaculars. From then until today it has been more widely read by Christians than any other religious work outside of the Bible. The *Imitation* urges its readers to participate in one religious ceremony—the sacrament of the Eucharist—but otherwise it emphasizes inward piety. According to its teachings, the individual Christian is best able to become the "partner" of Jesus Christ both by taking communion and also by engaging in biblical meditation and leading a simple, moral life.

*Heterodox and orthodox
mysticism*

A third distinct form of late-medieval piety was outright religious protest or heresy. In England and Bohemia especially, heretical movements became serious threats to the Church. The founder of heresy in late-medieval England was an Oxford theologian named John Wyclif (c. 1330–1384). Wyclif's rigorous adherence to the theology of St. Augustine led him to believe that a certain number of humans were predestined to be saved while the rest were irrevocably damned. He thought the predestined would naturally live simply, according to the standards of the New Testament, but in fact he found most members of the Church hierarchy indulging in splendid extravagances. Hence he concluded that most Church officials were damned. For him the only solution was to have secular rulers appropriate ecclesiastical wealth and reform the Church by replacing corrupt priests and bishops with men who would live according to apostolic standards. This position was obviously attractive to the aristocracy of England, who may have looked forward to enriching themselves with Church spoils and at least saw nothing wrong with using Wyclif as a bulldog to frighten the pope and the local clergy. Thus Wyclif at first received influential aristocratic support. But toward the end of his life he moved from merely calling for reform to attacking some of the most basic institutions of the Church, above all the sacrament of the Eucharist. This radicalism frightened off his influential protectors, and Wyclif probably would have been formally condemned for heresy had he lived longer. His death brought no respite for the Church, however, because he had attracted numerous lay followers—called Lollards—who zealously continued to propagate some of his most radical ideas. Above all, the Lollards taught that pious Christians should shun the corrupt Church and instead study the Bible and rely as far as possible on their individual consciences. Lollardy gained many adherents in the last two decades of the fourteenth century, but after the introduction in England of the death penalty for heresy in 1399 and the failure of a Lollard uprising in 1414 the heretical wave greatly receded. Nonetheless, a few Lollards did continue to survive underground, and their descendants helped contribute to the Protestant Reformation of the sixteenth century.

John Hus

Much greater was the influence of Wyclifism in Bohemia. Around 1400, Czech students who had studied in Oxford brought back Wyclif's ideas to the Bohemian capital of Prague. There Wyclifism was enthusiastically received by an eloquent preacher named John Hus (c. 1373–1415), who had already been inveighing in well-attended sermons against "the world, the flesh, and the devil." Hus employed Wyclifite theories to back up his own calls for the end of ecclesiastical corruption, and rallied many Bohemians to the cause of reform in the years between 1408 and 1415. Never alienating anyone as Wyclif had done by criticizing the doctrine of the Eucharist, Hus gained support from many different directions. The politics of the Great Schism prompted the king of Bohemia to lend Hus his protection, and influential aristocrats supported Hus for motives similar to those of their English counterparts. Above all, Hus gained a mass following because of his eloquence and concern for social justice. Accordingly, most of Bohemia was behind him when Hus in 1415 agreed to travel to the Council of Constance to defend his views and try to convince the assembled prelates that only thoroughgoing reform could save the Church. But although Hus had been guaranteed his personal safety, this assurance was revoked as soon as he arrived at the Council: rather than being given a fair hearing, the betrayed idealist was tried for heresy and burned.

Hus's supporters in Bohemia were justifiably outraged and quickly raised the banner of open revolt. The aristocracy took advantage of the situation to seize Church lands, and poorer priests, artisans, and peasants rallied together in the hope of achieving Hus's goals of religious reform and social justice. Between 1420 and 1424 armies of lower-class Hussites, led by a brilliant blind general, John Zizka, amazingly defeated several invading forces of well-armed "crusading" knights from Germany. In 1434 more conservative, aristocratically dominated Hussites overcame the radicals, thereby ending attempts to initiate a purified new religious and social dispensation. But even the conservatives refused to return to full orthodoxy. Thus Bohemia never came back to the Catholic fold until after the Catholic Reformation in the seventeenth century. The Hussite declaration of religious independence was both a foretaste of what was to come one hundred years later with Protestantism and the most successful late-medieval expression of dissatisfaction with the government of the Church.

The Hussite revolt

4. POLITICAL CRISIS AND RECOVERY

The story of late-medieval politics at first seems very dreary because throughout most of the period there was incessant strife. Almost everywhere neighbors fought neighbors and states fought states. But on closer inspection it becomes clear that despite the turmoil there was ultimate improvement in almost all the governments of Europe. In the course of the fifteenth century peace returned to most of the continent, the national monarchies in particular became stronger, and the period ended on a new note of strength just as it had from the point of view of economics.

Progress in late-medieval politics despite turmoil

Starting our survey with Italy, it must first be explained that the Kingdom of Naples in the extreme south of the Italian peninsula was sunk in endemic warfare or maladministration more or less without interruption throughout the fourteenth and fifteenth centuries. Otherwise, Italy emerged from the prevailing political turmoil of the late Middle Ages earlier than any other part of Europe. The fourteenth century was a time of troubles for the Papal States, comprising most of central Italy, because forces representing the absent or divided pa-

The political situation in Italy

pacy were seldom able to overcome the resistance of refractory towns and rival leaders of marauding military bands. But after the end of the Great Schism in 1417 the popes concentrated more on consolidating their own Italian territories and gradually became the strong rulers of most of the middle part of the peninsula. Farther north some of the leading city-states—such as Florence, Venice, Siena, and Genoa—had experienced at least occasional and most often prolonged social warfare in the fourteenth century because of the economic pressures of the age. But sooner or later the most powerful families or interest groups overcame internal resistance. By around 1400 the three leading cities of the north—Venice, Milan, Florence—had fixed definitively upon their own different forms of government: Venice was ruled by a merchant oligarchy, Milan by a dynastic despotism, and Florence by a complex, supposedly republican system that was actually controlled by the rich. (After 1434 the Florentine republic was in practice dominated by the banking family of the Medici.)

Peace established in the fifteenth century

Having settled their internal problems, Venice, Milan, and Florence proceeded from about 1400 to 1454 to expand territorially and conquer almost all the other northern Italian cities and towns except Genoa, which remained prosperous and independent but gained no new territory. Thus, by the middle of the fifteenth century Italy was divided into five major parts: the states of Venice, Milan, and Florence in the north; the Papal States in the middle; and the backward Kingdom of Naples in the south. A treaty of 1454 initiated a half-century of peace between these states: whenever one threatened to upset the "balance of power," the others usually allied against it before serious warfare could break out. Accordingly, the last half of the fifteenth century was a fortunate age for Italy. But in 1494 a French invasion initiated a period of renewed warfare in which the French attempt at dominating Italy was successfully countered by Spain.

Germany: the triumph of the princes

North of the Alps political turmoil prevailed throughout the fourteenth century and lasted longer into the fifteenth. Probably the worst instability was experienced in Germany. There the virtually independent princes continually warred with the greatly weakened emperors, or else they warred with each other. Between about 1350 and 1450 near-anarchy prevailed, because while the princes were warring and subdividing their inheritances into smaller states, petty powers such as free cities and knights who owned one or two castles were striving to shake off the rule of the princes. Throughout most of the German west these attempts met with enough success to fragment political authority more than ever, but in the east after about 1450 certain stronger German princes managed to assert their authority over divisive forces. After they did so they started to govern firmly over middle-sized states on the model of the larger national monarchies of England and France. The strongest princes were those who ruled in eastern territories such as Bavaria, Austria, and Brandenburg, because there towns were fewer and smaller and the princes had earlier been able to take advantage of imperial weakness to preside over the colonization of large tracts of land. Especially the Habsburg princes of Austria and the Hohenzollern princes of Brandenburg—a territory joined in the sixteenth century with the easternmost lands of Prussia—would be the most influential powers in Germany's future.

The great nation-states did not escape unscathed from the late-medieval turmoil either. France was strife-ridden for much of the period, primarily in the form of the Hundred Years' War between France and England. The Hundred Years' War was actually a series of conflicts that lasted for even more than one hundred years—from 1337 to 1453. There were several different causes for this prolonged struggle. The major one was the long-standing problem of French territory held by the English kings. At the beginning of the fourteenth century the English kings still ruled much of the rich southern French lands of Gascony and Aquitaine as vassals of the French crown. The French, who since the reign of Philip Augustus had been expanding and consolidating their rule, obviously hoped to expel the English, making war inevitable. Another cause for strife was that the English economic interests in the woolen trade with Flanders led them to support the frequent attempts of Flemish burghers to rebel against French rule. Finally, the fact that the direct Capetian line of succession to the French throne died out in 1328, to be replaced thereafter by the related Valois dynasty, meant that the English kings, who themselves descended from the Capetians as a result of intermarriage, laid claim to the French crown itself.

France: causes of the Hundred Years' War

France should have had no difficulty in defeating England at the start: it was the richest country in Europe and outnumbered England in population by some fifteen million to fewer than four million. Nonetheless, throughout most of the first three-quarters of the Hundred Years' War the English won most of the pitched battles. One reason for this was that the English had learned superior military tactics, using well-disciplined archers to fend off and scatter the heavily armored mounted French knights. In the three greatest battles of the long conflict—Crécy (1346), Poitiers (1356), and Agincourt (1415)—the outnumbered English relied on tight discipline and effective use of the longbow to inflict crushing defeats on the French. Another reason for English success was that the war was always fought on French soil. That being the case, English soldiers were eager to fight because they could look forward to rich plunder, while their own homeland suffered none of the disasters of war. Worst of all for the French was the fact that they often were badly divided. The French crown had always had to fear provincial attempts to assert autonomy: especially during the long period of warfare, when there were several highly inept kings and the English encouraged internal French dissensions, many aristocratic provincial leaders took advantage of the confusion to ally with the enemy and seek their own advantage. The most dramatic and fateful instance was the breaking away of Burgundy,

The course of the war: factors in the initial English success

Joan of Arc

whose dukes from 1419 to 1435 allied with the English, an act which called the very existence of an independent French crown into question.

It was in this dark period that the heroic figure of Joan of Arc came forth to rally the French. In 1429 Joan, an illiterate but extremely devout peasant girl, sought out the uncrowned French ruler, Charles VII, to announce that she had been divinely commissioned to drive the English out of France. Charles was persuaded to let her take command of his troops, and her piety and sincerity made such a favorable impression on the soldiers that their morale was raised immensely. In a few months Joan had liberated much of central France from English domination and had brought Charles to Rheims, where he was crowned king. But in May 1430 she was captured by the Burgundians and handed over to the English, who accused her of being a witch and tried her for heresy. Condemned in 1431 after a predetermined trial, she was publicly burned to death in the market square at Rouen. Nonetheless, the French, fired by their initial victories, continued to move on the offensive. When Burgundy withdrew from the English alliance in 1435, and the English king, Henry VI, proved to be totally incompetent, there followed an uninterrupted series of triumphs for the French side. In 1453 the capture of Bordeaux, the last of the English strongholds in the southwest, finally brought the long war to an end. The English now held no land in France except for the Channel port of Calais, which they ultimately lost in 1558.

More than merely expelling the English from French territory, the Hundred Years' War resulted in greatly strengthening the powers of the French crown. Although many of the French kings during the long war had been ineffective personalities—one, Charles VI, was even insane—the monarchy demonstrated remarkable staying power because it provided France with the strongest institutions it knew and therefore offered the only realistic hope for lasting stability and peace. Moreover, warfare emergencies allowed the kings to gather new powers, above all, the rights to collect national taxes and maintain a standing army. Hence after Charles VII succeeded in defeating the English, the crown was able to renew the high-medieval royal tradition of ruling the country assertively. In the reigns of Charles's successors, Louis XI (1461–1483) and Louis XII (1498–1515), the monarchy became ever stronger. Its greatest single achievement was the destruction of the power of Burgundy in 1477 when the Burgundian duke, Charles the Bold, fell in the battle of Nancy at the hands of the Swiss, whom Charles had been trying to dominate. Since Charles died without a male heir, Louis XI of France was able to march into Burgundy and reabsorb the breakaway duchy. Later, when Louis XII gained Brittany by marriage, the French kings ruled powerfully over almost all of what is today included in the borders of France.

Although the Hundred Years' War was fought on French instead of English soil, England also experienced great turmoil during the later

Louis XI of France. A portrait by Fouquet.

Middle Ages because of internal instability. Indeed, England was a hot-bed of insurrection: of the nine English kings who came to the throne between 1307 and 1485, five died violently because of revolts or con-spiracies. Most of these slain kings had proven themselves to be in-capable rulers, but there were other reasons for England's political troubles as well. One was that the crown had been too ambitious in trying both to hold on to its territories in France and also to subdue Scotland. This policy often made it necessary to resort to heavy taxa-tion and to grant major political concessions to the aristocracy. When English arms in France were successful, the crown rode the crest of popularity and the aristocracy prospered from military spoils and ran-soms; but whenever the tides of battle turned to defeat, the crown be-came financially embarrassed and thrown on the political defensive. To make matters worse, the English aristocracy was particularly un-ruly throughout the period, not just because the aristocrats often had reason to distrust the inept kings, but because the economic pressures of the age made them seek to enlarge their agricultural estates at the expense of each other. This led to factionalism, and factionalism often led to civil war.

After the English presence in France was virtually eradicated and the aristocracy could no longer hope to enrich itself on the spoils of foreign warfare, England's political situation became particularly des-perate. As bad luck would have it, the reigning king, Henry VI (1422–1461), was one of the most incompetent that England has ever had. According to one recent authority, Henry "paralyzed and con-fused the whole process of English government with a royal irrespon-sibility and inanity which had no precedent." Henry's willfullness helped provoke the Wars of the Roses that flared on and off from 1455 to 1485. These wars received their name from the emblems of the two competing factions: the red rose of Henry's family of Lancaster and the white rose of the rival house of York. The Yorkists for a time gained the kingship, under such monarchs as Richard III, but in 1485 they were replaced by a new dynasty, that of the Tudors, who began a new period in English history. The first Tudor king, Henry VII, steadily eliminated rival claimants to the throne, avoided expensive foreign wars, built up a financial surplus, and gradually reasserted royal power over the aristocracy. When he died in 1509 he was there-fore able to pass on to his son, Henry VIII (1509–1547), a royal power as great as it had ever been before.

It is tempting to view the entire period of English history between 1307 and the accession of Henry VII in 1485 as one long, dreary inter-regnum which accomplished nothing positive. But that would not quite be doing justice to the time: in the first place, the fact that Eng-land did not entirely fall apart during the recurrent turbulence was an accomplishment in itself. Remarkably, the rebellious aristocrats of the later Middle Ages never tried to proclaim the independence of any of their regions; only once, in 1405, did they seek unsuccessfully to divide the country between them. Discounting that insignificant exception, aristocratic rebels always sought to control the central government rather than destroy or break away from it. Thus when Henry VII came to the throne, he did not have to win back any English territories as Louis XI of France had had to win back Burgundy. More than that, the antagonisms of the Hundred Years' War had the ultimately beneficial effect of enhancing an English sense of national identity. From the Norman Conquest until deep into the fourteenth century, French was the preferred language of the English crown and aristocracy, but mounting anti-French sentiment contributed to the complete triumph of English by around 1400. The loss of lands in France was also ultimately beneficial because thereafter the crown was freed from the inevitability of war with the French. This freedom gave England more diplomatic maneuverability in sixteenth-century continental politics and later helped strengthen England's ability to invest its energies in overseas expansion in America and elsewhere. Yet another positive development was the steady growth of effective governmental institutions; despite the shifting fortunes of kings, the central governmental administration expanded and became more sophisticated. Parliament too became stronger, largely because both the crown and the aristocracy believed that they could use it for their own ends. In 1307 Parliament had not yet become a regular part of the English governmental system, but by 1485 it definitely had. Later kings who tried to govern without it ran into severe difficulties.

The consolidation of royal power in Spain

Around the time when Louis XI of France and Henry VII of England were reasserting royal power in their respective countries, the Spanish monarchs, Ferdinand and Isabella, were doing the same on the Iberian peninsula. In the latter area there had also been incessant strife in the later Middle Ages; Aragon and Castile had often fought each other, and aristocratic factions within those kingdoms had continually fought the crown. But in 1469 Ferdinand, the heir of Aragon, married Isabella, the heiress of Castile, and thereby created a union which laid the basis for modern Spain.

Ferdinand and Isabella

Although Spain did not become a fully united nation until 1716 because Aragon and Castile retained their separate institutions, at least warfare between the two previously independent kingdoms ended and the new country was able to embark on united policies. Isabella and Ferdinand, ruling respectively until 1504 and 1516, annexed Granada, the last Muslim state in the peninsula, expelled the Jews, whom they regarded as a divisive element in their society, and thoroughly subdued their aristocracies. Having dealt with their major internal obstacles, the Spanish rulers also started to embark on an ambitious foreign policy: not only did they turn to overseas expansion, as most famously in their support of Christopher Columbus, but they also entered decisively into the arena of Italian politics. Enriched by the influx of American gold and silver after the conquest of Mexico and Peru, and nearly invincible on the battlefields, Spain quickly became Europe's most powerful state in the sixteenth century.

Ultimately the clearest result of political developments throughout Europe in the late Middle Ages was the preservation of basic high-medieval patterns. The areas of Italy and Germany which had been politically divided before 1300 remained politically divided thereafter. The emergence of middle-sized states in both of these areas in the fifteenth century brought more stability than had existed before, but events would show that Italy and Germany would still be the prey of the Western powers. The latter were clearly much stronger because they were consolidated around stronger national monarchies. The trials of the later Middle Ages put the existence of these monarchies to the test, but after 1450 they emerged stronger than ever. The clearest illustration of their superiority is shown by the history of Italy in the years immediately following 1494. Until then the Italian states appeared to be relatively well governed and prosperous. They experimented with advanced techniques of administration and diplomacy. But when France and Spain invaded the peninsula the Italian states fell over like houses of cards. The Western monarchies could simply draw on greater resources and thus inherited the future of Europe.

5. THE FORMATION OF THE EMPIRE OF RUSSIA

Just as the half century after 1450 witnessed the definitive consolidation of the power of the western European nation-states, so it saw the rise to prominence of the state that henceforth was to be the dominant power in the european East—Russia. But Russia was not at all like a Western nation-state; rather, by about 1500 Russia had taken the first decisive steps on its way to becoming Europe's leading Eastern-style empire.

Had it not been for a combination of late-medieval circumstances, one or several Russian states might well have developed along typical Western lines. Indeed, the founders of the first political entity located in the territories of modern-day Russia were themselves Westerners— Swedish Vikings who in the tenth century established a principality centered around Kiev for the purposes of protecting their lines of trade between Scandinavia and Constantinople. (The very word *Rus* is Slavic for Swede.) Within two or three generations these Vikings became linguistically assimilated by their Slavic environment, but the Kievan state they founded remained until about 1200 very much part of the greater European community of nations. Since Kiev lay on the westernmost extremity of the Russian plain (properly speaking, Kiev is not in Russia at all but is the center of a territory known as the Ukraine) it was natural for the Kievan state of the High Middle Ages to maintain close and cordial diplomatic and trading relations with western

A Swedish Viking. An elk-horn carving showing the sort of Viking warrior who founded the Kievan state.

The Kievan state's ties to the West

Europe. For example, in the eleventh century King Henry I of France was married to a Kievan princess, Anne, and their son was consequently given the Kievan name of Philip, a christening that marked the introduction of this hitherto foreign first name into the West. Aside from such direct links with Western culture, Kievan government bore some similarity to Western limited monarchy inasmuch as the ruling power of the Kievan princes was limited by the institution of the *veche*, or popular assembly.

Reasons for retreat from the West: (1) the Mongol conquests in Russia

But after 1200 three epoch-making developments conspired to drive a wedge between Russia and western European civilization. The first was the conquest of most of Russia by the Mongols, or Tartars, in the thirteenth century. As early as the mid–twelfth century Kiev had been buffeted by the incursions of an Asiatic tribe known as Cumans, but Kiev and other loosely federated Russian principalities ultimately managed to hold the Cumans at bay. The utterly savage Mongols, who crossed the Urals from Asia into Russia in 1237, however, were quite another matter. Commanded by Batu, a grandson of the dreaded Genghis Khan, the Mongols cut such swaths of devastation as they advanced westward that, according to one contemporary, "no eye remained open to weep for the dead." In 1240 the Mongols overran Kiev, and two years later they created their own state on the lower Volga River—the Khanate of the Golden Horde—that exerted suzerainty over almost all of Russia for roughly the following two centuries. Unwilling or unable to institute governmental arrangements that would permit them to rule the vast expanses of Russia directly, the Mongol Khans instead tolerated the existence of several native Russian states, from whom they demanded obeisance and regular monetary tribute. Under this "Tartar yoke," the normal course of Russian political development was inevitably impeded.

The native Russian principality which finally emerged to defeat the Mongols and unify much of Russia in the fifteenth century was the Grand Duchy of Moscow, situated deep in the northeastern Russian

Kievans Chasing Cumans. From a fifteenth-century Russian manuscript.

interior. Inasmuch as Moscow was located very far away from the Mongol power base on the lower Volga, the Muscovite dukes had greater freedom of initiative to consolidate their strength free from Mongol interference than did some of their rivals, and when the Mongol Khans began to realize what was happening, it was too late to stem the Muscovite tide. But Moscow's remote location also placed it extremely far from western Europe: about 600 miles (often snow covered) farther away from France or Italy than the distance separating those countries from Kiev. This added distance alone would have presented an appreciable obstacle to the establishment of close relations between Moscow and the West, but, to make matters far worse, the rise of Poland-Lithuania after 1386 and the fall of Constantinople in 1453 rendered cordial relations all but impossible.

(2) the emergence of Moscow as a unifying force

Throughout most of the Middle Ages the Kingdom of Poland had been a second-rate power, usually on the defensive against German encroachments. But in the fourteenth century that situation changed dramatically, partly because German strength had by then become a ghost of its former self, and above all because the marriage in 1386 of Poland's reigning queen, Jadwiga, to Jagiello, grand duke of Lithuania, more than doubled Poland's size and enabled it to become a major expansionist state. Even before 1386 the Grand Duchy of Lithuania had begun to carve out an extensive territory for itself, not just on the shores of the Baltic where the present territory of Lithuania lies, but in the western Russian regions of Byelorussia and the Ukraine. Obviously, Lithuania's expansionist momentum increased after the union with Poland: in 1410 combined Polish-Lithuanian forces inflicted a stunning defeat on the German military order of Teutonic Knights who ruled neighboring Prussia at the battle of Tannenberg, and Poland-Lithuania extended its borders so far east in the early fifteenth century that the new power seemed on the verge of conquering all of Russia. But Poland-Lithuania subscribed to Roman Catholicism in religion, whereas many of the Russian peoples it had conquered were Eastern Orthodox who accordingly resented the sway of their new rulers. Eastern Orthodox Moscow was the obvious beneficiary of such discontent, becoming a center of religious resistance to Poland. Thus when Moscow was able to move on the offensive against Poland-Lithuania in the late fifteenth century, it appealed to religious as well as national sentiments. Prolonged warfare ensued, greatly exacerbating antagonisms, and since Poland-Lithuania stood in the Muscovites' minds for all the West, Moscow's attitude toward all of Western civilization became ever more etched by hostility.

(3) resentment of Catholic Poland's expansion

Finally, interrelated with this trend were the incalculable effects wrought by the fall of Constantinople to the Turks in 1453. We have seen in Chapter 10 that missionaries from the Byzantine Empire had been responsible for converting Russia to the Eastern Orthodox faith in the late tenth century. During the Kievan period Russia's commitment to Eastern Orthodoxy posed no barrier to cordial communica-

The impact of the fall of Constantinople

NORWAY

SWEDEN

WHITE
SEA

• Archangel

FINLAND

U R A L   M O U N T A I N S

BALTIC SEA

LIVONIA

TEUTONIC
ORDERS

REP. OF NOVGOROD
• Novgorod

KAZAN

TEUTONIC
ORDER
PRUSSIA

LITHUANIA

KAZAN

• Tannenberg

BYELORUSSIA

• Smolensk

DUCHY OF
MOSCOW

Nizhny
Novgorod

• Kazan

POLAND

KINGDOM OF POLAND
AND LITHUANIA

Moscow

• Cracow

UKRAINE

• Kiev

Dnieper R.

KHANATE OF
THE GOLDEN HORDE

HUNGARY

MOLDAVIA

Volga R.

VALLACHIA

CRIMEA

ASTRAKHAN

BLACK SEA

CASPIAN
SEA

OTTOMAN

Constantinople

EMPIRE

	Moscow c. 1300
	Expansion to 1389
	Expansion to 1462
	Expansion to 1505
▬ ▬ ▬	Kievan Russia (10-11th centuries)

RUSSIA TO 1505

tions with western Europe because there was as yet no insuperable religious enmity between Orthodox Byzantium and the West. But embittered hatred is the only expression to describe Byzantine attitudes toward Rome after 1204 when the Western Fourth Crusaders sacked Constantinople. Eastern Orthodox Russians came to sympathize with their Byzantine mentors thereafter, and felt all the more that they had extraordinarily good reason to shun the "Roman infection" after the debacle of 1453. This was because in 1438 the Byzantines in Constantinople, sensing correctly that a mighty Turkish onslaught was in the offing, swallowed their pride and agreed to a submissive religious compromise with the papacy in the hope that this might earn them Western military support for their last-ditch stand. But despite this submission, no Western help was forthcoming and Constantinople fell to the Turks in 1453 without any Roman Catholic knight lifting a hand. Meanwhile, however, the Orthodox hierarchy of Moscow had refused to follow Byzantium in its religious submission for the obvious reason that Moscow was in no way threatened by the Turks. Once Constantinople fell, therefore, the Muscovites reached the conclusion that the Turkish victory was a divine chastisement for the Byzantines' religious perfidy and the Muscovite state became the center of a particularly zealous anti-Roman ideology.

It is against this backdrop that we can examine the reign of the man who did the most to turn the Grand Duchy of Moscow into the nascent empire of Russia, Ivan III (1462–1505), customarily known as Ivan the Great. Ivan's immediate predecessor, Vasily II, had already gained the upper hand in Moscow's struggle to overthrow the domination of the Mongols, but Ivan was the one who completed this process by formally renouncing all subservience to the Mongol Khanate in 1480, by which time the Mongols were too awed by Muscovy's strength to offer any resistance. Concurrently, between 1462 and 1485, Ivan annexed one by one all the independent Russian principalities that remained between Moscow and Poland-Lithuania. And finally, as the result of two successive invasions of Lithuania (1492 and 1501), the mighty conqueror wrested away a whole stretch of Byelorussian and Ukranian territory along his western border. Thus when Ivan the Great died in 1505, it had become clear that Muscovy was a power to be reckoned with on the European scene.

Ivan the Great

But it also would have been clear to any observer that Russian culture and government were now almost completely non-Western. Having been divorced from the West for all practical purposes since about 1200, Russia had not kept up with the most basic Western intellectual and cultural developments. For example, there was virtually no secular literature, arithmetic was barely known, Arabic numerals were not used, and merchants made their calculations with the abacus. Nor were manners and customs comparable to those of the West. Women of the upper classes were veiled and secluded, and flowing beards and skirted garments were universal for men.

Russia's isolation from the West

Perhaps most important, during the reign of Ivan III Russia was evolving in the direction of Eastern-style political autocracy and imperialism. This can be seen most clearly in Ivan's assumption of the title "tsar of all the Russias." The word *tsar* (sometimes spelled czar) is Russian for Caesar, and Ivan's appropriation of it meant that he was claiming to be the successor of the defunct Byzantine emperors, who themselves had been heirs of the Roman Caesars. To reinforce this claim, Ivan married the niece of the last Byzantine ruler, adopted as his insignia the Byzantine double-headed eagle, encouraged his churchmen to proclaim Moscow as "the third Rome," and rebuilt Moscow's fortified princely residence, the Kremlin, in magnificent style to manifest his imperial splendor. Ivan's appropriation of the Byzantine model was fateful for Russia's future political development because it enabled him and his successors to imitate the Byzantine emperors in behaving like Oriental despots who assumed without discussion that "what pleases the prince has the force of law." Moreover, as "tsar of all the Russias," Ivan conceived of himself as the autocratic potentate not just of the Russians of Moscow but of all Russians, and even of Byelorussians and Ukrainians. As the subsequent course of events would show, this was the beginning of an expansionist policy by which future Russian tsars would incorporate both Russian and a wide variety of non–Russian peoples into Europe's largest empire.

6. THOUGHT, LITERATURE, AND ART

Although it might be guessed that the extreme hardships of the later Middle Ages in western Europe should have led to the decline or stagnation of intellectual and artistic endeavors, in fact the period was an extremely fruitful one in the realms of thought, literature, and art. In this section we will postpone treatment of certain developments most closely related to the early history of the Italian Renaissance, but will discuss some of western Europe's other important late-medieval intellectual and artistic accomplishments.

Theology and philosophy after about 1300 faced a crisis of doubt. This doubt did not concern the existence of God and His supernatural powers, but was rather doubt about human ability to comprehend the supernatural. Whereas St. Thomas Aquinas and other Scholastics in the High Middle Ages had serenely delimited the number of "mysteries of the faith" and believed that everything else, both in heaven and earth, could be thoroughly understood by humans, the floods, frosts, wars, and plagues of the fourteenth century helped undermine such confidence in the powers of human understanding. Once human beings experienced the universe as arbitrary and unpredictable, fourteenth-century thinkers began to wonder whether there was not far more in heaven and earth than could be understood by their philosophies. The result was a thoroughgoing reevaluation of the prior theological and philosophical outlook.

The leading late-medieval abstract thinker was the English Franciscan William of Ockham, who was born around 1285 and died in 1349, apparently from the Black Death. Traditionally, Franciscans had always had greater doubts than Dominicans like St. Thomas concerning the abilities of human reason to comprehend the supernatural; Ockham, convinced by the events of his age, expressed these most formidably. He denied that the existence of God and numerous other theological matters could be demonstrated apart from scriptural revelation, and he emphasized God's freedom and absolute power to do anything He wished. In the realm of human knowledge per se Ockham's searching intellect drove him to look for absolute certainties instead of mere theories. In investigating earthly matters he developed the position, known as *nominalism,* that only individual things, but not collectivities, are real, and that one thing therefore cannot be understood by means of another: to know a chair one has to see and touch it rather than just know what several other chairs are like. Ockham also formulated a logic which was based upon the assumption that words stood only for themselves rather than for real things. Such logic might not say much about the real world, but at least it could not be refuted, since it was as internally valid in its own terms as Euclidean geometry.

William of Ockham; nominalism

Ockham's outlook, which gained widespread adherence in the late-medieval universities, today often seems overly methodological and verging on the arid, but it had several important effects on the development of Western thought. Ockham's concern about what God *might* do led to the raising by his followers of some of the seemingly absurd questions for which medieval theology has been mocked, for example, asking whether God can undo the past, or whether an infinite number of pure spirits can simultaneously inhabit the same place (the nearest medieval thinkers actually came to asking how many angels can dance on the head of a pin). Nonetheless, Ockham's emphasis on preserving God's autonomy led to a stress on divine omnipotence that became one of the basic presuppositions of sixteenth-century Protestantism. Further, Ockham's determination to find certainties in the realm of human knowledge ultimately helped make it possible to discuss human affairs and natural science without reference to supernatural explanations—one of the most important foundations of the modern scientific method. Finally, Ockham's opposition to studying collectivities and his refusal to apply logic to real things helped encourage *empiricism,* or the belief that knowledge of the world should rest on sense experience rather than abstract reason. This too is a presupposition for scientific progress: thus it is probably not coincidental that some of Ockham's fourteenth-century followers made significant advances in the study of physics.

The significance of Ockham's thought

Ockham's search for reliable truths finds certain parallels in the realm of late-medieval literature, although Ockham surely had no direct influence in that field. The major trait of the best late-medieval literature was *naturalism,* or the attempt to describe things the way they really are. This was more a development from high-medieval precedents—such as the explorations of human conduct pursued by Chrétien de Troyes, Wolfram von Eschenbach, and Dante—than a reaction against them. The steady growth of a lay reading public furthermore encouraged authors to avoid theological and philosophical abstractions and seek more to entertain by portraying people realistically with all their strengths and foibles. Another main characteristic of late-medieval literature, the predominance of composition in the European vernaculars instead of Latin, also developed out of high-medieval precedents but gained great momentum in the later Middle Ages for two different reasons. One was that international tensions and hostilities, including the numerous wars of the age and the trials of the universal papacy, led to need for security and a pride of self-identification reflected by the use of vernacular tongues. Probably more important was the fact that continued spread of education for the laity greatly increased a public that could read in a given vernacular language but not in Latin. Hence although much poetry was written during the High Middle Ages in the vernacular, in the later Middle Ages use of the vernacular was widely extended to prose. Moreover, countries such as Italy and England, which had just begun to cultivate their own vernacular literatures around 1300, subsequently began to employ their native tongues to the most impressive literary effect.

The greatest writer of vernacular prose fiction of the later Middle Ages was the Italian Giovanni Boccaccio (1313–1375). Although Boccaccio would have taken an honored place in literary history for some of his lesser works, which included courtly romances, pastoral poems, and learned treatises, by far the most impressive of his writings is the *Decameron,* written between 1348 and 1351. This is a collection of one hundred stories, mostly about love and sex, adventure, and clever trickery, supposedly told by a sophisticated party of seven young ladies and three men who are sojourning in a country villa outside Florence in order to escape the ravages of the Black Death. Boccaccio by no means invented all one hundred plots, but even when he borrowed the outlines of his tales from earlier sources he retold the stories in his own characteristically exuberant, masterful, and extremely witty fashion. There are many reasons why the *Decameron* must be counted as epoch-making from a historical point of view. The first is that it was the earliest ambitious and successful work of vernacular creative literature ever written in western Europe in narrative prose. Boccaccio's prose is "modern" in the sense that it is brisk, for unlike the medieval authors of flowery romances, Boccaccio purposely wrote in an unaffected, colloquial style. Simply stated, in the *Decameron* he was less interested in being "elevated" or elegant than in being unpretentiously entertaining. From the point of view of content, Boccaccio wished to portray men and women as they really are rather than as they ought to be. Thus when he wrote about the clergy he showed them to be as susceptible to human appetites and failings as other mortals. His women are not pallid playthings, distant goddesses, or steadfast virgins, but flesh-and-blood creatures with intellects, who interact more comfortably and naturally with men and with each other than any women in Western literature had ever done before. Boccaccio's treatment of sexual relations is often graphic, often witty, but never demeaning. In his world the natural desires of both women and men are not meant to be thwarted. For all these reasons the *Decameron* is a robust and delightful appreciation of all that is human.

Similar in many ways to Boccaccio as a creator of robust, naturalistic vernacular literature was the Englishman Geoffrey Chaucer (c. 1340–1400). Chaucer was the first major writer of an English that can still be read today with relatively little effort. Remarkably, he was both a founding father of England's mighty literary tradition and one of the four or five greatest contributors to it: most critics rank him just behind Shakespeare, and in a class with Milton, Wordsworth, and Dickens. Chaucer wrote several highly impressive works, but his masterpiece is unquestionably the unfinished *Canterbury Tales,* dating from the end of his career. Like the *Decameron,* this is a collection of stories held together by a frame, in Chaucer's case the device of having a group of people tell stories while on a pilgrimage from London to Canterbury. But there are also differences between the *Decameron* and the *Canterbury Tales.* Chaucer's stories are told in sparkling verse instead of prose and they are recounted by people of all different classes—from a chivalric knight to a dedicated university student to a thieving miller with a wart on his nose. Lively women are also represented, most memorably the gap-toothed, oft-married "Wife of Bath," who knows all "the remedies of love." Each character tells a story which is particularly illustrative of his or her own occupation and outlook on the world. By this device Chaucer is able to create a highly diverse "human comedy." His range is therefore greater than Boccaccio's and although he is as witty, frank, and lusty as the Italian, he is sometimes more profound.

Chaucer

As naturalism was a dominant trait of late-medieval literature, so it was of late-medieval art. Already by the thirteenth century Gothic sculptors were paying far more attention than their Romanesque predecessors had done to the way plants, animals, and human beings really looked. Whereas medieval art had previously emphasized abstract design, the stress was now increasingly on realism: thirteenth-century carvings of leaves and flowers must have been done from direct observation and are the first to be clearly recognizable as distinct species. Statues of humans also gradually became more naturally proportioned and realistic in their portrayals of facial expressions. By around 1290 the concern for realism had become so great that a sculptor working on a tomb-portrait of the German Emperor Rudolf of Habsburg allegedly made a hurried return trip to view Rudolf in person, because he

Naturalism in late-medieval art

had heard that a new wrinkle had appeared on the emperor's face.

In the next two centuries the trend toward naturalism continued in sculpture and was extended to manuscript illumination and painting. The latter was in certain basic respects a new art. Ever since the caveman, painting had been done on walls, but walls of course were not easily movable. The art of wall-painting continued to be cultivated in the Middle Ages and long afterward, especially in the form of *frescoes,* or paintings done on wet plaster. But in addition to frescoes, Italian artists in the thirteenth century first started painting pictures on pieces of wood or canvas. These were first done in tempera (pigments mixed with water and natural gums or eggwhites), but around 1400 painting in oils was introduced in the European north. These new technical developments created new artistic opportunities. Artists were now able to paint religious scenes on altarpieces for churches and for private devotions practiced by the wealthier laity at home. Artists also painted the first Western portraits, which were meant to gratify the self-esteem of monarchs and aristocrats. The earliest surviving example of a naturalistic painted portrait is one of a French king, John the Good, executed around 1360. Others followed quickly, so that within a short time the art of portraiture done from life was highly developed. Visitors to art museums will notice that some of the most realistic and sensitive portraits of all time date from the fifteenth century.

The most pioneering and important painter of the later Middle Ages was the Florentine Giotto (c. 1267–1337). He did not engage in individual portraiture, but he brought deep humanity to his religious images done on both walls and movable panels. Giotto was preeminently a naturalist, i.e., an imitator of nature. Not only do his human beings and animals look more natural than those of his predecessors, they seem to do more natural things. When Christ enters Jerusalem on Palm Sunday, boys climb trees to get a better view; when St. Francis is laid out in death, one onlooker takes the opportunity to see whether the saint had really received Christ's wounds; and when the Virgin's parents, Joachim and Anna, meet after a long separation, they actually embrace and kiss—perhaps the first deeply tender kiss in Western art. It was certainly not true, as one fanciful storyteller later reported, that an onlooker found a fly Giotto had painted so real that he attempted to brush it away with his hand, but Giotto in fact accomplished something more. Specifically, he was the first to conceive of the painted space in fully three-dimensional terms: as one art historian has put it, Giotto's frescoes were the first to "knock a hole into the wall." After Giotto's death a reaction in Italian painting set in. This was probably caused by a new reverence for the awesomely supernatural brought about by the horrors of the plague. Whatever the explanation, artists of the mid–fourteenth century briefly moved away from naturalism and painted stern, forbidding religious figures who seemed to float in space. But by around 1400 artists came back down to earth and started

See color plates facing page 448 for *The Flight into Egypt* by Giotto

The Meeting of Joachim and Anna at the Golden Gate. A fresco by Giotto. Note how the haloes merge: this old and barren couple will soon miraculously have a child, none other than Mary, the mother of Jesus.

to build upon Giotto's influence in ways that led to the great Italian renaissance in painting.

In the north of Europe painting did not advance impressively beyond manuscript illumination until the early fifteenth century, but then it suddenly came very much into its own. The leading northern European painters were Flemish, first and foremost the brothers Hubert and Jan van Eyck (c. 1366–1426; c. 1380–1441), Roger van der Weyden (c. 1400–1464), and Hans Memling (c. 1430–1494). The van Eycks used to be credited with the invention of oil painting; while that is now open to question, they certainly were its greatest early practitioners. The use of oils allowed them and the other fifteenth-century Flemish painters to engage in brilliant coloring and sharp-focused realism. The van Eycks and van der Weyden excelled most at two things: communicating a sense of deep religious piety and portraying minute details of familiar everyday experience. These may at first seem incompatible, but it should be remembered that contemporary manuals of practical mysticism such as *The Imitation of Christ* also sought to link deep piety with everyday existence. Thus it was by no means blasphemous when a Flemish painter would portray behind a tender Madonna and Child a vista of contemporary life with people going about their usual business and a man even urinating against a wall. This union between the sacred and profane tended to fall apart in the work of Memling, who excelled in either straightforward religious pictures or secular portraits, but it would return in the work of the greatest painters of the Low Countries, Brueghel and Rembrandt.

The Flemish painters

See color plates facing page 384 for *The Virgin and Chacellor Rollin* by Jan van Eyck

7. ADVANCES IN TECHNOLOGY

No account of enduring late-medieval accomplishments would be complete without mention of certain epoch-making technological advances. Sadly, but probably not unexpectedly, treatment of this subject has to begin with reference to the invention of artillery and firearms. The prevalence of warfare stimulated the development of new weaponry. Gunpowder itself was a Chinese invention, but it was first put to particularly devastating uses in the late-medieval West. Heavy cannons, which made terrible noises "as though all the dyvels of hell had been in the way," were first employed around 1330. The earliest cannons were so primitive that it often was more dangerous to stand behind than in front of them, but by the middle of the fifteenth century they were greatly improved and began to revolutionize the nature of warfare. In one year, 1453, heavy artillery played a leading role in determining the outcome of two crucial conflicts: the Ottoman Turks used German and Hungarian cannons to breach the defenses of Constantinople—hitherto the most impregnable in Europe—and the French used heavy artillery to take the city of Bordeaux, thereby ending the Hundred Years' War. Cannons thereafter made it difficult for rebellious aristocrats to hole up in their stone castles, and thus they aided in the consolidation of the national monarchies. Placed aboard ships, cannons enabled European vessels to dominate foreign waters in the subsequent age of overseas expansion. Guns, also invented in the fourteenth century, were gradually perfected afterward. Shortly after 1500 the most effective new variety of gun, the musket, allowed foot-soldiers to end once and for all the earlier military dominance of heavily armored mounted knights. Once lance-bearing cavalries became outmoded and fighting could more easily be carried on by all, the monarchical states that could turn out the largest armies completely subdued internal resistance and dominated the battlefields of Europe.

Other late-medieval technological developments were more life-enhancing. Eyeglasses, first invented in the 1280s, were perfected in the fourteenth century. These allowed older people to keep on reading when nearsightedness would otherwise have stopped them. For example, the great fourteenth-century scholar Petrarch, who boasted excellent sight in his youth, wore spectacles after his sixtieth year and was thus enabled to complete some of his most important works. Around 1300 the use of the magnetic compass helped ships to sail farther away from land and venture out into the Atlantic. One immediate result was the opening of direct sea commerce between Italy and the North. Subsequently, numerous improvements in shipbuilding, map making, and navigational devices contributed to Europe's ability to start expanding overseas. In the early fourteenth century the Azores and Cape Verde Islands were reached; then, after a long pause caused

Cannons Being Used to Breach the Walls of a Castle. This scene depicts a late engagement of the Hundred Years' War.

by Europe's plagues and wars, the African Cape of Good Hope was rounded in 1487, the West Indies discovered in 1492, India reached by the sea route in 1498, and Brazil discovered in 1500. Partly as a result of technology the world was thus suddenly made much smaller.

Among the most familiar implements of our modern life that were invented by Europeans in the later Middle Ages were clocks and printed books. Mechanical clocks were invented shortly before 1300 and proliferated in the years immediately thereafter. The earliest clocks were too expensive for private purchase, but towns quickly vied with each other to install the most elaborate clocks in their prominent public buildings. These clocks not only told the time but showed the courses of sun, moon, and planets, and performed mechanical tricks on the striking of the hours. The new invention ultimately had two profound effects. One was the further stimulation of European interest in complex machinery of all sorts. This interest had already been awakened by the high-medieval proliferation of mills, but clocks ultimately became even more omnipresent than mills because after about 1650 they became quite cheap and were brought into practically every European home. Household clocks served as models of marvelous machines. Equally if not more significant was the fact that clocks began to rationalize the course of European daily affairs. Until the advent of clocks in the late Middle Ages time was flexible. Men and women had only a rough idea of how late in the day it was and rose and retired more or less with the sun. Especially people who lived in the country performed different jobs at different rates according to the rhythm of the seasons. Even when hours were counted, they were measured at different lengths according to the amount of light in the

(3) mechanical clocks

Horloge de Sapience. This miniature, from an early–fifteenth-century French manuscript, reflects the growing fascination with machines of all sorts and clocks in particular.

different seasons of the year. In the fourteenth century, however, clocks first started relentlessly striking equal hours through the day and night. Thus they began to regulate work with new precision. People were expected to start and end work "on time" and many came to believe that "time is money." This emphasis on time-keeping brought new efficiencies but also new tensions: Lewis Carroll's white rabbit, who is always looking at his pocket watch and muttering, "how late it's getting," is a telling caricature of time-obsessed Western man.

(4) the invention of printing

The invention of printing with movable type was equally momentous. The major stimulus for this invention was the replacement of parchment by paper as Europe's primary writing material between 1200 and 1400. Parchment, made from the skins of valuable farm animals, was extremely expensive: since it was possible to get only about four good parchment leaves from one animal, it was necessary to slaughter between two to three hundred sheep or calves to gain enough parchment for a Bible! Paper, made from rags turned into pulp by mills, brought prices down dramatically. Late-medieval records show that paper sold at one-sixth the price of parchment. Accordingly, it became cheaper to learn how to read and write. With literacy becoming ever more widespread, there was a growing market for still cheaper books, and the invention of printing with movable type around 1450 fully met this demand. By greatly saving labor, the invention made printed books about one-fifth as expensive as handwritten ones within about two decades.

The effects of printing

As soon as books became easily accessible, literacy increased even more and book-culture became a basic part of the European way of life. After about 1500 Europeans could afford to read and buy books of all sorts—not just religious tracts, but instructional manuals, light entertainment, and, by the eighteenth century, newspapers. Printing ensured that ideas would spread quickly and reliably; moreover, revolutionary ideas could no longer be easily extinguished once they were set down in hundreds of copies of books. Thus the greatest religious reformer of the sixteenth century, Martin Luther, gained an immediate following throughout Germany by employing the printing press to run off pamphlets: had printing not been available to him, Luther might have died like Hus. The spread of books also helped stimulate the growth of cultural nationalism. Before printing, regional dialects in most European countries were often so diverse that people who supposedly spoke the same language often could barely understand each other. Such a situation hindered governmental centralization because a royal servant might be entirely unable to communicate with inhabitants of the provinces. Shortly after the invention of printing, however, each European country began to develop its own linguistic standards which were disseminated uniformly by books. The "King's English" was what was printed in London and carried to Yorkshire or Wales. Thus communications were enhanced and governments were able to operate ever more efficiently.

In conclusion it may be said that clocks and books as much as guns and ocean-going ships helped Europe to dominate the globe after 1500. The habits inculcated by clocks encouraged Europeans to work

Left: *Paper-Making at a Paper Mill*. Right: *A Printing Press*. From a title page of a Parisian printer, 1520.

efficiently and to plan precisely; the prevalence of books enhanced communications and the flow of progressive ideas. Once accustomed to reading books, Europeans communicated and experimented intellectually as no other peoples in the world. Thus it was not surprising that after 1500 Europeans could start to make the whole world their own.

SELECTED READINGS

• *Items so designated are available in paperback editions.*

Breisach, E., *Renaissance Europe, 1300–1517*, New York, 1973. The best college-level textbook on the period.

Bridbury, A. R., *Economic Growth: England in the Later Middle Ages*, 2nd ed., New York, 1975. A controversial argument against the dominant theory of economic depression.

• Brucker, G., *Renaissance Florence*, New York, 1969. An excellent introduction by one of America's foremost experts.

• Cipolla, C. M., *Clocks and Culture, 1300–1700*, London, 1967. Treats both technological developments and the importance of clocks as items of trade.

• Cole, Bruce, *Giotto and Florentine Painting, 1280–1375*, New York, 1976. A clear and stimulating introduction.

Dollinger, P., *The German Hansa*, Stanford, Calif., 1970.

Florinsky, M. T., *Russia: A History and Interpretation*, Vol. I, New York, 1961. The best narrative in English of early Russian developments.

Hale, John R., et al., *Europe in the Late Middle Ages*, Evanston, Ill., 1965. Specialized essays on numerous subjects.

Herlihy, David, *Medieval and Renaissance Pistoia: The Social History of an Italian Town*, New Haven, Conn., 1967. Important for its use of statistical evidence.

• Holmes, George, *The Later Middle Ages, 1272–1485*, New York, 1962.

• Huizinga, J., *The Waning of the Middle Ages*, London, 1924. An evocatively written classic on forms of thought and art in the Low Countries.

• Johnson, Jerah, and W. Percy, *The Age of Recovery: The Fifteenth Century*, Ithaca, N.Y., 1970.

Kaminsky, H., *A History of the Hussite Revolution*, Berkeley, Calif., 1967. Detailed and difficult but far and away the best treatment of the subject.

• Lerner, R. E., *The Age of Adversity: The Fourteenth Century*, Ithaca, N.Y., 1968.

Lewis, P. S., *Later Medieval France: The Polity*, London, 1968.

McFarlane, K. B., *The Nobility of Later Medieval England*, Oxford, 1973. An excellent collection of essays by a late master of the field.

• Meiss, M., *Painting in Florence and Siena After the Black Death*, Princeton, N.J., 1951. A stimulating attempt to relate art history to the spirit of an age.

• Miskimin, H. A., *The Economy of Early Renaissance Europe, 1300–1460*, Englewood Cliffs, N.J., 1969. The best short work on the subject.

Mollat, G., *The Popes at Avignon, 1305–1378*, London, 1963.

Mollat, M., and P. Wolff, *The Popular Revolts of the Late Middle Ages*, London, 1973.

Oakley, F., *The Western Church in the Later Middle Ages*, Ithaca, N.Y., 1979.

• Panofsky, E., *Early Netherlandish Painting*, 2 vols., Cambridge, Mass., 1953. A brilliant specialized history by a master art historian.

• Pernoud, R., *Joan of Arc*, New York, 1966. Joan viewed through the eyes of her contemporaries.

Perroy, E., *The Hundred Years War*, Bloomington, Ind., 1959. The standard account.

Scaglione, A., *Nature and Love in the Late Middle Ages*, Berkeley, Calif., 1963.

• Smart, Alastair, *The Dawn of Italian Painting, 1250–1400*, Ithaca, N.Y., 1978. More detailed than Cole.

Trinkaus, C., and H. A. Oberman, eds., *The Pursuit of Holiness in Late Medieval and Renaissance Religion*, Leiden, 1974. Essays that reveal the most recent trends in research.

Vaughan, Richard, *Valois Burgundy*, London, 1975.

SOURCE MATERIALS

Allmand, C. T., ed., *Society at War: The Experience of England and France During the Hundred Years War*, Edinburgh, 1973. An outstanding collection of documents.

• Boccaccio, G., *The Decameron*, tr. M. Musa and P. E. Bondanella, New York, 1977.

• Chaucer, G., *The Canterbury Tales*. (Many editions.)

Colledge, E., ed., *The Mediaeval Mystics of England*, New York, 1961.

• Froissart, J., *Chronicles*, tr. G. Brereton, Baltimore, 1968. A selection from the most famous contemporary account of the Hundred Years' War. Reads more like a novel than like history.

The Imitation of Christ, tr. L. Sherley-Price, Baltimore, 1952.

John Hus at the Council of Constance, tr. M. Spinka, New York, 1965. The translation of a Czech chronicle with an expert introduction and appended collection of documents.

Meister Eckhart, tr. R. B. Blakney, New York, 1941.

Memoirs of a Renaissance Pope: The Commentaries of Pius II (abridged ed.), tr. F. A. Gragg, New York, 1959. A fascinating insight into the Renaissance papacy.

A Parisian Journal, 1405–1449, tr. J. Shirley, Oxford, 1968. A marvelous panorama of Parisian life recorded by an eyewitness.

• Pitti, B., and G. Dati, *Two Memoirs of Renaissance Florence*, tr. J. Martines, New York, 1967.

Part Four

THE EARLY-MODERN WORLD

Historians tend to agree that the Middle Ages ended sometime roughly around 1500 and were followed by an "early-modern" period of European history that lasted until the concurrent outbreaks of the French and Industrial Revolutions at the very end of the eighteenth century. As early as about 1350 in Italy representatives of a new cultural movement, usually called the Renaissance, began to challenge certain basic medieval assumptions and offer alternatives to medieval modes of literary and artistic expression. By around 1500 Renaissance ideals had not only triumphed fully in Italy, but they were also spreading to northern Europe where they were reconceived to produce the highly influential movement of Christian humanism. At the same time, in the early sixteenth century western Europe lost much of its medieval appearance by expanding and dividing. Intrepid mariners and conquista-dores ended Europe's millennium of geographical self-containment by venturing onto the high seas of the Atlantic and Indian Oceans and by planting Europe's flag throughout the world. Concurrently, however, Europe lost its religious uniformity as a result of the Protestant Reformation, which divided the continent up into hostile religious camps. Thereafter, from about 1560 to about 1660 western Europe experienced a period of grave economic, political, and spiritual crisis but emerged from this century of testing with renewed energy and confidence. A commercial revolution spurred the development of overseas colonies and trade, and encouraged agricultural and industrial expansion. Though monarchs continued to meet with opposition from the various estates within their realms, they asserted their power as absolute rulers, stabilizing domestic unrest by continually expanding state bureaucracies.

Warfare remained the chief instrument of their foreign policies; yet by the end of the period, the mutually recognized goal of those policies was more often the maintenance of a general balance of power than the pursuit of unrestrained aggrandizement. Finally, in the later seventeenth century the scientific revolution, initiated earlier by Copernicus, was completed by Sir Isaac Newton, and was followed during the eighteenth century by the "Enlightenment," or enthronement of a new secular faith in humanity's ability to master nature and better itself by its own efforts.

The Early Modern World

POLITICS	PHILOSOPHY AND SCIENCE	
	Civic humanism in Italy, c. 1400–c. 1450	**1400**
	Lorenzo Valla, 1407–1457	
Renaissance popes, 1447–1521	Florentine Neoplatonism, c. 1450–c. 1600	
French invade Italy, 1494	Erasmus, c. 1467–1536	
	Machiavelli, 1469–1527	
Henry VIII of England, 1509–1547	Nicholas Copernicus, 1473–1543	**1500**
	Andreas Vasalius, 1514–1564	
Charles V, Holy Roman Emperor, 1519–1546	More's *Utopia*, 1516	
Troops of Charles V sack Rome, 1527		
Spanish gain supremacy in Italy, 1529	Jean Bodin, 1530–1596	
	Michel de Montaigne, 1533–1592	
Philip II of Spain, 1556–1598		
Elizabeth I of England, 1558–1603		
Revolt of the Netherlands, 1566–1609	Francis Bacon, 1561–1626	
Defeat of Spanish Armada, 1588	Galileo, 1564–1642	
Henry IV of France, 1589–1610	Johann Kepler, 1571–1630	
	William Harvey, 1578–1657	
Edict of Nantes, 1598	Thomas Hobbes, 1588–1679	
	René Descartes, 1596–1650	
Thirty Years' War, 1618–1648	Bacon's *Novum Organum*, 1620	**1600**
Supremacy of Richelieu in France, 1624–1642	Blaise Pascal, 1623–1662	
	John Locke, 1632–1704	
English Civil War, 1642–1649	Descartes' *Discourse on Method*, 1637	
Fronde revolts in France, 1648–1653	Isaac Newton, 1642–1727	
Commonwealth and Protectorate in England, 1649–1660		
Louis XIV of France, 1651–1715		
Frederick William, Elector of Brandenburg, 1640–1688		
Louis XIV of France, 1643–1715		
Leopold I, Habsburg emperor, 1658–1705		
Restoration of Stuart dynasty in England, 1660		
Charles II of England, 1660–1685		
Peter the Great of Russia, 1682–1725		
Revocation of the Edict of Nantes, 1685		
James II of England, 1685–1688		
"Glorious" revolution in England, 1688	Newton's *Mathematical Principles of Natural Philosophy*, 1687	
War of the League of Augsburg, 1688–1697	Montesquieu, 1689–1755	
John Locke, *Two Treatises of Government*, 1690		
War of the Spanish Succession, 1702–1714	Voltaire, 1694–1778	
Jacques Bossuet, *Politics Drawn from the Very Words of Holy Scripture*, 1708		**1700**
Treaty of Utrecht, 1713	Linnaeus, 1707–1778	
Frederick William I of Prussia, 1713–1740	David Hume, 1711–1776	
Louis XV of France, 1715–1774	Diderot, 1713–1784	
Ascendency of Robert Walpole as Britain's "first minister," 1720–1743		
Frederick the Great of Prussia, 1740–1786		
Maria Theresa of Austria, 1740–1780	Condorcet, 1743–1794	
Seven Years' War, 1756–1763	Antoine Lavoisier, 1743–1794	
George III of Britain, 1760–1820	French *Encyclopedia*, 1751–1772	
Catherine the Great of Russia, 1762–1796	Edward Jenner introduces vaccination, 1796	
Louis XVI of France, 1774–1792		
War of American Independence, 1776–1783		
Joseph II of Austria, 1780–1790		
Beginning of the French Revolution, 1789		

The Early Modern World (continued)

ECONOMICS	RELIGION	ARTS AND LETTERS
		Francis Petrarch, 1304–1374
		Italian Renaissance, c. 1350– c. 1550
1400 Portugal gains control of East Indian spice trade, 1498–1511		Masaccio, 1401–1428
	Martin Luther, 1483–1546	Botticelli, 1444–1510
	Ulrich Zwingli, 1484–1531	Leonardo da Vinci, 1452–1519
	Ignatius Loyola, 1491–1556	Erasmus, c. 1467–1536
		Albrecht Dürer, 1471–1528
		Ariosto, 1474–1533
		Raphael, 1483–1520
1500	John Calvin, 1509–1564	Michelangelo, 1485–1564
	Letters of Obscure Men, 1515	Rabelais, c. 1494–1553
	Erasmus's Greek New Testament, 1516	Michelangelo's main work on Sistine Chapel, 1508–1512
	Luther attacks indulgences, 1517	Peter Brueghel, c. 1525–1569
		Palestrina, c. 1525–1594
Spain gains control of Central and South America, c. 1520–c. 1550	Henry VIII of England breaks with Rome, 1527–1534	El Greco, c. 1541–c. 1614
	Anabaptists seize Münster, 1534	Cervantes, 1547–1616
	Loyola's Society of Jesus approved by Pope Paul III, 1540	Shakespeare, 1564–1616
	Calvin takes over Geneva, 1541	Claudio Monteverdi, 1567–1643
	Council of Trent, 1545–1563	Rubens, 1577–1640
	Peace of Augsburg divides Germany into Lutheran and Catholic areas, 1555	Bernini, 1598–1680
"Price Revolution" in Europe, c. 1560–c. 1600	Elizabethan religious compromise in England, c. 1558– c. 1570	Velásquez, 1599–1660
Economic decline of Italy, c. 1580–c. 1700		
1600 Chartering of English East India Company, 1600		Rembrandt, 1606–1669
English Poor Law, 1601		John Milton, 1608–1674
Chartering of Dutch East India Company, 1602		Molière, 1622–1673
Settlement of Jamestown, 1607		Christopher Wren, 1632–1723
Height of mercantilism in Europe, 1650–1750		
Colbert's economic reforms in France, 1664–1683		Watteau, 1684–1721
Founding of Bank of England, 1694		J. S. Bach, 1685–1750
1700 Introduction of maize and potato crops in Europe, c. 1700		G. F. Handel, 1685–1759
Mississippi Bubble, 1715	John Wesley, 1703–1789	Voltaire, 1694–1778
South Sea Bubble, 1720		The Enlightenment, c. 1700– c. 1790
Last appearance of bubonic plague in western Europe, 1720		Henry Fielding, 1707–1754
Enclosure movement in England, 1730–1810		
General European population increase beginning 1750		Joseph Haydn, 1732–1809
		Edward Gibbon, 1737–1794
Adam Smith, *The Wealth of Nations,* 1776		W. A. Mozart, 1756–1791
		Jane Austen, 1775–1817

Chapter 14

THE CIVILIZATION
OF THE RENAISSANCE
(c. 1350—c. 1550)

Now may every reflecting spirit thank God he has chosen to live in this new age, so full of hope and promise, which already exults in a greater array of nobly-gifted souls than the world has seen in the thousand years before.

—Matteo Palmieri, *On the Civil Life,* c. 1435

Whatever was done by man with genius and with a certain grace he held to be almost divine.

—L. B. Alberti, *Self-Portrait,* c. 1460

The prevalent modern notion that a "Renaissance period" followed western Europe's medieval age was first expressed by numerous Italian writers who lived between 1350 and 1550. According to them, one thousand years of unrelieved darkness had intervened between the Roman era and their own times. During these "dark ages" the Muses of art and literature had fled Europe before the onslaught of barbarism and ignorance. Almost miraculously, however, in the fourteenth century the Muses suddenly returned and Italians happily collaborated with them to bring forth a glorious "renaissance of the arts."

"A renaissance of the arts"

Ever since this periodization was advanced historians have taken for granted the existence of some sort of "Renaissance," intervening between medieval and modern times. Indeed, in the late nineteenth and early twentieth centuries many scholars went so far as to argue that the Renaissance was not just an epoch in the history of learning and culture but that a unique "Renaissance spirit" transformed all aspects of life—political, economic, and religious, as well as intellec-

Limits of the term "Renaissance"

tual and artistic. Today, however, most experts no longer accept this characterization because they find it impossible to locate any truly distinctive "Renaissance" politics, economics, or religion. Instead, scholars tend to agree that the term "Renaissance" should be reserved to describe certain exciting trends in thought, literature, and the arts that emerged in Italy from roughly 1350 to 1550 and then spread to northern Europe during the first half of the sixteenth century. That is the approach that will be followed here: accordingly, when we refer to a "Renaissance period" in this chapter we mean to limit ourselves to an epoch in intellectual and cultural history.

Further qualifications

Granted this restriction, some further qualifications are still necessary. Since the word "renaissance" literally means "rebirth," it is sometimes thought that after about 1350 certain Italians who were newly cognizant of Greek and Roman cultural accomplishments initiated a classical cultural rebirth after a long period of "death." In fact, however, the High Middle Ages witnessed no "death" of classical learning. St. Thomas Aquinas, for example, considered Aristotle to be "the Philosopher" and Dante revered Virgil. Similarly, it would be completely false to oppose an imaginary "Renaissance paganism" to a medieval "age of faith" because however much most Renaissance personalities loved the classics, none went so far as to worship classical gods. And finally, all discussions of the postmedieval Renaissance must be qualified by the fact that there was no single Renaissance position on any given subject.

*The continuing
rediscovery and spread of
classical learning*

Nonetheless, in the realms of thought, literature, and the arts important distinguishing traits may certainly be found which make the concept of a "Renaissance" meaningful for intellectual and cultural history. First, regarding knowledge of the classics, there was indubitably a significant quantitative difference between the learning of the Middle Ages and that of the Renaissance. Medieval scholars knew many Roman authors, such as Virgil, Ovid, and Cicero, but in the Renaissance the works of others such as Livy, Tacitus, and Lucretius were rediscovered and made familiar. Equally if not more important was the Renaissance discovery of the literature of classical Greece. In the twelfth and thirteenth centuries Greek scientific and philosophical treatises were made available to Westerners in Latin translations, but none of the great Greek literary masterpieces and practically none of the major works of Plato were yet known. Nor could more than a handful of medieval Westerners read the Greek language. In the Renaissance, on the other hand, large numbers of Western scholars learned Greek and mastered almost the entire Greek literary heritage that is known today.

*New uses for classical
learning*

Second, Renaissance thinkers not only knew many more classical texts than their medieval counterparts, but they used them in new ways. Whereas medieval writers tended to employ their ancient sources for the purposes of complementing and confirming their own preconceived Christian assumptions, Renaissance writers customarily drew on the classics to reconsider their preconceived notions and alter their modes of expression. Firm determination to learn from classical antiquity, moreover, was even more pronounced in the realms of architecture and art, areas in which classical models contributed most strikingly to the creation of fully distinct "Renaissance" artistic styles.

Third, although Renaissance culture was by no means pagan, it certainly was more secular in its orientation than the culture of the Middle Ages. The evolution of the Italian city-states in the fourteenth and fifteenth centuries created a supportive environment for attitudes that stressed the attainment of success in the urban political arena and living well in this world. Inevitably such secular ideals helped create a culture that was increasingly nonecclesiastical. To be sure, the Church retained its wealth and some of its influence, but it adjusted to the spread of secularity by becoming more secular itself.

A secular Renaissance culture

One word above all comes closest to summing up the most common and basic Renaissance intellectual ideals, namely humanism. This word has two different meanings, one technical and one general, but both apply to the cultural goals and ideals of a large number of Renaissance thinkers. In its technical sense humanism was a program of studies which aimed to replace the medieval Scholastic emphasis on logic and metaphysics with the study of language, literature, history, and ethics. Ancient literature was always preferred: the study of the Latin classics was at the core of the curriculum, and, whenever possible, the student was expected to advance to Greek. Humanist teachers argued that Scholastic logic was too arid and irrelevant to the practical concerns of life; instead, they preferred the "humanities," which were meant to make their students virtuous and prepare them for contributing best to the public functions of the state. (Women, as usual, were generally ignored, but sometimes aristocratic women were given humanist training in order to make them appear more polished.) The broader sense of humanism lies in a stress on the "dignity" of man as the most excellent of all God's creatures below the angels. Some Renaissance thinkers argued that man was excellent because he alone of earthly creatures could obtain knowledge of God; others stressed man's ability to master his fate and live happily in the world. Either way, Renaissance humanists had a firm belief in the nobility and possibilities of the human race.

Humanism

1. THE ITALIAN BACKGROUND

The Renaissance originated in Italy for several reasons. The most fundamental was that Italy in the later Middle Ages encompassed the most advanced urban society in all of Europe. Unlike aristocrats north of the Alps, Italian aristocrats customarily lived in urban centers rather than in rural castles and consequently became fully involved in urban public affairs. Moreover, since the Italian aristocracy built its palaces

The erosion of distinctions between the aristocracy and upper bourgeoisie in Italy

in the cities, the aristocratic class was less sharply set off from the class of rich merchants than in the north. Hence whereas in France or Germany there was never any appreciable variation from the rule that aristocrats lived off the income from their landed estates while rich town dwellers (*bourgeois*) gained their living from trade, in Italy so many town-dwelling aristocrats engaged in banking or mercantile enterprises and so many rich mercantile families imitated the manners of the aristocracy that by the fourteenth and fifteenth centuries the aristocracy and upper bourgeoisie were becoming virtually indistinguishable. The noted Florentine family of the Medici, for example, emerged as a family of physicians (as the name suggests), made its fortune in banking, and rose imperceptibly into the aristocracy in the fifteenth century. The results of these developments for the history of education are obvious: not only was there a great demand for education in the skills of reading and counting necessary to become a successful merchant, but the richest and most prominent families sought above all to find teachers who would impart to their offspring the knowledge and skills necessary to argue well in the public arena. Consequently, Italy produced a large number of secular educators, many of whom not only taught students but demonstrated their learned attainments in the production of political and ethical treatises and works of literature. The schools of these educators, moreover, created the best educated upper-class public in all of Europe and inevitably therewith a considerable number of wealthy patrons who were ready to invest in the cultivation of new ideas and new forms of literary and artistic expression.

The special appeal of the classical past

A second reason why late-medieval Italy was the birthplace of an intellectual and artistic Renaissance lay in the fact that it had a far greater sense of rapport with the classical past than any other territory in western Europe. Given the Italian aristocratic commitment to an educational curriculum which stressed success in urban politics, the best teachers understandably sought inspiration from ancient Latin and Greek texts because politics and political rhetoric were classical rather than medieval arts. Elsewhere, resort to classical knowledge and classical literary style might have seemed intolerably antiquarian and artificial, but in Italy the classical past appeared most "relevant" because ancient Roman monuments were omnipresent throughout the peninsula and ancient Latin literature referred to cities and sites that Renaissance Italians recognized as their own. Moreover, Italians became particularly intent on reappropriating their classical heritage in the fourteenth and fifteenth centuries because Italians then were seeking to establish an independent cultural identity in opposition to a Scholasticism most closely associated with France. Not only did the removal of the papacy to Avignon for most of the fourteenth century, and then the prolonged Great Schism from 1378 to 1415, heighten antagonisms between Italy and France, but during the fourteenth century there was an intellectual reaction against Scholasticism on all fronts which made it natural for Italians to prefer the intellectual alternatives offered by classical literary sources. Naturally too, once Roman literature and learning became particularly favored in Italy, so did Roman art and architecture, for Roman models could help Italians create a splendid artistic alternative to French Gothicism just as Roman learning offered an intellectual alternative to French Scholasticism.

Finally, the Italian Renaissance obviously could not have occurred without the underpinning of Italian wealth. Oddly enough, the Italian economy as a whole was probably more prosperous in the thirteenth century than it was in the fourteenth and fifteenth. But late-medieval Italy was wealthier in comparison to the rest of Europe than it had been before, a fact which meant that Italian writers and artists were more likely to stay at home than seek employment abroad. Moreover, in late-medieval Italy unusually intensive investment in culture arose from an intensification of urban pride and the concentration of per capita wealth. Although these two trends overlapped somewhat, most scholars tend to agree that a phase of predominantly public urban support for culture came first in Italy from roughly 1250 to about 1400 or 1450, depending on place, with the private sector taking over thereafter. In the first phase the richest cities vied with each other in building the most splendid public monuments and in supporting writers whose role was to glorify the urban republics in letters and speeches as full of magniloquent Ciceronian prose as possible. But in the course of the fifteenth century, when most Italian city-states succumbed to the hereditary rule of princely families, patronage was monopolized by the princely aristocracy. It was then that the great princes—the Visconti and Sforza in Milan; the Medici in Florence; the Este in Ferrara; and the Gonzaga in Mantua—patronized art and literature in their courts to glorify themselves, while lesser aristocratic families imitated those princes on a smaller scale. Not least of the great princes in Italy from about 1450 to about 1550 were the popes in Rome, who were dedicated to a policy of basing their strength on temporal control of the Papal States. Hence the most worldly of the Renaissance popes—Alexander VI (1492–1503); Julius II (1503–1513); and Leo X (1513–1521), son of the Florentine ruler Lorenzo de' Medici—obtained the services of the greatest artists of the day and for a few decades made Rome the unrivaled artistic capital of the Western world.

Patronage of the arts rooted in urban pride and private wealth

2. THE RENAISSANCE OF THOUGHT AND LITERATURE IN ITALY

In surveying the greatest accomplishments of Italian Renaissance scholars and writers it is natural to begin with the work of Francis Petrarch (1304–1374), the earliest of the humanists in the technical

Pope Julius II. A portrait by Raphael.

*Petrarch, the first
humanist*

Civic humanism

*The civic humanists and
classical Greek studies*

sense of the term. Petrarch was a deeply committed Christian who believed that Scholasticism was entirely misguided because it concentrated on abstract speculation rather than teaching people how to behave properly and attain salvation. Petrarch thought that the Christian writer must above all cultivate literary eloquence so that he could inspire people to do good. For him the best models of eloquence were to be found in the ancient literary classics, which he thought repaid study doubly inasmuch as they were filled with ethical wisdom. So Petrarch dedicated himself to searching for undiscovered ancient Latin texts and writing his own moral treatises in which he imitated classical style and quoted classical phrases. Thereby he initiated a program of "humanist" studies that was to be influential for centuries. Petrarch also has a place in purely literary history because of his poetry. Although he prized his own Latin poetry over the poems he wrote in the Italian vernacular, only the latter have proved enduring. Above all, the Italian sonnets—later called Petrarchan sonnets—which he wrote for his beloved Laura in the chivalrous style of the troubadours, were widely imitated in form and content throughout the Renaissance period.

Because he was a very traditional Christian, Petrarch's ultimate ideal for human conduct was the solitary life of contemplation and asceticism. But in subsequent generations, from about 1400 to 1450, a number of Italian thinkers and scholars, located mainly in Florence, developed the alternative of what is customarily called "civic humanism." Civic humanists like the Florentines Leonardo Bruni (c. 1370–1444) and Leon Battista Alberti (1404–1472) agreed with Petrarch on the need for eloquence and the study of classical literature, but they also taught that man's nature equipped him for action, for usefulness to his family and society, and for serving the state—ideally a republican city-state after the classical or contemporary Florentine model. In their view ambition and the quest for glory were noble impulses which ought to be encouraged. They refused to condemn the striving for material possessions, for they argued that the history of human progress is inseparable from mankind's success in gaining mastery over the earth and its resources. Perhaps the most vivid of the civic humanists' writings is Alberti's *On the Family* (1443), in which he argued that the nuclear family was instituted by nature for the well-being of humanity. Not surprisingly, however, Alberti consigned women to purely domestic roles within this framework, for he believed that "man [is] by nature more energetic and industrious," and that woman was created "to increase and continue generations, and to nourish and preserve those already born."

In addition to differing with Petrarch in their preference for the active over the solitary or contemplative life, the civic humanists went far beyond him in their study of the ancient literary heritage. Many of them discovered important new Latin texts, but far more important was their success in opening up the field of classical Greek studies. In this they were greatly aided by the cooperation of several Byzantine scholars who had migrated to Italy in the first half of the fifteenth century. These men gave instruction in the Greek language and taught about the achievements of their ancient forebears. In doing so they inspired Italian scholars to make trips to Constantinople and other cities in the Near East in search of Greek manuscripts. In 1423 one Italian humanist, Giovanni Aurispa, alone brought back 238 manuscript books, including works of Sophocles, Euripides, and Thucydides. In this way most of the Greek classics, particularly the writings of Plato, the dramatists, and the historians, were first made available to western Europe.

Related in his textual interests to the civic humanists, but by no means a full adherent of their movement, was the atypical yet highly influential Renaissance thinker, Lorenzo Valla (1407–1457). Born in Rome and active primarily as a secretary in the service of the king of Naples, Valla had no inclination to espouse the ideas of republican political engagement as the Florentine civic humanists did. Instead, he preferred to advertise his skills as an expert in grammar, rhetoric, and the painstaking analysis of Greek and Latin texts by showing how the thorough study of language could discredit old verities. Most decisive in this regard was Valla's brilliant demonstration that the so-called Donation of Constantine was a medieval forgery. Whereas papal propagandists had argued ever since the early thirteenth century that the papacy possessed rights to temporal rule in western Europe on the grounds of a charter purportedly granted by the Emperor Constantine in the fourth century, Valla proved beyond dispute that the document in question was full of nonclassical Latin usages and anachronistic terms. Hence he concluded that the "Donation" was the work of a medieval forger whose "monstrous impudence" was exposed by the "stupidity of his language." This demonstration not only discredited a prize specimen of "medieval ignorance," but, more importantly, introduced the concept of anachronism into all subsequent textual study and historical thought. Valla also employed his skills in linguistic analysis and rhetorical argumentation to challenge a wide variety of philosophical positions, but his ultimate goals were by no means purely destructive, for he revered the literal teachings of the Pauline Epistles. Accordingly, in his *Notes on the New Testament* he applied his expert knowledge of Greek to elucidating the true meaning of St. Paul's words, which he believed had been obscured by the Latin Vulgate translation. This work was to prove an important link between Italian Renaissance scholarship and the subsequent Christian humanism of the north.

From about 1450 until about 1600 dominance in the world of Italian thought was assumed by a school of Neoplatonists, who sought to blend the thought of Plato, Plotinus, and various strands of ancient mysticism with Christianity. Foremost among these were Marsilio Ficino (1433–1499) and Giovanni Pico della Mirandola (1463–1494),

*Lorenzo Valla and
linguistic analysis*

*Renaissance
Neoplatonism: Ficino and
Pico*

both of whom were members of the Platonic Academy founded by
Cosimo de' Medici in Florence. The academy was a loosely organized
society of scholars who met to hear readings and lectures. Their hero
was unquestionably Plato: sometimes they celebrated Plato's birthday
by holding a banquet in his honor, after which everybody gave
speeches as if they were characters in a Platonic dialogue. Ficino's
greatest achievement was the translation of Plato's works into Latin,
thereby making them widely available to western Europeans for the
first time. It is debatable whether Ficino's own philosophy may be
called humanist because he moved away from ethics to metaphysics
and taught that the individual should look primarily to the other world.
In Ficino's opinion, "the immortal soul is always miserable in its mortal body." The same problem holds for Ficino's disciple Giovanni Pico
della Mirandola, whose most famous work is the *Oration on the Dignity of Man.* Pico was certainly not a civic humanist since he saw little
worth in mundane public affairs. But he did believe that there is
"nothing more wonderful than man" because he believed that man is
endowed with the capacity to achieve union with God if he so wills.

Hardly any of the Italian thinkers between Petrarch and Pico were
really original: their greatness lay mostly in their manner of expression, their accomplishments in technical scholarship, and their popu-
larization of different themes of ancient thought. The same, however,
can by no means be said of Renaissance Italy's greatest political philosopher, Niccolò Machiavelli (1469–1527), who belonged to no school
and stood in a class by himself. No man did more than Machiavelli to
overturn all earlier views of the ethical basis of politics or to pioneer
in the dispassionate direct observation of political life. Machiavelli's
writings reflect the unhappy condition of Italy in his time. At the end
of the fifteenth century Italy had become the cockpit of international
struggles. Both France and Spain had invaded the peninsula and were
competing with each other for the allegiance of the Italian states. The
latter, in many cases, were torn by internal dissension which made
them easy prey for foreign conquerors. In 1498 Machiavelli entered
the service of the newly founded republic of Florence as second chancellor and secretary. His duties largely involved diplomatic missions
to other states. While in Rome he became fascinated with the achievements of Cesare Borgia, son of Pope Alexander VI, in cementing a
solidified state out of scattered elements. He noted with approval Cesare's combination of ruthlessness with shrewdness and his complete
subordination of morality to political ends. In 1512 the Medici returned
to overthrow the republic of Florence, and Machiavelli was deprived
of his position. Disappointed and embittered, he spent the remainder
of his life in exile, devoting his time primarily to writing. In his *Dis-
courses on Livy* he praised the ancient Roman republic as a model for
all time. He lauded constitutionalism, equality, liberty, in the sense of
freedom from outside interference, and subordination of religion to
the interests of the state. But Machiavelli also wrote *The Prince* in

*The political thought of
Machiavelli*

Niccolò Machiavelli.

which he described the policies and practices of government, not in accordance with some lofty ideal, but as they actually were. The supreme obligation of the ruler, he avowed, was to maintain the power and safety of the country over which he ruled. No consideration of justice or mercy or the sanctity of treaties should be allowed to stand in his way. Cynical in his views of human nature, Machiavelli maintained that all men are prompted exclusively by motives of self-interest, particularly by desires for personal power and material prosperity. The head of the state should therefore not take for granted the loyalty or affection of his subjects. The one ideal Machiavelli kept before him in his later years was the unification of Italy. But this he believed could only be achieved through ruthlessness.

Far more congenial to contemporary tastes than the shocking political theories of Machiavelli were the guidelines for proper aristocratic conduct offered in *The Book of the Courtier* (1516) by the diplomat and count Baldesar Castiglione. This cleverly written forerunner of modern handbooks of etiquette stands in sharp contrast to the earlier civic humanist treatises of Bruni and Alberti, for whereas they taught the sober "republican" virtues of strenuous service in behalf of the city-state and family, Castiglione, writing in an Italy dominated by magnificent princely courts, taught how to attain the elegant and seemingly effortless qualities necessary for acting like a "true gentleman." More than anyone else, Castiglione popularized the ideal of the "Renaissance man": one who is accomplished in many different pursuits and is also brave, witty, and "courteous," meaning civilized and learned. By no means ignoring the female sex, Castiglione, much unlike Alberti, was silent about woman's role in "hearth and home," but stressed instead the ways in which court ladies could be "gracious entertainers." Thereby he was one of the first European male writers to offer women an independent role outside of the household, a fact which should not be underrated even though he was offering such a role merely to the richest of the rich and even though his stress on "pleasing affability" today seems demeaning. Widely read throughout Europe for over a century after its publication, Castiglione's *Courtier* spread Italian ideals of "civility" to princely courts north of the Alps, resulted in the ever-greater patronage of art and literature by the European aristocracy, and gave currency to the hitherto novel proposition that all women other than nuns were not fated to be passive vessels of reproduction and nutrition.

*Castiglione's ideal courtier
and court lady*

Had Castiglione's ideal courtier wished to show off his knowledge of contemporary Italian literature, he would have had many works from which to choose, for sixteenth-century Italians were highly accomplished in the creation of imaginative prose and verse. Among the many impressive writers who might be mentioned, Machiavelli himself wrote a delightful short story, "Belfagor," and an engaging bawdy play, *Mandragola;* the great artist Michelangelo wrote many moving sonnets; and the most eminent of sixteenth-century Italian

*Other sixteenth-century
Italian literary
achievements*

The Expulsion of Adam and Eve from the Garden of Eden. Masaccio built on the artistic tradition established by Giotto in stressing emotion and psychological study.

Italian painting in the fifteenth century

epic poets was Ludovico Ariosto (1474–1533), author of a lengthy verse narrative called *Orlando Furioso* (*The Madness of Roland*). Although woven substantially from materials taken from the medieval Charlemagne cycle, this work differed radically from any of the medieval epics because it introduced elements of lyrical fantasy and above all because it was totally devoid of heroic idealism. Ariosto wrote to make readers laugh and to charm them with felicitous descriptions of the quiet splendor of nature and the passions of love. His work represents the disillusionment of the late Renaissance, the loss of hope and faith, and the tendency to seek consolation in the pursuit of pleasure and aesthetic delight.

3. THE ARTISTIC RENAISSANCE IN ITALY

Despite numerous intellectual and literary advances, the most long-lived achievements of the Italian Renaissance were made in the realm of art. Of all the arts, painting was undoubtedly supreme. We have already seen that around 1300 very impressive beginnings were made in the history of Italian painting by the artistic genius of Giotto, but it was not until the fifteenth century that Italian painting began to attain its majority. One reason for this was that in the early fifteenth century the laws of linear perspective were discovered and first employed to give the fullest sense of three dimensions. Fifteenth-century artists also experimented with effects of light and shade (*chiaroscuro*) and for the first time carefully studied the anatomy and proportions of the human body. By the fifteenth century, too, increase in private wealth and the partial triumph of the secular spirit had freed the domain of art to a large extent from the service of religion. As we have noted above, the Church was no longer the only patron of artists. While subject matter from biblical history was still commonly employed, it was frequently infused with nonreligious themes. The painting of portraits for the purpose of revealing the hidden mysteries of the soul now became popular. Paintings intended to appeal primarily to the intellect were paralleled by others whose main purpose was to delight the eye with gorgeous color and beauty of form. The fifteenth century was characterized also by the introduction of painting in oil, probably from Flanders. The use of the new technique doubtless had much to do with the artistic advance of this period. Since oil does not dry so quickly as fresco pigment, the painter could now work more leisurely, taking time with the more difficult parts of the picture and making corrections if necessary as he went along.

The majority of the painters of the fifteenth century were Florentines. First among them was the precocious Masaccio (1401–1428). Although he died at the age of twenty-seven, Masaccio inspired the work of Italian painters for a hundred years. Masaccio's greatness as a painter is based on his success in "imitating nature," which became a primary value in Renaissance painting. To achieve this effect he employed perspective, perhaps most dramatically in his fresco of the *Trinity;* he also used *chiaroscuro* with originality, leading to a dramatic and moving outcome. In the *Expulsion of Adam and Eve from the Garden,* he records the shame and guilt felt by the individuals in the biblical story.

The best known of the painters who directly followed the tradition begun by Masaccio was the Florentine Sandro Botticelli (1444–1510), who depicted both religious and classical themes. Botticelli's work excels in beautiful and accurate depiction of natural detail; he is a master, for example, at painting the female nude. But his major contribution to Renaissance painting derives from the philosophical basis of much of his work, for he was closely associated with the Florentine Neoplatonists. Two of his most famous paintings are *The Allegory of Spring* and *The Birth of Venus,* which illustrate Neoplatonic concepts regarding the classical goddess of love, Venus or Aphrodite. Later in his life Botticelli became a follower of the evangelical priest Savonarola, who came to Florence from Ferrara to preach fire-and-brimstone sermons against worldiness. Botticelli's *Mystic Nativity* was probably painted as a result of Savonarola's influence; it is a profoundly moving religious painting, in which he anticipates the end of the world. The last years of Botticelli's life are shadowy; his popularity declined and it is believed he died in poverty.

Botticelli

See color plates facing page 448 for *The Birth of Venus*

Perhaps the greatest of the Florentine artists was Leonardo da Vinci (1452–1519), one of the most versatile geniuses who ever lived. Leonardo was practically the personification of the "Renaissance man": he was a painter, architect, musician, mathematician, engineer, and inventor. The illegitimate son of a lawyer and a peasant woman, Leonardo set up an artist's shop in Florence by the time he reached twenty-five and gained the patronage of the Medici ruler of the city, Lorenzo the Magnificent. But if Leonardo had any weakness, it was his slowness in working and difficulty in finishing anything. This naturally displeased Lorenzo and other Florentine patrons, who thought an artist was little more than an artisan, commissioned to produce a certain piece of work of a certain size for a certain price on a certain date. Leonardo, however, strongly objected to this view because he considered himself to be no menial craftsman but an inspired creator. Therefore in 1482 he left Florence for the Sforza court of Milan where he was given freer rein in structuring his time and work. He remained there until the French invaded Milan in 1499; after that he wandered about Italy, finally accepting the patronage of the French king, Francis I, under whose auspices Leonardo lived and worked in France until his death.

Leonardo da Vinci

Lorenzo de' Medici. The leading patron of Florentine art and literature in the latter part of the fifteenth century.

The paintings of Leonardo da Vinci began what is known as the High Renaissance in Italy. His approach to painting was that it should be the most accurate possible imitation of nature. Leonardo was like a naturalist, basing his work on his own detailed observations of a blade

Studies of the Shoulder by Leonardo da Vinci

See color plates following page 448 for the *Virgin on the Rocks,* the *Last Supper,* and the *Mona Lisa*

The Venetian painters

See color plates following page 448 for *Pope Paul III and His Nephews* and *Charles V* by Titian

of grass, the wing of a bird, a waterfall. He obtained human corpses for dissection—by which he was breaking the law—and reconstructed in drawing the minutest features of anatomy, which knowledge he carried over to his paintings. Leonardo worshiped nature, and was convinced of the essential divinity in all living things. It is not surprising, therefore, that he was a vegetarian, and that he went to the marketplace to buy caged birds which he released to their native habitat.

It is generally agreed that Leonardo's masterpieces are the *Virgin of the Rocks* (which exists in two versions), the *Last Supper,* and the *Mona Lisa.* The first represents not only his marvelous technical skill but also his passion for science and his belief in the universe as a well-ordered place. The figures are arranged in geometric composition with every rock and plant depicted in accurate detail. The *Last Supper,* painted on the walls of the refectory of Santa Maria delle Grazie in Milan, is a study of psychological reactions. A serene Christ, resigned to his terrible fate, has just announced to his disciples that one of them will betray him. The purpose of the artist is to portray the mingled emotions of surprise, horror, and guilt revealed in the faces of the disciples as they gradually perceive the meaning of their master's statement. The third of Leonardo's major triumphs, the *Mona Lisa,* reflects a similar interest in the varied moods of the human soul. Although it is true that the *Mona Lisa* is a portrait of an actual woman, the wife of Francesco del Giocondo, a Neapolitan, it is more than a mere photographic likeness. The distinguished art critic Bernard Berenson has said of it, "Who like Leonardo has depicted . . . the inexhaustible fascination of the woman in her years of mastery? . . . Leonardo is the one artist of whom it may be said with perfect literalness: 'Nothing that he touched but turned into a thing of eternal beauty.' "

The beginning of the High Renaissance around 1490 also witnessed the rise of the so-called Venetian school, the major members of which were Giovanni Bellini (c. 1426–1516), Giorgione (1478–1510), and Titian (c. 1477–1576). The work of all these men reflected the luxurious life and the pleasure-loving interests of the thriving commercial city of Venice. Most Venetian painters had little of the concern with philosophical and psychological themes that characterized the Florentine school. Their aim was to appeal primarily to the senses rather than to the mind. They delighted in painting idyllic landscapes and gorgeous symphonies of color. For their subject matter they chose not merely the natural beauty of Venetian sunsets and the shimmering silver of lagoons in the moonlight but also the artificial splendor of sparkling jewels, richly colored satins and velvets, and gorgeous palaces. Their portraits were invariably likenesses of the rich and the powerful. In the subordination of form and meaning to color and elegance there were mirrored not only the sumptuous tastes of wealthy merchants, but also definite traces of Eastern influence which had filtered through from Byzantium during the Middle Ages.

The remaining great painters of the High Renaissance all accomplished their most important work in the first half of the sixteenth century. It was in this period that Renaissance Italian art reached its peak. Rome was now the major artistic center of the Italian peninsula, although the traditions of the Florentine school still exerted a potent influence. Among the eminent painters of this period at least two must be given more than passing attention. One was Raphael (1483–1520), a native of Urbino, and perhaps the most beloved artist of the entire Renaissance. The lasting appeal of his style is due primarily to his ennobling humanism, for he portrayed the members of the human species as temperate, wise, and dignified beings. Although Raphael was influenced by Leonardo da Vinci and copied many features of his work, he cultivated a much more symbolical or allegorical approach. His *Disputà* symbolized the dialectical relationship between the Church in heaven and the Church on earth. In a wordly setting against a brilliant sky, theologians debate the meaning of the Eucharist, while in the clouds above, saints and the Trinity repose in the possession of a holy mystery. Raphael's *School of Athens* is an allegorical representation of the conflict between the Platonist and Aristotelian philosophies. Plato (painted as a portrait of Leonardo) is shown pointing upward to emphasize the spiritual basis of his world of Ideas, while Aristotle gestures toward the earth to exemplify his belief that concepts or ideas are inseparably linked with their material embodiments. Raphael is noted also for his portraits and Madonnas. To the latter, especially, he gave a softness and warmth that seemed to endow them with a sweetness and piety quite different from the enigmatic and somewhat distant Madonnas of Leonardo da Vinci.

The last towering figure of the High Renaissance was Michelangelo (1475–1564) of Florence. If Leondardo was a naturalist, Michelangelo was an idealist; where the former sought to recapture and interpret

The painters of the late Renaissance: Raphael

See color plates following page 448 for the *Madonna of the Chair* by Raphael

Michelangelo

The School of Athens by Raphael

The Creation of Adam by Michelangelo. One of a series of frescoes on the ceiling of the Sistine Chapel in Rome. Suggesting philosophical inquiries into the meaning of life and the universe, it represents Renaissance realism at its height.

fleeting natural phenomena, Michelangelo, who embraced Neoplatonism as a philosophy, was more concerned with expressing enduring, abstract truths. Michelangelo was a painter, sculptor, architect, and poet—and he expressed himself in all these with a similar power and in a similar manner. At the center of all of his paintings is the human figure, which is always powerful, colossal, magnificent. If man, and the potential of the individual, lay at the center of Italian Renaissance culture, then Michelangelo, who depicted the human, and particularly the male, figure without cease, is the supreme Renaissance artist.

The Sistine Chapel

Michelangelo's greatest achievements in painting appear in a single location—the Sistine Chapel in Rome—yet conveniently enough for the spectator they are products of two different periods in the artist's life and consequently exemplify two different artistic styles and outlooks on the human condition. Most famous are the sublime frescoes Michelangelo painted on the ceiling of the Sistine Chapel from 1508 to 1512, depicting scenes from the book of Genesis. All the panels in this series, including *God Dividing the Light from Darkness, The Creation of Adam,* and *The Flood,* exemplify the younger artist's commitment to classical Greek aesthetic principles of harmony, solidity, and dignified restraint. Correspondingly, all exude as well a sense of sublime affirmation regarding Creation and the heroic qualities of mankind. (When one considers that Michelangelo executed these magnificent scenes while lying on his back on a scaffold, one can begin to imagine the exalted mood of creativity that must have possessed him.) But a quarter of a century later, when Michelangelo returned to work in the Sistine Chapel, both his style and mood had changed dramatically. In the enormous *Last Judgment,* a fresco done for the

See color plates following page 448 for detail from the *Last Judgement*

Sistine Chapel's altar wall in 1536, Michelangelo repudiated classical restraint and substituted a style that emphasized tension and distortion in order to communicate the older man's pessimistic conception of a humanity wracked by fear and bowed by guilt.

In the realm of sculpture the Italian Renaissance took a great step forward by creating statues that were no longer carved as parts of columns or doorways on church buildings or as effigies on tombs. Instead, Italian sculptors for the first time since antiquity carved free-standing statues "in the round." These freed sculpture from its bondage to architecture and established its status as a separate art frequently devoted to secular purposes.

The first great master of Renaissance sculpture was Donatello (c. 1386?–1466). He emancipated his art from Gothic mannerisms and introduced a new vigorous note of individualism. His bronze statue of David triumphant over the body of the slain Goliath, the first free-standing nude since antiquity, established a precedent of glorifying the life-size nude. Donatello's *David,* moreover, represents a first step in the direction of imitating classical sculpture, not just in the depiction of a nude body but also in the subject's posture of resting his weight on one leg. Yet this David is clearly a lithe adolescent rather than a muscular Greek athlete. Later in his career, Donatello more fully imitated ancient statuary in his commanding portrayal of the proud warrior Gattamelata—the first monumental equestrian statue in bronze executed in the West since the time of the Romans. Here, in addition to drawing very heavily on the legacy of antiquity, the sculptor most clearly expressed his dedication to immortalizing the earthly accomplishments of a contemporary secular hero.

Certainly the greatest sculptor of the Italian Renaissance—indeed, probably the greatest sculptor of all time—was Michelangelo. Believ-

David by Donatello. The first free-standing nude statue executed in the West since antiquity.

Gattamelata by Donatello. Note the debt to the Roman equestrian statue of Marcus Aurelius, shown above, p. 186.

David by Michelangelo. Over thirteen feet high, this serenely self-confident affirmation of the beauty of the human form was placed prominently by the Florentine government in front of Florence's city hall to proclaim the city's humanistic values.

ing with Leonardo that the artist was an inspired creator, Michelangelo pursued this conviction to the conclusion that sculpture was the most exalted of the arts because it allowed the artist to imitate God most fully in recreating human forms. Furthermore, in Michelangelo's view the most God-like sculptor disdained slavish naturalism, for anyone could make a plaster cast of a human figure, but only an inspired creative genius could endow his sculpted figures with a sense of life. Accordingly, Michelangelo subordinated naturalism to the force of his imagination and sought restlessly to express his ideals in ever more arresting forms.

As in his painting, Michelangelo's sculpture followed a course from classicism to anticlassicism, that is, from harmonious modeling to dramatic distortion. The sculptor's most noted early work, his *David,* executed in 1501 when he was just twenty-six, is surely his most perfect classical statue in style and inspiration. Choosing, like Donatello, to depict a life-size male nude, Michelangelo nonetheless decided to make his own *David* heroic rather than merely graceful and hence conceived his nude in the purest, well-proportioned Greek terms. The resulting portrait in marble epitomizes for many the Italian Renaissance's facility for employing classical style to express the serenest confidence in human attainments. Deep serenity, however, is no longer

Left: *Moses* by Michelangelo. Far less classical in style than Michelangelo's *David,* this statue stresses a sense of drama. (Moses was depicted with horns in medieval and renaissance art on account of a faulty translation of a passage from the Book of Exodus.) Right: *Descent from the Cross* by Michelangelo. This portrayal of tragedy was made by the sculptor for his own tomb. Note the distortion for effect exemplified by the elongated body and left arm of the figure of Christ. The figure in the rear is Nicodemus, but was probably intended to represent Michelangelo himself. The original is in the cathedral of Florence.

St. Peter's, Rome. Built to a square cross plan originally conceived by Bramante and revised by Michelangelo. Completed in 1626, the church rises to a total height of 450 feet.

prominent in the works of Michelangelo's middle period; rather, in a work such as the *Moses* of about 1515, the sculptor has begun to explore the use of anatomical distortion to create effects of emotional intensity—in this case the biblical prophet's righteous rage. While such statues remain awesomely heroic, as Michelangelo's life drew to a close he experimented ever more with exaggerated stylistic mannerisms for the purpose of communicating moods of brooding pensiveness or outright pathos. The culmination of this trend in Michelangelo's statuary is his moving *Descent from the Cross,* a depiction of the Virgin Mary grieving over the body of the dead Christ, intended for the artist's own tomb.

To a much greater extent than either sculpture or painting, Renaissance architecture had its roots in the past. The new building style was eclectic, a compound of elements derived from the Middle Ages and from antiquity. It was not the Greek or the Gothic, however, but the Roman and the Romanesque which provided the inspiration for the architecture of the Italian Renaissance. Neither the Greek nor the Gothic had ever found a congenial soil in Italy. The Romanesque, by contrast, was able to flourish there, since it was more in keeping with Italian traditions, while the persistence of a strong admiration for Latin culture made possible a revival of the Roman style. Accordingly, the great architects of the Renaissance generally adopted their building plans from the Romanesque churches and monasteries and copied their decorative devices from the ruins of ancient Rome. The result was an architecture based on the cruciform floor plan of transept and nave and embodying the decorative features of the column and arch, or the column and lintel, the colonnade, and frequently the dome. Horizontal lines predominated; and, though many of the buildings were churches, the ideals they expressed were the secular ones of joy in this

The eclecticism of Renaissance architecture

The Villa Rotonda of Palladio. A highly influential Renaissance private dwelling near Vicenza. Note how Palladio drew for inspiration on the Roman Pantheon, pictured above, p. 189.

life and pride in human achievement. Renaissance architecture also emphasized harmony and proportion because Italian builders, under the influence of Neoplatonism, concluded that perfect proportions in man reflect the harmony of the universe, and that, therefore, the parts of a building should be related to each other and to the whole in the same way as the parts of the human body. A fine example of Renaissance architecture is St. Peter's Basilica in Rome, built under the patronage of Popes Julius II and Leo X and designed by some of the most celebrated architects of the time, including Donato Bramante (c. 1444–1514) and Michelangelo. Equally impressive are the artfully proportioned aristocratic country houses of the northern Italian architect Andrea Palladio (1518–1580), who redesigned ancient temples, such as the Roman Pantheon, to create secular miniatures meant to glorify the aristocrats who dwelled within them.

4. THE WANING OF THE ITALIAN RENAISSANCE

Political factors in the decline of the Italian Renaissance: the French invasion of 1494

Around 1550 the Renaissance in Italy began to decline after some two hundred glorious years. The causes of this decline were varied. Perhaps at the head of the list should be placed the French invasion of 1494 and the incessant warfare that ensued. The French king Charles VIII, who ruled the richest and most powerful kingdom in Europe, viewed Italy as an attractive prey for his grandiose ambitions. Accordingly, in 1494 he led an army of 30,000 well-trained troops across the Alps. The Medici of Florence fled before him, abandoning their city to immediate capture. Halting only long enough to establish peace with a subservient new republican government, the French resumed their advance and conquered Naples. By so doing, however, they aroused the suspicions of the rulers of Spain, who feared an attack on their own possession of Sicily. An alliance among Spain, the Papal States, the Holy Roman Empire, Milan, and Venice finally forced Charles to withdraw whence he had come. Yet upon his death his successor, Louis XII, launched a second invasion, and from 1499 until

1529 warfare in Italy was virtually uninterrupted. Alliances and counteralliances followed each other in bewildering succession, but they only managed to prolong the hostilities. The French won a great victory at Marignano in 1515, but they were decisively defeated by the Spanish at Pavia in 1525. The worst disaster came in 1527 when unruly Spanish and German troops, nominally under the command of the Spanish ruler and Holy Roman Emperor Charles V, but in fact entirely out of control, sacked the city of Rome, causing irreparable destruction. Only in 1529 did Charles finally manage to gain control over most of the Italian peninsula, putting the fighting to an end for a time. Once triumphant, Charles retained two of the largest portions of Italy for Spain—the Duchy of Milan and the Kingdom of Naples—and installed favored princes as the rulers of almost all the other Italian political entities exclusive of Venice and the Papal States. These protégés of the Spanish crown continued to preside over their own courts, to patronize the arts, and to adorn their cities with luxurious buildings, but in fact they were puppets of a foreign power and unable to inspire their retinues with a sense of vigorous cultural independence.

To the Italian political disasters was added a waning of Italian prosperity. Whereas Italy's virtual monopoly of trade with Asia in the fifteenth century had been one of the chief economic supports for the cultivation of Italian Renaissance culture, the gradual shifting of trade routes from the Mediterranean to the Atlantic region following the overseas discoveries of around 1500 slowly but surely cost Italy its supremacy as the center of world trade. Since the incessant warfare of the sixteenth century also contributed to Italy's economic hardships, as did Spanish financial exactions in Milan and Naples, there was gradually less and less of a surplus to support artistic endeavors.

The waning of Italian prosperity

The Entrance of Charles VIII into Florence. A painting by Francesco Granacci.

THE STATES OF ITALY DURING THE RENAISSANCE c. 1494

Giordano Bruno

A final cause of the decline of the Italian Renaissance was the Counter-Reformation. During the sixteenth century the Roman Church sought increasingly to exercise firm control over thought and art as part of a campaign to combat worldliness and the spread of Protestantism. In 1542 the Roman Inquisition was established; in 1564 the Council of Trent issued the first Index of Prohibited Books. The extent of ecclesiastical interference in cultural life was enormous. For example, Michelangelo's great *Last Judgment* in the Sistine Chapel was criticized by some straitlaced fanatics for looking like a bordello because it showed too many naked bodies. Therefore, Pope Paul IV ordered a second-rate artist to paint in clothing wherever possible. (The unfortunate artist was afterward known as "the underwear-maker.") While this incident may appear merely grotesquely humorous, the determination of ecclesiastical censors to enforce doctrinal uniformity could lead to death, as in the case of the unfortunate Neoplatonic philosopher Giordano Bruno, whose insistence on maintaining that there may be more than one world in contravention of the book of Genesis resulted in his being burned at the stake by the Roman Inquisition in 1600.

The most notorious example of inquisitorial censorship of free intellectual speculation was the disciplining of the great scientist Galileo, whose achievements we will discuss in more detail later on. In 1616 the Holy Office in Rome condemned the new astronomical theory that the earth moves around the sun as "foolish, absurd, philosophically false, and formally heretical." Accordingly, the Inquisition proceeded immediately against Galileo when he published a brilliant defense of the heliocentric system in 1632. In short order the Inquisition made Galileo recant his "errors" and sentenced him to house arrest for the duration of his life. Galileo was not willing to face death for his beliefs, but after he publicly retracted his view that the earth revolves around the sun he supposedly whispered, "despite everything, it still moves." Not surprisingly, Galileo was the last great Italian contributor to the development of astronomy and physics until modern times.

In conclusion, it should be emphasized that cultural and artistic achievement was by no means extinguished in Italy after the middle of the sixteenth century. On the contrary, an impressive new artistic style known as Mannerism was cultivated between about 1550 and 1600 by painters who drew on traits found in the later work of Michelangelo, and in the seventeenth century Mannerism was supplanted by the dazzling Baroque style, which was born in Rome under ecclesiastical auspices. Similarly, Italian music registered enormous accomplishments virtually without interruption from the sixteenth to the twentieth century. But whatever seemed threatening to the Church could not be tolerated and the free spirit of Renaissance culture was found no more.

5. THE RENAISSANCE IN THE NORTH

It was inevitable that after about 1500 the Renaissance which originated in Italy should have spread to other European countries. Throughout the fifteenth century a continuous procession of northern European students had come down to Italy to study in Italian universities such as Bologna or Padua, and an occasional Italian writer or artist traveled briefly north of the Alps. Such interchanges helped spread ideas, but only after around 1500 did most of northern Europe become sufficiently prosperous and politically stable to provide a truly congenial environment for the widespread cultivation of art and literature. Intellectual interchanges, moreover, became much more extensive after 1494, when France and Spain started fighting on Italian battlefields. The result of this development was that more and more northern Europeans began to learn what the Italians had been accomplishing (Spain's forces came not just from Spain but also from Germany and the Low Countries). Then too leading Italian thinkers and artists, like Leonardo, began to enter the retinues of northern kings or aristocrats. Accordingly, the Renaissance became an international movement and

continued to be vigorous in the north even as it started to wane on its
native ground.

The Renaissance outside Italy, however, was by no means identical
to the Renaissance within Italy. Above all, the northern European
Renaissance was generally less secular. The main explanation for this
difference lies in the different social and cultural traditions Italy and
northern Europe had inherited from the Middle Ages. As we have
seen, late-medieval Italy's vigorous urban society fostered a secular
educational system which led, in union with a revival of classicism, to
the evolution of new and more secular forms of expression. The north,
on the other hand, had a far less mercantile and urban-oriented economy than did Italy and no northern cities ever attained the political
dominance of their surrounding countrysides as did Florence, Venice,
and Milan. Instead, political power was coalescing around the nation-
states (or in Germany the princedoms), whose rulers were willing until
about 1500 to acknowledge the educational and cultural hegemony of
the clergy. Consequently, northern European universities tended to
specialize in theological studies, and the most prominent buildings in
almost all the leading northern towns were cathedrals.

Simply stated, the northern Renaissance was the product of an
engrafting of certain Italian Renaissance ideals upon preexisting northern traditions. This can be seen very clearly in the case of the most
prominent northern Renaissance intellectual movement, *Christian
humanism*. Agreeing with Italian humanists that medieval Scholasticism was too ensnarled in logical hair-splitting to have any value for
the practical conduct of life, northern Christian humanists nonetheless
looked for practical guidance from purely biblical, religious precepts.
Like their Italian counterparts, they sought wisdom from antiquity,
but the antiquity they had in mind was Christian rather than in any
way pagan—the antiquity, that is, of the New Testament and the early
Christian fathers. Similarly, northern Renaissance artists were moved
by the accomplishments of Italian Renaissance masters to turn their
backs on medieval Gothic artistic styles and became determined instead
to learn how to employ classical techniques. Yet these same artists
depicted classical subject matter far less frequently than did the Italians, and, inhibited by the greater northern European attachment to
Christian asceticism, virtually never dared to portray completely
undressed nudes.

Any discussion of northern Renaissance accomplishments in the
realm of thought and literary expression must begin with the career
of Desiderius Erasmus (c. 1467–1536), "the prince of the Christian
humanists." The illegitimate son of a priest, Erasmus was born near
Rotterdam in Holland, but later, as a result of his wide travels, became
in effect a citizen of all northern Europe. Placed as a teenager against
his will into a monastery, the young Erasmus found there little religion or formal instruction of any kind but plenty of freedom to read
what he liked. He devoured all the classics he could get his hands on

and the writings of many of the church fathers. When he was about thirty years of age, he obtained permission to leave the monastery and enroll in the University of Paris, where he completed the requirements for the degree of bachelor of divinity. But Erasmus subsequently rebelled against what he considered the arid learning of Parisian Scholasticism. In one of his later writings he reported the following exchange: "Q. Where do you come from? A. The College of Montaigu. Q. Ah, then you must be bowed down with learning. A. No, with lice." Erasmus also never entered into the active duties of a priest, choosing rather to make his living by teaching and writing. Ever on the lookout for new patrons, he changed his residence at frequent intervals, traveling often to England, staying once for three years in Italy, and residing in several different cities in the Netherlands before settling finally toward the end of his life in Basel, Switzerland. By means of a voluminous correspondence he kept up with learned friends he made wherever he went, Erasmus became the leader of a northern European humanist coterie. And by means of the popularity of his numerous publications, he became the arbiter of "advanced" northern European cultural tastes during the first quarter of the sixteenth century.

Erasmus's many-sided intellectual activity may best be appraised from two different points of view: the literary and the doctrinal. As a Latin prose stylist, Erasmus was probably without peer since the days *Erasmus's literary* of Cicero. Extraordinarily learned and witty, he revelled in tailoring *accomplishments* his mode of discourse to fit his subject, creating dazzling verbal effects when appropriate, and coining puns that took on added meaning if one knew Greek as well as Latin. Above all, Erasmus excelled in the deft use of irony, poking fun at all and sundry, including himself. For example, in his *Colloquies* (Latin for *Discussions*) he had a fictional character lament the evil signs of the times thus: "kings make war, priests strive to line their pockets, theologians invent syllogisms, monks roam outside their cloisters, the commons riot, and Erasmus writes colloquies."

But although Erasmus's urbane Latin style and wit earned him a wide audience for purely literary reasons, he by no means thought of himself as a mere entertainer. Rather, he intended everything he wrote *His "philosophy of* to propagate in one form or another what he called the "philosophy *Christ"* of Christ." The essence of Erasmus's Christian humanist convictions was his belief that the entire society of his day was caught up in corruption and immorality as a result of having lost sight of the simple teachings of the Gospels. Accordingly, he offered to his contemporaries three different categories of publication: clever satires meant to show people the error of their ways, serious moral treatises meant to offer guidance toward proper Christian behavior, and scholarly editions of basic Christian texts.

In the first category belong the works of Erasmus that are still most widely read today—the *Praise of Folly* (1509), in which he pilloried

Knight, Death, and Devil by Dürer. This engraving of 1513 illustrates the ideal figure of Erasmus's *Handbook of a Christian Knight*. The steadfast knight is able to advance through the world on his charger, his loyal dog at his side, despite intimations of mortality and the snares of the devil.

Scholastic pedantry and dogmatism as well as the ignorance and superstitious credulity of the masses; and the *Colloquies* (1518), in which he held up contemporary religious practices for examination in a more serious but still pervasively ironic tone. In such works Erasmus let fictional characters do the talking, and hence his own views can only be determined by inference. But in his second mode Erasmus did not hesitate to speak clearly in his own voice. The most prominent treatises in this second genre are the quietly eloquent *Handbook of the Christian Knight* (1501), which urged the laity to pursue lives of serene inward piety, and the *Complaint of Peace* (1517), which pleaded movingly for Christian pacifism.

The satires and moral treatises

Despite this highly impressive literary production, however, Erasmus probably considered his textual scholarship his single greatest achievement. Revering the authority of the early Latin Fathers, Augustine, Jerome, and Ambrose, he brought out reliable editions of all their works, and revering the authority of the Bible most of all, he applied his extraordinary skills as a student of Latin and Greek to producing a reliable edition of the New Testament. After reading Lorenzo Valla's *Notes on the New Testament* in 1505, Erasmus became convinced that nothing was more imperative than divesting the text of the entire New Testament of the myriad errors in transcription and translation that had piled up during the Middle Ages, for no one could

Erasmus's edition of the New Testament

be a good Christian without being certain of exactly what Christ's message really was. Hence he spent ten years studying and comparing all the best early Greek biblical manuscripts he could find in order to establish an authoritative text. Finally appearing in 1516, Erasmus's Greek New Testament, published together with explanatory notes and his own new Latin translation, was one of the most important landmarks of biblical scholarship of all time.

One of Erasmus's closest friends, and a close second to him in distinction among the ranks of the Christian humanists, was the Englishman Sir Thomas More (1478–1535). Following a successful career as a lawyer and as speaker of the House of Commons, in 1529 More was appointed lord chancellor of England. He was not long in this position, however, before he incurred the wrath of his royal master, King Henry VIII, because More, who was loyal to Catholic universalism, opposed the king's design to establish a national church under subjection to the state. Finally, in 1534, when More refused to take an oath acknowledging Henry as head of the Church of England, he was thrown into the Tower, and a year later met his death on the scaffold as a Catholic martyr. Much earlier, however, in 1516, long before More had any inkling of how his life was to end, he published the one work for which he will ever be best remembered, the *Utopia*. Creating the subsequently popular genre of "utopian fiction," More's *Utopia* expressed an Erasmian critique of contemporary society. Purporting

Sir Thomas More and Utopia

A Map of Thomas More's Imaginary Island of Utopia. "Utopia's" fictional discoverer, Hythlodaeus, whose name means "dispenser of nonsense" in Greek, points to the island of Utopia, which means "no place." From an early edition.

to describe an ideal community on an imaginary island, the book is really an indictment of the glaring abuses of the time—of poverty undeserved and wealth unearned, of drastic punishments, religious persecution, and the senseless slaughter of war. The inhabitants of Utopia hold all their goods in common, work only six hours a day so that all may have leisure for intellectual pursuits, and practice the natural virtues of wisdom, moderation, fortitude, and justice. Iron is the precious metal "because it is useful," war and monasticism are abolished, and toleration is granted to all who recognize the existence of God and the immortality of the soul. Although More advanced no explicit arguments in his *Utopia* in favor of Christianity, he clearly meant to imply that if the "Utopians" could manage their society so well without the benefit of Christian Revelation, Europeans who knew the Gospels ought to be able to do even better.

Ulrich von Hutten and the Letters of Obscure Men

Whereas Erasmus and More were basically conciliatory in their temperaments and preferred to express themselves by means of wry understatements, a third representative of the Christian humanist movement, Erasmus's German disciple Ulrich von Hutten (1488–1523) was of a much more combative disposition. Dedicated to the cause of German cultural nationalism, von Hutten in translations from the Roman historian Tacitus employed his command of classical scholarship to demonstrate how "proud and free" Germanic tribes had once triumphed heroically over Roman legions. In other writings he spoke up truculently in his own words to defend the German people against foreigners. But von Hutten's chief claim to fame was his collaboration with another German humanist, Crotus Rubianus, in the authorship of the *Letters of Obscure Men* (1515), one of the most stinging satires in the history of literature. This was written as part of a propaganda war in favor of a scholar named Johann Reuchlin who wished to pursue his study of Hebrew writings, above all, the Talmud. When Scholastic theologians from the University of Cologne and the German inquisitor general tried to have all Hebrew books in Germany destroyed, Reuchlin and his party strongly opposed the move. After a while it became apparent that direct argument was accomplishing nothing, so Reuchlin's supporters resorted to ridicule. Von Hutten and Rubianus published a series of letters, written in intentionally bad Latin, purportedly by some of Reuchlin's Scholastic opponents from the University of Cologne. These were given such ridiculous names as Goatmilker, Baldpate, and Dungspreader, and shown to be learned fools who paraded forth examples of absurd religious literalism or grotesque erudition. Heinrich Sheep's-mouth, for example, the supposed writer of one of the letters, professed to be worried that he had sinned grievously by eating on Friday an egg that contained the yolk of a chick. The author of another boasted of his "brilliant discovery" that Julius Caesar could not have written Latin histories because he was too busy with his military exploits ever to have learned Latin. Although immediately banned by the Church, the letters circulated nonetheless and were widely read, giving ever more currency to the Erasmian proposition that Scholastic theology and Catholic religious ritual had to be set aside in favor of the most earnest dedication to the pursuit of apostolic Christianity.

With Erasmus, More, and von Hutten the list of energetic and eloquent Christian humanists is by no means exhausted, for the Englishman John Colet (c. 1467–1519), the Frenchman Jacques Lefèvre d'Étaples (c. 1455–1529), and the Spaniards Cardinal Francisco Ximénez de Cisneros (1436–1517) and Juan Luis Vives (1492–1540), among still many others, all made signal contributions to the collective enterprise of editing biblical and early Christian texts and expounding Gospel morality. But despite a host of achievements, the Christian humanist movement, which possessed such an extraordinary degree of international solidarity and vigor from about 1500 to 1525, was thrown into disarray by the rise of Protestantism and subsequently lost its momentum. The irony here is obvious, for the Christian humanists' emphasis on the literal truth of the Gospels and their devastating criticisms of clerical corruption and excessive religious ceremonialism certainly helped pave the way for the Protestant Reformation initiated by Martin Luther in 1517. But, as will be seen in the following chapter, very few Christian humanists were willing to go the whole route with Luther in rejecting the most fundamental principles on which Catholicism was based, and the few who did became such ardent Protestants that they lost all the sense of quiet irony that earlier had been a hallmark of Christian humanist expression. Most Christian humanists tried to remain within the Catholic fold while still espousing their ideal of nonritualistic inward piety, but as time went on the leaders of Catholicism had less and less tolerance for them because lines were hardening in the war with Protestantism and any suggestion of internal criticism of Catholic religious practices seemed like giving covert aid to "the enemy." Erasmus himself, who remained a Catholic, died early enough to escape opprobrium, but several of his less fortunate followers lived on to suffer as victims of the Spanish Inquisition.

Yet if Christian humanism faded rapidly after about 1525, the northern Renaissance continued to flourish throughout the sixteenth century in primarily literary and artistic forms. In France, for example, the highly accomplished poets Pierre de Ronsard (c. 1524–1585) and Joachim du Bellay (c. 1525–1560) wrote elegant sonnets in the style of Petrarch, and in England the poets Sir Philip Sidney (1554–1586) and Edmund Spenser (c. 1552–1599) drew impressively on Italian literary innovations as well. Indeed, Spenser's *The Faerie Queene*, a long chivalric romance written in the manner of Ariosto's *Orlando Furioso*, communicates as well as any Italian work the gorgeous sensuousness typical of Italian Renaissance culture.

More intrinsically original than any of the aforementioned poets was the French prose satirist François Rabelais (c. 1494–1553), probably the best loved of all the great European creative writers of the sixteenth century. Like Erasmus, whom he greatly admired, Rabelais was educated as a monk, but soon after taking holy orders he left his monastery to study medicine. Becoming thereafter a practicing physician in Lyons, Rabelais from the start interspersed his professional activities with literary endeavors of one sort or another. He wrote almanacs for the common people, satires against quacks and astrologers, and burlesques of popular superstitions. But by far his most enduring literary legacy consists of his five volumes of "chronicles" published under the collective title of *Gargantua and Pantagruel*.

Rabelais' account of the adventures of Gargantua and Pantagruel, originally the names of legendary medieval giants noted for their fabulous size and gross appetites, served as a vehicle for his lusty humor and his penchant for exuberant narrative as well as for the expression of his philosophy of naturalism. To some degree, Rabelais drew on the precedents of Christian humanism. Thus, like Erasmus, he satirized religious ceremonialism, ridiculed Scholasticism, scoffed at superstitions, and pilloried every form of bigotry. But much unlike Erasmus, who wrote in a highly cultivated classical Latin style comprehensible to only the most learned readers, Rabelais chose to address a far wider audience by writing in an extremely down-to-earth French, often loaded with the crudest vulgarities. Likewise, Rabelais wanted to avoid seeming in any way "preachy" and therefore eschewed all suggestions of moralism in favor of giving the impression that he wished merely to offer his readers some rollicking good fun. Yet, aside from the critical satire in *Gargantua and Pantagruel*, there runs through all five volumes a common theme of glorifying the human and the natural. For Rabelais, whose robust giants were really life-

Chambord. Built in the early sixteenth century by an Italian architect in the service of King Francis I of France, this magnificent Loire Valley château combines Gothic and Renaissance architectural traits.

The West Side of the Square Court of the Louvre by Pierre Lescot. The enlargement of the Louvre, begun by Lescot in 1546, took more than a century to complete. Drawing on the work of Bramante (see above, p. 432), he achieved a synthesis of the traditional château and the Renaissance palace.

loving human beings writ very large, every instinct of humanity was healthy, provided it was not directed toward tyranny over others. Thus in his ideal community, the utopian "abbey of Thélème," there was no repressiveness whatsoever, but only a congenial environment for the pursuit of life-affirming, natural human attainments, guided by the single rule of "do what thou wouldst."

Were we to imagine what Rabelais' fictional abbey of Thélème might have looked like, we would do best to picture it as resembling one of the famous sixteenth-century French Renaissance châteaux built along the River Loire, for the northern European Renaissance had its own distinctive architecture that often corresponded in certain essentials to its literature. Thus, just as Rabelais recounted stories of medieval giants in order to express an affirmation of Renaissance values, so French architects who constructed such splendid Loire châteaux as Amboise, Chenonceaux, and Chambord, combined elements of the late-medieval French flamboyant Gothic style with an up-to-date emphasis on classical horizontality to produce some of the most impressively distinctive architectural landmarks ever constructed in France. Yet much closer architectural imitation of Italian models occurred in France as well, for just as Ronsard and du Bellay modeled their poetic style very closely on Petrarch, so Pierre Lescot, the French architect who began work on the new royal palace of the Louvre in Paris in 1546, hewed closely to the classicism of Italian Renaissance masters in constructing a facade that emphasized classical pilasters and pediments.

Northern Renaissance architecture

It only remains to treat the accomplishments of northern Renaissance painting, another realm in which links between thought and art can be discerned. Certainly the most moving visual embodiments of

Left: *St. Jerome in his Study* by Dürer. St. Jerome, a hero for both Dürer and Erasmus, represents inspired Christian scholarship. Note how the scene exudes contentment, even down to the sleeping lion which seems rather like an overgrown tabby cat. Right: *The Four Apostles* by Dürer. This painting in two separate panels is a moving statement of the artist's intense religious faith.

Albrecht Dürer

See color plates facing page 449 for the *Self-Portrait* by Dürer

the ideals of Christian humanism were conceived by the foremost of northern Renaissance artists, the German Albrecht Dürer (1471–1528). From the purely technical and stylistic points of view, Dürer's greatest significance lies in the fact that, returning from his native Nuremberg after a trip to Venice in 1494, he became the first northerner to master Italian Renaissance techniques of proportion, perspective, and modeling. Dürer also shared with contemporary Italians a fascination with reproducing the manifold works of nature down to the minutest details and a penchant for displaying various postures of the human nude. But whereas Michelangelo portrayed his naked David or Adam entirely without covering, Dürer's nudes are seldom lacking their fig leaves, in deference to more restrained northern traditions. Moreover, Dürer consistently refrained from abandoning himself to the pure classicism and sumptuousness of much Italian Renaissance art because he was inspired primarily by the more traditionally Christian ideals of Erasmus. Thus Dürer's serenely radiant *St. Jerome* expresses the sense of accomplishment that Erasmus or any other contemporary Christian humanist may have had while working quietly in his study, his *Knight, Death, and Devil* offers a stirring visual depiction of Erasmus's ideal Christian knight, and his *Four Apostles* intones a solemn hymn to the dignity and penetrating insight of Dürer's favorite New Testament authors, Saints Paul, John, Peter, and Mark.

Dürer would have loved nothing more than to have immortalized Erasmus in a major painted portrait, but circumstances prevented him from doing this because the paths of the two men crossed only once, and after Dürer started sketching his hero on that occasion his work was interrupted by Erasmus's press of business. Instead, the accomplishment of capturing Erasmus's pensive spirit in oils was left to the second greatest of northern Renaissance artists, the German Hans Holbein the Younger (1497–1543). As good fortune would have it, during a stay in England Holbein also painted an extraordinarily acute portrait of Erasmus's friend and kindred spirit, Sir Thomas More, which enables us to see clearly why a contemporary called More "a man of . . . sad gravity; a man for all seasons." These two portraits in and of themselves point up a major difference between medieval and Renaissance culture because whereas the Middle Ages produced no convincing naturalistic likenesses of any leading intellectual figure, Renaissance culture's greater commitment to recapturing the essence of human individuality created the environment in which Holbein was able to make Erasmus and More come to life.

Sir Thomas More. Portrait by Hans Holbein the Younger.

6. RENAISSANCE DEVELOPMENTS IN MUSIC

Music in western Europe in the fifteenth and sixteenth centuries reached such a high point of development that it constitutes, together with painting and sculpture, one of the most brilliant aspects of Renaissance endeavor. While the visual arts were stimulated by the study of ancient models, music flowed naturally from an independent evolution which had been in progress in medieval Christendom. As earlier, leadership came from men trained in the service of the Church, but secular music was now valued as well, and its principles were combined with those of sacred music to bring a decided gain in color and emotional appeal. The distinction between sacred and profane became less sharp; most composers did not restrict their activities to either field. Music was no longer regarded merely as a diversion or an adjunct to worship but came into its own as a serious independent art.

The evolution of music as an independent art

See color plates facing page 449 for Erasmus by Holbein

Different sections of Europe vied with one another for musical leadership. As with the other arts, advance was related to the generous patronage afforded by the prosperous cities of Italy and the northern European princely courts. During the fourteenth century a pre- or early Renaissance musical movement called Ars Nova (new art) flourished in Italy and France. Its outstanding composers were Francesco Landini (c. 1325–1397) and Guillaume de Machaut (1300–1377). The madrigals, ballads, and other songs composed by the Ars Nova musicians testify to a rich secular art, but the greatest achievement of the

Leadership provided by Italy and France

Renaissance Trumpeters and Singers. Reliefs by Luca della Robbia.

period was a highly complicated yet delicate contrapuntal style adapted for ecclesiastical motets. Machaut, moreover, was the first known composer to provide a polyphonic version for the singing of the Mass.

The fifteenth century was ushered in by a synthesis of French, Flemish, and Italian elements that took place in the ducal court of Burgundy. This music was melodious and gentle, but in the second half of the century it hardened a little as northern Flemish elements gained in importance. As the sixteenth century opened, Franco-Flemish composers appeared in every important court and cathedral all over Europe, gradually establishing regional-national schools, usually in attractive combinations of Flemish with German, Spanish, and Italian musical cultures. The various genres thus created show a close affinity with Renaissance art and poetry. In the second half of the sixteenth century the leaders of the nationalized Franco-Flemish style were the Flemish Roland de Lassus (1532–1594), the most versatile composer of the age, and the Italian Giovanni Pierluigi da Palestrina (c. 1525–1594), who specialized in highly intricate polyphonic choral music written for Catholic church services under the patronage of the popes in Rome. Music also flourished in sixteenth-century England, where the Tudor monarchs Henry VIII and Elizabeth I were active in patronizing the arts. Not only did the Italian madrigal, imported toward the end of the sixteenth century, take on remarkable new life

Synthesis of national elements

in England, but songs and instrumental music of an original cast antic-ipated future developments on the Continent. In William Byrd (1543–1623) English music produced a master fully the equal of the great Flemish and Italian composers of the Renaissance period. The general level of musical proficiency seems to have been higher in Queen Elizabeth's day than in ours: the singing of part-songs was a popular pastime in homes and at informal social gatherings, and the ability to read a part at sight was expected of the educated elite.

In conclusion, it may be observed that while accomplishments in counterpoint were already very advanced in the Renaissance period, our modern harmonic system was still in its infancy, and thus there was much room for later experimentation. At the same time one should realize that the music of the Renaissance constitutes not merely a stage in evolution but a magnificent achievement in itself, with masters who rank among the great of all time. The composers Lassus, Palestrina, and Byrd are as truly representative of the artistic triumph of the Renaissance as are the painters Leonardo, Raphael, and Michelangelo. Their heritage, long neglected, has within recent years begun to be appreciated, largely by means of phonograph records, and is now gaining in popularity as interested groups of musicians devote themselves to its revival.

The greatness of the Renaissance musical achievement

7. THE SCIENTIFIC ACCOMPLISHMENTS OF THE RENAISSANCE PERIOD

Some extraordinarily important accomplishments were made in the history of science during the sixteenth and early seventeenth centuries, but these were not preeminently the achievements of Renaissance humanism. The educational program of the humanists placed a low value on science because it seemed irrelevant to their aim of making people more eloquent and moral. Science for humanists like Petrarch, Leonardo Bruni, or Erasmus was part and parcel of the "vain speculation" of the Scholastics which they attacked and held up to ridicule. Accordingly, none of the great scientists of the Renaissance age belonged to the humanist movement.

The nonscientific orientation of Renaissance humanism

Nonetheless, at least two intellectual trends of the period did prepare the way for great new scientific advances. One was the currency of Neoplatonism. The importance of this philosophical system to science was that it proposed certain ideas, such as the central position of the sun and the supposed divinity of given geometrical shapes, that would help lead to crucial scientific breakthroughs. It is ironic that Neoplatonism seems very "unscientific" from the modern perspective because it emphasizes mysticism and intuition instead of empiricism or strictly rational thought. Yet it helped scientific thinkers to reconsider older notions which had impeded the progress of medieval science; in

Renaissance foundations of modern science: (1) Neoplatonism

A *Cannon Foundry* by Leonardo da Vinci

other words, it helped them to put on a new "thinking cap." Among the most important of the scientists who were influenced by Neoplatonism were Copernicus and Kepler.

A second trend that contributed to the advance of science was very different: the growth in popularity of a *mechanistic* interpretation of the universe. Renaissance mechanism owed its greatest impetus to the publication in 1543 of the works of the great Greek mathematician and physicist Archimedes. Not only were his concrete observations and discoveries among the most advanced and reliable in the entire body of Greek science, but Archimedes taught the view that the universe operates on the basis of mechanical forces, like a great machine. Because his view was diametrically opposed to the occult outlook of the Neoplatonists, who saw the world inhabited by spirits and driven by supernatural forces, it took some time to gather strength. Nonetheless, mechanism did gain some very important late-Renaissance adherents, foremost among whom was the Italian scientist Galileo. Ultimately mechanism played an enormous role in the development of modern science because it insisted upon finding observable and measurable causes and effects in the world of nature.

One other Renaissance development which contributed to the rise of modern science was the breakdown of the medieval separation between the realms of theory and practice. In the Middle Ages Scholastically trained clerics theorized about the natural world but never for a moment thought of tinkering with machines or dissecting corpses because this empirical approach to science lay outside the Scholastic framework. On the other hand, numerous technicians who had little formal education and knew little of abstract theories had much practical expertise in various aspects of mechanical engineering. Theory and practice began to come together in the fifteenth century. One reason for this was that the highly respected Renaissance artists bridged both areas of endeavor: not only were they marvelous craftsmen, but they advanced mathematics and science when they investigated the laws of perspective and optics, worked out geometric methods for supporting the weight of enormous architectural domes, and studied the dimensions and details of the human body. In general, they helped make science more empirical and practically oriented than it had been earlier. Other reasons for the integration were the decline in prestige of the overly theoretical universities and a growing interest in alchemy and astrology among the leisured classes. Here again we can see some irony: alchemy and astrology are today properly dismissed as unscientific superstitions, but in the sixteenth and seventeenth centuries their vogue led some wealthy amateurs to start building laboratories and measuring the courses of the stars. Thereby scientific practice was rendered eminently respectable. When that happened modern science was on the way to some of its greatest triumphs.

The actual scientific accomplishments of the Renaissance period were international in scope. The achievement par excellence in astronomy—the formulation and proof of the heliocentric theory that the earth revolves around the sun—was primarily the work of the Pole Copernicus, the German Kepler, and the Italian Galileo. Until the sixteenth century the Ptolemaic theory that the earth stands still at the center of the universe went virtually unchallenged in western Europe. Nicholas Copernicus (1473–1543), a Polish clergyman who had absorbed Neoplatonism while studying in Italy, was the first to posit an alternative system. Copernicus made few new observations, but he thoroughly reinterpreted the significance of the old astronomical evidence. Inspired by the Neoplatonic assumptions that the sphere is the most perfect shape, that motion is more nearly divine than rest, and that the sun sits "enthroned" in the midst of the universe, "ruling his children the planets which circle around him," Copernicus worked out a new heliocentric theory. Specifically, in his *On the Revolutions of the Heavenly Spheres*—which he completed around 1530 but did not publish until 1543—he argued that the earth and the planets move around the sun in concentric circles. Copernicus's system itself was still highly imperfect: by no means did it account without difficulties for all the known facts of planetary motion. Moreover, it asked people to reject their commonsense assumptions that the sun moves because observation shows it moving across the sky and that the earth stands still because no movement can be felt. More serious, Copernicus contradicted passages in the Bible, such as the one wherein Joshua commands the sun to stand still. As a result of such problems, believers in Copernicus's heliocentric theory remained distinctly in the minority until the early seventeenth century.

It was Kepler and Galileo who ensured the triumph of Copernicus's revolution in astronomy. Johann Kepler (1571–1630), a mystical thinker who was in many ways more like a magician than a modern scientist, studied astronomy in order to probe the hidden secrets of God. His basic conviction was that God had created the universe according to mathematical laws. Relying on the new and impressively accurate astronomical observations of the Dane Tycho Brahe (1546–1601), Kepler was able to recognize that two assumptions about planetary motion that Copernicus had taken for granted were simply not in accord with the observable facts. Specifically, Kepler replaced Copernicus's belief in uniform planetary velocity with his own "First Law" that the speed of planets varies with their distance from the sun, and he replaced Copernicus's view that planetary orbits were circular with his "Second Law" that the earth and the other planets travel in *elliptical* paths around the sun. He also argued that magnetic attractions between the sun and the planets keep the planets in orbital motion. That approach was rejected by most seventeenth-century mechanistic scientists as being far too magical, but in fact it paved the way for the law of universal gravitation formulated by Isaac Newton at the end of the seventeenth century.

As Kepler perfected Copernicus's heliocentric system from the

Progress in astronomy: Copernicus's heliocentric theory

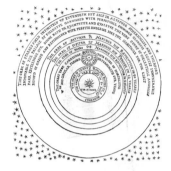

"A Perfect Description of the Celestial Orbes." A diagram by Copernicus, showing the relationship of stars, the planets, and the sun.

Kepler's laws of planetary motion

Galileo's confirmation of the Copernican revolution

Galileo

Leonardo da Vinci and Galileo as physicists

point of view of mathematical theory, so Galileo Galilei (1564–1642) promoted acceptance for it by gathering further astronomical evidence. With a telescope which he manufactured himself and raised to a magnifying power of thirty times, he discovered the moons of Jupiter, the rings of Saturn, and spots on the sun. He was able also to determine that the Milky Way is a collection of celestial bodies independent of our solar system and to form some idea of the enormous distances of the fixed stars. Though many held out against them, these discoveries of Galileo gradually convinced the majority of scientists that the main conclusion of Copernicus was true. The final triumph of this idea is commonly called the Copernican Revolution. Few more significant events have occurred in the intellectual history of the world, for it overturned the medieval worldview and paved the way for modern conceptions of mechanism, skepticism, and the infinity of time and space. Some thinkers believe that it contributed also to the degradation of man, since it swept man out of his majestic position at the center of the universe and reduced him to a mere particle of dust in an endless cosmic machine.

In the front rank among the physicists of the Renaissance were Leonardo da Vinci and Galileo. If Leonardo da Vinci had failed completely as a painter, his contributions to science would still entitle him to considerable fame. Not the least of these were his achievements in physics. Though he actually made few complete discoveries, his conclusion that "every weight tends to fall toward the center by the shortest way" contained the kernel of the law of gravity. In addition, he worked out the principles of an astonishing variety of inventions, including a diving board, a steam engine, an armored tank, and a helicopter. Galileo is especially noted as a physicist for his law of falling bodies. Skeptical of the traditional theory that bodies fall with a speed directly proportional to their weight, he taught that bodies dropped from various heights would fall at a rate of speed which increases with the square of the time involved. Rejecting the Scholastic notions of absolute gravity and absolute levity, he taught that these are purely relative terms, that all bodies have weight, even those which, like the air, are invisible, and that in a vacuum all objects would fall with equal velocity. Galileo seems to have had a broader conception of a universal force of gravitation than Leonardo da Vinci, for he perceived that the power which holds the moon in the vicinity of the earth and causes the satellites of Jupiter to circulate around that planet is essentially the same as the force which enables the earth to draw bodies to its surface. He never formulated this principle as a law, however, nor did he realize all of its implications, as did Newton some fifty years later.

The record of Renaissance achievements in medicine and anatomy is also a most impressive one. Attention must be called above all to the work of the German Theophrastus von Hohenheim, known as Paracelsus (1493–1541), the Spaniard Michael Servetus (1511–1553), and the Belgian Andreas Vesalius (1514–1564). The physician Paracelsus resembled Copernicus and Kepler in believing that spiritual rather than material forces governed the workings of the universe. Hence he was a firm believer in alchemy and astrology. Nevertheless, Paracelsus relied on observation for his knowledge of diseases and their cures. Instead of following the teachings of ancient authorities, he traveled widely, studying cases of illness in different environments and experimenting with many drugs. Above all, his insistence on the close relationship of chemistry and medicine foreshadowed and sometimes directly influenced important modern achievements in pharmacology and healing. Michael Servetus, whose major interest was theology, but who practiced medicine for a living, discovered the lesser or pulmonary circulation of the blood, in an attempt to prove the veracity of the Virgin birth. He described how the blood leaves the right chambers of the heart, is carried to the lungs to be purified, then returns to the heart and is conveyed from that organ to all parts of the body. But Servetus had no idea of the return of the blood to the heart through the veins, a discovery that was made by the Englishman William Harvey in the early seventeenth century.

Purely by coincidence the one sixteenth-century scientific treatise that came closest to rivaling in significance Copernicus's work in astronomy, Vesalius's *On the Structure of the Human Body,* was published in 1543, the same year that saw the issuance of Copernicus's

Michael Servetus

Two Plates from Vesalius's On the Structure of the Human Body. *On the left is a portrait of Vesalius himself displaying the sinews of the forearm. Note the striking similarity to the anatomical drawings of Leonardo, shown above, p. 426. On the right we see "the human skeleton shown from the side." The presence of the sarcophagus with the Latin warning "we live by the spirit, all else will die" shows that scientific illustrations still had to be justified by moralistic sententiousness in the early-modern period.*

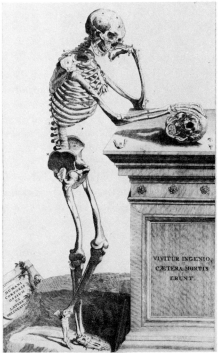

Revolutions of the Heavenly Spheres. Vesalius, a cosmopolitan who was born in Brussels and studied in Paris but later migrated to Italy where he taught anatomy and surgery at the University of Padua, approached his research from the correct point of view that much of ancient anatomical doctrine was in error. For him the ancient anatomy of Galen (so to speak, the Ptolemy of medicine) could only be corrected on the basis of direct observation. Hence he applied himself to frequent dissections of human corpses to see how various parts of the body actually appear when the skin covering is stripped away. Not content with merely describing in words what he saw, Vesalius then collaborated with an artist—Jan van Calcar, a fellow Belgian who had come to Italy to study under the Renaissance master Titian—in portraying his observations in detailed engravings. Art historians are uncertain as to whether van Calcar was directly inspired in executing his illustrations for Vesalius by knowledge of earlier anatomical drawings of Leonardo da Vinci, but even if not, he certainly relied on a cumulative tradition of expert anatomical depiction bequeathed to him by Italian Renaissance art. Gathered in Vesalius's *Structure of the Human Body* of 1543, van Calcar's plates offered a new map of the human anatomy just when Copernicus was laying out a new map of the heavens. Since Vesalius in the same work offered basic explanations of how parts of the body move and interact in addition to discussing and illustrating how they look, he is often counted as the father of modern physiology as well as the father of modern anatomy. With his landmark treatise we come to a fitting end to our survey of Renaissance accomplishments inasmuch as his *Structure of the Human Body* represented the fullest degree of fruitful international intellectual exchanges as well as the fullest merger of theory and practice, and art and science.

SELECTED READINGS

• *Items so designated are available in paperback editions.*

Baker, Herschel, *The Image of Man: A Study of the Idea of Human Dignity in Classical Antiquity, the Middle Ages, and the Renaissance,* Cambridge, Mass., 1947. An outstanding and engagingly written survey from the perspective of a modern liberal.
• Baxandall, Michael, *Painting and Experience in Fifteenth Century Italy,* Oxford, 1972.
Benesch, O., *The Art of the Renaissance in Northern Europe,* rev. ed., New York, 1965.
• Berenson, B., *The Italian Painters of the Renaissance,* New York, 1952.
• Boas, Marie, *The Scientific Renaissance: 1450–1630,* New York, 1962. An excellent, straightforward survey.
• Burckhardt, J., *The Civilization of the Renaissance in Italy,* many eds. The nineteenth-century work that formulated the modern view of the Renaissance.

Burke, Peter, *Culture and Society in Renaissance Italy, 1420–1540*, New York, 1972.

• Bush, D., *The Renaissance and English Humanism*, Toronto, 1939.

Butterfield, H., *The Origins of Modern Science*, London, 1949. Clear and wide ranging. Shows how science developed from major changes in intellectual orientations.

Chabod, F., *Machiavelli and the Renaissance*, London, 1958.

• Chambers, R. W., *Thomas More*, London, 1936. A spirited defense of the view that More was a life-long committed Catholic.

• Clark, Kenneth M., *Leonardo da Vinci*, 2nd ed., Cambridge, 1952.

De Tolnay, C., *Michelangelo: Sculptor, Painter, Architect*, Princeton, N.J., 1975.

Ferguson, W., ed., *The Renaissance: Six Essays*, rev. ed., New York, 1962.

Fox, Alistair, *Thomas More: History and Providence*, Oxford, 1982. More reliable in its judgments than Chambers.

• Gilmore, M., *The World of Humanism*, New York, 1952. A well-written survey.

Gould, Cecil, *An Introduction to Italian Renaissance Painting*, London, 1957.

Hale, J. R., *Machiavelli and Renaissance Italy*, New York, 1960.

• ———, *Renaissance Europe: The Individual and Society, 1480–1520*, London, 1971. A different kind of survey that does not treat the great events but examines the quality of life.

• Hay, D., ed., *The Renaissance Debate*, New York, 1965. A collection of readings on the question of how to define the Renaissance.

• Kearney, H., *Science and Change, 1500–1700*, New York, 1971. Supplements Butterfield in arguing that science progressed as the result of contributions made by three different "schools."

• Kristeller, P. O., *Eight Philosophers of the Italian Renaissance*, Stanford, Calif., 1964. Admirably clear.

• ———, *Renaissance Thought: The Classic, Scholastic, and Humanist Strains*, New York, 1961. Very helpful in defining main trends of Renaissance thought.

• Kuhn, Thomas S., *The Copernican Revolution: Planetary Astronomy in the Development of Western Thought*, Cambridge, Mass., 1957. Admirably clear.

Larner, John, *Culture and Society in Italy, 1290–1420*, New York, 1971.

• Levey, M., *Early Renaissance (Style and Civilization)*, Baltimore, 1967. Art history.

• Martines, L., *Power and Imagination: City-States in Renaissance Italy*, New York, 1979. An expert account of the interrelationships between political and material circumstances and cultural expressions.

Panofsky, E., *Albrecht Dürer*, 3rd ed., Princeton, N.J., 1948.

• ———, *Renaissance and Renascences in Western Art*, Stockholm, 1960. A difficult but rewarding attempt to distinguish the Italian Renaissance from its medieval predecessors.

Phillips, Margaret M., *Erasmus and the Northern Renaissance*, London, 1949.

Pope-Hennessy, J., *The Portrait in the Renaissance*, Princeton, N.J., 1966.

• Ralph, Philip L., *The Renaissance in Perspective*, New York, 1973. Both a useful summary and a stimulus to thought.

Reese, Gustave, *Music in the Renaissance*, rev. ed., New York, 1959. The leading work on the subject.

• Rice, E. F., Jr., *The Foundations of Early Modern Europe, 1460–1559,* New York, 1970.

Seigel, J., *Rhetoric and Philosophy in Renaissance Humanism,* Princeton, N.J., 1968. Treats a basic tension in the thought of early Renaissance thinkers.

Stechow, W., *Northern Renaissance Art: 1400–1600,* Englewood Cliffs, N.J., 1966.

Tracy, James, *Erasmus: The Growth of a Mind,* Geneva, 1972. The best intellectual biography.

Whitfield, J. H., *A Short History of Italian Literature,* Baltimore, 1960.

• Wittkower, R., *Architectural Principles in the Age of Humanism,* rev. ed., New York, 1965. An art-historical classic.

SOURCE MATERIALS

Alberti, Leon Battista, *The Family in Renaissance Florence,* tr. R. N. Watkins, Columbia, S.C., 1969.

• Cassirer, E., et al., eds., *The Renaissance Philosophy of Man,* Chicago, 1948. Leading works of Petrarch, Pico, etc.

• Castiglione, B., *The Book of the Courtier,* tr. C. S. Singleton, New York, 1959.

• Erasmus, D., *The Praise of Folly,* tr. J. Wilson, Ann Arbor, Mich., 1958.

• ———, *Ten Colloquies,* tr. C. R. Thompson, Indianapolis, 1957.

• Kohl, B. G., and R. G. Witt, eds., *The Earthly Republic: Italian Humanists on Government and Society,* Philadelphia, 1978. New translations with excellent introductions.

• Machiavelli, N., *The Prince,* tr. R. M. Adams, New York, 1976. In addition to Machiavelli's text, this edition provides related documents and an excellent selection of scholarly interpretations.

• Montaigne, M. de, *Essays,* tr. J. M. Cohen, Baltimore, 1958.

• More, Sir Thomas, *Utopia,* tr. R. M. Adams, New York, 1975. In the same series as Adams's translation of Machiavelli's *Prince;* provides background materials and selected scholarly interpretations as well as the text.

• Rabelais, F., *Gargantua and Pantagruel,* tr. J. M. Cohen, Baltimore, 1955. A robust modern translation.

Chapter 15

EUROPE EXPANDS AND DIVIDES: OVERSEAS DISCOVERIES AND PROTESTANT REFORMATION

Formerly we were at the end of the world, and now we are in the middle
of it, with an unprecedented change in our fortunes.
> —Hernán Pérez de Oliva, addressing the city fathers
> of Cordova, Spain, 1524

Since then your serene majesty and your lordships seek a simple answer,
I will give it in this manner, neither horned nor toothed: unless I am
convinced by the testimony of Scripture or by clear reason . . . I am
bound by the Scripture I have quoted, and my conscience is captive to the
Word of God. I cannot and I will not retract anything, since it is neither
safe nor right to violate one's conscience. I cannot do otherwise, here I
stand, may God help me. Amen.
> —Martin Luther, addressing the Diet of Worms, 1521

Much as the civilization of the Renaissance made fundamental contributions toward the shaping of the modern world, the two most dramatic developments in the transition from the Middle Ages to the early-modern period of western European history were the overseas ventures of Spain and Portugal, and the Protestant Reformation. More or less overnight, these two developments changed the course of European history forever. Whereas European Christian civilization had been geographically self-contained throughout the thousand years of its prior history (excepting the relatively brief Crusade episode), in just a few decades, from about 1490 to about 1520, Europeans sailed out on the open seas to take commanding positions in Southeast Asia and lay claim to the whole Western Hemisphere. Ever since, the course of European history has been inseparable from interactions between events on the landmass of Europe and European engagements in the rest of the world.

Overseas expansion of Spain and Portugal

But just when Europe was expanding it was also dividing. Up until the early sixteenth century, despite growing national differences, there remained a distinct European "Community of Christendom," presided over by the pope. Wherever one traveled one could hear the same Latin mass, see infants baptized and couples wed according to the same ecclesiastical formulae, and receive blessings from priests who were all ordained by virtue of the same papal authority. As quickly as Europeans took hold of the world, however, they lost their spiritual unity. The Protestant Reformation initiated by Martin Luther in 1517, as well as the Catholic response to it, were both to have numerous progressive effects, but the most obvious immediate results were that Europe rapidly became divided along several different religious lines and that Europeans quickly started warring with one another in the name of faith.

Although the overseas discoveries and Protestant Reformation were roughly contemporaneous, it is important to recognize that in their origins they had nothing directly to do with each other. The early explorers sailed prior to or in disregard of European religious dissensions, and the early Protestants gave little thought to the opening up of new trade routes or the discovery of continents. Yet there is warrant for treating the discoveries, the Protestant Reformation, and the Catholic Counter-Reformation all in the same chapter because their effects very quickly became interrelated and also because all these movements were full of incidents of great heroism. As Columbus sailed fearlessly into the unknown and Balboa viewed a new ocean, "silent, upon a peak in Darien," so Luther struggled fearlessly for a new understanding of "the justice of God" and the crippled soldier Ignatius Loyola found inspiration by inward "spiritual exercises," thereby opening up new vistas of their own.

1. THE OVERSEAS DISCOVERIES AND CONQUESTS OF PORTUGAL AND SPAIN

At first glance the speed with which Europeans in the years around 1500 began to traverse the high seas appears bewildering and almost incomprehensible. With good reason most contemporaries perceived Christian civilization to be on the defensive, not the offensive, in the second half of the fifteenth century. In 1453 Constantinople, a hitherto impregnable barrier to Islamic advance, fell to the Turks, commanded by Sultan Muhammad II "the Conqueror"; Serbia was lost in 1459 and Albania followed in 1470. Most frightening of all to western Europeans was a Turkish landing on the Italian peninsula itself in 1480, which saw the city of Otranto occupied and half the inhabitants slaughtered. Only the death of Sultan Muhammad in 1481 caused the Turks to abandon their Italian foothold, but many feared that the "Infidels" might soon return. In the midst of an unsuccessful attempt to organize united European resistance to the Turks, Pope Pius II (1458–1464) observed: "I see nothing good on the horizon."

Yet Pius II could hardly have been more wrong, for while Christians remained on the defensive against the Turks in eastern Europe until the later sixteenth century, Portuguese and Spanish sailing ships on the Atlantic horizon soon made Christians lords of the world. A few facts speak eloquently for themselves: in 1482 the Portuguese built a fortress at Elmina, in modern-day Ghana, which quickly dominated trade on the West African "Gold Coast"; in 1492 Columbus sighted the West Indies; in 1500 the Portuguese established their first trading base on the west coast of India; and in the two years from 1519 to 1521 the Spaniard Cortés seized hold of the Mexican empire of Montezuma.

How did this all happen so quickly? Two different schools of scholarly interpretation offer substantially different responses. Proponents of what may be called the "Renaissance School" point out that the Portuguese and Spanish voyages of discovery occurred at the same time as the spread of Renaissance civilization (Columbus was a direct contemporary of Leonardo da Vinci) and argue that European overseas expansion can only be explained as a manifestation of allegedly new Renaissance principles of curiosity and self-reliance in practical affairs. But this interpretation assumes falsely that medieval people were not curious and self-reliant. Proponents of the Renaissance school also call attention to the fact that many of the mariners who sailed for Portugal and Spain were Italian born, but here they dodge the reality that some Italian voyagers, like Columbus himself, came from Genoa, a city which hardly participated in Italian Renaissance civilization. More important, the Renaissance interpretation seems weak because the leading Italian Renaissance states did not patronize the voyages of discovery at all. Undeniably some bits of classical geographical knowledge acquired in Italy by Renaissance humanists strengthened the resolve of some explorers to pursue certain ocean routes, but otherwise the alternative to the Renaissance explanation, namely the view that the movement of overseas expansion came from medieval preparations, seems far preferable.

Simply stated, the motives, the knowledge, and the wherewithal for the great discoveries were all essentially medieval. Certainly the single most dominant motive for the oceanic voyages was economic— the quest for Asiatic spices and other luxury goods. Pepper, cinnamon, nutmeg, ginger, and cloves could all be grown only in the tropical climates of Southeast Asia, and all were greatly prized throughout the High and late Middle Ages because of their preservative qualities. (Imagine a civilization without refrigeration and one can easily understand why wealthy Europeans hankered after tangy spices to keep their food from putrifying and to relieve the monotony of salt.) In the late Middle Ages, Asiatic spices, as well as luxury cloths and precious gems, reached European households by means of the enterprise of Islamic,

Sudden overseas expansion

Explanations for voyages: "Renaissance School"

Medieval background to voyages: economic motives

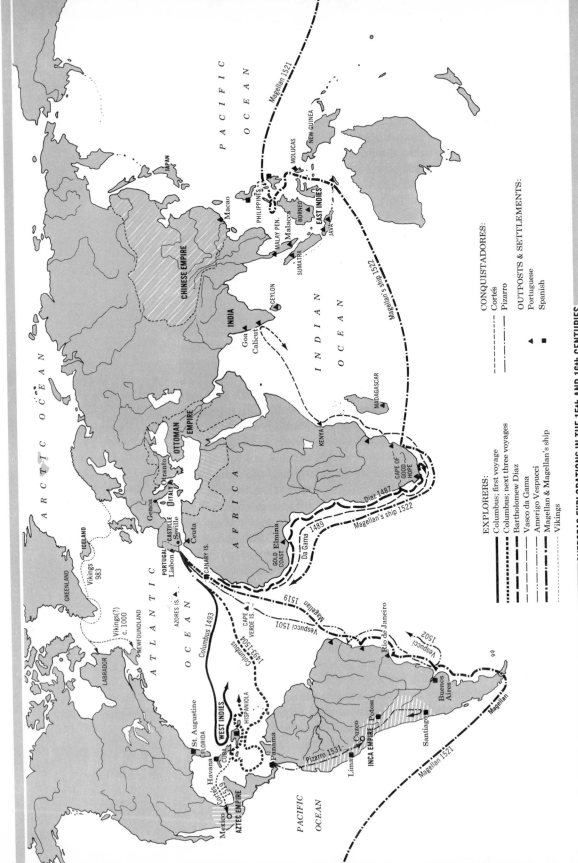

OVERSEAS EXPLORATIONS IN THE 15th AND 16th CENTURIES

EXPLORERS:

Columbus; first voyage
Columbus; next three voyages
Bartholomew Diaz
Vasco da Gama
Amerigo Vespucci
Magellan & Magellan's ship
Vikings

CONQUISTADORES:

Cortés
Pizarro

OUTPOSTS & SETTLEMENTS:

Portuguese
Spanish

Venetian, and Genoese middlemen, but the costs were exorbitant and a fortune was to be made by anyone who could go directly to the source by sea. (Land routes were out of the question because turbulent conditions in central Asia made them extremely unsafe; moreover, until the invention of railroads it normally was vastly more expensive to transport goods by land than by water.) Complementing the economic motives for overseas exploration were religious ones—hopes for converting unbaptized heathens and of finding imagined "lost Christians" in the East who might serve as allies against Islam. Needless to say, these hopes, like the lust for spices, flourished in the Middle Ages quite independently of the Italian Renaissance.

Then too the most important knowledge that lay behind the great discoveries and also the technological means to execute them were as medieval as the motivations. The popular notion that Europeans before Columbus believed the earth to be flat is simply a mistake: it would have been impossible after the twelfth century to have found an educated person or a mariner who did not accept the fact that the earth is a sphere. Nor did this knowledge remain solely in the realm of theory. As early as 1291 two Genoese, the Vivaldi brothers, sailed out on the Atlantic with the aim of reaching the East Indies by a "westward route." Although the Vivaldis never came back, by the middle of the fourteenth century Portuguese mariners were sailing regularly back and forth on the Atlantic as far west as the Azores Islands. These Portuguese sailings offer proof that by about 1350 European shipbuilding and navigational technology were fully up to the challenge of reaching new continents: since the Azores are one-third of the distance between Europe and America, from the strictly technological point of view any ship that could sail from Portugal to the Azores could have sailed all the way to the New World.

*Medieval background to
voyages: technology*

Why, then, was America not discovered a century before it actually was? Historians are at their greatest disadvantage in trying to explain things that did not happen, but two hypotheses may be offered. One relates to the fact that the fourteenth and fifteenth centuries were times of acute economic depression and political turmoil throughout western Europe. Since the major states of the Atlantic—France, England, and Castile (the dominant kingdom on the Spanish peninsula)—were all weakened by economic contraction and caught up in seemingly interminable wars, it is no wonder that none of them commissioned expensive and risky sailing ventures to the west. The second, less speculative hypothesis pertains to the change in routes pursued by Portugal, the one Atlantic state already deeply involved in ambitious seaward expeditions. After establishing colonies in the second half of the fourteenth century on the Atlantic islands of the Azores and Madeira that yielded a lucrative trade in sugar and wine, the Portuguese in the early fifteenth century quite understandably turned their attention to exploring the coast of West Africa because Africa promised even greater wealth in gold and slaves. Thereafter one Portuguese African

*Timing of voyages of
discovery*

Prince Henry the Navigator. By a fifteenth-century Portuguese painter.

discovery led to another until the Cape of Good Hope was rounded in 1487 and the race for Asiatic spices that led to the most dramatic of European overseas exploits had begun. Thus seen from the perspective of late-medieval Portuguese sailing and trading history, the great discoveries look much less startlingly revolutionary than they do at first glance.

The fifteenth-century Portuguese voyages that served as the major connecting link to the dramatic achievements of the years around 1500 were commissioned by Portugal's Prince Henry "the Navigator" from 1418 until his death in 1460. Starting from an initial base of Ceuta in North Africa, Portuguese ships advanced steadily southward along the West African coastline, braving the ever-hotter sun and establishing forts and trading posts as they went. The extraordinary heroism of the sailors on these ships can easily be appreciated from a mid–fifteenth-century account, according to which four galleys "were provisioned for several years and were away three years, but only one galley returned and even on that galley most of the crew had died. And those which survived could hardly be recognized as human. They had lost flesh and hair, the nails had gone from hands and feet. Their eyes were sunk deep in their heads and they were as black as Moors. They spoke of heat so incredible that it was a marvel that ships and crews were not burnt. They said also that they found no houses or land and they could sail no farther. The farther they sailed, so the sea became more furious and the heat grew more intense. They thought that the other ships had sailed too far and it was impossible that they should be able to return." But return they did, and despite the terrifying tales that such crews told, new expeditions continually were sent out that ventured still farther.

After Henry the Navigator's death in 1460 some slackening in the Portuguese enterprise ensued, but it regained vigor with the accession of King John II (1481–1495). Inasmuch as the Portuguese had already gained full control of the African Gold Coast and slave trade, they naturally began to set their sights on reaching the wealth of Asia. The literal as well as figurative turning point in this effort was the accidental rounding of the tip of southernmost Africa by the Portuguese captain Bartholomew Dias in 1487. Since Dias had only accomplished this feat by being caught in a gale, he pessimistically called this promontory the "Cape of Storms," but John II took a more optimistic view of the matter and renamed it the Cape of Good Hope. Furthermore, John resolved to organize a major naval expedition designed to travel beyond the cape all the way to India.

After several delays John's successor, Manuel I (1495–1521), finally sent off a fleet in 1497 captained by Vasco da Gama which accomplished all that was planned. Da Gama's exploits were so heroic that they later became the basis for the Portuguese national epic, *The Lusiad.* After four months beyond sight of land the intrepid captain rounded Africa, sailed up Africa's east coast to Kenya, and then crossed the

Discovery of Cape of Good Hope

Vasco da Gama's voyage to India

Left: *The Tower of Belem.* Right: *A Portuguese Galleon.* The Tower of Belem, a fifteenth-century fort, stands at the beach where Vasco da Gama departed in 1497 to sail beyond the Cape of Good Hope to India. The galleon shown at the right is the sort of ship da Gama might have sailed in.

Indian Ocean to western India, where he loaded his ships with spices. Two years after his departure da Gama returned, having lost half of his fleet and one-third of his men. But his pepper and cinnamon were so valuable that they made his losses seem worthwhile. Now master of the quickest route to riches in the world, King Manuel swiftly capitalized on da Gama's accomplishment. After 1500 Portuguese trading fleets sailed regularly to India; by 1510 Portuguese arms had established full control of the western Indian coastline, and in 1511 Portuguese ships seized Malacca, a center of the spice trade on the Malay peninsula. The Cape of Good Hope thus had lived up to John II's prophetic name and Europeans had arrived in the Far East to stay.

The decision of the Spanish rulers to underwrite Columbus's famous voyage was directly related to the progress of the Portuguese ventures. Specifically, given the strong likelihood that the Portuguese would dominate the sea lanes leading to Asia by the east in the wake of Dias's successful return in 1488, the only alternative for Portugal's Spanish rivals was to finance someone bold enough to try to reach Asia by sailing west. The popular image of Christopher Columbus (1451–1506) as a visionary who struggled to convince hardened ignoramuses that the world was round does not bear up under scrutiny. In fact Columbus was not "right" but "wrong" insofar as the sphericity of the earth was never in doubt and the stubborn Genoese seaman who had settled in Spain erred in vastly underestimating the distance westward from Europe to Asia. Had Columbus known the actual circum-

Reasons for Columbus's westward voyage

ference of the earth, even he would not have dared to set out because he would have realized that the distance to Asia, assuming no barriers lay between, was too great for ships of his day to traverse. America, then, was discovered as the result of a colossal error in reckoning, but when Columbus, with the financial backing of Queen Isabella of Castile, reached what we know today as the Bahamas and the island of Hispaniola in 1492 after only a month's sailing, he felt fully vindicated.

*The "discovery" of
America*

Strictly speaking, it cannot be said that Columbus "discovered America" for two reasons. In the first place, experts now agree that the earliest Europeans to reach the Western Hemisphere were the Vikings, who touched on present-day Newfoundland, Labrador, and perhaps New England in voyages made around the year 1000. Second, Columbus did not "discover America" because he never knew what he found, dying in the conviction that all the new land he encountered was merely the outer reaches of Asia. Yet neither of these arguments diminishes Columbus's achievement because the Viking landings had been forgotten or ignored throughout Europe for hundreds of years, and if Columbus did not know what he had found, others, following immediately in his path, came to the realization soon thereafter. Although Columbus brought back no Asiatic spices from his voyage of 1492, he did return with some small samples of gold and a few natives who gave promise of entire tribes that might be enslaved. (Columbus and all his contemporaries saw no conflict between converting heathen to Christianity and enslaving them.) This provided sufficient incentive for the Spanish monarchs, Ferdinand and Isabella, to finance three more expeditions by Columbus and many more by others. Soon the mainland was discovered as well as islands, and although Columbus refused until his death to accept the truth, the conclusion quickly became inescapable around 1500 that a new world had indeed been found. Since the recognition that Columbus had really stumbled upon a new world was most widely publicized by the Italian geographer Amerigo Vespucci (one of Vespucci's writings of 1504 was actually called *Mundus novus* or *A New World*), the Western Hemisphere soon became known as "America" after Vespucci's first name.

*The search for a
"southwest passage" to
Asia*

One might well think that the discovery of a new world around 1500 would have delighted the Spanish rulers who had invested in it, but in fact it came as a disappointment, for with a major landmass standing between Europe and Asia, Spain hardly could hope to beat Portugal in the race for spices. Any remaining doubt that two vast oceans separated Europe from East Asia instead of one was completely removed when Vasco Nuñez de Balboa first viewed the Pacific from the Isthmus of Panama in 1513. Not entirely admitting defeat, Ferdinand and Isabella's grandson King Charles accepted Ferdinand Magellan's offer in 1519 to see whether a feasible route to Asia could be found by sailing around South America. But Magellan's voyage merely demonstrated that the perils of a journey around southern Argentina

Ferdinand and Isabella Worshiping the Virgin. A contemporary Spanish painting: the royal pair are shown with two of their children in the company of saints from the Dominican order.

were simply too great: of five ships that left Spain, only one returned three years later, having been forced to circumnavigate the globe. Nor did Magellan himself live to tell this tale; instead, eighteen survivors out of an original crew of two hundred eighty reported that most of their comrades had died from scurvy or starvation and that their captain had been killed in a skirmish with East Indian natives. After this fiasco, all hope for an easy "southwest passage" came to an end.

But if it was disappointing that America loomed as a barricade to the East, it gradually became clear to the Spanish that the New World had much wealth of its own. From the start Columbus's gold samples, in themselves rather paltry, had nurtured hopes that somewhere in America gold might lie piled in ingots, and rumor fed rumor until a few Spanish adventurers really did strike it rich beyond their most avaricious imaginings. At first riches were seized by dint of astonishing feats of arms. In two years, from 1519 to 1521, the *conquistador* (Spanish for conqueror) Hernando Cortés, commanding six hundred men, subjugated the Aztec empire of Mexico numbering a million, and carried off all of the Aztecs' fabulous wealth. Then in 1533 another *conquistador,* Francisco Pizarro, this time with a mere hundred eighty men, plundered the fabled gold of the Incas in conquering Peru. Cortés and Pizarro had the advantage of some cannon and a few horses, but they achieved their victories primarily by sheer courage, treachery, and cruelty. Never before or since have so few men won such great realms against such enormous odds, but seldom have men acted in so ruthless and repugnant a manner.

The conquistadors *plunder the New World for gold*

Left: *The Aztec Ruler Montezuma Coming Forth to Meet Cortés.* Although Cortés here holds out his hand in friendship, he would soon destroy Montezuma and enslave the Aztec nation. From a German book of 1599. Right: *The Silver-mines of Potosí (Bolivia).* A French engraving of 1602: some of the miners work naked because of the heat.

Economic rewards for Spain in the New World

Cortés, Pizarro, and their fellow *conquistadors* fought only for themselves, not for Spain, and knew only how to plunder, not produce, but by the middle of the sixteenth century the Spanish crown had taken governmental control of all Central and South America (except for Brazil, which was colonized by Portugal), and great quantities of bullion were being mined instead of stolen. Most important by far was the mining of silver. Gold, of course, was the more sought-after metal, but after quickly hauling off the stores of gold amassed for centuries by pre-Columbian native civilizations, the Spanish were able to mine only small quantities of gold on their own. On the other hand, however, they soon realized that in areas of Bolivia and Mexico they were sitting on some of the richest silver deposits in the world. By means of forced native labor and new refining techniques, Spanish overlords produced such vast quantities of silver bars by the second half of the sixteenth century that the relative lack of gold was hardly a disappointment. Since livestock farming and the production of sugarcane in sixteenth-century Spanish America also became highly remunerative, the Spanish crown could have had no regrets after all that Columbus had lighted on a new world instead of Asia.

Consequences of European expansion overseas

Subsequent chapters will pursue the continued development of European overseas expansion and colonization; here it may be said that the overall results of the initial achievements were extremely profound in their implications for at least three reasons. First of all, the emergence of Portugal and Spain as Europe's leading long-distance traders in the sixteenth century permanently moved the center of gravity of European economic power away from Italy and the Mediterranean toward the Atlantic. Deprived of their role as conduits of Oriental trade, Genoa became Spain's banker and Venice gradually a tourist attraction, while Atlantic ports bustled with vessels and shone with wealth. Admittedly the prosperity of Portugal and Spain themselves was fleeting, but the other Atlantic states of England, Holland, and France quickly inherited their mantle as the preeminent economic powers of the world. Second, throughout Europe the increase in the circulation of imported goods and the sudden influx of bullion stimulated entrepreneurial ambitions. Simply stated, the opening of the seas around 1500 provided marvelous opportunities for people with ability and daring to make new fortunes, inspiring a sense that success could only lead to success. Thus not only were many enterprising individuals enriched overnight, but the entire sixteenth century was one of great overall economic growth for western Europe.

Unfortunately, however, the enormous riches of America were gained only at an appalling cost in human life. Although exact figures are not available, of an estimated indigenous population of 250,000 on the island of Hispaniola in 1492, only about 500 remained in 1538. As for the far larger population of Mexico, it declined by about 90 percent in the first century of Spanish rule. Not all this loss of life was due to conscious ruthlessness; on the contrary, huge numbers of natives died from epidemic diseases such as small pox and measles introduced by the Europeans to which they had no biological resistance. But countless innocent people also died as the result of merciless exploitation— literally worked so hard by their conquerors that they expired from exhaustion and lack of care. Thus however much Europeans profited from their colonization of the New World, for the original inhabitants the appearance of the white man was an unmitigated disaster.

The human costs

A Spaniard Kicking an Indian. As this sixteenth-century drawing makes clear, the Spanish treatment of the indigenous American population was brutal.

2. THE LUTHERAN UPHEAVAL

Martin Luther. A portrait by
Lucas Cranach.

Causes of the Lutheran
Reformation

Background to Luther's
revolt: superstition

While the Portuguese and Spanish were plowing new paths on the
seas, a German monk named Martin Luther (1483–1546) was searching
for a new path to the understanding of human salvation, and though
his discoveries were made in the quiet of a monastic cell rather than in
exotic tropical climes, their effects were no less momentous. Indeed,
many Europeans felt the impact of Luther's activities much more
immediately and directly than they did the results of the overseas discoveries, because once the German monk started attacking the institutions of the contemporary Roman Church he set off a chain reaction
which rapidly resulted in the secession of much of northern Europe
from the Catholic faith, thereby quickly affecting the religious practices of millions.

In searching for the causes of the Lutheran revolt in Germany, three
main questions need to be dealt with: (1) why Martin Luther happened
to instigate a break with Rome; (2) why large numbers of Germans
rallied to his cause; and (3) why several ruling German princes decided
to put the Lutheran Reformation into effect. Reduced to the barest
essentials, the answers to these questions are that Luther himself broke
with Rome because of his doctrine of justification by faith, that the
German masses followed him primarily because they were swept away
by a surge of religious nationalism, and that the princes were moved
to institute Lutheranism above all because of their desire for absolute
governmental sovereignty. Within a decade preacher, populace, and
princes, so to speak, would all sing the same stirring Lutheran hymn,
"A Mighty Fortress Is Our God," in the same church, but it should
be emphasized that they arrived there by rather different paths.

Many people think that Luther rebelled against Rome because he
was disgusted with contemporary religious abuses—superstitions,
frauds, and the offer of salvation for money—but that is only part of
the story. Certainly abuses in Luther's day were grave and intensely
upsetting to religious idealists. In a world beset by disease and disaster, frail mortals clutched at supernatural straws to seek health on earth
and salvation in the hereafter. Some superstitious men and women,
for example, believed that viewing the consecrated host during Mass
in the morning would guard them from death throughout the day,
and others neglected to swallow the consecrated wafer so that they
could use it later either as a charm to ward off evil, an application to
cure the sick, or a powder to fertilize their crops. Similarly, belief in
the miraculous curative powers of saints was hard to distinguish from
belief in magic. Every saint had his or her specialty: "for botches and
biles, Cosmas and Damian; St. Clare for the eyes, St. Apolline for
teeth, St. Job for pox. And for sore breasts, St. Agatha." Because
alleged relics of Christ and the saints were thought to radiate marvelous healing effects, traffic in relics boomed. Even Luther's patron, the

Elector Frederick the Wise of Saxony, had a collection in his castle church at Wittenberg of 17,000 relics, including a supposed remnant of Moses's burning bush, pieces of the holy cradle, shreds from Christ's swaddling clothes, and thirty-three fragments of the holy cross. As Mark Twain once sardonically observed, there were indeed enough splinters of the holy cross throughout Europe "to shingle a barn."

Superstitions and gross credulity were offensive enough to religious idealists of Luther's stamp, but worse still were the granting of dispensations and the promises of spiritual benefits for money. If a man wished to marry his first cousin, for example, he could usually receive an official religious dispensation allowing the marriage for a fee, and annulments of marriage—divorce being prohibited—similarly came for a price. Most malodorous to many, however, was the sale of indulgences. In Catholic theology, an indulgence is a remission by papal authority of all or part of the temporal punishment due for sin— that is, of the punishment in this life and in purgatory—after the guilt of sin itself is absolved by sacramental confession. As we have seen, the practice of granting indulgences began at the end of the eleventh century as an incentive for encouraging men to become Crusaders. Once it became accepted in the course of the High Middle Ages that the pope could dispense grace from a "Treasury of Merits" (that is, a storehouse of surplus good works piled up by Christ and the saints), it soon was taken for granted that the pope could promise people time off in purgatory as well. But indulgences originally granted for extraordinary deeds gradually came to be sold for money; by the fourteenth century, popes started granting indulgences to raise money for any worthy cause whatsoever, such as the building of cathedrals or hospitals; and finally, in 1476 Pope Sixtus IV (the patron of the Sistine chapel) took the extreme step of declaring that the benefits of indulgences could be extended to the dead already in purgatory as well as to the living. Money, then, could not only save an individual from works of penance but could save his dearest relatives from eons of agonizing torments after death.

Certainly Luther was horrified by the traffic in relics and the sale of indulgences; indeed, the latter provided the immediate grounds for his revolt against Rome. But it was by no means the abuses of the late-medieval Church so much as medieval Catholic theology itself that he came to find thoroughly unacceptable. To this degree the term "Lutheran Reformation" is misleading, for Luther was no mere "reformer" who wanted to cleanse the current religious system of its impurities. Many Christian humanists of Luther's day were reformers in just that sense, but they shrank from breaking with Rome because they had no objections to the basic principles of medieval Catholicism. Luther, on the other hand, by no means would have been satisfied with the mere abolition of abuses because it was the entire Catholic "religion of works" that appalled him.

Simply stated, Luther preferred a rigorously Augustinian system of

Background to Luther's revolt: sale of dispensations and indulgences

Luther's opposition to medieval Catholic theology

theology to a medieval Thomistic one. As we have seen, around the year 400 St. Augustine of Hippo had formulated an uncompromising doctrine of predestination which maintained that God alone determined human salvation and that His decisions concerning whom to save and whom to damn were made from eternity, without any regard to merits that given humans might show while sojourning on earth. This extreme view, however, left so little room for human freedom and responsibility that it was modified greatly in the course of the Middle Ages. Above all, during the twelfth and thirteenth centuries theologians such as Peter Lombard and St. Thomas Aquinas (hence the term "Thomistic") set forth an alternative belief system which rested on two assumptions: (1) since God's saving grace is not irresistible, humans can freely reject God's advances and encompass their own doom; and (2) since the sacramental ministrations of the Church communicate ongoing grace, they help human sinners improve their chances of salvation. Except in emergencies, none of the sacraments could be administered by persons other than priests. Having inherited this power from the Apostle Peter, the members of the clergy alone had the authority to cooperate with God in forgiving sins and in performing the miracle of the Eucharist, whereby the bread and wine were transubstantiated into the body and blood of the Saviour. All of this amounted, in Luther's opinion, to saying that humans could be saved by the performance of "good works," and it was this theology of works that he became prepared to resist even unto death.

*Augustinian and
Thomistic theological
systems*

Martin Luther may ultimately have been a source of inspiration for millions, but at first he was a terrible disappointment to his father. The elder Luther, who had risen from Thuringian German peasant stock and gained prosperity by leasing some mines, wanted his son Martin to rise still further. The father thus sent young Luther to the University of Erfurt to study law, but while there in 1505, possibly as the result of unconscious psychological rebellion against parental pressure, Martin shattered his father's ambitions by becoming a monk instead. Afterward, throughout his life Martin Luther was never to "put on airs." Even at the time of his greatest fame he lived simply and always expressed himself in the vigorous and sometimes earthy vernacular of the German peasantry.

Luther's early life

Like many great figures in the history of religion, Luther arrived at what he conceived to be the truth by a dramatic conversion experience. Once a monk, young Martin zealously pursued all the traditional medieval means for achieving his own salvation. Not only did he fast and pray continuously, but he confessed so often that his exhausted confessor would sometimes jokingly say that his sins were actually trifling and that if he really wanted to have a rousing confession he should go out and do something dramatic like committing adultery. Yet, try as he might, Luther could find no spiritual peace because he feared that he could never perform enough good deeds to

*Luther's search for
religious solace*

placate an angry God. But then, in 1513 he hit upon an insight that granted him relief and changed the course of his life.

Luther's guiding insight pertained to the problem of the justice of God. For years he had worried that God seemed unjust in issuing commandments that He knew men would not observe and then in punishing them with eternal damnation for not observing them. But after becoming a professor of biblical theology at the University of Wittenberg (many members of his monastic order were expected to teach), he was led by the Bible to a new understanding of the problem. Specifically, while meditating on the words in the Psalms "deliver me in thy justice," it suddenly struck him that God's justice had nothing to do with His disciplinary power but rather with His mercy in saving sinful mortals through faith. As Luther later wrote, "At last, by the mercy of God, I began to understand the justice of God as that by which God makes us just in his mercy and through faith . . . and at this I felt as though I had been born again, and had gone through open gates into paradise." Since the fateful moment of truth came to Luther in the tower room of his monastery, it is customarily called his "tower experience."

After that, everything seemed to fall into place. Lecturing on the Pauline Epistles in Wittenberg in the years immediately following 1513, Luther dwelled on the text of St. Paul to the Romans (1:17) "the just shall live by faith" to reach his central doctine of "justification by faith alone." By this he meant that God's justice does not demand endless good works and religious ceremonies, for no one can hope to be saved by his own works. Rather, humans are "justified"—that is, granted salvation—by God's saving grace alone, offered as an utterly unmerited gift to those predestined for salvation. Since this grace is manifested in humans in thoroughly passive faith, men and women are justified from the human perspective by faith alone. In Luther's view those who had faith would do good works anyway, but it was the faith that came first. Although the essence of this doctrine was not original but harked back to the predestinarianism of St. Augustine, it was new for Luther and the early sixteenth century, and if followed to its conclusions could only mean the dismantling of much of the contemporary Catholic religious structure.

At first Luther remained merely an academic lecturer, teaching within the realm of theory, but in 1517 he was goaded into attacking some of the actual practices of the Church by a provocation that was too much for him to bear. The story of the indulgence campaign of 1517 in Germany is colorful but unsavory. The worldly Albert of Hohenzollern, archbishop of Mainz and youngest brother of the elector of Brandenburg, had sunk himself into enormous debt for several discreditable reasons. In 1513 he had to pay large sums for gaining dispensations from the papacy to hold the bishoprics of Magdeburg and Halberstadt concurrently, and for assuming these offices even

His "tower experience"

Justification by faith

The scandalous indulgence campaign

though at twenty-three he was not old enough to be a bishop at all. Not satisfied, when the see of Mainz fell vacant in the next year, Albert gained election to that too, even though he knew full well that the costs of becoming archbishop of Mainz meant still larger payments to Rome. Obtaining the necessary funds by loans from the German banking firm of the Fuggers, he then struck a bargain with Pope Leo X (1513–1521). According to this, Leo proclaimed an indulgence in Albert's ecclesiastical territories on the understanding that half of the income raised would go to Rome for the building of St. Peter's Basilica, with the other half going to Albert so that he could repay the Fuggers. Luther did not know the sordid details of Albert's bargain, but he did know that a Dominican friar named Tetzel soon was hawking indulgences throughout much of northern Germany with Fugger banking agents in his train, and that Tetzel was deliberately giving people the impression that the purchase of an indulgence regardless of contrition in penance was an immediate ticket to heaven for oneself and one's dear departed in purgatory. For Luther this was more than enough because Tetzel's advertising campaign flagrantly violated his own conviction that people are saved by faith, not works. So on October 31, 1517, the earnest theologian nailed a statement of ninety-five theses objecting to Catholic indulgence doctrine onto the door of the castle church of Wittenberg, an act by which the Protestant Reformation is conventionally thought to have begun.

*Luther's theses and break
with Rome*

It is seldom realized that in posting his theses Luther by no means intended to bring his criticism of Tetzel to the public. Quite to the contrary, he wrote his objections in Latin, not German, and meant them only for academic dispute within the confines of Wittenberg University—the castle church door serving as something like the university's bulletin board. But some unknown person translated and published Luther's theses, an event which immediately gained the hitherto obscure monk wide notoriety. Since Tetzel and his allies outside the university did not mean to let the matter rest, Luther was immediately called upon to withdraw his theses or defend himself. At that point, far from backing down, he became ever bolder in his attacks on the government of the Church. In 1519 in public disputation before throngs in Leipzig, Luther defiantly maintained that the pope and all clerics were merely fallible men and that the highest authority for an individual's conscience was the truth of Scripture. Thereupon Pope Leo X responded by charging the monk with heresy, and after that there was no alternative for Luther but to break with the Catholic faith entirely.

*Theology of the new
Lutheran faith*

Luther's year of greatest creative activity came in 1520 when, in the midst of the crisis caused by his defiance, he composed three seminal pamphlets formulating the outlines of what was soon to become the new Lutheran religion. In these writings he put forth his three theological premises: justification by faith, the primacy of Scripture, and "the priesthood of all believers." We have already examined the meaning of the first. By the second he simply meant that the literal meaning of Scripture was always to be preferred to the accretions of tradition, and that all beliefs (such as purgatory) or practices (such as prayers to saints) not explicitly grounded in Scripture were to be rejected. As for "the priesthood of all believers," that meant that the true spiritual estate was the congregation of all the faithful rather than a special club of ordained priests.

From these premises a host of practical consequences followed. Since works themselves had no intrinsic value for salvation, Luther discarded such formalized practices as fasts, pilgrimages, and the veneration of relics. Far more fundamentally, he recognized only baptism and the Eucharist as sacraments (in 1520 he also included penance, but he later changed his mind on this), denying that even these had any supernatural effect in bringing down grace from heaven. For Luther, Christ was really present in the consecrated elements of the Lord's Supper, but there was no grace in the sacrament as such; rather, faith was essential to render the Eucharist effective as a means for aiding the believer along the road to eternal life. To make the meaning of the ceremony clear to all, Luther proposed the substitution of German for Latin in church services, and, to emphasize that those who presided in churches had no supernatural authority, he insisted on calling them merely ministers or pastors rather than priests. On the same grounds there was to be no ecclesiastical hierarchy since neither the pope nor anyone else was a custodian of the keys to heaven, and monasticism was to be abolished since it served no purpose whatsoever. Finally, firm in the belief that no sacramental distinction existed between clergy and laity, Luther argued that ministers could marry, and in 1525 took a wife himself.

Practical implications

Luther and his Wife, Katherine von Bora. Portraits done by Cranach for the couple's wedding in 1525.

Widely disseminated by means of the printing press, Luther's pamphlets of 1520 electrified much of Germany, gaining him broad and enthusiastic popular support. Because this response played a crucial role in determining the future success of the Lutheran movement—emboldening Luther to persevere in his defiance of Rome and soon encouraging some ruling princes to convert to Lutheranism themselves—it is appropriate before continuing to inquire into its causes. Of course, different combinations of motives influenced different people to rally behind Luther, but the uproar in Germany on Luther's behalf was above all a national religious revolt against Rome.

Ever since the high Middle Ages many people throughout Europe had resented the centralization of Church government because it meant the interference of a foreign papacy in local ecclesiastical affairs and the siphoning off of large amounts of ecclesiastical fees and commissions to the papal court. But certain concrete circumstances made Germany in the early sixteenth century particularly ripe for religious revolt. Perhaps greatest among these was the fact that the papacy of that time had clearly lost the slightest hint of apostolic calling but was demanding as much, if not more money from German coffers as before.

Susceptibility of Germany to religious rebellion

Left: *Luther with Dove and Halo.* Right: *Luther as German Hercules.* These two engravings, both executed before the end of 1522 while Luther was still garbed as a monk, exemplify the style of artistic propaganda that helped fuel the Lutheran movement in its earliest years. At the left, the artist Hans Baldung Grien has conceived Luther as a saint inspired by the Holy Spirit in the form of a dove. At the right, an engraving by Hans Holbein the Younger depicts Luther as the "German Hercules," smiting a Catholic theologian. Scholastic authorities such as Aristotle, St. Thomas (Aquinas), and Ockham already lie overwhelmed at Luther's feet.

Although great patrons of the arts, successive popes of Luther's day were worldly scoundrels or sybarites. As Luther was growing up, the Borgia pope, Alexander VI (1492–1503), bribed the cardinals to gain the papacy, used the money raised from the jubilee of 1500 to support the military campaigns of his son Cesare, and was so lascivious in office that he was suspected of seeking the sexual favors of his own daughter Lucrezia. Alexander's scandals could hardly have been outdone, but his successor, Julius II (1503–1515), was interested only in enlarging the papal states by military means (a contemporary remarked that he would have gained the greatest glory had he been a secular prince), and Leo X, the pope obliged to deal with Luther's defiance, was a self-indulgent esthete who, in the words of a modern Catholic historian, "would not have been deemed fit to be a doorkeeper in the house of the Lord had he lived in the days of the apostles." Under such circumstances it was bad enough for Germans to know that fees sent to Rome were being used to finance papal politics and the upkeep of luxurious courts, but worse still to pay money in the realization that Germany had no influence in Italian papal affairs, for Germans, unlike French or Spaniards, were seldom represented in the College of Cardinals and practically never gained employment in the papal bureaucracy.

In this overheated atmosphere, reformist criticisms voiced by both traditional clerical moralists and the new breed of Christian humanists exacerbated resentments. Ever since about 1400 prominent German critics of the papacy had been saying that the entire Church needed to be reformed "in head and members," and as the fifteenth century progressed, anonymous prophecies mounted to the effect, for example, that a future heroic emperor would reform the Church by removing the papacy from Rome to the Rhineland. Then in the early years of the sixteenth century, Christian humanists began to chime in with their own brand of satirical propaganda. Most eloquent of these humanists, of course, was Erasmus, who lampooned the religious abuses of his day with no mercy for Rome. Thus in the *Praise of Folly*, first published in 1511 and frequently reprinted, Erasmus stated that if popes were ever forced to lead Christlike lives, no one would be more disconsolate than themselves, and in his more daring pamphlet called *Julius Excluded*, published anonymously in Basel in 1517, the clever satirist imagined a dialogue held before the pearly gates in which Pope Julius II was locked out of heaven by Saint Peter because of his transgressions.

In addition to the objective reality of a corrupt Rome and the circulation of anti-Roman propaganda, a final factor that made Germany

Pope Leo X. A portrait by the Italian Renaissance master, Raphael.

Pope Alexander VI: "Appearance and Reality." Even before Luther initiated the German Reformation, anonymous critics of the dissolute Alexander VI surreptitiously spread propaganda showing him to be a devil. By lifting a flap Alexander is transformed into a monster who proclaims "I am the pope."

*The role of the German
universities*

ready for revolt in Luther's time was the belated growth of universities. All revolts need to have some general headquarters; universities were the most natural centers for late-medieval religious revolts because groups of enthusiastic, educated young people assembled in universities who were accustomed to working together, who could formulate doctrinal positions with assurance, and who could turn out militant manifestoes at a moment's notice. There had hardly been any universities on German soil until a spate of new foundations between 1450 and 1517 provided many spawning grounds for cultural nationalism and religious resistance to Rome. Luther's own University of Wittenberg was founded as late as 1502, but soon enough it had become the cradle of the Lutheran Reformation, offering immediate support to its embattled hero.

*Luther's inflammatory
pamphlets*

Still, of course, there would have been no Lutheran Reformation without Luther himself, and the daring monk did the most to enflame Germany's dry kindling of resentment in his pamphlets of 1520, above all in one entitled *To the Christian Nobility of the German Nation*. Here, in highly intemperate colloquial German, Luther stated that "if the pope's court were reduced ninety-nine percent it would still be large enough to give decisions on matters of faith"; that "the cardinals have

Left: *The Seven-Headed Papal Beast*. Right: *The Seven-headed Martin Luther*. Around 1530 a Lutheran cartoon was circulated in Germany which turned the papacy into the "seven-headed beast" of the Book of Revelation. The papacy's "seven heads" consist of pope, cardinals, bishops, and priests; the sign on the cross reads "for money, a sack full of indulgences"; and a devil is seen emerging from an indulgence treasure chest below. In response, a German Catholic propagandist showed Luther as Revelation's "beast." In the Catholic conception Luther's seven heads show him by turn to be a hypocrite, a fanatic, and "Barabbas"—the thief who should have been crucified instead of Jesus.

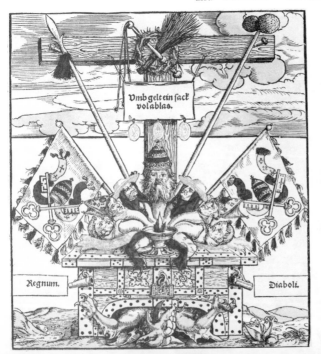

sucked Italy dry and now turn to Germany"; and that, given Rome's corruption, "the reign of Antichrist could not be worse." Needless to say, once this savage indictment was lodged, everyone wanted to read it. Whereas the average press run of a printed book before 1520 had been one thousand copies, the first run of *To the Christian Nobility* was four thousand, and these copies were sold out in a few days with many more thousands following.

Meanwhile, even as Luther's pamphlets were selling so rapidly, his personal drama riveted all onlookers. Late in 1520 the German rebel responded to Pope Leo X's bull ordering his recantation by casting not only the bull but all of Church law as well onto a roaring bonfire in front of a huge crowd. With the lines so drawn, events moved with great swiftness. Since Luther in the eyes of the Church was now a stubborn heretic, he was formally "released" to his lay overlord, the Elector Frederick the Wise, for proper punishment. Normally this would have meant certain death at the stake, but in this case Frederick was loath to silence the pope's antagonist. Instead, claiming that Luther had not yet received a fair hearing, he brought him early in 1521 to be examined by a "diet" (that is, a formal assembly) of the princes of the Holy Roman Empire convening in the city of Worms.

His appearance at the Diet of Worms

At Worms the initiative lay with the presiding officer, the newly elected Holy Roman Emperor, Charles V. Charles was not a German; rather, as a member of the Habsburg family by his paternal descent, he had been born and bred in his ancestral holding of the Netherlands. Since he additionally held Austria, and as grandson of Ferdinand and Isabella by his maternal descent, all of Spain, including extensive Spanish possessions in Italy and America, the emperor had primarily international rather than national interests and surely thought of Catholicism as a sort of glue necessary to hold together all his far-flung territories. Thus from the start Charles had no sympathy for Luther, and since Luther fearlessly refused to back down before the emperor, declaring instead "here I stand," it soon became clear that Luther would be condemned by the power of state as well as by Church. But just then Frederick the Wise once more intervened, this time by arranging a "kidnapping" whereby Luther was spirited off to the elector's castle of the Wartburg and kept out of harm's way for a year.

Luther vs. the Emperor Charles V

Thereafter Luther was never again to be in danger of his life. Although the Diet of Worms did issue an edict shortly after his disappearance proclaiming him an outlaw, the Edict of Worms was never properly enforced because, with Luther in hiding, Charles V soon left Germany to conduct a war with France. In 1522 Luther returned in triumph from the Wartburg to Wittenberg to find that all the changes in ecclesiastical government and ceremonial he had called for had spontaneously been put into practice by his university cohorts. Then, in rapid succession, several German princes formally converted to Lutheranism, bringing their territories with them. Thus by around

Lutheranism triumphant

The Wartburg. The castle in central Germany where Luther was hidden after the Diet of Worms.

1530 a considerable part of Germany had been brought over to the new faith.

Importance of German princely support

At this point, then, the last of the three major questions regarding the early history of Lutheranism arises: Why did German princes, secure in their own powers, heed Luther's call by establishing Lutheran religious practices within their territories? The importance of this question should by no means be underestimated, because no matter how much intense admiration Luther may have gained from the German populace, his cause surely would have failed had it not been for the decisive intervention and support of constituted political authorities. There had been heretics aplenty in Europe before, but most of them had died at the stake, as Luther would have without the intervention of Frederick the Wise. And even had Luther lived, spontaneous popular expressions of support alone would not have succeeded in instituting Lutheranism because such could easily have been put down by the power of the state. In fact, although in the early years of Luther's revolt he was more or less equally popular throughout Germany, only in those territories where rulers formally established Lutheranism (mostly in the German north) did the new religion prevail, whereas in the others Luther's sympathizers were forced to flee, face death, or conform to Catholicism. In short, the word of the prince in religious matters was simply law.

This distinction between populace and princes, however, should not obscure the fact that the motivations of both for turning to Lutheranism were similar, with the emphasis on the princely side being the search for sovereignty. As little as common people liked the idea of money being pumped off to Rome, princes liked it less: German princes assembled at the Diet of Augsburg in 1500, for example, went so far as to demand the refund of some of the ecclesiastical dues sent to Rome on the grounds that Germany was being drained of its coin. Since such demands fell on deaf ears, many princes were quick to perceive that if Lutheranism were adopted, ecclesiastical dues would not be sent to support ill-loved foreigners and much of the savings would directly or indirectly wind up in their own treasuries.

Economic motives for adoption of Lutheranism

Yet the matter of taxation was only part of the larger issue of the search for absolute governmental sovereignty. Throughout Europe the major political trend in the years around 1500 was toward making the state omnicompetent in all walks of life, religious as well as secular. Hence rulers sought to control the appointments of Church officials in their own realms and to limit or curtail the independent jurisdictions of Church courts. Because the papacy in this period had to fight off the attacks of internal clerical critics who wanted recognition of the "conciliarist" principle that general councils of prelates rather than popes should rule the Church (see Chapter 13), many popes found it advantageous to sign concordats with the most powerful rulers in the West—primarily the kings of France and Spain—whereby they granted the rulers much of the sovereignty they wanted in return for support against conciliarism. Thus in 1482 Sixtus IV conceded to the Spanish monarchs Ferdinand and Isabella the right to name candidates for all major Church offices; in 1487 Innocent VIII consented to the establishment of a Spanish Inquisition controlled by the crown which gave the rulers extraordinary powers in dictating religious policies; and in 1516, by the Concordat of Bologna, Leo X granted the choice of bishops and abbots in France to the French king, Francis I. In Germany, however, primarily because there was no political unity, princes were not strong enough to gain such concessions. Hence what they could not achieve by concordats some decided to wrest by force.

Political motives

In this determination they were fully abetted by Luther. Certainly as early as 1520 the fiery reformer recognized that he could never hope to institute new religious practices without the strong arm of the princes behind him, so he implicitly encouraged them to disappropriate the wealth of the Catholic church as an incentive for creating a new order. At first the princes bided their time, but when they realized that Luther had enormous public support and that Charles V would not act swiftly to defend the Catholic faith, several moved to introduce Lutheranism into their territories. Motives of personal piety cannot be discounted from case to case, but the common aim of gaining sovereignty by naming pastors, cutting off fees to Rome, and curtailing the jurisdiction of Catholic church courts ultimately must have been the most decisive consideration. Given the added fact that under Lutheranism monasteries could be shut down and their wealth simply pocketed by the princes, the temptation to ordain the new faith regardless of any deeply felt religious convictions must have been simply overwhelming.

The princes seize their opportunity

*Luther's growing political
and social conservatism*

Once safely ensconced in Wittenberg as the protégé of princes, Luther began to express ever more vehemently his own profound conservatism in political and social matters. In a treatise of 1523, *On Temporal Authority,* he insisted that "godly" rulers must always be obeyed in all things and that even ungodly ones should never be actively resisted since tyranny "is not to be resisted but endured." Then, in 1525, when peasants throughout Germany rose up in economic revolt against their landlords—in some places encouraged by the religious radical Thomas Münzer (c. 1490–1525), who urged the use of fire and sword against "ungodly" powers—Luther responded with intense hostility. In his vituperative pamphlet of 1525, *Against the Thievish, Murderous Hordes of Peasants,* he went so far as to urge all who could to hunt the rebels down like mad dogs, to "strike, strangle, stab secretly or in public, and remember that nothing can be more poisonous than a man in rebellion." Once the princes had ruthlessly put down the Peasants' Revolt of 1525, the firm alliance of Lutheranism with the powers of the state helped ensure social peace. In fact, after the bloody punishment of the peasant rebels there was never again to be a mass lower-class uprising in Germany.

Luther's last years

As for Luther himself, he concentrated in his last years on debating with younger, more radical, religious reformers, and on offering spiritual counsel to all who sought it. Never tiring in his amazingly prolific literary activity, he wrote an average of one treatise every two weeks for twenty-five years. To the end Luther was unswerving in his faith: on his deathbed in 1546 he responded to the question "Will you stand firm in Christ and the doctrine which you have preached?" with a resolute "Yes."

3. THE SPREAD OF PROTESTANTISM

*Other forms of
Protestantism*

Originating as a term applied to Lutherans who "protested" an action of a German Imperial Diet of 1529, the word "Protestant" has come to mean any non-Catholic, non–Eastern Orthodox Christian. In fact it was soon applied to non-Lutherans after 1529 because the particular form of Protestantism developed by Luther did not prove to be popular much beyond its native environment of Germany. To be sure, Lutheranism was instituted as the state religion of Denmark, Norway, and Sweden by official decrees of rulers made during the 1520s, and remains the religion of most Scandinavians today. But elsewhere early Protestantism spread in different forms. In England a break with Rome was introduced from above, just as in Germany and Scandinavia, but since Lutheranism appeared too radical for the reigning English monarch, a compromise variety of religious belief and practice, subsequently known as Anglicanism (in America, Episcopalianism), was worked out. On the other extreme, Protestantism spread more spontaneously in several cities of Switzerland and there soon took on forms that were more radical than Lutheranism.

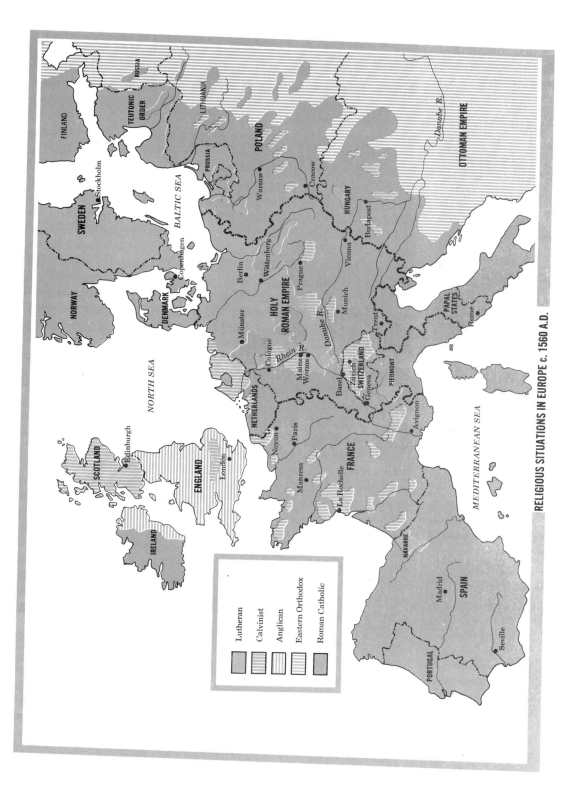

RELIGIOUS SITUATIONS IN EUROPE c. 1560 A.D.

FINLAND

RUSSIA

TEUTONIC ORDER

LITHUANIA

PRUSSIA

POLAND

Warsaw

Cracow

HUNGARY

Budapest

Danube R.

OTTOMAN EMPIRE

Stockholm

BALTIC SEA

SWEDEN

Copenhagen

Wittenberg

Berlin

Prague

Vienna

NORWAY

DENMARK

Münster

HOLY ROMAN EMPIRE

Munich

Trent

PAPAL STATES

Rome

NORTH SEA

Cologne

Rhein R.

Danube R.

Mainz

Worms

Basel

Zürich

SWITZERLAND

Geneva

PIEDMONT

Avignon

MEDITERRANEAN SEA

SCOTLAND

Edinburgh

ENGLAND

London

NETHERLANDS

Noyon

Paris

FRANCE

Manresa

La Rochelle

IRELAND

NAVARRE

Madrid

SPAIN

Seville

PORTUGAL

Lutheran

Calvinist

Anglican

Eastern Orthodox

Roman Catholic

Henry VIII. Portrait by Hans
Holbein.

Although the original blow against the Roman Church in England was struck by the head of the government, King Henry VIII (1509–1547), in breaking with Rome the English monarch had the support of most of his subjects. For this there were at least three reasons. First, in England, as in Germany, many people in the early sixteenth century had come to resent Rome's corruption and the siphoning off of the country's wealth to pay for the worldly pursuits of foreign popes. Second, England had already been the scene for some time of protests against religious abuses voiced by John Wyclif's heretical followers known as Lollards. The Lollards had indeed been driven underground in the course of the fifteenth century, but numbers of them survived in pockets throughout England, where they promulgated their anti-clerical ideas whenever they could and enthusiastically welcomed Henry VIII's revolt from Rome when it occurred. Finally, soon after the outbreak of the Reformation in Germany, Lutheran ideas were brought into England by travelers and by the circulation of printed tracts. As early as 1520 a Lutheran group was meeting at the University of Cambridge, and Lutheranism began to gain more and more clandestine strength as the decade progressed.

*King Henry VIII's
divorce suit*

Despite all this, England would never have broken with Rome had Henry VIII not issued the command because of his marital difficulties. In 1527 the imperious Henry had been married for eighteen years to Ferdinand and Isabella's daughter, Catherine of Aragon, yet all the offspring of this union had died in infancy, save only the Princess Mary. Since Henry needed a male heir to preserve the succession of his Tudor dynasty, and since Catherine was now past childbearing age, Henry had good reasons of state to rid himself of her, and in 1527 an immediate incentive arose when he became infatuated with the dark-eyed lady-in-waiting, Anne Boleyn, who would not give in to his advances out of wedlock. The king hence appealed to Rome to allow the severance of his marriage to Catherine so that he could make Anne his queen. Although the law of the Church did not sanction divorce, it did provide that a marriage might be annulled if proof could be given that conditions existing at the time of the wedding had made it unlawful. Accordingly, the king's representatives, recalling that Queen Catherine had previously been married to Henry's older brother, who had died shortly after the ceremony was performed, rested their case on a passage from the Bible which pronounced it "an unclean thing" for a man to take his brother's wife and cursed such a marriage with childlessness (Leviticus 20:31).

Henry's break with Rome

Henry's suit put the reigning pope, Clement VII (1523–1534), in a quandary. If he rejected the king's appeal, England would probably be lost to Catholicism, for Henry was indeed firmly convinced that the Scriptural curse had blighted his chances of perpetuating his dynasty. On the other hand, if the pope granted the annulment he would provoke the wrath of the Emperor Charles V, Catherine of Aragon's nephew, for Charles was then on a military campaign in

Italy and threatening the pope with a loss of his temporal power. There seemed nothing for Clement to do but to procrastinate. At first he made a pretense of having the question settled in England, empowering his officials to hold a court of inquiry to determine whether the marriage to Catherine had been legal. Then, after a long delay, he suddenly transferred the case to Rome. But meanwhile Henry had lost patience and resolved to take matters into his own hands. In 1531 the king obliged an assembly of English clergy to recognize him as "the supreme head" of the English Church. Next he induced Parliament to enact a series of laws abolishing all payments to Rome and proclaiming the English Church an independent, national unit, subject alone to royal authority. With the passage of the parliamentary Act of Supremacy (1534), declaring "the King's highness to be supreme head of the Church of England [having] the authority to redress all errors, heresies, and abuses," the last bonds uniting the English Church to Rome had been cut.

Yet these enactments did not yet make England a Protestant country. Quite to the contrary, although the break with Rome was followed by the dissolution of all England's monasteries, with their lands and wealth being sold to many of the king's loyal supporters, the system of Church government by bishops (episcopalianism) was retained, and the English Church remained Catholic in doctrine. The Six Articles, promulgated by Parliament in 1539 at Henry VIII's behest, left no room for doubt as to official orthodoxy: oral confession to priests, masses for the dead, and clerical celibacy were all confirmed; moreover, the Catholic doctrine of the Eucharist was not only confirmed but its denial made punishable by death.

The conservative nature of the Henrician Reformation

Nonetheless, the influence of Protestantism in the country at large at this time was growing, and during the reign of Henry's son, Edward VI (1547–1553), Protestantism gained the ascendancy. Since the new king (born from Henry's union with his third wife, Jane Seymour) was only nine years old when he inherited the crown, it was inevitable that the policies of the government should be dictated by powers behind the throne. The men most active in this regard were Thomas Cranmer, archbishop of Canterbury, and the dukes of Somerset and Northumberland, who successfully dominated the regency. Inasmuch as all three had strong Protestant leanings, the creeds and ceremonies of the Church of England were soon drastically altered. Priests were permitted to marry; English was substituted for Latin in the services; the veneration of images was abolished; and new articles of belief were drawn up repudiating all sacraments except baptism and communion and affirming the Lutheran doctrine of justification by faith alone. Thus when the youthful Edward died in 1553 it seemed as if England had definitely entered the Protestant camp.

The consolidation of English Protestantism

But Edward's pious Catholic successor, Mary (1553–1558), Henry VIII's daughter by Catherine of Aragon, thought otherwise. Because Mary associated the revolt against Rome with her mother's humilia-

The Burning of Archbishop Cranmer. In this Protestant conception an ugly Catholic, "Friar John," directs the proceedings, while the martyred Cranmer repeats Christ's words, "Lord, receive my spirit." John Foxe's *Book of Martyrs* (1563), in which this engraving first appeared, was an extraordinarily successful piece of English Protestant propaganda.

Popular resistance to Queen Mary's Catholicism

tions and her own removal from direct succession, upon coming to the throne she attempted to turn the clock back. Not only did she restore the celebration of the Mass and the rule of clerical celibacy, but she prevailed upon Parliament to vote the unconditional return of England to papal allegiance. Yet her policies ended in failure for several reasons. First of all, not only had Protestantism by then already sunk in deeply among the English masses, but many of the leading families which had profited from Henry VIII's dissolution of the monasteries had become particularly committed to Protestantism because a restoration of Catholic monasticism would have meant the loss of their newly acquired wealth. Then too, although Mary ordered the burning of Cranmer and a few hundred Protestant extremists, these executions were insufficient to wipe out religious resistance—indeed, Protestant propaganda about "Bloody Mary" and the "fires of Smithfield" soon actually hardened resistance to Mary's rule, making her seem like a vengeful persecutor. But perhaps the most serious cause of Mary's failure was her marriage to Philip, Charles V's son and heir to the Spanish throne. Although the marriage treaty stipulated that in the event of Mary's death Philip could not succeed her, patriotic Englishmen never trusted him. Hence when the queen allowed herself to be drawn by Philip into a war with France on Spain's behalf, in which England lost Calais, its last foothold on the European continent, the nation became highly disaffected. No one knows what might have happened next because death soon after ended Mary's troubled reign.

The question of whether England was to be Catholic or Protestant was thereupon settled definitively in favor of Protestantism by Elizabeth I (1558–1603). Daughter of Anne Boleyn and one of the most capable and popular monarchs ever to sit on the English throne, Elizabeth was predisposed in favor of Protestantism by the circumstances of her father's marriage as well as by her upbringing. But Elizabeth was no zealot, and wisely recognized that ordaining radical Protestantism in England posed the danger of provoking bitter sectarian strife because some English people were still Catholic and others resisted extremism. Accordingly, she presided over what is customarily known as "the Elizabethan compromise." By a new Act of Supremacy (1559), Elizabeth repealed all of Mary's Catholic legislation, prohibited the exercise of any authority by foreign religious powers, and made herself "supreme governor" of the English Church—a more Protestant title than Henry VIII's "supreme headship" insofar as most Protestants believed that Christ alone was the head of the Church. At the same time she accepted most of the Protestant ceremonial reforms instituted in the reign of her brother Edward. On the other hand, she retained Church government by bishops and left the definitions of some controversial articles of the faith, especially the meaning of the Eucharist, vague enough so that all but the most extreme Catholics and Protestants could accept them. Long after Elizabeth's death this settlement remained in effect. Indeed, as a result of the Elizabethan compromise, the Church of England today is broad enough to include such diverse elements as the "Anglo-Catholics," who differ from Roman Catholics only in rejecting papal supremacy, and the "low-church" Anglicans, who are as thoroughgoing in their Protestant practices as members of most other modern Protestant denominations.

The Elizabethan religious settlement

Philip of Spain and Mary Tudor. This double portrait was done on the occasion of the royal marriage.

*Protestantism in
Switzerland*

Zwinglianism

Anabaptism

If the English compromise came about through royal decision-making, in Switzerland more spontaneous movements to establish Protestantism resulted in the victory of greater radicalism. In the early sixteenth century Switzerland was neither ruled by kings nor dominated by all-powerful territorial princes; instead, prosperous cities there were either independent or on the verge of becoming so. Hence when the leading citizens of a Swiss municipality decided to adopt Protestant reforms no one could stop them, and Protestantism in Switzerland could usually take its own course. Although religious arrangements tended at first to vary in detail from city to city, the three main forms of Protestantism that emerged in Switzerland from about 1520 to 1550 were Zwinglianism, Anabaptism, and, most fateful for Europe's future, Calvinism.

Zwinglianism, founded by Ulrich Zwingli (1484–1531) in Zürich, was the most moderate form of the three. At first a somewhat indifferent Catholic priest, around 1516 Zwingli was led by close study of the Bible, as Luther was, to conclude that contemporary Catholic theology and religious observances conflicted with the Gospel. But he did not speak out until Luther set the precedent. Then, in 1522, Zwingli started attacking the authority of the Catholic church in Zürich, and soon all Zürich and much of northern Switzerland had accepted his leadership in instituting reforms that closely resembled those of the Lutherans in Germany. Yet Zwingli did differ from Luther concerning the theology of the Eucharist: whereas Luther believed in the real presence of Christ's body, for Zwingli Christ was present merely in spirit. Thus for him the sacrament conferred no grace at all and was to be retained merely as a memorial service. This disagreement may seem trifling to many of us today, but then it sufficed to prevent Lutherans and Zwinglians from uniting in a common Protestant front. Going his way, Zwingli fell in battle against Catholic forces in 1531, whereupon his successors in Zürich lost their leadership over Swiss Protestantism, and the Zwinglian movement was soon after absorbed by the far more radical Protestantism of John Calvin.

Before that happened, however, the phenomenon of Anabaptism briefly flared up in Switzerland and also Germany. The first Anabaptists were members of Zwingli's circle in Zürich, but they quickly broke with him around 1525 on the issues of infant baptism and their conception of an exclusive church of true believers. The name Anabaptism means "rebaptism," and stemmed from the Anabaptists' conviction that baptism should only be administered to adults because infants had no understanding of the meaning of the service. Yet this was only one manifestation of the Anabaptists' main belief that men and women were not born into any church. Although Luther and Zwingli alike taught the "priesthood of all believers," they still insisted that everyone, believer or not, should attend services and be part of one and the same officially instituted religious community. But the Anabaptists were sectarians or separatists, firm in the conviction that joining the true Church should be the product of an individual's inspired decision. For them, one had to follow the guidance of one's own "inner light" in opting for Church membership, and the rest of the world could go its own way. Since this was a hopelessly apolitical doctrine in an age when almost everyone assumed that Church and state were inextricably connected, Anabaptism was bound to be anathema to the established powers, both Protestant and Catholic. Yet in its first few years the movement did gain numerous adherents in Switzerland and Germany, above all because it appealed to sincere religious piety in calling for extreme simplicity of worship, pacifism, and strict biblical morality.

Unhappily for the fortunes of Anabaptism, a highly unrepresentative group of Anabaptist extremists managed to gain control of the city of Münster in northwestern Germany in 1534. When fellow extremists from surrounding areas came pouring in, Münster became a new Jerusalem where all the vagaries of the lunatic fringe of the movement were put into practice. The property of unbelievers was confiscated and polygamy was introduced. A former tailor named John of Leyden assumed the title of king, proclaiming himself the successor of David, with a mission to conquer the world and destroy the heathen. But after a little more than a year Münster was recaptured by Catholic forces and the leaders of Zion were put to death by excruciating tortures. Given that Anabaptism was already proscribed by many govern-

The turning point at Münster

The Anabaptists' Cages, Then and Now. After the three Anabaptist leaders who had reigned in Münster for a year were executed in 1535, their corpses were prominently displayed in cages hung from a tower of the marketplace church. As can be seen from the photo on the right, the bones are now gone but the iron cages remain to this very day as a grisly reminder of the horrors of sixteenth-century religious strife.

The Siege of Münster in 1534

ments, this episode thoroughly discredited the movement and all of
its adherents were subjected to ruthless persecution throughout Germany, Switzerland, and wherever else they could be found. Among
the few who survived were some who banded together in the Men-
nonite sect, named for its founder, the Dutchman Menno Simons
(1492–1559). This sect, dedicated to the pacifism and simple "religion
of the heart" of original Anabaptism, has continued to exist until the
present. Various Anabaptist tenets were also revived later by religious
groups such as the Quakers and different Baptist and Pentecostal sects.

A year after events in Münster sealed the fate of Anabaptism, a
twenty-six-year-old French Protestant named John Calvin (1509–1564),

John Calvin

who had fled to the Swiss city of Basel to escape religious persecution,
published the first version of his *Institutes of the Christian Religion,* a
work which was soon to prove the single most influential systematic
formulation of Protestant theology ever written. Born in Noyon in
northern France, Calvin originally had been trained for the law and
around 1533 was studying the Greek and Latin classics while living
off the income from a Church benefice. But then, as he later wrote,
while he was "obstinately devoted to the superstitions of Popery," a
stroke of light made him feel that God was extricating him from "an
abyss of filth," and he thereupon opted for becoming a Protestant
propagandist. Though some of these details resemble the early career
of Luther, there was one essential difference: namely, whereas Luther
was always a highly volatile personality, Calvin remained a cool French

John Calvin. A recently discovered anonymous portrait.

legalist through and through. Thus, whereas Luther never wrote systematic theology but only responded to given problems as they arose
or as the mood struck him, Calvin resolved in his *Institutes* to set forth
all the principles of Protestantism comprehensively, logically, and consistently. Accordingly, after several revisions and enlargements (the

definitive edition appeared in 1559), Calvin's *Institutes of the Christian Religion* became the most theologically authoritative statement of basic Protestant beliefs and the nearest Protestant equivalent of St. Thomas Aquinas's *Summa Theologica*.

The hallmark of Calvin's rigorous theology in the *Institutes* is that he started with the omnipotence of God and worked downward. For Calvin the entire universe is utterly dependent on the will of the Almighty, who created all things for his greater glory. Because of the original fall from grace, all human beings are sinners by nature, bound hand and foot to an evil inheritance they cannot escape. Nevertheless, the Lord for reasons of His own has predestined some for eternal salvation and damned all the rest to the torments of hell. Nothing that human beings may do can alter their fate; their souls are stamped with God's blessing or curse before they are born. But this does not mean, in Calvin's opinion, that Christians should be indifferent to their conduct on earth. If they are among the elect, God will implant in them the desire to live right. Upright conduct is a sign, though not an infallible one, that whoever practices it has been chosen to sit at the throne of glory. Public profession of faith and participation in the sacrament of the Lord's Supper are also presumptive signs of election to be saved. But most of all, Calvin required an active life of piety and morality as a solemn obligation resting upon members of the Christian commonwealth. For him, good Christians should conceive of themselves as chosen instruments of God with a mission to help in the fulfillment of His purposes on earth, not striving for their souls' salvation but for the glory of God. In other words, Calvin clearly did not encourage his readers to sit with folded hands, serene in the knowledge that their fate was sealed.

Calvin's theology

Although Calvin always acknowledged a great theological debt to Luther, his religious teachings differed from those of the Wittenberg reformer in several essentials. First of all, Luther's attitude toward proper Christian conduct in the world was much more passive than Calvin's: for the former, the good Christian should merely endure the trials of this life in suffering, whereas for the latter the world was to be mastered in unceasing labor for God's sake. Second, Calvin's religion was more legalistic and more nearly an Old Testament faith than Luther's. This can be illustrated in the attitude of the two men toward Sabbath observance. Luther's conception of Sunday was similar to that which prevails among most Christians today. He insisted, of course, that his followers attend church, but he did not demand that during the remainder of the day they refrain from all pleasure or work. Calvin, on the other hand, revived the Jewish Sabbath with its strict taboos against anything faintly resembling worldliness. Finally, the two men differed explicitly on basic matters of Church government and ritual. Although Luther broke with the Catholic system of a gradated ecclesiastical hierarchy, Lutheran district superintendents were not unlike bishops, and Luther also retained a good many features of Roman worship such as altars and vestments (special clothing for the

Calvinism and Lutheranism compared

Services in a Calvinist Church. "Four bare walls and a sermon."

clergy). On the other hand, Calvin utterly rejected everything that smacked to him of "popery." Thus he argued for the elimination of all traces of the hierarchical system, instead having congregational election of ministers and assemblies of ministers and "elders" (laymen responsible for maintaining proper religious conduct among the faithful) governing the entire Church. Further, he insisted on the barest simplicity in church services, prohibiting all ritual, vestments, instrumental music, images, and stained-glass windows. When these teachings were put into practice, Calvinist services became little more than "four bare walls and a sermon."

Not content with mere theory, Calvin was intent upon putting his teachings into practice. Sensing an opportunity to influence the course of events in the French-speaking Swiss city of Geneva, then in the throes of combined political and religious upheaval, he moved there late in 1536 and began preaching and organizing immediately. In 1538 his activities caused him to be expelled, but in 1541 he returned to Geneva, and this time soon had both the government and the religion of the city completely under his sway. Under Calvin's guidance Geneva's government became theocratic. Supreme authority in the city was vested in a "Consistory," made up of twelve lay elders and five ministers. (Although Calvin himself was seldom the presiding officer, he usually dominated the Consistory's decisions until his death in 1564.) In addition to passing on legislation submitted to it by a congregation of ministers, the Consistory had as its main function the supervision of morals. This activity was carried out not merely by the punishment of antisocial conduct but by a persistent snooping into the private life

Calvinist theocracy in Geneva

of every individual. Geneva was divided into districts, and a committee of the Consistory visited every household without warning to check on the habits of its members. Even the mildest forms of self-indulgence were strictly prohibited. Dancing, card-playing, attending the theater, working or playing on the Sabbath—all were outlawed as works of the devil. Innkeepers were forbidden to allow anyone to consume food or drink without first saying grace, or to permit any patron to stay up after nine o'clock. Needless to say, penalties were severe. Not only were murder and treason classified as capital crimes, but also adultery, "witchcraft," blasphemy, and heresy. During the first four years after Calvin gained control in Geneva, there were no fewer than 58 executions out of a total population of only 16,000.

As reprehensible as such interference in the private sphere may seem today, in the middle of the sixteenth century Calvin's Geneva appeared as a beacon-light of thoroughgoing Protestantism to thousands throughout Europe. Calvin's disciple John Knox, for example, who brought Calvinism to Scotland, declared that Geneva under Calvin was "the most perfect school of Christ that ever was on earth since the days of the Apostles." Accordingly, many foreigners flocked to the "perfect school" for refuge or instruction, and usually returned home to become ardent proselytizers of Calvinism. Moreover, since Calvin himself thought of Geneva as merely a way station for bringing Calvinism to France and the rest of the world, he encouraged the dispatching of missionaries and propaganda into hostile territories, with the result that from about the middle of the sixteenth century Geneva became the center of a concerted and militant attempt to spread the new faith far and wide. Soon Calvinists became a majority in Scotland, where they were known as Presbyterians; a majority in Holland, where they founded the Dutch Reformed Church; a substantial minority in France, where they were called Huguenots; and a substantial minority in England, where they were called Puritans. In addition, Calvinist preachers zealously tried to make converts in most other parts of Europe. But just as the Calvinists were fanning out through Europe, the forces of Catholicism were hardening in their determination to head off any further Protestant advances. The result, as we will see in the next chapter, was that many parts of a hitherto united Christendom became mired in bloody religious wars for decades after.

4. THE PROTESTANT HERITAGE

Inasmuch as Luther's revolt from Rome and the spread of Protestantism occurred after the height of the civilization of the Renaissance and before some particularly fundamental advances in modern European political, economic, and social development, it is tempting to think of historical events unfolding in an inevitably cumulative way: Renaissance, Reformation, "Triumphs of the Modern World." But history

Calvin as Seen by His Friends and His Enemies. Above, an idealized contemporary portrait of Calvin as a pensive scholar. Below, a Catholic caricature in which Calvin's face is a composite made from fish, a toad, and a chicken drumstick.

The place of Protestantism in Europe's historical development

is seldom as neat as that. Although scholars will continue to disagree on points of detail, most agree that the Protestant Reformation inherited little from the civilization of the Renaissance, that indeed in certain basic respects Protestant principles were completely at odds with major assumptions of Renaissance humanists. As for the relationship between "Protestantism and Progress," the most apt formulation appears to be a statement from a book of that title by the great German religious historian Ernst Troeltsch, according to which "Protestantism has furthered the rise of the modern world . . . [but nowhere] does it appear as its actual creator."

In considering the relationship between the Renaissance and the origins of the Protestant Reformation, it would admittedly be false to say that the one had absolutely nothing to do with the other. Certainly, criticisms of religious abuses by Christian humanists helped prepare Germany for the Lutheran revolt. Furthermore, close humanistic textual study of the Bible led to the publication of new, reliable biblical editions used by the Protestant reformers. In this regard a direct line ran from the Italian humanist Lorenzo Valla to Erasmus to Luther insofar as Valla's *Notes on the New Testament* inspired Erasmus to produce his own Greek edition and accompanying Latin translation of the New Testament in 1516, and that in turn enabled Luther in 1518 to reach some crucial conclusions concerning the literal biblical meaning of penance. For these and related reasons, Luther addressed Erasmus in 1519 as "our ornament and our hope."

But in fact Eramus quickly showed that he had no sympathy whatsoever with Luther's first principles, and most other Christian humanists shunned Protestantism as soon as it became clear to them what Luther and other Protestant reformers actually were teaching. The reasons for this were that most humanists believed in free will while Protestants believed in predestination, that humanists tended to think of human nature as basically good while Protestants found it unspeakably corrupt, and that most humanists favored urbanity and tolerance while the followers of Luther and Calvin emphasized faith and conformity. Thus when Erasmus, for example, defended *The Freedom of the Will* in a treatise of 1524, Luther attacked it vehemently in his *Bondage of the Will* of the following year, insisting that original sin makes all humans "bound, wretched, captive, sick, and dead." And when Henry VIII introduced the Reformation into England, England's foremost Christian humanist, Sir Thomas More, resisted the break with Rome even unto martyrdom, mounting the scaffold with some stirring words about the primacy of the individual conscience.

If the Protestant Reformation, then, was by no means the natural outgrowth of the civilization of the Renaissance, it very definitely contributed to certain traits most characteristic of modern European historical development. Foremost among these was the rise of the untrammeled powers of the sovereign state. As we have seen, those German princes who converted to Protestantism were moved to do so primarily by the search for sovereignty, and the kings of Denmark, Sweden, and England followed suit for the same reasons. Not at all accidentally, the earliest act of the English Parliament announcing Henry VIII's break with Rome, the Act in Restraint of Appeals of 1533, put forth the earliest official statement that England is a completely independent country, "governed by one supreme head and king," possessed of "plenary, whole, and entire power. . . . to render and yield justice and final determination to all manner of folk." Since Protestant leaders—Calvin as well as Luther—preached absolute obedience to "godly" rulers, and since the state in Protestant countries assumed direct control of the Church, the spread of Protestantism definitely resulted in the growth of state power. But, as we have also seen, the power of the state was growing anyway, and it continued to grow in Catholic countries like France and Spain where kings were granted most of the same rights over the Church that were forcibly seized by Lutheran German princes or Henry VIII.

As for the growth of nationalism, a sense of national pride was already present in sixteenth-century Germany that Luther played upon in his appeals of 1520. But Luther himself then did the most to foster German cultural nationalism by translating the entire Bible into a vigorous German idiom. Up until then Germans from some regions spoke a language so different from that of Germans from other areas that they could not understand each other, but the form of German given currency by Luther's Bible soon became the linguistic standard for the entire nation. Religion did not help to unite the German nation politically because the non-German Charles V opposed Lutheranism and as a result Germany soon became politically divided into Protestant and Catholic camps. But elsewhere, as in Scotland and Holland, where Protestants fought successfully against Catholic overlords, Protestantism enhanced a sense of national identity. And perhaps the most familiar case of all is that of England, where a sense of nationhood had existed before the advent of Protestantism even more markedly than it had in Germany, Scotland, or Holland, but where the new faith, as we shall see, helped underpin the greatest accomplishments of the Elizabethan age.

The problem of Protestantism's relationship to modern commercial and industrial economic development is more controversial. Around 1900 the great German sociologist Max Weber, noticing that the economically advanced territories of England, Holland, and North America had all been Protestant, argued that Protestantism, particularly in its Calvinist forms, was especially conducive to acquisitive economic enterprise. According to Weber, this was because Calvinistic theology, as opposed to Catholicism, sanctified the ventures of profit-oriented traders and moneylenders, and gave an exalted place in its ethical system to the business virtues of thrift and diligence. But historians have found shortcomings in Weber's thesis. Although Calvin did indeed praise diligence and acknowledge that merchants could

Catholic and Protestant Views of a Cardinal. A genuine papal medal (shown above) depicted a cardinal (right-side up) merged with a bishop (upside down). In response, a Protestant replica (shown below), probably struck in the Netherlands, depicted a cardinal merged with a grinning fool.

Protestantism and modern economic development

be "sanctified in their calling," he no more approved of exorbitant interest rates than Catholics did. Moreover Calvin argued vehemently that people should put their excess wealth at the service of the poor rather than piling up capital for the sake of gain or subsequent investments. Thus it appears that the "work ethic" necessary for economic success in commercial ventures did have some Calvinistic roots, but that Calvin's ideal merchant would by no means have been a great speculator or maker of fortunes. Bearing in mind that the European economy had already made great strides forward in the High Middle Ages and was advancing again in the early-modern period, not least because of the overseas ventures initiated by the Catholic powers of Portugal and Spain, Calvinism thus was at most just one of many contributory factors to the triumph of modern capitalism and the Industrial Revolution.

*Protestantism's effects on
relations between the sexes*

Finally, there arises the subject of Protestantism's effects on social relationships, specifically those between the sexes. As opposed to the question of Protestantism and economic development, this topic is still relatively unstudied. What is certain is that Protestant men as individuals could be just as ambivalent about women as Catholics, heathens, or Turks. John Knox, for example, inveighed against the Catholic regent of Scotland, Mary Stuart, in a treatise called *The First Blast of the Trumpet Against the Monstrous Regiment of Women,* yet maintained deeply respectful relationships with women of his own faith. But if one asks how Protestantism as a belief system rising above individual vagaries affected women's lot, the answer appears to be that it enabled women to become just a shade more equal to men, albeit still clearly within a subject status. Above all, since Protestantism, with its stress on the primacy of Scripture and the priesthood of all believers, called on women as well as men to undertake serious Bible study, it sponsored primary schooling for both sexes and thus enhanced female as well as male literacy. But Protestant male leaders never hesitated to insist that women were naturally inferior to men and thus should always defer to men in case of arguments. As Calvin himself said, "let the woman be satisfied with her state of subjection and not take it ill that she is made inferior to the more distinguished sex." Both Luther and Calvin appear to have been happily married, but that clearly meant being happily married on their own terms.

5. CATHOLIC REFORM

The historical novelty of Protestantism in the sixteenth century inevitably tends to cast the spotlight on such religious reformers as Luther and Calvin, but it must be emphasized that a powerful internal reform movement within the Catholic church exercised just as profound an effect on the course of European history as Protestantism did. Historians differ about whether to call this movement the "Catholic Ref-

*Catholic reform before and
after Luther*

ormation" or the "Counter-Reformation." Some prefer the former term because they wish to show that significant efforts to reform the Catholic church from within antedated the posting of Luther's theses and that therefore Catholic reform in the sixteenth century was no mere counterattack to check the growth of Protestantism. Others, however, insist quite properly that for the main part sixteenth-century Catholic reformers were indeed inspired primarily by the urgency of resisting what they regarded as heresy and schism. Fortunately the two interpretations are by no means irreconcilable, for they allude to two complementary phases: a Catholic Reformation that came before Luther and a Counter-Reformation that followed.

The Catholic Reformation beginning around 1490 was primarily a movement for moral and institutional reform inspired by the principles of Christian humanism and carried on with practically no help from the dissolute Renaissance papacy. In Spain around the turn of the fifteenth century, reform activities directed by Cardinal Francisco Ximénes de Cisneros (1436–1517) with the cooperation of the monarchy led to the imposition of strict rules of behavior for Franciscan friars and the elimination of abuses prevalent among the diocesan clergy. Although Ximénes aimed primarily at strengthening the Church in its rivalry with Jews and Muslims, his work had considerable effect in regenerating the spiritual life of the nation. In Italy there was no similarly centralized reform movement, but a number of earnest clerics in the early sixteenth century labored on their own to make the Italian Church more worthy of its calling. The task was a difficult one on account of the entrenchment of abuses and the example of profligacy set by the papal court, but despite these obstacles, the Italian reformers did manage to establish some new religious orders dedicated to high ideals of piety and social service. Finally, it cannot be forgotten that such leading Christian humanists as Erasmus and Thomas More were in their own way Catholic reformers, for in criticizing abuses and editing sacred texts, men like these certainly helped to enhance spirituality.

The Catholic Reformation

Once Protestantism began threatening to sweep over Europe, however, Catholic reform of the earlier variety clearly became inadequate to defend the Church, let alone turn the tide of revolt. Thus a second, more aggressive, phase of reform under a new style of vigorous papal leadership gained momentum during the middle and latter half of the sixteenth century. The leading Counter-Reformation popes—Paul III (1534–1549), Paul IV (1555–1559), St. Pius V (1566–1572), and Sixtus V (1585–1590)—were collectively the most zealous crusaders for reform who had presided over the papacy since the High Middle Ages. All led upright personal lives. Indeed, some were so grimly ascetic that contemporaries were unsure whether they were not too holy: as a Spanish councillor wrote in 1567, "We should like it even better if the present Holy Father were no longer with us, however great, inexpressible, unparalleled, and extraordinary his holiness may be." But in

The Counter-Reformation popes

A Session of the Council of Trent. The pope is not present, but the cardinals who represent him are enthroned, facing the semicircle of bishops. The orator with a raised right hand is a theologian advancing an opinion.

The Council of Trent: doctrinal matters

the circumstances of the Protestant onslaught, a pope's reputation for excessive asceticism was vastly preferable to a reputation for profligacy. More than that, becoming fully dedicated to activist revitalization of the Church, the Counter-Reformation popes reorganized their finances and filled ecclesiastical offices with bishops and abbots as renowned for austerity as themselves, and these appointees in turn set high standards for their own priests and monks.

These papal activities were supplemented by the actions of the Council of Trent, convoked by Paul III in 1545 and meeting at intervals thereafter until 1563. This general council was one of the most important in the history of the Church. Concerning basic matters of doctrine, the Council of Trent without exception reaffirmed all the tenets challenged by the Protestant Reformers. Good works were held to be as necessary for salvation as faith. The theory of the sacraments as indispensable means of grace was upheld. Likewise, transubstantiation, the apostolic succession of the priesthood, the belief in purgatory, the invocation of saints, and the rule of celibacy for the clergy were all confirmed as essential elements in the Catholic system. On the question as to the proper source of Christian belief, the Bible and the traditions of apostolic teaching were held to be of equal authority. Not only was papal supremacy over every bishop and priest expressly maintained, but the supremacy of the pope over the Church council itself was taken for granted in a way that left the monarchical government of the Church undisturbed. The Council of Trent also reaffirmed the doctrine of indulgences which had touched off the Lutheran revolt, although it did condemn the worst scandals connected with the selling of indulgences.

The legislation of Trent was not confined to matters of doctrine, but also included provisions for the elimination of abuses and for reinforcing the discipline of the Church over its members. Bishops and priests were forbidden to hold more than one benefice, so that absentees could not grow rich from a plurality of incomes. To eliminate the evil of an ignorant priesthood, it was provided that a theological seminary must be established in every diocese. Toward the end of its deliberations the council decided upon a censorship of books to prevent heretical ideas from corrupting those who still remained in the faith. A commission was appointed to draw up an index or list of writings which ought not to be read. The publication of this list in 1564 resulted in the formal establishment of the Index of Prohibited Books as a part of the machinery of the Church. Later, a permanent agency known as the Congregation of the Index was set up to revise the list from time to time. Altogether more than forty such revisions have been made. The majority of the books condemned have been theological treatises, and probably the effect in retarding the progress of learning has been slight. Nonetheless, the establishment of the Index must be viewed as a symptom of the intolerance which had come to infect both Catholics and Protestants.

The Council of Trent: practical reform and discipline

In addition to the independent activities of popes and the legislation of the Council of Trent, a third main force propelling the Counter-Reformation was the foundation of the Society of Jesus, commonly known as the Jesuit order, by St. Ignatius Loyola (1491–1556). In the midst of a youthful career as a worldly soldier, the Spanish nobleman Loyola was wounded in battle in 1521 (the same year in which Luther defied Charles V at Worms), and while recuperating, decided to change his ways and become a spiritual soldier of Christ. Shortly afterward he lived as a hermit in a cave near the Spanish town of Manresa for ten months, during which, instead of reading the Bible as a Luther or a Calvin might have done, he experienced ecstatic visions and worked out the principles of his subsequent meditational guide, *The Spiritual Exercises*. This manual, completed in 1535 and first published in 1541, offered practical advice on how to master one's will and serve God by a systematic program of meditations on sin and the life of Christ. Soon made a basic handbook for all Jesuits, and widely studied by numerous Catholic laypeople as well, Loyola's *Spiritual Exercises* had an influence second only to Calvin's *Institutes* of all the religious writings of the sixteenth century.

St. Ignatius Loyola

Nonetheless, St. Ignatius's foundation of the Jesuit order itself was certainly his greatest single accomplishment. Originating as a small group of six disciples who gathered around Loyola in Paris in 1534 to serve God in poverty, chastity, and missionary work, Ignatius's Society of Jesus was formally constituted as an order of the Church by Pope Paul III in 1540, and by the time of Loyola's death already numbered fifteen hundred members. The Society of Jesus was by far the most militant of the religious orders fostered by the Catholic reform move-

Ignatius Loyola. Engraving by Lucas Vorstiman, 1621.

ments of the sixteenth century. It was not merely a monastic society but a company of soldiers sworn to defend the faith. Their weapons were not to be bullets and spears but eloquence, persuasion, instruction in the right doctrines, and, if necessary, more worldly methods of exerting influence. The organization was patterned after that of a military company, with a general as commander-in-chief and iron discipline enforced on all members. Individuality was suppressed, and a soldierlike obedience to the general was exacted of the rank and file. The Jesuit general, sometimes known as "the black pope" (from the color of the order's habit), was elected for life and was not bound to take advice offered by any other member. But he did have one clear superior, namely the Roman pope himself, for in addition to the three monastic vows of poverty, chastity, and obedience, all senior Jesuits took a "fourth vow" of strict obedience to the Vicar of Christ and were held to be at the pope's disposal at all times.

*Jesuit militancy;
educational
accomplishments*

The activities of the Jesuits consisted primarily of proselytizing not just heathens but Christians, and establishing schools. Originally founded with the major aim of engaging in missionary work abroad, the early Jesuits by no means abandoned this goal, preaching to the heathen reached by the voyages of discovery in India, China, and Spanish America. For example, one of St. Ignatius's closest early associates, St. Francis Xavier (1506–1552), baptized thousands of natives and covered thousands of miles missionizing in the Indies. Yet, although Loyola had not at first conceived of his society as comprising shock-troops against Protestantism, that is what primarily became of it as the Counter-Reformation mounted in intensity. Working by means of preaching and diplomacy—sometimes at the risk of their lives—Jesuits in the second half of the sixteenth century fanned out through Europe in direct confrontation with Calvinists. In many places the Jesuits succeeded in keeping rulers and their subjects loyal to Catholicism, in others they met martyrdom, and in some others—notably Poland and parts of Germany and France—they actually succeeded in regaining territory temporarily lost to the Protestant faith. And wherever they were allowed to settle, the Jesuits set up schools and colleges, for they firmly believed that a vigorous Catholicism could rest only on widespread literacy and education. Indeed their schools were often so efficient that, after the fires of religious hatred began to subside, upper-class Protestants would sometimes send their children to receive a Jesuit education.

*Results of the
Counter-Reformation*

From the foregoing it should be self-evident that there is a "Counter-Reformation Heritage" every bit as much as there is a Protestant one. Needless to say, for committed Catholics, the greatest achievement of sixteenth-century Catholic reform was the defense and revitalization of the faith. Without any question, Catholicism would not have swept over the globe and reemerged in Europe as the vigorous spiritual force it remains today had it not been for the heroic efforts of the sixteenth-century reformers. But there were more practical results stemming

The Triumph of the Counter-Reformation. In this early–seventeenth-century fresco from the cathedral of Naples the Virgin intercedes for the faithful while personifications of Protestantism are trampled below.

from the Counter-Reformation as well. One was the spread of literacy in Catholic countries due to the educational activities of the Jesuits, and another was the growth of intense concern for acts of charity. Since Counter-Reformation Catholicism continued to emphasize good works as well as faith, charitable activities took on an extremely important role in the revived religion: hence spiritual leaders of the Counter-Reformation such as St. Francis de Sales (1567–1622) and St. Vincent de Paul (1576–1660) urged alms-giving in their sermons and writings, and a wave of founding orphanages and houses for the poor swept over Catholic Europe.

Two other areas in which the Counter-Reformation had less dramatic but still noteworthy effects were in the realm of women's history and intellectual developments. Whereas Protestantism encouraged female literacy for the purpose of making women just a little bit more like men in the ability to read the Bible, reinvigorated Catholicism pursued a different course. Most Catholic women were kept in a more subordinate position in the life of the faith than women under Protestantism, but Catholicism fostered a distinctive role for a female religious elite—countenancing the mysticism of a St. Teresa of Avila (1515–1582), or allowing the foundation of new orders of nuns such as the Ursulines and the Sisters of Charity. Under both Protestantism and Catholicism women remained subordinate, but in the latter model they were able to pursue their religious impulses more independently.

Effects of the Counter-Reformation on women

Finally, it unfortunately cannot be said that the Counter-Reformation perpetuated the tolerant Christianity of Erasmus, for Christian humanists lost favor with Counter-Reformation popes and all of Erasmus's writings were immediately placed on the Index. But sixteenth-

The Counter-Reformation and reason

century Protestantism was just as intolerant as sixteenth-century Catholicism, and far more hostile to the cause of rationalism. Indeed, because Counter-Reformation theologians returned for guidance to the scholasticism of Saint Thomas Aquinas, they were much more committed to acknowledging the dignity of human reason than their Protestant counterparts who emphasized pure Scriptural authority and blind faith. Thus although a hallmark of the subsequent seventeenth-century Scientific Revolution was the divorce between spirituality of any variety and strict scientific work, it does not seem entirely coincidental that René Descartes, one of the founders of the scientific revolution who coined the famous phrase "I think, therefore I am," was trained as a youth by the Jesuits.

SELECTED READINGS

• Items so designated are available in paperback editions.

OVERSEAS EXPANSION

Boxer, C. R., *The Portuguese Seaborne Empire, 1415–1825,* New York, 1969. The standard work on the subject.

Elliott, J. H., *The Old World and the New, 1492–1650,* Cambridge, 1970. A superb short analysis of the many ways in which the discovery of the New World affected life in the Old.

• Hale, J. R., *Renaissance Exploration,* New York, 1968. A scintillating brief introduction. Highly recommended as a point of departure.

• Morison, S. E., *Christopher Columbus, Mariner,* New York, 1955. A convenient abridgment of the master storyteller's definitive biography of Columbus, *Admiral of the Ocean Sea* (1942).

• Parry, J. H., *The Age of Reconnaissance,* London, 1963. Probably the best one-volume survey of the entire subject of early-modern European expansion; particularly strong on details of shipbuilding and navigation.

———, *The Spanish Seaborne Empire,* London, 1966. The counterpart to Boxer for the early Spanish colonial experience.

• Penrose, B., *Travel and Discovery in The Renaissance, 1420–1620,* Cambridge, Mass., 1960. Engrossing narratives of the major voyages.

PROTESTANT REFORMATION

• Bainton, R. H., *Here I Stand: A Life of Martin Luther,* Nashville, Tenn., 1950. The best introductory biography in English: absorbing and authoritative, though clearly partisan in Luther's favor.

———, *Women of the Reformation,* 3 vols., Minneapolis, 1970–1977. Full of interesting narrative, but little analysis.

• Brandi, K., *The Emperor Charles V,* New York, 1939. The standard narrative biography of the emperor who faced Luther and ruled much of Europe as well.

• Davis, Natalie Z., *Society and Culture in Early Modern France,* Stanford, Calif., 1975. A collection of pioneering essays in historical anthropology, including a brilliant piece on the role of women in sixteenth-century religious movements.

• Dickens, A. G., *The English Reformation*, New York, 1964. The best introduction.

————, *Reformation and Society in Sixteenth-Century Europe*, London, 1966. A highly stimulating introductory survey, with the added advantage of being profusely illustrated.

• Erikson, E. H., *Young Man Luther*, New York, 1958. A classic psychobiography that analyzes the young Luther's "identity crisis."

Grimm, Harold J., *The Reformation Era: 1500–1650*, 2nd ed., New York, 1973. The best college-level text; consistently informative, balanced, and reliable.

• Harbison, E. H., *The Age of Reformation*, Ithaca, N.Y., 1955. A magnificent elementary introduction by a master of the field.

————, *The Christian Scholar in the Age of the Reformation*, New York, 1956. Discusses the relationship between Christian humanism and early Protestantism.

• Hillerbrand, H., *The World of the Reformation*, London, 1975. A stimulating overview.

• Hurstfield, Joel, ed., *The Reformation Crisis*, London, 1965. Lively essays on all major aspects of Reformation history.

• McNeill, John T., *The History and Character of Calvinism*, New York, 1945. A basic, reliable, older work.

Monter, E. William, *Calvin's Geneva*, New York, 1967. Standard on the history of Calvin's Geneva.

Mullett, M., *Radical Religious Movements in Early Modern Europe*, London, 1980. Thematic analysis of some of the major effects of Protestantism, with as much attention given to the seventeenth as to the sixteenth century. Contains a particularly valuable annotated bibliography.

Oberman, H. A., *Masters of the Reformation*, Cambridge, 1981. A challenging study of the emergence of Protestantism as seen from the perspective of activities at the University of Tübingen. For more advanced readers.

Samuelsson, K., *Religion and Economic Action*, New York, 1961. The standard critical evaluation of Max Weber's thesis that Calvinism fostered the modern "spirit of capitalism."

• Skinner, Q., *The Foundations of Modern Political Thought: 2. The Age of Reformation*. In a class by itself as the best analysis of Reformation and Counter-Reformation trends in political theory.

• Smith, Lacey B., *Henry VIII: The Mask of Royalty*, Boston, 1971. A breathtaking interpretation of the last years of Henry VIII and the age in which he lived.

• Spitz, Lewis W., ed. *The Reformation: Basic Interpretations*, 2nd ed., Lexington, Mass., 1972. A collection of readings on points of scholarly dispute.

Tawney, R. H., *Religion and the Rise of Capitalism*, New York, 1926. The most sophisticated and elegantly written defense of the "Weber thesis."

Troeltsch, E., *Protestantism and Progress*, New York, 1931. An enduring classic.

Wendel, F., *Calvin*, London, 1963. A standard biography.

Williams, George H., *The Radical Reformation*, 1962. Detailed account of Anabaptism and the "left wing" of the Protestant Reformation.

CATHOLIC REFORM

Broderick, James, *The Origin of the Jesuits*, London, 1940. An older work, but still unsurpassed.

Delumeau, J., *Catholicism between Luther and Voltaire: A New View of the Counter-Reformation*, Philadelphia, 1977. A sympathetic account stressing the positive aspects of Reformed Catholicism.

• Dickens, A. G., *The Counter Reformation*, London, 1968. A splendid counterpart to Dickens's *Reformation and Society;* like its companion, profusely illustrated.

Janelle, P., *The Catholic Reformation*, Milwaukee, 1949. A reliable brief introduction.

Jedin, H., *A History of the Council of Trent*, 2 vols., London, 1957–1961. Authoritative and exhaustive.

Knowles, D., *From Pachomius to Ignatius: A Study in the Constitutional History of the Religious Orders*, Oxford, 1966. In less than one hundred masterful pages Knowles places the organizational principles of the Jesuits in historical perspective.

SOURCE MATERIALS

Dillenberger, J., ed., *John Calvin: Selections from His Writings*, Garden City, N.Y., 1971.

————, *Martin Luther: Selections from His Writings*, Garden City, N.Y., 1961.

Hillerbrand, H. J., ed., *The Protestant Reformation*, New York, 1967.

St. Ignatius Loyola, *The Spiritual Exercises*, tr. R. W. Gleason, Garden City, N.Y., 1964.

Ziegler, D. J., *Great Debates of the Reformation*, New York, 1969.

Chapter 16

A CENTURY OF CRISIS FOR EARLY-MODERN EUROPE
(c. 1560—c. 1660)

I do not wish to say much about the customs of the age in which we live. I can only state that this age is not one of the best, being a century of iron.

—R. Mentet de Salmonet, *History of the Troubles in Great Britain* (1649)

What in me is dark
Illumine, what is low raise and support.

—John Milton, *Paradise Lost*

O n the night before St. Bartholomew's Day in August of 1572 the Catholic queen mother of France, Catherine de Medici, authorized the ambush of French Protestant leaders who happened to be in Paris to attend a wedding. Thereupon, during the hours after midnight, unsuspecting people found themselves awakened to be stabbed in bed or thrown out of windows. Soon all the targeted Protestants were eliminated, but the killing did not stop because roving bands of Parisian Catholics seized the opportunity of licensed carnage to slaughter at will any enemies they happened upon, Protestant or otherwise. By morning the River Seine was clogged with corpses and scores of bodies hung from gibbets in witness to an event known ever since as the Massacre of St. Bartholomew's Day.

A massacre in Paris

Had this lamentable incident been an isolated event it hardly would be worth mentioning, but in fact throughout the hundred years from roughly 1560 to roughly 1660 outbreaks of religious mayhem—with Protestants the ruthless killers in certain cases as Catholics were in others—recurred in many parts of Europe. Moreover, to make matters far worse, economic hardships and prolonged wars accompanied religious riots to result in a century of pronounced crisis for European civilization.

A century of crisis

The St. Bartholomew's Day Massacre. A contemporary painting depicts the merciless slaughter of Huguenots in Paris. At the top left (in front of the large gate next to the Seine) the Queen Mother Catherine looks over a pile of naked dead bodies; to the right a Huguenot leader is being pushed out of a window.

In many respects Europe's early-modern period of crisis resembled the terrible times of the late Middle Ages, but the early-modern crisis was much less uniform in its nature and extent. From the economic point of view, there were two different major difficulties—first a dramatic price inflation lasting from about 1560 to 1600 that hurt the poor far worse than it did the rich, and then a period of overall economic stagnation which was marked, however, by significant exceptions from place to place. Similarly, although the main theme of political history during the entire era was intense warfare, the causes of war differed greatly according to place and time, with some areas occasionally even managing to bask in intervals of peace. Nonetheless, seen from the broadest perspective the period from 1560 to 1660 was western Europe's "iron century"—an age of enormous turbulence and severe trials.

Lack of uniformity in causes and effects

1. ECONOMIC, RELIGIOUS, AND POLITICAL TESTS

Europe's time of troubles crept up on contemporaries unawares. For almost a century before 1560 most of the West had enjoyed steady economic growth, and the discovery of the New World seemed to harbinger even greater prosperity to come. Political trends too seemed auspicious, since most western European governments were becoming ever more efficient and providing more internal peace for their

Impending crisis

subjects. Yet around 1560 thunderclouds were gathering in the skies that would soon burst into terrible storms.

Although the causes of these storms were interrelated, each may be examined separately, starting with the great price inflation. Nothing like the upward price trend which affected western Europe in the second half of the sixteenth century had ever happened before. The cost of a measure of wheat in Flanders, for example, tripled from 1550 to 1600, grain prices in Paris quadrupled, and the overall cost of living in England advanced well over 100 percent during the same period. Certainly the twentieth century has seen even more dizzying inflations than this, but since the skyrocketing of prices in the later sixteenth century was a novelty, most historians agree on calling it the "price revolution." *Soaring prices*

If experts agree on the terminology, however, very few of them agree on the exact combination of circumstances that caused the price revolution, for early-modern statistics are patchy and many areas of economic theory remain under dispute. Nonetheless, for present purposes two widely accepted dominant explanations for the great inflation may be offered with confidence. The first is demographic. Starting in the later fifteenth century, Europe's population began to mount again after the plague-induced fall-off: roughly estimated, there were about 50 million people in Europe around 1450 and 90 million around 1600. Since Europe's food supply remained more or less constant owing to the lack of any noteworthy breakthrough in agricultural technology, food prices inevitably were driven sharply higher by greater demand. In contrast, the prices of manufactured goods did not rise as steeply because there was a greater match between supply and demand. Yet prices of manufactured items did rise nonetheless, especially in cases where the supply of agricultural raw materials crucial to the manufacturing process remained relatively inelastic. *Causes of inflation: (1) population increase*

Population trends therefore explain much, but since Europe's population did not grow nearly as rapidly in the second half of the sixteenth century as prices, complementary explanations for the great inflation are still necessary, and foremost among these is the enormous influx of bullion from Spanish America. Around 1560 a new technique of extracting silver from silver ore made the working of newly discovered mines in Mexico and Bolivia highly practical, soon transforming the previous trickle of silver entering the European economy into a flood. Whereas in the five years between 1556 and 1560 roughly 10 million ducats worth of silver passed through the Spanish entry point of Seville, between 1576 and 1580 that figure had doubled, and between 1591 and 1595 it had more than quadrupled. Inasmuch as most of this silver was used by the Spanish crown to pay its foreign creditors and its armies abroad or by private individuals to pay for imports from other countries, Spanish bullion quickly circulated throughout Europe, where much of it was minted into coins. This dramatic increase in the volume of money in circulation further fueled the spiral of rising prices. *(2) influx of silver*

Aggressive entrepreneurs and landlords profited most from the changed economic circumstances, while the masses of laboring people were hurt the worst. Obviously, merchants in possession of sought-after goods were able to raise prices at will, and landlords either could profit directly from the rising prices of agricultural produce or, if they did not farm their own lands, could always raise rents. But laborers in country and town were caught in a squeeze because wages rose far more slowly than prices, owing to the presence of a more than adequate labor supply. Moreover, because the cost of food staples rose at a sharper rate proportionately than the cost of most other items of consumption, poor people had to spend an ever-greater percentage of their paltry income on necessities. In normal years they barely managed to survive, but when disasters such as wars or poor harvests drove grain prices out of reach, some of the poor literally starved to death. The picture that thus emerges is one of the rich getting richer and the poor getting poorer—splendid feasts enjoyed amid the most appalling suffering.

In addition to these direct economic effects, the price inflation of the later sixteenth century had significant political effects as well because higher prices placed new pressures on the sovereign states of Europe. The reasons for this were simple. Since the inflation depressed the real value of money, fixed incomes from taxes and dues in effect yielded less and less. Thus merely to keep their incomes constant governments would have been forced to raise taxes. But to compound this problem, most states needed much more real income than previously because they were undertaking more wars, and warfare, as always, was becoming increasingly expensive. The only recourse, then, was to raise taxes precipitously, but such draconian measures incurred great resentments on the part of subject populations—especially the very poor who were already strapped more than enough by the effects of the inflation. Hence governments faced continuous threats of defiance and potential armed resistance.

Less need be said about the economic stagnation that followed the price revolution because it interfered little with most of the trends just discussed. When population growth began to ease and the flood of silver from America began to abate around 1600, prices soon leveled off. Yet because the most lucrative economic exploitation of the New World only began in the late seventeenth century and Europe experienced little new industrial development, the period from about 1600 to 1660 was at best one of very limited overall economic growth, even though a few areas—notably Holland—bucked the trend. Within this context the rich were usually able to hold their own, but the poor as a group made no advances since the relationship of prices to wages remained fixed to their disadvantage. Indeed, if anything, the lot of the poor in many places deteriorated because the mid–seventeenth century saw some particularly expensive and destructive wars, causing helpless civilians to be plundered either by rapacious tax collectors, looting soldiers, or sometimes by both.

It goes without saying that most people would have been far better off had there been fewer wars during Europe's iron century, but given prevalent attitudes, newly arisen religious rivalries made wars inevitable. Simply stated, until religious passions began to cool toward the end of the period, most Catholics and Protestants viewed each other as minions of Satan who could not be allowed to live. Worse, sovereign states attempted to enforce religious uniformity on the grounds that "crown and altar" offered each other mutual support and in the belief that governments would totter where diversity of faith prevailed. Rulers on both sides felt certain that religious minorities, if allowed to survive in their realms, would inevitably engage in sedition; nor were they far wrong since militant Calvinists and Jesuits were indeed dedicated to subverting constituted powers in areas where they had not yet triumphed. Thus states tried to extirpate all potential religious resistance, but in the process sometimes provoked civil wars in which both sides tended to assume there could be no victory until the other was exterminated. And of course civil wars might become international in scope when one or more foreign powers resolved to aid embattled religious allies elsewhere.

Compounding the foregoing problems were more strictly political ones: namely, while strapped by price trends and racked by religious wars, governments brought certain provincial and constitutional grievances down upon themselves. Regarding the provincial issue, most of the major states of early-modern Europe had been built up by conquests or dynastic marital accretions, with the result that many smaller territories had been subjected to absentee rule. At first some degree of provincial autonomy was usually preserved and hence the inhabitants of such territories did not object too much to their annexation. But in the iron century, when governments were making evergreater financial claims on all their subjects or trying to enforce religious uniformity, rulers customarily moved to destroy all semblances of provincial autonomy in order to implement their financial or religious policies. Naturally the province-dwellers were usually not inclined to accept total subjugation without a fight, so rebellions might break out on combined patriotic and economic or religious grounds. Nor was that all, since most governments seeking money and/or religious uniformity tried to rule their subjects with a firmer hand than before, and thus sometimes provoked armed resistance in the name of traditional constitutional liberties. Given this bewildering variety of motives for revolt, it is by no means surprising that the century between 1560 and 1660 was one of the most turbulent in all European history.

2. A HALF CENTURY OF RELIGIOUS WARS

Despite the multiplicity of overlapping causes for instability, the greatest single cause of warfare in the first half of Europe's iron cen-

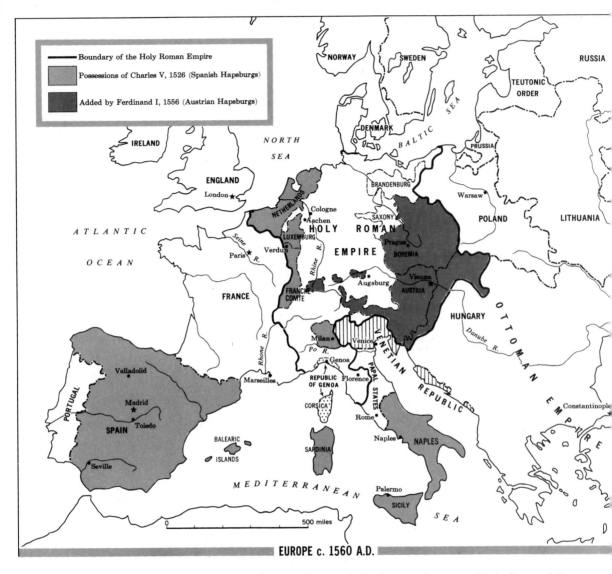

EUROPE c. 1560 A.D.

Legend:
— Boundary of the Holy Roman Empire
Possessions of Charles V, 1526 (Spanish Hapsburgs)
Added by Ferdinand I, 1556 (Austrian Hapsburgs)

Religious wars in Germany until the Peace of Augsburg

tury was religious rivalry. Indeed, wars between Catholics and Protestants began as early as the 1540s when the Catholic Holy Roman Emperor Charles V tried to reestablish Catholic unity in Germany by launching a military campaign against several German princes who had instituted Lutheran worship in their principalities. At times thereafter it appeared as if Charles was going to succeed in reducing his German Protestant opponents to complete submission, but since he was also involved in fighting against France, he seldom was able to devote concerted attention to affairs in Germany. Accordingly, religious warfare sputtered on and off until a compromise settlement was reached in the Religious Peace of Augsburg (1555). This rested on the principle of *"cuius regio, eius religio"* ("as the ruler, so the religion"), which meant that in those principalities where Lutheran princes ruled,

Lutheranism would be the sole state religion, and the same for those with Catholic princes. Although the Peace of Augsburg was a historical milestone inasmuch as Catholic rulers for the first time acknowledged the legality of Protestantism, it boded ill for the future in assuming that no sovereign state larger than a free city (for which it made exceptions) could tolerate religious diversity. Moreover, in excluding Calvinism it ensured that Calvinists would become aggressive opponents of the *status quo*.

Even though wars in the name of religion were fought in Europe before 1560, those that raged afterward were far more brutal, partly because the combatants had become more fanatical (intransigent Calvinists and Jesuits customarily took the lead on their respective sides), and partly because the later religious wars were aggravated by political and economic resentments. Since Geneva bordered on France, since Calvin himself was a Frenchman who longed to convert his mother country, and since Calvinists had no wish to displace German Lutherans, the next act in the tragedy of Europe's confessional warfare was played out on French soil. Calvinist missionaries had already made much headway in France in the years between Calvin's rise to power in Geneva in 1541 and the outbreak of religious warfare in 1562. Of the greatest aid to the Calvinist (Huguenot) cause was the conversion to Calvinism of many aristocratic French women because such women usually won over their husbands, who in turn maintained large private armies. The foremost example is that of Jeanne d'Albret, queen of the tiny Pyrenean kingdom of Navarre, who brought over to Calvinism her husband, the prominent French aristocrat Antoine de Bourbon, and her brother-in-law, the prince de Condé. Not only did Condé take command of the French Huguenot party when civil war broke out in 1562, but he later was succeeded in this capacity by Jeanne's son, Henry of Navarre, who came to rule all of France at the end of the century as King Henry IV. In addition to aristocrats, many people from all walks of life became Huguenots for a variety of motives, with Huguenot strength greatest in areas of the south which had long resented the dominance of northern rule from Paris. In short, by 1562 Calvinists comprised between 10 and 20 percent of France's population of roughly 16 million, and their numbers were swelling every day.

Jeanne D'Albret

Since both Catholics and Protestants assumed that France could have only a single *roi, foi,* and *loi* (king, faith, and law), civil war was inevitable, and no one was surprised when a struggle between the Huguenot Condé and the ultra-Catholic duke of Guise for control of the government during a royal minority led in 1562 to a show of arms. Soon all France was aflame. Churches were ransacked and local scores were settled by rampaging mobs who often were incited on both sides by members of their clergy. After a while it became clear that the Huguenots were not strong or numerous enough to gain victory, but they were also too strong to be defeated. Hence, despite intermittent truces, warfare dragged on at great cost of life until 1572. Then, during an interval of peace, the cultivated queen mother Catherine de Medici, normally a woman who favored compromise, plotted with members of the Catholic Guise faction to kill all the Huguenot leaders while they were assembled in Paris for the wedding of Henry of Navarre. In the early morning of St. Bartholomew's Day (August 24) most of the Huguenot chiefs were murdered in bed and two to three thousand other Protestants were slaughtered in the streets or drowned in the Seine by Catholic mobs. When word of the Parisian massacre spread to the provinces, some ten thousand more Huguenots were killed in a frenzy of blood lust that swept through France.

*Henry IV establishes
French religious peace*

The St. Bartholomew's Day episode effectively broke the back of Huguenot resistance, but even then warfare did not cease because the neurotic King Henry III (1574–1589) tried to play off Huguenots against the dominant Catholic Guise family and because die-hard Huguenots sometimes were able to ally with Catholics revolting against overburdensome taxes or inequities in tax assessments. Only when the politically astute Henry of Navarre succeeded to the French throne as Henry IV[1] (1589–1610), initiating the Bourbon dynasty that would rule until 1792, did civil war finally come to an end. In 1593 Henry abjured his Protestantism in order to placate France's Catholic majority ("Paris is worth a mass") and then, in 1598, offered limited religious freedom to the Huguenots by the Edict of Nantes. According to the terms of this proclamation, Catholicism was recognized as the official religion, but Huguenot nobles were allowed to hold Protestant services privately in their castles, other Huguenots were allowed to worship at specified places (excluding Paris and all cities where bishops and archbishops resided), and the Huguenot party was permitted to fortify some towns, especially in the south, for military defense if the need arose. Thus, although the Edict of Nantes certainly did not counte-

[1]Here, as elsewhere, dates following a ruler's name refer to dates of reign.

The Assassination of Henry IV. This contemporary engraving shows Henry seated in an open carriage without any concern for his personal danger while his assassin climbs on the spoke of the carriage wheel to attack him. The entire composition conveys a vivid impression of early-modern Paris.

The Emperor Charles V. This portrait by the Venetian painter Titian depicts the emperor in a grandiloquent equestrian pose. (Another depiction of Charles V by Titian appears in the section of color plates following p. 448.)

nance absolute freedom of worship, it nevertheless represented a major stride in the direction of toleration. With religious peace established, France quickly began to recover from decades of devastation, but Henry IV himself was cut down by the dagger of a Catholic fanatic in 1610.

Contemporaneous with the religious warfare in France was equally bitter religious strife between Catholics and Protestants in the neighboring Netherlands, where national resentments gravely compounded religious hatreds. For almost a century the Netherlands (or Low Countries), comprising modern-day Holland in the north and Belgium in the south, had been ruled by the Habsburg family. Particularly the Belgian part of the Netherlands prospered greatly from trade and manufacture: southern Netherlanders had the greatest per capita wealth of all Europe and their metropolis of Antwerp was northern Europe's leading commercial and financial center. Moreover, the half-century-long rule of the Habsburg Charles V (1506–1556) had been extremely popular because Charles, who had been born in the Belgian city of Ghent, felt a sense of rapport with his subjects and allowed them a large degree of local self-government.

Habsburg rule in the Netherlands

But around 1560 the good fortune of the Netherlands began to ebb. When Charles V retired to a monastery in 1556 (dying two years later) he ceded all his vast territories outside of the Holy Roman Empire and Hungary—not only the Netherlands, but Spain, Spanish America, and close to half of Italy—to his son Philip II (1556–1598). Unlike Charles, Philip had been born in Spain, and thinking of himself as a Spaniard, made Spain his residence and the focus of his policy. Thus he viewed the Netherlands primarily as a potentially rich source of income necessary for pursuing Spanish affairs. (Around 1560 silver was only

Philip II and the impending crisis

Philip II of Spain. Titian's portrait shows Philip's resemblance to his father, Charles V,
particularly in the protruding
lower jaw of the Habsburgs.

beginning to flood through Seville.) But in order to tap the wealth of
the Netherlands Philip had to rule it more directly than his father had,
and such attempts were naturally resented by the local magnates who
until then had dominated the government. To make matters worse, a
religious storm also was brewing, for after a treaty of 1559 ended a
long war between France and Spain, French Calvinists had begun to
stream over the Netherlandish border, making converts wherever they
went. Soon there were more Calvinists in Antwerp than in Geneva, a
situation that Philip II could not tolerate because he was an ardent
Catholic who subscribed wholeheartedly to the goals of the Counter-
Reformation. Indeed, as he wrote to Rome on the eve of conflict:
"rather than suffer the slightest harm to the true religion and service
of God, I would lose all my states and even my life a hundred times
over because I am not and will not be the ruler of heretics."

Evidence of the complexity of the Netherlandish situation is found
in the facts that the leader of resistance to Philip, William the Silent,
was at first not a Calvinist and that the territories which ultimately
succeeded in breaking away from Spanish rule were at first the most
Catholic ones in the Low Countries. William "the Silent," a prominent nobleman with large landholdings in the Netherlands, was in fact
very talkative, receiving his nickname rather from his ability to hide
his true religious and political feelings when the need arose. In 1566,
when still a nominal Catholic, he and other local nobles not formally
committed to Protestantism appealed to Philip to allow toleration for
Calvinists. But while Philip momentarily temporized, radical Protestant mobs proved to be their own worst enemy—ransacking Catholic
churches throughout the country, methodically desecrating hosts,
smashing statuary, and shattering stained-glass windows. Though local
troops soon had the situation under control, Philip II nonetheless

*Protestants Ransacking a Catholic
Church in the Netherlands*. The
"Protestant fury" of 1566 was
responsible for the large-scale
destruction of religious art and
statuary in the Low Countries,
provoking the stern repression
of Philip II.

decided to dispatch an army of ten thousand commanded by the steely Spanish duke of Alva to wipe out Protestantism in the Low Countries forever. Alva's tribunal, the "Council of Blood," soon examined some twelve thousand persons on charges of heresy or sedition, of whom nine thousand were convicted and one thousand executed. William the Silent fled the country and all hope for a free Netherlands seemed lost.

But the tide turned quickly for two related reasons. First, instead of giving up, William the Silent converted to Protestantism, sought help from Protestants in France, Germany, and England, and organized bands of sea-rovers to harass Spanish shipping on the Netherlands coast. And second, Alva's tyranny helped William's cause, especially when the hated Spanish governor attempted to levy a repressive 10 percent sales tax. With internal disaffection growing, in 1572 William, for tactical military reasons, was able to seize the northern Netherlands even though the north until then had been predominantly Catholic. Thereafter geography played a major role in determining the outcome of the conflict. Spanish armies repeatedly attempted to win back the north, but they were stopped by a combination of impassable rivers and dikes which could be opened to flood out the invaders. Although William the Silent was assassinated by a Catholic in 1584, his son continued to lead the resistance until the Spanish crown finally agreed by a truce in 1609 to stop fighting and thus implicitly recognized the independence of the northern Dutch Republic. Meanwhile, the pressures of war and persecution had made the whole north Calvinistic, whereas the south—which remained Spanish—returned to uniform Catholicism.

The Duke of Alva. The gaunt Spanish general who attempted in vain to extirpate Calvinism in the Netherlands.

Predictably, religious strife which could take the form of civil war, as in France, or war for national liberation, as in the Netherlands, could also take the form of warfare between sovereign states, as in the case of the late-sixteenth-century struggle between England and Spain. After narrowly escaping domination by the Catholic Queen Mary and her Spanish husband Philip II, English Protestants rejoiced in the rule of Queen Elizabeth I (1558–1603) and naturally harbored great antipathy for Philip II and the Counter-Reformation. Furthermore, English economic interests were directly opposed to those of the Spanish. A seafaring and trading people, the English in the later sixteenth century were steadily making inroads into Spanish naval and commercial domination, and were also determined to resist any Spanish attempt to block England's lucrative trade with the Low Countries. But the greatest source of antagonism lay in naval contests in the Atlantic, where English privateers, with the tacit consent of Queen Elizabeth, could not resist raiding silver-laden Spanish treasure ships. Beginning around 1570, and taking as an excuse Spanish oppression of Protestants in the Netherlands, English admirals or pirates (the terms were really interchangeable) such as Sir Francis Drake and Sir John Hawkins began plundering Spanish vessels on the high seas. In a particularly dramatic sailing exploit lasting from 1577 to 1580, lust for booty and prevailing winds propelled Drake all the way around the world, to

Antagonism between England and Spain

Left: *The Defeat of the Spanish Armada*. Right: *Queen Elizabeth I*. The contemporary English oil painting of the great sea battle gives only a schematic idea of its turbulence. Note, however, the prominence of the papal insignia (tiara over crossed keys of St. Peter) on the ship in the middle foreground: Englishmen were convinced that had they not defeated the Spanish Armada in 1588 the pope would have planted his banner on their shores. At the right is a typically overblown portrait of Queen Elizabeth, known to her admiring subjects as "Gloriana," standing on a map of England.

return with stolen Spanish treasure worth twice as much as Queen Elizabeth's annual revenue.

All this would have been sufficient provocation for Philip II to have retaliated against England, but because he had his hands full in the Netherlands he resolved to invade the island only after the English openly allied with the Dutch rebels in 1585. And even then Philip did not act without extensive planning and a sense of assurance that nothing could go wrong. Finally, in 1588 he dispatched an enormous fleet, confidently called the "Invincible Armada," to punish insolent Britannia. After an initial standoff in the English Channel, however, English fireships outmaneuvered the Spanish fleet, setting some Spanish galleons ablaze and forcing the rest to break formation. "Protestant gales" did the rest and a battered flotilla soon limped home with almost half its ships lost.

The defeat of the Spanish Armada

The defeat of the Spanish Armada was one of the most decisive battles of Western history. Had Spain conquered England it is quite likely that the Spanish would have gone on to crush Holland and perhaps even to destroy Protestantism everywhere. But, as it was, the Protestant day was saved, and not long afterward Spanish power began to decline, with English and Dutch ships taking ever-greater command of the seas. Moreover, in England itself patriotic fervor became intense. Popular even before then, "Good Queen Bess" was virtually revered

The salvation of Protestantism

The Crucifixion, Tintoretto (1518–1594). This Venetian master of Mannerism combined typically Venetian richness of color with an innovative concern for movement and emotion. (Scala)

Saint Andrew and St. Francis, El Greco (c. 1541–1614). A striking exemplification of the artist's penchant for elongation as well as his profound psychological penetration. (The Prado)

View of Toledo, El Greco. One of the most awesomely mysterious paintings in the entire Western tradition. (MMA)

The Maids of Honor, Diego Velásquez (1599–1660). The artist himself is at work on an idealized double portrait of the king and queen of Spain (who may be seen in the rear mirror), but reality is more obvious in the foreground in the persons of the delicately impish princess, her two maids, and a misshapen dwarf. The twentieth-century Spanish artist Picasso gained great inspiration from this work. (The Prado)

Pope Innocent X, Velásquez. A trenchant portrait of a decisive man of affairs. (Doria–Pamphili Collection)

England and Scotland Crowning Charles I, Peter Paul Rubens (1577–1640). A typical piece of Baroque propaganda, in this case painted to glorify the English monarch of the Stuart family in the years before his ill-fated demise. (Minneapolis Institute of Art)

The Horrors of War, Rubens. The war god Mars here casts aside his mistress Venus and threatens humanity with death and destruction. In his old age Rubens took a far more critical view of war than he did for most of his earlier career. (Gall. Palatina)

Aristotle Contemplating the Bust of Homer, Rembrandt van Rijn (1606–1669). One of the greatest painters' view of one of the greatest of philosophers caught up by the aura of one of the greatest poets. (MMA)

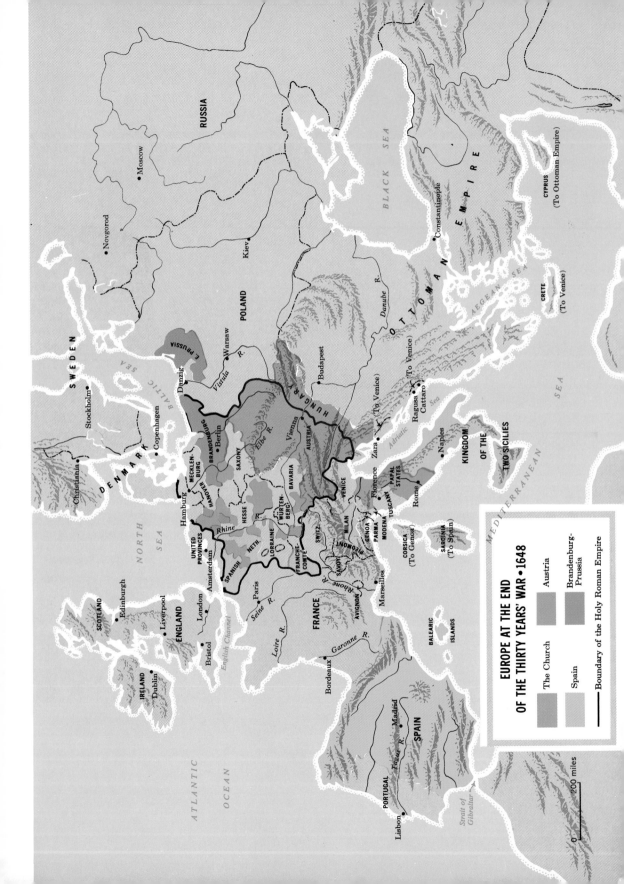

RUSSIA

• Moscow

• Novgorod

• Kiev

SWEDEN

• Stockholm

BALTIC SEA

• Christiania

DENMARK

• Copenhagen

POLAND

• Warsaw

Vistula R.

E. PRUSSIA

• Danzig

BRANDENBURG

• Berlin

MECKLEN-BURG

HANOVER

• Hamburg

SAXONY

Elbe R.

HESSE

WÜRTEN-BERG

BAVARIA

R.

Rhine

UNITED PROVINCES

• Amsterdam

SPANISH NETH.

LORRAINE

FRANCHE-COMTÉ

SWITZ.

HUNGARY

AUSTRIA

• Vienna

• Budapest

Danube R.

OTTOMAN EMPIRE

BLACK SEA

• Constantinople

CYPRUS
(To Ottoman Empire)

AEGEAN SEA

CRETE
(To Venice)

(To Venice)

Zara
(To Venice)

Ragusa
Cattaro

Adriatic Sea

VENICE

• Florence

TUSCANY

PAPAL STATES

• Rome

• Naples

KINGDOM
OF THE
TWO SICILIES

MEDITERRANEAN SEA

MILAN

PIEDMONT

SAVOY

GENOA

PARMA

MODENA

CORSICA
(To Genoa)

SARDINIA
(To Spain)

Rhône R.

• Marseilles

FRANCE

• Paris

Seine R.

Loire R.

Garonne R.

• Bordeaux

BALEARIC
ISLANDS

SCOTLAND

• Edinburgh

ENGLAND

• Liverpool

• London

• Bristol

English Channel

IRELAND

• Dublin

ATLANTIC
OCEAN

NORTH SEA

PORTUGAL

SPAIN

• Madrid

Tagus R.

• Lisbon

Strait of
Gibraltar

**EUROPE AT THE END
OF THE THIRTY YEARS' WAR • 1648**

| The Church | Austria |
| Spain | Brandenburg-Prussia |

—— Boundary of the Holy Roman Empire

0   200 miles

by her subjects until her death in 1603, and England embarked on its golden "Elizabethan Age" of literary endeavor. War with Spain dragged on inconclusively until 1604, but the fighting never brought England any serious harm and was just lively enough to keep the English people deeply committed to the cause of their queen, their country, and the Protestant religion.

3. YEARS OF TREMBLING

With the promulgation of the Edict of Nantes in 1598, the peace between England and Spain of 1604, and the truce between Spain and Holland of 1609, religious warfare tapered off and came to an end in the early seventeenth century. But in 1618 a major new war broke out, this time in Germany. Since this struggle raged more or less unceasingly until 1648 it bears the name of the Thirty Years' War. Meanwhile, far from returning to enduring peace, Spain and France became engaged in the Thirty Years' War and war with each other, and internal resentments in Spain, France, and England flared up in the decade of the 1640s in concurrent outbreaks of uprisings and civil turmoil. As an English preacher said in 1643, "these are days of shaking, and this shaking is universal." He might have added that while in some instances religion remained one of the contested issues, secular disputes about powers of government were now becoming predominant.

A new phase of turmoil

The clearest example is that of the Thirty Years' War, which began in a welter of religious passions as a war between Catholics and Protestants but immediately raised basic German constitutional issues and ended as an international struggle in which the initial religious dimension was almost entirely forgotten. Between the Peace of Augsburg

The Thirty Years' War

Two Artistic Broadsides from the Thirty Years' War. On the left the German peasantry is ridden by the soldiery; on the right is an allegorical representation of "the monstrous beast of war."

in 1555 and the outbreak of war in 1618, Calvinists had replaced
Lutherans in a few German territories but the overall balance between
Protestants and Catholics within the Holy Roman Empire had
remained undisturbed. In 1618, however, when a Protestant uprising
against Habsburg Catholic rule in Bohemia (not a German territory,
but nonetheless part of the Holy Roman Empire) threatened to upset
the balance, German Catholic forces ruthlessly counterattacked, first
in Bohemia and then in Germany proper. Led by Charles V's Habsburg descendant Ferdinand II, who was archduke of Austria, king of
Hungary, and from 1619 to his death in 1637, Holy Roman Emperor,
a German Catholic league seized the military initiative and within a
decade seemed close to extirpating Protestantism throughout Germany. But Ferdinand, who was intent on pursuing political goals as
well, imposed firm direct rule in Bohemia in order to build up the
strength of his own Austro-Hungarian state, and attempted to revive
the faded authority of the Holy Roman Empire in whatever ways he
could.

Thus when the Lutheran king of Sweden, Gustavus Adolphus,
marched into Germany in 1630 to champion the nearly lost cause of
Protestantism, he was welcomed by several German Catholic princes
who preferred to see the former religious balance restored rather than
stand the chance of surrendering their sovereignty to Ferdinand II. To
make matters still more ironic, Gustavus's Protestant army was secretly
subsidized by Catholic France, then governed by a cardinal of the
Church, because Habsburg Spain had been fighting in Germany on
the side of Habsburg Austria and France's Cardinal Richelieu was
determined to resist any possibility of being surrounded by a strong
Habsburg alliance on the north, east, and south. In the event, the military genius Gustavus Adolphus started routing the Habsburgs, but
when the Swedish king fell in battle in 1632, Cardinal Richelieu had
little choice but to send ever-greater support to the remaining Swedish
troops in Germany, until in 1639 French armies entered the war directly
on Sweden's side. From then until 1648 the struggle was really one of
France and Sweden against Austria and Spain, with most of Germany
a helpless battleground.

*The involvement of
Sweden and France*

The result was that Germany suffered more from warfare in the
terrible years between 1618 and 1648 than it ever did before or after
until the twentieth century. Several German cities were besieged and
sacked nine or ten times over, and soldiers from all nations, who often
had to sustain themselves by plunder, gave no quarter to defenseless
civilians. With plague and disease adding to the toll of outright butchery, some parts of Germany lost more than half their populations,
although it is true that others went relatively unscathed. Most horri-
fying was the loss of life in the last four years, when the carnage continued unabated even while peace negotiators had already arrived at
broad areas of agreement and were dickering over subsidiary clauses.

*The toll of warfare in
Germany*

Nor did the Peace of Westphalia, which finally ended the Thirty

A Swearing of Oaths at the Peace of Westphalia, 1648

Years' War in 1648, do much to vindicate anyone's death, even though it did establish some abiding landmarks in European history. Above all, from the international perspective the Peace of Westphalia marked the reemergence of France as the predominant power on the continental European scene, replacing Spain—a position France was to hold for two centuries more. In particular, France moved its eastern frontier directly into German territory by taking over large parts of Alsace. As for strictly internal German matters, the greatest losers were the Austrian Habsburgs, who were forced to surrender all the territory they had gained in Germany and to abandon their hopes of using the office of Holy Roman Emperor to dominate central Europe. Otherwise, something very close to the German *status quo* of 1618 was reestablished, with Protestant principalities in the north balancing Catholic ones in the south and Germany so hopelessly divided that it could play no united role in European history until the nineteenth century.

The Peace of Westphalia

See color map facing page 513

Still greater losers from the Thirty Years' War than the Austrian Habsburgs were their Spanish cousins, for Spain had invested vast sums in the struggle it could not afford and ceased being a great power forever after. The story of Spain's swift fall from grandeur is almost like a Greek tragedy in its relentless unfolding. Even after the defeat of the "Invincible Armada," around 1600 the Spanish empire—comprising all of the Iberian peninsula (including Portugal, which had been annexed by Philip II in 1580), half of Italy, half of the Netherlands, all of Central and South America, and even the Philippine Islands—was the mightiest power not just in Europe but in the world. Yet a bare half century later this empire on which the sun never set had come close to falling apart.

The decline of Spain

Spain's greatest underlying weakness was economic. At first this may seem like a very odd statement considering that in 1600, as in the

*Economic causes of
Spain's decline*

three or four previous decades, huge amounts of American silver were being unloaded on the docks of Seville. Yet as contemporaries themselves recognized, "the new world that Spain had conquered was conquering Spain in turn." Lacking either rich agricultural or mineral resources, Spain desperately needed to develop industries and a balanced trading pattern as its rivals England and France were doing. But since the dominant Spanish nobility had prized ideals of chivalry over practical business ever since the medieval days when it was engaged in winning back Spanish territory from the Muslims, the Spanish governing class was only too glad to use American silver to buy manufactured goods from other parts of Europe in order to live in splendor and dedicate itself to military exploits. Thus bullion left the country as soon as it entered, virtually no industry was established, and when the influx of silver began to decline after 1600 the Spanish economy remained with nothing except increasing debts.

*Spain's continued
aggressiveness*

Nonetheless, the crown, dedicated to supporting the Counter-Reformation and maintaining Spain's international dominance, would not cease fighting abroad. Indeed, the entire Spanish budget remained on such a warlike footing that even in the relatively peaceful year of 1608 four million out of a total revenue of seven million ducats were paid for military expenditures. Thus when Spain became engaged in fighting France during the Thirty Years' War it fully overextended itself. The clearest visible sign of this was that in 1643 outnumbered French troops at Rocroi inflicted a stunning defeat on the famed Spanish infantry, the first time that a Spanish army had been overcome in battle since the reign of Ferdinand and Isabella. Yet worse still was the fact that by then two territories belonging to Spain's European empire were in open revolt.

*Internal revolts against the
Castilian government*

In order to understand the causes of these revolts one must recognize that in the seventeenth century the real "nation of Spain" was Castile—all else was acquired territory. After the marriage of Isabella of Castile and Ferdinand of Aragon in 1469, geographically central Castile emerged as the dominant partner in the Spanish union, becoming even more dominant when Castile conquered the Muslim kingdom of Granada in southern Spain in 1492 and annexed Portugal in 1580. In the absence of any great financial hardships, semi-autonomous Catalonia (the most fiercely independent part of Aragon) endured Castilian hegemony. But in 1640, when the strains of warfare induced Castile to limit Catalonian liberties in order to raise more money and men for combat, Catalonia revolted. Immediately afterward the Portuguese learned of the Catalonian uprising and revolted as well, followed by southern Italians who revolted against Castilian viceroys in Naples and Sicily in 1647. At that point only the momentary inability of Spain's greatest external enemies, France and England, to take advantage of its plight saved the Spanish empire from utter collapse. Nothing if not determined, the Castilian government quickly put down the Italian revolts and by 1652 also brought Catalonia to heel. But

The Escorial. Philip II of Spain ordered the building between 1563 and 1584 of this somber retreat—part royal residence, part monastery—on an isolated spot, well removed from Madrid. Conceived on a grid-iron plan to honor the grid-iron martyrdom of St. Lawrence (on whose feast day Philip had won a decisive victory against the French), the Escorial symbolizes for many the Spanish crown's dedication to the ideals of the Counter-Reformation as well as its attempt to impose rationalized central government on the refractory outlying provinces of the Iberian Peninsula and Spanish Empire.

Portugal retained its independence forever, and by the Peace of the Pyrenees, signed with France in 1659, Spain in effect conceded that it would entirely abandon its ambitions of dominating Europe.

A comparison between the fortunes of Spain and France in the first half of the seventeenth century is highly instructive because some striking similarities existed between the two countries, but in the end differences turned out to be most decisive. Spain and France were of almost identical territorial extent and both countries had been created by the same process of accretion. Just as the Castilian crown had gained Aragon in the north, Granada in the south, and then Portugal, so the kingdom of France had grown by adding on such diverse territories as Languedoc, Dauphiné, Provence, Burgundy, and Brittany. Since the inhabitants of all these territories cherished traditions of local independence as much as the Catalans or Portuguese, and since the rulers of France, like those of Spain, were determined to govern their provinces ever more firmly—especially when the financial stringencies of the Thirty Years' War made ruthless tax collecting urgently necessary—a direct confrontation between the central government and the provinces in France became inevitable, just as in Spain. But France weathered the storm whereas Spain did not, a result largely attributable to France's greater wealth and the greater prestige of the French crown.

In good times most French people, including those from the outlying provinces, tended to revere their king. Certainly they had excellent reason to do so during the reign of Henry IV. Having established religious peace in 1598 by the Edict of Nantes, the affable Henry, who declared that there should be a chicken in every French family's pot each Sunday, set about to restore the prosperity of a country devastated by four decades of civil war. Fortunately France had enormous

Spain and France compared

The reign of Henry IV

Cardinal Richelieu. A contemporary portrait emphasizing the cardinal's awesome bearing.

Cardinal Richelieu

The Fronde

economic resiliency, owing primarily to its extremely rich and varied agricultural resources. Unlike Spain, which had to import food, France normally had been able to export it, and Henry's finance minister, the duke of Sully, quickly saw to it that France became a food exporter once more. Among other things, Sully distributed throughout the country free copies of a guide to recommended farming techniques and financed the rebuilding or new construction of roads, bridges, and canals to help expedite the flow of goods. In addition, Henry IV was not content to see France rest its economic development on agricultural wealth alone; instead he ordered the construction of royal factories to manufacture luxury goods such as crystal glass and tapestries, and he also supported the growth of silk, linen, and woolen cloth industries in many different parts of the country. Moreover, Henry's patronage allowed the explorer Champlain to claim parts of Canada as France's first foothold in the New World. Thus Henry IV's reign certainly must be counted as one of the most benevolent and progressive in all French history.

Far less benevolent was Henry's *de facto* successor as ruler of France, Cardinal Richelieu (1585–1642), yet Richelieu fully managed to maintain France's forward momentum. The cardinal, of course, was never the real king of France—the actual title was held from 1610 to 1643 by Henry IV's ineffectual son Louis XIII. But as first minister from 1624 to his death in 1642 Richelieu governed as he wished, and what he wished most of all was to enhance centralized royal power at home and expand French influence in the larger theater of Europe. Accordingly, when Huguenots rebelled against restrictions placed on them by the Edict of Nantes, Richelieu put them down with an iron fist and emended the Edict in 1629 by depriving them of all their military rights. Since his armed campaigns against the Huguenots had been very costly, the cardinal then moved to gain more income for the crown by abolishing the semi-autonomy of Burgundy, Dauphiné, and Provence so that he could introduce direct royal taxation in all three areas. Later, to make sure all taxes levied were efficiently collected, Richelieu instituted a new system of local government by royal officials known as *intendants* who were expressly commissioned to run roughshod over any provincial obstructionism. By these and related methods Richelieu made French government more centralized than ever and managed to double the crown's income during his rule. But since he also engaged in an ambitious foreign policy directed against the Habsburgs of Austria and Spain, resulting in France's costly involvement in the Thirty Years' War, internal pressures mounted in the years after Richelieu's death.

A reaction against French governmental centralization manifested itself in a series of revolts between 1648 and 1653 collectively known as "the slingshot tumults," or in French, the *Fronde*. By this time Louis XIII had been succeeded by his son Louis XIV, but because the latter was still a boy, France was governed by a regency consisting of Louis's mother Anne of Austria and her paramour Cardinal Mazarin. Considering that both were foreigners (Anne was a Habsburg and Mazarin originally an Italian adventurer named Giulio Mazarini), it is not surprising that many of their subjects, including some extremely powerful nobles, hated them. Moreover, nationwide resentments were greater still because the costs of war and several consecutive years of bad harvests had brought France temporarily into a grave economic plight. Thus when cliques of nobles expressed their disgust with Mazarin for primarily petty and self-interested reasons, they found much support throughout the country, and uncoordinated revolts against the regency flared on and off for several years.

France, however, was not Spain, and thus did not come close to falling apart. Above all, the French crown itself, which retained great reservoirs of prestige owing to a well-established national tradition and the undoubted achievements of Henry IV and Richelieu, was by no means under attack. On the contrary, neither the aristocratic leaders of the *Fronde* nor the commoners from all ranks who joined them in revolt claimed to be resisting the young king but only the alleged corruption and mismanagement of Mazarin. Some of the rebels, it is true, insisted that part of Mazarin's fault lay in his pursuance of Richelieu's centralizing, antiprovincial policy. But since most of the aristocrats who led the *Fronde* were merely "outs" who wanted to be "in," they often squabbled among themselves—sometimes even arranging agreements of convenience with the regency or striking alliances with France's enemy, Spain, for momentary gain—and proved completely unable to rally any unified support behind a common program. Thus when Louis XIV began to rule in his own name in 1651 and pretexts for revolting against "corrupt ministers" no longer existed, all opposition was soon silenced. As so often happens, the idealists and poor people paid the greatest price for revolt: in 1653 a defeated leader of popular resistance in Bordeaux was broken on a wheel and not long afterward a massive new round of taxation was proclaimed. Remembering the turbulence of the *Fronde* for the rest of his life, Louis XIV resolved never to let his aristocracy or his provinces get out of hand again and ruled as the most effective royal absolutist in all of French history.

French absolutism triumphant

Compared to the civil disturbances of the 1640s in Spain and France, those in England proved the most momentous in their results for the history of limited government. Whereas all that the revolts against Castile accomplished was the achievement of Portuguese independence and the crippling of an empire that was already in decline, and all that happened in France was a momentary interruption of the steady advance of royal power, in England a king was executed and barriers were erected against royal absolutism for all time.

The case of England

England around 1600 was caught up in a trend toward the growth of centralized royal authority characteristic of all western Europe. Not only had Henry VIII and Elizabeth I brought the English Church fully

James I. "The wisest fool in
Christendom."

under royal control, but both monarchs employed so-called prerogative courts wherein they could proceed against subjects in disregard of traditional English legal safeguards for the rights of the accused. Furthermore, although Parliament met regularly during both reigns, members of Parliament were far less independent than they had been in the fifteenth century: any parliamentary representative who might have stood up to Henry VIII would have lost his head, and almost all parliamentarians were so charmed by Elizabeth that they were glad to do her bidding. Thus when the Stuart dynasty succeeded Elizabeth, the last of the Tudors, it was only natural that the Stuarts would try to increase royal power still more. And indeed they might have succeeded had it not been for their ineptness and an extraordinary combination of forces ranged against them.

Lines of contention were drawn immediately at the accession of Elizabeth's nearest relative, her cousin James VI of Scotland, who in 1603 retained his Scottish crown but also became king of England as James I (1603–1625). Homely but vain, addled but erudite, James fittingly was called by Henry IV of France "the wisest fool in Christendom," and presented the starkest contrast to his predecessor. Whereas Elizabeth knew how to gain her way with Parliament without making a fuss about it, the schoolmasterish foreigner insisted on lecturing parliamentarians that he was semi-divine and would brook no resistance: "As it is atheism and blasphemy to dispute what God can do, so it is presumption and high contempt in a subject to dispute what a king can do." Carrying these sentiments further, in a speech to Parliament of 1609 he proclaimed that "kings are not only God's lieutenants on earth . . . but even by God Himself they are called gods."

That such extreme pretentions to divine authority would arouse strong opposition was a result even James should have been able to foresee, for the English were still intensely committed to the theory of parliamentary controls on the crown. Yet not just theory was at stake since the specific policies of the new king antagonized large numbers of his subjects. For one, James insisted upon supplementing his income by modes of money-raising which had never been sanctioned by Parliament; and when the leaders of that body remonstrated, he angrily tore up their protests and dissolved their sessions. Worse, he interfered with the freedom of business by granting monopolies and lucrative privileges to favored companies. And, worst of all in the eyes of most patriotic Englishmen, James quickly put an end to the long war with Spain and refused thereafter to become involved in any foreign military entanglements. Today many of us might think that James's commitment to peace was his greatest virtue; certainly his pacifism was well advised financially since it spared the crown enormous debts. But in his own age James was hated particularly for his peace policy because it made him seem far too friendly with England's traditional enemy, Spain, and because "appeasement" meant leaving seemingly heroic Protestants in Holland and Germany in the lurch.

Although almost all English people (except for a small minority of clandestine Catholics) objected to James I's pacific foreign policy, those who hated it most were a group destined to play the greatest role in overthrowing the Stuarts, namely, the Puritans. Extremist Calvinistic Protestants, the Puritans believed that Elizabeth I's religious compromises had not broken fully enough with the forms and doctrines of Roman Catholicism. Called Puritans from their desire to "purify" the English Church of all traces of Catholic ritual and observance, they most vehemently opposed the English "episcopal system" of church government by bishops. But James I was as committed to retaining episcopalianism as the Puritans were intent on abolishing it because he viewed royally appointed bishops as one of the pillars of a strong monarchy: "No bishop, no king." Since the Puritans were the dominant party in the House of Commons and many Puritans were also prosperous businessmen who opposed James's monopolistic policies and money-raising expediencies, throughout his reign James remained at loggerheads with an extremely powerful group of his subjects for a combination of religious, constitutional, and economic reasons.

The Puritans

Nonetheless, James survived to die peacefully in bed in 1625, and had it not been for mistakes made by his son Charles I (1625–1649), England might have gone the way of absolutistic France. Charles held the same inflated notions of royal power and consequently was quickly at odds with the Puritan leaders of Parliament. Soon after his accession to the throne Charles became involved in a war with France and needed revenue desperately. When Parliament refused to make more than the customary grants, he resorted to forced loans from his subjects, punishing those who failed to comply by quartering soldiers in their homes or throwing them into prison without a trial. In reaction to this, Parliament forced the Petition of Right on the king in 1628. This document declared all taxes not voted by Parliament illegal, condemned the quartering of soldiers in private houses, and prohibited arbitrary imprisonment and the establishment of martial law in time of peace.

Charles I

Angered rather than chastened by the Petition of Right, Charles I soon resolved to rule entirely without Parliament—and nearly succeeded. From 1629 to 1640 no Parliaments were called. During this "eleven-years' tyranny." Charles's government lived off a variety of makeshift dues and levies. For example, the crown sold monopolies at exorbitant rates, revived highly antiquated medieval financial claims, and admonished judges to collect the stiffest of fines. Though technically not illegal, all of these expedients were deeply resented. Most controversial was the collection of "ship money," a levy taken on the pretext of a medieval obligation of English seaboard towns to provide ships (or their worth in money) for the royal navy. Extending the payment of ship money from coastal towns to the whole country, Charles threatened to make it a regular tax in contravention of the Petition of Right, and was upheld in a legal challenge of 1637 brought against him on these grounds by the Puritan squire John Hampden.

Charles I. This portrait by Van Dyck vividly captures the ill-fated monarch's arrogance.

The Scottish uprising

By such means the king managed to make ends meet without the aid of taxes granted by Parliament. But he became ever more hated by most of his subjects, and above all the Puritans, not just because of his constitutional and financial policies but also because he seemed to be pursuing a course in religion that came much closer to Catholicism than to Calvinism. Whether the English Puritans would have risen up in revolt on their own is a moot question, but they were ultimately emboldened to do so by a chain of events beginning with a revolt in Scotland. The uprising in Scotland of 1640 against the policy of an English king was not unlike those in Catalonia and Portugal of the same year against the Spanish crown except that the Scottish rising was not just nationalistic but also explicitly religious in nature. Like his father, Charles believed in the adage "no bishop, no king" and hence foolhardily decided to introduce episcopalian church government into staunchly Presbyterian Scotland. The result was armed resistance by Charles's northern subjects and the first step toward civil war in England.

*The convening of
Parliament*

In order to obtain the funds necessary to punish the Scots, Charles had no other choice but to summon Parliament and soon found himself the target of pent-up resentments. Knowing full well that the king was helpless without money, the Puritan leaders of the House of Commons determined to take England's government into their own hands. Accordingly, they not only executed the king's first minister, the earl of Strafford, but they abolished ship money and the prerogative courts which ever since the reign of Henry VIII had served as instruments of arbitrary rule. Most significantly, they enacted a law forbidding the crown to dissolve Parliament and requiring the convening of sessions at least once every three years. After some indecision, early in 1642 Charles replied to these acts with a show of force. He marched with his guard into the House of Commons and attempted to arrest five of its leaders. All of them escaped, but an open conflict between crown and Parliament could no longer be avoided. Both parties collected troops and prepared for an appeal to the sword.

*Civil war: the Cavaliers
vs. the Roundheads*

These events initiated the English Civil War, a conflict at once political and religious, which lasted from 1642 to 1649. Arrayed on the royal side were most of England's most prominent aristocrats and largest landowners, who were almost all "high-church" Anglicans. Opposed to them, the followers of Parliament included smaller landholders, tradesmen, and manufacturers, the majority of whom were Puritans. The members of the king's party were commonly known by the aristocratic name of Cavaliers. Their opponents, who cut their hair short in contempt for the fashionable custom of wearing curls, were derisively called Roundheads. At first the royalists, having obvious advantages of military experience, won most of the victories. In 1644, however, the parliamentary army was reorganized, and soon afterward the fortunes of battle shifted. The Cavalier forces were badly beaten, and in 1646 the king was compelled to surrender.

The struggle would now have ended had not a quarrel developed within the parliamentary party. The majority of its members, who had allied with the Presbyterian Scots, were ready to restore Charles to the throne as a limited monarch under an arrangement whereby a uniform Calvinistic Presbyterian faith would be imposed on both Scotland and England as the state religion. But a radical minority of Puritans, commonly known as Independents, distrusted Charles and insisted upon religious toleration for themselves and all other non-Presbyterian Protestants. Their leader was Oliver Cromwell (1599–1658), who had risen to command the Roundhead army. Taking advantage of the dissension within the ranks of his opponents, Charles renewed the war in 1648, but after a brief campaign was forced to surrender. Cromwell now resolved to end the life of "that man of blood," and, ejecting all the Presbyterians from Parliament by force of arms, obliged the remaining so-called Rump Parliament to vote an end to the monarchy. On 30 January 1649 Charles I was beheaded, a short time later the hereditary House of Lords was abolished, and England became a republic.

Oliver Cromwell

But founding a republic was far easier than maintaining one, and the new form of government, officially called a Commonwealth, did not last long. Technically the Rump Parliament continued as the legislative body, but Cromwell, with the army at his command, possessed the real power and soon became exasperated by the attempts of the legislators to perpetuate themselves in office and to profit from confiscating the wealth of their opponents. Accordingly, in 1653 he marched a detachment of troops into the Rump, and, saying "Come, I will put an end to your prating," ordered the members to disperse. Thereby the Commonwealth ceased to exist and was soon followed by the "Protectorate" or virtual dictatorship established under a constitution drafted by officers of the army. Called the Instrument of Government, this text was the nearest approximation of a written constitution England has ever had. Extensive powers were given to Cromwell as Lord Protector for life, and his office was made hereditary. At first a Parliament exercised limited authority in making laws and levying taxes, but in 1655 its members were abruptly dismissed by the Lord Protector. Thereafter the government became a thinly disguised autocracy, with Cromwell now wielding a sovereignty even more absolute then any the Stuart monarchs would have dared to claim.

Given the choice between a Puritan military dictatorship and the old royalist regime, when the occasion arose England unhesitatingly opted for the latter. Above all, years of Calvinistic austerities such as the prohibition of any public recreation on Sundays—then the workingperson's only holiday—had discredited the Puritans, making most people long for the milder Anglicanism of the original Elizabethan settlement. Thus not long after Cromwell's death in 1658, one of the deceased Protector's generals seized power and called for elections for a new Parliament which met in the spring of 1660 and proclaimed as

The Stuart Restoration

Cromwell Felling the Royal Oak of England. A Royalist print of 1656 which portrays Oliver Cromwell as a destructive villain.

king Charles I's exiled son, Charles II. With the reign of Charles II (1660–1685) Anglicanism was immediately restored, but by no means the same was true for untrammelled monarchical power. Rather, stating with characteristic good humor that he did not wish to "resume his travels," Charles agreed to respect Parliament and observe the Petition of Right. Of greatest constitutional significance was the fact that all the legislation passed by Parliament immediately before the outbreak of the Civil War, including the requirement to hold Parliaments at least once every three years, remained as law. Thus in striking contrast to absolutistic France, England became a limited monarchy. Putting its constitutional struggles behind it after one brief further test in the late seventeenth century, the realm of England would soon live up to the poet Milton's prediction of "a noble and puissant nation rousing herself like a strong man after sleep."

4. QUESTS FOR LIGHT OUT OF DARKNESS

Witchcraft and philosophy

Caught up in economic uncertainty, religious rivalries, and political turmoil, many Europeans between 1560 and 1660 understandably cast about for emotional or intellectual resolutions of their most pressing problems. Sometimes, as in the case of the great witchcraft delusion, this quest led merely to an intensification of hysteria. But in the case of more dispassionate reflections, the search for ways of resolving Europe's crises led to some of the most enduring statements of moral and political philosophy of all time.

Although no one simple explanation can be offered for the outbreak of western Europe's fearful witchcraft hysteria that reached its peak between 1580 and 1660, it is certain that persecutions of witches in those years were fiercest during times of greatest disaster and that people who burned witches genuinely thought they were fighting the powers of darkness. Looking for the origins of the great early-modern witchcraft delusion, historians recognize that peasant culture throughout the Middle Ages included belief in the possibilities of sorcery. In other words, most simple rural people assumed that certain unusual individuals could practice good, or "white," magic in the form of healing, divination for lost objects, and fortune-telling, or perhaps also evil, "black" magic that might, for example, call up tempests or ravage crops. Yet only in the later Middle Ages did learned authorities begin to insist on theological grounds that black magic could be practiced only as a result of pacts with the devil. Naturally, once this belief became accepted, judicial officers soon found it urgent to prosecute all "witches" who practiced black magic because warfare against the devil was paramount to Christian society and "the evil one" could not be allowed to hold any sway. Accordingly, as early as 1484 Pope Innocent VIII ordered papal inquisitors to root out alleged witchcraft with all the means at their disposal, and the pace of witch hunts gained momentum in the following decades. Nor were witch trials curtailed in areas that broke with Rome, for Protestant reformers believed in the insidious powers of Satan just as much as Catholics did. Indeed, Luther himself once threw an inkpot at a supposed apparition of the devil and Calvin saw Satan's evil workings wherever he looked. Thus both urged that alleged witches be tried more peremptorily and sen-

The origins of the witchcraft delusion

Supposed Witches Worshiping the Devil in the Form of a Billy-Goat. In the background other "witches" ride bareback on flying demons. This is one of the earliest visual conceptions of witchcraft, dating from around 1460.

*Witchcraft hysteria and the
European crisis*

tenced with less leniency than ordinary criminals, and persecutions of innocent people continued apace in Protestant as well as Catholic lands.

Yet the outbreak of a real mania for catching and killing "witches" did not begin until about 1580. Therefore it can only be supposed that the witchcraft hysteria was connected in some way with Europe's general crisis—all the more since it continued for about as long as the age of crisis itself and was most severe in just those localities where warfare or economic dislocation was most intense. In such places, whenever crops failed or cattle sickened people assumed that a "witch"—usually a defenseless old woman—was responsible, and rushed to put her to death. If not always old, the victims were most frequently women, no doubt in part because preachers had encouraged their flocks to believe that evil had first come into the world with Eve and in part because men in authority felt psychologically most ambivalent about members of the opposite sex. Pure sadism certainly cannot have been the original motive for such proceedings, but once trials began, horrendous sadism very often was unleashed. Thus old women, young girls, and sometimes even mere children might be brutally tortured by having needles driven under their nails, fires placed at their heels, or their legs crushed under weights until marrow spurted from their bones, in order to make them confess to having had filthy orgies with demons. The final death toll will never be known, but in the 1620s there was an average of one hundred burnings a year in the German cities of Würzburg and Bamberg, and around the same time it was said the town square of Wolfenbüttel "looked like a little forest, so crowded were the stakes."

The end of the witch hunts

Why persecution quickly ended in the years immediately after 1660 will remain a matter for scholarly speculation. Aside from the fact that better times returned to most of Europe around then, probably the best explanation is that shortly after 1660 educated magistrates began to adhere to a mechanistic view of the universe. In other words, once the leaders of society came to believe that storms and epidemics arose from natural rather than supernatural causes, they ceased to countenance witch hunts.

Burning of Witches at Dernberg in 1555. From a sixteenth-century German pamphlet denouncing witchcraft.

Fortunately, other attempts of Europeans between 1560 and 1660 to master the darkness around them were not in themselves so dark. Indeed, one of the most "enlightened" of all European moral philosophers was the Frenchman Michel de Montaigne (1533–1592), who wrote during the height of the French wars of religion. The son of a Catholic father and a Huguenot mother of Jewish ancestry, the well-to-do Montaigne retired from a legal career at the age of thirty-eight to devote himself to a life of leisured reflection. The *Essays* which resulted were a new literary form originally conceived as "experiments" in writing (French *essai* simply means "trial"). Because they are extraordinarily well written as well as being searchingly reflective, Montaigne's *Essays* ever since have ranked securely among the most enduring classics of French literature and thought.

Although the range of subjects of the *Essays* runs a wide gamut from "The Resemblance of Children to Their Fathers" to "The Art of Conversing," two main themes are dominant. One is a pervasive skepticism. Making his motto "Que sais-je?" (What do I know?), Montaigne decided that he knew very little for certain. According to him, "it is folly to measure truth and error by our own capacities" because our capacities are severely limited. Thus, as he maintained in one of his most famous essays, "On Cannibals," what may seem indisputably true and proper to one nation may seem absolutely false to another because "everyone gives the title of barbarism to everything that is not of his usage." From this Montaigne's second main principle followed—the need for tolerance. Since all people think they know the perfect religion and the perfect government, no religion or government is really perfect and consequently no belief worth fighting for to the death.

If the foregoing description makes Montaigne sound surprisingly modern, it must be emphasized that he was by no means a rationalist. On the contrary, he believed that "reason does nothing but go astray in everything," and that intellectual curiosity "which prompts us to thrust our noses into everything" is a "scourge of the soul." Moreover, concerning practical affairs Montaigne was a fatalist who thought that in a world governed by unpredictable "fortune" the best human strategy is to face the good and the bad with steadfastness and dignity. Lest people begin to think too highly of their own abilities, he reminded them that "sit we upon the highest throne in the world, yet we do sit upon our own behinds." Nonetheless, despite his passive belief that "fortune, not wisdom, rules the life of mankind," the wide circulation of Montaigne's *Essays* did help combat fanaticism and religious intolerance in his own and subsequent ages.

If Montaigne sought refuge from the trials of his age in skepticism, tolerance, and resigned dignity, his contemporary, the French lawyer Jean Bodin (1530–1596), looked for more light to come out of darkness from the powers of the state. Like Montaigne, Bodin was particularly troubled by the upheavals caused by the religious wars in

Montaigne

Montaigne's Essays: *skepticism and tolerance*

Antirationalism and fatalism

Jean Bodin

France—he had even witnessed the frightful St. Bartholomew's Day Massacre of 1572 in Paris. But instead of shrugging his shoulders about the bloodshed, he resolved to offer a political plan to make sure turbulence would cease. This he did in his monumental *Six Books on the Commonwealth* (1576), the earliest fully developed statement of governmental absolutism in Western political thought. According to Bodin, the state arises from the needs of collections of families, but once constituted should brook no opposition, for the maintenance of order is paramount. Whereas writers on law and politics before him had groped toward a theory of governmental sovereignty, Bodin was the first to offer a succinct definition; for him, sovereignty was "the most high, absolute, and perpetual power over all subjects," consisting principally in the power "to give laws to subjects without their consent." Although Bodin acknowledged the theoretical possibility of government by aristocracy or democracy, he assumed that the nation-states of his day would be ruled by monarchs and insisted that such monarchs could in no way be limited, either by legislative or judicial bodies, or even by laws made by their predecessors or themselves. Expressing the sharpest opposition to contemporary Huguenots who were saying (in contravention of the original teachings of Luther and Calvin) that subjects had a right to resist "ungodly princes," Bodin maintained that a subject must trust in his ruler's "mere and frank good will." Even if the ruler proved a tyrant, Bodin insisted that the subject had no warrant to resist, for any resistance would open the door "to a licentious anarchy which is worse than the harshest tyranny in the world." Since in his own day Bodin knew much "licentious anarchy" but had hardly any notion of how harsh the "harshest tyranny" could be, his position is somewhat understandable. Yet in the next century his *Commonwealth* would become the point of departure for justifications of an increasingly oppressive French royal absolutism.

Quite understandably, just as the French civil wars of the sixteenth century provoked a variety of responses, so did the English Civil War of the seventeenth. Drawing on a tradition of resistance to untrammelled state power expressed by French Huguenots and earlier English parliamentarians and Puritans, the great English Puritan poet John Milton enunciated a stirring defense of freedom of the press in his *Areopagitica* (1644). Similarly bold upholders of libertarianism were a party of Milton's Puritan contemporaries known as Levellers, the first exponents of democracy since Greek times. Organizing themselves as a pressure group within Cromwell's army in the later 1640s when Charles I's monarchy seemed clearly doomed, the Levellers—who derived their name from their advocacy of equal political rights for all classes—agitated in favor of a parliamentary republic based on nearly universal manhood suffrage. For them, servants and other wage-laborers had no right to vote because they formed part of their employer's "family" and allegedly were represented by the family head. Moreover, the Levellers did not even deign to argue about women's rights. Otherwise, however, in the immortal words of one of their spokesmen, they argued that "the poorest He that is in England hath a life to live as the greatest He, and therefore . . . every man that is to live under a government ought first by his own consent to put himself under that government." But since Oliver Cromwell, who believed that the only grounds for suffrage was sufficient property, would have none of this, once Cromwell assumed virtually dictatorial powers the Leveller party disintegrated. More radical still were the communistic Diggers, so called from their attempts to cultivate common lands in 1649. Claiming to be "true Levellers," the Diggers argued that true freedom lies not in votes, but "where a man receives his nourishment," and hence argued for the redistribution of property. Cromwell, however, dispersed them quickly and thus the Diggers have merely historical interest as vanguards of movements to come.

Far to the other extreme of the libertarian Puritans was the political philosopher Thomas Hobbes (1588–1679), whose reactions to the English Civil War led him to become the most forceful advocate of unrestrained state power of all time. Like Bodin, who was moved by the events of St. Bartholomew's Day to formulate a doctrine of political absolutism, Hobbes was moved by the turmoil of the English Civil War to do the same in his classic of political theory entitled *Leviathan* (1651). Yet Hobbes differed from Bodin in several respects. For one, whereas Bodin assumed that the absolute sovereign power would be a royal monarch, the more radical Hobbes, writing without any respect for tradition in Cromwell's England two years after the beheading of a king, thought the sovereign could be any ruthless dictator whatsoever. Then too, whereas Bodin defined his state as "the lawful government of families" and hence did not believe that the state could abridge private property rights because families could not exist without property, Hobbes's state existed to rule over atomistic individuals and thus was licensed to trample over both liberty and property.

But the most fundamental difference between Bodin and Hobbes lay in the latter's uncompromisingly pessimistic view of human nature. Whereas Bodin was pessimistic about mankind only by implication, Hobbes posited that the "state of nature" which existed before civil government came into being was a condition of "war of all against all." For Hobbes, since man naturally behaves as "a wolf" toward man, and hence increasing fear of violent death in the state of nature made human life "solitary, poor, nasty, brutish, and short," people for their own good at some purely theoretical point in time surrendered their liberties to a sovereign ruler in exchange for his agreement to keep the peace. Having thus granted away their liberties, subjects have no right whatsoever to seek them back, and the sovereign can tyrannize as he likes—free to oppress his charges in any way other than to kill them, an act which would negate the very purpose of his

The Title Page of Hobbes's Leviathan

Hobbes's pessimism

rule. It is a measure of the relentless logic and clarity of Hobbes's abstract exposition that his *Leviathan* is widely regarded as one of the four or five greatest political treatises ever written, for practically nobody really likes what he says. Indeed, even in his own age Hobbes's views were vastly unpopular—libertarians detested them for obvious reasons, and royalists hated them as much because Hobbes was contemptuous of dynastic claims based on blood lineage and rationalized absolutistic rule not on the grounds of powers granted from God, as most royalists did, but on powers surrendered by society. Yet because many important thinkers felt compelled to argue against Hobbes, he had enormous influence, if only in provoking the responses of others.

Perhaps fittingly, the most moving and in certain ways most modern attempt to bring light out of pervasive darkness was that of the seventeenth-century French moral and religious philosopher Blaise Pascal (1623–1662). In certain superficial ways Pascal's most enduring legacy, his *Pensées* (*Thoughts*), resemble Montaigne's *Essays* because both are highly introspective collections of informal short pieces written with great literary power. But Pascal, who turned away in a conversion experience from scientific rationalism to become a firm adherent of Jansenism (the most puritanical wing of French Catholicism), was as ardent a religious believer as Montaigne was a cool skeptic. Thus while Pascal agreed with Montaigne that human life on earth was fraught with peril—he defined man as "a thinking reed"—he had no doubt that a just Providence ruled the world and he believed as firmly as did Luther or Calvin that faith alone could show the way to salvation. Yet, recognizing that skeptics or secular rationalists could never be brought to the true faith by dogmatic authority, he hoped to convert doubters by appealing simultaneously to their intellects and their emotions in a major defense of Christianity. Unfortunately, premature death prevented him from accomplishing this ambitious goal, but the *Pensées* survive as previews of his approach. In these he conceded his own sense of terror and anguish in the face of evil and eternity, but made the awe itself a sign of the existence of God. Individuals today will be moved by Pascal's *Pensées* in varying degrees according to their own convictions, but few people of any persuasion will dispute Pascal's famous paradox that "man knows he is wretched; he is therefore wretched because he is so; but he is very great because he knows it."

Blaise Pascal

5. LITERATURE AND THE ARTS

*Major statements
concerning the human
condition*

The combined wretchedness and greatness of humanity may be taken as the theme for the extraordinary profusion of towering works of literature and art produced during western Europe's period of crisis from 1560 to 1660. Of course not every single writing or painting of the era expressed the same message. During a hundred years of extraordinary literary and artistic creativity, works of all genres and sentiments were produced, ranging from the frothiest farces to the darkest tragedies, the serenest still lifes to the most grotesque scenes of religious martyrdom. Nonetheless, the greatest writers and painters of the period all were moved by a realization of the ambiguities and ironies of human existence not unlike that expressed in different ways by Montaigne and Pascal. They all were fully aware of the horrors of war and human suffering so rampant in their day, and all were directly or indirectly aware of the Protestant conviction that men are "vessels of iniquity"; but they also inherited a large degree of Renaissance affirmativeness, and most of them accordingly preferred to view life on earth as a great dare.

From the host of remarkable writers who flourished during what was probably the most extraordinary century in the entire history of western European poetry and drama, we may take the very greatest: Cervantes, the Elizabethan dramatists—Shakespeare to the fore—and John Milton. Although Miguel de Cervantes (1547–1616) was not strictly speaking either a poet or a dramatist, his masterpiece, the satirical romance *Don Quixote,* exudes great lyricism and drama. The plot recounts the adventures of a Spanish gentleman, Don Quixote of La Mancha, who has become slightly unbalanced by constant reading of chivalric epics. His mind filled with all kinds of fantastic adventures, he sets out at the age of fifty upon the slippery road of knight-errantry, imagining windmills to be glowering giants and flocks of sheep to be armies of infidels whom it is his duty to rout with his spear. In his distorted fancy he mistakes inns for castles and serving girls for courtly ladies on fire with love. Set off in contrast to the "knight-errant" is the figure of his faithful squire, Sancho Panza. The latter represents the ideal of the practical man, with his feet on the ground and content with the modest but substantial pleasures of eating, drinking, and sleeping. Yet Cervantes clearly does not wish to say that the realism of a Sancho Panza is categorically preferable to the "quixotic" idealism of his master. Rather, the two men represent different facets of human nature. Without any doubt, *Don Quixote* is a devastating satire on the anachronistic chivalric mentality that would soon help hasten Spain's decline. But for all that, the reader's sympathies remain with the protagonist, the man from La Mancha who dares to "dream the impossible dream."

Directly contemporaneous with Cervantes were the English Elizabethan dramatists who collectively produced the most glorious age of theater known in the Western world. Writing after England's victory over the Spanish Armada, when national pride was at a peak, all exhibited great exuberance but none was by any means a facile optimist. In fact a strain of reflective seriousness pervades all their best works, and a few, like the tragedian John Webster (c. 1580–c. 1625), who "saw the skull beneath the skin," were if anything morbid pessimists. Literary critics tend to agree that of a bevy of great Elizabe-

Cervantes

Miguel de Cervantes

Elizabethan drama

than playwrights the most outstanding were Christopher Marlowe (1564–1593), Ben Jonson (c. 1573–1637), and, of course, William Shakespeare (1564–1616). Of the three, the fiery Marlowe, whose life was cut short in a tavern brawl before he reached the age of thirty, was the most youthfully energetic. In plays such as *Tamburlaine* and *Doctor Faustus* Marlowe created larger-than-life heroes who seek and come close to conquering everything in their path and feeling every possible sensation. But they meet unhappy ends because, for all his vitality, Marlowe knew that there are limits on human striving, and that wretchedness as well as greatness lies in the human lot. Thus though Faustus asks a reincarnated Helen of Troy, conjured up by Satan, to make him "immortal with a kiss," he dies and is damned in the end because immortality is not awarded by the devil or found in earthly kisses. In contrast to the heroic tragedian Marlowe, Ben Jonson wrote corrosive comedies which expose human vices and foibles. In the particularly bleak *Volpone* Jonson shows people behaving like deceitful and lustful animals, but in the later *Alchemist* he balances an attack on quackery and guillibility with admiration for resourceful lower-class characters who cleverly take advantage of their supposed betters.

William Shakespeare

Incomparably the greatest of the Elizabethan dramatists, William Shakespeare, was born into the family of a tradesman in the provincial town of Stratford-on-Avon. His life is enshrouded in more mists of obscurity than the careers of most other great people. It is known that he left his native village, having gained little formal education, when he was about twenty, and that he drifted to London to find employment in the theater. How he eventually became an actor and still later a writer of plays is uncertain, but by the age of twenty-eight he had definitely acquired a reputation as an author sufficient to excite the jealousy of his rivals. Before he retired to his native Stratford about 1610 to spend the rest of his days in ease, he had written or collaborated in writing nearly forty plays, over and above 150 sonnets and two long narrative poems.

*Shakespeare's three
periods: (1) confidence*

As everyone knows, Shakespeare's plays rank as a kind of secular Bible wherever the English language is spoken. The reasons lie not only in the author's unrivaled gift of expression, and in his scintillating wit, but most of all in his profound analysis of human character seized by passion and tried by fate. Shakespeare's dramas fall rather naturally into three groups. Those written during the playwright's earlier years are characterized by a sense of confidence. They include a number of history plays, which recount England's struggles and glories leading up to the triumph of the Tudor dynasty; the lyrical romantic tragedy *Romeo and Juliet;* and a wide variety of comedies including the magical *Midsummer Night's Dream* and Shakespeare's greatest creations in the comic vein—*Twelfth Night, As You Like It,* and *Much Ado about Nothing.* Despite the last-named title, few even of the plays of Shakespeare's early, lightest period are "much ado about nothing." Rather, most explore with wisdom as well as wit fundamental problems of psychological identity, honor and ambition, love and friendship. Occasionally they also contain touches of deep seriousness, as in *As You Like It,* when Shakespeare has a character pause to reflect that "all the world's a stage, and all the men and women merely players" who pass through seven "acts" or stages of life.

Such touches, however, never obscure the restrained optimism of Shakespeare's first period, whereas the plays from his second period are far darker in mood. Apparently around 1601 Shakespeare underwent a crisis during which he began to distrust human nature profoundly and indict the whole scheme of the universe. The result was a group of dramas characterized by bitterness, frequent pathos, and a troubled searching into the mysteries of things. The series begins with the tragedy of indecisive idealism represented by *Hamlet,* goes on to the cynicism of *Measure for Measure* and *All's Well That Ends Well,* and culminates in the cosmic tragedies of *Macbeth* and *King Lear,* wherein characters assert that "life's but a walking shadow . . . a tale told by an idiot, full of sound and fury signifying nothing," and that "as flies to wanton boys are we to the gods; they kill us for their sport." Despite all this gloom, however, the plays of Shakespeare's second period generally contain the dramatist's greatest flights of poetic grandeur.

(2) crisis

Although *Macbeth* and *Lear* suggest an author in the throes of deep depression, Shakespeare managed to resolve his personal crisis and end his dramatic career with a third period characterized by a profound spirit of reconciliation. Of the three plays (all idyllic romances) written during this final period, the last, *The Tempest,* is the greatest.

(3) reconciliation

Mr. WILLIAM
SHAKESPEARES
COMEDIES,
HISTORIES, &
TRAGEDIES.

Published according to the True Originall Copies.

William Shakespeare. Portrait made for the First Folio edition of his works, 1623.

John Milton. From the First Edition of his poems, 1645.

*Italian and Spanish
Mannerism*

Here ancient animosities are buried and wrongs are righted by a combination of natural and supernatural means, and a wide-eyed, youthful heroine rejoices on first seeing men with the words "O brave new world, that has such people in it!" Here, then, Shakespeare seems to be saying that for all humanity's trials life is not so unrelentingly bitter after all, and the divine plan of the universe is somehow benevolent and just.

Though less versatile than Shakespeare, not far behind him in eloquent grandeur stands the Puritan poet John Milton (1608–1674). The leading publicist of Oliver Cromwell's regime, Milton wrote the official defense of the beheading of Charles I as well as a number of treatises justifying Puritan positions in contemporary affairs. But he was also a man full of contradictions who loved the Greek and Latin classics at least as much as the Bible. Hence he could write a perfect pastoral elegy, *Lycidas,* mourning the loss of a dear friend in purely classical terms. Later, when forced into retirement by the accession of Charles II, Milton, though now blind, embarked on writing a classical epic, *Paradise Lost,* out of material found in Genesis concerning the creation of the world and the fall of man. This magnificent poem, which links the classical tradition to Christianity more successfully than any literary work written before or since, is surely one of the greatest epics of all time. Setting out to "justify the ways of God to man," Milton in *Paradise Lost* first plays "devil's advocate" by creating the compelling character of Satan, who defies God with boldness and subtlety. But Satan is more than counterbalanced in the end by the real "epic hero" of *Paradise Lost,* Adam, who learns to accept the human lot of moral responsibility and suffering, and is last seen leaving Paradise with Eve, the world "all before them."

The ironies and tensions inherent in human existence also were portrayed with extraordinary eloquence and profundity by several immortal masters of the visual arts who flourished between 1560 and 1660. The dominant style in painting in Italy and Spain in the second half of the sixteenth century was Mannerism. Originally a term of opprobrium for alleged imitators—supposedly second-rate artists who painted in the "manner" of Michelangelo's late phase—the term *Mannerism* in current analysis has come to mean much more than that; indeed art historians now rank some Mannerist painters among the West's greatest masters. Unquestionably Mannerism did take as its point of departure Michelangelo's tendency toward anticlassicism and distortion of nature for emotional effects, but Mannerist painters went so much further in emphasizing restlessness, imbalance, and distortion that they left Michelangelo far behind. Admittedly many of them lacked skill and depth of vision, contenting themselves with portraying brawn instead of muscle, melodrama instead of drama. But some others fully succeeded in balancing great artistic virtuosity with the communication of radiant inner light.

Of the latter, the two most outstanding are the Venetian Tintoretto (1518–1594) and the Spaniard El Greco (c. 1541–1614). Combining Manneristic distortion and restlessness with a traditionally Venetian taste for rich color, Tintoretto produced an enormous number of monumentally large canvases devoted to religious themes that still inspire awe with their broodingly shimmering light and gripping theatricality. More emotional still is the work of Tintoretto's disciple, El Greco. Born Domenikos Theotokopoulos on the Greek island of Crete, this extraordinary painter absorbed some of the stylized elongation characteristic of Greco-Byzantine icon painting before traveling to Italy to learn from great contemporary Mannerist painters such as Tintoretto and then finally settling in Spain, where he was nicknamed "El Greco"—Spanish for "the Greek." El Greco's paintings were too bizarre to be greatly appreciated in his own age, and even now they often appear so unbalanced as to seem the work of one almost deranged. Yet such a view slights El Greco's deeply mystical Catholic fervor as well as his technical achievements. Best known today is his transfigured landscape, the *View of Toledo,* with its somber but awesome light breaking where no sun shines, but equally inspiring are his swirling religious allegories such as *The Burial of the Count of Orgaz* (thought by the painter to be his masterpiece), and his myriad stunning portraits in which gaunt, dignified Spaniards radiate a rare blend of austerity and spiritual insight.

Fray Felix Hortensio Paravicino, by El Greco. More restrained in composition than most of the artist's other work, this portrait nonetheless communicates a sense of deep spiritual intensity.

The dominant artistic school of southern Europe succeeding Mannerism was that of the Baroque, a school not just of painting but of sculpture and architecture lasting from about 1600 until the early eighteenth century. The term *Baroque* is derived from a Portuguese word for an irregular, rough pearl, and this reveals much about its meaning.

See color plates following page 512 for the *Crucifixion* by Tintoretto and the *View of Toledo* by El Greco

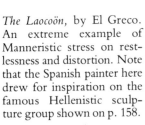

The Laocoön, by El Greco. An extreme example of Manneristic stress on restlessness and distortion. Note that the Spanish painter here drew for inspiration on the famous Hellenistic sculpture group shown on p. 158.

The Church of S. Carlo alle Quattro Fontane, Rome. Built by Bernini's contemporary Francesco Borromini in 1665, the facade of S. Carlo well exemplifies the frontage "in depth" characteristic of Baroque architecture.

Picking up where Mannerism left off, the Baroque style emphasized the emotional, the antinaturalistic, and the swirling as much as Mannerism, but Baroque works of art characteristically were less shrouded by somber mystery and were far more affirmative than Manneristic paintings. One major explanation for this is that Baroque art in all genres was usually semi-propagandistic. Originating in Rome as an expression of the ideals of the Counter-Reformation papacy and the Jesuit order, Baroque architecture in particular aimed to gain adherence for a specific worldview. Similarly, Baroque painting often was done in the service of the Counter-Reformation Church, which at its high tide around 1620 seemed everywhere to be on the offensive, and when Baroque painters were not celebrating Counter-Reformation ideals, most of them worked in the service of monarchs who sought their own glorification.

Indubitably the most imaginative and influential figure of the original Roman Baroque was the architect and sculptor Gianlorenzo Bernini (1598–1680), a frequent employee of the papacy who created one of the most magnificent celebrations of papal grandeur in the sweeping colonnades leading up to St. Peter's basilica. Breaking with the serene Renaissance classicism of Palladio, Bernini's architecture retained the use of classical elements such as columns and domes, but combined them in ways meant to express both aggressive restlessness and great power. In addition Bernini was one of the first to experiment with church facades built "in depth"—building frontages, that is, not conceived as continuous surfaces but which jutted out at odd angles

Left: *David*, by Bernini. Whereas the earlier conceptions of David by the Renaissance sculptors Donatello and Michelangelo were reposeful (see pp. 429 and 430), the Baroque sculptor Bernini chose to portray his young hero at the peak of physical exertion. Right: *St. Theresa in Ecstasy*, by Bernini. As David is seen at the peak of bodily exertion, St. Theresa is shown at the peak of spiritual transport.

The Surrender of Breda, by Velásquez. Celebrating a Spanish victory over the Dutch in an early phase of the Thirty Years' War, the Spanish lances point proudly skyward in contrast to the desolate Dutch smoke, but the Spanish commander displays magnanimity for the defeated enemy.

and seemingly invaded the open space in front of them. If the purpose of these innovations was to stir the viewer and draw him emotionally into the ambit of the work of art, the same may be said for Bernini's aims in sculpture. Harking back to the restless motion of Hellenistic statuary—particularly the Laocoön group—and building on tendencies already present in the later sculpture of Michelangelo, Bernini's statuary emphasizes drama and incites the viewer to respond to it rather than serenely observe.

Since most Italian Baroque painters lacked Bernini's artistic genius, to view the very greatest masterpieces of southern European Baroque painting one must look to Spain and the work of Diego Velásquez (1599–1660). Unlike Bernini, Velásquez, a court painter in Madrid just when Spain hung on the brink of ruin, was not an entirely typical exponent of the Baroque style. Certainly many of his canvases display a characteristically Baroque delight in motion, drama, and power, but Velásquez's best work is characterized by a more restrained thoughtfulness than usually found in the Baroque. Thus his famous *Surrender at Breda* shows muscular horses and splendid Spanish grandees on the one hand, but un-Baroque humane and deep sympathy for defeated, disarrayed troops on the other. Moreover, Velásquez's single greatest painting, *The Maids of Honor,* done around 1656 after Spain's collapse, radiates thoughtfulness rather than drama and is one of the most probing artistic examinations of illusion and reality ever executed.

Southern Europe's main northern rival for artistic laurels in the "iron century" was the Netherlands, where three extremely dissimilar painters all explored the theme of the greatness and wretchedness of

See color plates following page 512 for the *Maids of Honor* and *Pope Innocent X* by Velásquez

A Dwarf, by Velásquez. The great Spanish artist had an enduring fascination with the less favored of the earth.

*Painting in the
Netherlands: (1) Peter
Brueghel*

See color plates facing
page 449 for the
Harvesters by Breughel

man to the fullest. The earliest, Peter Brueghel (rhymes with frugal) (c. 1525–1569), worked in a vein related to earlier Netherlandish realism. But unlike his predecessors, who favored quiet urban scenes, Brueghel exulted in portraying the busy, elemental life of the peasantry. Most famous in this respect are his rollicking *Peasant Wedding* and *Peasant Wedding Dance,* and his spacious *Harvesters,* in which guzzling and snoring fieldhands are taking a well-deserved break from their heavy labors under the noon sun. Such vistas give the impression of uninterrupted rhythms of life, but late in his career Brueghel became appalled by the intolerance and bloodshed he witnessed during the time of the Calvinist riots and the Spanish repression in the Netherlands and expressed his criticism in an understated yet searing manner. In *The Blind Leading the Blind,* for example, we see what happens when ignorant fanatics start showing the way to each other. More powerful still is Brueghel's *Massacre of the Innocents,* which from a distance looks like a snug scene of a Flemish village buried in snow. In fact, however, heartless soldiers are methodically breaking into homes and slaughtering babies, the simple peasant folk are fully at their mercy, and the artist—alluding to a Gospel forgotten by warring Catholics and Protestants alike—seems to be saying "as it happened in the time of Christ, so it happens now."

Vastly different from Brueghel was the Netherlandish Baroque painter Peter Paul Rubens (1577–1640). Since the Baroque, unlike

The Massacre of the Innocents. This painting by Brueghel shows how effectively art can be used as a means of social commentary. Many art historians believe that Brueghel was tacitly depicting the suffering of the Netherlands at the hands of the Spanish in his own day.

The Triumph of the Eucharist, by Rubens. A typical Baroque work, this painting proclaims the victory of the Cross and the Eucharistic Chalice, symbols of Counter-Reformation Catholicism.

Mannerism, was an international movement closely linked to the spread of the Counter-Reformation, it should offer no surprise that Baroque style was extremely well represented in just that part of the Netherlands which, after long warfare, had been retained by Spain. In fact, Rubens of Antwerp was a far more typical Baroque artist than Velásquez of Madrid, painting literally thousands of robust canvases that glorified resurgent Catholicism or exalted second-rate aristocrats by portraying them as epic heroes dressed in bearskins. Even when Rubens's intent was not overtly propagandistic he customarily revelled in the sumptuous extravagance of the Baroque manner, being perhaps most famous today for the pink and rounded flesh of his well-nourished nudes. But unlike a host of lesser Baroque artists, Rubens was not entirely lacking in subtlety and was a man of many moods. His gentle portrait of his son Nicholas catches unaffected childhood in a moment of repose, and though throughout most of his career Rubens had celebrated martial valor, his late *Horrors of War* movingly portrays what he himself called "the grief of unfortunate Europe, which, for so many years now, has suffered plunder, outrage, and misery."

In some ways a blend of Brueghel and Rubens, the greatest of all Netherlandish painters, Rembrandt van Rijn (1606–1669), defies all attempts at facile characterization. Living across the border from the Spanish Netherlands in staunchly Calvinistic Holland, Rembrandt belonged to a society which was too austere to tolerate the unbuckled realism of a Brueghel or the fleshy Baroque pomposity of a Rubens. Yet Rembrandt managed to put both realistic and Baroque traits to new uses. In his early career he gained fame and fortune as the painter of biblical scenes which lacked the Baroque's fleshiness but retained its grandeur in their swirling forms and stunning experiments with

(2) Peter Paul Rubens

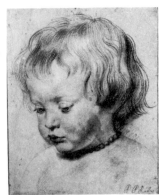

Rubens's Portrait of his Son Nicholas.

See color plates following page 512 for the *Horrors of War* and *England and Scotland Crowning Charles I* by Rubens

The Polish Rider, by Rembrandt. Unlike Titian's equestrian Charles V (above, p. 509), Rembrandt's rider is self-reflective and hence more humane.

(3) Rembrandt

See color plates following page 512 for *Aristotle Contemplating the Bust of Homer* by Rembrandt

light. In this early period too Rembrandt was active as a realistic portrait painter who knew how to flatter his self-satisfied subjects by emphasizing their Calvinistic steadfastness, to the great advantage of his purse. But gradually his prosperity faded, apparently in part because he grew tired of flattering and definitely because he made some bad investments. Since personal tragedies also mounted in the painter's middle and declining years his art inevitably became far more pensive and sombre, but it gained in dignity, subtle lyricism, and awesome mystery. Thus his later portraits, including those of himself, are imbued with introspective qualities and a suggestion that only the half is being told. Equally moving are explicitly philosophical paintings such as *Aristotle Contemplating the Bust of Homer,* in which the supposedly earthbound philosopher seems spellbound by the otherworldy luminous radiance of the epic poet, and the *The Polish Rider,* in which realistic and Baroque elements merge into a higher synthesis portraying a pensive young man setting out fearlessly into a perilous world. Like Shakespeare, Rembrandt knew that life's journey is full of perils, but his most mature paintings suggest that these can be mastered with poetry and courage.

SELECTED READINGS

- Items so designated are available in paperback editions.
- Ashton, Robert, *The English Civil War: Conservatism and Revolution, 1603–1649,* New York, 1978. A highly scholarly account: very informative, but not for beginners.

Aston, T., ed., *Crisis in Europe: 1560–1660,* London, 1965. A collection of highly valuable essays.

• Braudel, F., *The Mediterranean and the Mediterranean World in the Age of Philip II,* New York, 1972. One of the most brilliant history books of our age. Treats life in the Mediterranean regions in the second half of the sixteenth century with particular emphasis on how geography determines the course of human history.

• Chute, M., *Shakespeare of London,* New York, 1949. The best popular biography.

• Dean, Leonard F., ed., *Shakespeare: Modern Essays in Criticism,* New York, 1957. A variety of scholarly appraisals.

• Dunn, Richard S., *The Age of Religious Wars, 1559–1715,* 2nd ed., New York, 1979. The best college-level text on this period. Extremely well written.

• Elliot, J. H., *Imperial Spain, 1469–1716,* London, 1963. A masterpiece of sophisticated synthesis.

• ———, *Europe Divided: 1559–1598,* London, 1968. An extremely lucid narrative of complex events.

• Elton, G. R., *England under the Tudors,* 2nd ed., London, 1977. Engagingly written and authoritative.

• Ford, Boris, ed., *The Age of Shakespeare,* Baltimore, 1955. A good shorter handbook.

Frame, D., *Montaigne: A Biography,* New York, 1965. By far the best study in English.

Fraser, Lady Antonia, *Oliver Cromwell,* London, 1973. A popular biography.

Held, J. S., and D. Posner, *17th and 18th Century Art: Baroque Painting, Sculpture, Architecture,* New York, 1979. The most complete introductory review of the subject in English.

• Hibbard, Howard, *Bernini,* Baltimore, 1965. The basic study in English of this central figure of Baroque artistic activity.

• Hill, Christopher, *A Century of Revolution: 1603–1714,* 2nd ed., New York, 1982. A valuable survey of English developments that holds narrative to a minimum and stresses economic and social trends.

• Kahr, M. M., *Velázquez: The Art of Painting,* New York, 1976.

Kamen, Henry, *The Iron Century: Social Change in Europe, 1559–1660,* New York, 1971. One of the most detailed and persuasive statements of the view that there was a "general crisis" in many different aspects of European life.

Le Roy Ladurie, E., *Carnival in Romans,* New York, 1979. A closeup view of social turmoil in France in 1580.

• Mattingly, Garrett, *The Armada,* Boston, 1959. Fascinating narrative; thoroughly reliable but reads like a novel.

• Monter, E. W., ed., *European Witchcraft,* New York, 1969. Selected readings with fine introductions by one of the world's leading experts.

Parker, Geoffrey, *The Dutch Revolution,* Ithaca, N.Y., 1977. Now the standard survey in English on the revolt of the Netherlands.

• ———, *Europe in Crisis: 1598–1648,* Brighton, Sussex, 1980. A primarily political narrative of war and revolution in Europe exclusive of England.

• Pennington, D. H., *Seventeenth-Century Europe,* London, 1970. An extremely thorough and reliable survey that follows the conventional periodization of treating a century bounded by the round numbers 1600 and 1700.

Pierson, Peter, *Philip II of Spain,* London, 1975. An absorbing attempt to study Philip's personality and actions in terms of the dominant assumptions of his age.

• Rabb, T. K., *The Struggle for Stability in Early Modern Europe,* New York, 1975. A stimulating essay arguing for a shift from crisis to stability around 1660.

Roots, Ivan, ed., *Cromwell, A Profile,* New York, 1973. A collection of readings on problems in interpretation; complements Fraser.

• Rosenberg, Jakob, *Rembrandt, Life and Work,* London, 1964.

• Russell, Conrad, *The Crisis of Parliaments: English History, 1509–1660,* New York, 1971. The best survey covering this broad range of time.

• Shearman, John, *Mannerism,* Baltimore, 1967. Treats trends in late-sixteenth-century architecture and sculpture as well as Manneristic painting.

• Steinberg, S. H., *The Thirty Years' War and the Conflict for European Hegemony, 1600–1660,* New York, 1966. The best scholarly account.

• Stone, Lawrence, *The Causes of the English Revolution, 1529–1642,* New York, 1972. A judicious analysis by one of the foremost social historians of our age.

• Thomas, Keith, *Religion and the Decline of Magic,* London, 1971. A marvelously insightful study of popular belief in England.

• Trevor-Roper, H. R., *The Crisis of the Seventeenth Century: Religion, the Reformation and Social Change,* New York, 1968. A collection of path-breaking essays including one on the witch craze.

• Walzer, Michael, *The Revolution of the Saints: A Study in the Origins of Radical Politics,* Cambridge, Mass., 1965. An attempt by a political scientist to demonstrate that English Puritanism was the earliest form of modern political radicalism.

• Wedgwood, C. V., *William the Silent,* London, 1944. A laudatory and urbanely written biography.

———, *Richelieu and the French Monarchy,* New York, 1950. A somewhat slight but still useful introduction.

SOURCE MATERIALS

• Cervantes, Miguel de, *Don Quixote,* tr. Walter Starkie, New York, 1957.

Hobbes, Thomas, *Leviathan,* abridged by F. B. Randall, New York, 1964.

Montaigne, Michel de, *Essays,* tr. J. M. Cohen, Baltimore, 1958.

Pascal, Blaise, *Pensées,* French-English ed., H. F. Stewart, London, 1950.

Sprenger, Jakob, and H. Kramer, *The Malleus Maleficarum,* tr. M. Summers, 2nd ed., London, 1948. A frightful yet fascinating work, the *Malleus* ("The Hammer of Witches") was the most frequently used handbook of early-modern witchcraft prosecutors.

Chapter 17

THE ECONOMY AND SOCIETY
OF EARLY-MODERN EUROPE

We ought to esteem and cherish those trades which we have in remote or far countries, for besides the increase in shipping and mariners thereby, the wares also sent thither and received from thence are far more profitable unto the kingdom than by our trades near at hand.

—Thomas Mun, *England's Treasure by Foreign Trade,* 1630

In nearly every state in Europe citizens are divided into the three orders of nobles, clergy, and people. . . . Even Plato, although he intended all his citizens to enjoy an equality of rights and privileges, divided them into the three orders of guardians, soldiers and labourers. All this goes to show that there never was a commonwealth, real or imaginary, even if conceived in the most popular terms, where citizens were in truth equal in all rights and privileges. Some always have more, some less than the rest.

—Jean Bodin, *Six Books of the Commonwealth,* 1570

A ny study of early-modern European society must concern itself with change, with the factors that in the two hundred years after 1600 were powerful enough to produce the political upheaval of the French Revolution and the economic stimulus for the Industrial Revolution. Unquestionably, the most profound change during that period was economic. By the latter part of the eighteenth century, the freebooting overseas expansionism that had begun in the sixteenth century with the Spanish conquistadors had ended with Europe at the center of a vast system of worldwide trade. Commerce on this increasingly global scale had given birth to institutions fashioned for its support, and had altered patterns of living among those caught up in its overpowering dynamic. Banks and joint-stock companies financed international commercial ventures. New urban workshops responded to the intensified demand for manufactured goods.

Economic change

As international banking developed into a highly sophisticated profession, its practitioners became powerful men. As urban workshops imposed new conditions and habits, the urban artisan was forced to bend uncomfortably to unfamiliar demands.

European society as a whole found bending no more comfortable. Change was imposed upon national communities which, in many cases, were still defined according to the hierarchies of the Middle Ages: landlord and peasant, nobleman and serf. Each order was expected to acknowledge its inherent obligations and responsibilities, as each was assumed to be part of an organic and divinely sanctioned communal whole. Where, within this preordained structure, was the independent commercial entrepreneur or the dispossessed laborer supposed to fit? Tension of this sort between old forms and new realities was further exacerbated by the general crisis that we analyzed in the preceding chapter. Change produced by economic expansion and dislocation occurred against the background of civil and religious turmoil that tore much of Europe to pieces in the seventeenth century, and against an equally disruptive cycle of demographic swings caused by warfare and disease, by good weather one year, bad weather—and hence famine—the next. Those were the changes closest to the lives of most Europeans, the men and women still bound to the land, for whom, as the French historian Pierre Goubert has observed, "death was at the center of life, just as the graveyard was at the center of the village." The concerns of this chapter are thus both the economic and social circumstances that represented change, and the habits and traditions that were making change complex and difficult.

1. CAPITALISM, MERCANTILISM, AND THE COMMERCIAL REVOLUTION

The early-modern world of commerce and industry was governed by the assumptions of capitalism and mercantilism. Reduced to its simplest terms, capitalism may be defined as a system of production, distribution, and exchange, in which accumulated wealth is invested by private owners for the sake of gain. Its essential features are private enterprise, competition for markets, and business for profit. Generally it involves also the wage system as a method of payment of workers; that is, a mode of payment based not on the amount of wealth they create, but rather upon their ability to compete with one another for jobs. Capitalism represented a direct challenge to the semi-static economy of the medieval guilds, in which production and trade were supposed to be conducted for the benefit of society and with only a reasonable charge for the service rendered, instead of unlimited profits. Capitalism is a system designed to encourage commercial expansion beyond the local level, on a national and international scale. Guildmasters had neither the money (capital) to support nor the knowledge to organize and direct commercial enterprises beyond their own towns. Activity on that wider scale demanded the resources and expertise of wealthy and experienced entrepreneurs. These men, who usually started as merchants operating over a wide area and ended as bankers, could afford to invest in large quantities of manufactured goods, and if necessary, to hold them unsold until they could command a high price. The capitalist entrepreneur studied patterns of international trade. He knew where markets were and how to manipulate them to his advantage.

Capitalism is a system designed to reward the individual. In contrast, mercantilist doctrine emphasized direct governmental intervention in economic policy to increase the general prosperity of the state. Mercantilism was by no means a new idea. It was in fact a variation on the medieval notion that the populace of any particular town comprised a community with a common wealth, and that the economic well-being of such communities depended on the willingness of that populace to work at whatever task God or their rulers assigned them to benefit the community as a whole. Membership in a particular order within the community ensured to men and women the privileges of that order. In the case of the poor, this meant no more than protection from unfair prices and from starvation. In return for such protection, members of the community willingly placed themselves under the regimentation that guild restrictions and town ordinances imposed.

*The medieval origins of
mercantilism*

The mercantilism of the seventeenth and eighteenth centuries translated this earlier concept of community as a privileged, but regimented, economic unit from the level of towns to the level of the entire state. This translation represented not so much a complete change as it did the extension and elaboration of theories and practices that had governed the policies of earlier rulers. The conquest and subsequent plundering of the New World by Spain was an instance of mercantilism at work on a grand scale. The Statute of Artificers, passed by the English Parliament in 1563, which established a customary "fair" wage scale applicable to all laborers, instituted economic privilege and regimentation at the national level.

Mercantilism and the state

Mercantile theory held that a state's power depended on its actual, calculable wealth, expressed in terms of the amount of gold and silver bullion in its possession at any given time. A state amassed bullion by ensuring itself as favorable a balance of trade as possible. Hence the degree to which a state could remain self-sufficient, importing as little as necessary while exporting as much as possible, was the clearest gauge not only of its economic prosperity but of its power. This doctrine had profound effects on state policy. First, it led to the establishment and development of overseas colonies. Colonies, mercantilists reasoned, would, as part of the national community, provide it with raw materials, including precious metals in some instances, which would otherwise have to be obtained outside the community. Second,

Definition of wealth

it inspired state governments to encourage industrial production and trade, both sources of revenue which would increase the state's income. And finally, it persuaded policy-makers to discourage domestic consumption, since goods purchased on the home market reduced the goods available for export. Government policy was thus to keep wages low, so that laborers would not have money to spend for more than it took to provide them with basic food and shelter.

Although most western European statesmen were prepared to endorse mercantilist goals in principle, the degree to which their policies reflected those goals varied according to national circumstance. Spain, despite its insistence on closed colonial markets and its determination to amass a fortune in bullion, never succeeded in attaining the economic self-sufficiency that mercantilist theory demanded. The Spaniards therefore found it necessary to exchange their bullion for Flemish, French, and English manufactured goods which they were unable to supply to either their home market or to their colonies. Madrid's mercantilism, however, had little appeal in Amsterdam. The Dutch rejected the governmental centralization implicit in the mercantilist notion of the sovereign state as an economic unit which they associated with the hated regime of Philip II of Spain. They further recognized that the United Provinces were too small to permit them to achieve economic self-sufficiency. Throughout the seventeenth and eighteenth centuries the Dutch remained dedicated in principle and practice to free trade, often investing, contrary to mercantilist doctrine, in the commercial enterprises of other countries and promoting national prosperity by encouraging the rest of Europe to rely upon Amsterdam as a hub of international finance and trade. The Dutch commitment to free trade did not extend to their colonial preserves which remained closed to their commercial rivals. It was the French and the English who combined, in differing degrees, governmental centralization and independent commercial enterprise most consistently and effectively and who became the most successful practitioners of mercantilism in early-modern Europe.

The goal of capitalism was a commercial system that would make individuals rich. The goal of mercantilism was a system that would make the state powerful. Though they differed as to ends, the two systems functioned compatably together for most of the early-modern period. Together, governments and entrepreneurs designed new institutions that facilitated the expansion of global commerce during the seventeenth and eighteenth centuries and effected what has come to be called a Commercial Revolution.

Enterprise on this new scale depended on the availability of capital for investment. And that capital was generated primarily by a gradual increase in agricultural prices throughout much of the period. Had that increase been sharp, it would probably have produced enough hunger and suffering to retard rather than stimulate economic growth.

Merchants' Houses in Seventeenth-Century Amsterdam. This engraving depicts
not only the opulence of middle-class life in a thriving commercial capital,
but also the spirit of civic unity, expressed by the crowds gathered for a public
celebration. (Several of the principal thoroughfares of Amsterdam are canals.)

Had there been no increase, however, the resulting stagnation produced by marginal profits would have proved equally detrimental to
expansion. Agricultural entrepreneurs had surplus capital to invest in
trade; bankers put that surplus to use to expand their commercial
enterprises. Together, capitalist investors and merchants profited.

Banks played a vital role in the history of this expansion. Strong
religious and moral disapproval of lending money at interest meant
that banking had enjoyed a dubious reputation in the Middle Ages. *(2) the rise of banking*
Because the Church did come to allow profit-making on commercial
risks, however, banks in Italy and Germany were organized under
family auspices, the most notable examples being the fourteenth- and
fifteenth-century operations of the Medici in Florence and the Fuggers
of Augsburg. The Fuggers lent money to kings and bishops, and served
as broker to the pope for the sale of indulgences. The rise of these
private financial houses was followed by the establishment of government banks, reflecting the mercantilist goal of serving the monetary
needs of the state. The first such institution, the Bank of Sweden, was
founded in 1657. The Bank of England was established in 1694, at a
time when England's emergence as a world commercial power guaranteed that institution a leading role in international finance.

The growth of banking was necessarily accompanied by the adoption of various aids to financial transactions on a large scale, further

evidence of a commercial revolution. Credit facilities were extended in such a way that a merchant in Amsterdam could purchase goods from a merchant in Venice by means of a bill of exchange issued by an Amsterdam bank. The Venetian merchant would obtain his money by depositing the bill of exchange in his local bank. Later, the two banks would settle their accounts by comparing balances. Among the other facilities for the expansion of credit were the adoption of a system of payment by check in local transactions and the issuance of bank notes as a substitute for gold and silver. Both of these devices were invented by the Italians and were gradually adopted in northern Europe. The system of payment by check was particularly important in increasing the volume of trade, since the credit resources of the banks could now be expanded far beyond the actual amounts of cash in their vaults.

*(3) expansion of credit
facilities*

International commercial expansion called forth larger units of business organization. The prevailing unit of production and trade in the Middle Ages was the shop or store owned by an individual or a family. Partnerships were also quite common, in spite of the grave disadvantage of unlimited liability of each of its members for the debts of the entire firm. Obviously no one of these units was well adapted to business involving heavy risks and a huge investment of capital. The attempt to devise a more suitable business organization resulted in the formation of *regulated companies.* The regulated company was an association of merchants banded together for a common venture. Members did not pool their resources but agreed merely to cooperate for their mutual advantage and to abide by certain definite regulations. Usually the purpose of the combination was to maintain a monopoly of trade in some part of the world. Assessments were often paid by the members for the upkeep of docks and warehouses and especially for protection against "interlopers," as those traders were called who attempted to break into the monopoly. A leading example of this type of organization was an English company known as the Merchant Adventurers, established for the purpose of trade with the Netherlands and Germany.

*(4) changes in business
organization; the growth
of regulated companies*

The Commercial Revolution was facilitated in the seventeenth century when the regulated company was largely superseded by a new type of organization at once more compact and broader in scope. This was the *joint-stock company,* formed through the issuance of shares of capital to a considerable number of investors. Those who purchased the shares might or might not take part in the work of the company. Whether they did or not, they were joint owners of the business and therefore entitled to share in its profits in accordance with the amount they had invested. The joint-stock company had numerous advantages over the partnership and the regulated company. First, it was a permanent unit, not subject to reorganization every time one of its members died or withdrew. And second, it made possible a much larger accumulation of capital, through a wide distribution of shares.

Joint-stock companies

In short, it possessed nearly every advantage of the modern corporation except that it was not a person in the eyes of the law with the rights and privileges guaranteed to individuals. While most of the early joint-stock companies were founded for commercial ventures, some were organized later in industry. A number of the outstanding trading combinations were also *chartered companies*. They held charters from the government granting a monopoly of the trade in a certain locality and conferring extensive authority over the inhabitants, and were thus an example of the way capitalist and mercantilist interests might coincide. Through a charter of this kind, the British East India Company undertook the exploitation of vast territories on the Indian subcontinent, and remained virtual ruler there until the end of the eighteenth century.

A final important feature of the Commercial Revolution was the development of a more efficient money economy. Money had been used widely since the revival of trade in the eleventh century. Nevertheless, there were few coins with a value that was recognized other than locally. By 1300, the gold ducat of Venice and the gold florin of Florence had come to be accepted in Italy and also in the international markets of northern Europe. But no country could be said to have had a uniform monetary system. Nearly everywhere there was great confusion. Coins issued by kings circulated side by side with the money of foreign states. Moreover, the types of currency were modified frequently, and the coins themselves were often debased. A common method by which kings expanded their own personal revenues was to increase the proportion of cheaper metals in the coins they minted. But the growth of trade and industry in the Commercial Revolution accentuated the need for more stable and uniform monetary systems. The problem was solved by the adoption of a standard system of money by every important state to be used for all transactions within its borders. Much time elapsed, however, before the reform was complete. England began the construction of a uniform coinage during the reign of Queen Elizabeth, but the task was not finished until late in the seventeenth century. Indeed, the French did not succeed in reducing their money to its modern standard of simplicity and convenience until the early nineteenth century.

(5) a money economy

The Commercial Revolution, although it contributed to the prosperity of both individuals and states, was accompanied by serious risks and consequences occasionally disastrous to investors and to national economies. One major result of overseas expansion was the severe inflation caused by the increase in the supply of silver, which plagued Europe at the end of the sixteenth century (see above, p. 503). Price fluctuations, in turn, produced further economic instability. Businessmen were tempted to expand their enterprises too rapidly; bankers extended credit so liberally that their principal borrowers, especially nobles, often defaulted on loans. Spain and Italy were among the first to suffer setbacks. In both, failure of wages to keep pace with rising

The dangers of expansion

prices brought severe and continuing hardships to the lower classes. Impoverishment was rife in the cities, and bandits flourished in the rural areas. In Spain, some ruined aristocrats were not too proud to join the throngs of vagrants who wandered from city to city. At the end of the fifteenth century the great Florentine bank of the Medici closed its doors. The middle of the century that followed saw numerous bankruptcies in Spain and the decline of the Fuggers in Germany. Meanwhile, England, Holland, and to some extent France waxed prosperous. This prosperity was especially characteristic of the "age of silver," which lasted from about 1540 to 1620. In the seventeenth century decline set in once more after inflation had spent its force, and as a consequence of religious and international wars and civil strife.

The South Sea Bubble

The alternation of booms and recessions was followed by outbreaks of feverish speculation. These reached their climax early in the eighteenth century. The most notorious were the South Sea Bubble and the Mississippi Bubble. The former was the result of inflation of the stock of the South Sea Company in England, whose offer to assume the national debt led to unwarranted confidence in the company's future. When buoyant hopes gave way to fears, investors made frantic attempts to dispose of their shares for whatever they would bring. A crash which came in 1720 was the inevitable result.

The Night-Share Crier and His Magic Lantern. A Dutch caricature of John Law's Mississippi Bubble, correctly suggesting that its promised financial rewards were illusory.

During the years when the South Sea Bubble was being inflated in England, the French were going through a similar wave of speculative madness. In 1715 a Scotsman by the name of John Law, who had been compelled to flee from British soil for killing his rival in a love intrigue, settled in Paris, after various successful gambling adventures in other cities. He persuaded the regent of France to adopt his scheme for paying off the national debt through the issuance of paper money and to grant him the privilege of organizing the Mississippi Company for the colonization and exploitation of Louisiana. As the government loans were redeemed, those who received the money were encouraged to buy stock in the company. Soon the shares began to soar, ultimately reaching a price forty times their original value. Nearly everyone who could scrape together a bit of surplus cash rushed forward to participate in the scramble for riches. Stories were told of butchers and tailors who were supposed to have become millionaires by buying a few shares and holding them for a rise in price. But as the realization grew that the company would never be able to pay more than a nominal dividend on the stock at its inflated value, the more cautious investors began selling their holdings. The alarm spread, and soon all were as

The Mississippi Bubble

anxious to sell as they had been to buy. In 1720 the Mississippi Bubble burst in a wild panic. Thousands of people who had sold good property to buy the shares at fantastic prices were ruined.

The role of the state

Joint-stock companies in France were more directly dependent on the state than was the case elsewhere, a reflection of French dedication to mercantilist theory. In most cases French companies were floated under governmental auspices; courtiers—and the king himself—were heavy investors. Agents of the state played a direct role in their management, sometimes to the company's ultimate disadvantage. The French East India Company, for example, was compelled by state direction to govern its colonies in accordance with the laws of Paris, a fact which, one historian has remarked, "reminds one of the complaint that French progress in the Sahara was retarded by the refusal of the camel to accommodate its habits to administrative regulations made in Paris."[1] Even though companies elsewhere were less subject to governmental regulation than they were in France, government and commerce generally worked to promote each other's interests. In time of war, governments called upon commercial capitalists to assist in the financing of their campaigns. When England went to war against France in 1689, for example, the government had no long-range borrowing mechanism available to it; during the next quarter century the merchant community, through the Bank of England, assisted the government in raising over £170 million and in stabilizing the national debt at £40 million. In return, trading companies used the war to increase long-distance commercial traffic at the expense of their French enemy, and exerted powerful pressure on the government to secure treaties that would work to their commercial advantage.

2. COLONIZATION AND OVERSEAS TRADE

Spanish colonization

The institutions of the Commercial Revolution—banks, credit facilities, joint-stock companies, monetary systems—were designed specifically to assist both capitalist entrepreneurs and mercantilist policymakers in the development and exploitation of overseas colonies and trading posts, the most visible evidence of the economic expansionism of early-modern Europe. Following the exploits of the conquistadors, the Spanish established colonial governments in Peru and in Mexico, which they controlled from Madrid in proper mercantilist fashion by a Council of the Indies. In return for a protection fee, as distinct from the royalty of one-fifth of all bullion extracted from the colonies, the Spanish navy attempted to protect treasure ships from attacks by the French, English, and Dutch. The mercantilist governments of Philip II and his successors were determined to defend their monopoly in the New World. They issued trading licenses to none but Spanish merchants; exports and imports passed only through the port of Seville (later the more navigable port of Cadiz), where they were registered at the government-operated Casa de Contratación, or customs house.

These precautions did not deter other countries from attempting to win a share of the treasure for themselves. Probably the boldest challengers were the English, and their leading buccaneer the "sea dog" Sir Francis Drake, who three times raided the east and west coasts of

[1]G. N. Clark, *The Seventeenth Century* (New York, 1961), p. 39.

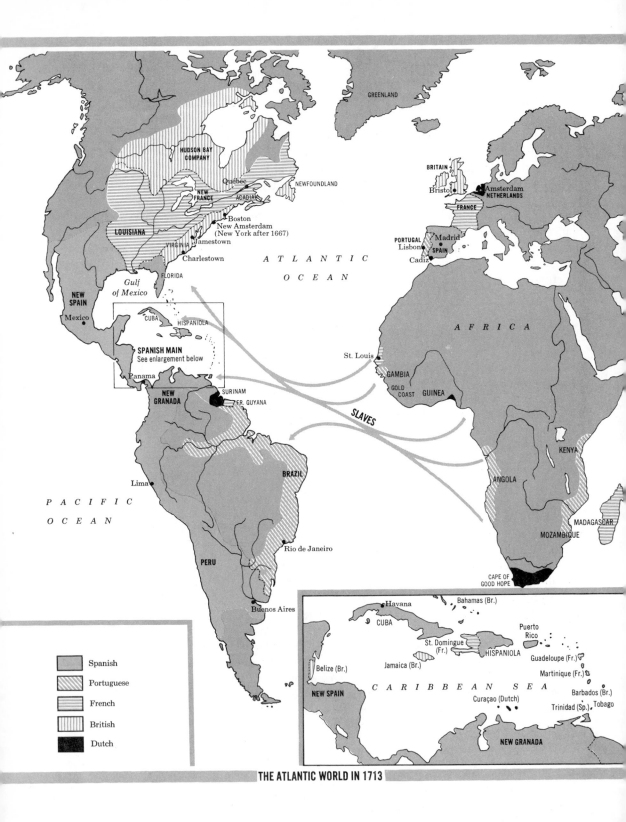

GREENLAND

HUDSON BAY
COMPANY

Québec

NEW
FRANCE ACADIA

NEWFOUNDLAND

LOUISIANA

Boston
New Amsterdam
(New York after 1667)

VIRGINIA Jamestown

Charlestown

Gulf
of Mexico

FLORIDA

NEW
SPAIN

Mexico

CUBA

HISPANIOLA

SPANISH MAIN
See enlargement below

Panama

NEW
GRANADA SURINAM
FR. GUYANA

BRAZIL

Lima

PACIFIC
OCEAN

PERU

Rio de Janeiro

Buenos Aires

ATLANTIC
OCEAN

BRITAIN

Bristol

Amsterdam
NETHERLANDS

FRANCE

PORTUGAL Madrid
Lisbon SPAIN

Cadiz

AFRICA

St. Louis

GAMBIA
GOLD
COAST GUINEA

SLAVES

KENYA

ANGOLA

MADAGASCAR

MOZAMBIQUE

CAPE OF
GOOD HOPE

Havana
Bahamas (Br.)

CUBA

Puerto
Rico

St. Domingue
(Fr.)
HISPANIOLA Guadeloupe (Fr.)

Belize (Br.)

Jamaica (Br.)

Martinique (Fr.)

CARIBBEAN SEA
Barbados (Br.)

NEW SPAIN
Curaçao (Dutch)
Trinidad (Sp.) Tobago

NEW GRANADA

Spanish

Portuguese

French

British

Dutch

THE ATLANTIC WORLD IN 1713

Spanish America and who, in 1587, the year before the Armada set sail on its ill-fated voyage north, "singed the beard of the Spanish king" by attacking the Spanish fleet at its anchorage in Cadiz harbor. Yet despite dashing heroics of that sort, the English could do no more than dent the Spanish trade. Reluctantly foresaking the search for the quick profits Spain was extracting from its colonial gold and silver mines, English colonists began to establish agricultural settlements in North America and the Caribbean basin. The first permanent, though ultimately unsuccessful, colony was established at Jamestown, in Virginia, in 1607. Over the next forty years, 80,000 English emigrants founded over twenty autonomous settlements in the New World. At first, English governments did far less than the Spanish to control these enterprises by means of mercantilist-inspired policies. Agriculture did not seem to promise rewards large enough to warrant state regulation. In addition, since many of the colonies were settled by religious dissenters escaping the attempts of James I and Charles I to impose religious uniformity, those monarchs were not disposed to encourage their economic prosperity by direct subsidy, or by the introduction of tariffs to prevent foreign competitors from underselling the colonists in the English home market.

English colonization

By the mid–seventeenth century, however, English policy had changed. Agricultural colonies were producing crops in high demand throughout Europe. The profits of colonial planters encouraged the governments of both Oliver Cromwell and Charles II to intervene in the management of their overseas economy. Navigation Acts, passed in 1651 and 1660, and rigorously enforced thereafter, decreed that all exports from English colonies to the mother country be carried in English ships, and forbade the direct exporting of certain "ennumerated" products directly from the colonies to continental ports.

*The growth of English
colonial regulation*

The most valuable of those products were sugar and tobacco. Sugar, virtually unknown in Europe earlier, had become a popular luxury by the end of the sixteenth century. Where once it had been considered no more than a medicine, one observer now noted that the wealthy were "devouring it out of gluttony." Sugarcane was raised in the West Indies after 1650 in rapidly increasing amounts. In the eighteenth century, the value of the sugar that England imported from its small island colonies there—Barbados, Jamaica, St. Kitts, and others— exceeded the value of its imports from the vast subcontinents of China and India. Although the tobacco plant was imported into Europe by the Spaniards about fifty years after the discovery of America, another half century passed before Europeans contracted the habit of smoking. At first the plant was believed to possess miraculous healing powers and was referred to as "divine tobacco" and "our holy herb nicotian." (The word "nicotine" derives from the name of the French ambassador to Portugal, Jean Nicot, who brought the tobacco plant to France.) The practice of smoking was popularized by English explorers, especially by Sir Walter Raleigh, who had learned to smoke

Sugar and tobacco

The Dutch East India Company Warehouse and Timber Wharf at Amsterdam. The substantial warehouse, the stockpiles of lumber, and the company ship under construction in the foreground illustrate the degree to which overseas commerce could stimulate economy of the mother country.

while living among the Indians of Virginia. It spread rapidly through all classes of European society. Governments at first joined the Church in condemning the use of tobacco because of its socially and spiritually harmful effects, but by the end of the seventeenth century, having realized the profits to be made from its production, they were encouraging its use.

The Dutch in the Far East

The Dutch were even more successful than the English in establishing a flourishing commercial empire in the seventeenth century. Their joint-stock East India Company, founded in 1602, rivaled its English counterpart in Asia, gaining firm control of Sumatra, Borneo, and the Moluccas, or Spice Islands, and driving Portuguese traders from an area where they had heretofore enjoyed an undisturbed commercial dominion. The result was a Dutch monopoly in pepper, cinnamon, nutmeg, mace, and cloves. The Dutch also secured an exclusive right to trade with the Japanese, and maintained outposts in China and India as well. In the Western hemisphere, their achievements were less spectacular. Following a series of trade wars with England, they surrendered their North American colony of New Amsterdam (subsequently renamed New York) in 1667, retaining Surinam, off the northern coast of South America, as well as the islands of Curaçao and Tobago in the West Indies in compensation.

The French in America

French colonial policy matured during the administration of Louis XIV's mercantilist finance minister, Jean Baptiste Colbert (1619–1683), who perceived of overseas expansion as an integral part of state economic policy. He organized joint-stock companies to compete with those of the English. He encouraged the development of lucrative sugar-producing colonies in the West Indies, the largest of which was St. Dominique (present-day Haiti). France also dominated the interior of the North American continent. Frenchmen traded furs and preached Christianity to the Indians in a vast territory that stretched from Acadia and the St. Lawrence River in the northeast to Louisiana in the west. Yet the financial returns from these lands was hardly commensurate with their size. Furs, fish, and tobacco were exported to home markets, but not in sufficient amounts to match the profits from the sugar colonies of the Caribbean or from the line of trading posts the French maintained in India.

The fortunes of these commercial empires rose and fell in the course of the seventeenth and eighteenth centuries. The Spanish, mired in a persistent economic lassitude and embroiled in a succession of expensive wars and domestic rebellions, were powerless to preserve the sanctity of their empire. Their merchant marine, once a match for cunning pirate-admirals like Drake, was by the middle of the seventeenth century unable to protect itself from attack by its more spirited commercial rivals. In a war with Spain in the 1650s, the English captured not only the island of Jamaica but treasure ships lying off the Spanish harbor of Cadiz. Further profit was obtained by bribing Spanish customs officials on a grand scale. During the second half of the century, two-thirds of the imported goods sold in Spanish colonies were smuggled in by Dutch, English, and French traders. By 1700, though Spain still possessed a colonial empire, it was one which lay at the mercy of its more dynamic rivals. Portugal, too, found it impossible to prevent foreign penetration of its colonial economies. The English worked diligently and successfully to win commercial advantages. They obtained concessions to export woolens duty-free into Portugal itself in return for similar preferential treatment for Portuguese wines. (The notorious affection of the English upper class for port wine dates from the signing of the Treaty of 1703.) English trade with the mother country led in time to English trade with the Portuguese colony of Brazil, indeed to the opening of commercial offices in Rio de Janeiro.

"The Solid Enjoyment of Bottle and Friend." An eighteenth-century English satire on the drinking habits of the upper classes.

The Dutch, whose merchant fleet of over 16,000 vessels was the largest in seventeenth-century Europe, continued to dominate world trade until eclipsed by the French and British after the late seventeenth century. Dutch ships—about half the European total—not only sailed the high seas, but dominated the European coastal carrying trade as well. The Dutch merchant marine force ensured the position of Amsterdam as the world's premier trading center, the volume of Dutch commerce allowing Amsterdam merchants to undersell their English and French rivals. During the eighteenth century a growing Anglo-French rivalry in India stole the commercial spotlight from the Dutch spice monopoly in the Far East. The French and English East India Companies employed mercenaries to establish and expand trading areas such as Madras, Bombay, and Pondichéry. By exploiting indigenous industries, European capitalists continued to increase the flow of fine cotton textiles, tea, and spices which passed through these commercial depots on their way to Europe. The struggle for economic dominance in India was resolved in mid-century in England's favor following a series of military clashes. As a sign of France's defeat, in 1769 the French East India Company was dissolved.

*Increasing dominance of
western trade routes*

Despite the commercial importance of India, however, patterns of world trade came increasingly to be dominated by western routes that had developed in response to the lucrative West Indian sugar industry, and to the demand for slaves from Africa to work the plantations in the Caribbean. Here Britain, again, eventually assumed the lead. Typically, an English ship might begin its voyage with a consignment of Jamaican rum and sail to Africa, where the rum would be exchanged for a cargo of slaves. From the west coast of Africa the ship would then cross the South Atlantic to the sugar colonies of Jamaica or Barbados, where slaves would be traded for molasses, which would make the final leg of the journey to New England. A variant triangle might see cheap manufactured goods move from Bristol or Liverpool, in England, to Africa, where they would be traded for slaves. Those slaves would then be shipped to Virginia and exchanged for tobacco, which would be shipped to England and processed there for sale in continental markets. Other eighteenth-century trade routes were more direct: the Spanish, French, Portuguese, and Dutch all engaged in the slave trade between Africa and Central and South America; the Spanish attempted, vainly, to retain a mercantilist monopoly on direct trade between Cadiz and their South American colonies; others sailed from England, France, or North America to the Caribbean and back again. And of course trade continued to flourish between Europe and the Near and Far East. But the triangular western routes, dictated by the grim economic symbiosis of sugar and slaves, remained dominant.

The slave trade

The cultivation of sugar and tobacco depended on slave labor; and as demand for those products increased, so did the traffic in black slaves, without whose labor those products could not be raised or harvested. At the height of the Atlantic slave trade in the eighteenth century, somewhere between 75,000 and 90,000 blacks were shipped across the Atlantic yearly: six million in the eighteenth century, out of a total of over nine million for the entire history of the trade. About 35 percent went to English and French Caribbean plantations, 5 percent (roughly 450,000) to North America, and the rest to the Portuguese colony of Brazil and to Spanish colonies in South America. Although run in the sixteenth and early seventeenth centuries as a monopoly by various governments, in its heyday the slave trade was open to private entrepreneurs, who operated ports on the West African coast. Traders exchanged cheap Indian cloth, metal goods, rum, and firearms with African slave merchants in return for their human cargo. Already disoriented and degraded by their capture at the hands

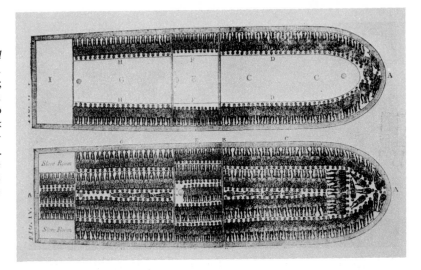

How Slaves Were Stowed Aboard Ship during the Middle Passage. Men were "housed" on the right; women on the left; children in the middle. The human cargo was jammed onto platforms six feet wide without sufficient headroom to permit an adult to sit up. This diagram is from evidence gathered by English abolitionists and depicts conditions on the Liverpool slave ship *Brookes.*

of rival tribes, black men, women, and children were packed by the hundreds into the holds of slave ships for the gruesome "middle passage" across the Atlantic (so called to distinguish it from the ship's voyage from Europe to Africa, and from the slave colony back to Europe again). Shackled to the decks, without sanitary facilities, the black "cargo" suffered horribly; the mortality rate, however, remained at about 10 or 11 percent, not much higher than the rate for a normal sea voyage of one hundred days or more. Since traders had to invest as much as £10 per slave in their enterprise, they ensured that their consignment would reach its destination in good enough shape to be sold for a profit.

Not until the very end of the eighteenth century did Europeans protest this ghastly traffic. Though the trade was risky, dependent as it was on a good wind and fair weather, profits often reached as much as 300 percent. Demand for slaves remained high throughout the eighteenth century. By the 1780s, there were over 500,000 slaves on the largest French plantation island, St. Dominique, and 200,000 or more on the English counterpart, Jamaica. Those numbers reflected the expanding world market for slave-grown crops. As long as demand for the crops cultivated by slaves continued to rise—as long as the economy relied to the extent it did upon slave labor—governments would remain unwilling to put an end to the system that, as one Englishman wrote in 1749, provided "an unexhaustible fund of wealth to this nation." Philosophers argued that though there was reason to rejoice that slavery had been banished from the continent of Europe (forgetting, apparently, the extent to which it continued to exist east of the Elbe in the form of serfdom), it remained a necessity in other parts of the world. Public pressure, first from Quakers and then from others motivated either by religious or humanitarian zeal, helped put an end to the trade in England in 1807, and to slavery itself in British

The ending of the trade

colonies in 1833. Slavery in French colonies was abolished in 1793, but only after slaves had risen in massive revolt on St. Dominique. Elsewhere, in Latin and North America, slavery lasted well into the nineteenth century—in the United States, until the Civil War of 1861–1865.

The slave trade is an integral part of the history of the dramatic rise of English and French commerce during the eighteenth century. France experienced a striking rise in trade. French colonial trade, valued at 25 million livres in 1716, rose to 263 million livres in 1789. In England, during roughly the same period, foreign trade increased in value from £10 million to £40 million, the latter amount more than twice that for France. These figures suggest the degree to which statecraft and private enterprise were bound to each other. If merchants depended on their government to provide a navy to protect and defend their overseas investments, governments depended equally on entrepreneurship, not only to generate money to build ships, but to sustain the trade upon which national power had come to rely so heavily.

3. AGRICULTURE AND INDUSTRY

The pace of industrial change in early-modern Europe was not as dynamic as that of the Commercial Revolution and the expansion of overseas colonization and trade. Changes did occur, but less uniformly and dramatically than those we have been tracing. This is not surprising, since the major economic enterprise remained agricultural production, which, throughout much of the period, was generally carried on according to traditional techniques that kept the volume of production low. Yet by the end of the eighteenth century, tradition was beginning to yield to innovation, with the result that production in some areas was increasing dramatically.

Most of the agricultural regions of seventeenth-century Europe were farmed in open fields. In the north, these fields were usually large sections of land, divided into long, narrow strips; in the south, the strips tended to reflect the more irregular shape of local landscapes. Although one or two rich aristocrats might own as much as three-fourths of the land in an open-field village, that land did not comprise one solid block. Instead it was made up of a great many plots, seldom contiguous, within the various open fields that surrounded the village. A large property owner's *desmesne* farm—which he worked with hired laborers for his own direct profit—and his tenant farms—those which he leased out to peasants—all consisted of these bits and pieces of land which lay alongside other bits and pieces that belonged to other landowners—very often small peasant proprietors. Each large open field thus resembled a patchwork quilt. Under these circumstances, in order for the fields to be cultivated with any degree of efficiency, all the "patches" had to be planted with the same crop, and sown, cultivated, and harvested together. Once the harvest was in, livestock was often turned into the fields to graze. One consequence of this practice was that crops were cut with a primitive sickle, which left more stubble for sheep and cattle, rather than with the far more efficient scythe. Inefficiency was indeed the hallmark of the open-field system, an inefficiency which those who owned large tracts of land grew more and more unwilling to tolerate. The Commercial Revolution encouraged landlords, particularly those in England and Holland, to compete for markets as capitalist agricultural entrepreneurs. In doing so, they looked for ways to improve the yield on their lands.

By the end of the eighteenth century a great many had resolved the problem of low production by adopting a full range of innovative farming techniques, the most drastic of which was the enclosure of open fields to allow for more systematic and therefore more productive farming. "Enclosure" was the term for land reorganization within a traditional village community. The earliest enclosures in England took place in the fifteenth and sixteenth centuries and entailed the conversion of lands into fenced-off sheep meadows. Because of the great profits to be accrued from wool, some landlords decided to convert common pastures that hitherto had supported peasant livestock into their own preserves for sheep-raising. Sometimes they also succeeded in converting grain fields into sheep pastures by evicting peasants whose leaseholds were none too secure. This caused grave hardships for the peasants concerned. As Thomas More wrote in his *Utopia* (1516), "sheep that used to be so meek and eat so little now are becoming so greedy and wild that they devour men themselves . . . for they leave no land free for the plough." The humanitarian More, however, was exaggerating somewhat. In fact, no more than about 3 percent of arable land had been enclosed before 1525 and part of that was not for sheep pasturage.

Enclosure

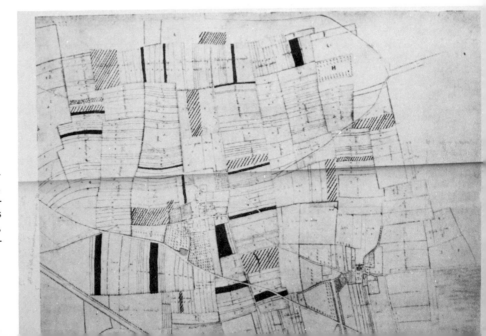

The Open-Field System in Northern France, 1738. Note the subdivision of large tracts into narrow strips, each owned by different proprietors.

Scientific farming

*Improved farming
techniques*

The process of enclosure

The really dramatic enclosure movement in England took place between 1710 and 1810 and aimed not to free land for sheep but to increase the efficiency of crop-raising. In this period landlords became convinced of the necessity for "scientific farming." Above all, they realized that by introducing new crops and farming methods they could reduce the amount of fallow lands and bring in higher yields, and thus higher profits. Some of the important new crops with which they experimented were clover, alfalfa, and related varieties of leguminous plants. These reduced fertility much less than cereal grains and actually helped to improve the quality of the soil by gathering nitrogen and making the ground more porous. Another new crop that had a similar effect was the turnip. The greatest propagandist for the planting of this unattractive vegetable was Viscount Charles Townshend (1674–1738), a prominent aristocrat and politician, who toward the end of his life left the royal court to experiment with agriculture. In this he became a model for subsequent aristocratic interest in scientific farming. Townshend gained the nickname of "Turnip" Townshend because he was so dedicated to converting people to the use of the turnip in new crop-rotation systems.

Clover, alfalfa, and turnips not only helped in doing away with the fallow but they provided excellent winter food for animals, thereby aiding the production of more and better livestock. And more livestock also meant more manure. Accordingly, intensive manuring became another way in which scientific farmers could eliminate the need for letting land lie fallow. Other improvements in farming methods introduced in the period were more intensive hoeing and weeding, and the use of the seed drill for planting grain. The latter eliminated the old wasteful method of sowing grain broadcast by hand, most of it remaining on top to be eaten by birds.

Scientific farming dictated the necessity of enclosures because the "improving" landlord needed flexibility to experiment as he wished. He simply could not try to plant one narrow open strip with turnips while peasants were continuing to rotate all the contiguous areas on the basis of the age-old three-field system. Instead, it was necessary for him to have fenced-off compact plots to leave no doubt as to which territory was his own, to maximize efficiency in experimentation, and to keep away stray grazing animals. When the enclosure movement gathered momentum, landlords were not above using the principle of reorganizing and enclosing territories to gain new lands from freeholders that hitherto had in no way belonged to them. In all this they had the government on their side. Parliament stopped trying to prohibit enclosures in 1640 and actually started directing them in 1710, not surprising in view of the fact that Parliament was dominated by large landowners. Thereafter, throughout the eighteenth century, parliamentary "acts of enclosure" provided that all the lands of a given village be completely redistributed into compact, fenced parcels, with the leading landlords of an area gaining far and away the most land.

Here was a change that had major social consequences where it occurred. Village life under the open-field system was communal, since decisions as to which crops were to be grown where and when had to be arrived at jointly. Often land was held under customary right by the village as a whole; and this common land afforded the poor not only a place to tether a cow, to fish, or to gather firewood, but to breathe at least a bit of the air of social freedom. In most cases the acts of enclosure included the common land in the redistribution. Hence enclosure cost villagers their modest freedoms, as well as the traditional right to help determine how the community's subsistence economy was to be managed. Cottagers (very small landholders) and squatters, who had over generations established a customary right to the use of common lands, were reduced to the rank of landless laborers.

The social consequences of enclosure

On the Continent, except for Holland, there was nothing comparable to the English advance in scientific farming. Nor, with the notable exception of Spain, was there a pronounced enclosure movement as in England and the Low Countries. Wherever small peasant proprietorship was firmly entrenched, as in France and in some areas of Germany, enclosure was successfully opposed. Yet despite that fact, European food production became increasingly capitalistic in the seventeenth and eighteenth centuries. Landlords leased farms to tenants and reaped profits as rent. Often they allowed tenants to pay rent in the form of half their crops. This system of sharecropping was most prevalent in France, Italy, and Spain. Farther east, in Prussia, Poland, Hungary, and Russia, landowners continued to rely on unpaid serfs to till the land. Wherever the market economy replaced the economy of local self-sufficiency, it brought change in its wake.

The increasingly capitalistic basis of European agriculture

The eighteenth century saw the introduction of two crops from the New World, maize (Indian corn) and the potato, that eventually resulted in the provision of a more adequate diet for the poor. Since maize can only be grown in areas with substantial periods of sunny and dry weather, its cultivation spread through Italy and the southeastern part of the Continent. Whereas an average ear of grain would yield only about four seeds for every one planted, an ear of maize would yield about seventy or eighty. That made it a "miracle" crop, filling granaries where they had been almost empty before. The potato was an equally miraculous innovation for the European north. Its advantages were numerous: potatoes could be grown on the poorest, sandiest, or wettest of lands where nothing else could be raised; they could be fitted into the smallest of patches. Raising potatoes even in small patches was profitable because the yield of potatoes was extraordinarily abundant. Finally, the potato provided an inexpensive means of improving the human diet. It is rich in calories, and contains many vitamins and minerals. Northern European peasants initially resisted growing and eating potatoes. Some feared the plant because it is not mentioned in the Bible. Some claimed that it transmitted leprosy. Still

Introduction of maize and potatoes

others insisted that it was a cause of flatulence, a property acknowl-edged by the French *Encyclopédie* in 1765, although the writers added: "What is a little wind to the vigorous organs of the peasants and workers?" Yet in the course of the eighteenth century the poor grew accustomed to the potato, although sometimes after considerable pressure. Frederick the Great of Prussia at first practically forced pota-toes down his peasants' throats until the crop achieved acceptence and became a staple throughout much of northern Germany. By about 1800 the average north German peasant family ate potatoes as a main course at least once a day. In the same period the potato was also introduced into Ireland and England. In the 1840s, it was all that stood between millions of Irish and starvation.

Agriculture was, of course, not the only commercial enterprise in early-modern rural Europe. Increasingly, manufactured goods—par-ticularly textiles—were being produced in the countryside, as entre-preneurs battled to circumvent artisanal and guild restrictions that limited production in urban manufacturing centers. The so-called put-ting-out system, which had grown increasingly common since the sixteenth century, was used by entrepreneurs as a way of realizing the highest profit on their investments. Unhampered by guild regula-tions, which in medieval times had restricted the production and dis-tribution of textiles to maintain price levels, merchants would buy up a stock of raw material, most often wool or flax, which they would then "put out," or supply, to rural workers for carding (combing the fibers) and spinning. Once spun, the yarn or thread was collected by the merchant and passed to rural weavers, who wove it into cloth. Collected once more, the material was processed by other workers at bleaching or dyeing shops, and collected for a final time by the entre-preneur who then either sold it to a wholesaler or directly to retail customers.

Rural workers accepted the putting-out system as a means of stav-ing off poverty, or possible starvation in years of particularly bad har-vests. Domestic textile production involved the entire family. Even the youngest children could participate in the process of cleaning the raw wool. Older children carded. Wives and husbands spun or wove. Spinning, until the invention of the jenny at the end of the eighteenth century (see below, p. 719) was a far more time-consuming process than weaving, which was speeded considerably by the invention of the fly-shuttle by the Englishman John Kay in the early eighteenth century, a mechanical device that automatically returned the shuttle to its starting place after it had been "thrown" across the loom.

In addition to extra income, the putting-out system provided other advantages to rural homeworkers. They could regulate the pace of their labor to some degree, and could abandon it altogether when farm work was available during the planting and harvest seasons. Their ability to work at home was not an unmixed blessing, for conditions in cottages that were wretchedly built and poorly ventilated were often exceedingly cramped and unpleasant, especially when they were com-

*Rural manufacturing: the
putting-out system*

Family production

Advantages of putting-out

Left: *"Rustic Courtship."* This detail from an etching (1785) by the English satirist Thomas Rowlandson suggests the advantages of doorstep domestic industry: natural lighting, improved ventilation, and a chance to converse with visitors. Work under these self-paced conditions, though usually long and hard, was carried on to a personal rhythm. Right: *Artisan and Family* by Gerard ter Borch. This seventeenth-century wheelwright, though a skilled artisan, is nevertheless depicted as living on the brink of poverty. Sickness, a bad harvest, unemployment—any of these might easily drive him and his family over the edge.

pelled to accommodate a bulky loom within their already crowded living quarters. But domestic labor, however unpleasant, was preferable in the minds of most to work away from home in a shop, where conditions might be even more oppressive under the watchful eye of an unsympathetic master. There were also advantages for the merchant-entrepreneur, who benefited not only from the absence of guild restrictions, but from the fact that none of his capital was tied up in expensive equipment. (Spinners usually owned their spinning wheels; weavers either owned or rented their looms.) Governments appreciated the advantages of the system too, viewing it as one way to alleviate the ever-present problem of rural poverty. The French abolished the traditional privileges of urban manufacturers in 1762, acknowledging by law what economic demand had long since established: the widespread practice of unrestricted rural domestic production. By that time, the putting-out system prevailed not only in northern France, but in the east and northeast of England, in Flanders, and in much of northern Germany—all areas where a mixed agricultural and manufacturing economy made economic sense to those engaged in it as entrepreneurs and producers.

Later generations, looking back nostalgically on the putting-out system, often compared it favorably to the factory system which displaced it. Life within the system's "family economy" was seldom other

*Quality of life under the
family system*

than hard, however. While workers could set their own pace to some extent, they remained subject to the demands of small, often inexperienced entrepreneurs who, misjudging their markets, might overload spinners and weavers with work at one moment, then abandon them for lack of orders the next. Though it often kept families from starvation, putting-out did little to make their lives anything other than monotonous and harsh. The pressures of the system are crudely if eloquently expressed in an English ballad, in which the weaver husband responds to his wife's complaint that she has no time to sit at the "bobbin wheel," what with the washing and baking and milking she must do. No matter, the husband replies. She must "stir about and get things done./ For all things must aside be laid,/ when we want help about our trade."

*Other rural manufacturing
activities*

Textiles were not the only manufactured goods produced in the countryside. In France, for example, metal-working was as much a rural as an urban occupation, with migrant laborers providing a workforce for small, self-contained shops. In various parts of Germany, the same sort of unregulated domestic manufacturing base prevailed: in the Black Forest for clock making, in Thuringia for toys. English production of coal increased from 200,000 tons a year in the 1550s to more than three million tons by the end of the seventeenth century; that of iron, another essentially rural enterprise, grew fivefold in the same period.

*Rudimentary
transportation systems*

Rural industry flourished despite the fact that for most of the early-modern period transportation systems remained rudimentary. In all but a very few cases, roads were little more than ill-defined tracks, full of holes as much as four feet deep, and all but impassible in the rain, when carts and carriages might stay mired in deep ruts for days.

Roadside Inn by Thomas Rowlandson. Coaching inns brought the outside world into the lives of isolated villagers. Note the absence of any clearly defined roadway.

The Duke of Bridgewater Canal

One of the few paved roads was that from Paris to Orléans, the main river port of France, but that was a notable exception. In general, no one could travel more than twelve miles an hour—"post haste" at a gallop on horseback—and speed such as that could be achieved only at the expense of fresh horses at each stage of the ride. A journey of 60 miles over good roads could be accomplished in twenty-four hours, provided that the weather was fair. To travel by coach from Paris to Lyons, a distance of approximately 250 miles, took ten days. Merchants ran great risks when they shipped perishable goods. Breakables were not expected to survive for more than fifteen miles. Transportation of goods by boat along coastal routes was far more reliable than shipment overland. In 1675, English merchants calculated that it was cheaper to ship coal 300 miles by water than to send it fifteen miles overland, so impassable were the roads to heavy transport. In 1698, a bronze statue of Louis XIV was sent on its way from the river port of Auxerre, southeast of Paris, to the town of Dijon. The cart in which it was dispatched was soon stuck in the mud, however, and the statue remained marooned in a wayside shed for twenty-one years, until the road was improved to the point that it could continue its belated journey.

Gradually in the eighteenth century transportation improved. The French established a Road and Bridge Corps of civil engineers, with a separate training school, in 1747. Work began in 1777 on a series of canals which eventually linked the English Channel to the Mediterranean. By the end of the century, France was spending seven million livres a year on road construction. In England, private investors, spearheaded by that inveterate canal builder the duke of Bridgewater, constructed a network of waterways and turnpikes linking provincial

Transportation improvements

towns to each other and to London. With improved roads came stage-coaches, feared at first for their speed and recklessness much as automobiles were feared in the early twentieth century. People objected to being crowded into narrow carriages designed to reduce the load pulled by the team of horses. "If by chance a traveller with a big stomach or wide shoulders appears," an unhappy passenger lamented, "one has to groan or desert." Improvements such as stagecoaches and canals, much as they might increase the profits or change the pattern of life for the wealthy, meant little to the average European. Barges plied the waterways from the north to the south of France, but most men and women traveled no farther than to their neighboring market town, on footpaths or on rutted cart tracks eight feet wide, which had served their ancestors much as they served them.

*Urban manufacturing
centers*

That industry flourished to the extent it did, despite the hazards and inefficiencies of transport, is a measure of the strength of Europe's ever-increasing commercial impulse. Rural "putting-out" did not prevent the growth of important urban manufacturing centers. In northern France, many of the million or so men and women employed in the textile trade lived and worked in cities such as Amiens, Lille, and Rheims. The eighteenth-century rulers of Prussia made it their policy to develop Berlin as a manufacturing center, taking advantage of an influx of French Protestants to establish the silk-weaving industry there. Even in cities, however, work was likely to be carried out in small shops, where anywhere from five to twenty journeymen labored under the supervision of a master to manufacture the particular products of their craft. Despite the fact that manufacturing was centered in homes and workshops, by 1700 these industries were increasing significantly in scale as many workshops grouped together to form a single manufacturing district. Textile industries led this trend, but it was true as well of brewing, distilling, soap and candle making, tanning, and the manufacturing of various chemical substances for the bleaching and dying of cloth. These and other industries might often employ several thousand men and women congregated together into towns—or larger communities of several towns—all dedicated to the same occupation and production.

*Response to changing
machinery and techniques*

Techniques in some crafts remained much as they had for centuries. In others, however, inventions changed the pattern of work as well as the nature of the product. Mechanically powered saws were introduced into shipyards and elsewhere across Europe in the seventeenth century. The technique of calico printing, the application of colored designs directly to textiles, was imported from the Far East. New and more efficient printing presses appeared, first in Holland and then elsewhere. The Dutch invented a machine, called a "camel," by which the hulls of ships could be raised in the water so that they could be more easily repaired.

Innovations of this kind were not readily accepted by workers. Labor-saving machines such as mechanical saws threw men out of work. Artisans, especially those organized into guilds, were by nature conservative, anxious to protect not only their restrictive "rights," but the secrets of their trade. Often, too, the state would intervene to block the widespread use of machines if they threatened to increase unemployment. The Dutch and some German states for example, prohibited the use of what was described as a "devilish invention," a ribbon loom capable of weaving sixteen or more ribbons at the same time. Sometimes the spread of new techniques was curtailed by states in order to protect the livelihood of powerful commercial interest groups. On behalf of both domestic textile manufacturers and importers of Indian goods, calico printing was for a time outlawed in both France and England. The cities of Paris and Lyons, and several German states banned the use of indigo dyes because they were manufactured abroad. Changes in manufacturing processes, like changes in agriculture, though they promised greater profits to enterpreneurs, threatened the livelihood of workers and their families. Facing the disruptions that capitalism and the Commercial Revolution were producing, they tried to cling to a pattern of life they knew, which, if harsh, was at least predictable.

Adverse reaction to new machinery and processes

4. POPULATION PATTERNS

The patterns of life for most seventeenth-century Europeans centered on the struggle to stay alive. They lived and worked within a subsistence economy, considering themselves extremely fortunate if they could grow or earn what it took to survive. In most instances their enemy was not an invading army, but famine. At least once a decade, climatic conditions—usually a long period of summer rainfall—would produce a devastatingly bad harvest, which in turn would result in widespread malnutrition often leading to serious illness and death. A family might survive for a time by eating less; but eventually, with its meager stocks exhausted and the cost of grain high, the human costs would mount. The substitution of grass, nuts, and tree bark for grain on which the peasants depended almost entirely for nourishment was as inadequate for them as it appears pathetic to us.

The threat of famine

Widespread crop failures occurred at fairly regular intervals—the worst in France, for example, about every thirty years (1597, 1630, 1662, 1694). They helped to produce the series of population crises that are the outstanding feature of early-modern demographic history. Poor harvests and the high prices produced by a scarcity of grain meant not only undernourishment and possible starvation, but increasing unemployment: with fewer crops to be harvested, more money was spent on food and, consequently, less on manufactured goods. The despair such conditions could easily breed would in turn contribute to a postponement of marriage and of births, and thus to a

Population crises

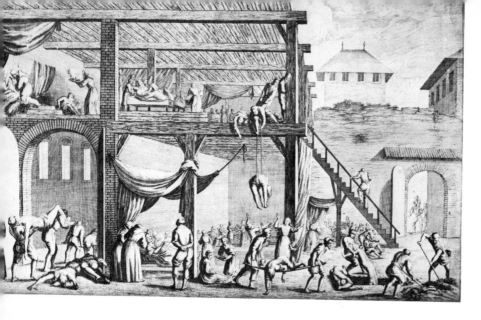

A Plague Hospital in Vienna. The efforts to contain outbreaks of plague by gathering the sick in establishments such as this and burying the dead on the site proved unsuccessful.

Health and sanitation

"Summer Amusement: Bugg Hunting." In this joking treatment of one of the facts of everyday life the bedbugs meet sudden death in a full chamber pot.

population decline. The patterns of marriages and births revealed in local parish registers indicate that throughout Europe the populations of individual communities rose and fell dramatically in rhythm with the fortunes of the harvest.

An undernourished population is a population particularly susceptible to disease. Bubonic plague had ravaged seventeenth-century Europe. Severe outbreaks occurred in Seville in 1649, in Amsterdam in 1664, and in London the following year. By 1700 it had all but disappeared; it last appeared in western Europe in a small area of southern France in 1720. But Moscow suffered an outbreak as late as 1771. Despite the gradual retreat of the plague, however, other diseases took a dreadful toll, in an age when available medical treatment was little more than crude guesswork, and in any event, beyond the reach of the poor. Epidemics of dysentery, smallpox, and typhus occurred with savage regularity. As late as 1779, over 100,000 people died of dysentery in the French province of Brittany. Most diseases attacked rich and poor impartially. Water supplies in towns and in the country were contaminated by heedless disposal of human waste and by all manner of garbage and urban filth. Bathing, feared at one time as a method of spreading disease, was by no means a weekly habit, whatever the social status of the household. Samuel Pepys, a prosperous servant of the crown in seventeenth-century London, recorded in his diary that his housemaid was in the habit of picking the lice from his scalp, that he took his first bath only after his wife had taken hers and experienced the pleasures of cleanliness, and that he had, on occasion, thought nothing of using the fireplace in his bedroom as a toilet, the maid having failed to provide him with a chamberpot. If such was Pepys's attitude toward hygiene and sanitation, imagine that of the poverty-stricken and ignorant peasant, and the threat to health implicit in such attitudes.

The precariousness of life encouraged most men and women in early-modern Europe to wed much later than in other traditional societies in Asia and Africa. This exceptional pattern found women marrying, on average, at twenty-five years of age, men at twenty-seven or twenty-eight, by which time they hoped to have accumulated sufficient resources to establish a household. Young couples lived on their own, and not, as in societies elsewhere, as part of "extended" families of three generations. In those extended families, a farm might pass from father to son before the death of the former. But in Europe this was not the custom. Since a son could not inherit until his father died, he was compelled to establish himself independently, and to postpone starting his own family until he had done so. Late marriage helped to control the birth rate. Once married, however, generally produced their first child within a year. Although subsequent children appeared with annual or biannual regularity, long periods of breast-feeding, which tends to reduce the mother's fertility, and community disapproval of extramarital sexual relations went some way toward limiting childbirth.

*Implications of the
European marriage pattern*

Until the middle of the eighteenth century, populations continued to chart their rise and fall according to the outbreak of warfare, famine, and disease. From about 1750 on, however, there was a steady and significant population increase, with almost all countries experiencing major growth. In Russia, where territorial expansion added further to the increases, the population rate may have tripled in the second half of the eighteenth century. Gains elsewhere, while not usually as spectacular, were nevertheless significant. The population of Prussia and Spain doubled; Hungary's more than tripled; and England's population, which was about 5.5 million in 1700, reached 9 million in 1800. France, already in 1700 the most heavily populated country in Europe (about 20 million), added a further 6 million before 1790. Although reasons for the population increase remain something of mystery, historians are inclined to agree that it was the cumulative result of a very gradual decline in the death rate, due in large measure to an equally gradual increase in the food supply. Better transportation facilitated the shipment of food over greater distances. Land clearances, particularly in England, and in Prussia and Russia, where territories were opened to colonization, provided an essential ingredient for increased production. New staples—the potato and maize—supplemented the diets of the very poor. And although evidence here is only fragmentary, it appears that whereas the climate of seventeenth-century Europe was abnormally bad, that of the succeeding hundred years was on the whole favorable.

Population growth

Population increase brought with it new problems and new attitudes. For example, the decline in the death rate among infants—along with an apparent increase in illegitimacy at the end of the eighteenth century—created a growing population of unwanted babies among the poor. Some desperate women resorted to infanticide, though since

*New problems and
attitudes*

children murdered at birth died without benefit of baptism, the crime was stigmatized as especially heinous by the Church as well as by society in general. More often, babies were abandoned at the door of foundling hospitals. As an English benefactor of several such institutions, Jonas Hanway, remarked in 1766, "it is much less difficult to the human heart and the dictates of self-preservation to drop a child than to kill it." In Paris during the 1780s from seven to eight thousand children were being abandoned out of a total of thirty thousand new births. Paradoxically, some historians now argue that during this same period the decrease in infant and child mortality encouraged many parents to lavish care and affection on their offspring in a way that they had not when the repeated early deaths of their sons and daughters had taught them the futility of that emotional bond. The eighteenth century witnessed the rise of the children's book industry; in England between 1750 and 1814, over 2400 titles were published. Toy shops appeared in cities and towns; dolls and dollhouses began to be mass produced for the first time. All of this suggests the willingness of parents to invest in a new relationship that was the result of major demographic change.

5. LIFE WITHIN A SOCIETY OF ORDERS

*Orders, privilege, and
freedom*

Despite the economic and demographic alterations that were occurring in early-modern Europe, it remained a society divided into traditional orders. Jean Bodin, the French philosopher, wrote in 1570 that the division of the citizenry into "the three orders of nobles, clergy and people" was no more than natural. "There never was a commonwealth, real or imaginary, where citizens were in truth equal in all rights and privileges. Some always have more, some less than the rest." And some had none. Orders were demarcated by those rights and privileges. "Freedom" was understood as one such privilege, as a benefit, bestowed not upon all men and women, but upon special groups whose position "freed" them to do certain things others could not do, or freed them from the burden of doing certain things that were required of others. An English landowner was, because of the position his property conferred upon him, privileged, and therefore "free," to participate directly in the election of his government. A French nobleman was privileged, and therefore "free," to avoid the heavy burden of taxation levied upon the unprivileged orders. A German tailor who had served out his seven-year apprenticeship was free to set up his own shop for profit, something an unapprenticed man could not do, no matter what his degree of skill with needle and thread. The master tailor's position conferred this freedom, just as the position of aristocrat and property owner conferred theirs.

The members of the higher orders attempted at all times to live their lives in a particular style which accorded with their rank. The nobility

Middle-Class Fashion. In this seventeenth-century portrait of a Dutch burgo-master and his family, the patriarch and his wife are wearing the costume of an earlier generation, while the children are clothed in the current style. All display the opulence characteristic of their prosperous class.

The theater of a society of orders

was taught from birth to consider itself a class apart. Merchants and manufacturers were just as insistent upon maintaining the traditional marks of privilege that separated them from artisans and peasants. Sumptuary laws decreed what could be worn and by whom. An edict promulgated in the German principality of Brunswick in 1738, for example, forbade servant girls to use silk dress materials, to wear gold or silver ornaments, or shoes of anything but plain black leather. A similar law in the Polish city of Posen prohibited the wives of burgh-ers from wearing capes or long hair. Style was not simply a matter of current whim. It was a badge of status and was carefully adhered to as such. An aristocratic lady powdered her hair and rouged her cheeks as a sign that she was an aristocrat. Life within a society of orders demanded a certain degree of theatricality, especially from those at the top of the social hierarchy. Aristocrats "acted" their part in a calculat-edly self-conscious way. Their manner of speech, their dress, the cer-emonial sword they were privileged to wear, the title by which they were addressed, were the props of a performance which constantly emphasized the distinctions between those above and those below. Noble families lived in castles, chateaux, or country houses whose size and antiquity were a further proclamation of superiority. When they built new mansions, as the *nouveau riche* capitalist English gentry did in the eighteenth century, they made certain their elaborate houses and spacious private parks declared their newfound power. The English politician Robert Walpole had an entire village moved to improve the view from his grand new residence.

The vast majority of men and women defined and understood social

Banquet Given in Paris by the Spanish Duke of Alva in Honor of the Prince of Asturias. The scene illustrates the ostentatious display this powerful nobleman believed suitable to his rank and fortune.

hierarchy in terms of the rural communities in which they lived. At the head of those communities, in all likelihood, stood a representative of the noble elite. Aristocrats probably numbered about 3 percent of the total population of Europe. The percentage was higher in Russia, Poland, Hungary, and Spain; lower in Germany, France, and England. Land was the hallmark of aristocratic position. And, generally speaking, the more land one possessed, the higher one stood within the aristocracy. In Hungary, five noble families owned about 14 percent of the entire country; the greatest of these, Prince Esterházy, controlled the lives of over half a million peasants. Most noblemen were not nearly so rich and powerful. Some, indeed, could rely on little more than inherited privilege to distinguish themselves from peasants.

The nobility

The pattern of noble life varied considerably from country to country. In England and Prussia, the nobility tended to reside on its estates; in south and west Germany, and in France, aristocrats were more likely to leave the management of their estates to stewards and to live at the royal court. Although the nobility claimed to disdain commerce, by the end of the eighteenth century they were involving themselves in increasing numbers in a variety of commercial enterprises. Some exploited mineral deposits on their estates; others invested in overseas trade. In France, two of the four largest coal mines were owned and operated by noblemen, while the duke of Orléans was an important investor in the newly established chemical dye industry. In eastern Europe, because there were few middle-class merchants, aristocrats frequently undertook to market their agricultural produce themselves.

Nobility and commerce

In no country was the aristocracy a completely closed order. Men who proved of use to the crown as administrators or lawyers, men who amassed large fortunes as a consequence of judicious—and often legally questionable—financial transactions, moved into the ranks of the nobility with increasing frequency during the late seventeenth and eighteenth century. Joseph II of Austria was making financiers into noblemen by the dozen in the late eighteenth century. In France, it was possible to attain nobility through the purchase of expensive offices from the crown. There was also a growing legal nobility of the "robe," headed by members of the thirteen provincial *parlements* whose function it was to record, and thereby sanction, the laws of the kingdom.

An "open" nobility

In time, severe tensions arose, most particularly in France but elsewhere as well, between the older nobility and those much more active and frequently more intelligent men of a new noble order, whom aristocrats with a longer pedigree considered upstarts. Tradition had it that noble service meant military service, that the ideal of noble honor involved heroism on the battlefield, not cunning at the law courts or conniving in palace antechambers.

Rivalry between the old and new nobility

Whether recently enobled or members of one of those ancient families that existed throughout Europe and which the French called—simply and eloquently—*les grandes,* most aristocrats owned large landed estates. Landownership helped them not only to establish their position but to define it as well, by bringing them into direct relationship with the peasants and laborers who worked that land and over whose lives the aristocracy exercised dominion. The status of the peasantry varied greatly across the face of rural Europe. In the East—Russia, Poland, Hungary, and in parts of Germany beyond the Elbe—the desire for profit in agriculture and the collusion of the state with the aristocracy led to the growth of a "second serfdom," a serf system much stronger than that which had existed during the Middle Ages. In East Prussia, serfs often had to work from three to six days a week for their lord, and some had only late evening or night hours to cultivate their own lands.

The peasantry

Peasants throughout eastern Europe found their destinies controlled in almost all respects by their masters. Noble landlords dispensed justice in manorial courts and even ruled in cases to which they were themselves interested parties. These men were a combination of sheriff, chief magistrate, and police force in one, able to sentence their "subjects" to corporal punishment, imprisonment, exile, or in many cases death, without right of appeal. Peasants could not leave their land, marry, or learn a trade unless permitted to do so by their lord. In Russia, where half the land was owned by the state, peasants were bound to work in mines or workshops if their masters so ordered, and could be sold to private owners. Although Russian peasant serfs were said to possess a "legal personality" that distinguished them from slaves, the distinction was obscured in practice.

Peasant subordination in eastern Europe

In western Europe, the position of the peasantry reflected the fact that serfdom had all but disappeared by the sixteenth century. Peas-

NE' POUR LA PEINE

A French Peasant. Tattered and overworked, this peasant farmer is shown feeding his livestock as the tax collector at his door relieves him of all of his profits.

Poverty and the peasantry

Peasant bread and board

ants might theoretically own land, although the vast majority were either tenants or laborers. Hereditary tenure was in general more secure than in the East; peasants could dispose of their land and had legal claim to farm buildings and implements. Although far freer than their eastern European counterparts, the peasantry of western Europe still lived to a great degree under the domination of landowners. They were in many cases responsible for the payment of various dues and fees: an annual rent paid to landlords by those who might otherwise own their land outright; a special tax on recently cleared land; a fee, often as much as one-sixth of the assessed value of the land, collected by the manorial lord whenever peasant property changed hands; and charges for the use of the lord's mill, bakery, or wine press. In France, peasants were compelled to submit to the *corvée,* a requirement that they labor for several weeks a year maintaining local roads. Even access to the often questionable justice meted out in the manorial courts, which endured throughout the early-modern period in almost all of western Europe, was encumbered with fees and commissions. To many peasants, however, the most galling badge of their inferiority was their inability to hunt within the jurisdiction of their landlord's manor. The slaughter of game was a privilege reserved to the nobility, a circumstance generating sustained resentment on the part of a population that looked upon deer and pheasant not as a symbol of aristocratic status but as a necessary supplement to its meager diet. Noble landlords rarely missed an opportunity to extract all the money they could from their peasants while constantly reminding them of the degree to which their destiny was controlled by the lord of the manor.

That destiny was shaped as well by the level of economic prosperity a particular peasant might enjoy. A few were genuinely independent, literate, influential members of the communities where they lived, owning not only land but considerable livestock. Most, however, were far less fortunate. Those with claim to a small piece of land usually worked it into infertility in the course of one or two generations as they scrambled to make it produce as much as possible. Each time a peasant proprietor died, his property was divided among his male heirs, encouraging the sort of marginal economic existence that was the fate of most rural laborers.

Poor peasants often lived, contrary to the biblical injunction, by bread alone—two pounds a day if they were lucky, the dark dough a mixture of wheat and rye flour. Bread was supplemented by peas and beans, beer, wine, or, far less often, skimmed milk. Their houses usually contained no more than one or two rooms, and were constructed of wood, plastered with mud or clay. Roofs were most often thatched with straw, which was used as fertilizer when replaced, and provided fodder for animals at times of scarcity. Furnishings seldom consisted of more than a table, benches, pallets for sleeping, a few earthenware plates, and simple tools—an axe, a wooden spade, a knife.

Left: *"Russian Soup."* Interior of a sparcely furnished peasant's cottage. Note the cradle suspended from the ceiling. Right: *Market Scene* by Jean Michelin. Peasant women and children bringing produce to a nearby market town.

Wives of peasants tended livestock and vegetables, and managed the dairy, if there was one. Wives of agricultural laborers went out themselves as field workers, or worked at home at knitting, spinning, or weaving in order to augment the family income. A popular seventeenth-century poem has a laborer's wife lamenting her lot with a refrain that has echoed down the ages: ". . . my labor is hard,/ And all my pleasures are debarr'd;/ Both morning, evening, night and noon,/ I'm sure a woman's work is never done."

Although somewhere between 80 and 90 percent of the population lived in small rural communities, towns and cities were coming to play an increasingly important role in the life of early-modern Europe. One must speak of the "rise" of towns and cities with some caution, however, since the pace of urbanization varied greatly across the Continent. Russia remained almost entirely rural: only 2.5 percent of its population lived in towns in 1630, and that percentage had increased by only 0.5 percent by 1774. In Holland, on the other hand, 59 percent of the population was urban centered in 1627 and 65 percent in 1795.

As the fortunes of towns and cities rose and fell, so did their populations. Capital cities grew dramatically. By the middle of the eighteenth century, Madrid, Berlin, and St. Petersburg all had populations of over 100,000. London grew from 674,000 in 1700 to 860,000 a century later. Paris a city of approximately 180,000 in 1600, increased to over half a million by 1800. Berlin presents a particularly interesting example of urban expansion. From a population of 6500 in 1661, it swelled to 60,000 in 1721 and 140,000 in 1783. Its increase was due in

The peasant wife

The growth of urban centers

Urban populations

part to the fact that successive Prussian rulers undertook to improve its position as a trade center by the construction of canals which linked it with Breslau and Hamburg. Its population rose as well, however, because of the marked increase in Prussian army and bureaucratic personnel based in the capital city. Of the 140,000 citizens of Berlin in 1783, approximately 65,000 were state employees or members of their families.

The population of other cities was related to the growth of trade. Amsterdam, the hub of early-modern international commerce, grew from 30,000 in 1530 to 115,000 in 1630 and 200,000 by 1800. Naples, the busy Mediterranean port, went from a population of 300,000 in 1600 to nearly half a million by the late eighteenth century. Populations could fluctuate considerably as a result of economic growth or decline. For example, that of Norwich, in England, increased when the manufacture of woolen goods shifted away from older industrial centers on the English Channel to the north. That of the important German market center of Frankfurt declined during and after the period of the Thirty Years' War, when difficulties of communication and the general instability caused by frequent military campaigns diverted much of its former business to Amsterdam.

Those towns and cities that grew did so because of the decline in the death rate, but also because commerce, industry, and government were attracting new urban recruits from the countryside. An eighteenth-century commentator noted that the laborers in Paris were "almost all foreigners"—that is, men and women born outside the city: carpenters from Savoy, water carriers from Auvergne, porters from Lyons, stonecutters from Normandy, wigmakers from Gascony, shoemakers from Lorraine. In the case of industries such as textile manufacturing, whose workshops required more space than was available inside the medieval walls of the city center, new workers settled in industrial suburbs. In capital cities, suburbs also served as fashionable neighborhoods for the ruling elite, places "where the want of London smoke is supplied by the smoke of Virginia tobacco," as one Englishman remarked wryly. Houses in areas inhabited by the wealthy were increasingly built of brick and stone, which replaced the wood, lath, and plaster of the Middle Ages. This change was a response to the constant danger of fire. The great fire of London in 1666, which destroyed three-quarters of the town—12,000 houses—was the largest of the conflagrations that swept cities with devastating regularity. Urban dwellings of the laboring poor remained firetraps. Workers' quarters were badly overcrowded; entire families lived in one-room accommodations in basements and attics that were infested with bugs and fleas.

Urban society was, like its rural counterpart, a society of orders. In capital cities, noble families occupied the highest social position, as they did in the countryside, living a parasitic life of conspicuous consumption at court. The majority of cities and towns were dominated by a nonnoble *bourgeoisie*. That French term originally designated a burgher or townsman who was a long-term, resident property owner or leaseholder and taxpayer. By the eighteenth century it had come to mean a townsman of some means who aspired to be recognized as a person of local importance, and evinced a willingness to work hard, whether at counting-house or government office, and a desire to live a comfortable, if by no means extravagant, existence. A bourgeois gentleman might derive his income from rents; he might, as well, be an industrialist, banker, or merchant, a professional, lawyer, or physician. If he served in the central bureaucracy, he would consider himself the social superior of those provincials whose affairs he administered. Yet he would himself be looked down upon by the aristocracy, who tended to think of the *bourgeoisie* as a class of vulgar social climbers. The French playwright Molière's comedy *The Bourgeois Gentleman* (1670) reflected this attitude, ridiculing the manners of the commercial class who were trying to ape their betters. "Bourgeois," another French writer observed, "is the insult given by noblemen to anybody they deem slow-witted or out of touch with the court." The *bourgeoisie* usually constituted about 20 to 25 percent of a town's population. As its economic elite, these men were almost always its governing elite as well. Municipal offices were considered a privilege of this order and were distributed accordingly.

Urban society: the bourgeoisie

Next within the urban hierarchy was a vast middle range of shopkeepers and artisans. Many of the latter continued to learn and then to practice their craft as members of guilds, which in turn contained their own particular ascending hierarchy of apprentice, journeyman, and master, thus preserving a society of orders. Throughout the early-modern period, however, commercial expansion threatened the rigid hierarchy of the guild structure. The expense and curtailed output resulting from restrictive guild practices met with serious opposition in big cities such as Paris and London, where expanding markets called for cheaper and more readily available goods. Journeymen tailors and shoemakers in increasing numbers set up shops without benefit of mastership and produced cheaper coats and shoes in defiance of guild regulations. In the silk workshops of Lyons, both masters and journeymen were compelled to labor without distinction of status for piece rates (wages paid per finished article, rather than per hour) set by merchandising middlemen far below an equitable level in the opinion of the silk workers. Artisans like these, compelled to work for low wages at the behest of profiteering middlemen, grew increasingly restive. In France and Germany, journeymen's associations had originated as social and mutual-aid organizations for young men engaged in "tramping" the country to gain experience in their trade. In some instances, however, these associations fostered the development of a trade consciousness that led to strikes and boycotts against masters and middlemen

Urban society: shopkeepers and artisans

over the issues of wages and working conditions. An imperial law passed in Germany in 1731 deprived the associations of their right to organize, and required journeymen to carry a certificate of identification as testimony of their respectability during their travels.

Urban society: the poor

At the bottom of urban society was a mass of semi-skilled and unskilled workers: carters and porters; stevedores and dockers; water carriers and sweepers; seamstresses, laundresses, cleaners, and domestic servants. These men and women, like their rural counterparts, lived on the margins of urban life, constantly battling the trade cycles, seasonal unemployment, and epidemics that threatened their ability to survive. A number lived in shanties on the edge of towns and cities. In Genoa, the homeless poor were sold as galley slaves each winter. In Venice, the poor lived on decrepit barges under the city's bridges. A French ordinance of 1669 ordered the destruction of all houses "built on poles by vagabonds and useless members of society." Derpived of the certainty of steady work, these people were prey not only to economic fluctuations and malevolent "acts of God," but to a social system that left them without any "privilege" or "freedom" whatsoever.

Attitudes toward poverty

Attitudes toward poverty varied from country to country. Most localities extended the concept of orders to include the poor: "the deserving"—usually orphans, the insane, the aged, the infirm; and "the undeserving"—able-bodied men and women who were out of work or who, even though employed, could not support themselves and their families. The authorities tended to assume in the latter case that poverty was the result of personal failings; few made a connection between general economic circumstances and the plight of the individual poor. For the deserving, private charitable organizations, such as those in France, founded by the order of St. Vincent de Paul and by

Beggars at the Doorway by Louis LeNain. A seventeenth-century depiction of poverty, sentimentalized so as to celebrate the virtues of deference.

Hanging Thieves. This seventeenth-century engraving is designed to teach a lesson. Troops stand by and priests shave the heads of the condemned criminals as they are executed by the dozen. "At last," the engraver's caption reads, "these infamous lost souls are hung like unhappy fruit."

the Sisters of Charity, provided assistance. For the undeserving, there was harsh treatment at the hands of the state whose concern to alleviate extreme deprivation arose more from a desire to avert public disorder than from motives of human charity. Food riots were common occurrences. In times of scarcity the French government frequently intervened to reduce the price of grain, hoping thereby to prevent an outbreak of rioting. Yet riots nevertheless occurred. When property damage resulted, the ringleaders were always severely punished, usually by hanging, but the remainder of the crowd was usually left untouched by the law, a fact suggesting the degree to which governments were prepared to tolerate rioting itself as a means of dealing with the chronic problem of poverty. Poor vagrants were perceived as a serious threat to social tranquility. They were therefore frequently rounded up at harvest time to keep them from plundering the fields.

Vagrants and other chronically unemployed persons were placed in poorhouses where conditions were little better than those in prisons. Often the very young, the very old, the sick, and the insane were housed together with hardened criminals. Poor relief in England was administered parish by parish in accordance with a law passed in 1601. Relief was tied to a "law of settlement," which stipulated that paupers might receive aid only if still residing in the parish of their birth. An unemployed weaver who had migrated fifty miles in search of work could thus expect assistance only if he returned home again. In the late eighteenth century, several European countries established modest public works programs in an attempt to relieve poverty by reducing unemployment. France, for example, undertook road-building projects in the 1770s under the auspices of its progressive finance minister.

The treatment of paupers

Louis XIV Visiting the French Academy of Sciences. Royal patronage sustained such academies by guaranteeing members rewards suitable to their station.

Turgot. But generally speaking, indigence was perceived not as a social ill for which a remedy might be sought, but as an indelible stigma demarking the lowest of a community's social orders.

Early-modern Europe fashioned its institutions to reflect the patterns of social hierarchy. Nowhere was this more apparent than in the field of education. One barrier—a knowledge of Latin—separated aristocrats and a fair number of scholars and professionals from the commercial middle ranks; a second—the ability to read and write—separated the middle from the rest. Noblemen were generally educated by private tutors; though they might attend university for a time, they did so not in preparation for a profession but to receive further educational "finishing." Indeed during the late seventeenth and eighteenth centuries universities more or less surrendered intellectual leadership to various academies established with royal patronage by European monarchs to enhance their own reputations as well as to encourage the advancement of science and the arts: the Royal Society of London, founded by Charles II in 1660; the French Academy of Sciences, a project upon which Louis XIV lavished a good deal of ostentatious attention; and the Berlin Royal Academy of Science and Letters, patronized by Frederick the Great of Prussia in the eighteenth century. Few noblemen had the interest or the intelligence to participate in the activities of these august organizations, which were not, in any case, teaching institutions. Far better suited to their needs and inclinations was "the grand tour," often of many months' duration,

Education in a society of orders: the nobility

which led the aristocrat through the capitals of Europe, and during which he was expected to acquire a kind of international *politesse*.

Endowed, fee-charging schools for the training of a governmental elite existed in France (the *collège*) and Spain (the *collegio mayor*) and in Germany and Austria (the *gymnasium*). Here the emphasis was by no means on "practical" subjects such as modern language or mathematics, but on the mastery of Greek and Latin translation and composition, the intellectual badge of the educated elite. An exception was the Prussian University of Halle, designed to teach a professional elite; a contemporary described that institution as teaching only what was "rational, useful, and practical."

Training for government service

Male children from the middle orders destined to enter the family business or profession as a rule attended small private academies where the curriculum included the sort of "useful" instruction ignored in the *collèges* and *gymnasia*. Female children, from both the upper and middle orders, were almost invariably educated at home, receiving little more than rudimentary instruction in gentlewomanly subjects such as modern language, belles lettres, and music, if from the noble ranks, and a similar, if slightly more practical training, if from the bourgeoisie.

Education for the middle orders

No European country undertook the task of providing primary education to all its citizens until the mid–eighteenth century, when Frederick the Great in Prussia and the Habsburg monarchs Maria Theresa and her son Joseph II in Austria instituted systems of compulsory attendance. Available evidence suggests that their results fell far short of expectation. An early–nineteenth-century survey from the relatively enlightened Prussian province of Cleves revealed dilapidated schools, poorly attended classes, and an incompetent corps of teachers. Educational conditions were undoubtedly worse in most other European communities.

Education for the poor

Although educational opportunities for peasants and workers remained meager by modern standards, available evidence suggests that literacy rates increased considerably in the seventeenth and eighteenth centuries; in England, from one in four males in 1600 to one in two by 1800; in France, from 29 percent of the male population in 1686 to 47 percent in 1786. Literacy among women increased as well, though their rate of increase generally lagged behind that of men: only 27 percent of the female population in France was literate in 1786. Naturally, such rates varied according to particular localities and circumstances, and from country to country. Literacy was higher in urban areas which contained a large proportion of artisans. In rural eastern Europe, literacy remained extremely low (20–30 percent) well into the nineteenth century. Notwithstanding state-directed efforts in Prussia and Austria, the rise in literacy was largely the result of a growing determination on the part of religiously minded reformers to teach the poor to read and write as a means of encouraging obedience to divine and secular authority. A Sunday-school movement in eigh-

Increasing literacy

teenth-century England and similar activities among the Christian Brotherhood in France are clear evidence of this trend.

Though the majority of the common people were probably no more than barely literate, they possessed a flourishing culture of their own. Village life, particularly in Roman Catholic countries, centered about the church, to which men and women would go on Sundays not only to worship but to socialize. Much of the remainder of their day of rest would be devoted to participation in village games. Religion provided the opportunity for association and for a welcome break from the daily work routines. Pilgrimages, for example, to a nearby shrine would include a procession of exuberant villagers led by one of their number carrying an image of the village's patron saint and accompanied by drinking, dancing, and picnicking. In towns, Catholics joined organizations, called confraternities in France, Italy, Austria, and the Netherlands, which provided mutual aid and a set of common rituals and traditions centered upon a patron saint. Religious community was expressed as well in popular Protestant movements which arose in the eighteenth century: Pietism on the Continent and Methodism in England. Both emphasized the importance of personal salvation through faith and the potential worth of every human soul regardless of station. Both therefore appealed particularly to people whose position within the community had heretofore been presumed to be without any value. Though Methodism's founder, John Wesley (1703–1791), preached obedience to earthly authority, his willingness to rely on working men and women as preachers and organizers gave them a new sense of personal importance.

While much popular culture was directly linked to religious traditions and practices, much was now growing secular. Carnival, that vibrant prelenten celebration indigenous not only to Mediterranean

Cockfight by William Hogarth. This London scene suggests the degree to which men from different social orders came together for sport, drinking, and adventure. Here a clergyman and a young gentleman consort with the London riff-raff.

French Tavern. Often located outside the city limits so as to avoid the payment of municipal taxes, taverns such as this provided a gathering place for workers to drink, gossip, and relax after the day's labors. The tavern also served as a convenient place for public readings and for airing common grievances.

Europe but to Germany and Austria as well, represented an opportunity for common folk to cast aside the burdens and restraints imposed upon their order by secular authority. Performances and processions celebrated a "world turned upside down," a theme popular throughout much of Europe from the Later Middle Ages, appealing to commoners for a variety of ambiguous psychological reasons, but in large part, certainly, as a way of avenging symbolically the economic and social oppression under which they lived. For a few days, the oppressed played the role of the oppressor and rulers were made to look like fools and knaves. In parades, men dressed as kings walked barefoot while peasants rode on horseback or in carriages; the poor threw pretend money to the rich. Annual harvest festivals, once sponsored by the church, were also increasingly secular celebrations of release from backbreaking labor, punctuated by feasting, drinking, sporting, and lovemaking. Fairs and traveling circuses brought something of distant places and people into lives bound to one spot. The drudgery of everyday life was also relieved by horseraces, cock fights, and bear baiting. Taverns played an even more constant role in the daily life of the village, providing a place for men to gather over tobacco and drink to gossip and gamble.

Carnival and other amusements

Laboring men and women depended on an oral tradition of myth, legend, and superstition to steady their lives, and give them point and purpose. Stories in books sold at fairs by peddlers were passed on by those who could read. They told of heroes and saints, and of kings like Charlemagne whose paternal concern for his common subjects led him into battle against his selfish nobility. Belief in villains matched

The role of the oral tradition

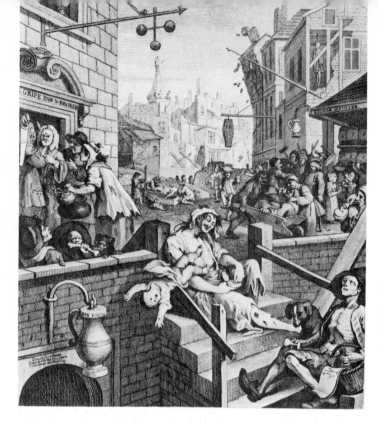

Gin Lane by William Hogarth. Hogarth believed in portraying human nature as he found it. In this famous engraving, he is preaching a sermon against the gin trade, one of the besetting evils of eighteenth-century London.

belief in heroes. Witchcraft, as we have seen, was a reality for much of the period to superstitious men and women. So was Satan. So was any supernatural force, whether for good or evil, which could help them make sense of a world in which they, more than any, were victims of events beyond their control.

Stability and change

Though increasingly secularized, popular customs, celebrations, and beliefs remained a stabilizing force in early-modern Europe. They were the cultural expression of that social order to which the vast majority of Europeans belonged. Popular culture in the main tended to reinforce the traditions and assumptions of order and hierarchy. As such, it helped to bind men and women to what civilization had been, as capitalism and mercantilism impelled them in the direction of what it would become.

SELECTED READINGS

• *Items so designated are available in paperback editions.*
• Blum, Jerome, *Lord and Peasant in Russia*, Princeton, N.J., 1961. A good study of Russian society.
• Braudel, F., *Capitalism and Material Life, 1400–1800*, London, 1973. A fascinating review of evidence pertaining to the entire world by one of the greatest of living historians.

————, *The Structures of Everyday Life: The Limits of the Possible*, New York, 1981. A survey of the material conditions of life; profusely illustrated.

• Burke, Peter, *Popular Culture in Early Modern Europe*, London, 1978. Synthesizes the most recent work on the period between 1500 and 1800; fascinating.

Chambers, J. D., and G. E. Mingay, *The Agricultural Revolution, 1750–1880*, London, 1966. Now the standard work.

• Cipolla, C. M., *Before the Industrial Revolution: European Society and Economy, 1000–1700*, 2nd ed., New York, 1980. Wide-ranging and full of deft observations.

• Curtin, Philip D., *The Atlantic Slave Trade*, Madison, Wisc., 1969. Reinterprets the character of the trade.

• Davis, Natalie Z., *Society and Culture in Early Modern France*, Stanford, Calif., 1975. Eight scintillating essays by a pioneer in the use of anthropological methods for the study of early-modern European history.

Forster, Robert, *The Nobility of Toulouse in the Eighteenth Century*, Baltimore, Md., 1960. A careful analysis of the extent and nature of aristocratic power.

Glass, D. V., and D. E. C. Eversley, eds., *Population in History*, New York, 1965. Contains useful essays on demographic patterns.

Hafton, Olwen H., *The Poor of Eighteenth Century France*, Oxford, 1974. One of the first studies of a preindustrial "underclass."

Heckscher, E., *Mercantilism*, rev. ed., 2 vols., London, 1955. The most influential, but controversial, work on the subject.

Kamen, Henry, *The Iron Century: Social Change in Europe, 1560–1660*, New York, 1971. Especially suggestive and interesting in its exploration of the bleak side of life.

Kaplow, Jeffry, *The Names of Kings: The Parisian Laboring Poor in the Eighteenth Century*, New York, 1972. A valuable study of the urban poor.

• Laslett, Peter and Richard Wall, eds., *Household and Family in Past Times*, New York, 1972. A suggestive collection of essays.

LeRoy Ladurie, Emmanual, *The Peasants of Languedoc*, Urbana, Ill., 1974. A classic on peasant life and demography.

Levine, David, *Family Formation in an Age of Nascent Capitalism*, New York, 1977. A thoughtful, recent treatment of patterns of social formation.

Mousnier, R., *Peasant Uprisings in Seventeenth-Century France, Russia and China*, New York, 1970. A comparative analysis.

• Ranum, Orest, *Paris in the Age of Absolutism*, New York, 1968. A useful view of urban life.

Rich, E. E., and C. H. Wilson, eds., *The Cambridge Economic History of Europe*: Volume 5, *The Economic Organization of Early Modern Europe*, New York, 1977. An indispensable guide to the study of the period's economy and society.

• Stone, Lawrence, *The Family, Sex and Marriage in England, 1500–1800*, New York, 1977. An important, controversial book which argues important changes in attitudes over the course of three centuries.

Wilson, Charles, *England's Apprenticeship, 1603–1763*, London, 1965. A reliable economic survey.

• Wrigley, E. A., *Population and History*, New York, 1969. A good introduction to family history.

SOURCE MATERIALS

Barnett, G. E., ed., *Two Tracts by Gregory King,* Baltimore, 1936. An introduction to the work of the modern world's first real statistician.

• Goubert, P., *The Ancien Régime: French Society, 1600–1750,* London, 1973. Particularly strong in its descriptions of rural life. Includes selections from illuminating documents.

Young, Arthur, *Travels in France during the Years 1787, 1788, 1789,* London, 1912. Vivid observations by an English traveler.

Chapter 18

THE AGE OF ABSOLUTISM
(1660-1789)

There are four essential characteristics or qualities of royal authority.
First, royal authority is sacred.
Second, it is paternal.
Third, it is absolute.
Fourth, it is subject to reason.

　　—Jacques Bossuet, *Politics Drawn from the Very Words of Holy Scripture*

T he period from the accession to personal rule of Louis XIV of France until the French Revolution is known as the age of absolutism. The label is accurate if we define absolutism as the conscious extension of the legal and administrative power of state sovereigns over their subjects, and over the vested interests of the social and economic orders in which those subjects were ranked. The dates are suggestive in that for the period as a whole the activities of French monarchs most clearly expressed the doctrines of absolutist government. Yet both the dates and the label need to be treated with some caution. We have already noted that from about 1500 on, a general trend to make the state omnicompetent had manifested itself in England and on the Continent. Sixteenth-century kings saw in Protestantism a way of asserting the sovereignty of their states as a challenge to papal and aristocratic power. And political thinkers such as Bodin were championing absolutist theory in ther writings well before Louis XIV assumed personal rulership of France. By establishing the French monarchs as prototypical early-modern rulers, we risk ignoring variant modes of centralized government instituted by the rulers of Prussia, Russia, and Austria. And we exclude the crucially important exception of England, where after 1688 absolutist tendencies gave way to oligarchy, and political power was shared among monarchy, aristocracy, and plutocracy.

Absolutism defined

The limits of absolutism

Finally, the term "absolutism" needs qualification. As practiced by western European eighteenth-century rulers, absolutism was not despotism. They did not understand it as a license for untrammeled and arbitrary rule, such as that practiced by Oriental potentates. Despite the best efforts of these European monarchs to consolidate their authority, they could not issue irresponsible decrees and achieve lasting compliance. Aristocrats, churchmen, merchants, and entrepreneurs remained strong enough within their respective orders to ensure that kings and queens would need to justify the actions they took. Moreover, rulers tended to respect not only the strength of their political adversaries but the processes of law; they quarreled openly and broke with tradition only under exceptional circumstances. No matter how "absolute" monarchs might wish to be, they were limited as well by rudimentary systems of transportation and communication from interfering with any degree of consistency and efficiency in the daily lives of their subjects. In this chapter we will measure the extent of royal power throughout Europe in the late seventeenth and eighteenth centuries, examine the varieties of absolutism as instituted and practiced by different monarchs, and take note of the way in which the centralization of power contributed to the rise of an international state system.

1. THE APPEAL AND JUSTIFICATION OF ABSOLUTISM

Absolutism's appeal

Absolutism appealed to many Europeans for the same reason that mercantalism did. In theory and practice, it expressed a desire for an end to the constant alarms and confusions of Europe's "iron century." The French religious wars, the Thirty Years' War in Germany, and the English Civil War all had produced great turbulence. The alternative, domestic order, absolutists argued, could come only with strong, centralized government. Just as mercantilists maintained that economic stability would result from regimentation, so absolutists contended that social and political harmony would be realized when subjects recognized their duty to obey their divinely sanctioned rulers.

The duties of the monarch

Absolutist monarchs insisted, in turn, upon *their* duty to teach their subjects, even against their will, how to order their domestic affairs. As Margrave Karl Friedrich, eighteenth-century ruler of the German principality of Baden, expressed it: "We must make them, whether they like it or not, into free, opulent and law-abiding citizens." Looking back to the seventeenth-century wars that had torn Europe apart, rulers can be excused for believing that absolutism's promise of stability and prosperity—"freedom and opulence"—presented an attractive as well as an imperative alternative to disorder. Louis XIV of France remembered the experience of the *Fronde* as a threat to the welfare of the nation which he had been appointed by God to rule wisely and justly. When marauding Parisians entered his bedchamber one night in 1651 to discover if he had fled the city with Mazarin, Louis saw the intrusion as a horrid affront not only to his own person, but to the state. Squabbles among the nobility and criticisms of royal policy in the Paris Parlement during his minority left him convinced that he must exercise his powers and prerogatives rigorously if France was to survive and prosper as a great European state.

In order to achieve that objective, absolutist monarchs worked to control the disposition of the state's armed forces, the administration of its legal system, and the collection and distribution of its tax revenues. This ambitious goal required an efficient bureaucracy that owed its primary allegiance not to some particular social or economic order with interests antithetical to the monarchy, but to the institution of the monarchy itself. One hallmark of absolutist policy was its determination to construct a set of institutions strong enough to withstand, if not destroy, the privileged interests that had stood in the path of royal power in the past. The church and the nobility, the semi-autonomous regions, and the would-be independent representative bodies (the English Parliament and the French Estates-General) were all obstacles to the achievement of strong, centralized monarchical government. And the history of absolutism is, as much as anything, the history of the attempts of various rulers to bring these institutions to heel.

In those major European countries where Roman Catholicism still remained the state religion—France, Spain, and Austria—successive monarchs throughout the eighteenth century made various attempts to "nationalize" the Church and its clergy. We have already noted the way in which in the fifteenth and sixteenth centuries, popes had conceded certain powers to the temporal rulers of France and Spain. Later absolutists, building on those earlier precedents, wrested further power from the Church in Rome. Even Charles III, the devout Spanish king who ruled from 1759 to 1788, pressed successfully for a papal concordat granting the state control over ecclesiastical appointments, and established his right to sanction the proclamation of papal bulls. Powerful as the Church was, it did not rival the aristocracy as an opponent of a centralized state. Monarchs combatted the noble orders in various ways. Louis XIV controlled the ancient French aristocracy by depriving it of political power while increasing its social prestige. Peter the Great, the talented and erratic tsar of early eighteenth-century Russia, coopted the nobility into government service. Later in the century, Catherine II struck a bargain whereby in return for the granting of vast estates and a variety of social and economic privileges such as exemption from taxation, the Russian aristocracy virtually surrendered the administrative and political power of the state into the empress's hands. In Prussia under Frederick the Great, the army was staffed by nobles: again, as in Peter's Russia, a case of cooption. Yet in late–eighteenth-century Austria, the emperor Joseph II adopted a policy of confrontation rather than accommodation, denying the nobility exemption from taxation and deliberately blurring the distinctions between nobles and commoners.

These struggles between monarchs and nobles had implications for the additional struggle between local privileges and centralized power. Absolutists in France waged constant war against the autonomy of provincial institutions, often headed by aristocrats, much as Spanish rulers in the sixteenth century had battled independent-minded nobles in Aragon and Catalonia. Prussian rulers intruded into the governance of formerly "free" cities, assuming police and revenue powers over their inhabitants. These various campaigns, constantly waged and usually successful for a time, were evidence of the nature of absolutism and of its continuing success.

Absolutism had its theoretical apologists as well as its able practitioners. In addition to the political philosophies of men such as Bodin, defenders of royal power could rely on treatises such as Bishop Jacques Bossuet's *Politics Drawn from the Very Words of Scripture* (1708), written during the reign of Louis XIV, to sustain the case for extended monarchical control. Bossuet argued that absolute government was not the same as arbitrary government, since God, in whom "all strength and all perfection were united," was united as well with the person of the king. "God is holiness itself, goodness itself, and power itself. In these things lies the majesty of God. In the image of these things lies the majesty of the prince." It followed that the king was answerable to no one but God himself, and that the king was as far above other mortals as God was above the king. "The prince, as prince, is not regarded as a private person; he is a public personage, all the state is in him. . . .

Bishop Jacques Bossuet

The Château of Versailles. Dramatically expanded by Louis XIV in the 1660s from a hunting lodge to the principal royal residence and the seat of government, the château became a monument to the international power and prestige of the Grand Monarch.

Louis XIV, the Sun King. This portrait by Rigaud illustrates the degree to which absolute monarchy was defined in terms of studied performance.

As all perfection and all strength are united in God, all the power of individuals is united in the Person of the prince. What grandeur that a simple man should embody so much." What grandeur indeed! Bossuet's treatise was the most explicit and extreme statement of the theory of the divine right of kings, the doctrine that James I had tried to foist upon the English. Unlikely as it may sound to modern ears, the political philosophy of Bossuet was comforting to men and women who craved peace and stability after a century or more of international and domestic turmoil.

2. THE ABSOLUTISM OF LOUIS XIV

Examine a portrait of Louis XIV [1] (1643–1715) in court robes; it is all but impossible to discern the human being behind the facade of the absolute monarch. That facade was carefully and artfully constructed by Louis, who recognized, perhaps more clearly than any other early-modern ruler, the importance of theater as a means of establishing authority. Well into the eighteenth century, superstitious commoners continued to believe in the power of the king's magic "touch" to cure disease. Louis and his successors used this belief to enhance their position as divine-right rulers endowed with God-like powers and far removed from common humanity.

    The advantages of strategic theater were expressed most clearly in Louis's palace at Versailles, the town out side of Paris to which he

Absolutism as theater: Louis XIV

---

[1]Here, as elsewhere, dates following a ruler's name refer to dates of reign.

One of the 1400 Fountains in the Gardens at Versailles. The grounds as well as the palace were part of the backdrop for the theater of absolutism.

moved his court. The building itself was a stage, upon which Louis mesmerized the aristocracy into obedience by his performance of the daily rituals of absolutism. The main facade of the palace was a third of a mile in length. Inside, tapestries and paintings celebrated French military victories and royal triumphs. Outside, in gardens containing 1400 fountains, statues of Apollo, god of the sun, recalled Louis's claim to be the "Sun King" of the French. Noblemen vied to attend him when he arose from bed, ate his meals (usually stone-cold, having traveled the distance of several city blocks from royal kitchen to royal table), strolled in his gardens, or rode to the hunt. As Louis called himself the Sun King, so his court was the epicenter of his royal effulgence. Its glitter, in which France's leading aristocrats were required by their monarch to share, was deliberately manufactured so as to blind them to the possibility of disobedience to the royal will. Instead of plotting some sort of minor treason on his estate, a marquis enjoyed the pleasure of knowing that on the morrow he was to be privileged to engage the king in two or three minutes of vapid conversation as the royal party made its stately progress through the vast palace halls (whose smells were evidence of the absence of sanitation facilities and of the seamy side of absolutist grandeur).

Louis understood this theater as part of his duty as sovereign, a duty which he took with utmost seriousness. Though far from brilliant, he was hard-working and conscientious. Whether or not he actually remarked "L'état, c'est moi" ("I am the State"), he believed himself personally responsible for the well-being of his subjects. "The deference and the respect that we receive from our subjects," he wrote in a memoir he prepared for his son on the art of ruling, "are not a free gift from them but payment for the justice and the protection that they

Versailles

Louis XIV on his duties

expect from us. Just as they must honor us, we must protect and defend them."

Louis defined this responsibility in absolutist terms: as a need to concentrate royal power so as to produce general domestic tranquility. While taming the aristocracy, he conciliated the upper bourgeoisie by enlisting its members to assist him in the task of administration. He appointed them as intendants, responsible for the administration and taxation of the thirty-six *generalités* into which France was divided. Intendants never served in the regions where they were born, and were thus unconnected with the local elites over which they exercised authority. They held office at the king's pleasure, and were clearly "his" men. Other administrators, often from families newly ennobled as a result of administrative service, assisted in directing affairs of state from Versailles. These men were not actors in the theater of Louis the Sun King; they were the hard-working assistants of Louis the royal custodian of his country's welfare. Much of the time and energy of Louis's bureaucrats was expended on the collection of taxes, necessary above all in order to finance the large standing army on which France's ambitious foreign policy depended. In addition to the *taille,* or land tax, which increased throughout the seventeenth century and upon which a surtax was levied as well, the government introduced a capitation tax, payable by all, and pressed hard for the collection of indirect taxes such as that on salt (the *gabelle*) and on wine and tobacco. Since the nobility was exempt from the *taille,* its burden fell most heavily on the peasantry, whose periodic local revolts Louis easily crushed.

The administration of French absolutism: intendants and revenue

Regional opposition—and indeed regionalism generally—was curtailed during Louis's reign. Although intendants and lesser administrators came from afar, did not speak the local dialect, ignored local custom, and were therefore despised, they were generally obeyed. The semi-autonomous outer provinces of Brittany, Languedoc, and Franche Comté (a part of that territory known collectively as the *pays d'état*) came to heel as central administration crippled their provincial Estates. To put an end to the power of regional *parlements* (the courts responsible for registering laws), Louis decreed that members of those bodies which vetoed legislation would be summarily exiled. The Estates-General, the national French representative assembly last summoned in 1614 during the troubled regency following the death of Henry IV, did not meet again until 1789.

Curbing regional opposition

Louis was equally determined, for reasons of state and of personal conscience, to impose religious unity upon the French. That task proved to be difficult and time-consuming. The Huguenots were not the only source of theological heterodoxy. Jesuits, Quietists, and Jansenists—all three claiming to represent the "true" Roman faith—battled among themselves for adherents to their particular brand of Catholicism. Jesuits served Louis's interests best, since they advocated obedience to the secular power of the French state. Quietists preached

Louis XIV's religious policies

a retreat into personal mysticism. Jansenism—a movement named for its founder Cornelius Jansen, a seventeenth-century bishop of Ypres—was a French version of Calvinism which stressed the doctrine of original sin and rejected the belief in free will that was central to Jesuit teaching. Louis, adhering to the absolutist doctrine of *un roi, une loi, une foi* (one king, one law, one faith) which had served as a rallying cry for both Catholics and Protestants in France during the preceding century, took drastic steps to achieve religious conformity as part of his program of national unification. He persecuted Quietists and Jansenists, offering them the choice of recanting or of prison and exile. Against the Huguenots he waged an even sterner war. Protestant churches and schools were destroyed; Protestant families were forced to convert. In 1685, Louis revoked the Edict of Nantes, the legal foundation of the toleration Huguenots had enjoyed since 1598. French Protestants were thereafter denied civil rights, and their clergy was exiled. Thousands of religious refugees fled France for England, Holland, the Protestant states of Germany, and America, where their particular professional and artisanal skills made a significant contribution to economic prosperity. (The silk industry of Berlin and of Spitalfields, an urban quarter of London, was established by Huguenots.)

Jean Baptiste Colbert

Louis's drive for unification and centralization was assisted by his ability to rely upon increased revenues to fuel the domestic and military machinery of his absolutist monarchy. Those revenues were largely the result of policies and programs initiated by Jean Baptiste Colbert (1619–1683), the country's finance minister from 1664 until his death. Colbert was an energetic and committed mercantilist who believed that until France could put its fiscal house in order it could not achieve economic greatness. Colbert assumed office at a time when France, because of costly wars, was deeply in debt. Although he could not rid the country of that burden, he did for a time establish an interest rate of no higher than 5 percent, significantly lower than those the government had been accustomed to paying, and began negotiating directly with major creditors, rather than relying, as in the past, on fee-charging middlemen. Meanwhile, he tightened the process of tax collection, hounding corrupt officials who skimmed off a share of the taxes for themselves. He eliminated wherever possible the practice of tax farming, the system whereby collection agents were permitted to withhold a certain percentage of what they gathered for themselves. When Colbert assumed office, only about 25 percent of the taxes collected throughout the kingdom was reaching the treasury. By the time he died, that figure had risen to 80 percent.

The financial policies of Colbert

Colbert as mercantilist

As a mercantilist, Colbert did all he could to increase the nation's income by means of protection and regimentation. Tariffs he imposed in 1667 and 1668 were designed to discourage the importation of foreign goods into France. He invested in the improvement of France's roads and waterways. And he used state money to promote the growth of national industry, and in particular the manufacture of goods such as silk, lace, tapestries, and glass, which had long been imported. Yet Colbert's efforts to achieve national economic stability and self-sufficiency could not withstand the insatiable demands of Louis XIV's increasingly expensive wars. Nor did his overseas trading companies ever achieve the stature of those of England and Holland. Unquestionably, however, France's economy was generally healthier as a result of his policies. And his championing of industrial enterprise did much to enhance the image of businessmen and entrepreneurs in the eyes of a nation which in the past had tended to disdain commerce and manufacturing.

3. ABSOLUTISM IN CENTRAL AND EASTERN EUROPE, 1660–1720

The degree of success enjoyed by Louis XIV as an absolutist monarch was in part the result of his own abilities, and of those of his advisors. Yet it was due as well to the fact that he could claim to stand as supreme embodiment of the will of all his people. Despite its internal division into territories and orders that continued to claim some right to independence, France was already unified before the accession of Louis XIV, possessed of a sense of itself as a nation. In this, it differed from the empires, kingdoms, and principalities to the east, where rulers faced an even more formidable task than did Louis as they attempted to weld their disparately constructed monarchies into a united, centralized whole. The Thirty Year's War had delivered a final blow to the pretensions of the Holy Roman Empire, which the French philosopher Voltaire dubbed neither holy, Roman, nor an empire. Power, in varying degrees, passed to the over three hundred princes, bishops, and magistrates who governed the assorted states of Germany throughout the remainder of the seventeenth and eighteenth centuries.

Absolutism and national unity

Despite the minute size of their domains, many of these petty monarchs attempted to establish themselves as absolutists in miniature, building lesser versions of Louis XIV's Versailles, maintaining standing armies, and paying for their expensive pretensions by tariffs and tolls that severely hampered the development of any sort of economic unity within the region as a whole. Although these rulers often prided themselves on their independence from imperial control, in many instances they were client states of France. A sizable portion of the money Louis devoted to the conduct of foreign affairs went to these German princelings. States like Saxony, Brandenburg-Prussia, and Bavaria, which were of a size to establish themselves as truly independent, were not averse to forming alliances against their own emperor.

Absolutism in the German states

Most notable among these middle-sized German states was Brandenburg-Prussia, whose emergence as a power of consequence during this period was the result of the single-minded determination of its rulers, principally Frederick William, elector of Brandenburg from

1640 to 1688, whose abilities have earned him the title of "Great Elector." The rise of Brandenburg-Prussia from initial insignificance, poverty, and devastation in the wake of the Thirty Years' War resulted from three basic achievements that can be credited to the Great Elector. First, he pursued an adroit foreign policy which enabled him to establish effective sovereignty over the widely dispersed and underdeveloped territories under his rule: Brandenburg, a large but not particularly productive territory in north-central Germany; Prussia, a duchy to the east that was dangerously exposed on three sides to Poland; and a sprinkling of tiny states—Cleves, Mark, and Ravensberg—to the west. By siding with Poland in a war against Sweden in the late 1650s, the Great Elector obtained the Polish king's surrender of nominal overlordship in East Prussia. And by some crafty diplomatic shuffling in the 1670s, he secured his western provinces from French interference by returning Pomerania, captured in a recent war, to France's Swedish allies.

Frederick William's second achievement was the establishment of a large standing army, the primary instrument of his diplomatic successes. By 1688, Brandenburg-Prussia had 30,000 troops permanently under arms. That he was able to sustain an army of this size in a state with comparatively limited resources was a measure of the degree to which the army more than repaid its costs. It ensured the elector and

Prussians Swearing Allegiance to the Great Elector at Königsberg, 1663. The occasion upon which the Prussian estates first acknowledged the overlordship of their ruler, this ceremony marked the beginning of the centralization of the Prussian state.

his successors absolute political control by fostering obedience among the populace, an obedience they were prepared to observe if their lands might be spared the devastation of another Thirty Years' War.

The third factor contributing to the emergence of the Great Elector's state as an international power was his imposition of an effective system of taxation and his creation of a government bureaucracy to administer it. Here he struck an important bargain with the powerful and privileged landlords (*Junkers*) without whose cooperation his programs would have had no chance of success. In return for an agreement which allowed them to reduce their peasant underlings to the status of serfs, the Junkers gave away their right to oppose a permanent tax system, provided, of course, that they were made immune from the payment of taxes themselves. (As in other European countries, taxes in Prussia fell most heavily on the peasantry.)

Henceforth, the political privileges of the landlord class diminished; secure in their right to manage their own estates as they wished, the Junkers were content to surrender management of the Hohenzollern possessions into the hands of a centralized bureaucracy. Its most important department was a military commissariat, whose functions included not only the dispensing of army pay and matériel, but the development of industries to manufacture military equipment. Frederick William's success was due primarily to his ability to gain the active cooperation of the Junker class, something he needed even more than Louis XIV needed the support of the French nobility. Without it, Frederick William could never have hammered together his absolutist state from the disparate territorial pieces that were his political raw material. To obtain it, he used the army not only to maintain order, but as a way of coopting Junker participation. The highest honor that could befall a Brandenburg squire was commission and promotion as a military servant of the state.

Like Brandenburg–Prussia, the Habsburg monarch was confronted with the task of transforming three different regions into a cohesive state. In the case of Austria, this effort was complicated by the fact that these areas were ethnically and linguistically diverse: the southernmost Germanic lands that roughly comprised the present-day state of Austria; the northern Czech- (Slavic-) speaking provinces of Bohemia and Moravia; the German-speaking Silesia, inherited in 1527; and Hungary, where the Magyar population spoke a non-Slavic, Finno-Ugric language, also acquired in 1527 but largely lost to Turkish invasion just a few years afterward. For the next 150 years the Habsburgs and the Turks vied for control of Hungary. Until 1683 Turkish pashas ruled three-fourths of the Magyar kingdom, extending to within eighty miles of the Habsburg capital of Vienna. In 1683 the Turks besieged Vienna itself, but were repulsed by the Austrians, assisted by a mixed German and Polish army under the command of King John Sobieski of Poland. This victory was a prelude to the Habsburg reconquest of virtually all of Hungary by the end of the century.

Bargaining with Bohemia and Moravia

The task of constructing an absolutist state from these extraordinarily varied territories was tackled with limited success by the seventeenth-century Habsburg emperors Ferdinand III (1637–1657) and Leopold I (1658–1705). Most of their efforts were devoted to the establishment of productive agricultural estates in Bohemia and Moravia, and to taming the independent nobility there and in Hungary. Landlords were encouraged to farm for export, and were supported in this effort by a government decree which compelled peasants to provide three days of unpaid *robot* service per week to their masters.[2] For this support, Bohemian and Moravian landed elites exchanged the political independence that had in the past expressed itself in the activities of their territorial legislative Estates.

Problems with the Hungarian nobility

Habsburg rulers tried to effect this same sort of bargain in Hungary as well. But there the tradition of independence was stronger and died harder. Hungarian (or Magyar) nobles in the west claimed the right to elect their king, a right they eventually surrendered to Leopold in 1687. But the central government's attempts to further reduce the country by administering it through the army, by granting large tracts of land to German aristocrats and settlers, and by persecuting non-Catholics were an almost total failure. The result was a powerful nobility which, while it insisted upon its right to exploit its serfs as it saw fit, nevertheless remained fiercely determined to retain its traditional constitutional and religious "liberties." The Habsburg emperors could boast that they too, like absolutists elsewhere, possessed a large standing army and an educated (in this case German-speaking) bureaucracy. But the exigencies imposed by geography and ethnicity kept them at some distance from the absolutist goal of a unified, centrally controlled and administered state.

Peter the Great. An eighteenth-century mosaic.

Undoubtedly the most dramatic episode in the history of early-modern absolutist rule was the dynamic reign of Tsar Peter I of Russia (1682–1725). Peter's accomplishments alone would clearly have earned him his history-book title, Peter the Great. But his gigantic height—he was nearly seven feet tall—as well as his mercurial personality—jesting one moment, raging the next—certainly helped. Peter is best remembered as the tsar whose policies brought Russia into the world of western Europe. Previously the country's rulers had set their faces firmly against the West, disdaining a civilization at odds with the Eastern Orthodox, semi-Oriental culture that was their heritage, while laboring to keep the various ethnic groups—Russians, Ukrainians, and a wide variety of nomadic tribes—within their ever-growing empire from destroying not only each other but the tsarist state itself. Since 1613 Russia had been ruled by members of the Romanov dynasty, who had attempted with some success to restore political stability following the chaotic "time of troubles" that had occurred after the death of the bloodthirsty, half-mad Tsar Ivan the Terrible in 1584. The early Romanovs' severest test had come between 1667 and 1671, when a

---

[2] The English usage of the term *robot* derives from the Czech designation of a serf.

Cossack leader (the Russian Cossacks were semi-autonomous bands of peasant cavalrymen) named Stenka Razin led much of southeastern Russia into rebellion. Stenka Razin's uprising found widespread support from hordes of serfs who had been oppressed by their masters as well as from non-Russian tribes in the lower Volga area who longed to cast off domination from Moscow. But ultimately Tsar Alexis (1645–1676) and the Russian nobility whose interests were most at stake were able to raise an army capable of defeating Razin's zealous but disorganized bands. Before the rebellion was finally crushed, over 100,000 rebels had been slaughtered.

Russian absolutism: the situation before Peter the Great

This campaign was but a prelude to the deliberate and ruthless drive to absolutist power launched by Peter after he overthrew the regency of his half-sister Sophia and assumed personal control of the state in 1689. Within ten years he had scandalized aristocrats and churchmen alike by traveling to Holland and England to recruit highly skilled foreign workers and to study the craft of shipbuilding. Upon his return he distressed them still further by declaring his intention to Westernize Russia, and initiating this campaign by cutting off the "Eastern" beards and flowing sleeves of leading noblemen at court. Determined to "civilize" the nobility, he published a book of manners which forbade spitting on the floor and eating with one's fingers, and encouraged the cultivation of the art of polite conversation between the sexes.

Peter Cutting a Nobleman's Beard. In this Russian woodcut Peter the Great is portrayed as a diminutive pest.

Much as Peter wished to consider himself a Westerner, his particular brand of absolutism differed from that of other contemporary monarchs. As we have seen, the autocracy imposed by Ivan III in the fifteenth cetury had a decidedly Eastern caste. Peter was the willing heir to much of that tradition. He considered himself above the law

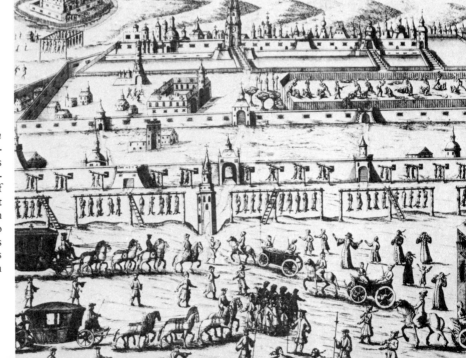

Peter the Great's Execution of the Streltsy. This contemporary print shows scores of corpses gibbeted outside the walls of the Kremlin. Peter kept the rotting bodies on display for months to discourage his subjects from opposing his efforts to Westernize Russian society.

and thus his own absolute master to a degree that was alien to the absolutist theories and traditions of the Habsburgs and Bourbons. Autocrat of all the Russias, he ruled despotically, with a ferocious individual power that western European rulers did not possess. Armed with such arbitrary power in theory, and intent on realizing its full potential in practice, Peter set out to turn Russia to the West and to modernize his state. He would brook no opposition.

The suppression and reconstruction of the army

Confronted with a rebellion among the *streltsy,* the politically active, elite corps of the army who were most opposed to his innovations and who favored the restoration of his half-sister to the throne, Peter reacted with a savagery that astonished his contemporaries. Roughly 1200 suspected conspirators were summarily executed, many of them gibbeted outside the walls of the Kremlin, where their bodies remained for months as a graphic reminder of the fate awaiting those who would dare to challenge his absolute authority. Applying a lesson from the West, Peter proceeded to create a large standing army recruited from the ranks of the peasantry and scrupulously loyal to the tsar. One of every twenty males was conscripted for lifelong service. He financed his army, as did other absolutists, by increasing taxes, with their burden falling most heavily on the peasantry. To equip his new military force, he fostered the growth of the iron and munitions industries. Factories were built and manned by peasant laborers whose position was little better than that of slaves. Serfs were also commandeered for other public works projects, such as road and canal building, necessary for the modernization of the state.

Absolutism and the new bureaucracy

In an effort to further consolidate his absolute power, he replaced the Duma—the nation's rudimentary national assembly—with a rubber-stamp senate, and appointed a procurator, dependent directly on him, to manage the affairs of the tradition-bound Russian Orthodox church, which essentially became an extension of the state. At the same time, Peter was fashioning new, larger, and more efficient administrative machinery to cope with the demands of his modernization program. Although he preferred to draw "new" men, whose loyalty to the tsar would be unerring, into the bureaucracy, he was compelled to rely upon the services of the aristocrat—or *boyar*—class as well, rewarding them by increasing their control over their serfs. Nevertheless, membership in his new bureaucracy did not depend on birth. One of his principal advisers, Alexander Menshikov, began his career as a cook and finished as a prince. Bureaucratic status replaced noble rank as the key to power. The administrative machinery devised by Peter furnished Russia with its ruling class for the next two hundred years.

The influence of foreign and domestic policy

Peter the Great's Eurocentric worldview also manifested itself in his foreign policy, as witnessed by his bold drive to gain a Russian outlet on the Baltic Sea. To this end he engaged in a war with Sweden's meteoric soldier-king Charles XII (1697–1718), who devoted most of his reign to campaigns in the field against the Danes, the Poles, and

The St. Petersburg Palaces. The first of six versions of the Winter Palace here depicted (left) was erected in 1711. It quickly proved to be too modest for Peter's needs. Within a decade he had created a far more elaborate complex called Peterhof (right), complete with fountains fashioned after those of Versailles.

the Russians. By defeating Charles decisively at the Battle of Poltava in 1709, Peter was able to secure his window to the West. He promptly outdid his absolutist counterparts to the West, who moved their courts the outskirts of their capital cities, by moving the capital itself from Moscow to an entirely new city on the Gulf of Finland. An army of serfs was employed to erect the baroque city of St. Petersburg around a palace intended to imitate and rival Louis XIV's Versailles. It was not enough that Peter looked to the West; he wanted the Russian people to share the view.

Not surprisingly, Peter's drastic programs met with concerted resistance. Resentment smoldered under his imposing hand, even within the palace. His son Alexis, who had dared to declare himself opposed to his father's innovations, became a rallying point for the forces of resistance to the tsar and his policies, and died under torture inflicted at his father's command in 1718. Upon Peter's death in 1725, *boyar* determination to undo his reforms surfaced during the succession struggle. A series of ineffective tsars followed Peter, thus allowing the resentful nobles to rescind many of his reforms, until, in 1762, the crown passed to Catherine II, a ruler whose ambitions and determination were equal to those of her august predecessor.

Peter's successors

Peter the Great of Russia, Leopold I of Austria, Frederick William of Brandenburg-Prussia, and above all Louis XIV of France: these were the "great" seventeenth-century absolutists. Elsewhere, the fortunes of absolutism fared far less well. The ineffectual, weak-minded

The failure of absolutism to take root elsewhere

Spanish monarch Charles II found himself besieged by rebellions in Portugal and Sicily. In 1668, after years of fighting, he was forced to recognize Portuguese independence. In Sweden, Charles X and Charles XI managed to extend their territories at the expense of the Danes and to quell the independence of the aristocracy by confiscating their fiefdoms. During the reign of Charles XII, however, that legacy was dissipated by an adventurous but ultimately unproductive foreign policy. The opposition of the landed gentry—or *szlachta*—to any form of centralized government in Poland produced a political stalemate that amounted to little more than anarchy. Foreign powers took advantage of this situation to intervene in Polish affairs and, in the eighteenth century, to carve up the country and distribute it among themselves.

4. THE ENGLISH EXCEPTION

The policies of Charles II

But what of England, which had experienced a taste of absolutist centralization under the Tudors and early Stuarts, and indeed under Oliver Cromwell, but which possessed in its Parliament the longest tradition and most highly developed form of representative government in western Europe? England's political history in the late seventeenth century provides the most striking contrast to continental absolutism. Charles II, son of the beheaded Charles I, who returned from exile and ascended the throne in 1660, was initially welcomed by most English men and women. He pledged himself not to reign as a despot, but to respect Parliament and to observe Magna Carta and the Petition of Right, for he admitted that he was not anxious to "resume his travels." His delight in the unbuttoned moral atmosphere of his court and the culture it supported (risque plays, dancing, and marital infidelity) mirrored a public desire to forget the restraints of the puritan past. The wits of the time suggested that Charles, "that known enemy to virginity and chastity," played his role as the father of his country to the fullest. However, as Charles's admiration of things French grew to include the absolutism of Louis XIV, he came to be regarded as a threat to more than English womanhood by a great many powerful Englishmen who, however anxious they were to restore the monarchy, were not about to surrender their traditional rights to another Stuart autocrat. By the late 1670s, the country found itself divided politically into those who supported the king (called by their opponents "Tories," a popular nickname for Irish Catholic bandits) and those opposed to him (called by *their* opponents "Whigs," a similar nickname for Scottish Presbyterian rebels).

Charles II of England

Religion and the political reaction

As the new party labels suggest, religion remained an exceedingly divisive national issue. Charles was sympathetic to Roman Catholicism, even to the point of a deathbed conversion in 1685. He therefore opposed the stiff code of ecclesiastical regulations, known as the Clarendon Code, which had reestablished Anglicanism as the official state religion and which penalized Roman Catholics and Protestant dissenters. In 1672, Charles suspended the Clarendon Code, although the public outcry against this action compelled him to retreat. This controversy, and rising opposition to the probable succession of Charles's ardent Roman Catholic brother James, led to a series of Whig electoral victories between 1679 and 1681. But Charles found that increased revenues, plus a secret subsidy he was receiving from Louis XIV, enabled him to govern without resort to Parliament, to which he would otherwise have had to go for money. In addition to ignoring Parliament, Charles further infuriated and alarmed Whig politicians by arranging the execution of several of their most prominent leaders on charges of treason, and by remodeling local government in such a way as to make it more dependent on royal favor. Charles died in 1685 with his power enhanced; but he left behind him a political and religious legacy that was to be the undoing of his successor.

James II was the very opposite of his brother. A zealous Catholic convert, he alienated his Tory supporters, all of whom were of course Anglicans, by dismissing them in favor of Roman Catholics, and by once again suspending the penal laws against Catholics and dissenters. His stubbornness, as one historian has remarked, made it all but impossible for him to take "yes" for an answer. Whereas Charles had been content to defeat his political enemies, James was determined to humiliate them. Like Charles, James interfered in local government, but his appointments were so personally distasteful and so mediocre as to arouse active opposition. James made no attempt to disguise his Roman Catholicism. He publically declared his wish that all his subjects might be converted, and paraded papal legates through the streets of London. When, in June 1688, he ordered all Anglican clergymen to read his decree of toleration from their pulpits, seven bishops refused and were clapped into prison on charges of seditious libel. At their trial, however, they were declared not guilty, to the vast satisfaction of the English populace.

James II as religious zealot

The trial of the bishops was one event that brought matters to a head. The other was the birth of a son to James and his second wife, the Roman Catholic daughter of the duke of Modena. This male infant, who was to be raised a Roman Catholic, replaced James's much older Protestant daughter Mary as heir to the British throne. Despite a rumor that the baby boy was an imposter smuggled into the royal bedchamber in a warming pan, political leaders of both parties were prepared not only to believe in the legitimacy of the child but to take active steps to prevent the possibility of his succession. A delegation of Whigs and Tories crossed the channel to Holland with an invitation to Mary's husband William of Orange, the *stadholder* or chief executive of the United Provinces and the great-grandson of William the Silent. William was asked to cross to England with an invading army to restore

The succession question

William III

A "glorious" revolution?

1688 as a defense of status quo

English religious and political freedom. As leader of a continental coalition determined to put a spoke in Louis XIV's expansionist policies, he accepted, welcoming the chance such a move represented to bring England into active opposition to the French (see below, p. 609).

William's conquest was a bloodless coup. James fled the country, thereby allowing Parliament to declare the throne vacant and clearing the way for the accession of William and Mary as joint sovereigns of England. A Bill of Rights, passed by Parliament and accepted by the new king and queen, reaffirmed English civil liberties such as trial by jury, habeas corpus (guaranteeing the accused a speedy trial), and the right of petition and redress, and established that the monarchy was subject to the law of the land. An Act of Toleration, passed in 1689, granted dissenters the right to worship, though not the right to full political protection. In 1701, with the son of the exiled James II now reaching maturity in France, an Act of Succession ordained that the English throne was to pass first to Mary's childless sister Anne, who ruled from 1702 to 1714, and then to George, elector of the German principality of Hanover, who was the great-grandson of James I. The connection was a distant one, but the Hanoverian dynasty was Protestant, and George reputed to be a capable enough ruler. The act was further evidence of the degree to which Parliament could dictate its terms. Henceforth, all English sovereigns were to be communicants of the Church of England. If foreign born, they could not engage England in the defense of their native land, nor leave the country, without Parliamentary consent.

The events of 1688 and 1689 were soon referred to by the English as "the Glorious Revolution." Glorious for the English in that it occurred without bloodshed (although James is reputed to have been suffering from a nosebleed at the moment of crisis). Glorious, too, for defenders of Parliamentary prerogative. Although William and Mary and their royal successors continued to enjoy a large measure of executive power, after 1688 no king or queen attempted to govern without Parliament, which met annually from that time on. Parliament strengthened its control over the collection and expenditure of public money. Future sovereigns were henceforth unable to conduct the country's business without recourse to the House of Commons for the funds to do so. Glorious, finally, for advocates of the civil liberties now guaranteed within the Bill of Rights.

Yet 1688 was not all glory. It was a revolution that consolidated the position of large property holders, local magnates whose political and economic power base in their rural constituencies and on their estates had been threatened by the interventions of Charles II and James II. If it was a revolution, it was one designed to restore the *status quo* on behalf of a wealthy social and economic order that would soon make itself even wealthier as it drank its fill of government patronage and war profits. And it was a revolution that brought nothing but misery to the Roman Catholic minority in Scotland, which joined with England and Wales in the union of Great Britain in 1701, and the Catholic majority in Ireland where, following the Battle of the Boyne in 1690, repressive military forces imposed the exploitive will of a self-interested Protestant minority upon the Catholic majority.

Although the "Glorious Revolution" was an expression of immediate political circumstance, it was a reflection as well of anti-absolutist theories that had risen in the late seventeenth century to challenge the ideas of writers such as Bodin, Hobbes, and Bossuet. Chief among these opponents of absolutism was the Englishman John Locke (1632–1704), whose *Two Treatises of Civil Government* (1690) was used to justify the events of the previous two years. Locke maintained that originally all humans had lived in a theoretical state of nature in which absolute freedom and equality prevailed, and in which there was no government of any kind. The only law was the law of nature, which each individual enforced for himself in order to protect his natural rights to life, liberty, and property. It was not long, however, before men began to perceive that the inconveniences of the state of nature greatly outweighed its advantages. With individuals attempting to enforce their own rights, confusion and insecurity were the unavoidable results. Accordingly, the people agreed among themselves to establish a civil society, to set up a government, and to surrender certain powers to it. But they did not make that government absolute. The only power they conferred upon it was the executive power of the law of nature. Since the state was nothing but the joint power of all the members of society, its authority could "be no more than those persons had in a state of nature before they entered into society, and gave it up to the community." All powers not expressly surrendered were reserved to the people themselves. If the government exceeded or abused the authority explicitly granted in the political contract, it became tyrannical; the people then had the right to dissolve it or to rebel against it and overthrow it.

Locke condemned absolutism in every form. He denounced despotic monarchy, but he was no less severe in his strictures against the absolute sovereignty of parliaments. Though he defended the supremacy of the law-making branch, with the executive primarily an agent of the legislature, he nevertheless refused to concede to the representatives of the people an unlimited power. Arguing that state government was instituted among people for the preservation of property, he denied the authority of any political agency to invade the natural rights of a single individual. The law of nature, which embodied these rights, was an automatic limitation upon every branch of the government. Locke's theoretical defense of political liberties emerged in the late eighteenth century as an important element in the intellectual background of the French Revolution. In 1688, however, it served a far less radical purpose. The landed magnates responsible for the

John Locke

Defense of 1688: the political theories of John Locke

Locke and limited sovereignty

exchange of James II for William and Mary could read Locke as an apoligia for their conservative revolution. James II, rather than protecting their property and liberties, had encroached upon them; hence their right to overthrow the tyranny he had established and replace it with a government that would, by ensuring their rights, defend their interests.

5. WARFARE AND DIPLOMACY: THE EMERGENCE OF A STATE SYSTEM

Emergence of state interests

The rise of absolutist monarchies in the late seventeenth century resulted in the emergency of an international state system. To the extent that absolutists succeeded in attaining their goals of unification and centralization, their states took shape as individual, identifiable political and economic entities. Although the achievements of various monarchs in this regard were limited, they were significant enough to encourage diplomats to speak more commonly than in the past of the "interests" of a particular state, as if that state somehow had a corporate personality of its own, and of the way in which those interests might coincide or conflict with the interests of another state. Often the interests of a monarch might clash with those of the country over which he ruled. Bourbon kings and Habsburg emperors worried about the future of their family dynasties to the detriment of the future of France or Austria. Religion, the factor that had torn Europe apart in the preceding century, remained an international issue in 1700. But increasingly, both dynasty and religion were superseded by newer "interests"—commerce and international balance and stability. The emergence of something approaching the modern state was to result, by 1715, in a significant redefinition of the aims and calculations of diplomacy and warfare.

The growth of diplomacy

The organization of diplomatic bureaucracies was a major accomplishment of absolutist monarchies. Had most foreign ministers and ambassadors read the Dutchman Hugo Grotius's treatise on *The Law of War and Peace* (1625), they would have agreed with him about the necessity of establishing a body of rules that would help to bring reason and order to relations between governments. In practice, of course, reason and order gave way to bribery and improvisation. Yet the rationalization of diplomatic processes and the establishment of foreign ministries and embassies in European capitals, with their growing staffs of clerks and ministers, reflected a desire to bring order out of the international chaos that had gripped Europe during its "war century." International relations in the late seventeenth century was, among other things, a history of diplomatic coalitions, an indication of the degree to which negotiation was now a weapon in the armory of the absolutist state.

The Capture of Cambrai by Louis XIV in 1677. This print illustrates the tactics of siege warfare as practiced by early-modern armies. Louis is shown receiving an emissary from the city, whose walls have been breeched by siege guns.

Warfare, however, continued to play an integral and almost constant role in the international arena. The armies of the period grew dramatically. When Louis XIV acceded to power in 1661, the French army numbered 20,000 men; by 1688, it stood at 290,000; by 1694, 400,000. These armies were increasingly professional organizations, controlled directly by the state, and under the command of trained officers recruited from the nobility. In Prussia, common soldiers were mostly conscripts; in other European countries they were volunteers, either native or foreign, though often "volunteers" in no more than name, having been coerced or tricked into service. Increasingly, however, enlistment was perceived by common soldiers as an avenue to a career, one which included the possibility of promotion to corporal or sergeant, and in the case of France, the promise of a small pension at the end of one's service. However recruited, common soldiers became part of an increasingly elaborate and efficient fighting force. The maneuvers of infantry, cavalry, and artillery were coordinated as never before. Soldiers were drilled with a thoroughness necessitated by tactics which depended on the accurate firepower of cannon and flintlock muskets. They were taught to stand their ground in formations of long, rigid lines in the face of direct enemy assault. They mastered the use of the bayonet (short steel spikes attached to the end of muskets, first manufactured in Bayonne, France, in the seventeenth century); the most effective procedure: stabbing the man

The growth of professional armies

in his left side as he raised his right arm to fire. Above all, they were made to understand the dire consequences of disobedience, breaking rank, or desertion. Soldiers were expected to obey instantly and unquestioningly. Failure to do so resulted in brutal punishment, often flogging, sometimes execution. Commissioned and noncommissioned officers carried sticks and prods with which to "encourage" correct military behavior in their men. Drill, not only on the battlefield but on the parade ground, in brilliant, elaborate uniforms and intricate formations, was designed to reduce individuals to automaton-like parts of an army whose regiments were moved across battlefields as a chess player moves pawns across the board—and with about the same concern for loss of human life.

The patterns of international relations during the period from 1660 to 1715 show European monarchs making use of the new machinery of diplomacy and warfare to resolve the conflicting interests of dynasty, stability, and commerce. At the center of that pattern, as at the center of Europe, stood Louis XIV. From 1661 until 1688, in a quest for glory, empire, and even revenge, he waged war across his northern and eastern frontiers on the pretext that the lands in question belonged both to the Bourbons and to the French by tradition, by former treaty, or by dynastic inheritance. His aggressively expansionist policies, alarming to other European rulers, led William of Orange, in 1674, to form an anti-French coalition with Austria, Spain, and various smaller German states. Yet Louis continued to push his frontiers eastward, invading territories that had been Germanic for centuries, and capturing Strassburg in 1681 and Luxembourg in 1684. Louis's seizure of Strassburg (subsequently called Strasbourg by the French), completing the conquest of the German-speaking province of Alsace begun in 1634 by Richelieu, irreversibly incorporated the seeds of a Franco-German animosity centered on this region that would bear bitter fruit in the great wars of the nineteenth and twentieth centuries. A second coalition, the so-called League of Augsburg—Holland, Austria, Sweden, and further German allies—was only somewhat more successful than the first.

These allies were concerned above all to maintain some sort of European balance of power. They feared an expansionist France would prove insatiable, as it pressed its boundaries farther and farther into Germany and the Low Countries. Louis, mistakenly expecting that William would be forced to fight an English army under James to establish his right to his new throne and would therefore be too preoccupied to devote his full attention to developments on the Continent, kept up the pressure. In September 1688 he invaded the Palatinate and occupied the city of Cologne. The following year the French armies crossed the Rhine and continued their eastward drive, burning Heidelberg and committing numerous atrocities throughout the middle Rhine area. Aroused at last to effective action, the coalition, led by

William and now including in addition to its former members both England and Spain, engaged Louis in a war that was to last until 1697.

The major campaigns of this War of the League of Augsburg were fought in the Low Countries. William managed to drive an army under his predecessor, James II, from Ireland in 1690; from that point on, he took command of the allied forces on the Continent. By 1694 Louis was being pressed hard, not only by his allied foes, but by a succession of disastrous harvests that crippled France. Fighting remained stalemated until a treaty was signed at Ryswick in Holland which compelled Louis to return most of France's post-1679 gains, except for Alsace, and to recognize William as the rightful king of England.

War of the League of Augsburg

Ryswick did nothing, however, to resolve the dynastic tangle known as the Spanish Succession. Since Charles II of Spain had no direct heirs, and since he appeared to be on his deathbed in 1699, European monarchs and diplomats were obsessed by the question of who would succeed to the vast domain of the Spanish Habsburgs: not only Spain itself, but also its overseas empire, as well as the Spanish Netherlands, Naples, Sicily, and other territories in Italy. Both Louis XIV and Leopold I of Austria were married to sisters of the decrepit, unstable Charles; and both, naturally, eyed the succession to the Spanish inheritance as an exceedingly tempting dynastic plum. Yet it is a measure of the degree to which even absolutists were willing to keep their ambitions within bounds that both Leopold and Louis agreed to William's suggestion that the lion's share of the Habsburg lands should go to six-year-old Joseph Ferdinand, the prince of Bavaria, who was Charles II's grandnephew. Unfortunately, in 1699 the child died. Though the chances of war increased, William and Louis were prepared to bargain further and arranged a second treaty that divided the Spanish empire between Louis's and Leopold's heirs. Yet at the same time, Louis's diplomatic agents in Madrid persuaded Charles to sign a will in which he stipulated that the entire Spanish Habsburg inheritance should pass to Louis's grandson Philip of Anjou. This option was welcomed by many influential Spaniards, willing to endure French hegemony in return for the protection France could provide to the Spanish empire. For a time, Louis contemplated an alternative agreement which would have given France direct control of much of Italy. When Charles finally died in November 1700, Louis decided to accept the will. As if this was not enough to drive his former enemies back to war, he sent troops into the Spanish Netherlands and traders to the Spanish colonial empire, while declaring the late James II's son—the child of the warming pan myth—the legitimate king of England.

The problem of the Spanish Succession

Once it was clear to the allies that Louis intended to treat Spain as if it were his own kingdom, they again united against him in the cause of balance and stability. William died in 1702, just as the War of the Spanish Succession was beginning. His position as first general of the coalition passed to two brilliant strategists, the English John Chur-

War: the battle of Blenheim

chill, duke of Marlborough, and his Austrian counterpart, Prince Eugene of Savoy, an upper-class soldier of fortune who had been denied a commission by Louis. Under their command the allied forces engaged in battle after fierce battle in the Low Countries and Germany, including an extraordinary march deep into Bavaria, where the combined forces under Marlborough and Eugene smashed the French and their Bavarian allies decisively at Blenheim (1704). While the allies pressed France's armies on land, the English navy captured Gibraltar and the island of Minorca, thus establishing a strategic and commercial foothold in the Mediterranean, and helping to open a fourth major military theater in Spain itself.

Military stalemate

The War of the Spanish Succession was a "professional" war that tested the highly trained armies of the combatants to the fullest. At the battle of Malplaquet in northeastern France in 1709, 80,000 French soldiers faced 110,000 allied troops. Though Marlborough and Eugene could claim to have won that battle, in that they forced the French to retreat, they suffered 24,000 casualties, twice those of the French. Neither Malplaquet nor other such victories brought the allies any closer to their final goal, which now appeared to be not the containment, but the complete destruction of the French military force. Queen Anne of England (Mary's sister and William's successor), once Marlborough's staunchest defender, grew disillusioned with the war and fired her general.

Dynastic changes and the pursuit of peace

More than war-weariness impelled the combatants toward negotiation, however. The War of the Spanish Succession had begun as a conflict about the balance of power in Europe and the world. Yet dynastic changes had by 1711 compelled a reappraisal of allied goals. Leopold I had died in 1705. When his elder son and successor Joseph I died in 1711, the Austrian monarchy fell to Leopold's youngest son, the Archduke Charles, who had been the allies' candidate for the throne of Spain. With Charles now the Austrian and the Holy Roman Emperor as Charles VI (1711–1740), the prospect of his accession to the Spanish inheritance conjured up the ghost of Charles V and threatened to give him far too much power. International stability therefore demanded an end to hostilities and diplomatic negotiation toward a solution that would reestablish some sort of general balance.

The Treaty of Utrecht

The Treaty of Utrecht, which settled the conflict in 1713 to the extent that it redistributed territory and power in equitable portions, was a serious attempt to do just that. No one emerged a major winner or loser. Philip, Louis's grandson, remained on the throne of Spain, but Louis agreed that France and Spain would never be united under the same ruler. Austria gained territories in the Netherlands and Italy. The Dutch, victims of French aggression during the war, were guaranteed protection of their borders against future invasion. The English retained Gibraltar and Minorca, as well as territory in America: Newfoundland, Acadia, Hudson Bay, and in the Caribbean, St. Kitts. Perhaps most valuable of all, the English extracted the *asiento* from Spain

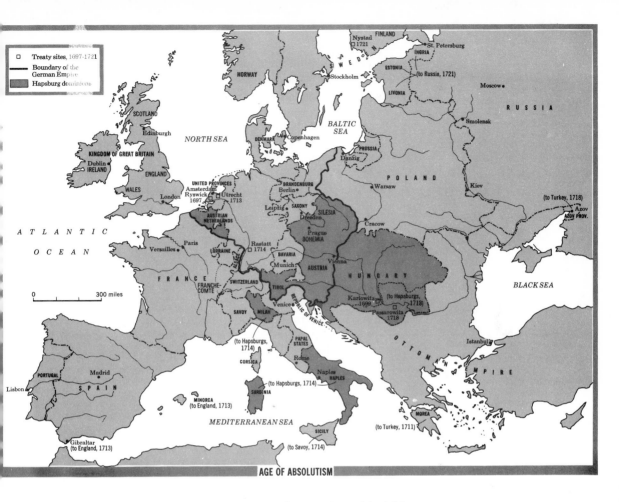

AGE OF ABSOLUTISM

which gave them the right to supply Spanish America with African slaves. The settlement reflected the degree to which new interests had superseded old. Balance of power and stability among states were the major goals of the negotiations, goals that reflected a departure from the world of seventeenth-century turmoil when religious fanaticism had been a major factor in international conflict. The eventual "winners" were undoubtedly the English, whose dynastic concerns were limited to a general acceptance of the Hanoverian settlement, and who could therefore concentrate their efforts on amassing overseas territories that would contribute to the growth of their economic prosperity and hence their international power.

6. ENLIGHTENED ABSOLUTISM AND LIMITED MONARCHY IN THE EIGHTEENTH CENTURY

Eighteenth-century absolutism was a series of variations on the dominant themes composed in the previous century by Louis XIV. That it has earned itself the historical distinction of "enlightened" absolut-

Louis XV

Absolutism under the successors of Louis XIV

ism suggests that those variations were of some consequence. Eighteenth-century rulers backed their sovereign claims not in the language of divine right, but in terms of their determination to act, as Frederick the Great of Prussia declared, as "first servant of the state." Enlightened rulers served their subjects by introducing reformist legislation and administration designed, at least in theory, to serve the well-being of the state community as a whole. They moved to curtail the privileges of old institutions. The Roman Catholic Church, for example, was compelled to suffer the expulsion of the Jesuits from most Catholic countries. Customary laws benefiting particular orders or interests were reformed. Serfdom was abolished or limited in some German states. Innovative policies in the areas of taxation, economic development, and education were instituted. As we shall see in Chapter 19, rational schemes of this sort reflected the spread of Enlightenment ideals as manifested in the writings of thinkers such as Beccaria, Diderot, and Voltaire. (The last was, in fact, a guest at Frederick's court for several years.) Assisting enlightened "first servants" in the implementation of these changes was a growing cadre of lesser servants: bureaucrats, often recruited from the nobility, but once recruited, expected to declare primary allegiance to their new master, the state. Despite innovation, "enlightened" absolutists continued to insist, as their predecessors had, that state sovereignty rested with the monarchy. Power remained their overriding concern, and to the extent that they combatted efforts by the estates of their realms to dilute that power, they declared their descent from their seventeenth-century forebears.

Louis XIV's successors, his great-grandson Louis XV (1715–1774) and that monarch's grandson Louis XVI (1774–1792), were unable to sustain the energetic drive toward centralization that had taken place under the Sun King. Indeed, during his last years, while fighting a desperate defensive war against his allied enemies, Louis XIV had seen his own accomplishments begin to crumble under the mounting pressure of military expenses. His heir was only five years old when he assumed the throne. As he grew up, Louis XV displayed little of his great-grandfather's single-minded determination to act the role of Sun King. The heroic, baroque grandeur of the main palace at Versailles yielded to the rococo grace of the Grand and Petit Trianons, pleasure pavillions built by Louis XV in the palace gardens. Both Louis XIV and Louis XV solaced themselves with the company of mistresses. The difference in their tastes, however, is a mark of the difference in their reigns. Madame de Maintenon, the Sun King's mistress, was a stern, devout Catholic, who interested herself directly in policies of state. Madame du Pompadour, Louis XV's favorite for many years, was a stylish, witty sensualist whose legacy was the elaborate hairstyle to which she bequeathed her name.

During the minority of Louis XV, the French *parlements,* those courts of record responsible for registering and thereby legalizing royal decrees, enjoyed a resurgence of power which they retained through-out the century. No longer tame adjuncts of absolutist governmental machinery as they had been under Louis XIV, these bodies now pro-claimed themselves the protectors of French "liberties." In fact they were protectors of little more than the privileges of the elite, although a growing number welcomed the *parlements'* willingness to block new taxes. In the late 1760s, hoping to emulate the success of his illustrious predecessor, and encouraged by his chancellor René Maupeou, Louis XV issued an edict effectively ending the right of *parlements* to reject decrees. Protest on the part of the magistrates resulted in their impris-onment or banishment. The *parlements* themselves were replaced by new courts charged not only with the responsibility of rubber-stamp-ing legislation but also with administering law more justly and less expensively. When Louis XVI ascended the throne in 1774, his min-isters persuaded him to reestablish the *parlements* as a sign of his will-ingness to conciliate his trouble-making aristocracy. This he did, with the result that government—particularly the management of finances—developed into a stalemated battle.

Resurgence of the
parlements

Stalemate was what the Prussian successors to Frederick William, the Great Elector, were determined to avoid. Absolutism, to thrive, needed to remain a dynamic force: precisely what it was in eighteenth-century Prussia. Frederick I (1688–1713), the Great Elector Frederick William's immediate successor, enhanced the appearance and cultural life of Berlin. As the Roman numeral by his name attests, he also succeeded in bargaining his support to the Austrians during the War of the Spanish Succession in return for the coveted right to style himself king.[3]

*The achievements of
Prussia*

Frederick William I(1713–1740), cared little for the embellishments his father had made to the capital city. His overriding concern was the building of a first-rate army. So single-minded was his attention to the military that he came to be called "the sergeant king." Military display became an obsession. His private regiment of "Potsdam Giants" was comprised exclusively of soldiers over six feet in height. The king traded musicians and prize stallions for such choice specimens and delighted in marching them about his palace grounds. Frederick Wil-liam I's success as the builder of a military machine can be measured in terms of numbers: 30,000 men under arms when he came to the throne; 83,000 when he died twenty-seven years later, commander of the fourth-largest army in Europe, after France, Russia, and Austria. Since he could hardly count on volunteers, most of his soldiers were conscripts, drafted from the peasantry for a period of years and required to attend annual training exercises lasting three months. Conscription was supplemented by the kidnapping of forced recruits in neighboring

Frederick William I

---

[3] The Austrian monarch was the Holy Roman Emperor and therefore had the right to create kings.

German lands. To finance his army, Frederick William I increased taxes and streamlined their collection through the establishment of a General Directory of War, Finance, and Domains. He instituted a system of administration by boards, hoping thereby to eliminate individual inefficiency through collective responsibility and surveillance. In addition, he created an inspectorate to uncover and report to him the mistakes and inefficiencies of his officialdom. Even then, he continued to supervise personally the implementation of state policy while shunning the luxuries of court life; for him, the "theater" of absolutism was not the palace but the office, which placed him at the helm of the state and the army. Perceiving the resources of the state to be too precious to waste, he pared costs at every turn to the point where, it was said, he had to invite himself to a nobleman's table in order to enjoy a good meal.

The apprenticeship of Frederick the Great

A hard, unimaginative man, Frederick William I had little use for his son, whose passion was not the battlefield but the flute, and who admired French culture as much as his father disdained it. Not surprisingly, young Frederick rebelled; in 1730, when he was eighteen, he ran away from court with a friend. Apprehended, the companions were returned to the king, who welcomed the fledgling prodigal with something other than a fatted calf. Before Frederick's eyes, he had the friend executed. The grisly lesson took. Thenceforward Frederick, though he never surrendered his love of music and literature, bound himself to his royal duties, living in accordance with his own image of himself as "first servant of the state," and earning himself history's title of Frederick the Great.

Frederick the Great and Voltaire. Although Frederick offered asylum to the French *philosophe,* this "enlightened despot" did not permit his intellectual pursuits to interfere with matters of state.

Frederick William I's zealous austerity and his compulsion to build an efficient army and administrative state made Prussia a lean, strong state. Frederick the Great, building on the work of his father, raised his country to the status of a major power. As soon as he became king in 1740, Frederick mobilized the army his father had never taken into battle and occupied the poorly protected Austrian province of Silesia to which Prussia had no legitimate claim. Although he had earlier vowed to make morality rather than expediency the hallmark of his reign, he seemingly had little difficulty in sacrificing his youthful idealism in the face of an opportunity to make his Prussian state a leading member of the concert of nations. The remaining forty-five years of his monarchy were devoted to the consolidation of this first bold stroke.

The seizure of Silesia

Such a daring course required some adjustments within the Prussian state. The army had to be kept at full strength, and to this end, Frederick staffed its officer corps with young noblemen. In expanding the bureaucracy, whose financial administration kept his army in the field, he relied on the nobility as well, reversing the policy of his father, who had recruited his civil servants according to merit rather than birth. But Frederick was not one to tolerate mediocrity; he fashioned the most highly professional and efficient bureaucracy in all of Europe. The degree to which both army and bureaucracy were staffed by the nobility is a measure of his determination to secure the unflagging support of the most privileged order in his realm, in order to ensure a united front against Prussia's external foes.

*The Prussian army and
the nobility*

Frederick's domestic policies reflected that same strategy. In matters where he ran no risk of offending the aristocracy, he followed his own rationalist bent, prohibiting the torture of accused criminals, putting an end to the bribing of judges, and establishing a system of elementary schools. He promoted religious toleration, declaring that he would happily build a mosque in Berlin if he could find enough Muslims to fill it. (Yet he was strongly anti-Semitic, levying special taxes on Jews and making efforts to close the professions and the civil service to them.) On his own royal estates he was a model "enlightened" monarch. He abolished capital punishment, curtailed the forced labor services of his peasantry, and granted them long leases on the land they worked. He fostered scientific forestry and the cultivation of new crops. He opened new lands in Silesia and brought in thousands of immigrants to cultivate them. When wars ruined their farms, he supplied the peasants with new livestock and tools. Yet he never attempted to extend these reforms to the estates of the Junker elite, since to have done so would have alienated that social and economic group upon which Frederick was most dependent.

*Frederick the Great as an
enlightened absolutist*

Although the monarchs of eighteenth-century Austria eventually proved themselves even more willing than Frederick the Great to undertake significant social reform, the energies of Emperor Charles VI (1711–1740) were concentrated on guaranteeing the future dynastic

*Charles VI and the
"pragmatic sanction"*

Maria Theresa of Austria

*"Enlightened" absolutism
in Austria*

and territorial integrity of the Habsburg lineage and domain. Without a male heir, Charles worked to secure the right of his daughter Maria Theresa to succeed him as eventual empress. By his death in 1740 Charles had managed to persuade not only his subjects but all the major European powers to accept his daughter as his royal heir—a feat known as the "pragmatic sanction." Yet his painstaking efforts were only partially successful. As we have seen, Frederick the Great used the occasion of Charles's death to sieze Silesia. The French, unable to resist the temptation to grab what they could, entered the lists in this War of the Austrian Succession against the new empress, Maria Theresa (1740–1780).

With most of her other possessions already occupied by her enemies, Maria Theresa appealed successfully to the Hungarians for support. The empress was willing to play the role of the wronged woman when, as on this occasion, it suited her interests to do so. Hungary's vital troops combined with British financial assistance helped to enable her to battle Austria's enemies to a draw, although she never succeeded in regaining Silesia. The experience of those first few years of her reign persuaded Maria Theresa, who was both capable and tenacious, to reorganize her dominions along the tightly centralized lines characteristic of absolutist Prussia and France. Ten new administrative districts were established, each with its own "war commissar" appointed by and responsible to the central administration in Vienna—an Austrian equivalent of the French intendant. Property taxes were increased to finance an expanded army, which was modernized and professionalized so as to remain on a par with the military establishments of the other great powers. Centralization, finances, army: once more those three crucial elements in the formula of absolute rule came into play.

Austrian absolutism did not stop there, however. Together Maria Theresa and her son Joseph II, with whom she ruled jointly from 1765 to 1780, and who then succeeded her for another ten years, instituted a series of social reforms which has earned them their reputation as "enlightened" absolutists. Although both mother and son were devout Roman Catholics, they moved to assert control of the church, removing the clergy's exemption from taxation and decreeing the state's ability to block the publication of papal bulls in Austria. In 1773, following the papal suppression of the Jesuits, they used the order's assets to finance a program of state-wide primary education. Although the General Schools Ordinance of 1774 never achieved anything like a universally literate population, it did succeed in educating hundreds of thousands, and in financing not only schools for children but schools as well for those who taught the children. Joseph followed these reforms with an "Edict on Idle Institutions" in 1780, which resulted in the closing of hundreds of monastic houses, whose property went to support charitable institutions now under state control. These

Joseph II of Austria Visiting a Farm. The royal estates provided Joseph with the opportunity to experiment with agrarian reforms by raising the serfs to the status of free peasants.

reforms and others—rationalization of criminal procedures, a relaxation of censorship, and an attempt to eradicate superstition by curbing the practice of pilgrimages and celebration of saint's days—made Joseph more enemies than friends, among both the noble elite and the common people. Joseph's brother Leopold II, who succeeded him in 1790, attempted to maintain the reformist momentum. His death two years later and the accession of his reactionary brother Francis II (1792–1835), put an end to liberalizing experiments. "Enlightened" though Joseph II was, however, he nevertheless remained a staunch absolutist, as concerned with the maintenance of a strong army and an efficient bureaucracy as with the need to educate his peasantry.

Unlike Joseph II, Catherine the Great of Russia (1762–1796) felt herself compelled to curry the favor of her nobility by involving them directly in the structure of local administration, by exempting them from military service and taxation, and probably most important, by granting them absolute control over the serfs on their estates. Her policy grew out of her strong ties to powerful nobles and her involvement in the conspiracy which led to the assassination of her husband, Tsar Peter III, the last of a series of weak rulers who followed Peter the Great. Catherine was herself a German, and prided herself on her devotion to Western principles of government. Ambitious to establish a reputation as an intellectual and enlightened monarch, she corresponded with French philosophers, wrote plays, published a digest of William Blackstone's *Commentaries on the Laws of England*, and even began a history of Russia. Her contributions to social reform did not extend much beyond the founding of hospitals and orphanages, and

Catherine the Great

Catherine the Great of Russia

the expression of a pious hope that someday the serfs might be liberated. Although she did summon a commission in 1767 to codify Russian law, its achievements were modest: a minor extension of religious toleration; a slight restriction of the use of torture by the state.

Any plans Catherine may have had for improving the lot of the peasants, however, were abruptly cancelled after their frustration with St. Petersburg's centralization efforts erupted in a violent peasant-serf rebellion in 1773–1774. Free peasants in the Volga valley region found themselves compelled to provide labor services to nobles sent by the crown to control them, Cossacks were subjected to taxation and conscription for the first time, and factory workers and miners were pressed into service in the state's industrial enterprises. These and other disparate but dissatisfied groups, including serfs, united under the rebel banner of Emelyan Pugachev, an illiterate Cossack who claimed to be the late Tsar Peter III. The hapless Peter spoke as a reformer in life, and in death became a larger-than-life hero for those opposed to the determined absolutism of his successor. As Pugachev marched, he encouraged his followers to strike out not only against the empress but also against the nobility and the church. Over 1500 landlords and priests were murdered and the ruling classes terrified as the revolt spread. While Catherine's forces initially had little success against the rebel army, the threat of famine plagued Pugachev's advance and finally led to disrray among his troops. Betrayed in 1774, he was captured and taken in an iron cage to Moscow, where he was tortured and killed. Catherine responded to this uprising with further centralization and tightening of aristocratic authority over the peasantry.

Emelyan Pugachev Shackled and Encaged after His Capture

The significance of Catherine the Great

The brutal suppression and punishment of the rebels reflected the ease with which the German-born Catherine took to the despotic authoritarianism that characterized Russian absolutism. She was as outsized in her tastes and personality as was Peter the Great. Her sexual appetite was voracious; her current chief officers of state as often as not were also her current lovers. Catherine's chief significance lies in her ability to continue the work of Peter the Great in introducing Russia to Western ideas, to come to terms with the nobility in a way that brought stability to the state, and to make the country a formidable power in European affairs by extending its boundaries to include not only most of Poland but lands on the Black Sea.

The absolutist worldview

Eighteenth-century absolutist monarchs shared a desire to pursue policies that would mark their regimes as modern, befitting a world that was leaving obscurantism and fanaticism behind. They were modern, also, in their determination to press ahead with the task, begun by their seventeenth-century predecessors, of building powerful, centralized states by continuing to eliminate or harness the ancient privileges of still-powerful noble orders and provincial estates. The notion of a limited monarchy, in which power was divided between local and central authorities and shared by monarchs, nobles, and legislative assemblies, struck them as a dangerous anachronism. Yet as the century progressed, they found that conviction challenged by the emergence of England, under limited monarchy, as the world's leading commercial and naval power.

England (or Britain, as the country was called after its union with Scotland in 1707) prospered as a state in which power was divided between the king and Parliament. This division of political power was guaranteed by a constitution which, though unwritten, was grounded in common law and strengthened by precedent and by particular legal settlements such as those that had followed the restoration of the Stuarts in 1660 and the overthrow of James II in 1688. The Hanoverians George I (1714–1727) and his son George II (1727–1760) were by no means political cyphers. Though George I could not speak English, he could converse comfortably enough with his ministers in French. The first two Georges made a conscientious and generally successful effort to govern within their adopted kingdom. They appointed the chief ministers who remained responsible to them for the creation and direction of state policy. Yet because Parliament, after 1688, retained the right to legislate, tax, and spend, its powers were far greater than those of any European parlement, estate, or diet. During the reign of the first two Hanoverians, politics was on most occasions little more than a struggle between factions within the Whig party, composed of wealthy—and in many cases newly rich—landed magnates who were making fortunes in an expanding economy based on commercial and agricultural capitalism.

The Tories, because of their previous association with the Stuarts, remained political "outs" for most of the century. To the Whigs,

George I of England

The House of Commons. Despite its architectural division into two "sides," the House was composed of men of property whose similar economic interests encouraged them to agree on political fundamentals.

Left: *Sir Robert Walpole with Members of His Cabinet.* Right: *Walpole as a Roman Emperor.*

Local government

national politics was no longer a matter of clashing principles. Those principles had been settled—to their satisfaction—in 1688. Nor was politics a matter of legislating in the national interest. Britain was governed locally, not from the center, as in an absolutist state. Aristocrats and landed gentry administered the affairs of the particular counties and parishes in which their estates lay, as lords lieutenant, as justices of the peace, as overseers of the poor, unhampered, to a degree unknown on the Continent, by legislation imposed uniformly throughout the kingdom. The quality of local government varied greatly. Some squires were as "allworthy" as Henry Fielding's fictional character of that name in the novel *Tom Jones*. Others cared for little beyond the bottle and the chase. A French traveler noted in 1747 that the country gentleman was "naturally a very dull animal" whose favorite afterdinner toast was "to all honest fox hunters in Great Britain." These men administered those general laws that did exist—the Poor Law, game laws—which were drawn in such a way as to leave their administrators wide latitude, a latitude which they exercised in order to enhance the appearance of their own local omnipotence. Thus in Britain there was no attempt to pass a law establishing a state-wide system of primary education. Centralizing legislation of that sort, the hallmark of absolutist states, was anathema to the British aristocracy and gentry. They argued that education, if it was to be provided, should be provided at their expense, in village schoolrooms by schoolmasters in their employ. Those instructors would make it their business to teach their pupils not only rudimentary reading, writing, and figuring, but the deferential behavior that bespoke the obligation of the poor to their rich benefactors.

Politics, then, was neither first principles nor national legislation. It was "interest" and "influence," the weaving of a web of obligations into a political faction powerful enough to secure jobs and favors—a third secretaryship in the foreign office from a minister, an Act of Enclosure from Parliament. The greatest master of this game of politics was Robert Walpole (1676–1745) who was England's leading minister from the early 1720s until 1742. Walpole is sometimes called Britain's first prime minister, a less than entirely accurate distinction, since officially that position did not exist until the nineteenth century. Prime minister or not, he wielded great political power. He took advantage of the king's frequent absences in Hanover to assert control over the day-to-day governance of the country. He ruled as chief officer of his cabinet, a small group of like-minded politicians whose collective name derived from the small room in which they met. In time the cabinet evolved into the policy-making executive arm of the British political system; Britain is governed today by cabinet and Parliament, the cabinet comprised of leading politicians from the majority party in Parliament. Walpole was a member of a Norfolk gentry family who had risen to national prominence on the fortune he amassed while serving as paymaster-general to the armed forces during the War of the Spanish Succession. Adept at bribery and corruption, he used his ability to reward his supporters with appointments to ensure himself a loyal political following. By the end of his career, grossly fat and stuffed, seemingly, with the profits of his years in office, he was being depicted by cartoonists and balladeers as Britain's most accomplished robber. "Little villains must submit to Fate," lamented a typical lampoon, "while great ones do enjoy the world in state." Walpole was no more corrupt, however, than the political process over which he presided. The majority of seats in Parliament's lower House of Commons were filled by representatives from boroughs which often had no more than two or three dozen electors. Hence it was a relatively simple task to buy votes, either directly or with promises of future favors. Walpole cemented political factions together into an alliance that survived for about twenty years. During that time, he worked to ensure domestic tranquility by refusing to press ahead with any legislation that might arouse national controversy. He withdrew what was perhaps his most innovative piece of legislation—a scheme to increase excise taxes and reduce import duties as a means of curbing smugglers—in the face of widespread popular opposition.

Other Whig politicians succeeded Walpole in office in the 1740s and 1750s, but only one, William Pitt, later elevated to the House of Lords as the earl of Chatham, commanded public attention as Walpole had. George III (1760–1820), who came to the throne as a young man in 1760, resented the manner in which he believed his royal predecessors had been treated by the Whig oligarchy. Whether or not, as legend has it, his mother fired his determination with the constant injunction "George, be king!" he began his reign convinced that he must assert his rightful prerogatives. He dismissed Pitt, and attempted to impose ministers of his own choosing on Parliament. King and Parliament battled this issue of prerogative throughout the 1760s. In 1770, Lord North, an aristocrat satisfactory to the king and with a large enough following in the House of Commons to ensure some measure of stability, assumed the position of first minister. His downfall occurred a decade later, as a result of his mismanagement of the overseas war which resulted in Britain's loss of its original thirteen North American colonies. A period of political shuffling was followed by the king's appointment, at the age of twenty-three, of another William Pitt, Chatham's son, and this Pitt directed Britain's fortunes for the next twenty-five years—a political reign even longer than Walpole's. Although the period between 1760 and 1780 witnessed a struggle between crown (as the king and his political following were called) and Parliament, it was a very minor skirmish compared with the titanic constitutional struggles of the seventeenth century. Britain saw the last of absolutism in 1688. What followed was the mutual adjustment of the two formerly contending parties to a settlement both considered essentially sound.

7. WAR AND DIPLOMACY IN THE EIGHTEENTH CENTURY

Diplomacy in mid-century: the "diplomatic revolution"

The history of European diplomacy and warfare after 1715 is one in which the twin goals of international stability and economic expansion remained paramount. The fact that those objectives often conflicted with each other set off further frequent wars, in which the ever-growing standing armies of absolutist Europe were matched against each other and in which the deciding factor often turned out to be not continental military strength, but British naval power. The major conflict at mid-century, known as the Seven Years' War in Europe and the French and Indian War in North America, reflects the overlapping interests of power balance and commercial gain. In Europe, the primary concern was balance. Whereas in the past Franch had seemed the major threat, now Prussia loomed—at least in Austrian eyes—as a far more dangerous interloper. Under these circumstances, in 1756 the Austrian foreign minister, Prince Wenzel von Kaunitz, effected the so-called diplomatic revolution, which put an end to the enmity between France and Austria, and resulted in a formidable threat to the Prussia of Frederick the Great. Frederick, meanwhile, was taking steps to protect his flanks. While anxious not to arouse his French ally, he nevertheless signed a neutrality treaty with the British, who were concerned to secure protection for their sovereign's Hanoverian domains. The French read Frederick's act as a hostile one, and thus fell all the more readily for Kaunitz's offer of an alliance. The French indeed perceived a pressing need for trustworthy European allies, since they were already engaged in an undeclared war with England in North America. By mid-1756 Kaunitz could count France, Russia, Sweden, and several German states as likely allies against Prussia. Rather than await retribution from his enemies, Frederick invaded strategic but neutral Saxony and then Austria itself, thus once again playing the role of aggressor.

The configurations in this diplomatic gavotte are undoubtedly confusing. They are historically important, however, because they indicate the way in which the power balance was shifting, and the attempts of European states to respond to those shifts by means of new diplomatic alliances. Prussia and Britain were the volatile elements: Prussia on the Continent; Britain overseas. The war from 1756 to 1763 in Europe centered upon Frederick's attempts to prevent the dismemberment of his domain at the hands of the French-Austrian-Russian alliance. Time and again the Prussian army's superiority and Frederick's own military genius frustrated his enemies' attacks. Ultimately, Prussia's survival against these overwhelming odds—"the miracle of the House of Brandenburg"—was ensured by the death of the Tsarina Elizabeth (1741–1762), daughter of Peter the Great, and by the accession of Peter III (1762), whose admiration for Frederick was as great as was his predecessor's hostility. Peter withdrew from the war, returning the conquered provinces of East Prussia and Pomerania to his country's erstwhile enemy. The peace that followed, though it compelled Frederick to relinquish Saxony, recognized his right to retain Silesia, and hence put an end to Austria's hope of one day recapturing that rich prize.

*Shifting power balances:
the Seven Year's War*

Overseas, fighting occurred not only in North America but in the West Indies and in India, where Anglo-French commercial rivalry had resulted in sporadic, fierce fighting since the 1740s. Ultimate victory would go to that power possessing a navy strong enough to keep its supply routes open—that is, to Britain. Superior naval forces resulted in victories along the North American Great Lakes, climaxing in the Battle of Québec in 1759 and the eventual surrender of all of Canada to the British. By 1762 the French sugar islands, including Martinique, Grenada, and St. Vincent, were in British hands. Across the globe in India, the defeat of the French in the Battle of Plassey in 1757 and the capture of Pondichéry four years later made Britain the dominant European presence on the subcontinent. In the Treaty of Paris in 1763 which brought the Seven Years' War to an end, France officially surrendered Canada and India to the British, thus affording them an extraordinary field for commercial exploitation.

*The British navy as key
to victory*

The success of the British in North America in the Seven Years' War was itself a major cause of the war which broke out between the mother country and her thirteen original colonies in 1775. To pay for

The Battle of Québec, 1759. Most often remembered for the fact that the British and French commanders, Generals Wolfe and Montcalm, were killed on the bluffs above the St. Lawrence River (the Plains of Abraham), this battle was most notable for the success of the British amphibious assault, a measure of Britain's naval superiority.

"Taxation without representation . . ."

the larger army the British now deemed necessary to protect their vastly expanded colonial possessions, they imposed unwelcome new taxes on the colonists. The North Americans protested that they were being taxed without representation. The home government responded that, like all British subjects, they were "virtually" if not actually represented by the present members of the House of Commons. Colonists thundered back that the present political system in Britain was so corrupt that no one but the Whig oligarchs could claim that their interests were being looked after.

The American Revolution

Meanwhile the British were exacting retribution for rebellious acts on the part of colonists. East India Company tea shipped to be sold in Boston at prices advantageous to the company was dumped in Boston harbor. The port of Boston was thereupon closed, and democratic government in the colony of Massachusetts curtailed. The British garrison clashed with colonial civilians. Colonial "minutemen" formed a counterforce. By the time war broke out in 1775, most Americans were prepared to sever ties with Britain and declare themselves an independent nation, which they did the following year. Fighting continued until 1781 when a British army surrendered to the colonists at Yorktown to the tune of a song entitled "A World Turned Upside Down." The French, followed by Spain and the Netherlands, were determined to do everything possible to inhibit the further growth of Britain's colonial empire, and allied themselves with the newly independent United States in 1778. A peace treaty signed in Paris in 1783 recognized the sovereignty of the new state. Though the British lost direct control of their former colonies, they reestablished their transatlantic commercial ties with America in the 1780s. Indeed, the brisk trade in raw cotton between the slave-owning southern states and Britain made possible the industrial revolution in textiles that began in the north of England at this time, and that carried Britain to worldwide preeminence as an economic power in the first half of the nineteenth century. This ultimately profitable arrangement lay in the future. At the time, the victory of the American colonists seemed to contemporary observers to right the world balance of commercial power, which had swung so far to the side of the British. In this instance, independence seemed designed to restore stability.

In eastern Europe, however, the very precariousness of Poland's independence posed a threat to stability and the balance of power. As an independent state, Poland functioned, at least in theory, as a buffer among the major central European powers—Russia, Austria, and Prussia. Poland was the one major central European territory whose landed elite had successfully opposed introduction of absolutist centralization and a consequent curtailment of its "liberties." The result, however, had not been anything like real independence for either the Polish nobility or the country as a whole. Aristocrats were quite prepared to accept bribes from foreign powers in return for their vote in elections for the Polish king. And their continued exercise of their constitutionally guaranteed individual veto (the "liberum veto") in the Polish Diet meant that the country remained in a perpetual state of weakness that made it fair game for the land-hungry absolutist potentates who surrounded its borders.

Poland and the balance of power in eastern Europe

In 1764 Russia intervened to influence the election of King Stanislaus Poniatowski, an able enough nobleman who had been one of Catherine the Great's lovers. Thereafter Russia continued to meddle in the affairs of Poland—and of Turkey as well—often protecting both countries' Greek Orthodox Christian minority. When war finally broke out with Turkey in 1769, resulting in large Russian gains in the Balkans, Austria made known its opposition to further Russian expansion, lest it upset the existing balance of power in eastern Europe. In the end Russia was persuaded to acquire territory in Poland instead, by joining Austria and Prussia in a general partition of that country's lands. Though Maria Theresa opposed the dismemberment of Poland, she reluctantly agreed to participate in the partition in order to maintain the balance of power, an attitude which prompted a scornful Frederick the Great to remark that "She weeps, but she takes her share." According to the agreement of 1772, Poland lost about 30 percent of its kingdom and about half of its population.

The first partition of Poland

Following this first partition, the Russians continued to exercise virtual control of Poland. King Stanislaus, however, took advantage of a new Russo-Turkish war in 1788 to press for a more truly independent state with a far stronger executive than had existed previ-

The second and third partitions of Poland

ously. A constitution adopted in May 1791 established just that; but this rejuvenated Polish state was to be short-lived. In January 1792, the Russo-Turkish war ended and Catherine the Great pounced. Together the Russians and Prussians took two more enormous bites in 1793, destroying the new constitution in the process. A rebellion under the leadership of Thaddeus Kosciuszko, who had fought in America, was crushed in 1794 and 1795. A final swallow by Russia, Austria, and Prussia in 1795 left nothing of Poland at all. After this series of partitions of Poland, each of the major powers was a good deal fatter; but on the international scales by which such things were measured, they continued to weigh proportionately the same.

European upheaval

The final devouring of Poland occurred at a time when the Continent was once again engaged in a general war. Yet this most recent conflict was not just another military attempt to resolve customary disputes over commerce or problems of international stability. It was the result of violent revolution that had broken out in France in 1789, that had toppled the Bourbon dynasty there, and that threatened to do the same to other monarchs across Europe. The second and third partitions of Poland were a final bravura declaration of power by monarchs who already feared for their heads. Henceforth, neither foreign nor domestic policy would ever again be dictated as they had been in absolutist Europe, by the convictions and determinations of kings and queens alone. Poland disappeared as Europe fell to pieces, as customary practice gave way to new and desperate necessity.

The Royal Cake. A contemporary cartoon showing the monarchs of Europe at work carving up a hapless Poland.

• *Items so designated are available in paperback editions.*

Anderson, M. S., *Peter the Great,* London, 1978. A good, thorough biography.

• Avrich, Paul, *Russian Rebels, 1600–1800,* New York, 1972. A study of revolts against absolutist power.

Baxter, Stephen, *William III,* New York, 1965. The best study of the Dutchman who became England's king.

Bernard, Paul, *Joseph II,* New York, 1968.

• Carsten, F. L., *The Origins of Prussia,* Oxford, 1954. A survey which focuses on the reign of the Great Elector.

Churchill, W. S., *Marlborough,* New York, 1968. An abridged edition of Churchill's magnificently written biography of his ancestor.

• Dorn, Walter, *The Competition for Empire, 1740–63,* New York, 1940. A standard survey, still valuable.

Dukes, Paul, *Catherine the Great and the Russian Nobility,* Cambridge, 1967. A study of the limits of absolutism.

• Dunn, Richard S., *The Age of Religious Wars, 1559–1715,* 2nd ed., New York, 1979. A detailed and up-to-date survey, useful for the history of late seventeenth- and early eighteenth-century absolutism.

Florinsky, M. T., *Russia: A History and an Interpretation,* Vol. 1, New York, 1955. A useful text. Reviews divergent interpretations and emphasizes politics.

Ford, Franklin, *Robe and Sword: The Regrouping of the French Aristocracy after Louis XIV,* Cambridge, Mass., 1953. An important social study of the nobility of the robe and its striving for dominance before the revolution.

• Fraser, Antonia, *Royal Charles: Charles II and the Restoration,* New York, 1979. A readable, reliable life of the king and his times.

• Gagliardo, John, *Enlightened Despotism,* New York, 1967. A useful study of eighteenth-century absolutism.

Gershoy, Leo, *From Despotism to Revolution, 1763–1789,* New York, 1944. Valuable for the tensions leading up to the revolutionary period.

• Goubert, Pierre, *Louis XIV and Twenty Million Frenchmen,* New York, 1972. A valuable study, the starting point for an understanding of the Sun King's reign.

• Hatton, R. N., *Europe in the Age of Louis XIV,* New York, 1969. Thoughtful interpretation of the period; excellent illustrations.

• Herr, Richard, *The Eighteenth Century Revolution in Spain,* Princeton, N.J., 1958. The best introduction to Spain in this period.

Holborn, Hajo, *The Age of Absolutism,* New York, 1964. The best survey for Germany. Second volume of Holborn's *History of Modern Germany.*

• Krieger, Leonard, *Kings and Philosophers, 1689–1789,* New York, 1970. A thorough survey of the political and intellectual developments of this century.

• Lewis, W. H., *The Splendid Century: Life in the France of Louis XIV,* New York, 1953. A delightfully written survey.

• Palmer, R. R., *The Age of the Democratic Revolution: A Political History of Europe and America, 1760–1800,* Vol. 1, Princeton, N.J., 1964. Argues in favor of a general European aristocratic reaction prior to 1789.

Plumb, J. H., *Sir Robert Walpole,* 2 vols., Boston, 1956, 1961. A well-written, sympathetic biography of England's leading eighteenth-century politician.

• Ritter, Gerhard, *Frederick The Great: A Historical Profile,* Berkeley, Calif., 1968. A readable biography.

• Rosenberg, Hans, *Bureaucracy, Aristocracy, and Autocracy: The Prussian Experience, 1660–1815,* Cambridge, Mass., 1958.

Rudé, George, *Europe in the Eighteenth Century: Aristocracy and the Bourgeois Challenge,* New York, 1972. A survey which stresses social stratification and tension.

• Speck, W. A., *Stability and Strife: England, 1714–1760,* Cambridge, Mass., 1977. A good, recent survey.

Spielman, John P., *Leopold I of Austria,* New Brunswick, N.J., 1977. The only biography of the monarch in English.

• Wangermann, Ernst, *The Austrian Achievement, 1700–1800,* London, 1973. A suggestive introductory survey.

• Wolf, John B., *Louis XIV,* New York, 1968. The standard biography in English.

• ———, *The Emergence of the Great Powers, 1685–1715,* New York, 1951. A useful general survey of this critical period.

• Woloch, Isser, *Eighteenth Century Europe: Tradition and Progress, 1715–1789,* New York, 1982. A thoughtful, well-organized survey.

SOURCE MATERIALS

• Locke, John, *Two Treatises of Government.* (Many editions.) The argument against absolutism.

Saint-Simon, Louis, *Historical Memoirs.* (Many editions.) A brilliant source for evidence about life at the court of Louis XIV.

RULERS OF PRINCIPAL EUROPEAN STATES SINCE 700 A.D.

The Carolingian Dynasty

Pepin, Mayor of the Palace, 714
Charles Martel, Mayor of the Palace, 715–741
Pepin I, Mayor of the Palace, 741; King, 751–768
Charlemagne, King, 768–814; Emperor, 800–814
Louis the Pious, Emperor, 814–840

WEST FRANCIA

Charles the Bald, King, 840–877; Emperor, 875
Louis II, King, 877–879
Louis III, King, 879–882
Carloman, King, 879–884

MIDDLE KINGDOMS

Lothair, Emperor, 840–855
Louis (Italy), Emperor, 855–875
Charles (Provence), King, 855–863
Lothair II (Lorraine), King, 855–869

EAST FRANCIA

Ludwig, King, 840–876
Carloman, King, 876–880
Ludwig, King, 876–882
Charles the Fat, Emperor, 876–887

Holy Roman Emperors

SAXON DYNASTY

Otto I, 962–973
Otto II, 973–983
Otto III, 983–1002
Henry II, 1002–1024

FRANCONIAN DYNASTY

Conrad II, 1024–1039
Henry III, 1039–1056
Henry IV, 1056–1106
Henry V, 1106–1125
Lothair II (of Saxony), King, 1125–1133; Emperor, 1133–1137

HOHENSTAUFEN DYNASTY

Conrad III, 1138–1152
Frederick I (Barbarossa), 1152–1190
Henry VI, 1190–1197
Philip of Swabia, 1198–1208 ⎱ Rivals
Otto IV (Welf), 1198–1215 ⎰
Frederick II, 1220–1250
Conrad IV, 1250–1254

INTERREGNUM, 1254–1273

EMPERORS FROM VARIOUS DYNASTIES
Rudolf I (Habsburg), 1273–1291

Adolf (Nassau), 1292–1298
Albert I (Hapsburg), 1298–1308
Henry VII (Luxemburg), 1308–1313
Ludwig IV (Wittelsbach), 1314–1347
Charles IV (Luxemburg), 1347–1378
Wenceslas (Luxemburg), 1378–1400
Rupert (Wittelsbach), 1400–1410
Sigismund (Luxemburg), 1410–1437

HABSBURG DYNASTY

Albert II, 1438–1439
Frederick III, 1440–1493
Maximilian I, 1493–1519
Charles V, 1519–1556
Ferdinand I, 1556–1564
Maximilan II, 1564–1576
Rudolf II, 1576–1612
Matthias, 1612–1619
Ferdinand II, 1619–1637
Ferdinand III, 1637–1657
Leopold I, 1658–1705
Joseph I, 1705–1711
Charles VI, 1711–1740
Charles VII (not a Habsburg), 1742–1745
Francis I, 1745–1765
Joseph II, 1765–1790
Leopold II, 1790–1792
Francis II, 1792–1806

Rulers of France from Hugh Capet

CAPETIAN KINGS

Hugh Capet, 987–996
Robert II, 996–1031
Henry I, 1031–1060
Philip I, 1060–1108
Louis VI, 1108–1137
Louis VII, 1137–1180
Philip II (Augustus), 1180–1223
Louis VIII, 1223–1226
Louis IX, 1226–1270
Philip III, 1270–1285
Philip IV, 1285–1314
Louis X, 1314–1316
Philip V, 1316–1322
Charles IV, 1322–1328

HOUSE OF VALOIS

Philip VI, 1328–1350
John, 1350–1364
Charles V, 1364–1380
Charles VI, 1380–1422
Charles VII, 1422–1461
Louis XI, 1461–1483
Charles VIII, 1483–1498
Louis XII, 1498–1515
Francis I, 1515–1547

Henry II, 1547–1559
Francis II, 1559–1560
Charles IX, 1560–1574
Henry III, 1574–1589

BOURBON DYNASTY

Henry IV, 1589–1610
Louis XIII, 1610–1643
Louis XIV, 1643–1715
Louis XV, 1715–1774
Louis XVI, 1774–1792

AFTER 1792

First Republic, 1792–1799
Napoleon Bonaparte, First Consul, 1799–1804
Napoleon I, Emperor, 1804–1814
Louis XVIII (Bourbon dynasty), 1814–1824
Charles X (Bourbon dynasty), 1824–1830
Louis Philippe, 1830–1848
Second Republic, 1848–1852
Napoleon III, Emperor, 1852–1870
Third Republic, 1870–1940
Pétain regime, 1940–1944
Provisional government, 1944–1946
Fourth Republic, 1946–1958
Fifth Republic, 1958–

Rulers of England

ANGLO-SAXON KINGS

Egbert, 802–839
Ethelwulf, 839–858
Ethelbald, 858–860
Ethelbert, 860–866
Ethelred, 866–871
Alfred the Great, 871–900
Edward the Elder, 900–924
Ethelstan, 924–940
Edmund I, 940–946
Edred, 946–955
Edwy, 955–959
Edgar, 959–975

Edward the Martyr, 975–978
Ethelred the Unready, 978–1016
Canute, 1016–1035 (Danish Nationality)
Harold I, 1035–1040
Hardicanute, 1040–1042
Edward the Confessor, 1042–1066
Harold II, 1066

HOUSE OF NORMANDY

William I (the Conqueror), 1066–1087
William II, 1087–1100
Henry I, 1100–1135
Stephen, 1135–1154

HOUSE OF PLANTAGENET

Henry II, 1154–1189
Richard I, 1189–1199
John, 1199–1216
Henry III, 1216–1272
Edward I, 1272–1307
Edward II, 1307–1327
Edward III, 1327–1377
Richard II, 1377–1399

HOUSE OF LANCASTER

Henry IV, 1399–1413
Henry V, 1413–1422
Henry VI, 1422–1461

HOUSE OF YORK

Edward IV, 1461–1483
Edward V, 1483
Richard III, 1483–1485

HOUSE OF TUDOR

Henry VII, 1485–1509
Henry VIII, 1509–1547
Edward VI, 1547–1553
Mary, 1553–1558
Elizabeth I, 1558–1603

HOUSE OF STUART

James I, 1603–1625
Charles I, 1625–1649

COMMONWEALTH AND PROTECTORATE, 1649–1659

HOUSE OF STUART RESTORED

Charles II, 1660–1685
James II, 1685–1688
William III and Mary II, 1689–1694
William III alone, 1694–1702
Anne, 1702–1714

HOUSE OF HANOVER

George I, 1714–1727
George II, 1727–1760
George III, 1760–1820
George IV, 1820–1830
William IV, 1830–1837
Victoria, 1837–1901

HOUSE OF SAXE-COBURG-GOTHA

Edward VII, 1901–1910
George V, 1910–1917

HOUSE OF WINDSOR

George V, 1917–1936
Edward VIII, 1936
George VI, 1936–1952
Elizabeth II, 1952–

Prominent Popes

Silvester I, 314–335
Leo I, 440–461
Gelasius I, 492–496
Gregory I, 590–604
Nicholas I, 858–867
Silvester II, 999–1003
Leo IX, 1049–1054
Nicholas II, 1058–1061
Gregory VII, 1073–1085
Urban II, 1088–1099
Paschal II, 1099–1118
Alexander III, 1159–1181

Innocent III, 1198–1216
Gregory IX, 1227–1241
Boniface VIII, 1294–1303
John XXII, 1316–1334
Nicholas V, 1447–1455
Pius II, 1458–1464
Alexander VI, 1492–1503
Julius II, 1503–1513
Leo X, 1513–1521
Adrian VI, 1522–1523
Clement VII, 1523–1534
Paul III, 1534–1549

Paul IV, 1555–1559
Gregory XIII, 1572–1585
Gregory XVI, 1831–1846
Pius IX, 1846–1878
Leo XIII, 1878–1903
Pius X, 1903–1914
Benedict XV, 1914–1922

Pius XI, 1922–1939
Pius XII, 1939–1958
John XXIII, 1958–1963
Paul VI, 1963–1978
John Paul I, 1978
John Paul II, 1978–

Rulers of Austria and Austria-Hungary

*Maximilian I (Archduke), 1493–1519
*Charles I (Charles V in the Holy Roman Empire),
  1519–1556
*Ferdinand I, 1556–1564
*Maximilian II, 1564–1576
*Rudolph II, 1576–1612
*Matthias, 1612–1619
*Ferdinand II, 1619–1637
*Ferdinand III, 1637–1657
*Leopold I, 1658–1705
*Joseph I, 1705–1711
*Charles VI, 1711–1740
Maria Theresa, 1740–1780

*Joseph II, 1780–1790
*Leopold II, 1790–1792
*Francis II, 1792–1835 (Emperor of Austria as
  Francis I after 1804)
Ferdinand I, 1835–1848
Francis Joseph, 1848–1916 (after 1867 Emperor
  of Austria and King of Hungary)
Charles I, 1916–1918 (Emperor of Austria and King
  of Hungary)
Republic of Austria, 1918–1938 (dictatorship
  after 1934)
Republic restored, under Allied occupation, 1945–1956
Free Republic, 1956–

*Also bore title of Holy Roman Emperor.

Rulers of Prussia and Germany

*Frederick I, 1701–1713
*Frederick William I, 1713–1740
*Frederick II (the Great), 1740–1786
*Frederick William II, 1786–1797
*Frederick William III, 1797–1840
*Frederick William IV, 1840–1861
*William I, 1861–1888 (German Emperor after 1871)

Frederick III, 1888
William II, 1888–1918
Weimar Republic, 1918–1933
Third Reich (Nazi Dictatorship), 1933–1945
Allied occupation, 1945–1952
Division into Federal Republic of Germany in west
  and German Democratic Republic in east, 1949–

*Kings of Prussia.

Rulers of Russia

Ivan III, 1462–1505
Vasily III, 1505–1533
Ivan IV, 1533–1584
Theodore I, 1584–1598
Boris Godunov, 1598–1605

Theodore II, 1605
Vasily IV, 1606–1610
Michael, 1613–1645
Alexius, 1645–1676
Theodore III, 1676–1682

Ivan V and Peter I, 1682–1689
Peter I (the Great), 1689–1725
Catherine I, 1725–1727
Peter II, 1727–1730
Anna, 1730–1740
Ivan VI, 1740–1741
Elizabeth, 1741–1762
Peter III, 1762

Catherine II (the Great), 1762–1796
Paul, 1796–1801
Alexander I, 1801–1825
Nicholas I, 1825–1855
Alexander II, 1855–1881
Alexander III, 1881–1894
Nicholas II, 1894–1917
Soviet Republic, 1917–

Rulers of Italy

Victor Emmanuel II, 1861–1878
Humbert I, 1878–1900
Victor Emmanuel III, 1900–1946
Fascist Dictatorship, 1922–1943
   (maintained in northern Italy until 1945)

Humbert II, May 9–June 13, 1946
Republic, 1946–

Rulers of Spain

Ferdinand { and Isabella, 1479–1504
           and Philip I, 1504–1506
           and Charles I, 1506–1516
Charles I (Holy Roman Emperor Charles V),
   1516–1556
Philip II, 1556–1598
Philip III, 1598–1621
Philip IV, 1621–1665
Charles II, 1665–1700
Philip V, 1700–1746
Ferdinand VI, 1746–1759
Charles III, 1759–1788
Charles IV, 1788–1808

Ferdinand VII, 1808
Joseph Bonaparte, 1808–1813
Ferdinand VII (restored), 1814–1833
Isabella II, 1833–1868
Republic, 1868–1870
Amadeo, 1870–1873
Republic, 1873–1874
Alfonso XII, 1874–1885
Alfonso XIII, 1886–1931
Republic, 1931–1939
Fascist Dictatorship, 1939–1975
Juan Carlos I, 1975–

ILLUSTRATIONS IN COLOR

ILLUSTRATIONS IN THE TEXT

Index

Guide to Pronunciation

The sounds represented by the diacritical marks used in this Index are illustrated by the following common words:

āle   ēve   īce   ōld   ūse   bōōt
ăt   ĕnd   ĭll   ŏf   ŭs   fŏŏt
fâtality   évent   ȯbey   ûnite
câre   fôrm   ûrn
ärm
ȧsk

Vowels that have no diacritical marks are to be pronounced "neutral," for example: Aegean = ê-je′an, Basel = bäz′el, Basil = bă′zil, common = kŏm′on, Alcaeus = ăl-sē′us. The combinations ou and oi are pronounced as in "out" and "oil."

Abbasid caliphate, 263-64, 275
Abdera, city of, 125, 126
Abdul Hamid II (äb′dul hä-mēd′), sultan of
    Turkey, 912
Abelard, Peter, 349-50, 354-55
abortion, 57, 66, 1050-51
Abraham, 68, 72
absolutism, 316, 673
    of Abbasid caliphate, 263
    Age of (c. 1660-1789), 587-628
    Bodin on, 528, 529
    Byzantine, 247
    Carbonari threat to, 770
    Cretan, 95
    of Cromwell, 523, 602
    despotism vs., 588
    Egyptian, 43
    enlightened, 611-22
    of Frederick II, 308
    of French monarchy, 519, 521, 524, 528,
        587, 588-89, 591-95, 638-39, 681, 775-76
    of Habsburg monarchy, 597-98
    Hobbes's advocacy of, 529-30
    of Near East civilizations, 144
    Persian, 69, 263
    responsibilities of, 592-93
    Rousseau vs., 680-81
abstract expressionism, 1053-54
Abu-Bakr (á-bōō′băk′ĕr), Caliph, 259-60
Abukir Bay, Battle of (1798), 699

Academy, Plato's, 129
Acadia, 555, 610
Achaean League, 149
Achilles (a-kĭl′ēz), 132
Acre, city of, 338
Act in Restraint of Appeals (England; 1533),
    491
Actium, Battle of (31 B.C.), 183, 208
Act of Succession (England; 1701), 604
Act of Supremacy (England; 1534), 481
Act of Supremacy (England; 1559), 483
Act of Toleration (England; 1689), 604
Addison, Joseph, 636
Addresses to the German Nation (Fichte), 795,
    798, 803
Adrianople, Battle of (378 A.D.), 224, 225
Adventures of Augie March, The (Bellow),
    1052
adversity theory of civilization, 17-18
advertising industry, 839, 986
Aegean Sea, 110, 113, 114, 151
Aelius Aristides, 165
Aeneid (Virgil), 187
aerial warfare:
    in First World War, 930
    in Second World War, 996, 998-99, 1003
    in Vietnam, 1038
Aeschylus (ĕs′kĭ-lus), 133, 134, 135, 136
Aesop, 360
Aetolian (ê-tō′lĭ-an) League, 149

Afghanistan, 1039
Africa, 16, 460, 1024, 1032-39
    black separatist movement and, 1046-47
    CIA intervention in, 1033, 1034
    colonization of, 457, 459-61, 847, 853-56
    Islam in, 256, 265
    Islamic trade with, 270
    Neolithic culture in, 12
    population explosion in, 1024
    see also Third World; *and specific countries*
African socialism, 1035
*Against the Thievish, Murderous Hordes of
    Peasants* (Luther), 478
Agamemnon, 98
Agincourt, Battle of (1415), 389
agnosticism, 635, 873
agriculture:
    Assyrian, 57
    Athenian, 118, 141-42
    Babylonian, 54
    in Byzantine Empire, 248
    Carolingian, 279, 286-87, 291
    development of, 6
    in early Middle Ages, 279
    in early-modern Europe, 558-62, 567
    Egyptian, 41
    in England, 286, 287, 291, 370, 373, 559-61
    in France, 319, 373, 678, 679
    in Germany, 223, 291, 292
    Great Depression and, 975-77

ii